PENGUIN CLASSICS

ADVISORY EDITOR: BETTY RADICE

THE HISTORIES

Few facts are known about the life of HERODOTUS. He was born around 490 BC in Halicarnassus, on the south-west coast of Asia Minor. He seems to have travelled widely throughout the Mediterranean world, including Egypt, Africa, the area around the Black Sea and throughout many Greek city-states, of both the mainland and the islands. A sojourn in Athens is part of the traditional biography, and there he is said to have given public readings of his work and been friends with the playwright Sophocles. He is said also to have taken part in the founding of the colony of Thurii in Italy in 443 BC. He probably died at some time between 425 and 420 BC. His reputation has varied greatly, but for the ancients and many moderns he well deserves the title (first given to him by Cicero) of 'the Father of History'.

AUBREY DE SÉLINCOURT, scholar and translator, translated Livy's *The Early History of Rome* (Books I–V) and *The War with Hannibal* (Books XXI–XXX), *The Histories* of Herodotus and *The Campaigns of Alexander* by Arrian, all for the Penguin Classics. He was born in 1896 and educated at Rugby, and University College, Oxford. A schoolmaster of genius for twenty-six years, he retired in 1947 to the Isle of Wight, where he lived until his death in 1962.

JOHN MARINCOLA was born in Philadelphia in 1954, and was educated at Swarthmore College, the University of Pennsylvania, and Brown University. He has taught at the College of the Holy Cross in Massachusetts, and at Union College in New York, and is currently an Associate Professor of Classics at New York University. From 1997 to 1999 he was Executive Director of the American Philological Association, and in 1999–2000 he was a Junior Fellow at the Center for Hellenic Studies in Washington, DC. He is the author of *Authority and Tradition in Ancient Historiography* (Cambridge, 1997), *Greek Historians* (*Greece and Rome New*

Surveys in the Classics 31, Oxford, 2001), and of several articles on the Greek and Roman historians. He is currently at work on a book on Hellenistic historiography.

HERODOTUS

The Histories

Translated by AUBREY DE SÉLINCOURT
Revised with Introduction and Notes by
JOHN MARINCOLA

PENGUIN BOOKS

PENGUIN BOOKS

Published by the Penguin Group
Penguin Books Ltd, 80 Strand, London WC2R ORL, England
Penguin Putnam Inc., 375 Hudson Street, New York, New York 10014, USA
Penguin Books Australia Ltd, 250 Camberwell Road, Camberwell, Victoria 3124, Australia
Penguin Books Canada Ltd, 10 Alcorn Avenue, Toronto, Ontario, Canada M4V 3B2
Penguin Books India (P) Ltd, 11, Community Centre, Panchsheel Park, New Delhi – 110 017, India
Penguin Books (NZ) Ltd, Cnr Rosedale and Airborne Roads, Albany, Auckland, New Zealand
Penguin Books (South Africa) (Pty) Ltd, 24 Sturdee Avenue, Rosebank 2196, South Africa

Penguin Books Ltd, Registered Offices: 80 Strand, London WC2R ORL, England

www.penguin.com

This translation first published 1954
Revised edition 1972
Revised edition with new introductory matter and Notes 1996
Further revised edition 2003

001

Translation copyright 1954 by Aubrey de Sélincourt
Revised edition with new introductory matter and Notes copyright © John Marincola, 1996, 2003
All rights reserved

The moral right of the editor has been asserted

Maps on pages xlvii–liii by Nigel Andrews

Set in 10.25/12.25 pt PostScript Adobe Sabon
Typeset by Rowland Phototypesetting Ltd, Bury St Edmunds, Suffolk
Printed in the United States of America

ISBN-13: 978–0–140–44908–2

Contents

Preface

For this further revised edition, I have limited myself mainly to corrections of the translation, and to a modest updating of the Introduction (especially sections 3 and 5), the Notes, and the Further Reading. For calling my attention to errors and infelicities in the earlier edition I thank Ernst Badian, Hugh Bowden, Michael Flower, Adolfo Gómez-Lobo, John Lenz, Philip Mayerson, and Peter Rhodes. I also thank Penguin Books and especially Laura Barber, the editor of the Penguin Classics, who suggested a revision of this edition and was most helpful in its execution. The failings that persist are my own.

May 2002   J. M.

PREFACE TO 1996 REVISED EDITION

In writing the notes I have had in mind the interested general reader and the beginning student of Greek history. The vast scope of Herodotus' work and the need to keep the notes within reasonable limits meant that I had to select rather drastically throughout. My procedure has been to comment briefly on matters about which a general reader might have questions and then to refer the reader to more detailed treatments. With very few exceptions I have limited myself to citing works in English, although the reader should be aware that much of the most important work done on Herodotus has been in other languages. I have tended towards comment on matters more traditionally historical but I have tried not to lose sight of Herodotus as an author in his own right. All dates in the book, unless otherwise noted, are BCE.

For help and advice I am indebted to Peter Lacovara, John Lenz and Mark Toher. I owe a special debt of thanks to Michael Flower, who read several drafts, corrected many errors and called my attention to bibliographic items I should otherwise have missed. Thanks are due to Union College for a leave to complete the work, and to my secretary, Mrs Marianne Snowden, for assistance in ways too numerous to mention. I thank, above all, my wife Michele, who has given intellectual, practical and moral support from beginning to end. For errors of omission and commission that remain, I alone am responsible.

November 1994   J.M.

Introduction

1. HERODOTUS' LIFE AND WORK

Not much is known of the life of Herodotus and the few items that have come down to us are not above suspicion. A late source, the eleventh-century Byzantine lexicon known as the *Suda*, preserves a number of biographical details: that Herodotus was born in Halicarnassus, the son of Lyxes and Dryo, and the brother of Theodorus; that he was the nephew or cousin of an epic poet Panyassis, who wrote on historical themes (such as the foundings of Ionian cities); that he was exiled by the tyrant of Halicarnassus, Lygdamis, to the island of Samos, where he learned the Ionic dialect of Greek (in which his *Histories* are composed); that he afterwards returned to Halicarnassus, assisted in expelling Lygdamis, and then, seeing himself hated by his fellow citizens, went into exile and joined in the foundation of Thurii, an Athenian-led pan-Hellenic colony in southern Italy; and that he died there or perhaps in Macedonia at Pella.

It is impossible to say how much of this is reliable. We know that the biographies composed of ancient poets were made up largely of inferences from remarks made in their writings, and much the same thing may have happened in Herodotus' case.[1] He may thus have been thought a tyrant-slayer because of his obvious love of freedom as evidenced in his work, and Samos was assumed to be the place of his exile because he shows a great deal of knowledge about the island and its monuments, and is favourably disposed towards the Samians in his work. (Indeed, the assertion that he learned Ionic Greek there is patently absurd, since his own Dorian community of Halicarnassus used the Ionic dialect for its public inscriptions.) Finally, the tradition of exile may be an explanation for the wide travels that Herodotus portrays in his work; and since exile was not uncommon for historians of later times (Thucydides, Xenophon, Polybius, to name a few), this may have been retrojected onto Herodotus, the 'father of history'.[2]

We hear that Herodotus approached both the Thebans and the Corinthians to request their patronage for his work but was rebuffed, and in return for this he wrote disparagingly of them in his history. By contrast, we are told, the people of Athens were so delighted with his work that they voted to give him the sum of ten talents – a fortune – from public funds to show their gratitude. These remarks, with their anachronistic notions of patronage and local pride, clearly come from a later time and are meant to explain why Herodotus wrote favourably towards one group and not another. Since ancient critics always maintained a keen eye for bias, it was not difficult for them to suppose that Herodotus' treatment of the participants was directly related to how he himself had been treated by them.[3]

A sojourn in Athens is also part of the traditional biography. In Athens Herodotus is said to have been a friend of the tragedian Sophocles: Plutarch records a poem that the playwright wrote for the historian and scholars have noted several correspondences between Herodotus' work and Sophocles' plays. There is a strong pro-Athenian bias in Herodotus' narrative, either in explicit praise or in implicit acceptance of the Athenian viewpoint in his evaluations of other states. Yet while there is no reason to doubt that he spent time in Athens, this does not mean (as is so often claimed) that he must have been friendly with the Alcmaeonids, a prominent Athenian clan, or that he must have admired and approved of the policies of Pericles, the Alcmaeonid who enjoyed an unparalleled influence in democratic Athens from 445 to his death in 429 BCE.[4]

Herodotus himself states that he came from Halicarnassus, a Dorian town on a promontory in the southwest corner of Asia Minor, the western coast of modern Turkey, which in antiquity was filled with Greek cities and Greek culture. There is abundant evidence that Halicarnassus, although a Greek city, had close

contact with the non-Greek Carians who occupied the hinterlands and were subject to Persia. It has been thought, not
improbably, that this less insular atmosphere influenced the
young Herodotus, broadening his inquisitiveness and tolerance
towards Persians and non-Greeks in general. The exact date of
his birth is unknown; the ancients put it in 484 and the date,
although conjecture, is nevertheless not likely to be far off.

Herodotus gives every indication in his work of having travelled widely throughout the Mediterranean. He claims explicitly
to have journeyed as far south as Elephantine at the first cataract
of the Nile (II. 29), and as far north as the Black Sea area in his
research on the Scythians (IV. 76–81). He says he visited
Dodona in northwest Greece (II. 55), Zacynthus off the western
coast of the Peloponnese (IV. 195) and Metapontum in southern
Italy (IV. 15). He inspected temples in Phoenicia and at Thasos
(II. 44), observed the remnants of a battle in the Egyptian Delta
(III. 12), inspected monuments in Palestine (II. 106) and viewed
the majestic Thessalian plain (VII. 129). By other remarks not
as explicit, he strongly suggests that he travelled as far east as
Babylon and as far west as Cyrene in Libya (I. 193; IV. 154).
He saw inscriptions in Theban temples (V. 59), and his descriptions of the treasures at Delphi and Miletus indicate that he saw
them for himself. Elsewhere he uses geographical comparisons
that demonstrate his knowledge of Athens and the Peloponnese
as well as Asia Minor (not surprisingly) and even the 'heel' of
Italy. Given the difficulty, danger and expense of travel in the
time of Herodotus, we should be justified in concluding that he
must have been from the upper class. Although some scholars
doubt the extent of Herodotus' travels (see below, pp. xxix–
xxxi), the general opinion is that he was a man of indefatigable
character, who spent many years researching the material that
he eventually brought together in his *Histories*.

What audience Herodotus envisioned and what form the
'publication' of his work took are not easy to determine.[5] He
certainly saw himself as writing for a pan-Hellenic audience,
and although better informed about some states than others,
he presents in his work numerous perspectives and traditions
without strict allegiance to any school of thought and for the

most part avoiding the promotion of any one group's political
claims. His work is not in any sense provincial, and this is even
more impressive when we consider the general insularity of the
individual Greek city-states. The form in which he communicated his researches was the recital or public performance. Since
he lived in a largely oral society where the level of functional
literacy cannot have been high,[6] most would have known of his
work from oral presentations or performances. We may imagine
that Herodotus gave readings from his work at religious festivals
or in smaller intellectual gatherings such as symposia, of the
sort familiar to us from Plato's *Symposium*.[7] In the earlier
books it is possible to see independent and almost detachable
'performance pieces', in which the author, with great emphasis,
criticizes previous treatments of a subject and with much fanfare
substitutes his own solution to a problem: the discussion of the
Nile's inundation (II. 19–27) or the revisionary account of
the Trojan War (II. 113–20) are good examples. This kind
of performance, which finds parallels in the philosophers and
medical writers of Herodotus' time, is part of the intellectual
ferment of the fifth century, where reciters would lay claim to
wisdom and openly debate issues before citizens and pro-
fessionals.[8]

There is some uncertainty whether the *Histories* as we have
them are complete. The chief grounds for doubt are three unfulfilled promises: two refer to a history of Assyria (I. 106; 184)
and one to the capture of a Greek traitor (VII. 213). The failure
to fulfil the promises may, however, be nothing more than lapses
of memory, since in Herodotus' day the physical act of writing
researches down would have involved long and cumbersome
rolls of papyrus, and it would have been difficult to go back and
revise once he had begun. Moreover, in supporting the argument
that the work is finished, one might adduce the ending, which
has a strong sense of thematic closure.[9]

The date of Herodotus' death is unknown. He makes several
unmistakable references to the Peloponnesian War, the great
war between Athens and Sparta that lasted from 431 to 404,
with a period of nominal but suspect peace (the so-called 'Peace
of Nicias') from 421 to about 414. The latest datable reference

in his work is to the year 430, and a remark that he makes about the Athenian *deme* of Decelea (IX. 73 with n.) implies that he was probably not alive in 413 (unless we assume that only this passage is unrevised). The traditional date for his death is some time between 430 and 425. The latter date is chosen because it is assumed that a passage from Aristophanes' *Acharnians* (performed in 425) is a parody of Herodotus, and that therefore the work must have been published before that date. Others find allusions to Herodotus in the same poet's *Birds* (performed 414) and suggest therefore that the *Histories* were published around 415. These assume, then, that Herodotus lived through the first part of the Peloponnesian War (known as the Archidamian War) and died during the Peace of Nicias, which would put his death somewhere between 421 and 415. Such notions as 'publication' are probably anachronistic, and both passages attest only that Herodotus' work was well known in Athens, no doubt as a result of his own reading of it there.[10]

Whatever date we assign to his death, it is more important to recognize that Herodotus was doing most of his research, writing and performances from the 450s up to the 420s. This was a time not only of exciting inquiry carried out in many fields (some of which finds its place in Herodotus' own work) but also of increasing conflict between Sparta and Athens, which were then the two great powers in the Greek world – the powers, in fact, that had combined not so long before, in 490 and again in 480–479, to repel the Persians and ensure Greek freedom. It was in this environment, and perhaps because of it, that Herodotus decided to look back from his time of growing tensions and internecine strife to an era when the major powers and many of the Greeks had united, even if only temporarily and uneasily, in a common and glorious enterprise.[11]

2. THE SUBJECT-MATTER OF
THE *HISTORIES*

The variety of wares at the Herodotean bazaar is truly stagger-
ing. Given the title *Histories*, the modern reader might expect to find a linear narrative of battles, rulers and political
upheavals. This description would barely do justice to the work
we have. Our word 'history' comes from the Greek *historia*,
which originally meant 'inquiry, investigation', and only later
came to be applied specifically to the investigation of the past.[12]
Herodotus, however, lived in a time when categories of knowledge had not been rigidly separated, and his work ranges over
many fields and includes geography, anthropology, ethnology,
zoology, even fable and folklore. His work defies easy categoriz-
ation: like Homer, Herodotus is a world unto himself.

In his preface he claims that he wishes to preserve 'human
achievements' (*ta genomena ex anthropon*), thus distinguishing
his work at the outset from epic poetry, where gods and humans
both are characters and act in concert with each other. He wants
also to be sure that the 'great and marvellous deeds' (*erga megala
te kai thomasta*) done by both Greeks and barbarians (by which
Herodotus means, without prejudice, non-Greeks) have their
proper share of glory. These 'great and marvellous deeds' are
not only those done on the battlefield, but include monuments,
temples, memorable actions by people in all situations – even
the works of nature, such as the Nile's flood and the gradual
creation of its Delta.[13]

In his search for great and memorable deeds, Herodotus
extended his view beyond the Greek world to the lives, ways
and beliefs of the people with whom the Greeks and the Persians
came into contact. When treating a people, it is Herodotus' habit
to comment on their monuments, religious beliefs, customs,
livelihoods and the natural wonders of their country. An interest
in foreign ways is evident in the earliest Greek literature, and
these descriptions, known as ethnographies, did not originate
with Herodotus.[14] But in Herodotus these descriptions are

woven into the historical narrative and form an integral part of his conception of the world and human action. More importantly, these ethnographies were a useful tool in helping the Greeks to define their own character and notion of themselves.[15] The Greek world, as we might expect, forms the norm used by Herodotus: those nations that differ the most receive the largest treatment, whereas nations rather similar to the Greeks are only briefly described.[16] Egypt, for example, receives an entire Book of its own, in part due to the Greek fascination (evidenced long before Herodotus) with that country: its wealth, its monuments, its astounding river and the antiquity of its civilization, in comparison with that of the Greeks, all contributed to its uniqueness. Scythia too receives extended treatment, because the Scythians' way of life was antithetical to that of the Greeks.[17]

A conceptual mapping of the world and the Greeks' place in it also motivates Herodotus' interest in geography and the natural world. There are long descriptions and explanations of such things as the sources of the Nile, the reasons for its flood, the rivers of Scythia or the oases of Africa. He discusses the number and nature of the continents, and what can be gathered about their size and relationship to one another. Here again, Herodotus was not the first in the field, and was only laying claim to the legacy of the Ionian natural scientists and travellers, who had also collected information about the natural world. But some of this material is part of Herodotus' attempt to include in his work what could be known of the entire *oikoumene* (the inhabited world) and to better his predecessors by introducing new information they did not have. Other lands, their positions and their relationship to Greece were all of importance in helping the Greeks to understand their own place in the world. This was true not least because a nation's geography and climate were felt to be important factors in the character of its people, as a reading of the roughly contemporary ethnographical essay *Airs, Waters, Places* (which is included in the Hippocratic medical corpus) shows.[18]

The reader will often find in Herodotus stories that can only be described as folktales, the type of literature known from the collections of the brothers Grimm. Stories of this kind, which

are found all over the world, often have a whiff of the marvellous
about them. One reads of the child who is supposed to be
destroyed at birth, but survives and grows up to be king; of the
clever thief who outwits all attempts to catch him, and who is
rewarded in the end with marriage to the king's daughter; of
the destructive promise, with someone being bound by necessity
to choose between equally bad alternatives; of magical recov-
eries and supernatural escapes. Herodotus was probably drawing here on a long tradition of Ionian story-telling, but he took
this and brought it to a level of inspired brilliance. Many of
Herodotus' readers can sense that whatever his shortcomings as
a historian (in the modern sense of the word), he is a story-teller
of the first rank.[19]

Herodotus' strong sense of the marvellous can be found as
well in his interest in the unusual or the fantastic. These marvels
can be of many types. In nature they are best seen in geographical
features or in the world of animals. Man-made marvels can be
extraordinary monuments, such as the Egyptian pyramids or
the Labyrinth, or the temple of Hera at Samos; they can be
ingenious inventions, like the boats of Babylon that sail down
the river but are then disassembled and carried back on donkeys.
They can even be human actions and actors who display great
wit, character or bravery. It is because of his love for marvels
and the unusual that his reputation, even in antiquity, was
tarnished, and he was often reproved as a tall-story teller: he
was both 'father of history' and 'father of lies'.[20]

Above all, Herodotus is the historian of Persia's wars with
Greece. He identifies this as an important concern at the conclusion of his preface, where he says that he will investigate
'especially why the two peoples fought with each other'. Herodotus' choice of the war as a subject was certainly due in part
to his admiration for the extraordinary achievement by which
a small and cantankerous group of city-states defeated not once
but several times the might of the Persians, the most powerful
empire that had existed up to that time. Nevertheless, Herodotus' *Histories* are not primarily a military narrative. Even his
accounts of the famous battles of Marathon, Thermopylae and
Salamis have little on strategy and tactics, and the battle descrip-

tions tend to focus on individual prowess and achievement or on interesting and unusual details. The focus here as elsewhere was on great and marvellous deeds, deeds that Herodotus wished to invest with fame.

Moreover, by choosing a war between east and west, Herodotus was consciously emulating the greatest of Greek poets, Homer, and his narrative of the Greek war against Troy. Herodotus' debt to Homer is profound, and may be seen in his choice of subject, his language, his conception of his task, as well as in many occasional observations and verbal echoes. At the outset of the work Herodotus says that he does not want the great deeds of Greeks and barbarians to be without their glory (*kleos*), a reference to the scene in the *Iliad* where Achilles takes pleasure in singing of the 'glories of men' (*klea andron*, IX. 189). Like the poet of the *Iliad*, Herodotus records and immortalizes the actions worthy of remembrance. These actions, however, were not those of heroes long ago, but rather of men whom Herodotus may have met and whose descendants were still to be found in the Greek city-states. By placing himself in this tradition, Herodotus makes the bold claim that the actions of the Persian Wars were every bit as glorious and memorable as those of Homeric conflict. Nor was Herodotus' debt to Homer limited to the *Iliad*; part of his work, like the *Odyssey*, is full of adventures and tales, and the historian himself, like Odysseus, is an experienced traveller.[21]

On one very important level Herodotus saw the Persian Wars as a conflict between freedom and slavery, between oriental and arbitrary despots on the one hand, and on the other hand free Greek communities in which men were required to persuade their fellow citizens and to be responsible for their actions.[22] In Herodotus the Persians are portrayed as driven on by the whip, while the Greeks fight for themselves. The portrait is subtle and without jingoism or malice, but its assumptions occasionally rise to the surface, as in the explanation of Demaratus to the Persian king Xerxes, who does not understand how the Spartans (and, by extension, the Greeks) can fight well if they do not put on, in Aeschylus' memorable phrase, the 'yoke of necessity'. Demaratus emphasizes that the Spartan master is Law – what the community has agreed upon and chosen to follow. And in Herodotus' account of the wars, that law is superior to one-man rule, no matter how great the disparity in numbers between the combatants.[23]

Lands, peoples, nature, war, memorable deeds: Herodotus' work is a vast canvas, filled with the variety of his own interests. We can be fairly certain that before Herodotus the Greeks already possessed narratives of the foundings of cities, accounts of the customs of non-Greek peoples, and even treatments of the events of the Persian Wars. There were geographical studies, which attempted to mark out the Greeks' place in the world. What makes Herodotus unique is the range of his interests and his attempt to unite human and natural phenomena, and in so doing to discover the causal interconnection of widely disparate events.

3. HERODOTUS' SOURCES AND METHOD

We naturally wish to know where and how Herodotus got his information for all this material. In antiquity Herodotus was seen as the last in a long line of chroniclers who had written histories of their individual city-states, a genre that Herodotus then subsumed and superseded.[24] In the extreme form in which it was found in the ancient sources, that approach must definitely be rejected: many of the supposed 'sources' named for Herodotus can be shown to have written later than he did. On the other hand, it is possible to identify several prose writers who were predecessors or contemporaries of Herodotus. Pride of place must be given to Hecataeus of Miletus (fl. c. 500), the most important prose-writer before Herodotus and the only one to whom Herodotus refers by name in his own work. A product of the intellectual ferment of Miletus, Hecataeus wrote two works rather different in character but both of profound importance for the future of historical writing in Greece. In the *Genealogies* (or *Histories*) Hecataeus tried to bring order to the various and contradictory genealogies that existed in the Greek mythic tradition.[25] His other work, entitled *Circuit of the Earth* and

divided into two Books, 'Europe' and 'Asia', described the
coastal settlements of the Mediterranean region, proceeding in
a clockwise direction and giving for each place some description
of the climate, people, customs and perhaps the hinterlands.[26]
What makes Hecataeus important, despite the sparse remains
of his work, is that he was the first Greek to attempt in prose to
order (not simply to chronicle) the mass of Greek traditions,
and to investigate the customs and peoples of the Mediterranean, using his own inquiry and rational analysis. Herodotus
learned the method and, we can be fairly certain, drew upon
some of the information which his predecessor had gathered.[27]

Besides Hecataeus, we may name the following, although the
reader should be aware that the dates for these authors are in
many cases uncertain. Dionysius of Miletus wrote in the early
fifth century a work entitled *Persian Matters* (*Persica*). The work
most likely covered some material from Persian history, and
there is no reason to think that it did not include the wars of
Darius and Xerxes, although almost certainly not on the scale
of Herodotus' treatment. Xanthus of Lydia wrote a four-book
work entitled *Lydian Matters* (*Lydiaca*), which may have been
known to Herodotus in writing his own brief treatment of
the Lydian kings. A later fourth-century historian, Ephorus of
Cyme, said that Xanthus had given Herodotus his 'starting-
point' (or perhaps 'spur'), but so little survives of Xanthus'
work that we cannot make any worthwhile judgement. Another
possible predecessor is Charon of Lampsacus, to whom are
attributed works on Ethiopia, Persia, and the foundations of
cities, but the fragments are meagre, and there is no evidence to
demonstrate that Herodotus used his works (which is not to say
that he did not use them). Finally, there is Hellanicus of Lesbos,
a polymath best known as the author of the first local history
of Athens, but who also wrote works entitled *Customs of the
Barbarians*, *Lydian Matters*, *Egyptian Matters*, and *Persian
Matters*. The intersection of Hellanicus' work with that of Herodotus is unclear, and it must suffice to note that Herodotus'
activity coincides with a flourishing interest in foreign nations,
particularly those of the Ancient Near East.[28]

There were also poetic treatments of historical themes on

which Herodotus may have drawn. The best known, Aeschylus' *Persians*, produced at Athens in 472, has within it a messenger's speech describing the engagement at the battle of Salamis in 480. Herodotus himself mentions Phrynichus' *Fall of Miletus* which recounted that city's fate at the end of the Ionian revolt in 494, and other poetic treatments of historical events include a history of Smyrna by Mimnermus, Xenophanes' *Foundation of Colophon*, Semonides of Amorgos on the early history of the Samians, Panyassis' *Ionian History* and Simonides' *Seabattle of Salamis, Seabattle of Artemisium* and *Battle of Plataea*. Of this last work in particular we have come to know something more because of the recent publication of papyrus fragments of the work. Each one of the lines of the poem is fragmentary, and the whole must be heavily restored. Caution is decidedly in order, since in restoring the fragments scholars have been largely dependent on Herodotus' text, and so the danger of circular argument is great. Nevertheless, it seems clear that Simonides made a correlation between the great heroes of the Trojan war with (specifically) the Spartans' performance at the battle of Plataea, and the tone, to the extent that it can be recovered, seems to have been encomiastic. Although Herodotus nowhere mentions this and the other poetic works, it can hardly be doubted that their contents were familiar to him.[29]

Predominantly, however, Herodotus based his work on his own observation, inquiry, conjecture and rational analysis. He is explicit about this only at times (II. 99, 142) but there is no doubt that he meant his audience to assume that this was his procedure throughout his work. Different matters, of course, would have called forth different methods. He could use his own eyes (autopsy) for geographical information, buildings, monuments, artworks and the observance of customs. For past deeds, however, and for people who lived at the edge of the known world, autopsy could not be employed, and he would have to turn to oral inquiry, to what reliable informants had to say. Sometimes the methods complement each other, and something seen – dedications of a king in a temple, the statue of a man riding a dolphin, the practice of circumcision – corroborates an account learned orally or formed by conjecture. Where data are lacking the historian may have recourse to analogy, to arguing from the known to the unknown. Sometimes he uses reasoned inferences, sometimes rather more tenuous opinion. All these are employed as needed, and their use marks Herodotus out as a pioneer in the field of historical research and method.[30]

Herodotus presents his work as a collection of oral traditions, and his method is frequently to allow native spokesmen to present their case: 'the Persians say', 'the Egyptians say', 'the Athenians do not agree', 'the Spartans alone maintain', and so on. More than once he refers to his role explicitly as 'to say what is said' and he cautions that he reports more than he believes (II. 123; VII. 152). These source-statements in most cases (Book II is the exception) are not meant to emphasize that he has heard these for himself (though he may well have), but rather that these are the traditions that exist in each of these cities or lands.[31] The Egyptians had written records of their past and the Persians a vast bureaucracy, but we must emphasize that Herodotus needed here and elsewhere to use intermediaries, for there is no evidence that he knew any language other than Greek. Occasionally, by the use of qualifiers – 'learned' Persians or the Heliopolitans who are 'the most devoted to memory' – Herodotus indicates people with a special knowledge of the past, an 'expert' as opposed to a layman.[32] Naturally, we wonder who these unnamed Persians or Phoenicians (or indeed even Athenians) are, and much scholarship has been concerned with identifying both general and specific sources of Herodotus.[33]

Written records in Greece, aside from the literary works mentioned earlier, would have been rare if they existed at all. Greek traditions would have been almost exclusively oral, preserved either by individual families or the community as a whole. Aristocratic clans would have maintained traditions about their founders or important ancestors, but we must not imagine that they had a monopoly, and there is sufficient evidence in Herodotus of traditions hostile to ruling families. Religious centres, too, such as Delphi and Didyma, preserved traditions, of varying accuracy, associated with the numerous dedications made by Greeks and non-Greeks alike in their sanctuaries.[34] Sometimes these traditions were contradictory, apologetic or exculpatory. On occasion Herodotus takes a stand, but in many cases he realized that there was no way to judge between irreconcilable traditions, and his solution was to place competing accounts side by side and allow his audience to choose.[35]

We must admit that if Herodotus, with few exceptions, did not use written sources, then his achievement is impressive indeed, for it was put together from vast researches done over the better part of a lifetime on travels throughout the Mediterranean world. These sources can be generally, if not specifically, identified, but what Arnaldo Momigliano wrote in 1960 is nevertheless still true today and likely to be true for some time to come: 'Herodotus' success in touring the world and handling oral traditions is something exceptional by any standard – something that we are not yet in a position to explain fully. The secrets of his workshop are not yet all out.'[36]

4. STRUCTURE AND THEMES IN THE *HISTORIES*

Perhaps the greatest challenge to Herodotus was to give order and structure to the mass of material that he had assembled. Here again it was Homer who provided a useful model for a monumental composition.[37] Herodotus decided to make the guiding thread of his work the advance of Persian power, but, like Homer, he gave variety and movement to an underlying linear structure. He moves forward and backward in time (usually a difficulty for the modern reader), while often stopping to examine people or events in detail. Few of these digressions are without importance, and behind the fiction of an informal style lies a recognizable and carefully articulated structure. The ethnographies, for example, are not randomly given, but usually placed where the relevant group comes into contact with the advance of Persia. Egypt is described on the eve of Cambyses' invasion, Scythia and Libya when Darius sets out against them. Other patterns suggest careful consideration by the author. In Book I, for example, the Lydian king Croesus in his quest for allies against the Persian king Cyrus sends inquiries to Sparta and Athens. This provides the occasion for Herodotus to say a little of Spartan and Athenian history to about 650 (the time of Croesus' inquiry). Later, in Book V, Aristagoras leads Ionia in a revolt from Persia. In his quest for allies he goes to Sparta and Athens and at this point Herodotus brings the history of those states down to about 500, shortly before the Persian invasion of the mainland.

Thematic patterning also gives structure: despite the enormity and variety of Herodotus' work, certain themes and concerns appear regularly enough to indicate the conscious choice of the historian. Many of these themes are interconnected, and the historian uses them to give order and meaning to the random and at times meaningless mass of historical actions.

The theme of retribution and vengeance – that those who commit evil deeds will pay for them now or in the future – pervades the *Histories* from first to last, and is deeply woven into Herodotus' view of human action and historical causation. His work begins with a series of abductions of women, first by men from Asia, then in retaliation by men from Europe (I. 1–5). Demands for satisfaction from the injured parties are unmet and keep the cycle of vengeance alive. Even Paris' seizure of Helen, the event that set off the Trojan War, is seen by Herodotus within this framework, for Paris was 'confident that he would not have to pay for the venture any more than the Greeks had done'. In the first story, that of the Lydian king Candaules and the usurper Gyges, the injured party is told by the Delphic oracle that they 'would have their revenge on Gyges in the fifth generation' (I. 13). This desire for retributive justice (*tisis*) motivates individuals and states. Herodotus presents the Persian attack on Athens in 490 as retribution for the Athenians' participation in the burning of the Persian provincial capital of Sardis in 498. In a memorable image, Darius, having heard of his city's destruction, 'called for his bow . . . set an arrow on the string, shot it up into the air and cried, "Grant, O God, that I may punish the Athenians"' (V. 105). Xerxes is later told by his general Mardonius that the Greeks 'will be brought to account for the injuries they have done you, now and in the past' (VIII.

100). The Athenians in turn portray their actions as a desire to pay back the Persians for their burning of the Acropolis and its temples (VIII. 144). This notion is so deeply ingrained in Herodotus' thought that it is carried over even into nature: when flying snakes mate, he says, the female latches on to the male's neck and kills him; but the female 'has to pay for her behaviour, for the young in her belly avenge their father by gnawing at her insides, until they end by eating their way out' (III. 109).[38]

Herodotus also shared the common Greek belief that any act of insolence or overweening pride (*hybris*) inevitably leads to some destruction (*nemesis*). Solon, who had written of these very things in one of his poems,[39] is the spokesman in Herodotus for this viewpoint, as he tells the wealthy Lydian king Croesus, in the first extended narrative of the *Histories*, that 'God is envious of human prosperity and likes to trouble us' (I. 32). The idea is expanded by Artabanus in his later warning to Xerxes: 'It is always the great buildings and the tall trees which are struck by lightning. It is God's way to bring the lofty low . . . For God tolerates pride in none but Himself' (VII. 10e). Herodotus even invokes *nemesis* to explain Croesus' fall from prosperity: 'After Solon's departure nemesis fell upon Croesus, presumably because God was angry with him for supposing himself the happiest of men' (I. 34). And most clearly of all, one can see in the destruction of Troy 'that great offences meet with great punishments at the hands of God' (II. 120).

In Herodotus *hybris* is frequently manifest in the expansion of empire. Often enough a campaign to a distant people involves some transgression of natural limits, as when Cyrus crosses the River Araxes to conquer the Massagetae at the ends of the earth (I. 205ff.), or Darius bridges the Danube to bring over the Scythians to his empire (IV. 83ff.), or (in the climax of the work) Xerxes yokes the Hellespont, joins Europe and Asia – which God had separated – in his attempt to conquer the Greeks (VII. 54ff.). All three expeditions fail and Themistocles after the Greek victory at Salamis comments explicitly that the gods and heroes 'were jealous that one man in his godless pride should be king of Asia and of Europe too' (VIII. 109). No doubt the thought was not original (there are strong traces of it in Aeschylus' *Persians*, e.g. 353–63, 472–3, 739–51); but in Herodotus this recurrent theme suggests the inevitable destruction of any far-reaching empire, while at the same time serving the practical purpose of giving a recognizable pattern to events.[40]

Related closely to this is the theme of the instability of human fortune. In delineating the scope of his work, Herodotus says that he will tell of small cities and great, for the cities 'which were great once are small today; and those which used to be small were great in my own time' – from which Herodotus judges that 'human prosperity never abides long in the same place' (I. 5). This belief is given substance again by Solon to the wealthy but short-sighted Lydian king Croesus. As Croesus prods Solon to concede that he is the happiest man whom Solon has ever seen, the Athenian warns that the sum total of a human life from beginning to end is necessary in order to calculate happiness, since 'often enough God gives a man a glimpse of happiness, and then utterly ruins him' (I. 32). Nor is it many pages later that Croesus has lost all and is about to be immolated by his Persian conqueror Cyrus. Here too it is the recognition by Cyrus of 'the instability of human things' that persuades him not to destroy 'another who had once been as prosperous as he' (I. 86). Motivated by the same knowledge, the Egyptian king Amasis renounces his alliance with the tyrant Polycrates, because he saw that Polycrates had unbroken good fortune and would therefore come to a miserable end (III. 43).

A recurring figure in Herodotus' stories of limits and the reversals of fortune is the 'tragic warner' or 'wise adviser'. These figures serve in the narrative to dramatize the important choices before individuals, to give advice to those who lack a larger perspective, and to suggest a proper way to behave. They appear at crucial points, and despite the usefulness of their advice they are usually ignored, and the disaster they warn of comes true. From Solon and Croesus to Artemisia and Xerxes, wise advisers are reminders of what might have been. They form part of the theme evident elsewhere in Herodotus that warnings are never believed until too late.[41]

Warnings are found as well in oracles and dreams. Despite Herodotus' focus on human actions and his occasional statements of ignorance about divine matters,[42] these oracles and dreams – which are supernatural and come from the gods – appear throughout the *Histories*. The most important oracle, both in the Greek world and in Herodotus' narrative, was that of Apollo at Delphi, and before taking any important action individuals and cities alike consulted what the god had to say through his priestess. Frequently Herodotus quotes these oracles in part or in full. Although the god always speaks truthfully, he often speaks ambiguously or metaphorically. When Croesus wishes to attack Persia he is told by the Delphic Oracle that 'he will destroy a mighty empire', but the headstrong king does not recognize the ambiguity in this pronouncement. Croesus is also warned of sufferings 'the day that a mule shall sit on the Median throne' (I. 55), but he fails to interpret the metaphor properly; whereas the Athenians, when advised to take refuge behind the 'wooden wall', are fortunate to have Themistocles, who understands that the god is indicating their navy (VII. 143). In these and many other cases the oracle speaks enigmatically, and it is the task of human beings to discern the actual, as opposed to apparent, meaning. In some cases the correct interpretation is discovered too late; in others, such as the wooden wall prophecy, a person of keen wit and insight may see into the god's meaning; not infrequently, individuals and whole communities suffer until they discern what the god wishes them to do. For in Herodotus the oracles are never wrong, even if their real meaning is misunderstood. They suggest a gulf between divine and human knowledge that can only partially and imperfectly be bridged.[43]

Dreams too come from the gods and, like oracles, urge some action or predict the future. Some dreams, like oracles, are couched in metaphor, as when, for example, the Median king Astyages dreams that his daughter urinates so greatly as to inundate all Asia: the dream indicates that her child will be king over the whole continent (I. 107). Cyrus dreams that Darius has wings on his shoulders and with them covers Europe and Asia, again a dream that indicates the enormous rule he shall have as

Persian king (I. 209). Like oracles, dreams come true: when Cambyses dreams that his brother Smerdis sits on his throne he executes him, unaware that a usurper who has the same name will take the throne (III. 64). In this type of dream the dreamer is alarmed and takes precautions based on his own or his experts' interpretation, but to no avail. Another type of dream urges a particular course of action, as when Xerxes is commanded to invade Greece (VII. 12ff.). This one is particularly notable in that the dream's purpose is to order the king not to try to avert 'that which must happen' (VII. 17).

Such a phrase suggests that Herodotus has some notion of a pre-existing divine ordinance, which for convenience we usually call 'fate'. Several times he explains that a character was 'doomed to a bad end', but in some cases this is the mark of a story-teller, pointing out for the audience the decisive moment, or fixing their attention on a fatal choice.[44] Yet in other cases, Herodotus certainly seems to have a notion of some pre-existing ordinance. When Apollo defends himself to Croesus, the god says that 'he had been unable to divert the course of destiny' (I. 91), a remark in keeping with the abilities of the gods as we see them in contemporary and earlier Greek literature: for although they manoeuvre and manipulate as best they can for humans they favour, the gods too, in the end, are beholden to fate and must yield to it. None the less, Herodotus allows an active role to gods and heroes, even if he avoids describing them within the narrative. When a violent storm destroys many Persian ships off Euboea, Herodotus comments that 'God was indeed doing everything possible to reduce the superiority of the Persian fleet and bring it down to the size of the Greek' (VIII. 13), a remark that reminds us of the jealous god who brings down those who become too great. When the Persians try to attack Delphi (VIII. 37) the weapons from the temple mysteriously appear outside it and the attacking Persians are struck by thunderbolts as a voice within is heard. Demaratus and Dicaeus see a mysterious cloud of dust from Eleusis, which indicates divine help coming to the Greeks (VIII. 65). In the battles themselves, Herodotus reports the stories of eyewitnesses who claimed that men of superhuman size – heroes – were assisting them. While Herodotus carefully distances himself from these occurrences by remarks such as 'it is said', he nevertheless includes the incidents and does nothing to lessen their credibility. His mixture of caution and belief in divine matters is neatly summed up in a remark he makes to explain why the bodies of none of the Persians who fell at Plataea were found in Demeter's sanctuary: 'My own view is – if one may have views at all about divine matters – that the Goddess herself would not let them in, because they had burnt her sanctuary at Eleusis' (IX. 65).[45]

It would, however, be a serious error to suggest that Herodotus has no sense of human choice. The vast majority of actions taken in his narrative are decided without divine intervention and with wholly human motives. Herodotus has been criticized for writing 'too theological' a history; perhaps so, to modern taste. But this level of religious explanation, and even the employment of 'fate', does not replace or cancel out human explanation and motivation. Rather, it parallels it, by furnishing the larger perspective within which human actions with their purely human motivations – fear, greed, desire, bravery, obedience to custom, love of glory – find their place. The greed of Cyrus in his urge to conquer the Massagetae explains his campaign against them, but it cannot explain why empires rise and fall, why human prosperity never abides long in the same place, why man, in Solon's words, is completely a creature of chance. Only a larger perspective can suggest answers to these profound questions.[46]

Finally, a word about narrative manner. In Herodotus, more than any other ancient historian, one finds a prominent use of the first person, and a narrator by no means reticent. The historian comments on himself and his findings, explains the structure of his composition, and directs the reader's attention and judgement to matters he deems important. By contrast, later historians (and their modern descendants) with few exceptions write primarily third-person narratives, and a historian such as Thucydides goes to great lengths to conceal his authorial presence.[47] Not so Herodotus. As the writer of the first prose work of such enormous size, he gave order and structure to the narrative not least by maintaining his own presence throughout it. To be sure, it is more pronounced in some places than in others, but it is never far from the surface.[48]

Despite this presence, the greater part of Herodotus' work employs imitation (*mimesis*): characters are presented to us as they act. This is a legacy from Homer. So too is the use of direct speech, by which characters defend their actions, reveal their intentions and motivate others to act. Unlike the speeches in Homer, however, which can be quite lengthy, Herodotus' speeches are usually short and dramatic. For most, if not all, of these speeches, it was Herodotus himself who invented the words and gave the structure. No doubt he was guided by intuition and imagination, by placing himself in the situation and reproducing what his characters 'must have said'. When he records speeches of a more public nature, he may have had more information on the gist of what was actually said. But even if he did, here too the structure and the actual words are those of Herodotus himself. These speeches mark one of the great differences between ancient and modern historiography, and yet they were a natural consequence of Herodotus' desire to do in prose what Homer had done in poetry.[49]

5. HERODOTUS' LATER REPUTATION

Herodotus' work was an immediate success, and its influence is already discernible in the next century. It was recopied through the ages and at some point it was divided into the nine books that appear in our editions. (Each of the books was given the name of one of the nine Muses.) Herodotus was for the ancients as well as for us the 'father of history', and he and Thucydides were considered by later Greeks and Romans to be the founders and best practitioners of the genre of history, the appropriate models to be emulated and imitated. But whereas Thucydides was rarely criticized in antiquity, no historian (except perhaps the dyspeptic Timaeus) was more censured than Herodotus. These criticisms took many forms: charges of inaccuracy, of bias, of telling tall tales and of general dishonesty.

Criticism began early: Thucydides uses two errors of Herodotus' as evidence that the majority of people spend little energy in investigating the past (I. 20). Thucydides did not name Herodotus; that was left for later writers. Most famous (or perhaps infamous) was Ctesias of Cnidus, who was court physician to the Persian king Artaxerxes II and who claimed to have used his position at court to study Persian records and correct Herodotus. His work (which does not survive) is summarized by a later reader in this way: 'in his Books VII–XIII, he goes through the events of the reigns of Cyrus and Cambyses and the Magus, and of Darius and Xerxes, writing things opposed to Herodotus on nearly every matter, refuting him as a liar in many things, and calling him a fable-monger (*logopoios*) as well.'[50] The tall tales – gold-digging ants, dog-headed men, people who never dream – were a common point of attack by later writers, who ignored Herodotus' careful withholding of his own belief when reporting such matters. After Thucydides, who was reserved in his treatment of marvels and generally confined his work to politics and war, Herodotus' approach seemed unserious by comparison. Yet there was often a certain hypocrisy in the complaints of later writers, since many of them, Ctesias included, had a love for the fabulous and went far beyond Herodotus in their stories of marvels and natural wonders.[51]

A different type of criticism may be seen in the essay *On the Malice of Herodotus* by the first-century CE biographer Plutarch.[52] In this work Herodotus is accused of slander, spite, partiality for the barbarian and general maliciousness. Plutarch's main concern is with Herodotus' treatment of the Persian Wars but he finds fault with the entire history, underlining what he sees to be Herodotus' prejudice and errors. Despite the fact that Plutarch cites much useful evidence, his account, with few exceptions, has nothing to add to Herodotus. This work, nevertheless, and the copious criticisms served up throughout antiquity, merely remind us of Herodotus' popularity and the fact that for all the criticism his work was read and debated, and no one ever replaced him.

In modern times, too, Herodotus' credibility has been questioned, but in a different way. Archaeology has given us new evidence for the cultures of Egypt and the Ancient Near East, which can then be used to test Herodotus' narrative. Early in the twentieth century doubts were raised that Herodotus ever went to Egypt, and more recently some have suspected that he never travelled anywhere at all. Detlev Fehling has argued in a wide-ranging study that Herodotus' source-citations ('the Persians say', 'the Spartans say'), which most scholars assume to be a report of a genuine native tradition, were invariably invented by Herodotus himself, who adorned his tale with the devices of a story-teller to give it greater credence. In his view, Herodotus is more a writer of fiction than of history. Working in a different way, O. K. Armayor has argued that Herodotus' presentation of foreign marvels and exotic peoples owes more to Greek influences – his predecessors such as Hecataeus and his literary models such as Homer – than it does to any serious research on his part into the real world of the Ancient Near East. And pursuing yet a third line of inquiry, François Hartog has claimed that Herodotus' account of the Scythians in Book IV is an idealized 'other', constructed by Herodotus as an opposite pole to his own Greek world of the city-state with its notions of permanence and fixity.

These works have predictably called forward an array of counter-arguments designed to show that Herodotus is an historian in our sense of the word, not a writer of fiction. One must observe, for example, that some evidence from the Near East or Greek sources supports Herodotus, and in some cases he is more reliable than later historians, who claimed to have access to more reliable traditions and sought to correct him. Unfortunately, both sides in the debate have painted with rather broad brushes, and have simplified what are complex issues of narrative and identity. Even so, it may be worthwhile to note that Fehling has identified a number of features of Herodotus' work that must raise some important questions about his work. For example, he demonstrates that Herodotus' source-citations follow predictable rules, and that they often occur just where the question of 'native' tradition is most problematic, when, for example, it is the Lydians who relate the story of Croesus saved on the pyre (I. 87) or the Persians, who report on Xerxes' dream (VII. 12) when he decides to invade Greece. Fehling has also pointed out that numbers in Herodotus follow certain patterns, and that certain numbers, such as 10, 30 and 300, may be called 'typical numbers'. Even if one does not follow Fehling in his particular interpretation of these phenomena, one must acknowledge that the phenomena are there, and they must at the very least give pause when we try to evaluate what Herodotus was doing.[53]

Some scholars have pointed to the importance of the fact that Herodotus was working in an oral tradition. The study of oral, or largely oral, societies by modern anthropologists has opened up a new world of possibilities and problems. The nature of oral tradition – the ways in which oral societies preserve, hand down and modify their traditions – is seen to be very different from that of written tradition. Assumptions that we make as members of a society where writing is an everyday part of life may be invalid when applied to the very different cultures of the ancient world. Those things that we find unusual in the traditions reported by Herodotus may owe much to the fact that they were preserved without the aid of writing. Moreover, it has come to be seen that the interaction between an inquirer and his source is not simple and straightforward but is conditioned by and dependent on the cultural presuppositions of both sides. Inquiry, it seems, is not a simple matter of asking questions and getting answers.[54] Yet explanation by recourse to oral tradition will not answer all of our questions, since oral societies, too, have clear notions of what is true and false. There is no reason to doubt that the question of Herodotus' reliability will continue to exercise scholars, and one expects that new studies with greater sophistication and nuance will be brought to the debate in the future.

Such studies should help us to arrive at a fairer estimation of Herodotus and his achievement. In the past he has too often suffered from inappropriate comparisons with his successor Thucydides and with modern notions of how history should be written. If, however, we eliminate these preconceptions and expectations, we may be better able to see Herodotus as a complex writer, who viewed the past not exclusively through the narrow prism of wars and politics, but in the variety and richness of what human beings had sought to achieve.[55] Of course, we are not the Greeks and Herodotus' world is not our world. And yet, as with any great writer, it is possible to enter that world, helped by the inclusiveness of the author's vision and the wide compass of his humanity. Herodotus called the deeds narrated in his history 'great and worthy of wonder': it is a description that just as easily applies to the historian himself. For he did nothing less than attempt to fashion for his contemporaries (and, in a different way, for those who still read him) a portrait of themselves and of others, and of the vast world, both physical and metaphysical, within which their actions take place.

NOTES

1. On the fictional lives of poets see M. Lefkowitz, *The Lives of the Greek Poets* (London and Baltimore 1981).
2. For H.'s life see HW i. 1–4; Evans (1982) 2–15; Gould 17–18; Myres 1–16; T. S. Brown, *Ancient World* 17 (1988) 3–15, 17–28, 67–75.
3. See Plut. *Mal. Her.* 26, 31; Dio Chrysostom, *Oration* 37 for the traditions mentioned; on bias as crucial in determining truth for ancient historians and critics, see Woodman, *passim*, esp. ch. 2; Marincola 158–74.
4. On H. and Sophocles see HW i. 7; S. West, 'Sophocles' *Antigone* and Herodotus Book III', in J. Griffin, ed., *Sophocles Revisited. Essays . . . H. Lloyd–Jones* (Oxford 1999) 109–36. Explicit praise of Athens: VII. 139; see also the speeches given to the Athenians at VIII. 143–4. Implicit assumptions: see H.'s remarks about the Aeginetans, Thebans and Corinthians: VII. n. 68, VIII. n. 33, IX. nn. 30, 34; the Alcmaeonids: HW i. 42, but this has been demolished by Fornara (1971) ch. III and Thomas 264–72. See also J. A. S. Evans, 'H. and Athens: the Evidence of the Encomium', *Ant. Class.* 48 (1979) 112–18.
5. On H.'s audience see S. Flory, 'Who Read H.'s *Histories*?', *AJP* 101 (1980) 12–28; Evans (1991) 94–104; cf. A. Momigliano, 'The Historians of the Classical World and their Audiences: Some Suggestions', *Sesto contributo alla storia degli studi classici e del mondo antico* (Rome 1980) 361–76.

6. On the oral society of Greece in H.'s day see R. Thomas, *Literacy and Orality in Ancient Greece* (Cambridge 1992) *passim*, esp. chs 5 and 6.

7. The second-century CE writer Lucian specifically says (*Hdt.* 1) that H. performed his *Histories* at the Olympic Games in order to get them known as quickly as possible, but the value of this testimony is small.

8. On wisdom contests and the performances of intellectuals, see G. E. R. Lloyd, *The Revolutions of Wisdom* (Berkeley and London 1987) ch. 2; on this milieu as important for H., see R. Thomas, 'Performance and Written Publication in H. and the Sophistic Generation', in: *Vermittlung und Tradierung von Wissen in der griechischen Kultur*, ed. W. Kullmann and J. Althoff (Tübingen 1993) 225–44. On symposia, see below, n. 29.

9. On the composition and genesis of the work there are many theories. Jacoby believed that H. developed from a geographer and ethnographer into a historian (in our sense of the word), and he equated the development of Greek historiography with H.'s maturation. For a similar developmental view see Fornara (1971); cf. K. von Fritz, 'H. and the Growth of Greek Historiography', *TAPA* 67 (1936) 315–40. For a summary of different theories see Myres 20–31. R. Lattimore, 'The Composition of the "History" of H.', *CP* 53 (1958) 9–21 assumes that our text of H. was written straight through from beginning to end without revisions. On the ending of the *Histories*, see the Notes to Book IX below, pp. 681–2.

10. A sample of the various arguments may be found in: Evans (1982) 15–18; id., 'Herodotus' Publication Date', *Athenaeum* 57 (1979) 145–9; C. W. Fornara, 'Evidence for the Date of Herodotus' Publication', *JHS* 91 (1971) 25–34; id., 'Herodotus' Knowledge of the Archidamian War', *Hermes* 109 (1981) 149–56. Evans (1991) 89–90 argues that our notions of publication are anachronistic.

11. On the influence of the Peloponnesian War on H. see Fornara (1971) *passim*.

12. The word's original meaning lives on in our 'natural history' which means the inquiry into nature.

13. See Immerwahr (1960). The Greek word *ergon* can mean both 'work' and 'deed'.

14. On ethnography as a genre, see Drews 37–9; Fornara (1983) 12–16. For arguments that the border between ethnography and history was fluid, see Fowler 62–9; J. Marincola, 'Genre, Convention, and Innovation in Greco-Roman Historiography', in C.S. Kraus, ed., *The Limits of Historiography* (Leiden 1999) 281–324.

15. On H.'s use of ethnography see Redfield; Lateiner 145–62; Gould 86–109.

16. The Lydians, for example, whose 'way of life is not unlike the Greek' (I. 94), are passed over in a few sentences.

17. On previous Greek treatments of Egypt see Lloyd i. 120–40. On H. and Egypt see Fornara (1971) ch. 2; T. S. Brown, *The Ancient World* 17 (1988) 77–98; on H. and Scythia see Hartog. On Greek attempts at self-definition see Cartledge (1993) ch. 3.

18. On geography in H. see Myres 32–43; for character and climate see Redfield 109–14, and the final story of the work, IX. 122 with n. *Airs, Waters, Places* can be found in *Hippocratic Writings*, ed. G. E. R. Lloyd (Harmondsworth 1970) 148–69.

19. For H. as heir to Ionian storytelling see Murray (1987); on folktales see W. Aly, *Volksmärchen, Sage und Novelle bei Herodot und seinen Zeitgenossen* (Göttingen 1921), and more generally S. Thompson, *The Folktale*; good remarks in Gould 32–9; cf. Flory 151–8 on anecdotal treatment of events.

20. For more on H.'s posthumous reputation see below, §5.

21. On Homer and historiography see H. Strasburger, *Homer und die Geschichtsschreibung* (Heidelberg 1972); G. Huxley, *Herodotos and the Epic* (Athens 1989). There is no full treatment in English of Homer's influence on H.; see the remarks in Fornara (1983) 31–2, 96–7; Gould 75–8, 119–20; Woodman 1–4; on H. as bestower of praise, G. Nagy, 'H. the *Logios*', *Arethusa* 20 (1987) 175–84; on Homer and other influences, J. Griffin, 'Die Ursprünge der Historien Herodots', in: *Memoria Rerum Veterum. Neue Beiträge z. Antiken Historiographie und Alten Geschichte. Festschrift . . . C. J. Classen*, ed. W. Ax (Stuttgart 1990) 51–82.

22. On the contrast between Greek/free and barbarian/slave in H. see Cartledge (1993) 143–5; see also Redfield 113–14.

23. Waters (1971) maintains that H. portrayed autocrats without obvious moralizing; but cf. Lateiner 181–5.

24. On the ancient tradition see Fornara (1983) 16–20. On H.'s predecessors see Brown ch. 1; Pearson *passim*; Drews 20–44; on Hecataeus see Drews 11–19; Pearson 25–108.

25. We have the opening words of this work and they reveal something of the author's confidence and method: 'Hecataeus of Miletus speaks thus: I write what follows as it seems to me to be true; for the stories of the Greeks are various and, as is manifest to me, ridiculous.' H. echoes these words at IV. 36 where he criticizes Hecataeus and others.

26. There is no evidence that Hecataeus gave an area's history, but this cannot be certain, because the majority of the fragments of his work that survive come from a late geographical lexicon.

27. On Hecataeus, see Brown ch. 1; West (1991).

28. On these writers, see Brown ch. 1; Fowler 62–9.

29. On historical epic see E. L. Bowie, 'Early Greek Elegy, Symposium, and Public Festival', *JHS* 106 (1986) 13–35; id., 'Ancestors of Historiography in Early Greek Elegiac and Iambic Poetry?', in Luraghi 45–66. For a text, translation and numerous essays on Simonides' Persian War poems, see D. Boedeker and D. Sider, eds., *The New Simonides: Contexts of Praise and Desire* (New York and Oxford 2001).

30. On H.'s historical methodology see Momigliano 211–20; H. Verdin, *De historisch-kritische Methode van Herodotus* (Brussels 1971); Lateiner; id., 'The Empirical Element in the Methods of Early Greek Medical Writers and Herodotus: A Shared Epistemological Response', *Antichthon* 20 (1986) 1–20; D. Müller, 'Herodot – Vater des Empirismus? Mensch und Erkenntnis im Denken Herodots', in: *Gnomosyne: Festschrift für Walter Marg* (Munich 1981) 299–318; G. Schepens, *L' 'autopsie' dans la méthode des historiens grecs du Ve siècle* (Brussels 1980); A. Corcella, *Erodoto e l'Analogia* (Palermo 1984); brief studies may be found in Lloyd i. 81–9; Gould 19–41.

31. See the important article of N. Luraghi, 'Local Knowledge in Herodotus' *Histories*', in Luraghi 138–61. See also below, §5, on the question of Herodotus' reliability.

32. Such qualifiers are limited to foreign nations.

33. On H.'s sources in general see Waters (1985) 76–95; Evans (1991) 107–13; Lateiner 91–108 (including list of H.'s disagreements with explicitly named sources); Gould 19–41; for attempts to define them more specifically see Lloyd i. 77–140 (on Egypt); Lewis (1984), (1985) and Murray (1987) 108–15 (on Persia and the east). And see next note.

34. It is rare that H. explicitly names individuals as sources for special accounts. In four passages he claims to have met sources himself: the priestesses Promeneia, Timarete and Nicandra at the oracle of Dodona (II. 55); the Spartan Archias who gave H. information about his grandfather who had fought against Samos (III. 55); Tymnes, an agent of Ariapithes, who gave him information about the Scythian Anacharsis (IV. 76); and Thersander, who gave H. details of a banquet of Thebans and Persians before Plataea (IX. 16). H. names individuals at VI. 117 and VIII. 65, who recount marvellous incidents that befell them in battle or elsewhere, but he does not claim to have met them. Scholars have proposed other individual sources for H., for example Demaratus, the exiled Spartan king, and Zopyrus, a deserter from Persia who was the grandson of the Zopyrus who helped Darius conquer Babylon (III. 160), but this must remain conjecture, and one must wonder why, if these were sources, H. failed to name them. Sometimes conjectures

have more certainty: H.'s treatment of the Halicarnassian queen Artemisia must certainly depend on the native tradition of H.'s own city.

35. For a list of variant versions in H. see Lateiner 76–90.

36. A. Momigliano, *Studies in Historiography* (London and New York 1966) 129–30.

37. There are numerous studies of the structure of H.'s work: see Myres 89–134; Immerwahr ch. 3; Waters (1985) ch. 5; H. Wood, *The Histories of H.* (The Hague 1972). J. Cobet, *Herodots Exkurse und die Frage der Einheit seines Werkes* (Wiesbaden 1971) is fundamental on the digressions and their contribution to the structure of the whole. For the reader's assistance, I have included a Structural Outline in this edition.

38. On retribution see Gould 89–92; Harrison 102–21.

39. Solon's words are quoted at *Ath. Pol.* 12. 2: 'For excess (*koros*) breeds insolence (*hybris*), when great prosperity comes to those who are of unsound mind.'

40. See Lateiner ch. 6.

41. See H. Bischoff, *Der Warner bei Herodot* (diss. Marburg 1932); R. Lattimore, 'The Wise Adviser in H.', *CP* 34 (1939) 24–35.

42. In his discussion of Greek and Egyptian gods, H. says: 'I am not anxious to repeat what I was told about the Egyptian religion . . . for I do not think that any one nation knows much more about such things than any other' (II. 3). But relative ignorance does not mean that the gods do not take part somehow in human history.

43. On oracles in H. see Harrison 122–57; cf. F. Hartog, 'Myth into *Logos*: the Case of Croesus or the Historian at Work', in R. Buxton, ed., *From Myth to Reason?* (Oxford 1999) 183–95, esp. 188–90, for the suggestion that the oracles in H. serve something of the same function as the divine epiphanies of Homer. On the consultation of oracles in general see R. Parker, 'Greek States and Greek Oracles', in P. Cartledge and F. Harvey, eds., *CRUX. Essays . . . G. E. M. de Ste Croix* (London 1985) 298–326.

44. Candaules, I. 8; Apries, II. 61; Scylas, IV. 79; Artaÿnte, IX. 109. For this type of narrative technique in H. see Gould 67–76.

45. For H.'s notions of fate and destiny, see Harrison 223–42.

46. For the parallel systems of explanation see Gould 63–85.

47. For the different narrative techniques of H. and his successors see Marincola 8–11, but cf. 95–117.

48. See Dewald (1987); C. Darbo-Peschanski, *Le discours du particulier* (Paris 1987); A. Beltrametti, *Erodoto. Una storia governata dal discorso* (Florence 1986).

49. On the speeches in H. see R. Heni, *Die Gespräche bei Herodot* (diss. Heidelberg 1976); Lateiner 19–26; on speeches in Greek historiography in general see F. W. Walbank, 'Speeches in Greek Historians', in: *Selected Papers* (Cambridge 1985) 242–62. H.'s technique of dramatization also owes something to Athenian drama: see J. L. Myres, 'H. the Tragedian', in: *A Miscellany Presented to J. L. Mackay* (Liverpool 1914) 88–96; K. Waters, 'The Purpose of Dramatisation in H.', *Historia* 15 (1966) 157–71.

50. T 8 (Jacoby) = Photius, *Bibliotheca* 72 p. 35 b 35.

51. On H.'s later reputation see K.-A. Riemann, *Das herodoteische Geschichtswerk in der Antike* (Munich 1967); O. Murray, 'Herodotus and Hellenistic Culture', *CQ* 22 (1972) 200–213; J. Evans, 'Father of History or Father of Lies: the reputation of H.', *CJ* 64 (1968) 11–17; Momigliano 127–42; id., *The Classical Foundations of Modern Historiography* (Berkeley and London 1991) ch. 2.

52. On Plutarch's work there is now the full commentary of Bowen.

53. One may follow the debate in Fehling, *passim*. On archaeology and H. see O. K. Armayor, 'Did H. Ever Go to Egypt?', *Journal of the American Research Center in Egypt* 15 (1978) 59–73; id., 'Sesostris and H.'s Autopsy of Thrace, Colchis, Inland Asia Minor, and the Levant', *HSCP* 84 (1980) 51–74; and his other works cited at II n. 82. For H.'s portrait of the Scythians see Hartog, *passim*. The most strident opponent of what he calls (inaccurately) the 'Liar School' of H. is Pritchett (1993), but this work must be used with caution. There are useful remarks on the debate in Fowler 80–86.

54. For H. and oral tradition in general see Murray (1987); repr. in Luraghi 16–44; id., 'H. and Oral History Reconsidered', in Luraghi 314–25; Evans (1991) 89–146; Gould 27–41. For the application to individual cases see Evans (1991) 110–14; Thomas 161–73, 238–82; H. I. Flower, 'H. and Delphic Traditions about Croesus', in: *Georgica. Studies ... G. L. Cawkwell*, ed. M. Flower and M. Toher (London 1991) 57–77. On the effect of the inquirer on the act of inquiry see the brief remarks in Redfield 97–101; Evans (1991) 132–46.

55. It is worthwhile mentioning that because of his wider interests in human beings, H. (unlike most other ancient historians) has much to say about women: see Dewald (1981); Sancisi-Weerdenburg; Cartledge (1993) 76–86.

Further Reading

Superscript numbers indicate the edition of the work.

1. BIBLIOGRAPHIC SURVEYS OF WORK ON HERODOTUS

L. Bergson, 'Herodotus 1937–1960', *Lustrum* 11 (1966) 71–138

P. MacKendrick, 'Herodotus, 1954–1963', *Classical World* 56 (1963) 269–75

——, 'Herodotus, 1963–1969', *Classical World* 63 (1969) 37–44

F. Hampl, 'Herodot: Ein kritischer Forschungsbericht nach methodischen Gesichtspunkten', *Grazer Beiträge* 4 (1975) 97–136

H. Verdin, 'Hérodot Historien? Quelques interprétations récentes', *L'Antiquité Classique* 44 (1975) 668–85

C. Dewald and J. Marincola, 'A Selective Introduction to Herodotean Studies', *Arethusa* 20 (1987) 9–40

F. Bubel, *Herodot-Bibliographie 1980–88* (Hildesheim 1991)

2. TEXTS AND COMMENTARIES

The standard Greek text of Herodotus is that of C. Hude, *Herodoti Historiae*, 2 vols (Oxford ³1927). A new Teubner text by H. B. Rosén is now complete: the first volume, containing Books I–IV, was published in 1987, the second in 1995.

The only complete commentary in English on Herodotus is still that of W. W. How and J. Wells, *A Commentary on Herodotus*, 2 vols (Oxford 1913, repr. with corrections 1928), now in many ways out of date. A complete French commentary may be found in the Budé series, 11 vols, one for each Book, together with the valuable *Introduction* volume by Ph.-E. Legrand (Paris ³1966) and the *Index analytique des neuf volumes* (²1966).

For commentaries on individual Books, the English reader is fortunate to have the comprehensive work of A. B. Lloyd on Book II (see §4 below). An ongoing Italian series published by Arnaldo Mondadore under the aegis of the Fondazione Lorenzo Valla will provide the most thorough and up-to-date treatment of Herodotus (an English translation of Books I–IV is forthcoming). In this series the commentaries by David Asheri on Books I and III are without peer: *Erodoto. Le Storie. Libro I. La Lidia e la Persia* (Milan 1989) and *Libro III. La Persia* (Milan 1991). There is also much of value in A. Corcella, *Libro IV. La Scizia e la Libia* (Milan 1993) and G. Nenci, *Libro VI. La Battaglia di Maratone* (1999). The other volumes already published in the series are those by A. Masaracchia for Books VIII and IX: *Libro VIII. La Battaglia di Salamina* (Milan 1977) and *Libro IX. La Sconfitta dei Persiani* (Milan 1979). For Books IV–IX there is the still acute work of R. W. Macan (below, §4). For Book IX see the commentary of M. Flower and J. Marincola, *Herodotus: Histories Book IX* (Cambridge 2002), the first in a new series promised by Cambridge University Press.

3. GENERAL TREATMENTS

The work of F. Jacoby (below, §4) is still fundamental and can be consulted with profit on nearly every aspect of Herodotus' life and work. The best introduction to Herodotus is that of D. Asheri in his commentary on Book I (cited above, §2), pp. ix–lxix (in Italian). See also M. Pohlenz, *Herodot. Der erste Geschichtsschreiber des Abendlandes* (Leipzig 1937; repr. Stuttgart 1961). Evans (1982) packs much information into its small compass and is valuable for its summary of individual books. Gould's study is particularly noteworthy because it brings a new sophistication to the analysis of Herodotus and tries to tie together the many aspects of Herodotus' work into an intelligible whole. J. Romm's *Herodotus* (New Haven and London 1998), which emphasizes the literary side of H.'s work, makes a nice complement to Gould's study. Other introductions include Waters (1985); and S. Stambler, 'Herodotus' in T. J. Luce, ed., *Ancient Writers* (New York 1982), vol. I, pp. 209–32.

For works on individual aspects of Herodotus, see notes to the Introduction.

4. WORKS FREQUENTLY CITED IN THE INTRODUCTION AND NOTES

A. Andrewes, *The Greek Tyrants* (London 1956)

O. K. Armayor (cited as 1978a), 'Did Herodotus Ever Go to the Black Sea?', *Harvard Studies in Classical Philology* 82 (1978) 45–62

—— (cited as 1978b), 'Herodotus' Catalogue of the Persian Empire in Light of the Monuments and the Greek Literary Tradition', *Transactions and Proceedings of the American Philological Association* 108 (1978) 1–9

M. M. Austin, *Greece and Egypt in the Archaic Age* (Cambridge 1970)

—— 'Greek Tyrants and the Persians, 546–479 BC', *Classical Quarterly* 40 (1990) 289–306

S. Benardete, *Herodotean Inquiries* (The Hague 1969)

John Boardman, *The Greeks Overseas. Their Early Colonies and Trade* (London and New York, 4th ed., 1999)

A. J. Bowen, *Plutarch: The Malice of Herodotus* (Warminster 1992)

P. Briant, *Histoire de L'empire Perse. De Cyrus à Alexandre* (Paris 1996)

T. S. Brown, *The Greek Historians* (Lexington, Mass. 1973)

W. Burkert, *Greek Religion. Archaic and Classical*, trans. J. Raffan (Oxford and Cambridge, Mass. 1985)

A. R. Burn, *Persia and the Greeks* (London 1962); repr. with a postscript by D.M. Lewis (London 1984)

S. Burstein, *Graeco-Africana: Studies in the History of Greek*

Relations with Egypt and Nubia (New Rochelle, NY 1995)

P. Cartledge, *Sparta and Lakonia* (London 1979)

—— *The Greeks. A Portrait of Self and Others* (Oxford and New York 1993)

J. M. Cook, *The Persian Empire* (London 1987)

N. Demand, *Thebes in the Fifth Century* (London and Boston 1982)

C. Dewald, 'Women and Culture in Herodotus' *Histories*', in: *Reflections on Women in Antiquity*, ed. H. Foley (New York 1981) 91–125

—— 'Narrative Surface and Authorial Voice in Herodotus' *Histories*', *Arethusa* 20 (1987) 147–70

R. Drews, *The Greek Accounts of Eastern History* (Cambridge, Mass. 1973)

J. A. S. Evans, *Herodotus* (Boston 1982)

—— *Herodotus. Explorer of the Past* (Princeton 1991)

D. Fehling, *Herodotus and his 'Sources'* (Leeds 1989), an expanded translation by J. G. Howie of *Die Quellenangaben bei Herodot. Studien zur Erzählkunst Herodots* (Berlin and New York 1971)

S. Flory, *The Archaic Smile of Herodotus* (Detroit 1987)

Charles W. Fornara, *Herodotus. An Interpretative Essay* (Oxford 1971)

—— *The Nature of History in Ancient Greece and Rome* (Berkeley, Calif. and London 1983)

W. G. Forrest, *The Emergence of Greek Democracy 800–400 BC* (London and New York 1966)

—— *A History of Sparta 950–192 BC* (London and New York 1968)

R. Fowler, 'Herodotus and his Contemporaries', *JHS* 116 (1996) 62–87

R. Frye, *The History of Ancient Iran* (Munich 1984)

J. Gould, *Herodotus* (London 1989)

T. Harrison, *Divinity and History: The Religion of Herodotus* (Oxford 2000)

F. Hartog, *The Mirror of Herodotus* (Berkeley and London

1988), translation by J. Lloyd of *Le Miroir d'Hérodote* (Paris 1980)

C. Hignett, *A History of the Athenian Constitution* (Oxford 1952)

—— *Xerxes' Invasion of Greece* (Oxford 1963)

H. Immerwahr, 'Historical Action in Herodotus', *TAPA* 85 (1954) 14–45

—— 'Aspects of Historical Causation in Herodotus', *TAPA* 87 (1956) 241–80

—— '*Ergon*: history as a monument in Herodotus and Thucydides', *American Journal of Philology* 81 (1960) 261–90

—— *Form and Thought in Herodotus* (Cleveland 1966)

F. Jacoby, 'Herodot', *Real-Encyclopädie der classischen Altertumswissenschaft*, Suppl.-Band II (1913) 205–520

A. Kuhrt, *The Ancient Near East, c. 3000–330 BC*, 2 vols (London and New York 1995)

D. Lateiner, *The Historical Method of Herodotus* (Toronto 1989)

R. Lattimore, 'The Wise Advisor in Herodotus', *Classical Philology* 34 (1939) 24–35

J. F. Lazenby, *The Defence of Greece 490–479 BC* (Warminster 1993)

D. Lewis, 'Postscript 1984', in Burn (above) 587–609

—— 'Persians in Herodotus', in: *The Greek Historians. Literature and History. Papers Presented to A. E. Raubitschek* (Saratoga, Calif. 1985) 101–17

A. B. Lloyd, *Herodotus. Book II*, (i) Introduction (Leiden 1975); (ii) Commentary on 1–98 (Leiden 1976); (iii) Commentary on 99–182 (Leiden 1988)

N. Luraghi (ed.), *The Historian's Craft in the Age of Herodotus* (Oxford 2001)

R. W. Macan, *Herodotus: The Fourth, Fifth and Sixth Books*, 2 vols (London 1895; repr. New York 1973)

—— *Herodotus: The Seventh, Eighth and Ninth Books*, 3 vols (London 1908; repr. New York 1973)

D. Macdowell, *Spartan Law* (Edinburgh 1986)

J. Marincola, *Authority and Tradition in Ancient Historiography* (Cambridge 1997)

H. Michell, *Sparta* (Cambridge 1964)

O. Murray, 'Herodotus and Oral History', in: *Achaemenid History Proceedings of the Groningen Achaemenid History Workshop* ii (1987) 93–115

—— *Early Greece* (London and Cambridge, Mass. ²1993)

J. L. Myres, *Herodotus. Father of History* (Oxford 1953)

J. Oates, *Babylon* (London 1979)

A. T. Olmstead, *A History of the Persian Empire* (Chicago 1948)

L. Pearson, *Early Ionian Historians* (Oxford 1939)

J. E. Powell, *The History of Herodotus* (Cambridge 1939)

W. K. Pritchett, 'Some recent critiques on the veracity of Herodotus', in: *Studies in Ancient Greek Topography* IV (Berkeley and Los Angeles, Calif. 1982) 234–85

—— *The Liar School of Herodotus* (Amsterdam 1993)

J. Redfield, 'Herodotus the Tourist', *Classical Philology* 80 (1985) 97–118

P. J. Rhodes, *A Commentary on the Aristotelian Athenaion Politeia* (Oxford 1981)

G. Roux, *Ancient Iraq* (Harmondsworth ³1992)

J. B. Salmon, *Wealthy Corinth* (Oxford 1984)

H. Sancisi-Weerdenburg, 'Exit Atossa: images of women in Greek historiography of Persia', in: *Images of Women in Antiquity*, ed. A. Cameron and A. Kuhrt (London 1983)

R. Sealey, *A History of the Greek City-States 700–338 BC* (Berkeley, Calif. and London 1978)

B. Shimron, *Politics and Belief in Herodotus* (Wiesbaden 1989)

G. Shipley, *A History of Samos 800–188 BC* (Oxford 1988)

R. Thomas, *Oral Tradition and Written Record in Classical Athens* (Cambridge 1989)

—— *Herodotus in Context. Ethnography, Science and the Art of Persuasion* (Cambridge 2000)

R. A. Tomlinson, *Argos and the Argolid* (London and Ithaca, NY 1972)

K. H. Waters, *Herodotus on Tyrants and Despots. A Study in Objectivity* (Wiesbaden 1971)

—— *Herodotos the Historian. His Problems, Methods, and Originality* (London and Norman, Okla. 1985)

S. West, 'Herodotus' Epigraphical Interests', *Classical Quarterly* 35 (1985) 278–305

—— 'Herodotus' Portrait of Hecataeus', *Journal of Hellenic Studies* III (1991) 174–90

A. J. Woodman, *Rhetoric in Classical Historiography* (London and Portland, Ore. 1988)

A Note on the Text

In revising A. de Sélincourt's translation, I have relied mainly on C. Hude's text in the Oxford Classical Texts series (3rd edn., 2 vols.; Oxford, 1927), with occasional consultation of H. B. Rosén's more recent Teubner text (2 vols.; Leipzig and Stuttgart, 1987–97).

Maps

Greece and Western Asia Minor

The Near East and North Africa

The Egyptian Delta

Attica and Environs

Herodotus

The Histories

BOOK ONE

Herodotus of Halicarnassus here displays his inquiry, so that human achievements may not become forgotten in time, and great and marvellous deeds – some displayed by Greeks, some by barbarians – may not be without their glory; and especially to show why the two peoples fought with each other.[1]

Learned Persians put the responsibility for the quarrel on the Phoenicians. These people came originally from the so-called Red Sea;[2] and as soon as they had penetrated to the Mediterranean and settled in the country where they are today, they took to making long trading voyages. Loaded with Egyptian and Assyrian goods, they called at various places along the coast, including Argos, in those days the most important place in the land now called Hellas.[3]

Here in Argos they displayed their wares, and five or six days later when they were nearly sold out, a number of women came down to the beach to see the fair. Amongst these was the king's daughter, whom Greek and Persian writers agree in calling Io, daughter of Inachus. These women were standing about near the vessel's stern, buying what they fancied, when suddenly the Phoenician sailors passed the word along and made a rush at them. The greater number got away; but Io and some others were caught and bundled aboard the ship, which cleared at once and made off for Egypt.

This, according to the Persian account (the Greeks have a different story), was how Io came to Egypt; and this was the first in a series of unjust acts.

Later on some Greeks, whose name the Persians fail to record – they were probably Cretans – put into the Phoenician port of

Tyre and carried off the king's daughter Europa, thus giving them tit for tat.

For the next outrage it was the Greeks again who were responsible. They sailed in an armed merchantman to Aea in Colchis on the river Phasis, and, not content with the regular business which had brought them there, they abducted the king's daughter Medea. The king sent to Greece demanding reparations and his daughter's return; but the only answer he got was that the Greeks had no intention of offering reparation, having received none themselves for the abduction of Io from Argos.[4]

3   The accounts go on to say that some forty or fifty years afterwards Paris, the son of Priam, was inspired by these stories to steal a wife for himself out of Greece, being confident that he would not have to pay for the venture any more than the Greeks had done. And that was how he came to carry off Helen.[5]

The first idea of the Greeks after the rape was to send a demand for satisfaction and for Helen's return. The demand was met by a reference to the seizure of Medea and the injustice of expecting satisfaction from people to whom they themselves had refused it, not to mention the fact that they had kept the girl.

4   Thus far there had been nothing worse than woman-stealing on both sides; but for what happened next the Greeks, they say, were seriously to blame; for it was the Greeks who were, in a military sense, the aggressors. Abducting young women, in their opinion, is not, indeed, a lawful act; but it is stupid after the event to make a fuss about avenging it. The only sensible thing is to take no notice; for it is obvious that no young woman allows herself to be abducted if she does not wish to be. The Asiatics, according to the Persians, took the seizure of the women lightly enough, but not so the Greeks: the Greeks, merely on account of a girl from Sparta, raised a big army, invaded Asia and destroyed the empire of Priam. From that root sprang their belief in the perpetual enmity of the Grecian world towards them – because the Persians claim Asia and the barbarian races dwelling in it as their own, Europe and the Greek states being, in their opinion, quite separate and distinct from them.

Such then is the Persian story. In their view it was the capture 5
of Troy that first made them enemies of the Greeks.

As to Io, the Phoenicians do not accept the Persians' account;
they deny that they took her to Egypt by force. On the contrary,
the girl while she was still in Argos went to bed with the
ship's captain, found herself pregnant, and, ashamed to face her
parents, sailed away voluntarily to escape exposure.

So much for what Persians and Phoenicians say; and I have
no intention of passing judgment on its truth or falsity. I prefer
to rely on my own knowledge, and to point out who it was in
actual fact that first injured the Greeks; then I will proceed with
my history, telling the story as I go along of small cities of men
no less than of great. For most of those which were great once
are small today; and those which used to be small were great in
my own time. Knowing, therefore, that human prosperity never
abides long in the same place, I shall pay attention to both alike.[6]

Croesus of Lydia, son of Alyattes, was tyrant of all the peoples 6
to the west of the river Halys, which runs northward into the
Black Sea and forms the boundary between Cappadocia and
Paphlagonia. He was the first foreigner so far as we know to
come into direct contact with the Greeks, both in the way of
conquest and alliance, forcing tribute from Ionians, Aeolians,
and Asiatic Dorians, and forming a pact of friendship with the
Lacedaemonians. Before Croesus' time all the Greeks had been
free; for the earlier Cimmerian attack on Ionia was not a conquest, but a mere plundering raid.[7]

The sovereignty of Lydia, which had belonged to the Hera- 7
clids, passed into the family of Croesus – the Mermnadae – in
the following way. Candaules, king of Sardis (the Greeks call
him Myrsilus),[8] was descended from Alcaeus, son of Heracles.
His father was Myrsus, and he was the last of the Heraclids to
reign at Sardis, the first being Agron, son of Ninus, grandson of
Belus, and great-grandson of Alcaeus. Before the time of Agron,
the reigning house had been of the family of Lydus, son of Atys:
hence the name 'Lydians', the people being previously known
as Maeonians. These princes turned over the management of
affairs to the Heraclids, the descendants of Heracles and a

slave-girl belonging to Iardanus; the Heraclids later had their power confirmed by an oracle. They reigned for twenty-two generations, a period in all of five hundred and five years, son succeeding father right down the line to Candaules, son of Myrsus.

8   Now Candaules conceived a passion for his own wife, and thought she was the most beautiful woman on earth. So, having in his bodyguard a fellow he particularly liked whose name was Gyges, son of Dascylus, Candaules not only discussed his most important business with him, but even used to make him listen to eulogies of his wife's beauty.

One day the king (who was doomed to a bad end) said to Gyges: 'It appears you don't believe me when I tell you how lovely my wife is. Well, a man always believes his eyes better than his ears; so do as I tell you – contrive to see her naked.'

Gyges gave a cry of horror. 'Master,' he said, 'what an improper suggestion! Do you tell me to look at the queen when she has no clothes on? No, no: "when she takes off her clothing, she does away with her shame" – you know what they say of women. Let us learn from experience. Right and wrong were distinguished long ago – and I'll tell you one thing that is right: a man should mind his own business. I do not doubt that your wife is the most beautiful of women; so for goodness' sake do not ask me to behave contrary to custom.'

9   Thus he did his utmost to decline the king's invitation, because he was afraid of what might happen if he accepted it.

The king, however, told him not to distress himself. 'There is nothing to be afraid of,' he said, 'either from me or my wife. I am not laying a trap for you; and as for her, I promise she will do you no harm. I'll manage so that she doesn't even know that you have seen her. Look: I will hide you behind the open door of our bedroom. My wife will follow me in to bed. Near the door there's a chair – she will put her clothes on it as she takes them off, one by one. You will be able to watch her with perfect ease. Then, while she's walking away from the chair towards the bed with her back to you, slip away through the door – and mind she doesn't catch you.'

10   Gyges, since he was unable to avoid it, consented, and when

bedtime came Candaules brought him to the room. Presently the queen arrived, and Gyges watched her walk in and put her clothes on the chair. Then, just as she had turned her back and was going to bed, he slipped softly out of the room. But the queen saw him.

At once she realized what her husband had done. But she did not betray the shame she felt by screaming, or even let it appear that she had noticed anything. Instead she silently resolved to have her revenge. For with the Lydians, as with most barbarian races, it is thought highly indecent even for a man to be seen naked.[9]

For the moment she kept her mouth shut and did nothing; but at dawn the next morning she sent for Gyges after preparing the most trustworthy of her servants for what was to come. There was nothing unusual in his being asked to attend upon the queen; so Gyges answered the summons without any suspicion that she knew what had occurred on the previous night. 11

'Gyges,' she said, as soon as he presented himself, 'there are two courses open to you, and you may take your choice between them. Kill Candaules and seize the throne, with me as your wife; or die yourself on the spot, so that never again may your blind obedience to the king tempt you to see what you have no right to see. One of you must die; either my husband, the author of this wicked plot; or you, who have outraged propriety by seeing me naked.'

For a time Gyges was too much astonished to speak. At last he found words and begged the queen not to force him to make so difficult a choice. But it was no good; he soon saw that he really was faced with the alternatives, either of murdering his master, or of being murdered himself. He made his choice – to live.

'Tell me,' he said, 'since you drive me against my will to kill the king, how shall we set on him?'

'We will attack him when he is asleep,' was the answer; 'and on the very spot where he showed me to you naked.'

All was made ready for the attempt. The queen would not let 12 Gyges go or give him any chance of escaping the dilemma: either Candaules or he must die. Night came, and he followed her into the bedroom. She put a knife into his hand, and hid him behind the same door as before. Then, when Candaules was asleep, he crept from behind the door and struck.

Thus Gyges usurped the throne and married the queen. This is the Gyges whom Archilochus of Paros mentions as a contemporary in his Satires.[10]

13   Later he had his power confirmed by an oracle from Delphi.[11] The Lydians, indignant at the murder of Candaules, were prepared to fight; however, they managed to agree with the supporters of Gyges that he should continue to reign if the oracle declared that he was really the king; if on the other hand the oracle should declare against him, he should restore the throne to the Heraclids.

The answer of the oracle was in favour of Gyges, so his royal power was established. Nevertheless the Priestess of the Shrine added that the Heraclids would have their revenge on Gyges in the fifth generation: a prophecy to which neither the Lydians nor their kings paid any attention, until it was actually fulfilled.

14   This was the way in which the Mermnadae got rid of the Heraclids and assumed sovereign power. Gyges, as soon as he had made himself supreme, sent a number of presents to the shrine at Delphi; indeed, most of the silver there came from him, and in addition he presented a vast number of vessels of gold of various kinds, the most noteworthy being six golden mixing-bowls. These bowls weigh in all nearly 2500 lb and stand in the Corinthian treasury – though to speak strictly it should not be called the public treasury of the Corinthians, but the treasury of Cypselus, son of Eëtion.

Gyges was the first foreigner we know of, after King Midas of Phrygia, son of Gordias, to dedicate offerings at Delphi. Midas presented the royal throne from which he used to give judgement; it stands with Gyges' bowls, and is well worth seeing.[12]

The Delphians call all this silver and gold which Gyges sent the Gygean Treasure, after the name of the donor.

Once established in power, Gyges sent a military expedition against Miletus and Smyrna and captured the citadel of Colophon. That, however, being his only act of any importance

during a reign of thirty-eight years, I will pass on without further 15
comment and mention his son Ardys who succeeded him.

Ardys took Priene and attacked Miletus; and during his reign
the Cimmerians, driven from their homes by nomadic Scythian
tribes, came to Asia and captured Sardis, except for its citadel.[13]

Next on the throne after Ardys, who reigned forty-nine years, 16
was his son Sadyattes, who reigned twelve years and was succeeded by Alyattes. Alyattes made war on the Medes under
Cyaxares, grandson of Deioces, expelled the Cimmerians from
Asia, captured Smyrna, a city which had been founded by people
from Colophon, and attacked Clazomenae – where he did not
succeed as he hoped, but met with disaster.

Furthermore – to continue the tale of what was most memorable during his reign – Alyattes carried on the war which he had 17
taken over from his father, against the Milesians. His custom
each year was to invade Milesian territory when the crops were
ripe, marching in to the music of pipes, harps, and treble and
tenor oboes. On arrival he never destroyed or burned the houses
in the country, or pulled their doors off, but left them unmolested. He would merely destroy the trees and crops, and then
retire. The reason for this was the Milesian command of the sea,
which made it useless for his army to attempt a regular siege.
The Lydians refrained from demolishing houses in order that
the Milesians, having somewhere to live, might continue to
work the land and sow their seed, with the result that they
themselves would have something to plunder each time they
invaded their country.

They employed this strategy for eleven consecutive years, 18
during which the Milesians suffered two serious defeats, one in
the neighbourhood of Limeneium in their own country, the
other in the plain of the Maeander.

For six out of the eleven years Sadyattes, son of Ardys, who
began the invasion of Milesia and was the originator of the war,
was still on the throne of Lydia; for the five which followed
Alyattes, who, as I have already mentioned, inherited it from
his father, carried it on with all possible energy.[14]

The Milesians received no help from any of the Ionians except
the men of Chios, who fought by their side in payment of a debt

of honour, the Milesians having previously assisted them right through their war against the Erythraeans.

19   In the twelfth year of the fighting, the burning of the crops was the cause of an accident. No sooner had the fire taken hold, than the wind drove the flames on to the temple of Athene at Assesus, which was set alight and burnt down. Nobody bothered much about this at the moment; but on the army's return to Sardis, Alyattes fell ill. For a considerable time he got no better; so either on somebody's advice, or because he thought it the sensible thing to do, he sent to Delphi to inquire of the god about his health. When the messengers arrived, the Priestess of Apollo refused to give an answer until the Lydians had rebuilt Athene's temple, which they had burnt down at Assesus. I know

20   this at first hand, for I heard it from the Delphians; the Milesians, however, have something to add to the story. They say that Periander, son of Cypselus, who was a very close friend of Thrasybulus, tyrant of Miletus at that time, got to know of what the Delphic Priestess had said to Alyattes' messengers, and had thereupon sent to tell Thrasybulus all about it, knowing that to be forewarned is to be forearmed.

21   Now Alyattes, as soon as he received the message from Delphi, sent a herald to Miletus in the hope of concluding a truce until the temple could be rebuilt. Off went the herald – and Thrasybulus, meanwhile, thought of a clever plan. On the strength of the information he had received, he had made a good guess at the line Alyattes was likely to take; so he had all the grain in the city, both from his own and from private stores, collected in the public square, and issued an order that everyone in the town, on a given signal, was to start drinking and revelling.

22   His object was to get the messenger from Sardis to tell Alyattes about the enormous quantity of grain he had seen poured recklessly out in the street, and how the townspeople were enjoying themselves.

This is just what happened. The messenger, having seen the merry-making and delivered his master's message to Thrasybulus, returned to Sardis, and, so far as my information goes, peace was concluded for no other reason than because Alyattes, expecting to find the Milesians reduced to extremities by famine, was told by the herald on his return to Sardis that this was not so: that the Milesians, in fact, were by no means hungry, but very much the reverse.

By the terms of the peace the two peoples afterwards became friends and allies; Alyattes built two temples for Athene at Assesus instead of one, and recovered his health.

This, then, is the story of Alyattes and his war with Thrasybulus and the Milesians.

Periander, who told Thrasybulus about the oracle, was the son of Cypselus, the despot of Corinth. The Corinthians tell of an extraordinary thing that occurred during his life, and the Lesbians confirm the truth of it. It concerns Arion of Methymna, the most distinguished musician of that date, and the man who first, so far as we know, composed and named the dithyramb, and trained choirs to perform it in Corinth. The tale is, that Arion rode on a dolphin's back to Taenarum. Most of his time Arion had spent with Periander, till he felt a longing to sail to Italy and Sicily. This he did; and after making a great deal of money in those countries, he decided to return to Corinth. He sailed from Tarentum in a Corinthian vessel, because he had more confidence in Corinthians than in anyone else. The crew, however, when the ship was at sea, hatched a plot to throw him overboard and steal his money. He got wind of their intention, and begged them to take his money, but spare his life. To no purpose, however; for the sailors told him either to kill himself if he wanted to be buried ashore, or to jump overboard at once.

Arion, seeing they had made up their minds, as a last resort begged permission to stand on the after-deck, dressed in his singing robes, and give them a song; the song over, he promised to kill himself. Delighted at the prospect of hearing a song from the world's most famous singer, the sailors all made their way forward from the stern and assembled amidships. Arion put on his full professional costume, took up his lute and, standing on the afterdeck, played and sang a lively tune. Then he leapt into the sea, just as he was, with all his clothes on.

The ship continued her voyage to Corinth, but a dolphin picked up Arion and carried him on its back to Taenarum. Here Arion landed, and made his way in his singing costume to

23

24

Corinth, where he told the whole story. Periander was not too ready to believe it; so he put Arion under strict supervision, keeping the ship's crew meanwhile carefully in mind. On their return he sent for them, and asked if they had anything to tell him about Arion. 'Oh yes,' they answered, 'we left him safe and sound at Tarentum in Italy.' But no sooner were the words out of their mouths than Arion himself appeared, just as he was when he jumped overboard. This was an unpleasant shock for the sailors. The lie was detected, and further denial useless.

That is the story as the Corinthians and Lesbians tell it. There is, moreover, at Taenarum today an offering of Arion's in the temple, a small bronze figure of a man on a dolphin.[15]

25   After bringing the war with Miletus to an end, Alyattes died, having reigned for fifty-seven years. He was the second of his family to send a present to Delphi, for in return for the recovery of his health he gave a large silver bowl, and a salver of welded iron – the most remarkable of all the offerings at Delphi. It was the work of Glaucus of Chios, the inventor of the art of welding.

26   Alyattes was succeeded by his son Croesus, a man of thirty-five. The first Greek city that Croesus attacked was Ephesus.[16] The Ephesians, when he laid siege to them, ran a rope from their walls to the temple of Artemis, putting the town, by means of this link, under the goddess' protection. The distance between the temple and the old town which was then under siege is just under a mile. Having started with the Ephesians, Croesus subsequently attacked all the Ionian and Aeolian cities in turn on various pretexts, substantial or trivial, according to what ground of complaint he could find against them. He forced all

27   the Asiatic Greeks to pay him tribute, and then turned his attention to ship-building in order to attack the islanders. However, when everything was ready to begin building, something happened which persuaded him to desist. A certain Bias, of Priene – or some say it was Pittacus, a Mytilenaean – came to Sardis, and in answer to Croesus' request for news from Greece, told him that the islanders were raising ten thousand horse to attack him in Sardis.

Croesus took the remark literally, and exclaimed: 'What? The islanders mean to attack the Lydians with cavalry? I only wish they would!'

'Sire,' the man replied, 'I think you are longing to catch the islanders on horseback on the continent. Indeed, you are perfectly justified. But they know your intention of building a fleet to attack them – and what do you think they want more than a chance of catching the Lydians at sea? It would give them their revenge for their brothers on the mainland, whom you have enslaved.'

This way of putting the matter tickled Croesus' fancy. Moreover, it seemed so much to the point, that he abandoned the idea of building a fleet, and formed a treaty of friendship with the Ionian islanders.[17]

In the course of time Croesus subdued all the peoples west of the river Halys, except the Cilicians and Lycians. The rest he kept in subjection – Lydians, Phrygians, Mysians, Mariandynians, Chalybians, Paphlagonians, Thracians (both Thynian and Bithynian), Carians, Ionians, Dorians, Aeolians, and Pamphylians. 28

When all these nations had been added to the Lydian empire, and Sardis was at the height of her wealth and prosperity, all the great Greek teachers of that epoch, one after another, paid visits to the capital. Much the most distinguished of them was Solon the Athenian, the man who at the request of his countrymen had made a code of laws for Athens. He was on his travels at the time, intending to be away ten years, in order to avoid the necessity of repealing any of the laws he had made. That, at any rate, was the real reason of his absence, though he gave it out that what he wanted was just to see the world. The Athenians could not alter any of Solon's laws without him, because they had solemnly sworn to give them a ten years' trial.[18] 29

For this reason, then – and also no doubt for the pleasure of foreign travel – Solon left home and, after a visit to the court of Amasis in Egypt, went to Sardis to see Croesus. 30

Croesus entertained him hospitably in the palace, and three or four days after his arrival instructed some servants to take him on a tour of the royal treasuries and point out the richness and magnificence of everything. When Solon had made as thorough an inspection as opportunity allowed, Croesus said: 'Well, my Athenian friend, I have heard a great deal about your wisdom, and how widely you have travelled in the pursuit of knowledge. I cannot resist my desire to ask you a question: who is the happiest man you have ever seen?'

The point of the question was that Croesus supposed himself to be the happiest of men. Solon, however, refused to flatter, and answered in strict accordance with his view of the truth. 'An Athenian,' he said, 'called Tellus.'

Croesus was taken aback. 'And what,' he asked sharply, 'is your reason for this choice?'

'There are good reasons,' said Solon; 'first, his city was prosperous, and he had fine sons, and lived to see children born to each of them, and all these children surviving; secondly, he had wealth enough by our standards; and he had a glorious death. In a battle with the neighbouring town of Eleusis, he fought for his countrymen, routed the enemy, and died like a brave man; and the Athenians paid him the high honour of a public funeral on the spot where he fell.'

31   All these details about the happiness of Tellus, Solon doubtless intended as a moral lesson for the king; Croesus, however, thinking he would at least be awarded second prize, asked who was the next happiest person whom Solon had seen.

'Two young men of Argos,' was the reply; 'Cleobis and Biton. They had enough to live on comfortably; and their physical strength is proved not merely by their success in athletics, but much more by the following incident. The Argives were celebrating the festival of Hera, and it was most important that the mother of the two young men should drive to the temple in her ox-cart; but it so happened that the oxen were late in coming back from the fields. Her two sons therefore, as there was no time to lose, harnessed themselves to the cart and dragged it along, with their mother inside, for a distance of nearly six miles, until they reached the temple. After this exploit, which was witnessed by the assembled crowd, they had a most enviable death – a heaven-sent proof of how much better it is to be dead than alive. Men kept crowding round them and congratulating them on their strength, and women kept telling the mother how lucky she was to have such sons, when, in sheer pleasure at this public recognition of her sons' act, she prayed the goddess Hera, before whose shrine she stood, to grant Cleobis and Biton, who had brought her such honour, the greatest blessing that can fall to mortal man.

'After her prayer came the ceremonies of sacrifice and feasting; and the two lads, when all was over, fell asleep in the temple – and that was the end of them, for they never woke again.

'The Argives, considering them to be the best of men, had statues made of them, which they sent to Delphi.'

Croesus was vexed with Solon for giving the second prize for happiness to the two young Argives, and snapped out: 'That's all very well, my Athenian friend; but what of my own happiness? Is it so utterly contemptible that you won't even compare me with mere common folk like those you have mentioned?'   32

'Croesus,' replied Solon, 'I know God is envious of human prosperity and likes to trouble us; and you question me about the lot of man. Listen then: as the years lengthen out, there is much both to see and to suffer which one would wish otherwise. Take seventy years as the span of a man's life: those seventy years contain 25,200 days, without counting intercalary months. Add a month every other year, to make the seasons come round with proper regularity, and you will have thirty-five additional months, which will make 1050 additional days. Thus the total of days for your seventy years is 26,250, and not a single one of them is like the next in what it brings. You can see from that, Croesus, that man is entirely a creature of chance. You seem to be very rich, and you rule a numerous people; but the question you asked me I will not answer, until I know that you have died happily. Great wealth can make a man no happier than moderate means, unless he has the luck to continue in prosperity to the end. Many very rich men have been unfortunate, and many with a modest competence have had good luck. The former are better off than the latter in two respects only, whereas the poor but lucky man has the advantage in many ways; for though the rich have the means to satisfy their appetites and to bear calamities, and the poor have not, the poor, if they are lucky, are more likely to keep clear of trouble, and will have besides the blessings of a sound body, health, freedom from trouble, fine children, and good looks.

'Now if a man thus favoured dies as he has lived, he will be just the one you are looking for: the only sort of person who deserves to be called happy. But mark this: until he is dead, keep the word "happy" in reserve. Till then, he is not happy, but only lucky.

'Nobody of course can have all these advantages, any more than a country can produce everything it needs: whatever it has, it is bound to lack something. The best country is the one which has most. It is the same with people: no man is ever self-sufficient – there is sure to be something missing. But whoever has the greatest number of the good things I have mentioned, and keeps them to the end, and dies a peaceful death, that man, Croesus, deserves in my opinion to be called happy.

'Look to the end, no matter what it is you are considering. Often enough God gives a man a glimpse of happiness, and then utterly ruins him.'

33   These sentiments were not of the sort to give Croesus any pleasure; he let Solon go with cold indifference, firmly convinced that he was a fool. For what could be more stupid than to keep telling him to look at the 'end' of everything, without any regard to present prosperity?

34   After Solon's departure nemesis fell upon Croesus, presumably because God was angry with him for supposing himself the happiest of men. It began with a dream he had about a disaster to one of his sons: a dream which came true. He had two sons: one with a physical disability, being deaf and dumb; the other, named Atys, as fine a young man as one can fancy. Croesus dreamt that Atys would be killed by a blow from an iron weapon. He woke from the dream in horror, and lost no time in getting his son a wife, and seeing to it that he no longer took the field with the Lydian soldiers, whom he used to command. He also removed all the weapons – javelins, spears and so on – from the men's rooms, and had them piled up in the women's quarters, because he was afraid that some blade hanging on the wall might fall on Atys' head.

The arrangements for the wedding were well in hand, when 35 there came to Sardis an unfortunate stranger who had been guilty of manslaughter. He was a Phrygian, and related to the Phrygian royal house. This man presented himself at the palace and begged Croesus to cleanse him from blood-guilt according to the laws of the country (the ceremony is much the same in Lydia as in Greece): and Croesus did as he asked. When the formalities were over, Croesus, wishing to know who he was and where he came from, said: 'What is your name, stranger, and what part of Phrygia have you come from, to take refuge with me? What man or woman did you kill?'

'Sire,' the stranger replied, 'I am the son of Gordias, and Midas was my grandfather. My name is Adrastus. I killed my brother by accident, and here I am driven from home by my father and stripped of all I possessed.'

'Your family and mine,' said Croesus, 'are friends. You have come to a friendly house. If you stay in my dominions, you shall have all you need. The best thing for you will be not to take your misfortune too much to heart.' Adrastus, therefore, took 36 up his residence in the palace.

Now it happened just at this time that Mt Olympus in Mysia was infested by a monstrous boar. This tremendous creature used to issue from his mountain lair and play havoc with the crops, and many times the Mysians had taken the field against him, but to no purpose. The unfortunate hunters received more damage than they were able to inflict. As a last resort the Mysians sent to Croesus.

'Sire,' the messengers said, 'a huge beast of a boar has appeared amongst us, and is doing fearful damage. We want to catch him, but we can't. Please, my lord, send us your son with a party of young men, and some dogs, so that we can get rid of the brute.'

Croesus had not forgotten his dream, and in answer to this request forbade any further mention of his son.

'I could not send him,' he said; 'he is just married, and that keeps him busy. But I will certainly send picked men, with a complete hunting outfit, and I will urge them to do all they can to help rid you of the animal.'

37   This answer satisfied the Mysians; but at that moment Atys, who had heard of their request, entered the room. The young man, finding that Croesus persisted in his refusal to let him join the hunting party, said to his father: 'Once honour demanded that I should win fame as a huntsman and fighter; but now, father, though you cannot accuse me of cowardice or lack of spirit, you won't let me take part in either of these admirable pursuits. Think what a figure I must cut when I walk between here and the place of assembly! What will people take me for? What must my young wife think of me? That she hasn't married much of a husband, I fear! Now, father, either let me join this hunt, or give me an intelligible reason why what you're doing is good for me.'

38   'My son,' said Croesus, 'of course you are not a coward or anything unpleasant of that kind. That is not the reason for what I'm doing. The fact is, I dreamt that you had not long to live – that you would be killed by an iron spearpoint. It was that dream that made me hasten your wedding; and the same thing makes me refuse to let you join in this enterprise. As long as I live, I am determined to protect you, and to rob death of his prize. You are my only son, for I do not count that one who is mute, your brother.'

39   'No one can blame you, father,' Atys replied, 'for taking care of me after a dream like that. Nevertheless there is something which you have failed to observe, and it is only right that I should point it out to you. You dreamt that I should be killed by an iron weapon. Very well: has a boar got hands? Can a boar hold this weapon you fear so much? Had you dreamt that I should be killed by a boar's tusk or anything of that sort, your precautions would be justified. But you didn't: it was a spearpoint which was to kill me. Let me go, then. It is only to hunt an animal, not to fight against men.'

40   'My boy,' said Croesus, 'I own myself beaten. You interpret the dream better than I did. I cannot but change my mind, and allow you to join the expedition.'

41   The king then sent for Adrastus the Phrygian, and said to him: 'Weighed down by misfortune, Adrastus, you came to me in great distress. I gave you ritual purification, welcomed you

to my house, and have spared no expense to entertain you. Now
I expect a fair return for my generosity: take charge of my son
on this boar-hunt; protect him from highwaymen and cut-
throats on the road. In any case it is your duty to go where you
can distinguish yourself: your family honour demands it, and
you are a stalwart fellow besides.'

'Sire,' Adrastus answered, 'under ordinary circumstances I   42
should have taken no part in this adventure. A man under a
cloud has no business to associate with those who are luckier
than himself. Indeed I have no heart for it, and there are many
reasons to prevent my going. But your wishes make all the
difference. It is my duty to gratify you in return for your kindness: so I am ready to do as you ask. So far as it lies in my power
to protect your son, you may count on his returning safe and
sound.'

When Adrastus had given his answer, the party set out, men,   43
dogs, and all. They made their way to Olympus and kept their
eyes open for the boar. As soon as they spotted him, they
surrounded him and let fly with spears – and then it was that
the stranger – Adrastus, the very man whom Croesus had
cleansed from the stain of blood – aimed at the boar, missed
him, and struck the king's son. Croesus' dream had come true.

A messenger hurried off to Sardis, and Croesus was told of
the encounter with the boar and the death of his son. The shock   44
of the news was dreadful; and the horror of it was increased by
the fact that the weapon had been thrown by the very man
whom the king had cleansed from the guilt of blood. In the
violence of his grief Croesus prayed to Zeus, calling on him as
God of Purification to witness what he had suffered at the hands
of his guest; he invoked him again under his title of Protector of
the Hearth, because he had unwittingly entertained his son's
murderer in his own house; and yet again as God of Guest-
Friendship, because the man he had sent to guard his son had
turned out to be his bitterest enemy.

Before long the Lydians arrived with the body, followed by   45
the killer. He took his stand in front of the corpse, and stretching
out his hands in an attitude of submission begged the king to
cut his throat there and then upon the dead body of his son.

'My former trouble,' he said, 'was bad enough. But now that I have ruined the man who absolved me of my guilt, I cannot bear to live.'

In spite of his grief Croesus was moved to pity by these words.

'Friend,' he said, 'as you condemn yourself to death, there is nothing more I can require of you. Justice is satisfied. This calamity is not your fault; you never meant to strike the blow, though strike it you did. Some god is to blame – some god who long ago warned me of what was to happen.'

Croesus buried his son with all proper ceremony; and as soon as everything was quiet after the funeral, Adrastus – the son of Gordias, the grandson of Midas: the man who had killed his brother and destroyed the host who gave him purification – convinced that he was the unluckiest of all the men he had ever known, stabbed himself and fell dead upon the tomb.

46   For two years Croesus grieved for the death of his son, until the news from Persia put an end to his mourning: Cyrus, son of Cambyses, had destroyed the empire of Astyages, and the power of Persia was steadily increasing. This gave Croesus food for thought, and he wondered if he might be able to check Persian expansion before it had gone too far. With this purpose in view he at once prepared to try out the oracles, and sent to Delphi, to Abae in Phocis, to Dodona, to the oracles of Amphiaraus and Trophonius, and to Branchidae in Milesia. These were the Greek ones which he consulted, but, not content with them, he sent also to the oracle of Ammon in Libya. His object was to test the knowledge of the oracles, so that if they should prove to be in possession of the truth he might send a second time and ask if he should undertake a campaign against Persia.

47   The Lydians whom Croesus sent to make the test were given the following orders: on the hundredth day, reckoning from the day on which they left Sardis, they were to consult the oracles, and inquire what Croesus, son of Alyattes and king of Lydia, was doing at that moment. The answer of each oracle was to be taken down in writing and brought back to Sardis. No one has recorded the answer of any of the oracles except that of Delphi; here, however, immediately the Lydians entered the shrine for

their consultation, the Priestess gave them, in hexameter verse, the following reply:

> I know the grains of sand on the beach and measure the sea;
> I understand the speech of the dumb and hear the voiceless.
> The smell has come to my sense of a hard-shelled tortoise
> Boiling and bubbling with lamb's flesh in a bronze pot:
> The cauldron underneath is of bronze, and of bronze the lid.

The Lydians took down the Priestess' answer and returned with it to Sardis.   48

When the other messengers came back with the answers they had received, Croesus opened all the rolls and read what they contained. None had the least effect upon him except the one which contained the answer from Delphi. But no sooner had this one been read to him than he accepted it with profound reverence, declaring that the oracle at Delphi was the only genuine one in the world, because it had succeeded in finding out what he had been doing. And indeed it had; for after sending off the messengers, Croesus had thought of something which no one would be likely to guess, and with his own hands, keeping carefully to the prearranged date, had cut up a tortoise and a lamb and boiled them together in a bronze cauldron with a bronze lid.

So much for the answer from Delphi. As to the oracle of Amphiaraus, there is no record of what answer the Lydians received when they had performed the customary rites in the temple; all I can say is, that Croesus believed this oracle too to be in possession of the truth.   49

Croesus now attempted to win the favour of the Delphian Apollo by a magnificent sacrifice. Of every kind of appropriate animal he slaughtered three thousand; he burnt in a huge pile a number of precious objects – couches overlaid with gold or silver, golden cups, tunics, and other richly coloured garments – in the hope of binding the god more closely to his interest; and he issued a command that every Lydian was also to offer a sacrifice according to his means. After this ceremony he melted down an enormous quantity of gold into one hundred and   50 seventeen ingots about eighteen inches long, nine inches wide, and three inches thick; four of the ingots were of refined gold weighing approximately a hundred and forty-two pounds each: the rest were alloyed and weighed about a hundred and fourteen pounds. He also caused the image of a lion to be made of refined gold, in weight some five hundred and seventy pounds. This statue, when the temple at Delphi was burnt down, fell from the gold bricks which formed its base and lies today in the Corinthian treasury. It lost about two hundred pounds weight in the fire, and now weighs only three hundred and seventy pounds.[19]

51   This was by no means all that Croesus sent to Delphi; there were also two huge mixing-bowls, one of gold which was placed on the right-hand side of the entrance to the temple, the other of silver, on the left. These also were moved at the time of the fire, and the golden one, which weighs nearly a quarter of a ton, now stands in the treasury of the Clazomenians, and the silver one, which holds over five thousand gallons, is in the corner of the ante-chapel. Its capacity is known because the Delphians use it for mixing wine at the festival called Theophania. It is a most remarkable piece of work, and I should say the Delphians are right in ascribing it to Theodorus of Samos.[20] In addition Croesus sent four silver casks, which are in the Corinthian treasury, and two sprinklers for lustral water, one of gold, the other of silver; the former has the name of the Lacedaemonians engraved upon it, and they claim to have presented it. But this is not true: Croesus presented it along with all the rest, and some Delphian (I know his name but will not mention it)[21] cut the inscription to please the Lacedaemonians. I admit that the boy through whose hand the water runs is a Lacedaemonian gift, but not either of the two sprinklers. There were many other gifts of no great importance, including round silver basins; but I must not forget to mention a figure of a woman, in gold, four and a half feet high, said by the Delphians to represent the woman who baked Croesus' bread. Lastly, he sent his own wife's neck-

52 laces and girdles. These, then, were the offerings which Croesus sent to Delphi; to the shrine of Amphiaraus, the story of whose valour and misfortune he knew, he sent a shield of solid gold

and a spear, also of solid gold throughout, both shaft and head; the shield and spear were still at Thebes in my own day, in the temple of Ismenian Apollo.[22]

The Lydians who were to bring the presents to the temples were instructed by Croesus to ask the oracles if he should undertake the campaign against Persia, and if he should strengthen his army by some alliance. On their arrival, therefore, they offered the gifts with proper ceremony and put their question in the following words: 'Croesus, King of Lydia and other nations, in the belief that these are the only true oracles in the world, has given you gifts such as your power of divination deserves, and now asks you if he should march against Persia and if it would be wise to seek an alliance.' To this question both oracles returned a similar answer; they foretold that if Croesus attacked the Persians, he would destroy a great empire, and they advised him to find out which of the Greek states was the most powerful, and to come to an understanding with it. 53

Croesus was overjoyed when he learnt the answer which the oracles had given, and was fully confident of destroying the power of Cyrus. To express his satisfaction he sent a further present to Delphi of two gold staters for every man, having first inquired how many men there were. The Delphians in return granted in perpetuity to Croesus and the people of Lydia the right of citizenship for any who wished, together with exemption from dues, front seats at state functions and priority in consulting the oracle. 54

When Croesus had given the Delphians their presents, he consulted the oracle a third time, for one true answer had made him greedy for more. On this occasion he asked if his reign would be a long one. The Priestess answered: 55

When comes the day that a mule shall sit on the Median throne,
Then, tender-footed Lydian, by pebbly Hermus
Run and abide not, nor think it shame to be a coward.

This reply gave Croesus more pleasure than anything he had yet heard; for he did not suppose that a mule was likely to become king of the Medes,[23] and that meant that he and his line 56

would remain in power for ever. He then turned his attention to finding out which of the Greek states was the most powerful, with a view to forming an alliance. His inquiries revealed that the Lacedaemonians were the most eminent of the Dorian peoples and the Athenians of the Ionian. These two, one originally Pelasgian the other Hellenic, were the most powerful of the Greek peoples. The Ionians are an indigenous race, but the Dorians on the contrary have been constantly on the move; their home in Deucalion's reign was Phthiotis and in the reign of Dorus son of Hellen the country known as Histiaeotis in the neighbourhood of Ossa and Olympus; driven from there by the Cadmeians they settled in Pindus and were known as Macednons; thence they migrated to Dryopis, and finally to the Pelo-
57 ponnese, where they got their present name of Dorians. Of the Pelasgian language I cannot speak with certainty, but that it was not Greek may be inferred from the language of those of Pelasgian race now living in Creston above the Tyrrhenians, who were neighbours of the people now known as Dorians when their home was in the country which we call Thessaliotis; also from the language of the Pelasgian peoples who settled at Placia and Scylace on the Hellespont and were fellow countrymen of the Athenians, and of the other Pelasgian towns which have since changed their names. Granted, then, that these are a fair sample of the Pelasgian race, one may conclude that the Athenians, being themselves Pelasgian, changed their language when they were absorbed into the Greek family of nations. In Creston and Placia the same language is spoken, but it is not the language of the surrounding country: which indicates that these people did not change their language when they changed
58 their home. I believe myself that the Greek peoples have always spoken the same language, but they were weak after their separation from the Pelasgians of whom they were a branch, and have since grown from small beginnings to their present numbers by the addition of various foreign elements, amongst which were the Pelasgians themselves. I do not think that the Pelasgians, a non-Greek people, ever became very numerous or powerful.[24]
59 Athens, he learned, had been split by faction and was now

under the tyranny of Pisistratus the son of Hippocrates. An extraordinary thing had occurred when Hippocrates, who held no public office, was present at the festival of Olympia: he had slaughtered the animals for his sacrifice, when the cauldrons with the flesh and water in them boiled over, though no fire had been lighted. Chilon the Lacedaemonian chanced to be present, and seeing this ominous sight advised Hippocrates not to marry and have children, or, if he was married already, to divorce his wife, or again, if he had a son, to disown him. Hippocrates refused to take Chilon's advice, and some time later Pisistratus, of whom I was speaking, was born. When there was strife in Attica between the coastal villages under the leadership of Megacles, son of Alcmaeon, and the inland settlements under Lycurgus, son of Aristoleides, Pisistratus with a view to seizing power for himself organized a third party. He collected adherents and coming forward as the professed champion of the hillmen, he devised the following ruse: he cut himself and his mules about the body and then drove his cart into the market square, and pretended that he had escaped from his enemies who tried to kill him as he was driving out of town. Then, relying on the reputation he had won during his command of the expedition against Megara, during which the capture of Nisaea was not the least of his distinguished services, he asked the people to give him a guard. The Athenians, who were taken in by the trick, consented, and told off a number of men for his bodyguard, who followed him armed with clubs instead of spears. With their assistance Pisistratus captured the Acropolis, and from that moment found himself master of Athens. In this way he ruled the Athenians, governing in accordance with custom, and neither eliminating the existing magistracies nor changing the laws. And he adorned the city well and beautifully.[25]

Not long afterwards the two parties under Megacles and Lycurgus agreed to combine, and drove Pisistratus out, so that in this first phase of his tyranny he lost his power before it had really taken root. His rivals, however, falling foul of one another once again, Megacles found himself so harassed that he made overtures to Pisistratus and promised to restore him to power if he would consent to marry his daughter. Pisistratus agreed to the terms which Megacles proposed, and then, to bring about his return to power, they devised between them what seems to me the silliest trick which history has to record. The Greeks have never been simpletons; for centuries past they have been distinguished from other nations by superior wits; and of all Greeks the Athenians are allowed to be the most intelligent: yet it was at the Athenians' expense that this ridiculous trick was played. In the village of Paeania there was a handsome woman called Phye, nearly six feet tall, whom they fitted out in a suit of armour and mounted in a chariot; then, after getting her to pose in the most striking attitude, they drove into Athens, where messengers who had preceded them were already, according to their instructions, talking to the people and urging them to welcome Pisistratus back, because the goddess Athene herself had shown him extraordinary honour and was bringing him home to her own Acropolis. They spread this nonsense all over the town, and it was not long before rumour reached the outlying villages that Athene was bringing Pisistratus back, and both villagers and townsfolk, convinced that the woman Phye was indeed the goddess, offered her their prayers and received Pisistratus with open arms.

61   After the recovery of his power in this way Pisistratus married Megacles' daughter, as he had agreed to do; but because of a story that Megacles' family, the Alcmaeonidae, had a curse upon it, and because he already had grown-up sons of his own, he did not want children from his new wife, and to prevent her from having any refused normal intercourse and lay with her in an unnatural way.[26] For a time his wife said nothing about this insult, but later – perhaps in answer to a question – she told her mother, and her mother told Megacles, who was so angry at the slight upon himself and his daughter, that he made up his quarrel with his political enemies. This new threat determined Pisistratus to get right out of the country. He went to Eretria and there discussed the situation with his sons. The view of Hippias that an attempt should be made to recover his lost position proved the most acceptable, and they began to collect contributions from the towns which were in any way under

obligation to them. Many towns gave large sums of money, but the contribution from Thebes was by far the most handsome. Time passed; they were joined by Argive mercenaries from the Peloponnese; a certain Lygdamis from Naxos freely offered his enthusiastic support, contributing both money and men; and at last – to cut the story short – everything was ready for the march on Athens. More than ten years had passed, when they left   62 Eretria and returned.[27]

The first place in Attica which they took was Marathon. Here they were joined in camp by their supporters in the city, and others who preferred tyranny to democracy trickled in from the villages to swell their force. While Pisistratus had been collecting supplies, and even after he occupied Marathon, the Athenians in the city ignored him; but the news that he was marching against Athens soon brought them into the field in full force against the returning exiles, and they were met by Pisistratus on his way from Marathon at the temple of Athene Pallenis, where the two armies halted and faced one another. Here it providentially occurred that Amphilytus, the soothsayer from Acarnania, accosted Pisistratus and made a prophecy to him in verse:

The net is cast and the meshes of it are spread wide;
In the moonlit night the tunnies will come darting through the sea.

Pisistratus understood the meaning of this inspired utterance   63 and, declaring that he accepted the oracle, gave the order to advance. Just at this time the Athenians from the city were taking their lunch, while others were following the meal by a game of dice or a siesta, so that the attack of Pisistratus' army met with no resistance. The Athenians fled, and Pisistratus by a clever stratagem prevented any subsequent rally and ensured that they should remain scattered: he told his son to ride on in advance, and they, each time they overtook a group of fugitives, spoke to them according to Pisistratus' instructions, urging every man to keep his spirits up and go home. The Athenians   64 did as they were bidden, and thus for the third time Pisistratus made himself master of the city.

He now proceeded to establish his power on a firm basis. He

hired bodyguards, raised revenue from various sources, partly in Attica, partly from property on the river Strymon, took as hostages and sent for safe keeping to Naxos (which he had captured and turned over to Lygdamis) the sons of those Athenians who had remained in the city and not immediately fled; and, finally, 'cleansed' the island of Delos. The object of this was to obey the injunctions of an oracle, and the method he adopted was to dig up all the dead bodies which were buried within sight of the temple and re-inter them in another part of the island.

Thus it was that Pisistratus won undisputed power in Athens. A number of the Athenians had been killed in the fighting, and others, including the Alcmaeonidae, had fled the country.[28]

65   The condition of Athens at the time when Croesus made his inquiry was such as I have described. He then proceeded to get information about Sparta. Here he found that the Lacedaemonians after a period of depression had been successful in their struggle with Tegea, which during the joint reign of Leon and Agasides had been the only town to hold out against their victorious arms. At an earlier date they had been the worst governed people in Greece, both in their internal and external relations – for they would have no dealings of any kind with strangers. How the change to good government came about I will now relate. Lycurgus, a distinguished Spartan, visited the Delphic oracle, and no sooner had he entered the shrine than he was greeted with these words:

> Hither to my rich temple have you come, Lycurgus,
> Dear to Zeus and to all gods that dwell in Olympus.
> I know not whether to declare you human or divine –
> Yet I incline to believe, Lycurgus, that you are a god.

There is a story that the Priestess also revealed to him the system of government which obtains at Sparta today, but the Lacedaemonians themselves say that Lycurgus brought it from Crete after he became guardian of his nephew Leobotas, king of Sparta, and acted as his regent; for it is a fact that as soon as he received this appointment he made fundamental changes in the laws, and took good care that the new ones should not be broken. Later he reorganized the army, introducing the system of messes and the new tactical divisions of squadrons and companies, in addition to the new civil offices of Ephor and Elder. By these changes Spartan government was put upon a sound basis, and when Lycurgus died a temple was built in his honour, and he is still regarded with profound reverence.[29] 66

Thanks to a good soil and a numerous population the Lacedaemonians soon shot up and flourished like a sturdy tree. No longer content to let things be, they took it into their heads that they were better men than the Arcadians, and consulted the oracle at Delphi with a view to the conquest of the whole of Arcadia. This was the answer they received:

> Arcady? Great is the thing you ask. I will not grant it.
> In Arcady are many men, acorn-eaters,
> And they will keep you out. Yet, for I am not grudging,
> I will give you Tegea to dance in with stamping feet
> And her fair plain to measure out with the line.

The Lacedaemonians failed to perceive the ambiguity of this oracle, and decided to leave the rest of Arcadia alone and march against Tegea: and so confident were they of reducing the men of Tegea to slavery, that they took the chains with them. But they lost the battle, and those who were taken prisoner were forced to wear on their own legs the chains they had brought, and to 'measure out with the line' the plain of Tegea as labourers. In my own lifetime the fetters they were bound with were still preserved in Tegea, hanging up round the temple of Athene Alea.

In this former war with Tegea the Spartans had continually the worst of it, but by the time of Croesus, under their kings Anaxandrides and Ariston, they had got the upper hand.[30] This is the story of their success: after a long series of reverses in the war they sent to Delphi and asked of which god they should beg favour in order to ensure their conquest of Tegea, and the Priestess promised them victory if they brought home the bones of Orestes, Agamemnon's son. Unable to find the tomb of 67

Orestes, they sent again to inquire where the body lay, and the messengers received this answer:

> In Arcady lies Tegea in the level plain,
> Where under strong constraint two winds are blowing;
> Smiting is there and counter-smiting, and woe on woe;
> There earth, the giver of life, holds Agamemnon's son.
> Bring him home, and you will prevail over Tegea.

This oracle brought them no nearer than the previous one to finding the body. They searched everywhere; but all in vain until Lichas, who was one of the Spartan special agents called 'Agathoergi', or 'good-service men', solved the riddle. The Agathoergi are the five eldest men who quit the cavalry each year, and it is their duty to spend the subsequent year in active employment on whatever service the state may require of them. 68 Lichas, as I have said, was one of them, and he it was who, by the aid of luck and his own wits, found the body in Tegea. Taking advantage of the better relations which existed at this time between the two towns, he went to Tegea and entered a forge where he watched some iron being hammered out, a process which caused him great surprise. The smith, seeing his astonishment, paused in his work and said: 'Well, my friend, your surprise at seeing me work in iron would be nothing to what you'd have felt, if you had seen what I saw. I wanted to make a well in the yard here, and as I was digging I came on a huge coffin – ten feet long! I couldn't believe that men were ever bigger than they are today, so I opened it – and there was the corpse, as big as the coffin! I measured it, and then shovelled the earth back.' Lichas turned over in his mind the smith's account of his discovery, and came to the conclusion that the oracle was fulfilled and that this was the body of Orestes. He found the explanation of the 'winds' in the smith's two pairs of bellows; the 'smiting and counter-smiting' were the hammer and anvil, and the 'woe on woe' the beaten iron – the inference being drawn from the fact that the discovery of iron was a bad thing for mankind. Confident that he had solved the puzzle, he returned to Sparta and told the whole story. The Spartans pretended that he had committed some crime, charged him with it and drove him out of the country; whereupon he went back to Tegea, told the smith what had happened to him, took from him a lease of the courtyard, as he refused to sell it, and having persuaded him took up his quarters there. Then he dug up the grave, collected the bones and took them away to Sparta; and ever since that day the Lacedaemonians in any trial of strength had by far the better of it. They had now subdued the greater part of the Peloponnese.

Now when Croesus had gathered all this information, he sent 69 messengers to Sparta with presents, to ask for an alliance. They were instructed what words to use, so on their arrival they said that they came from Croesus, king of Lydia and other nations, with the following message: 'Men of Lacedaemon, I the King have been advised by the oracle to make the Greek my friend, and because I am told that you are the most eminent of the Greeks, I am obeying the oracle in asking for your help. I wish to be your friend and ally, without deceit or underhand dealing.'

Now the Lacedaemonians, who had themselves heard about the oracle, were very glad that the Lydians had come with this proposal from Croesus, and made a pact of friendship and alliance with him.[31] This was partly in gratitude for a favour which Croesus had done them on a former occasion, when they had sent to Sardis to buy gold for a statue of Apollo (the one which now stands in the Laconian town of Thornax) and Croesus had given it to them as a gift. For this reason, then, and 70 also because Croesus had chosen them out of all the Greeks to be his friends, the Lacedaemonians consented to give him their help. Not only, moreover, were they ready to serve when he should call upon them, but wishing to make Croesus some return for his presents they had a bronze bowl made, large enough to hold two thousand five hundred gallons and covered with small figures round the outside of the rim. They meant to take this bowl to Croesus, but for one reason or another it never reached Sardis. The Lacedaemonians say that off Samos the islanders got wind of its presence and sailed out in their warships and stole it. But the Samians deny the theft: according to them, the Lacedaemonians who were taking the bowl to Sardis were too late, and when they heard that the city had fallen and Croesus was a prisoner, they sold it in Samos to some men who placed it as an offering in the temple of Hera. And indeed if they did sell it, it is not unlikely that on their return to Sparta they would pretend to have been robbed. So much for the story of the bowl.

71

Croesus, who had failed to grasp the true meaning of the oracle, now prepared an expedition against Cappadocia, sure of success in bringing down the power of Cyrus and the Persians. But while the preparations were going on, he received a piece of advice from a Lydian named Sandanis, who was already known for his good sense, and by the opinion he then expressed greatly increased his reputation amongst the Lydians. 'My lord,' he said, 'you are preparing to fight against men who dress in leather – both breeches and everything else. So rough is their country that they eat as much as they have, never as much as they want. They drink no wine but only water. They have no good things at all, not even figs for dessert. Now if you conquer this people, what will you get from them, seeing they have nothing for you to take? And if they conquer you, think how many good things you will lose; for once they taste the luxuries of Lydia they will hold on to them so tightly that nothing will make them let go. I am thankful myself that the gods have never put it into the Persians' heads to attack the Lydians.'

Croesus did not take this advice – though Sandanis was right: the Persians before their conquest of Lydia had no luxuries of any kind.

72

The Cappadocians are known by the Greeks as Syrians. Before the rise of Persian power they were subject to the Medes, but at this period to Cyrus. The boundary between the Median and Lydian empires was the river Halys, which flows from a mountain region in Armenia through Cilician territory, and then, passing between the Matieni and Phrygians, turns northward and forms the boundary between the Cappadocians to the east and the Paphlagonians to the west. The Halys is thus the boundary of nearly the whole of southern Asia Minor from the Mediterranean in the neighbourhood of Cyprus to the Black

Sea. This is where the neck of the peninsula lies, and it is five days' journey across for a man travelling light.[32]

Croesus had a craving to extend his territories, but there were two other reasons for his attack on Cappadocia: namely his trust in the oracle and his desire to punish Cyrus for his treatment of Astyages. Astyages, son of Cyaxares and king of Media, was Croesus' brother-in-law, and had been dethroned by Cyrus, son of Cambyses. I will now relate how this relationship arose. A number of nomad Scythians, driven out in a quarrel, emigrated to Media, which was at that time ruled by Cyaxares, son of Phraortes and grandson of Deioces. Cyaxares at first respected their dependence and treated them kindly, and even valued them so far as to make them guardians of some boys, whom they were to teach their language and the use of the bow. Now as time went on it so happened that the Scythians, who were continually out hunting and continually bringing in game, one day came home empty-handed. Cyaxares (who was, as he showed, a quick-tempered man) received them with insult and abuse. The Scythians, in revenge for treatment which they considered undeserved, decided to kill one of their young pupils, chop him up, dress the pieces in the ordinary way like meat, serve them to Cyaxares as a dish of game, and then make the best of their escape to the court of Alyattes in Sardis. This they actually did. Cyaxares and the guests at his table ate some of the meat, and the Scythians escaped to Sardis and threw themselves on the mercy of Alyattes. Cyaxares demanded that they should be given up; but when Alyattes refused, war subsequently broke out between the two countries and continued for five years, during which both Lydians and Medes won a number of victories. One battle was fought at night. But then, after five years of indecisive warfare, a battle took place in which the armies had already engaged when day was suddenly turned into night. This change from daylight to darkness had been foretold to the Ionians by Thales of Miletus, who fixed the date for it in the year in which it did, in fact, take place.[33] Both Lydians and Medes broke off the engagement when they saw this darkening of the day: they were more anxious than they had been to conclude peace, and a reconciliation was brought

73

74

about by Syennesis of Cilicia and Labynetus of Babylon,[34] who were the men responsible both for the pact to keep the peace and for the exchange of marriages between the two kingdoms. They persuaded Alyattes to give his daughter Aryenis to Astyages, son of Cyaxares – knowing that treaties seldom remain intact without powerful sanctions. These nations have the same form of oath as the Greeks, but for additional confirmation they make a shallow cut in their arms and lick each other's blood.

75   Astyages was Cyrus' maternal grandfather and had been attacked and defeated by him for a reason which I will explain later on. My point at the moment is that Croesus blamed Cyrus for his action, and therefore sent to ask the oracles about his invasion of Persia, and, when the ambiguous answer arrived, interpreted it in his own favour and began the war. When he reached the Halys, he crossed it by the existing bridge; that, at any rate, is my own belief in spite of the common Greek story that it was Thales of Miletus who contrived the crossing. This tale supposes that the bridge had not yet been built, and that while Croesus was wondering how his men were to get across, Thales, who was in camp with them, made the river flow on both sides of the army instead of only on the left. He managed this feat by digging a deep crescent-shaped channel, from a spot a little above the camp and thence round to the rear of it, for the purpose of diverting some of the water from the original bed, into which it would flow again once it had passed the camp. In this way the river was split in two, so that both parts at once became fordable. Some say that the original river-bed was completely dried up; but I do not believe this – for had it been so, how would they have crossed on their return journey?[35]

76   When the army was over the river and had reached the district called Pteria in Cappadocia (Pteria is the strongest place hereabouts and lies more or less in a line with Sinope on the Black Sea), Croesus encamped and began to devastate the crops on the Syrians' land. He captured the town, enslaved the inhabitants, and took all the neighbouring settlements, driving the innocent Syrians from house and home.

Cyrus meanwhile had collected his army and was on his way

to meet him, increasing his forces as he went by levying troops from all the peoples that lay on his route. Before starting he had sent representatives to the Ionians in an attempt to detach them from Croesus, but without success. He marched none the less to Pteria, and when he had pitched camp in the face of Croesus' army, there was a trial of strength between them. After a sharp struggle in which both sides lost heavily, night fell and the battle was broken off without a decision.

Croesus laid the blame for his lack of success upon the size of his army, which in that engagement was much smaller than the army of Cyrus; so when on the next day Cyrus did not advance to the attack, he marched back to Sardis with the intention of calling upon the Egyptians to assist him according to the pact which he had concluded with King Amasis before the treaty of alliance with Sparta; he meant also to summon the Babylonians (for with them too, under their king, Labynetus, he had previously formed an alliance), and, lastly, to call upon the Lacedaemonians to join him on a definite date. Thus, with all these reinforcements added to his own army, he proposed to wait until winter was over, and attack the Persians in the following spring. [77]

With this purpose in mind, Croesus, as soon as he reached home, sent instructions to his allies to send troops to Sardis after an interval of four months. All the mercenary troops which had been engaged with the Persians and had returned with him, he disbanded and sent home, for he did not for a moment suppose that Cyrus after so close a fight would venture to advance on Sardis. While he was thinking these arrangements over, he was surprised by an unusual occurrence: snakes swarmed into the suburbs of the town, and on their appearance the horses in the meadows stopped grazing and came and ate them. Croesus, quite rightly, took this extraordinary sight as an omen, and at once sent to Telmessus where there were men who interpreted such things. His messenger did indeed learn the significance of the omen from the men of Telmessus, but they never told Croesus what it was – for before their ship made Sardis on the return voyage, Croesus had been taken prisoner. This interpretation was that Croesus must expect the coming of a foreign [78]

army, which would subdue the people whose home was in
Sardis; for the snakes (so they explained it) sprang from the soil,
but horses were beasts of war and not native to the country.
The men of Telmessus who gave this answer had not yet had
the news from Sardis, though Croesus was already a prisoner.

79   When Croesus started for home after the battle in Pteria,
Cyrus was sure that he would disband his army as soon as he
arrived; so after consideration he found that his best course was
to press on to Sardis with all speed before the Lydian forces had
time to muster again. This was no sooner determined than done.
Indeed he was his own messenger – for so swift was his advance
into Lydia that Croesus had no news that he was on the way.
This unexpected turn of events put Croesus into a very difficult
position; however, he made an attempt to resist the invader. In
those days there were no stouter or more courageous fighters in
Asia than the Lydians. They were cavalrymen, excellent horsemen, and their weapon was the long spear.[36]

80   The armies met on the level ground in front of Sardis; it is a
broad expanse, bare of trees, and watered by the Hyllus and
other streams which join another and larger one called the
Hermus. The Hermus has its source in the mountains sacred to
the Phrygian Cybele, and flows into the sea near the town of
Phocaea. When Cyrus saw the Lydians take up battle positions
on this plain, his fear of their cavalry led him to adopt a suggestion of Harpagus, one of the Medes; this was to get together all
the camels (they were used as pack-animals to carry equipment
and stores), unload them and mount men armed as cavalrymen
on their backs. He then ordered them to advance as the first
line of attack against the cavalry of Croesus, with the infantry
following and his own cavalry bringing up the rear. Having
made his dispositions, he reminded his troops of their duty to
kill without mercy every Lydian they met – except Croesus.
Croesus was on no account to be killed, even if he tried to resist
capture.

The reason for confronting the Lydian cavalry with camels
was the instinctive fear which they inspire in horses. No horse
can endure the sight or smell of a camel. This is the fact upon
which the stratagem was based, and its object was to render

useless Croesus' cavalry, the very arm in which the Lydians expected to distinguish themselves. The ruse succeeded, for when the battle began, the horses turned tail the moment they smelt and saw the camels – and Croesus' chief ground of confidence was cut from under him. The Lydians, however, did not play the coward; seeing what had happened they leapt from the saddle and engaged the Persians on foot. Both sides suffered heavy losses, but finally the Lydians, forced to retire, were driven within the city walls, where they were besieged by the Persians.

Thus the siege of Sardis began, and Croesus, in the belief that it would last a long time, sent a second appeal for help to his allies. The first messenger had been sent to ask for reinforcements to be at Sardis after four months, but these, now that Croesus was already beleaguered, were to beg for immediate assistance. All the states which were in treaty with Croesus were applied to, but the most urgent request was to Sparta.

It happened that just at this time the Spartans were engaged in a quarrel with Argos over Thyreae, a place in Argive territory which the Spartans had cut off and occupied.[37] (The country to the west as far as Malea once belonged to the Argives, including Cythera and the other islands in that neighbourhood.) The Argives marched to recover their stolen property, and agreed in conference with the Spartans that three hundred picked men a side should fight it out, and that Thyreae should belong to the victors; the rest of the two armies were to go home without staying to watch the fight, lest either side, seeing its champions getting the worst of it, might be tempted to intervene. On these terms they parted, leaving behind the men chosen to represent them, and the battle began. So closely was it contested that of the six hundred men only three were left alive – two Argives, Alcenor and Chromios, and one Spartan, Othryades – and even these would have been killed had not darkness put an end to the fighting. The two Argives claimed the victory and hurried back to Argos; but the Spartan Othryades remained under arms and, having stripped the bodies of the Argive dead, carried their equipment to his own camp.

Both parties met again on the following day, when they had heard the result of the battle. For a while both Argives and

Spartans maintained that they had won, the former because they had the greater number of survivors, the latter because the two Argives had run away, whereas their own man had remained on the battlefield and stripped the bodies of the dead. The argument ended in blows, and a fresh battle began, in which after severe losses on both sides the Spartans were victorious. From that day the Argives, who were previously compelled by custom to wear their hair long, began to cut it short, and made it an offence against religion for any man to grow his hair, and for any woman to wear gold, until Thyreae was recovered. The Spartans also adopted a new custom, but in precisely the opposite sense: they used not to grow their hair long, but from that time they began to do so. It is said that Othryades, the sole survivor of the three hundred, was ashamed to return to Sparta after the death of his companions, and killed himself at Thyreae.

83   It was in the midst of these troubles that the messenger arrived at Sparta to ask for help in raising the siege of Sardis, and the Spartans in spite of their difficulties were eager to render assistance, when they heard what he had to say. But by the time their preparations were complete and their ships ready to sail, a second message brought the news that the city had fallen and that Croesus was a prisoner. They were much distressed to hear of his misfortune, but they could do no more.

84   This was how Sardis was taken. On the fourteenth day of the siege Cyrus sent officers to ride round his lines and tell the troops that he promised a reward for the first man to scale the wall. Following this an attempt was made in force, but it failed and was abandoned; then a Mardian called Hyroeades resolved to try at a point in the fortifications which was unguarded, because a successful attack there had never been supposed possible. It was a section of the central stronghold so precipitous as to be almost inaccessible. In old days the Telmessians had pronounced that Sardis would never be taken if Meles, who was king at that time, carried round the walls the lion which his concubine had borne him.[38] So far as the rest of the fortifications were concerned, where they were open to attack, Meles took their advice and had the lion carried round; but this one point

he neglected, thinking that the sheer drop was sufficient defence. It is on the side of the city which faces Tmolus.

On the previous day Hyroeades the Mardian had seen one of the Lydians fetch a helmet, which had rolled down this precipitous slope, and the sight of the man climbing down had set him thinking. He had then made the ascent himself, and other Persians followed; after them a great many more climbed up, and Sardis was taken and sacked.

What happened to Croesus remains to be told.[39] I have already mentioned his son who was dumb, but in other ways a fine enough young man. In the time of his prosperity – now gone – Croesus had done everything he could for the boy, not even omitting to ask advice from the Delphic oracle. The Priestess had replied:

> O Lydian lord of many nations, foolish Croesus,
> Wish not to hear the longed-for voice within your palace,
> That is, your son's voice: better for you were it otherwise;
> For his first word will he speak on a day of sorrow.

When the city was stormed, a Persian soldier was about to cut Croesus down, not knowing who he was. Croesus saw him coming; but because in his misery he did not care if he lived or died, he made no effort to defend himself. But this dumb son, seeing the danger, was so terrified by the fearful thing that was about to happen that he broke into speech, and cried: 'Do not kill Croesus, fellow!' Those were the first words he ever uttered – and he retained the power of speech for the rest of his life.

In this way Sardis was captured by the Persians and Croesus taken prisoner, after a reign of fourteen years and a siege of fourteen days. The oracle was fulfilled; Croesus had destroyed a mighty empire – his own.

The Persians brought their prisoner into the presence of the king, and Cyrus chained Croesus and placed him with fourteen Lydian boys on a great pyre that he had built; perhaps he intended them as a choice offering to some god of his, or perhaps he had made a vow and wished to fulfil it; or it may be that he had heard that Croesus was a godfearing man, and set him on

85

86

the pyre to see if any divine power would save him from being
burnt alive. But whatever the reason, that was what he did; and
Croesus, for all his misery, as he stood on the pyre, remembered
with what divine truth Solon had declared that no man could
be called happy until he was dead. Till then Croesus had not
uttered a sound; but when he remembered, he sighed bitterly and three times, in anguish of spirit, pronounced Solon's
name.

Cyrus heard the name and told his interpreters to ask who
Solon was; but for a while Croesus refused to answer the question and kept silent; at last, however, he was forced to speak.
'He was a man,' he said, 'who ought to have talked with every
king in the world. I would give a fortune to have had it so.' Not
understanding what he meant, they renewed their questions and
pressed him so urgently to explain, that he could no longer
refuse. He then related how Solon the Athenian once came to
Sardis, and made light of the splendour which he saw there, and
how everything he said had proved true, and not only for him
but for all men and especially for those who imagine themselves
fortunate – had in his own case proved all too true.

While Croesus was speaking, the fire had been lit and was
already burning round the edges. The interpreters told Cyrus
what Croesus had said, and the story touched him. He himself
was a mortal man, and was burning alive another who had once
been as prosperous as he. The thought of that, and the fear of
retribution, and the realization of the instability of human
things, made him change his mind and give orders that the
flames should at once be put out, and Croesus and the boys
brought down from the pyre. But the fire had got a hold, and
87   the attempt to extinguish it failed. The Lydians say that when
Croesus understood that Cyrus had changed his mind, and saw
everyone vainly trying to master the fire, he called loudly upon
Apollo with tears to come and save him from his misery, if any
of his gifts had been pleasant to him. It was a clear and windless
day; but suddenly in answer to Croesus' prayer clouds gathered
and a storm broke with such violent rain that the flames were
put out.

This was proof enough for Cyrus that Croesus was a good

man whom the gods loved; so he brought him down from the pyre and said, 'Tell me, Croesus, what man persuaded you to march against my country and be my enemy rather than my friend?'

'King,' Croesus replied, 'the luck was yours when I did it, and the loss was mine. The god of the Greeks encouraged me to fight you: the blame is his. No one is fool enough to choose war instead of peace – in peace sons bury fathers, but in war fathers bury sons. It must have been heaven's will that this should happen.'

Cyrus had his chains taken off and invited him to sit by his side. He made much of him and looked at him with wonder, as did everyone who was near enough to see. 88

For a while Croesus was deep in his thoughts and did not speak. Then he turned, and seeing that the Persians were sacking the town, said: 'Should I tell you, O king, what I have in my mind, or must I now keep silent?' Cyrus replied that he might say what he pleased without fear, so Croesus put another question: 'What is it,' he asked, 'that all those men of yours are so intent upon doing?'

'They are plundering your city and carrying off your treasures.'

'Not my city or my treasures,' Croesus answered. 'Nothing there any longer belongs to me. It is you they are robbing.'

Cyrus thought this carefully over; then he sent away all the company that was present, and asked Croesus what advice he saw fit to give him in the matter. 89

'Since the gods have made me your slave,' Croesus said, 'I think it my duty, if I have advice worth giving you, not to withhold it. The Persians are violent men; and they are poor. They are ransacking the town, and if you let them get possession of all that wealth you may be sure that whichever of them gets the most will rebel against you. So do what I advise – if you like the advice: put men from your guard on watch at every gate, and when anyone brings out anything of value, let the sentries take it and say that a tenth part of the spoil must be given to Zeus. If you do that, they will not hate you, as they certainly would if you confiscated the things by mere authority. They will admit that it is an act of justice, and be willing to give up what they have got.'

90   Cyrus was delighted with this advice, which he thought was excellent. With many compliments to Croesus he gave orders to the guard to put the proposal into practice. Then turning to Croesus, 'I see,' he said, 'that though you are a king you are ready to do me good service in word and deed. I should like to make you some return: ask, therefore, for whatever you wish, and it shall immediately be yours.'

'Master,' Croesus answered, 'you will please me best if you let me send these chains to the god of the Greeks, whom I most honoured, and ask if he is accustomed to cheat his benefactors.' Cyrus asked the reason for this request, whereupon Croesus repeated the whole story of what he had hoped to accomplish and of the answers of the oracles, and dwelt at length upon the rich gifts he had sent and on how his belief in the prophecies had emboldened him to invade Persia. Then he ended by repeating his request for permission to reproach Apollo for his deceit. Cyrus laughed, and told Croesus he should have what he wanted, and anything else he might ask for, no matter when. Croesus, therefore, sent to Delphi, and instructed his messengers to lay the chains on the threshold of the temple; then, pointing to the chains, they were to ask the god if, when such things were the fruits of war, he was not ashamed to have encouraged Croesus by his oracles to invade Persia in the confident hope of destroying the power of Cyrus. And they were also to ask if it was the habit of Greek gods to be ungrateful.

91   It is said that when the Lydian messengers reached Delphi and asked the questions they had been told to ask, the Priestess replied that not God himself could escape destiny. As for Croesus, he had expiated in the fifth generation the crime of his ancestor, who was a soldier in the bodyguard of the Heraclids, and, tempted by a woman's treachery, had murdered his master and stolen his office, to which he had no claim. The God of Prophecy was eager that the fall of Sardis might occur in the time of Croesus' sons rather than in his own, but he had been unable to divert the course of destiny. Nevertheless what little the Fates allowed, he had obtained for Croesus' advantage: he

had postponed the capture of Sardis for three years, so Croesus must realize that he had enjoyed three years of freedom more than was appointed for him. Secondly, the god had saved him when he was on the pyre. As to the oracle, Croesus had no right to find fault with it: the god had declared that if he attacked the Persians he would bring down a mighty empire. After an answer like that, the wise thing would have been to send again to inquire which empire was meant, Cyrus' or his own. But as he misinterpreted what was said and made no second inquiry, he must admit the fault to have been his own. Moreover, the last time he consulted the oracle he failed also to understand what Apollo said about the mule. The mule was Cyrus, who was the child of parents of different races – a nobler mother and a baser father. His mother was a Mede and daughter of Astyages, king of Media; but his father was a Persian, subject to the Medes, and had married his queen to whom he was in every way inferior.

When the Lydians returned to Sardis with the Priestess' answer and reported it to Croesus, he admitted that the god was innocent and he had only himself to blame.

Such are the facts about the reign of Croesus and the first conquest of Ionia. I must add that Croesus sent many offerings to Greek shrines in addition to those I have already mentioned: for instance a tripod of gold (now at Thebes in Boeotia) which he dedicated to Ismenian Apollo, the golden cows and most of the columns at Ephesus, and a large golden shield in the Pronaea at Delphi. All these were in existence in my own day, and there were others which have since disappeared. There were others, again, at Branchidae, near Miletus, similar in weight and kind, so far as my information goes, to those at Delphi.[40]

Everything which Croesus sent to Delphi and to the shrine of Amphiaraus came from his own treasure and what he had inherited from his father; but the other gifts were originally the property of an enemy, who had opposed him before his reign began and supported the claim of Pantaleon to the throne. Pantaleon was Croesus' brother, a son of Alyattes by a different woman – Croesus' mother being a Carian, Pantaleon's an Ionian. Croesus obtained the succession by his father's gift, and this fellow, who had plotted against him, he put to death by dragging him on a carding-comb; his property, which he had already vowed to confiscate, he then sent as offerings to the various shrines in the way I have already described.

I will now leave the subject of Croesus' dedicatory offerings, and go on to say a word about Lydia. The country, unlike some others, has few marvels of much consequence for a historian to describe, except the gold dust which is washed down from Tmolus; it can show, however, the greatest work of human hands in the world, apart from the Egyptian and Babylonian: I mean the tomb of Croesus' father Alyattes.[41] The base of this monument is built of huge stone blocks; the rest of it is a mound of earth. It was raised by the joint labour of the tradesmen, craftsmen, and prostitutes, and on the top of it there survived to my own day five stone phallic pillars with inscriptions cut in them to show the amount of work done by each class. Calculation revealed that the prostitutes' share was the largest. Working-class girls in Lydia prostitute themselves without exception to collect money for their dowries, and continue the practice until they marry. They choose their own husbands. The circumference of the tomb is nearly three-quarters of a mile, and its breadth about four hundred yards. Near it is a large lake, the lake of Gyges, said by the Lydians to be never dry. Apart from the fact that they prostitute their daughters, the Lydian way of life is not unlike the Greek. The Lydians were the first people we know of to use a gold and silver coinage and to introduce retail trade,[42] and they also claim to have invented the games which are now commonly played both by themselves and by the Greeks. These games are supposed to have been invented at the time when they sent a colony to settle in Tyrrhenia, and the story is that in the reign of Atys, the son of Manes, the whole of Lydia suffered from a severe famine. For a time the people lingered on as patiently as they could, but later, when there was no improvement, they began to look for something to alleviate their misery. Various expedients were devised: for instance, the invention of dice, knucklebones, and ball-games. In fact they claim to have invented all games of this sort except draughts. The way they used these inventions to help them endure their hunger was to eat and play on alternate days – one day playing so continuously that they had no time to think of food, and eating on the next without playing at all. They managed to live like this for eighteen years. There was still no remission of their suffering – indeed it grew worse; so the King divided the population into two groups and determined by drawing lots which should emigrate and which should remain at home. He appointed himself to rule the section whose lot determined that they should remain, and his son Tyrrhenus to command the emigrants. The lots were drawn, and one section went down to the coast at Smyrna, where they built vessels, put aboard all their household effects and sailed in search of a livelihood elsewhere. They passed many countries and finally reached Umbria in the north of Italy, where they settled and still live to this day. Here they changed their name from Lydians to Tyrrhenians, after the King's son Tyrrhenus, who was their leader.[43]

So far I have described the subjugation of Lydia by the Persians. The course of my story now leads me to Cyrus: who was this man who destroyed the empire of Croesus, and how did the Persians win their predominant position in Asia?[44] I could, if I wished, give three versions of Cyrus' history, all different from what follows; but I propose to base my account on those Persian authorities who seem to tell the simple truth about him without trying to exaggerate his exploits.

The Assyrians had been masters of upper Asia over a period of five hundred and twenty years, when the Medes set the example of revolt from their authority.[45] They took arms in the cause of liberty and fought with such gallantry that they shook off the Assyrian yoke and became a free people. Their lead was followed by the other nations within the Assyrian empire, until every people in that part of the continent had won its independence. But it was not to last, and they became once more subject to autocratic government. The change was brought about by Deioces, a Median, son of Phraortes, who was a man of great ability and ambitious for power. The Medes had established themselves in small settlements, and Deioces, who was already a man of mark in his own village, now entered wholeheartedly into the task of distinguishing himself for just dealing. In this he had a purpose; for throughout the country at that time there was no sort of organized government whatever, and he was well aware that injustice is the enemy of justice. The result was that the men of his own village, seeing his habit of fair dealing, chose him to arbitrate their disputes. Bent upon getting all power into his own hands, he performed this office with perfect integrity and thus won no small praise from the men of his village. His reputation for being the only man to settle a dispute according to strict justice spread to the other villages, where corrupt processes of law were causing much distress, so that once the news of Deioces' integrity got abroad, everyone was glad to submit cases to his judgement, until in the end he became the only person they would turn to. As the knowledge of his impartiality spread, so the number of his clients increased, and he himself realized the supremacy of his position. He then announced that he had had enough of it – he would no longer sit in the chair of judgement; he would hear no more suits. It was contrary to his interest to spend all his time settling his neighbours' quarrels to the neglect of his own affairs. The result was that robbery increased and the contempt of law throughout the country was worse than ever. The Medes discussed the situation at a general meeting, at which (I presume) the friends of Deioces did most of the talking. 'We cannot,' they said, 'continue to live in this country under the present intolerable conditions. Let us appoint one of our number to rule us so that we can get on with our work under orderly government, and not lose our homes altogether in the present lawlessness.' The argument prevailed and the assembly was persuaded to set up a monarchy. The next step was to propose candidates for the royal office, and as during the debate Deioces and his admirable qualities were on everybody's lips, he was the man they agreed to appoint.

Deioces' first act was to command his subjects to build a palace worthy of a king, and to grant him the protection of a private guard. The Medes complied; they built a large and well-defended palace on a site he himself indicated, and allowed him to select a bodyguard without restriction of choice.

Once firmly on the throne, Deioces compelled the Medes to

build a single great city to which, as the capital of the country, all other towns were to be held of secondary importance. Again they complied, and the city now known as Ecbatana was built, a place of great size and strength fortified by concentric walls, these so planned that each successive circle was higher than the one below it by the height of the battlements. The fact that it was built on a hill helped to bring about this effect, but still more was done by deliberate contrivance. The circles are seven in number, and the innermost contains the royal palace and treasury. The circuit of the outer wall is much the same in extent as at Athens.[46] The battlements of the five outer rings are painted in different colours, the first white, the second black, the third crimson, the fourth blue, the fifth orange; the battlements of the two inner rings are plated with silver and gold respectively. These fortifications were to protect the king and his palace; the people had to build their houses outside the circuit of the walls.

99

When the work of building was complete, Deioces introduced for the first time the ceremonial of royalty: admission to the king's presence was forbidden, and all communication had to be through messengers. Nobody was allowed to see the king, and it was an offence for anyone to laugh or spit in the royal presence. This solemn ceremonial was designed as a safeguard against his contemporaries, men as good as himself in birth and personal quality, with whom he had been brought up in earlier years. There was a risk that if they saw him habitually, it might lead to jealousy and resentment, and plots would follow; but if nobody saw him, he would be thought to be of a different order from mere men.

Once his sovereign power was firmly established, he con-   100
tinued his strict administration of justice. All suits were con-
veyed to him in the form of written documents, which he would send back after recording upon them his decisions. In addition to this there were other practices he introduced: if he heard of any act of arrogance or ostentation, he would send for the offender and punish him as the offence deserved, and his spies were busy watching and listening in every corner of his dominions.[47]

101   The achievement of Deioces, who reigned for fifty-three years, was to unite under his rule the people of Media – Busae, Parataceni, Struchates, Arizanti, Budii, Magi; beyond these he did not 102 extend his empire. His son Phraortes, however, who succeeded to the throne on his father's death, was not content to be king only of Media; he carried his military operations further afield, and the first country he attacked and brought into subjection was Persia.[48] By the combination of these two powerful peoples he proceeded to the systematic conquest of Asia, and finally attacked the Assyrians – the Assyrians of Nineveh, that is, who were formerly masters of all Asia, but at that time stood alone because of the desertion of their allies.[49] However, they were still powerful and prosperous, and in the campaign against them Phraortes and most of his army were killed. Phraortes reigned for twenty-two years and was succeeded by his son Cyaxares, 103 grandson of Deioces. This prince had a far greater military reputation than his father or grandfather. It was he who first organized the Asiatic armies by dividing them into separate units – spearmen, archers, and cavalry. Previously the different arms had all been mixed up in a mob. It was Cyaxares who fought the battle with the Lydians on the occasion when the day was darkened, and it was he who united all Asia beyond the Halys under his rule.[50]

    The first act of his reign was to march against Nineveh at the head of all his subject nations, with the object of destroying the town and avenging his father. He fought a successful battle against the Assyrians, but while he was besieging the town he was attacked by a large Scythian army under the command of King Madyas, son of Protothyes. The Scythians had entered Asia in pursuit of the Cimmerians whom they had expelled from Europe, a fact which explains their presence in Median territory 104 at this time. From the sea of Azov to the Phasis and the Colchians is a thirty days' journey for a quick traveller; but it is not far from Colchis to Media, and to reach it one has to pass through the country of only one intervening people, the Saspires. The Scythians, however, did not enter Media by this way, but took the much longer upper, or northern, route, keeping the Caucasus mountains on their right. A battle was fought, in which the

Medes were defeated and lost their power in Asia, which was taken over in its entirety by the Scythians.

The Scythians next turned their attention to Egypt, but were met in Palestine by Psammetichus the Egyptian king, who by earnest entreaties supported by bribery managed to prevent their further advance. They withdrew by way of Ascalon in Syria. The bulk of the army passed the town without doing any damage, but a small number of men got left behind and robbed the temple of Aphrodite Urania – the most ancient, I am told, of all the temples of this goddess. The one in Cyprus the Cyprians themselves admit was derived from it, and the one in Cythera was built by the Phoenicians, who belong to this part of Syria. The Scythians who robbed the temple at Ascalon were punished by the goddess with the infliction of what is called the 'female disease', and their descendants still suffer from it. This is the reason the Scythians give for this mysterious complaint, and travellers to the country can see what it is like. The Scythians call those who suffer from it 'Enarees'.[51]

During the twenty-eight years of Scythian supremacy in Asia, violence and neglect of law led to absolute chaos.[52] Apart from tribute arbitrarily imposed and forcibly exacted, they behaved like mere robbers, riding up and down the country and seizing people's property. At last Cyaxares and the Medes invited the greater number of them to a banquet, at which they made them drunk and murdered them, and in this way recovered their former power and dominion. They captured Nineveh (the story of the capture I will relate in another place[53]) and subdued the Assyrians, all except the territory belonging to Babylon. Then Cyaxares died, after a reign – including the period of Scythian domination – of forty years. He was succeeded by his son Astyages.

Astyages had a daughter called Mandane, and he dreamed one night that she urinated in such enormous quantities that it filled his city and swamped the whole of Asia. He told his dream to the Magi, whose business it was to interpret such things, and was much alarmed by what they said it meant. Consequently when Mandane was old enough to marry, he did not give her to some Mede of suitable rank, but was induced by his fear

of the dream's significance to marry her to a Persian named
Cambyses, a man he knew to be of good family and quiet habits
– though he considered him much below a Mede even of middle
rank.

108   Before Mandane and Cambyses had been married a year,
Astyages had another dream. This time it was that a vine grew
from his daughter's private parts and spread over Asia. As
before, he told the interpreters about this dream, and then sent
for his daughter, who was now pregnant. When she arrived, he
kept her under strict watch, intending to make away with her
child; for the fact was that the Magi had interpreted the dream
to mean that his daughter's son would usurp his throne. To
guard against this, Astyages, when Cyrus was born, sent for
his kinsman Harpagus, the steward of his property, whom
he trusted more than anyone, and said to him: 'I have some
instructions for you, Harpagus, and mind you pay attention to
them, whatever they may be. My safety depends upon you. If
you neglect it and prefer to serve others, the day will come when
you will be caught in your own trap. Get hold of Mandane's
child – take it home and kill it. Then bury it how you please.'[54]

'Sire,' Harpagus replied, 'you have never had cause to find
fault with me yet, and I will take care not to offend you in the
future. If this is your will, it is for me to do my duty and obey.'

109   The baby was dressed in grave-clothes and handed over to
Harpagus, who wept as he took it home. On his arrival, he told
his wife everything that Astyages had said, and she asked him
what he intended to do. 'Not,' Harpagus replied, 'what Astyages
has ordered. He can rage and rave as much as he likes – even
worse than he does now; but I will not consent to do what he
wants. Never will I take a hand in so brutal a murder. There are
many reasons why I will not do it – he is related to me by blood,
and Astyages is old and has no son. Suppose, when he dies,
Mandane – whose child I am to be the instrument of murdering
– should succeed to the throne: shouldn't I be in the utmost
peril? For my own safety's sake the baby must be killed. But one
of Astyages' servants must do it, not one of mine.'

110   He promptly sent a messenger to one of the king's herdsman,
who he knew had a stretch of pasture amongst mountains

ranged by wild beasts, and therefore most suitable to the purpose in hand. The fellow's name was Mitradates, and he lived with another of the king's slaves, a woman whose name in Greek would be Cyno, or Bitch (the Median form of it was Spaco – 'spaca' being the Median for bitch).[55] The foothills of the mountains where Mitradates pastured his oxen, lie to the north of Ecbatana in the direction of the Black Sea. Everywhere else Media is flat, but here, south of the country of the Saspires, it is very high, mountainous, and thickly wooded.

The herdsman made haste to answer the summons, and Harpagus said to him: 'The king's orders are that you must expose this infant in the wildest spot you know of amongst the hills, where it may soonest die. I am to tell you, moreover, that if you disobey and find some means of saving the child, the king will have you put to death in a way not pleasant to think of. I am commanded to see for myself that the child has been exposed.'

Mitradates picked up the baby and, returning by the way he had come, took it back to the shack where he lived. Fate had decreed that his wife, who had been daily expecting a child of her own, was on that very day brought to bed, while her husband was away in the city. Each had been worrying about the other, he in anxiety over his wife's confinement, and she because Harpagus had sent for her husband. What, she wondered, could be the meaning of that? In her fear she had hardly expected ever to see him again, so the instant he returned she asked him, before he could speak, why Harpagus had sent such an urgent message.

'My dear,' he said, 'I am sorry to say our masters in town are in trouble. I would give much not to have heard or seen what I saw there today. Why, in Harpagus' house there was nothing but sobs and tears – a most extraordinary thing. I went in, and no sooner was I inside than I saw a baby kicking and howling; it had lovely clothes on, too; all gold and bright colours. When Harpagus saw me, he told me to carry it off at once to the wildest spot in the mountains and leave it there. According to him it was the king's orders that I should do this – and he said he'd do dreadful things to me if I disobeyed. Of course I picked up the child and went off with it. It might have belonged to one

III

of the servants, for all I knew; though I *was* surprised at the gold and the grand clothes, and all those tears that nobody in the house was trying to hide – but I should never have guessed whose it really was, if the servant who put it into my arms, and showed me the way out of town, had not told me the whole story as we went along. Well, what do you think? it's the child of Mandane, the king's daughter, and Cambyses the son of Cyrus, and the king has given orders to make away with it. Look – here it is!'

112   As he said this, the herdsman uncovered the baby and showed it to his wife, who, seeing that it was a fine strong child, burst out crying, and put her arms round her husband's knees, imploring him to do anything rather than expose it. The man replied that he had no choice in the matter – for Harpagus would send people to see that it was done; and if he disobeyed, he would be put to death by torture. His wife therefore, seeing that her entreaties were in vain and that she could not dissuade her husband from exposing the baby, said that if the sight of the dead body was really necessary in order to prove that the deed was done, she had a suggestion to make.

'My own child,' she said, 'was born today – and it was born dead. Take the body and expose it, and let us bring up Mandane's son as our own. If we do this, no one will find out that you have disobeyed your masters. Moreover, we shall have managed pretty well for ourselves too: our dead baby will have a royal burial, and this live one will not be killed.'

113   Mitradates was pleased with his wife's proposal, and at once proceeded to act upon it. He took Mandane's child, which he had intended to kill, from the box in which he had brought it, stripped it of its fine clothes, and gave it to his wife, next he dressed his own dead child in the princely robes and put it in the box in place of the other. Then he took it to a lonely spot amongst the hills, and left it there.

When the child had lain there for two days, Mitradates went into town on the following morning, leaving one of his assistants on guard. Going to Harpagus' house, he said that he was ready to show him the child's corpse. Harpagus dispatched some trusty members of his guard, and through them obtained the proof he wanted, and had the herdsman's child buried. And so it came about that the herdsman's wife, when her own son was buried, brought up the child that was one day to be Cyrus, though she, of course, did not call him by that name.

When the boy was ten years old, his identity was revealed in the way I will now relate. He and some other boys were playing the game of 'Kings' in the street of the village, where Mitradates kept his oxen, and it so happened that Cyrus – the supposed son of the herdsman – was the one whom the boys picked as their king. In the course of their game, he was giving his subjects their various tasks – some to build houses, others to be his bodyguard, one to be the 'king's eye', and another his messenger – when one of the players, who happened to be the son of a distinguished Mede called Artembares, refused to do what King Cyrus commanded, and Cyrus ordered his arrest. The other boys accordingly seized him, and Cyrus beat him savagely with a whip. Furious at this indignity the boy, as soon as he was released, ran home to his father's house in the city and bitterly complained of his rough handling – saying, of course, that it was the son of Astyages' herdsman who had beaten him. He did not say it was Cyrus, because that was not yet his name. Artembares was very angry. He took his boy to Astyages, and reported the monstrous treatment he had received, showing the weals on his shoulders and complaining of the insult offered them both by a cowman's brat, a mere slave of the king. Seeing his raw shoulders, Astyages, when he had heard the story, was willing for the sake of the father's rank to give the boy his due; so he sent for the herdsman and his son. They came, and Astyages, fixing his eyes upon Cyrus, said: 'Had you – the son of a slave – the impudence to handle in this outrageous manner a boy whose father is my most distinguished subject?'

'Master,' Cyrus replied, 'there was nothing wrong in what I did to him. We boys in the village – and he was with us – were playing our game, and they made me king, because they thought I was the best man to hold the office. The others obeyed my orders, but *he* did not; he took no notice of me – until he was punished. That is what happened; and if I deserve to suffer for it, I am ready.'

116   Almost before he finished speaking, Astyages had guessed
who he was, for that was not the answer of a slave; moreover,
the cast of the boy's features seemed to resemble his own, and
he was just of an age to fit the date of the exposure. Deeply
troubled, for a long time Astyages did not speak; at last he
recovered himself and, wishing for an opportunity to examine
the herdsman privately, told Artembares that he would deal
with the matter so as to leave neither him nor his son any
cause for complaint; then he dismissed Artembares and told his
servants to take Cyrus into another room. When the two were
left alone, Astyages asked the herdsman how the child had come
into his possession, and the name of the man who had given it
him.

'The child is my own,' answered the herdsman, 'and its mother
is still my wife.'

Saying he was a fool if he wanted to have the truth dragged
out of him, Astyages signed to his guards, who seized Mitradates
and were about to take him off to the torture, when he revealed
what had actually happened.

He told the whole story truthfully from the beginning and
117   ended by begging the king for mercy. Once he had got the truth
from him, Astyages put the herdsman out of his mind and
transferred his wrath to Harpagus, whom he ordered his guard
to summon. As soon as he appeared, Astyages said: 'Harpagus,
when I gave you my daughter's child, how did you kill it?'
Harpagus, seeing that the herdsman was in the palace, made no
attempt to lie, for he knew that if he did he would be caught
and refuted. 'My lord,' he said, 'when I took the child, I considered how best I might fulfil your wishes and at the same time,
without offending you, avoid the guilt of killing with my own
hands your daughter's child – your own grandchild. What I did
was to employ this herdsman: I gave the child to him, and told
him it was your orders that it should be killed. And that was the
truth: it was indeed what you commanded. I gave him, moreover, careful instructions, telling him to expose it in a lonely
place amongst the hills, and to keep watch there until it was
dead. And I threatened him with all sorts of punishments if he
should disobey. He carried out my orders, and when the child

died, I sent the most trustworthy eunuchs I possess to witness for me that it was dead, and to have it buried. That, sire, is the fact of the matter, and that is how the child was made away with.'

Harpagus' tale was a straightforward one, and Astyages, concealing his anger, first repeated to him the herdsman's account of the affair, and then, when he had gone over the whole story, ended by saying that all was well and the child was still alive; he had been greatly distressed, he added, by what had been done to it, and seriously concerned at the hatred he could not have failed to arouse in his daughter. 'And now,' he said, 'since things have taken this lucky turn, I want you to send your own son to visit the young newcomer; and come to dinner with me yourself, as I intend to celebrate my grandson's deliverance by a sacrifice to the gods to whom such rites belong.'

Harpagus bowed low when he heard what the king said, and went home much pleased with his invitation to dinner on so happy an occasion: it was a great thing, he thought, to have come off so lightly. As soon as he reached home, he sent his son – his only son, a boy of about thirteen years old – to Astyages' palace, with instructions to do whatever the king should command. Then in high glee he told his wife everything that had occurred.

When Harpagus' son arrived at the palace, Astyages had him butchered, cut up into joints and cooked, roasting some, boiling the rest, and having the whole properly prepared for the table. Dinner-time came and the guests assembled, with Harpagus amongst them. Dishes of mutton were placed in front of Astyages and of everybody else – except Harpagus. To Harpagus was served the flesh of his son: all of it, except the head, the hands, and the feet, which had been put separately on a platter covered with a lid.

When Harpagus thought he had eaten as much as he wanted, Astyages asked him if he had enjoyed his dinner. He answered that he had enjoyed it very much indeed, whereupon those whose business it was to do so brought in the boy's head, hands, and feet in the covered dish, stood by Harpagus' chair and told him to lift the lid and take what he fancied. Harpagus removed the cover and saw the fragments of his son's body. As he kept control of himself and did not lose his head at the dreadful sight, Astyages asked him if he knew what animal it was whose flesh he had eaten. 'I know, my lord,' was Harpagus' reply; 'and for my part – may the king's will be done.' He said no other word, but took up what remained of the flesh and went home, intending, I suppose, to bury all of it together. And that was how Harpagus was punished.

Astyages now turned his attention to Cyrus, and summoning the Magi who had previously interpreted his dream, asked them again what they judged its meaning to be. They answered just as before, saying that the boy was certainly destined to be king, had he grown to manhood instead of meeting a too early death. 'The boy is not dead,' Astyages answered; 'he is alive and safe; and when he was living in the country, the village boys chose him as their king. He did to perfection everything that real kings do: he gave his playfellows their tasks as guards, sentries, messengers, and ruled them all. Tell me now – what do you think this signifies?'

'If he is alive,' said the Magi, 'and has already been a king by no contrivance of your own, then you may feel confident about him and need not lose heart. He has been king once and will never be so again. Even our regular prophecies are sometimes fulfilled in apparently small incidents, and as for dreams – they often work out in something quite trivial.'

'That is very much my own opinion,' Astyages answered. 'My dream has been fulfilled by the mere fact that the boy has been called king, and he is no longer a danger to me. Nevertheless I wish you to consider the position carefully, and give me your advice on what is likely to be the safest course for my family and yourselves.'

'Sire,' the Magi answered, 'for us too it is of the greatest moment that your rule should prosper. This boy is a Persian and a foreigner, and if the power passes into his hands, we, who are Medes and of a different race, will be despised and enslaved by the Persians; but you are our countryman, and with you on the throne we have our share of power and the positions of honour which you grant us. That is quite enough to ensure our deepest concern for you and your empire. If we saw danger in the present situation, we should tell you without reserve; but now that your dream has had this trifling conclusion, we feel quite comfortable and advise you not to be any more anxious than we are ourselves. We suggest, however, that you should send the boy to his parents in Persia, where he will be out of your sight.'

Astyages was much pleased by the Magi's advice. He called 121 Cyrus and said to him: 'I did you a wrong, my boy, because of a dream which was not fulfilled; but your own fortune saved you. Be off now to Persia – I will give you an escort on your way – and good luck to you. You will find a father and mother there of a different sort from Mitradates the herdsman and his wife.'

So Cyrus was dismissed, and on his return to Cambyses' 122 palace was received by his parents. When they found he was the son who they were sure had died long before, they greeted him with delight and asked how he had escaped death. Cyrus replied that it was only on the way thither that he had learnt his own history; previously he had known nothing and had made the mistake of supposing that he was the son of Astyages' herdsman. In the course of the journey, however, he had heard the whole truth from his guides, and he described how he had been brought up by Cyno the herdsman's wife. He was full of her praises, and through his story her name was continually on his tongue. The name Cyno – 'Bitch' – suggested to his parents a way of creating a legend amongst the Persians about the miraculous preservation of their son; so they put it about that a bitch had found him abandoned in the mountains and had suckled him. That 123 was the origin of this well-known tale.

When Cyrus grew up to be the bravest and most popular young man in Persia, Harpagus, who was burning for revenge upon Astyages, began to pay him court and send him presents. His own position, he thought, was inadequate to justify hopes of punishing the king without assistance; so when he saw Cyrus coming to maturity, he exerted himself to win his support, saying he had suffered injuries not unlike his own. He had already paved the way to his design by severally persuading the great Median nobles that it would be to their advantage, in view of the harshness of Astyages' rule, to dethrone him in favour of Cyrus. This done by way of preparation, Harpagus wished to inform Cyrus of his purpose; but, as Cyrus lived in Persia and the roads were guarded, there was only one way he could think of to get a message through to him: this was by slitting open a hare, without pulling the fur off, and inserting into its belly a slip of paper on which he had written what he wanted to say. He then sewed up the hare, gave it to a trusted servant, together with a net to make him look like a huntsman, and sent him off to Persia with orders to present the hare to Cyrus, and tell him by word of mouth to cut it open with his own hands, and 124 to let no one be present while he did so. The orders were obeyed. Cyrus received the hare, cut it open, found the letter inside and read it. 'Son of Cambyses,' it ran, 'since the gods watch over you – for without them you would never have been so fortunate – pay back Astyages, your would-be murderer. Had he achieved his purpose, you would have died; to the gods, and to me, you owe your deliverance. Doubtless you have long known what was done to you, and how Astyages punished me for giving you to the cowherd instead of killing you. Do now as I advise, and you will become master of the whole realm of Astyages. Persuade the Persians to revolt, and march against the Medes. It makes no odds whether I or any other Mede of distinction is appointed by the king to take command against you: you will succeed in either case, for the Median nobility will be the first to desert him and join you in the attempt to pull him down. All our preparations are made. Do what I advise, and do it quickly.'

125   The letter set Cyrus thinking of the means by which he could most effectively persuade the Persians to revolt, and his deliberations led him to adopt the following plan, which he found best suited to his purpose. He wrote on a roll of paper that Astyages had appointed him to command the Persian army; then he summoned an assembly of the Persians, opened the roll in their presence and read out what he had written. 'And now,' he added, 'I have an order for you: every man is to appear on parade with a sickle.' The Persian nation contains a number of

tribes, and the ones which Cyrus assembled and persuaded to revolt were the Pasargadae, Maraphii, and Maspii, upon which all the other tribes are dependent. Of these the Pasargadae are the most distinguished; they contain the clan of the Achaemenidae from which spring the Perseid kings. Other tribes are the Panthialaei, Derusiaei, Germanii, all of which are attached to the soil, the remainder – Dai, Mardi, Dropici, Sagartii – being nomadic.[56]

The order was obeyed. All the men assembled with their sickles, and Cyrus' next command was that before the day was out they should clear a certain piece of rough land full of thorn bushes, about eighteen or twenty furlongs square. This too was done, whereupon Cyrus issued the further order that they should present themselves again on the following day, after having taken a bath. Meanwhile Cyrus collected and slaughtered all his father's goats, sheep, and oxen in preparation for entertaining the whole Persian army at a banquet, together with the best wine and bread he could procure. The next day the guests assembled, and were told to sit down on the grass and enjoy themselves. After the meal Cyrus asked them which they preferred – yesterday's work or today's amusement; and they replied that it was indeed a far cry from the previous day's misery to their present pleasures. This was the answer which Cyrus wanted; he seized upon it at once and proceeded to lay bare what he had in mind. 'Men of Persia,' he said, 'listen to me: obey my orders, and you will be able to enjoy a thousand pleasures as good as this without ever turning your hands to servile labour; but, if you disobey, yesterday's task will be the pattern of innumerable others you will be forced to perform. Take my advice and win your freedom. I am the man destined to undertake your liberation, and it is my belief that you are a match for the Medes in war as in everything else. It is the truth I tell you. Do not delay, but fling off the yoke of Astyages at once.' 126

The Persians had long resented their subjection to the Medes. At last they had found a leader, and welcomed with enthusiasm the prospect of liberty. 127

When news of these events reached Astyages, he summoned

Cyrus to appear before him; but Cyrus' answer was to send the messenger back with the threat that he would be there a good deal sooner than Astyages liked. Astyages thereupon armed the Medes to a man, and so far lost his wits as to appoint Harpagus to command them – having apparently forgotten how he had treated him. The result was that when they took the field and engaged the Persian army, a few who were not in the plot did their duty, but of the remainder some deserted to the Persians and the greater number deliberately fought badly and took to

128 their heels. When Astyages learnt of the disgraceful collapse of the Median army, he swore that even so Cyrus should not get away with it so easily; then, having first impaled the Magi who had advised him to let Cyrus go, he armed all Medes, both under and over military age, who had been left in the city, led them out to battle and was defeated. His men were killed and he himself was taken alive.[57]

129 After the capture of Astyages, Harpagus came and jeered at him, the most bitter of his insults being a reference to the supper at which the king had regaled him with his son's flesh, followed by the question of what it felt like to be a slave instead of a king. Astyages looked at him and countered the question by another: did Harpagus, he asked, claim responsibility for what Cyrus had done? Harpagus replied that he most certainly did, for it was he who wrote the letter urging Cyrus to revolt.

'Then,' said Astyages, 'you are not only the wickedest but the most stupid of men: you are stupid, because when you might have been king yourself (if you really were responsible for what has happened) you gave another man the power; and you are wicked, because merely on account of that supper you have brought the Medes into slavery. If you had to hand the throne over to somebody else rather than keep it to yourself, it would have been more proper to give so fine a prize to a Mede than to a Persian; but as things are, the innocent Medes have become slaves instead of masters, and the Persians masters of the Medes though they were once their slaves.'

130 Astyages had reigned for thirty-five years before he was deposed in the manner I have described. Because of his harsh rule the Medes, who had been masters of Asia beyond the Halys

for a hundred and twenty-eight years except for the period of Scythian domination, were forced to bow before the power of Persia. At a later period they regretted their submission and revolted from Darius, but were defeated and again reduced.[58] On the present occasion the Persians under Cyrus rose against the Medes and from then onwards were masters of Asia.

Cyrus treated Astyages with great consideration and kept him at his court until he died.

That, then, is the story of the birth and upbringing of Cyrus, and of how he seized the throne. I have already related his subsequent success in resisting the aggression of Croesus, a victory which gave him control of the whole of Asia.

The following are certain Persian customs which I can describe from personal knowledge.[59] The erection of statues, temples, and altars is not an accepted practice amongst them, and anyone who does such a thing is considered a fool, because, presumably, the Persian religion is not anthropomorphic like the Greek. Zeus, in their system, is the whole circle of the heavens, and they sacrifice to him from the tops of mountains. They also worship the sun, moon, and earth, fire, water, and winds, which are their only original deities: it was later that they learned from the Assyrians and Arabians the cult of Uranian Aphrodite. The Assyrian name for Aphrodite is Mylitta, the Arabian Alilat, the Persian Mitra.[60]

As for ceremonial, when they offer sacrifice to the deities I mentioned, they erect no altar and kindle no fire; the libation, the flute-music, the garlands, the sprinkled meal – all these things they have no use for; but before a ceremony a man sticks a spray of leaves, usually myrtle leaves, into his headdress, takes his victim to some purified place and invokes the deity to whom he wishes to sacrifice. The actual worshipper is not permitted to pray for any personal or private blessing, but only for the king and for the general good of the community, of which he is himself a part. When he has cut up the animal and cooked it, he makes a little heap of the softest green-stuff he can find, preferably clover, and lays all the meat upon it. This done, a Magus (a member of this caste must be always present at sacrifices) utters an incantation over it in a form of words which is supposed to recount the Birth of the Gods. Then after a short interval the worshipper removes the flesh and does what he pleases with it.

133   Of all days in the year a Persian most distinguishes his birthday, and celebrates it with a dinner of special magnificence. A rich Persian on his birthday will have an ox or a horse or a camel or a donkey baked whole in the oven and served up at table, and the poor some smaller beast. The main dishes at their meals are few, but they have many sorts of dessert, the various courses being served separately. It is this custom that has made them say that the Greeks leave the table hungry, because they never have anything worth mentioning after the first course: they think that if the Greeks did, they should go on eating. They are very fond of wine, and no one is allowed to vomit or urinate in the presence of another person.

If an important decision is to be made, they discuss the question when they are drunk, and the following day the master of the house where the discussion was held submits their decision for reconsideration when they are sober. If they still approve it, it is adopted; if not, it is abandoned. Conversely, any decision they make when they are sober, is reconsidered afterwards when they are drunk.

134   When Persians meet in the streets one can always tell by their mode of greeting whether or not they are of the same rank; for they do not speak but kiss – their equals upon the mouth, those somewhat superior on the cheeks. A man of greatly inferior rank prostrates himself in profound reverence. After their own nation they hold their nearest neighbours most in honour, then the nearest but one – and so on, their respect decreasing as the distance grows, and the most remote being the most despised. Themselves they consider in every way superior to everyone else in the world, and allow other nations a share of good qualities decreasing according to distance, the furthest off being in their view the worst. By a similar sort of principle the Medes extended their system of administration and government during the period of their dominance: the various nations governed each other, the Medes being the supreme authority and concerning themselves specially with their nearest neighbours; these in their

turn ruling *their* neighbours, who were responsible for the next, and so on.

No race is so ready to adopt foreign ways as the Persian; for instance, they wear the Median costume because they think it handsomer than their own, and their soldiers wear the Egyptian corslet. Pleasures, too, of all sorts they are quick to indulge in when they get to know about them – a notable instance is pederasty, which they learned from the Greeks. Every man has a number of wives, and a much greater number of concubines. After prowess in fighting, the chief proof of manliness is to be the father of a large family of boys. Those who have most sons receive an annual present from the king – on the principle that there is strength in numbers. The period of a boy's education is between the ages of five and twenty, and they are taught three things only: to ride, to use the bow, and to speak the truth. Before the age of five a boy lives with the women and never sees his father, the object being to spare the father distress if the child should die in the early stages of its upbringing. In my view this is a sound practice. I admire also the custom which forbids even the king himself to put a man to death for a single offence, and any Persian under similar circumstances to punish a servant by an irreparable injury. Their way is to balance faults against services, and then, if the faults are greater and more numerous, anger may take its course. They declare that no man has ever yet killed his father or mother; in the cases where this has apparently happened, they are quite certain that inquiry would reveal that the son was either a changeling or born out of wedlock, for they insist that it is most improbable that the actual parent should be killed by his child. What they are forbidden to do, they are forbidden also to mention. They consider telling lies more disgraceful than anything else, and, next to that, owing money. There are many reasons for their horror of debt, but the chief is their conviction that a man who owes money is bound also to tell lies. Sufferers from the scab or from leprosy are isolated and forbidden the city. They say these diseases are punishments for offending the sun, and they expel any stranger who catches them: many Persians drive away even white doves, as if they, too, were guilty of the same offence. They have a

135

136

137

138

profound reverence for rivers: they will never pollute a river with urine or spittle, or even wash their hands in one, or allow
139 anyone else to do so. There is one other peculiarity which one notices about them, though they themselves are unaware of it: all their names, which express magnificence or physical qualities, end in the letter S (the Dorian 'san'). Inquiry will prove this in every case without exception.[61]

140 All this I am able to state definitely from personal knowledge. There is another practice, however, concerning the burial of the dead, which is not spoken of openly and is something of a mystery: it is that a male Persian is never buried until the body has been torn by a bird or a dog. I know for certain that the Magi have this custom, for they are quite open about it. The Persians in general, however, cover a body with wax and then bury it. The Magi are a peculiar caste, quite different from the Egyptian priests and indeed from any other sort of person. The Egyptian priests make it an article of religion to kill no living creature except for sacrifice, but the Magi not only kill anything, except dogs and men, with their own hands but make a special point of doing so; ants, snakes, crawling animals, birds – no matter what, they kill them indiscriminately. Well, it is an ancient custom, so let them keep it.[62]

141 I will now resume the thread of my story. The Ionians and Aeolians immediately after the Persian conquest of Lydia sent representatives to Cyrus at Sardis, to try to obtain from him the same terms as they had had under Croesus, their former master. Cyrus replied to their request by the story of the fluteplayer who saw some fish in the sea and played his flute to them in the hope that they would come ashore. When they refused to do so, he took a net, netted a large catch, and hauled them in. Seeing the fish jumping about, he said to them: 'It is too late to dance now: you might have danced to my music – but you would not.' The point of the story was, that when Cyrus had sent to the Ionians to ask them to revolt from Croesus, they had been unwilling to do so, though they were ready enough to offer their allegiance now that everything was settled in his favour. Cyrus was angry with them – and hence his reply.

When the news reached the various cities, the Ionians began

to erect defences and held meetings at the Panionium. The meetings were attended by all except the Milesians, who were the only ones to have obtained the same terms from Cyrus as from Croesus. The others came to a common agreement to apply for help to Sparta.

These Ionians to whom the Panionium belongs had the good fortune to establish their settlements in a region which enjoys a better climate than any other we know of. It does not resemble what is found either further north, where there is an excess of cold and wet, or further south, where the weather is both too hot and too dry. There are four different dialects of the Ionic language, distributed as follows: the most southerly of the Ionian towns is Miletus, with Myrus to the north of it, and then Priene, these three being in Caria and speaking the same dialect. Ephesus, Colophon, Lebedus, Teos, Clazomenae, and Phocaea are in Lydia, and share a common dialect completely distinct from what is spoken at the places previously mentioned. There are three other Ionian settlements, two being the islands of Samos and Chios and one, Erythrae, a mainland town. The two latter use the same dialect, Samos a peculiar one of its own. 142

The Milesians were in no danger from Cyrus, because of the treaty they had made with him; and of the other Ionians the islanders had nothing to fear, because the Phoenicians were not yet subject to Persia and Persia herself was not a sea power. 143

The reason for the separation of Miletus from the other Ionian towns was simply the general weakness of the Hellenic peoples at that date, and particularly of the Ionians, who of all the Greek races had least power and influence. There was no Ionian settlement of any consequence except Athens. The nation as a whole, including Athens and with the exception only of the twelve cities previously mentioned, took a dislike to the very name 'Ionian' and refused to admit to it – and even today I believe that most of them are ashamed of it. The twelve cities, on the contrary, were proud of it and marked their pride by building a temple for their own use which they called the Panionium, and by excluding from it all the other Ionians – though in point of fact only Smyrna ever applied for admission. Something similar can be seen in the case of the Dorian Pentapolis (or 144

Hexapolis as it used to be), where the Dorians are careful to exclude their neighbours from the use of their temple, the Triopium, and even went so far as to put a ban upon some of their own body who failed to observe the proprieties in regard to it. It used to be customary at the Games of the Triopian Apollo to give bronze tripods as prizes, and the winners were not allowed to take them away, but were required to dedicate them on the spot to the god. This ancient custom was openly defied by a Halicarnassian called Agasicles, who, after winning his tripod, took it home and fastened it up on the wall of his house. In punishment for this offence the five cities of Lindus, Ialyssus, Camirus, Cos, and Cnidus excluded Halicarnassus (which was the sixth) from the temple privileges.[63] The reason 145 why the Ionians chose the number twelve for their Asiatic settlements and refused to increase it, is, I fancy, the fact that they were divided into twelve states when they lived in the Peloponnese, just as the Achaeans, who drove them out, are today. Of the Achaean cities, that nearest Sicyon is Pallene; then comes Aegira, then Aegae on the Crathis, a stream which is never dry and gave its name to the Italian Crathis; then Bura and Helice (where the Ionians took refuge after their defeat by the Achaeans); then Aegium, Rhypes, Patres, Phares, and Olenus (on the large river Pirus); then Dyme and Tritaeës. Of these only 146 the last lies inland. Those, then, are the twelve divisions of what is now Achaea but used to be Ionia: and that is the reason, as I have said, why the Ionians founded twelve settlements in Asia. It is quite absurd to pretend that they are any more Ionian, or of purer blood than the Ionians generally; for a large section of them were actually Abantians from Euboea, who are not Ionians at all, even in name, to say nothing of the admixture of Minyae from Orchomenus and of Cadmeians, Dryopes, Phocians from various towns in Phocis, Molossians, Arcadian Pelasgi, Dorians from Epidaurus, and many others. Even those who started from the Council House in Athens and believe themselves to be of the purest Ionian blood, took no women with them but married Carian girls, whose parents they had killed. The fact that these women were forced into marriage after the murder of their fathers, husbands, and sons was the origin of the law, established by oath and passed down to their female descendants, forbidding them to sit at table with their husbands or to address them by name. It was at Miletus that this took place.

As to government, some of them took kings of Lycian nationality, descended from Glaucus the son of Hippolochus, others men of the Caucones from Pylus, descended from Codrus the son of Melanthus; and others, again, were ruled by men from both these families. But since these Ionians set more store by the name than the others, they may as well pass for the pure-bred ones. In point of fact, the name applies to all who originate from Athens and keep the festival of the Apaturia:[64] all the Ionians, that is, except the men of Ephesus and Colophon, who, because of some murder or other, are the only ones to be excluded from it.

The Panionium is a consecrated spot on the north side of Mycale, chosen by common consent of the Ionians and dedicated to Poseidon, who was previously worshipped at Helice. Mycale itself is a promontory of the mainland running out in a westerly direction towards Samos, and it is here that the Ionians gathered from their various cities to keep the festival called the Panionia. The names of festivals, not only amongst the Ionians but amongst all the Greeks, end, like the Persian proper names, in the same letter.

Those I have mentioned, then, are the twelve towns of the Ionians; the Aeolic towns are Cyme (also known as Phriconis), Larissa, Neon Tichus, Temnus, Cilla, Notium, Aegiroessa, Pitane, Aegaeae, Myrina, and Grynea. These are the eleven ancient towns of the Aeolians. Originally, indeed, they had twelve on the mainland, as the Ionians did, but one of them – Smyrna – the Ionians took from them. The soil of Aeolis is better than that of Ionia, but the climate is not so good.

The Aeolians lost Smyrna by treachery.[65] They had received into the town some men from Colophon, who had been defeated by the rival faction and expelled; the fugitives watched their chance and, when the people of Smyrna were celebrating a festival of Dionysus outside the walls, shut the gates and got possession of the town. The Aeolians of the other states came to their help, and terms were agreed to whereby the Ionians should surrender all moveable property but keep possession of the town. The people of Smyrna were then distributed amongst the other eleven Aeolian towns, where they were given civic rights. These, then, are the Aeolian settlements on the mainland, excluding those about Mt Ida which are not part of the confederacy. Of the island settlements, Lesbos has five (the sixth, Arisba, was taken by the Methymnaeans, their kinsmen, and the inhabitants enslaved), Tenedos one, and the so-called Hundred Isles one more. The Aeolians of Lesbos and Tenedos, like the Ionian islanders, had at this time nothing to fear. The other Aeolians came to a general agreement to follow the Ionians in whatever course they should take.

When the Aeolian and Ionian envoys reached Sparta (no time had been lost in the business) they chose Pythermus, a Phocaean, as their spokesman. In order to draw as large an audience as possible, he dressed himself in purple clothes and came forward to make a long speech asking for Spartan aid. The speech was a failure. The Spartans refused to help the Ionians, and the envoys left. Nevertheless, in spite of their rejection of the Ionian request, the Spartans dispatched a fifty-oared galley to the Asiatic coast, in order, I suppose, to watch Cyrus and what was going on in Ionia. The vessel put in at Phocaea, and the most distinguished of the men on board, a man called Lacrines, was sent to Sardis to forbid Cyrus, on behalf of the Lacedaemonians, to harm any Greek city or they would take action. The story goes that when Cyrus heard what the herald said, he asked some Greeks who happened to be with him who the Lacedaemonians were, and what were their numbers that they dared to send him such a command. On being informed, he gave the following answer to the Spartan herald: 'I have never yet been afraid of men who have a special meeting place in the centre of their city, where they swear this and that and cheat each other. Such people, if *I* have anything to do with it, will not have the troubles of Ionia to chatter about, but their own.' This was intended by Cyrus as a criticism of the Greeks generally, because they have markets for buying and selling, unlike the Persians who never buy in open market, and indeed have not a single market-place in the whole country. After this Cyrus left Tabalus, a Persian, as

governor of Sardis, entrusted to a Lydian named Pactyes the
task of collecting and conveying the treasure belonging to
Croesus and the other Lydians, and himself started eastwards
on his march to Ecbatana, taking Croesus with him. He did not
think the Ionians important enough to constitute a primary
objective, for his mind was on Babylon and the Bactrians and
the Sacae and the Egyptians, against whom he intended to lead
an expedition in person. Some other commander would suffice
to tackle the Ionians.

As soon as Cyrus had gone, Pactyes induced the Lydians to   154
rise against their Persian governor, and going down to the coast
was enabled by his possession of the Sardian gold to hire soldiers
and persuade the men from the coastal districts to support him.
He then marched against Sardis and laid siege to Tabalus, who
was shut up in the acropolis of the city. Cyrus, when the news   155
reached him on the road, asked Croesus what he thought would
be the end of it all. 'For I don't suppose,' he said, 'that the
Lydians will stop being a nuisance to me – and to themselves
too for that matter. I am not at all sure that the best thing would
not be to make slaves of them. As things are, I seem to have acted
like a man who kills a father and spares the sons; for you, who
were more than a father to the Lydians, are now my prisoner,
and to the Lydians themselves I have made a present of Sardis
– and then feel surprised because they are not loyal to me.'

When Croesus heard him give this expression to his thoughts,
he was afraid Sardis might be laid in ruins; so he replied: 'King,
your argument is reasonable enough; nevertheless I beg you not
to indulge your anger without restraint, or destroy an ancient
city which is not responsible for the present situation any more
than for what happened previously. The previous offence was
my own: I was the guilty one, and I am paying the penalty for
it; this time the villain is Pactyes, in whose charge you put Sardis.
So it is Pactyes you should punish. As for the Lydians, forgive
them – but at the same time, if you want to keep them loyal and
to prevent any danger from them in future, I suggest you put a
veto upon their possession of arms. Make them wear tunics
under their cloaks, and high boots, and tell them to teach their
sons to play the zither and harp, and to start shopkeeping. If

you do that, my lord, you will soon see them turn into women instead of men, and there will not be any more danger of their rebelling against you.'

156   Croesus gave this advice, because it seemed to him preferable from the Lydians' point of view to being sold into slavery. Moreover, he was aware that he would never induce Cyrus to change his mind, unless the suggestion he made was something worth listening to; and he was afraid that the Lydians, if they escaped the immediate danger, might nevertheless at some future date risk a rebellion against Persia and so come to grief. The proposal pleased Cyrus, and he promised to accept it; then, saying he was no longer angry, he sent for Mazares, a Mede, and ordered him to make a proclamation to the Lydians along the lines suggested by Croesus, and to sell into slavery everybody who had joined in the Lydian attack on Sardis. Pactyes himself

157   was at all costs to be taken alive and brought before him. Then, having given his orders, Cyrus continued his journey towards Persian territory.

Pactyes, when he learnt that an army was on his tracks and already near, took fright and fled to Cyme, and Mazares the Mede marched to Sardis with a detachment of Cyrus' troops. Finding Pactyes and his supporters gone, the first thing he did was to compel the Lydians to carry out Cyrus' orders – as a result of which they altered from that moment their whole way of life; he then sent a demand to Cyme that Pactyes should be surrendered, and the men of the town decided to consult the oracle at Branchidae as to whether they should obey. Branchidae is in Milesian territory close to the harbour of Panormus, and the oracle there, frequently consulted by the Ionians and Aeoli-

158   ans, is a very ancient one. The messengers from Cyme were instructed to ask how to deal with Pactyes in the way most likely to win the favour of the god, and the answer they received was that he must be give up to the Persians. The messengers returned home to report, and the citizens of Cyme were prepared in consequence to given up the wanted man. But just as they were about to do so, one of their number, a man of repute called Aristodicus, son of Heracleides, stopped them, because, as he said, he had his doubts about the oracle's answer and thought

the messengers had not reported it correctly. The result of this
was that another party, of which Aristodicus himself was a
member, left for Branchidae to repeat the question about
Pactyes. On their arrival Aristodicus, as spokesman, put to the
oracle this question: 'Lord Apollo, Pactyes the Lydian has fled
to us for safety, to escape violent death at the hands of the
Persians, who are now demanding that we should hand him
over. We do not dare to betray a suppliant, in spite of our fear
of Persian power, until we receive from you clear instructions
upon how we should act.' The answer to this second question
was the same as before: namely that Pactyes must be handed
over to the Persians.

Aristodicus, however, who had expected this answer, was not
yet satisfied. He went all round the outside of the temple, and
took from their nests the sparrows and other birds which had
built there; and the story goes that while he was doing it he heard
a voice from the innermost shrine, saying: 'Impious wretch, how
dare you do this wicked thing? Would you destroy those who
have come to my temple for protection?' Aristodicus, by no
means at a loss, replied: 'Lord Apollo, do you protect your
suppliants, yet tell the men of Cyme to abandon theirs?' 'Yes,'
answered the god; 'I do indeed, that you may suffer the sooner
for the sacrilege, and never come here again to consult my oracle
about handing over suppliants.'

This answer put the people of Cyme in a dilemma. They did
not want to come to grief as a result of surrendering their
suppliant, any more than to be besieged by the Persians as a
result of keeping him – so they sent him to Mytilene, and the
Mytilenaeans, on receiving a demand from Mazares, were about
to give him up in return for a sum of money (how much I cannot
say definitely, for it was never paid), when the people of Cyme,
hearing of these negotiations, sent a boat to Lesbos and took
Pactyes off to Chios. It was here that he was dragged by the
Chians from the temple of Athene the Guardian and surrendered
to the Persians. They were paid by getting in exchange the
district of Atarneus, a tract of land in Mysia opposite Lesbos.
So the Persians got hold of Pactyes and kept him under guard,
meaning to bring him before Cyrus.

159

160

For a considerable time after this no Chian would use barley meal from Atarneus to sprinkle on a sacrifice, or make any cake from the grain grown there; in fact they put a ban upon all the produce of the district so far as religious purposes were concerned.

161   After Pactyes had been given up by the Chians, Mazares began a campaign against the men who had taken part in besieging Tabalus. He sold the inhabitants of Priene into slavery, overran and plundered the district of Magnesia and the plain of the
162 Maeander. Then he fell ill and died. The command was taken over by Harpagus, another Mede – the same man who was given the abominable supper by the Median King Astyages, and helped to put Cyrus on the throne. On his appointment by Cyrus to the command, he marched into Ionia and set about taking the towns by means of earthworks. His method was to force the defenders inside their fortifications, raise a mound of earth close up against the wall, and so get an entrance and carry the town. The first Ionian town he attacked was Phocaea.

163   The Phocaeans were the first Greeks to make long sea voyages; it was they who showed the way to the Adriatic, Tyrrhenia, Iberia, and Tartessus. They used to sail not in deep, broad-beamed merchant vessels but in fifty-oared galleys. When they went to Tartessus they made themselves agreeable to Arganthonius, the king, who had ruled the place for eighty years, and lived to be a hundred and twenty. Indeed, this person took such a fancy to them that he asked them to quit Ionia permanently and settle wherever they liked on his own land; the Phocaeans, however, refused the offer, whereupon the king, hearing that the Median power was on the increase in their part of the world, gave them money to build a wall round their town. And he must have given a great deal, for the wall at Phocaea is of pretty considerable extent, and constructed of large stone blocks well fitted together.

164   Harpagus, then, brought his troops to Phocaea, whose defences were built in the way I have described, and began a siege, proclaiming to the Phocaeans that he would be satisfied if they consented to pull down a single tower in the fortifications and sacrifice one house. The Phocaeans, however, indignant at

the thought of slavery, asked for one day in which to consider
the proposal before answering; stipulating at the same time that
Harpagus should withdraw his forces during their deliberations.
This Harpagus consented to do, though he said he was perfectly
aware of their intention. So the troops were withdrawn, and
the Phocaeans at once launched their galleys, put aboard their
women and children and moveable property, including the
statues and other sacred objects from their temples – everything,
in fact, except paintings, and images made of bronze or marble
– and sailed for Chios. So the Persians on their return took
possession of an empty town.

The Phocaeans made an offer for the islands known as the 165
Oenussae, but the Chians, who were afraid that they might be
turned into a new centre of trade to the exclusion of their own
island, refused to sell; so the Phocaeans prepared to sail to
Corsica, where twenty years previously on the advice of an
oracle they had founded a city called Alalia. At the time Arganthonius was already dead. But before starting on the voyage,
they returned to Phocaea and killed the Persian garrison left
there by Harpagus. Then they laid fearful curses upon any man
who should fail to accompany them. They also dropped a lump
of iron into the sea and swore never to return to Phocaea until
it floated up again. But at the very beginning of the voyage to
Corsica more than half of them were seized with such passionate
longing to see their city and their old homes once more, that
they broke their oath and sailed back to Phocaea. The others
kept their oath, and continuing the voyage from the Oenussae,
arrived safely in Corsica. For five years they lived at Alalia with 166
the former settlers and built temples in the town; but during
that period they caused so much annoyance to their neighbours
by plunder and pillage, that the Tyrrhenians and Carthaginians
agreed to attack them with a fleet of sixty ships apiece. The
Phocaeans manned their own vessels, also sixty in number, and
sailed to meet them in the Sardinian sea, as it is called. In the
engagement which followed the Phocaeans won; but it was a
Cadmeian sort of victory with more loss than gain, for forty of
their vessels were destroyed and the remaining twenty had their
rams so badly bent as to render them unfit for service. The

survivors returned to Alalia, took aboard their women and
children and such of their property as there was room for,
167   and sailed from Corsica to Rhegium.[66] The Carthaginians and
Tyrrhenians drew lots for the possession of the prisoners from
the ships which were sunk. Of the Tyrrhenians, the people of
Agylla got by far the largest number, and they took them all
ashore and stoned them to death. The result of this outrage was
that when any living thing – sheep, ox, or man – subsequently
passed the place where the Phocaeans had lain, its body became
twisted and crippled by a paralytic stroke. Wishing to expiate
the crime of the murder, the men of Agylla sent to Delphi, and
were told by the Priestess to begin the custom, which they still
observe today, of honouring the dead men with a grand funeral
ceremony and the holding of athletic and equestrian contests.

Such was the fate of this section of the Phocaeans. Those
who went off to Rhegium made it the base from which they
afterwards sent men to found a new city in Oenotria. It is known
today as Velia. It was founded on the advice of a man of
Posidonia, who suggested that when the oracle said 'Cyrnus' –
or Corsica – it meant not the island but the hero of that name,
whose worship they were to institute.

168   So much for the Ionian city of Phocaea. The story of Teos
was not very different, for the Teians, when Harpagus took
their city by means of his mound, also took to their ships and
escaped by sea to Thrace. There they founded Abdera, a place
where Timesius of Clazomenae had previously tried to settle
but without success, as he was driven out by the Thracians. He
is honoured today as a hero by the Teians of Abdera.

169   The men of Phocaea and Teos were the only Ionians who
preferred voluntary exile to the prospect of slavery; the others
remained where they were. All of them, except the Milesians,
fought Harpagus as the Phocaeans and Teians had done, but in
spite of individual acts of great courage in defence of their homes
they were defeated; their towns were taken, and they were forced
to submit to their new masters. The Milesians, as I have already
mentioned, had already come to terms with Cyrus, so the war
did not affect them.

In this way Ionia was a second time reduced to subjection;

and after the defeat of the mainland towns by Harpagus, the islanders took fright and surrendered to Cyrus.

In spite of their defeat the Ionians continued the practice of meeting at the Panionium, and I am told that it was at one of these meetings that a man of Priene, called Bias, made a most admirable suggestion which, had they taken it, might have made them the most prosperous people in the Greek world. The proposal was that all the Ionians should unite and sail for Sardinia and settle together in a single community; there, living in the biggest island in the world, they would escape subjection, rule over their neighbours and be prosperous. If, on the other hand, they stayed in Ionia, there was little chance, so far as he could see, of ever regaining their freedom. This proposal was made by Bias after the Ionian defeat; but there was another, hardly less excellent, which had been made before it by Thales of Miletus, a Phoenician by remote descent: this was that the Ionians should set up a common centre of government at Teos, as that place occupied a central position; the other cities would continue as going concerns, but subject to the central government, in the relationship of outlying villages to the main city. Such were the two proposals.[67]

After the subjugation of Ionia, Harpagus attacked the Carians, Caunians, and Lycians, taking with him both Ionians and Aeolians in his army. The Carians, now a mainland people, were originally islanders. Long ago, when they inhabited the islands, they were known as Leleges and were subjects of Minos; but as far as I have been able to gather information on the subject, they never paid tribute in money but manned his ships whenever he had need of them; and in this way, because Minos had great military success and extended his conquests over a wide area, they became in his day by far the most famous of all nations. The Greeks are indebted to them for three inventions: fitting crests on helmets, putting devices on shields, and making shields with handles. Hitherto everyone who used a shield had managed it, not by a handle, but by means of a leather thong slung round the neck and left shoulder.[68] Long after this period the Carians were driven from the islands by the Dorians and Ionians, and settled on the mainland: that, at any rate, is the account the Cretans give – though the Carians themselves deny it, and claim to have been mainlanders from the first and never to have been known by any other name than their present one. In support of the claim to be aboriginals, they point to an ancient temple of the Carian Zeus at Mylasa, the use of which is shared by Mysians and Lydians as brother races of the Carians – Lydus and Mysus, according to them, having been the brothers of Car. These people, then, have the use of the temple; but others, even those which speak the same dialect as the Carians, are excluded from it.

172   The Caunians I believe myself to be of native stock, though by their own account they came originally from Crete.[69] As to dialect they have come to resemble the Carians – or the Carians them, for I cannot say definitely which way round it should be; but in their way of life they are very different from the Carians, and indeed from everybody else; for they think it the finest thing in the world for men, women, or children to organize large drinking parties of friends of similar age. Again, having decided on one occasion to reject certain foreign cults which had been established amongst them, and to worship only their own ancestral gods, all but the boys put on their armour and went as far as the boundary of Calynda, striking the air with their spears and saying they were driving out the foreign gods.

173   The Lycians came originally from Crete, which in ancient times was occupied entirely by non-Greek peoples. The two sons of Europa, Sarpedon and Minos, fought for the throne, and the victorious Minos expelled Sarpedon and his party. The exiles sailed for Asia and landed on Milyan territory, Milyas being the ancient name of the country where the Lycians live today, though it was occupied then by the Solymi. During the rule of Sarpedon, the Lycians were known as the Termilae, the name they had brought with them from Crete – and which is still in use amongst their neighbours; but after Lycus, son of Pandion, had been driven from Athens by *his* brother Aegeus, and had taken refuge with Sarpedon amongst the Termilae, in the course of time they adopted his name and came to be called Lycians. In their manners they resemble in some ways the Cretans, in others the Carians, but in one of their customs, that

of taking the mother's name instead of the father's they are unique. Ask a Lycian who he is, and he will tell you his own name and his mother's, then his grandmother's and great-grandmother's and so on. And if a free woman has a child by a slave, the child is considered legitimate, whereas the children of a free man, however distinguished he may be, and a foreign wife or mistress have no citizen rights at all.

The Carians were subdued by Harpagus, and neither they   174 nor any of the Greeks who lived in this country managed to distinguish themselves. Amongst the latter were the Cnidians, colonists from Lacedaemon, who occupy a district on the coast, called Triopium, adjoining the peninsula of Bybassus. All but a narrow neck is surrounded by water, the Ceramic gulf lying to the northward and the sea off Syme and Rhodes to the south-ward. The neck of the peninsula is about half a mile across, and while Harpagus was conquering Ionia, the Cnidians began to dig through it, with the intention of turning their country into an island. The isthmus they were trying to cut lies just where the Cnidian territory ends on the mainland side, so it is all contained within the peninsula. A large number of men worked at it, but it was observed that the workmen got hurt by splinters of stone in various places about the body, especially the eyes, more often than might have been expected. Indeed, there was something so unnatural about it, that they sent to Delphi to ask what it was that was hindering the work. Their own account is that the Priestess gave them the following answer in iambic verse:

> Do not fence off the isthmus; do not dig.
> Zeus would have made an island, had he willed it.

Having received their answer, the Cnidians stopped digging, and surrendered without a struggle on the approach of Harpagus and his army.

Inland, east of Halicarnassus, there were the men of Pedasus.   175 These people used to get warning of any impending disaster to them and their neighbours by the priestess of Athene growing a long beard, a thing which has actually happened on three occasions. They were the only Carians who resisted Harpagus for any length of time, and they did in fact cause him a good deal of trouble by holding out behind the defences they erected on Mount Lida. But the place was ultimately taken.

176

The fate of the Lycians of Xanthus makes a different story. When Harpagus advanced into the plain of Xanthus, they met him in battle, though greatly outnumbered, and fought with much gallantry; at length, however, they were defeated and forced to retire within their walls, whereupon they collected their women, children, slaves, and other property and shut them up in the citadel, set fire to it and burnt it to the ground. Then having sworn to do or die, they marched out to meet the enemy and were killed to a man. Most of the Lycians who now claim to be Xanthians are foreign immigrants, except eighty families who happened on that occasion to be away from home, and consequently survived. The people of Caunus followed in most respects the example of the Lycians, and their town fell into Harpagus' hands in much the same way as Xanthus did.

177

While Harpagus was turning upside-down the lower, or western, part of Asia, Cyrus was engaged with the north and east, bringing into subjection every nation without exception. Most of his minor conquests I will say nothing about, but mention only those of his campaigns which gave him the greatest trouble and are in themselves the most interesting.

178

Having subdued the rest of the continent, he turned his attention to Assyria, a country remarkable for the number of great cities it contained, and especially for the most powerful and renowned of them all – Babylon, to which the seat of government was transferred after the fall of Nineveh.[70] Babylon lies in a wide plain, a vast city in the form of a square with sides nearly fourteen miles long and a circuit of some fifty-six miles, and in addition to its enormous size it surpasses in splendour any city of the known world. It is surrounded by a broad deep moat full of water, and within the moat there is a wall fifty royal cubits wide and two hundred high (the royal cubit is three inches

179

longer than the ordinary cubit).[71] And now I must describe how the soil dug out to make the moat was used, and the method of building the wall. While the digging was going on, the earth that was shovelled out was formed into bricks, which were baked in ovens as soon as a sufficient number were made; then using hot bitumen for mortar the workmen began by revetting with brick each side of the moat, and then went on to erect the actual wall. In both cases they laid rush-mats between every thirty courses of brick. On the top of the wall they constructed, along each edge, a row of one-roomed buildings facing inwards with enough space between for a four-horse chariot to pass. There are a hundred gates in the circuit of the wall, all of bronze with bronze uprights and lintels.[72]

Eight days' journey from Babylon there is a city called Is on a smallish river of the same name, a tributary of the Euphrates, and in this river lumps of bitumen are found in great quantity. This was the source of supply for the bitumen used in building the wall of Babylon. The Euphrates, a broad, deep, swift river which rises in Armenia and flows into the Persian Gulf, runs through the middle of the city and divides it in two. The wall is brought right down to the water on both sides, and at right angles to the wall, there is a low fencing wall of baked bricks, stretching down each bank of the river. There are a great many houses of three and four storeys. The main streets and the side streets which lead to the river are all dead straight, and for every one of the side streets or alleys there was a bronze gate in the river wall by which the water could be reached.

180

The great wall I have described is the chief armour of the city; but there is a second one within it, hardly less strong though narrower. There is a fortress in the middle of each half of the city: in one the royal palace surrounded by a wall of great strength, in the other the temple of Bel, the Babylonian Zeus.[73] The temple is a square building, two furlongs each way, with bronze gates, and was still in existence in my time; it has a solid central tower, one furlong square, with a second erected on top of it and then a third, and so on up to eight. All eight towers can be climbed by a spiral way running round the outside, and about half-way up there are seats and a shelter for those who make the ascent to rest on. On the summit of the topmost tower stands a great temple with a fine large couch in it, richly covered, and a golden table beside it. The shrine contains no image and

181

no one spends the night there except, as the Chaldaeans who are the priests of Bel say, one Assyrian woman, all alone, whoever it

182   may be that the god has chosen. The Chaldaeans also say – though I do not believe them – that the god enters the temple in person and takes his rest upon the bed. There is a similar story told by the Egyptians at Thebes, where a woman always passes the night in the temple of the Theban Zeus and is forbidden, so they say, like the woman in the temple at Babylon, to have any intercourse with men; and there is yet another instance in the Lycian town of Patara, where the priestess who delivers the oracles when required (for there is not always an oracle there) is shut up in the temple during the night.

183   In the temple of Babylon there is a second shrine lower down, in which is a great sitting figure of Bel, all of gold on a golden throne, supported on a base of gold, with a golden table standing beside it. I was told by the Chaldaeans that, to make all this, more than twenty-two tons of gold were used. Outside the temple is a golden altar, and there is another one, not of gold, but of great size, on which full-grown sheep are sacrificed. (The golden altar is reserved for the sacrifice of sucklings only.) On the larger altar the Chaldaeans also offer something like twenty-eight and a half tons of frankincense every year at the festival of Bel. In the time of Cyrus there was also in this sacred building a solid golden statue of a man some fifteen feet high – I have this on the authority of the Chaldaeans, though I never saw it myself. Darius the son of Hystaspes had designs upon it, but he never carried it off because his courage failed him; Xerxes, however, did take it and killed the priest who tried to prevent the sacrilege.[74] In addition to the adornments I have described there are also many private offerings in the temple.

184   There have been many kings of Babylon who helped to fortify the city and adorn its temples, and I will tell their story in my History of Assyria.[75] There were also two queens, the earlier, Semiramis, preceding the later by five generations.[76] It was Semiramis who was responsible for certain remarkable embankments in the plain outside the city, built to control the river

185   which until then used to flood the whole countryside. The later of the two queens, Nitocris, was a woman of greater intelligence

than Semiramis, and not only left as a memorial of her reign the works which I will presently describe, but also, having her eye on the great and expanding power of the Medes and the many cities, including Nineveh itself, which had fallen before them, took every possible measure to increase her security.[77] For instance, she changed the course of the Euphrates, which flows through Babylon. Its course was originally straight, but by cutting channels higher upstream she made it wind about with so many twists and turns that now it actually passes a certain Assyrian village called Ardericca three separate times, so that anyone today who travels from the Mediterranean to Babylon and comes down the Euphrates finds himself three times over at Ardericca, on three different days. In addition to this she constructed embankments on both sides of the river of remarkable strength and height, and a long way above the city, close beside the river, dug a basin for a lake some forty-seven miles in circumference. The depth of the basin was governed by the point at which the workmen came to water as they dug down. The soil from the excavation was used for the embankments. When the basin was finished, the queen had stone brought to the place and built up the edge of it the whole way round. The purpose both of the excavation and of the diversion of the river was to cause the frequent bends to reduce the speed of the current, and to prevent a direct voyage downstream to the city. A boat would be faced with a devious course, and at the end of her trip she would have to make the tedious circuit of the lake. Moreover, these works lay in the neighbourhood of the approaches to Assyria and on the direct route to Media, and the intention of the queen was to discourage the Medes from mixing with the peoples of Babylon and thus getting to know what was going on there. Besides these defences she was responsible for another undertaking of a less important kind: the city, as I have said, being divided in two by the river, it was necessary under its previous rulers for anyone who wanted to get from one half to the other to cross over by boat and no doubt this was a tiresome business. Nitocris, however, when she was having the basin dug for the lake, had the foresight to make that work a means of getting rid of the inconvenience as well as of leaving

186

yet another monument of her reign. She ordered long stone blocks to be cut, and when they were ready and the excavation complete, she diverted the river into the basin; and while the basin was filling and the original bed of the stream was drying up, she built with burnt brick, on the same pattern as the wall, an embankment on each side of the river where it flowed through the city, and also along the descent to the water's edge from the gates at the end of the side streets; then, as near as possible to the centre of the city, she built a bridge over the river with the blocks of stone which she had had prepared, using iron and lead to bind the blocks together. Between the piers of the bridge she had squared baulks of timber laid down for the inhabitants to cross by – but only during daylight, for every night the timber was removed to prevent people from going over in the dark and robbing each other. Finally when the basin had been filled and the bridge finished, the river was brought back into its original bed, with the result that the basin had been made to serve the queen's purpose, and the people of the town had their bridge into the bargain.

187   This same queen was also the perpetrator of a grim practical joke. She had a tomb made for herself over one of the main gateways of the city, right high up above the actual entrance, and caused the following inscription to be cut on it: 'If any king of Babylon hereafter is short of money, let him open my tomb and take as much as he likes. But this must be done only in case of need. Whoever opens my tomb under any other circumstances will get no good of it.' The tomb remained undisturbed till the reign of Darius, who resented being unable to use one of the city gates – for he never did use the one under the tomb because, had he done so, he would have had to drive directly under the corpse; moreover, he thought it was absurd, when treasure was lying there asking to be taken, not to take it. So he opened the tomb. He found, however, not a penny inside – but only the body of the queen and another inscription, which read: 'If you had not been insatiably greedy and eager to get money by the most despicable means, you would never have opened the tomb of the dead.'[78] So much, then, for the tradition about the character of Nitocris.

The expedition of Cyrus was directed against her son, who,   188
like his father, was called Labynetus and was king of Assyria.[79]
When the Persian king goes to war, he is always well provided
not only with victuals from home and his own cattle, but also
with water from the Choaspes, a river which flows past Susa.
No Persian king ever drinks the water of any other stream, and
a supply of it ready boiled for use is brought along in silver jars
carried in a long train of four-wheeled mule waggons wherever
the king goes.

On his march to Babylon Cyrus came to the river Gyndes   189
which rises in the Matienian mountains, runs through the
country of the Dardanes and then joins the Tigris which passes
the city of Opis and flows into the Persian Gulf. Cyrus was
preparing to cross this river, for which boats were needed, when
one of his sacred white horses, a high-spirited creature, entered
the water and attempted to swim across but was swept under
by the rapid current and carried away. Cyrus was so furious
with the river for daring to do such a thing, that he swore he
would punish it by making it so weak that even a woman could
get over in future without difficulty and without wetting her
knees. He held up his march against Babylon, divided his army
into two parts, marked out on each side of the river a hundred
and eighty channels running off from it in various directions,
and ordered his men to set to work and dig. Having a vast
number of hands employed, he managed to finish the job, but
only at the cost of the whole summer wasted. Then, having   190
punished the Gyndes by splitting it into three hundred and sixty
separate channels, Cyrus, at the beginning of the following
spring, resumed his march to Babylon.

The Babylonians had taken the field and were awaiting his
approach. When he arrived near the city they attacked him, but
were defeated and forced to retire inside their defences; they
already knew of Cyrus' restless ambition and had watched his
successive acts of aggression against one nation after another,
and as they had taken the precaution of accumulating in Babylon
a stock of provisions sufficient to last many years, they were
able to regard the prospect of a siege with indifference. The siege
dragged on, no progress was made, and Cyrus was beginning to

191 despair of success. Then somebody suggested or he himself thought up the following plan: he stationed part of his force at the point where the Euphrates flows into the city and another contingent at the opposite end where it flows out, with orders to both to force an entrance along the riverbed as soon as they saw that the water was shallow enough. Then, taking with him all his non-combatant troops, he withdrew to the spot where Nitocris had excavated the lake, and proceeded to repeat the operation which the queen had previously performed: by means of a cutting he diverted the river into the lake (which was then a marsh) and in this way so greatly reduced the depth of water in the actual bed of the river that it became fordable, and the Persian army, which had been left at Babylon for the purpose, entered the river, now only deep enough to reach about the middle of a man's thigh, and, making their way along it, got into the town. If the Babylonians had learnt what Cyrus was doing or had seen it for themselves in time, they could have let the Persians enter and then, by shutting all the gates which led to the waterside and manning the walls on either side of the river, they could have caught them in a trap and wiped them out. But as it was they were taken by surprise. The Babylonians themselves say that owing to the great size of the city the outskirts were captured without the people in the centre knowing anything about it; there was a festival going on, and they continued to dance and enjoy themselves, until they learned the news the hard way. That, then, is the story of the first capture of Babylon.[80]

192 I will give several indications of the wealth and resources of Babylon, but the following is a specially striking one. Apart from normal tribute, the whole Persian empire is divided into regions for the purpose of furnishing supplies for the king and his army, and for four months out of the twelve the supplies come from Babylonian territory, the whole of the rest of Asia being responsible for the remaining eight. This shows that the resources of Assyria are a third part of the resources of Asia as a whole. It will be seen that the governorship (or satrapy, as the Persians call it) of Assyria is by far the most coveted of all their provincial posts, when one realizes that Tritantaechmes the son

of Artabazus, who held it from the king, received an *artaba* of silver every day – the *artaba* is a Persian dry measure of about five bushels, exceeding the Attic *medimnus* by three *choinikes*, or about five pints. He also had as his personal property, in addition to war horses, eight hundred stallions and sixteen thousand mares, twenty for each stallion, and so many Indian dogs that four large villages in the plain were exempted from other charges on condition of supplying them with food. This will give an idea of the wealth of the governor of Babylon.[81]

The rainfall of Assyria is slight and provides enough moisture   193
only to burst the seed and start the root growing, but to swell the grain and bring it to maturity artificial irrigation is used, not, as in Egypt, by the natural flooding of the river, but by hand-worked swipes.[82] Like Egypt, the whole country is intersected by dykes; the largest of them has to be crossed in boats and runs in a south-easterly direction from the Euphrates until it joins another river, the Tigris, on which Nineveh was built. As a grain-bearing country Assyria is the richest in the world. No attempt is made there to grow figs, grapes, or olives or any other fruit trees, but so great is the fertility of the grain fields that they normally produce crops of two-hundredfold, and in an exceptional year as much as three-hundredfold. The blades of wheat and barley are at least three inches wide. As for millet and sesame, I will not say to what an astonishing size they grow, though I know well enough; but I also know that people who have not been to Babylonia have refused to believe even what I have said already about its fertility. The only oil these people use is made from sesame; date-palms grow everywhere, mostly of the fruit-bearing kind, and the fruit supplies them with food, wine, and honey. The method of cultivation is the same as for figs, particularly in regard to the practice of taking the fruit of what the Greeks call the 'male' palm and tying it into the 'female' or date-bearing tree, to allow the gall-fly to enter the fruit and ripen it and prevent it from dropping off. For it is a fact that the male palms have the gall-fly in their fruit, like wild figs.

I will next describe the thing which surprised me most of all   194
in this country, after Babylon itself: I mean the boats which ply down the Euphrates to the city. These boats are circular in shape

and made of hide; they build them in Armenia to the northward
of Assyria, where they cut ribs of osiers to make the frames and
then stretch watertight skins taut on the under side for the body
of the craft; they are not fined-off or tapered in any way at bow
or stern, but quite round like a shield. The men fill them with
straw, put the cargo on board – mostly wine in palm-wood
casks – and let the current take them downstream. They are
controlled by two men; each has a paddle which he works
standing up, one in front drawing his paddle towards him, the
other behind giving it a backward thrust. The boats vary a great
deal in size; some are very big, the biggest of all having a capacity
of some hundred and thirty tons. Every boat carries a live
donkey – the larger ones several – and when they reach Babylon
and the cargoes have been offered for sale, the boats are broken
up, the frames and straw sold and the hides loaded on the
donkeys' backs for the return journey overland to Armenia. It
is quite impossible to paddle the boats upstream because of the
strength of the current, and that is why they are constructed of
hide instead of wood. Back in Armenia with their donkeys, the
men build another lot of boats to the same design.[83]

195   The dress of the Babylonians consists of a linen tunic reaching
to the feet with a woollen one over it, and a short white cloak
on top; they have their own fashion in shoes, which resemble
the slippers one sees in Boeotia. They grow their hair long, wear
turbans, and perfume themselves all over; everyone owns a seal
and a walking-stick specially made for him, with a device carved
on the top of it, an apple or rose or lily or eagle or something of
the sort; for it is not the custom to have a stick without some
such ornament. I will say no more about dress and so forth, but
196   will go on to describe some of their practices. The most ingenious
in my opinion is a custom which, I understand, they share with
the Eneti in Illyria. In every village once a year all the girls of
marriageable age used to be collected together in one place,
while the men stood round them in a circle; an auctioneer then
called each one in turn to stand up and offered her for sale,
beginning with the best-looking and going on to the second best
as soon as the first had been sold for a good price. Marriage was
the object of the transaction. The rich men who wanted wives

bid against each other for the prettiest girls, while the humbler folk, who had no use for good looks in a wife, were actually paid to take the ugly ones, for when the auctioneer had got through all the pretty girls he would call upon the plainest, or even perhaps a crippled one, to stand up, and then ask who was willing to take the least money to marry her – and she was offered to whoever accepted the smallest sum. The money came from the sale of the beauties, who in this way provided dowries for their ugly or misshapen sisters. It was illegal for a man to marry his daughter to anyone he happened to fancy, and no one could take home a girl he had bought without first finding a backer to guarantee his intention of marrying her. In cases of disagreement between husband and wife the law allowed the return of the purchase money. Anyone who wished could come even from a different village to buy a wife.

This admirable practice has now fallen into disuse and they have of late years hit upon another scheme, namely the prostitution of all girls of the lower classes to provide some relief from the poverty which followed upon the conquest with its attendant hardship and general ruin.

Next in ingenuity to the old marriage custom is their treatment 197
of disease. They have no doctors, but bring their invalids out into the street, where anyone who comes along offers the sufferer advice on his complaint, either from personal experience or observation of a similar complaint in others. Anyone will stop by the sick man's side and suggest remedies which he has himself proved successful in whatever the trouble may be, or which he has known to succeed with other people. Nobody is allowed to pass a sick person in silence; but everyone must ask him what is the matter. They bury their dead in honey, and their dirges for 198
the dead are like the Egyptian ones. When a Babylonian has had intercourse with his wife, he sits over incense to fumigate himself, with his wife opposite doing the same, and at daybreak they both wash. Before they have washed they will not touch any household utensils. In this they resemble the Arabians.

There is one custom amongst these people which is wholly 199
shameful: every woman who is a native of the country must once in her life go and sit in the temple of Aphrodite and there

give herself to a strange man. Many of the rich women, who are too proud to mix with the rest, drive to the temple in covered carriages with a whole host of servants following behind, and there wait; most, however, sit in the precinct of the temple with a band of plaited string round their heads – and a great crowd they are, what with some sitting there, others arriving, others going away – and through them all gangways are marked off running in every direction for the men to pass along and make their choice. Once a woman has taken her seat she is not allowed to go home until a man has thrown a silver coin into her lap and taken her outside to lie with her. As he throws the coin, the man has to say, 'In the name of the goddess Mylitta' – that being the Assyrian name for Aphrodite. The value of the coin is of no consequence; once thrown it becomes sacred, and the law forbids that it should ever be refused. The woman has no privilege of choice – she must go with the first man who throws her the money. When she has lain with him, her duty to the goddess is discharged and she may go home, after which it will be impossible to seduce her by any offer, however large. Tall, handsome women soon manage to get home again, but the ugly ones stay a long time before they can fulfil the condition which the law demands, some of them, indeed, as much as three or four years. There is a custom similar to this in parts of Cyprus.

200   In addition to the general practices I have mentioned, there is one which is peculiar to three of their clans: these people live entirely on fish which they catch and dry in the sun and then pound in a mortar: the smooth powder is then strained through muslin and eaten either kneaded into cakes or baked like a sort of bread, according to taste.

201   After the conquest of Assyria, Cyrus' next desire was to subdue the Massagetae, whose country lies far to the eastward beyond the Araxes, opposite the Issedones; they are reputed to be a numerous and warlike people and some suppose them to
202   be of Scythian nationality.[84] The Araxes is said by some to be bigger than the Danube, by others to be not so big.[85] It is also said to have a number of islands in it as large as Lesbos, where men live during summer on various kinds of roots which they dig up, and for their winter supplies pick as it ripens and put

into store any sort of tree-fruit which they have found to be suitable for food. They have also discovered another tree whose fruit has a very odd property: for when they have parties and sit round a fire, they throw some of it into the flames, and as it burns it smokes like incense, and the smell of it makes them drunk just as wine does the Greeks; and they get more and more intoxicated as more fruit is thrown on until they jump up and start dancing and singing. Such at least are the reports on how these people live.[86]

Like the Gyndes, which Cyrus divided into three hundred and sixty channels, the river Araxes rises in the country of the Matieni. It has forty mouths, all but one issuing into swamp and marshland, where men are said to live who eat raw fish and dress in seal-skins; by the remaining mouth it flows clear into the Caspian Sea. The Caspian is a sea in itself and has no connexion with the sea elsewhere, unlike the Mediterranean which the Greeks use, and what is called the Atlantic beyond the Pillars of Heracles, and the Indian Ocean, all of which are in reality parts of a single sea. The Caspian, however, is quite separate; in length it is a fifteen days' voyage, using the oars, and it is eight days' voyage across in its broadest part.[87] Along the west of it stretches the chain of the Caucasus, the longest and loftiest of all mountain ranges, inhabited by many different tribes, most of whom live off wild scrub. It is also said that there are trees here of which the leaves when crushed and mixed with water produce a dye with which the natives paint figures on their clothes, and the dye is so permanent that the designs never wash out but last as long as the material does, as if they had been woven into it when it was first made; and that these people copulate in the open like animals. 203

On the west, then, the Caspian is bounded by the Caucasus; eastwards lies an immense tract of flat country over which the eye wanders till it is lost in the distance. The greater part of this region is occupied by the Massagetae, whom Cyrus wished to attack. There were many things which roused his ambition and gave him courage to undertake this new war, the two most important being his belief in his superhuman origin and the success of all his previous campaigns; for it was a fact that till 204 then it had been impossible for any nation to escape, once he had marched against it.[88]

205   At this time Tomyris was queen of the Massagetae, her husband having died.[89] Cyrus sent to her and pretended to sue for her hand in marriage; but he was met with a refusal, for the queen was well aware that he was wooing not herself but her dominions. Cyrus, therefore, having failed to achieve his object by cunning, turned to open force, and advancing to the Araxes began his assault upon the Massagetae by bridging the river for his men to cross and constructing upper-works on the ferry
206 boats. While these works were still in hand, Tomyris sent him a message: 'King of the Medes,' it ran, 'I advise you to abandon this enterprise, for you cannot know if in the end it will do you any good. Rule your own people, and try to bear the sight of me ruling mine. But of course you will refuse my advice, as the last thing you wish for is to live in peace. Listen then – if you are so bent upon trying your strength against the Massagetae, give up the laborious task of building that bridge, and let my army withdraw three days' march from the river, and then come over yourself. Or, if you prefer it, retire the same distance yourselves, and let us meet you on your side of the river.'

    When he heard the queen's message, Cyrus called a meeting of his chief officers and laid the question before them, to get their opinions on which course to adopt. Every one of them
207 voted to let Tomyris and her army cross to their side. There was, however, one dissentient – Croesus the Lydian, who had attended the meeting of Persian officers and put forward a quite different view. 'My lord,' he said, 'I have already told you that since God has made me your servant I will do all I can to avert any danger which I see threatening your house; and I have learnt much from my own cruel misfortunes. Doubtless, if you think that you and your men are immortal, there is little point in my telling you my opinion; but if you recognize the fact that both you and the troops under your command are merely human, then the first thing I would tell you is that human life is like a revolving wheel and never allows the same people to continue long in prosperity. My view of the question you are discussing is the opposite of what the others have expressed. In my opinion,

if we allow the enemy to come over to this side of the river, the danger will be that in the event of defeat you may lose not only the battle but your whole empire as well; for obviously the Massagetae, if they are victorious, are not likely to run away home again: on the contrary, they will advance into your dominions. If on the other hand the fight goes in your favour, the victory will be less decisive than it might have been, had you crossed into their territory and followed it up by a pursuit of the beaten enemy. As you see, I balance what the Massagetae will do by what I am sure you will do yourself: namely that, in the event of victory, you will drive straight against the kingdom of Tomyris. And, apart from what I have already said, it would surely be an intolerable disgrace for Cyrus son of Cambyses to give ground before a woman. Here, then, is my advice: cross the river, advance to the limit of the enemies' withdrawal, and then try to get the better of them by a piece of strategy. I have heard that these people have no experience of such luxuries as the Persians enjoy and know nothing about the pleasures of life. Let us take advantage of this fact and set out a banquet in our camp on the most generous scale, with a great many sheep slaughtered and dressed, all sorts of other dishes, and bowls of strong wine in liberal quantities. Then when the banquet is all prepared, let us march back to the river, leaving only a detachment of inferior troops behind. Unless I am very much mistaken, when our enemies see all those good things, they will set to work upon them – and that will be our chance to distinguish ourselves by a bold stroke.'

When Cyrus had heard these two conflicting opinions, he   208
changed his mind in favour of Croesus, and sent a message to Tomyris to the effect that she should withdraw her troops, as he intended to cross the river himself. This she did according to her previous offer; and Cyrus, putting Croesus under the protection of his son Cambyses, whom he had named as his successor, with many injunctions to treat him with kindness and respect should the expedition end in disaster, sent the two back home to Persia and himself crossed the river with his army.

On the night after the crossing of the Araxes, when Cyrus   209
was lying asleep in the country of the Massagetae, he dreamed

that he saw the eldest son of Hystaspes with a pair of wings on his shoulders, with one of which he cast a shadow upon Asia and with the other upon Europe. The eldest son of Hystaspes and grandson of Arsames – Hystaspes belonged to the Achaemenid family – was Darius, a young man of about twenty at that time, who had been left behind in Persia as not yet old enough for campaigning. When Cyrus awoke, he thought over his dream and came to the conclusion that it was a serious matter; so he sent for Hystaspes and took him aside to speak to him. 'Hystaspes,' he said, 'I have discovered that your son is plotting against me and my throne, and I will tell you the source of my information, which admits of no doubt whatever. When I was asleep last night – and the gods, remember, watch over me and always warn me of approaching danger – I saw your eldest son with a pair of wings on his shoulders, shadowing Asia with one of them and Europe with the other. One cannot possibly get away from the fact that this dream means that he is plotting against me. You, therefore, must at once return to Persia and see to it that you can produce the young man for examination when I come home victorious after this war.'

210   Though Cyrus was so sure of Darius' treachery, the real meaning of the dream was not as he supposed: rather it was sent by God to warn him of his death then and there, and of the ultimate succession of Darius to the throne.

Hystaspes, when he heard about the dream, said, 'Heaven forbid, my lord, that any Persian alive should plot against you. If any does, may he die on the spot! Why – you found the Persians slaves and have made them free men; you found them subjects and have made them rulers. If a dream has told you that my son is planning treason, I make you a present of him to do with as you please.' And having given his answer, he crossed the Araxes and returned to Persia, to keep a watch on his son Darius in accordance with Cyrus' orders.

211   Cyrus now advanced a day's march from the river and proceeded to do what Croesus had proposed; then, leaving behind the feeblest portion of his men, he marched back again with his army thus purged. A detachment of the Massagetae, one-third of their whole force, fell upon the Persians who had been left

behind and killed them all, in spite of an attempt to resist; then, after this victory, they saw the splendid meal all ready laid out for them. At once they took their seats and began to regale themselves, and ate and drank so much that they went to sleep. This was the Persians' opportunity: they fell upon them, killed many, and took an even greater number of prisoners, amongst whom was Spargapises, the son of Tomyris the queen and general of the army.

When news of the defeat of her army and the capture of her son got through to the queen, she sent a message to Cyrus in the following terms: 'Glutton as you are for blood, you have no cause to be proud of this day's work, which has no smack of soldierly courage. Your weapon was the fruit of the vine, with which you fill yourselves till you are so mad that, as the liquor goes down, shameful words float up on the fumes of it – that is the poison you treacherously used to get my son into your clutches. Now listen to me and I will advise you for your good: give me back my son and get out of my country with your forces intact, and be content with your triumph over a third part of the Massagetae. If you refuse, I swear by the sun our master to give you more blood than you can drink, for all your gluttony.' 212

To this threat Cyrus paid not the least attention. The queen's son Spargapises, when he was sober again and able to realize his position, begged Cyrus to have his fetters removed. The request was granted, and, as soon as he had the use of his hands, he killed himself. The queen, on hearing that Cyrus ignored her terms, engaged him in the field with all the forces she possessed. The battle which followed I judge to have been more violent than any other fought between foreign nations. According to the information I have, the engagement began by the two armies coming to a halt within range of each other and exchanging shots with bows and arrows until their arrows were used up; after which there was a long period of close fighting with spears and daggers, neither side being willing to retreat. Finally, however, the Massagetae got the upper hand, the greater part of the Persian army was destroyed where it stood, and Cyrus himself was killed. He had been on the throne for twenty-nine years. 213 214

After the battle Tomyris ordered a search to be made amongst the Persian dead for the body of Cyrus; and when it was found she pushed his head into a skin which she had filled with human blood, and cried out as she committed this outrage: 'Though I have conquered you and live, yet you have ruined me by treacherously taking my son. See now – I fulfil my threat: you have your fill of blood.' There are many accounts of Cyrus' death; I have given the one which I think most plausible.[90]

215   In their dress and way of living the Massagetae are like the Scythians. Some ride, some do not – for they use both infantry and cavalry. They have archers and spearmen and are accustomed to carry the 'sagaris', or battle-axe. The only metals they use are gold and bronze: bronze for spearheads, arrow-points, and battle-axe, and gold for headgear, belts, and girdles. Similarly they give their horses bronze breastplates, and use gold about the bridle, bit, and cheek-pieces. Silver and iron are unknown to them, none being found in the country, though it

216   produces bronze and gold in unlimited quantity. As to their customs: every man has a wife, but all wives are used promiscuously. The Greeks believe this to be a Scythian custom; but it is not – it belongs to the Massagetae. If a man wants a woman, all he does is to hang up his quiver in front of her waggon and then enjoy her without misgiving. They have one way only of determining the appropriate time to die, namely this: when a man is very old, all his relatives give a party and include him in a general sacrifice of cattle; then they boil the flesh and eat it. This they consider to be the best sort of death. Those who die of disease are not eaten but buried, and it is held a misfortune not to have lived long enough to be sacrificed. They have no agriculture, but live on meat and fish, of which there is an abundant supply in the Araxes. They are milk-drinkers. The only god they worship is the sun, to which they sacrifice horses: the idea behind this is to offer the swiftest of mortal creatures to the swiftest of the gods.

BOOK TWO

Cyrus was succeeded by his son Cambyses, whose mother was 1
Pharnaspes' daughter Cassandane. Cassandane had died while
Cyrus was still alive, and he not only bitterly lamented her loss
but issued a proclamation that all his subjects should go into
mourning for her.

Cambyses, the son of Cyrus and of this princess, on the
ground that he had inherited his father's dominion over the
Ionians and Aeolians, included them amongst his other subjects
in the army he was preparing for an expedition against Egypt.[1]

The Egyptians before the reign of Psammetichus used to 2
think that of all races in the world they were the most ancient;
Psammetichus, however, when he came to the throne, took it
into his head to settle this question of priority, and ever since
his time the Egyptians have believed that the Phrygians surpass
them in antiquity and that they themselves come second.[2] Psammetichus, finding that mere inquiry failed to reveal which was
the original race of mankind, devised an ingenious method of
determining the matter. He took at random, from an ordinary
family, two newly born infants and gave them to a shepherd to
be brought up amongst his flocks, under strict orders that no
one should utter a word in their presence. They were to be kept
by themselves in a lonely cottage, and the shepherd was to bring
in goats from time to time, to see that the babies had enough
milk to drink, and to look after them in any other way that was
necessary. All these arrangements were made by Psammetichus
because he wished to find out what word the children would
first utter, once they had grown out of their meaningless baby-
talk. The plan succeeded; two years later the shepherd, who

during that time had done everything he had been told to do, happened one day to open the door of the cottage and go in, when both children, running up to him with hands outstretched, pronounced the word 'becos'. The first time this occurred the shepherd made no mention of it; but later, when he found that every time he visited the children to attend to their needs the same word was constantly repeated by them, he informed his master. Psammetichus ordered the children to be brought to him, and when he himself heard them say 'becos' he determined to find out to what language the word belonged. His inquiries revealed that it was the Phrygian for 'bread', and in consideration of this the Egyptians yielded their claims and admitted the superior antiquity of the Phrygians. That this was what really happened I myself learnt from the priests of Hephaestus at Memphis,[3] though the Greeks have various improbable versions of the story, such as that Psammetichus had the children brought up by women whose tongues he had cut out. The version of the priests, however, is the one I have given. There were other things, too, which I learnt at Memphis in conversation with the priests of Hephaestus, and I actually went to Thebes and Heliopolis for the express purpose of finding out if the priests in those cities would agree in what they told me with the priests at Memphis. It is at Heliopolis that the most learned of the Egyptians are said to be found.[4] I am not anxious to repeat what I was told about the Egyptian religion, apart from the mere names of their deities, for I do not think that any one nation knows much more about such things than any other; whatever I shall mention on the subject will be due simply to the exigencies of my story. As to human matters, they all agreed in saying that the Egyptians by their study of astronomy discovered the year and were the first to divide it into twelve parts – and in my opinion their method of calculation is better than the Greek; for the Greeks, to make the seasons work out properly, intercalate a whole month every other year, while the Egyptians make the year consist of twelve months of thirty days each and every year intercalate five additional days, and so complete the regular circle of the seasons.[5] They also told me that the Egyptians first brought into use the names of the twelve gods,[6] which the Greeks took over from them, and were the first to assign altars and images and temples to the gods, and to carve figures in stone. They proved the truth of most of these assertions, and went on to tell me that the first man to rule Egypt was Min, in whose time the whole country, except the district around Thebes, was marsh, none of the land below Lake Moeris – seven days' voyage up river from the sea – then showing above the water. I have little doubt that they were right in this; for it is clear to any intelligent observer, even if he has no previous information on the subject, that the Egypt to which the Greeks sail nowadays is, as it were, the gift of the river and has come only recently into the possession of its inhabitants.[7] The same is true of the country above the lake for the distance of a three days' voyage: the priests said nothing to me about it, but it is, in fact, precisely the same type of country.

The following is a general description of the physical features of Egypt. If you take a cast of the lead a day's sail off-shore, you will get eleven fathoms, muddy bottom – which shows how far out the silt from the river extends. The length of the Egyptian coastline (defining Egypt, as we usually do, from the gulf of Plinthine to Lake Serbonis which lies along the base of Mt Casius) is sixty *schoeni* – the *schoenus* being an Egyptian measure equivalent to sixty *stades*. The people there who own very little land measure it by fathoms; those not so poor, by *stades*, or furlongs; those with much land in *parasangs*, and those with vast estates in *schoeni*. The *parasang* is equal to thirty *stades*, the *schoenus*, as I have said, to sixty. Thus the coastline of Egypt is 3600 *stades* in length.[8] From the coast inland as far as Heliopolis – just about the same distance as along the road from the altar of the Twelve Gods in Athens to the temple of Olympian Zeus at Pisa – the country is broad and flat, with much swamp and mud. In point of fact these two distances – from Heliopolis to the sea, and from Athens to Pisa – are not exactly the same, but very nearly: careful reckoning would show that they differ by only fifteen *stades*. The latter is fifteen short of fifteen hundred: the former just the round number – fifteen hundred precisely.[9] Southward of Heliopolis the country narrows. It is confined on the one side by the range of the Arabian

mountains which run north and south and then continue without a break in the direction of the Arabian Gulf. In these mountains are the quarries where the stone was cut for the pyramids
at Memphis. This is the point where the range changes its
direction and bends away towards the Arabian Gulf. I learnt
that its greatest length from east to west is a two months'
journey, and that towards its eastern limit frankincense is produced. On the Libyan side of Egypt there is another range of
hills where the pyramids stand; these hills are rocky and covered
with sand, and run in a southerly direction like the Arabian
range before it bends eastward. Above Heliopolis, then, for a
distance of four days' voyage up the river Egypt is narrow, and
the extent of territory, for so important a country, is meagre
enough. Between the two mountain ranges – the Libyan and
Arabian – it is a level plain, in its narrowest part, so far as I
could judge, not more than about two hundred furlongs across.
South of this the country broadens again.

9   From Heliopolis to Thebes is a nine days' voyage up the
Nile, a distance of eighty-one *schoeni* or 4860 *stades*.[10] Putting
together the various measurements I have given, one finds that
the Egyptian coastline is, as I have said, about 420 miles in
length, and the distance from the sea inland to Thebes about
714 miles. It is another 210 miles from Thebes to Elephantine.[11]

10   My own observation bears out the statement made to me by
the priests that the greater part of the country I have described
has been built up by silt from the Nile. I formed the opinion
that the whole region above Memphis between the two ranges
of hills was originally a gulf of the sea, and resembles (if I may
compare small things with great) the country around Troy,
Teuthrania, Ephesus and the plain of the Maeander – not that
any of the rivers which have caused the alluvial deposits in those
neighbourhoods are comparable in size to any one of the five
mouths of the Nile. There are other rivers too I could mention,
much smaller than the Nile, which have effected great changes
in the coastline: for instance, the Achelous which flows through
Acarnania and has already joined to the mainland half the
islands of the Echinades group.

11   In Arabia not far from Egypt there is a very long narrow gulf

running up from the Red Sea[12] (as it is called). It is only half a day's voyage across in its narrowest part, but its length from its extreme limit to the open sea is a voyage of forty days for a vessel under oars. It is tidal. Now it is my belief that Egypt itself was originally some such arm of the sea – there were two gulfs, that is, one running from the Mediterranean southwards towards Ethiopia, and the other northwards from the Indian Ocean towards Syria, and the two almost met at their extreme ends, leaving only a small stretch of country between them. Suppose, now, that the Nile should change its course and flow into this gulf – the Red Sea – what is to prevent it from being silted up by the stream within, say, twenty thousand years? Personally I think even ten thousand would be enough. That being so, surely in the vast stretch of time which has passed before I was born, a much bigger gulf than this could have been turned into dry land by the silt brought down by the Nile – for the Nile is a great river and does, in fact, work great changes. So I not only believe the people who gave me this account of Egypt, but my own conclusions strongly support what they said. I have observed for myself that Egypt at the Nile Delta projects into the sea beyond the coast on either side; I have seen shells on the hills and noticed how salt exudes from the soil to such an extent that it affects even the pyramids; I have noticed, too, that the only hill where there is sand is the hill above Memphis, and – a further point – that the soil of Egypt does not resemble that of the neighbouring country of Arabia, or of Libya, or even of Syria (the Mediterranean coast of Arabia is inhabited by Syrians), but is black and friable as one would expect of an alluvial soil formed of the silt brought down by the river from Ethiopia. The soil of Libya is, as we know, reddish and sandy, while in Arabia and Syria it has a larger proportion of stone and clay. I had from the priests another striking piece of evidence about the origin of the country: namely that in the reign of Moeris the whole area below Memphis used to be flooded when the river rose only twelve feet – and when I got that information Moeris had been dead for less than nine hundred years. Today, however, the river never floods unless it rises at least twenty-three and a half, or twenty-four, feet. It seems to me therefore

that, if the land continues to increase at the same rate in height
and extent, the Egyptians who live below Lake Moeris in the
Delta and thereabouts will, if the Nile fails to flood, suffer
permanently the same fate as they said would some day overtake
the Greeks; for when they learned that all Greece is watered by
rain and not, as Egypt is, by the flooding of rivers, they remarked
that the day would come when the Greeks would be sadly
disappointed and starve – in other words, if God sees fit to send
no rain but afflicts the Greeks with a drought, they shall all die
from famine because they have no source of water other than
the rain which God chooses to grant them. All this is only too
true – but let me point out in answer how the case stands with
the Egyptians themselves: if, as I said before, the land below
Memphis (for this is the part which is always rising) continues
to increase in height at the same rate as in the past, is it not
obvious that when the river can no longer flood the fields – and
there is no chance of rain either – the people who live there will
have to go hungry? As things are at present these people get
their harvests with less labour than anyone else in the world,
the rest of the Egyptians included; they have no need to work
with plough or hoe, or to use any other of the ordinary methods
of cultivating their land; they merely wait for the river of its
own accord to flood their fields; then, when the water has
receded, each farmer sows his plot, turns pigs into it to tread in
the seed, and then waits for the harvest.[13] Pigs are used also for
threshing, after which the grain is put into store.

15   The Ionians maintain that Egypt proper is confined to the
Nile Delta, a stretch of country running along the coast from
what is known as Perseus' Watchtower to the Pelusian Salt-pans
– a distance of forty *schoeni* – and inland as far as Cercasorus,
where the Nile divides into the two branches which enter the
sea at Pelusium and Canopus.[14] The rest of what is usually called
Egypt belongs, according to this view, either to Libya or Arabia.
If, therefore, we accept it, we are forced to the conclusion that
there was a time when the Egyptians had no country at all; for
I am convinced – and the Egyptians themselves admit the fact –
that the Delta is alluvial land and has only recently (if I may so
put it) appeared above water. If, then, they once had no place

to live in, why did they make such a business of the theory that
they are the oldest race in the world? Surely there was no need
whatever to experiment with those two children to find out
what word they would utter first. But the fact is, I do not believe
that the Egyptians came into being at the same period as the
Delta (as the Ionians call it); on the contrary, they have existed
ever since men appeared upon the earth, and as the Delta
increased with the passage of time, many of them moved down
into the new territory and many remained where they originally
were. The name of Egypt was in ancient times given to Thebes,
the whole circumference of whose territory is only 6120 furlongs.[15] If, then, my judgement is correct, the Ionians are mis-   16
taken in their opinions about Egypt; if, on the other hand, the
Ionians are right, I am ready to prove that neither they nor
the rest of the Greeks know how to count: for they hold that
the world consists of three parts – Asia, Europe, and Libya –
whereas it is obvious that they should add a fourth, namely the
Egyptian Delta, since they do not include it in either Asia or
Libya. According to their theory the Nile is the boundary
between Asia and Libya; but the Nile splits at the apex of the
Delta and flows round it, thus making it a separate tract of land
lying between the two.

About the Ionians' opinion I have said enough; here now is   17
my own: Egypt, I consider, is the whole extent of territory
inhabited by Egyptians, just as Cilicia is the country occupied
by Cilicians or Assyria the country occupied by Assyrians. The
only true boundary between Asia and Libya is formed by the
frontiers of Egypt. By the usual Greek reckoning we should have
to suppose that Egypt, all the way from the Cataracts and
Elephantine, is cut in two, one half belonging to Libya and the
other to Asia; for the Nile divides, flowing from the Cataracts
to the sea right through the middle of the country – as far as
Cercasorus in a single stream, and below that city splitting into
three branches, of which one trends eastward and is known as
the mouth of Pelusium, and another trends westward and is
called the mouth of Canopus. There remains the third branch
which, coming down from the southward to the tip of the Delta,
flows straight on and cuts it in two on its course to the sea. This

branch, issuing at what is called the mouth of Sebennytus, is neither the least in volume, nor the least famous of the three. In addition to these there are two other mouths, the Saitic and Mendesian, which split off from the Sebennytic and so run into the sea. The Bolbitine and Bucolic mouths are not natural branches but excavated channels.

18   The opinion I have expressed about the extent of Egypt is supported by an oracle delivered from the shrine of Ammon which came to my notice after I had formed my own conclusions.[16] The people of Marea and Apis, on the Libyan frontier, took a dislike to certain religious observances, especially the prohibition against eating the flesh of heifers; accordingly, they sent to the shrine of Ammon and said they were in no way bound by Egyptian custom as they considered themselves not to be Egyptians at all, but Libyans; they lived outside the Delta, had nothing in common with Egypt, and wished to be allowed to eat what they pleased. The oracle, however, refused their request, and declared that all the country irrigated by the Nile was Egypt and all the people who lived below Elephantine and

19   drank the Nile's water were Egyptians. Now when the Nile overflows, it floods not only the Delta but parts of the territory on either side supposed to be Libyan and Arabian respectively, to a distance of two days' journey – in some places more, in some less.

About why the Nile behaves precisely as it does I could get no information from the priests or anyone else.[17] What I particularly wished to know was why the water begins to rise at the summer solstice, continues to do so for a hundred days, and then falls again at the end of that period, so that it remains low throughout the winter until the summer solstice comes round again in the following year. Nobody in Egypt could give me any explanation of this, in spite of my constant attempts to find out what was the peculiar property which made the Nile behave in the opposite way to other rivers, and why – another point on which I hoped for information – it was the only river to cause no breezes.

20   Certain Greeks, hoping to advertise how clever they are, have tried to account for the flooding of the Nile in three different

ways. Two of the explanations are not worth dwelling upon, beyond a bare mention of what they are: one is that the summer north winds cause the water to rise by checking the flow of the current towards the sea. In fact, however, these winds on many occasions have failed to blow, yet the Nile has risen as usual; moreover, if these winds were responsible for the rise, the other rivers which happen to run against them would certainly be affected in the same way as the Nile – and to a greater extent, in that they are smaller and have a less powerful current. There are many such rivers in Syria and Libya, but none of them are affected in the same way as the Nile. The second explanation is 21 less rational, being somewhat, if I may so put it, of a legendary character: it is that the Nile exhibits its remarkable character- istics because it flows from the Ocean, the stream of which encircles the world. The third theory is much the most plausible, 22 but at the same time furthest from the truth; according to this, the water of the Nile comes from melting snow, but as it flows from Libya through Ethiopia into Egypt, that is, from a very hot into a cooler climate, how could it possibly originate in snow? Obviously, this view is as worthless as the other two. Anyone who can use his wits about such matters will find plenty of arguments to prove how unlikely it is that snow is the cause of the flooding of the river: the strongest proof is provided by the winds, which blow hot from those regions; secondly rain and frost are unknown there – and after snow rain is bound to fall within five days. So that if there were snow in that part of the world, there would necessarily be rain too; thirdly, the natives are black because of the hot climate. Again, hawks and swallows remain throughout the year, and cranes migrate thither in winter to escape the cold weather of Scythia. But if there were any snow, however little, in the region through which the Nile flows and in which it rises, none of these things could possibly be; for they are contrary to reason. As to the writer 23 who mentions the Ocean in this connexion, his account is a mere fairy-tale depending upon an unknown quantity and cannot therefore be disproved by argument. I know myself of no river called Ocean, and can only suppose that Homer or some earlier poet invented the name and introduced it into poetry. If, after 24 criticizing these theories, I must express an opinion myself about a matter so obscure as the reason why the Nile floods in summer, I would say (to put the whole thing in the fewest words) that during winter the sun is driven out of his course by storms towards the upper parts of Libya. It stands to reason that the country nearest to, and most directly under, the sun should be most short of water, and that the streams which feed the rivers in that neighbourhood should most readily dry up.

25   But let me explain in somewhat greater detail my view of what happens when the sun passes across the upper regions of Libya. The atmosphere there is always clear, the land is open to the sun, and there are no cold winds to temper the heat; and the result of this is that the sun, as it passes over, has the same effect as it normally has elsewhere in summer on its passage through the mid-heaven: namely, it draws the water towards itself and then thrusts it into those parts of the country still further inland, where it comes under the influence of the winds which scatter and disperse it in vapour – so naturally the winds (the south and south-west) which blow from this region, are the most rainy. It seems to me, moreover, that not all the moisture drawn each year from the Nile is dispersed but that a certain amount is retained, as it were, in the neighbourhood of the sun. When the rough winter weather is over, the sun resumes its normal course in mid-heaven, and from then on exercises an equal attraction upon all rivers. In winter, then, all rivers but the Nile run in flood, because a great deal of rainwater is added to their volume – the rain cutting watercourses all over the country – but in summer, when the attraction of the sun's heat is added to the lack of rain, their volume is diminished. The Nile, on the other hand, behaves in the opposite way, and for an obvious reason: being subject to evaporation by the sun and having no rain to swell it, it is the only river which is much lower in winter than in summer – for in summer it is subject to the same force of solar attraction as other rivers, but in winter it is the only one to feel it. These, then, are my reasons for thinking that the sun

26 is the cause of this phenomenon, as also, I believe, of the dryness of the atmosphere in Egypt; the sun parching whatever lies in its path – so that in the upper parts of Libya it is always summer.

Suppose for a moment the relative positions of north and south were changed – suppose, that is, the north wind and the south wind each, so to speak, usurped that part of the heavens which now belongs to the other: if such a thing occurred, the sun, when driven from its normal course by the northerly gales of winter, would pass over the north of Europe instead of – as now – over the south of Libya, and I have no doubt that during its passage across Europe its effect upon the Danube would be precisely the same as its present effect upon the Nile. I mentioned the fact that no breeze blows from the Nile; I would suggest, in explanation of this, that the usual thing is for winds to originate in a cold region, not in a hot one.

Well, these things have been as they are since the beginning of time, and there is no changing them; so I will pass to another subject. Concerning the sources of the Nile, nobody I have spoken with, Egyptian, Libyan, or Greek, professed to have any knowledge, except the scribe who kept the register of the treasures of Athene in the Egyptian city of Sais.[18] But even this person, though he pretended to exact knowledge, seemed to me hardly serious. He told me that between Syene, near Thebes, and Elephantine there were two mountains of conical shape called Crophi and Mophi; and that the springs of the Nile, which were of fathomless depth, flowed out from between them. Half of the water flowed northwards towards Egypt and half southwards towards Ethiopia. The fact that the springs were bottomless he said had been proved by the Egyptian king Psammetichus, who had a rope made many thousands of fathoms long which he let down into the water without finding the bottom. I think myself that if there is any truth in this story of the scribe's, it indicates the presence of powerful whirlpools and eddies in the water, caused by its impact upon the mountains, and it was these eddies which prevented the sounding-line from reaching the bottom.

On this subject I could get no further information from anybody. As far as Elephantine I speak as an eye-witness, but further south from hearsay.[19] The most I could learn was that beyond Elephantine the country rises steeply; and in that part of the river boats have to be hauled along by ropes – one rope on each side – much as one drags an ox. If the rope parts, the boat is gone in a moment, carried away by the force of the stream. These conditions last over a four days' journey, the river all the time winding greatly, like the Maeander, and the distance to be covered amounting to twelve *schoeni*. After this one reaches a level plain, where the river is divided by an island named Tachompso. South of Elephantine the country is inhabited by Ethiopians who also possess half of Tachompso, the other half being occupied by Egyptians. Beyond the island is a great lake, and round its shores live nomadic tribes of Ethiopians. After crossing the lake one comes again to the stream of the Nile, which flows into it. At this point one must land and travel along the bank of the river for forty days, because sharp rocks, some showing above water and many just awash, make the river impracticable for boats. After the forty days' journey on land one takes another boat and in twelve days reaches a big city named Meroë, said to be the capital city of the Ethiopians. The inhabitants worship Zeus and Dionysus alone of the gods, holding them in great honour. There is an oracle of Zeus there, and they make war according to its pronouncements, taking from it both the occasion and the object of their various

30 expeditions.[20] Continuing upstream for the same length of time as it takes to travel from Elephantine to the capital, one comes to the Deserters – a people whose name is *Asmach*, a word which would mean in Greek 'those who stand on the left hand of the king'. They were a body of men two hundred and forty thousand strong, of the Egyptian warrior class, who went over to the Ethiopians during the reign of Psammetichus. The Egyptians had guard-posts in various parts of the country: one at Elephantine against the Ethiopians, another in Daphnae at Pelusium against the Arabians and Assyrians, and a third at Marea to keep a watch on Libya. The Persians have similar garrisons today both at Elephantine and Daphnae. Now it happened in Psammetichus' time that the Egyptians were kept on garrison duty for three years without being relieved, and this was the cause of their desertion. They discussed their grievances, came to a unanimous resolution, and went off in a body to Ethiopia. The king, on hearing the news, gave chase and overtook them;

and the story goes that when he besought them to return and used every argument to dissuade them from abandoning their wives and children and the gods of their country, one of their number pointed, in reply, to his private parts and said that wherever those were, there would be no lack of wives and children. So they continued their journey to Ethiopia and put themselves at the disposal of the Ethiopian king, by whom they were well rewarded, for he gave them permission to expel certain Ethiopians with whom he was on bad terms, and to settle on their land. The result of their living there was that the Ethiopians learned Egyptian manners and became more civilized.

The course of the Nile is, then, known not only where it 31 traverses Egypt but as much further southward as one can travel by land or water in four months; for calculation will show that that is the time it takes to go from Elephantine to the Deserters. At that point the river runs from west to east; beyond, nobody knows its course with any certainty, for the country is uninhabited because of the heat. I did, however, hear a story from some 32 people of Cyrene, who told me that during a visit to the oracle of Ammon they happened, in the course of conversation with Etearchus the Ammonian king, to get on to the subject of the Nile and the riddle of its source.[21] Etearchus told them that he had once had a visit from certain Nasamonians, a people who live in Syrtis and the country a little to the eastward. Being asked if there was anything more they could tell him about the uninhabited parts of Libya, these men declared that a group of wild young fellows, sons of chieftains in their country, had on coming to manhood planned amongst themselves all sorts of extravagant adventures, one of which was to draw lots for five of their number to explore the Libyan desert and try to penetrate further than had ever been done before. The whole Mediterranean coast of Libya from Egypt to Cape Soloeis, where it ends, is inhabited by many different tribes of Libyans, except the portion which is possessed by Greeks and Phoenicians; but in the inland parts lying to the southward of the inhabited coastal district only wild beasts are to be found, and further still to the southward there is a waterless and sandy desert without life of any kind. The story then was that the young men, sent off by their companions on their travels with a good supply of food and water, passed through the inhabited parts of the country to the region of wild beasts and then came to the desert, which they proceeded to cross in a westerly direction. After travelling for many days over the sand they saw some trees growing on a level spot; they approached and began to pick the fruit which the trees bore, and while they were doing so were attacked by some little men – of less than middle height – who seized them and carried them off. The speech of these dwarfs was unintelligible, nor could they understand the Nasamonians. They took their captives through a vast tract of marshy country, and beyond it came to a town, all the inhabitants of which were of the same small stature, and all black. A great river with crocodiles in it flowed past the town from west to east.[22]

33   I have said enough about Etearchus the Ammonian and his story, and will merely add his statement – which I repeat on the authority of the men from Cyrene – that the explorers got safely home again, and that the people whose country they visited were a nation of wizards. The river which flows past their town was supposed by Etearchus, reasonably enough, to be the Nile; for the Nile does in fact flow from Libya, dividing it in two and (to argue by analogy from the known to the unknown) I am willing to believe that it rises at the same distance from its mouth as the Danube, which has its source amongst the Celts near Pyrene and flows right through the middle of Europe, to reach the Black Sea at the Milesian colony of Istria. (The Celts live beyond the Pillars of Heracles, next to the Cynesians who are

34   the most westerly people of Europe.) Its course is quite familiar because it flows through inhabited country; but nobody, on the other hand, knows anything about the source of the Nile, because that river runs through a part of Libya which is uninhabited and desert. All I could possibly learn by inquiry about its course, I have here set down. It enters Egypt from the country beyond. Egypt is more or less opposite to, or south of, the mountainous part of Cilicia, from which the direct route to Sinope on the Black Sea takes five days for a man travelling light; and Sinope lies opposite the mouth of the Danube. It is my belief, then, that the Nile, as it traverses the whole of Libya,

is equal in length to the Danube – and on that subject I shall say no more.

About Egypt I shall have a great deal more to relate because 35 of the number of remarkable things which the country contains, and because of the fact that more monuments which beggar description are to be found there than anywhere else in the world.[23] That is reason enough for my dwelling on it at greater length. Not only is the Egyptian climate peculiar to that country, and the Nile different in its behaviour from other rivers elsewhere, but the Egyptians themselves in their manners and customs seem to have reversed the ordinary practices of mankind. For instance, women attend market and are employed in trade, while men stay at home and do the weaving. In weaving the normal way is to work the threads of the weft upwards, but the Egyptians work them downwards. Men in Egypt carry loads on their heads, women on their shoulders; women urinate standing up, men sitting down. To ease themselves they go indoors, but eat outside in the streets, on the theory that what is unseemly but necessary should be done in private, and what is not unseemly should be done openly. No woman holds priestly office, either in the service of goddess or god; only men are priests in both cases. Sons are under no compulsion to support their parents if they do not wish to do so, but daughters must, whether they wish it or not. Elsewhere priests grow their hair long; in Egypt 36 they shave their heads. In other nations the relatives of the deceased in time of mourning cut their hair, but the Egyptians, who shave at all other times, mark a death by letting the hair grow both on head and chin. They live with their animals – unlike the rest of the world, who live apart from them. Other men live on wheat and barley, but any Egyptian who does so is blamed for it, their bread being made from spelt, or *Zea* as some call it. Dough they knead with their feet, but clay with their hands – and even handle dung. They practise circumcision, while men of other nations – except those who have learnt from Egypt – leave their private parts as nature made them. Men in Egypt have two garments each, women only one. The ordinary practice at sea is to make sheets fast to ring-bolts fitted outboard; the Egyptians fit them inboard. In writing or calculating, instead of going, like the Greeks, from left to right, the Egyptians go from right to left – and obstinately maintain that theirs is the dexterous method, ours being left-handed and awkward.[24] They

37 have two sorts of writing, the sacred and the common. They are religious to excess, beyond any other nation in the world, and here are some of the customs which illustrate the fact: they drink from brazen cups which they scour every day – everyone, without exception. They wear linen clothes which they make a special point of continually washing. They circumcise themselves for cleanliness' sake, preferring to be clean rather than comely. The priests shave their bodies all over every other day to guard against the presence of lice, or anything else equally unpleasant, while they are about their religious duties; the priests, too, wear linen only, and shoes made from the papyrus plant – these materials, for dress and shoes, being the only ones allowed them. They bathe in cold water twice a day and twice every night – and observe innumerable other ceremonies besides. Their life, however, is not by any means all hardship, for they enjoy advantages too: for instance, they are free from all personal expense, having bread made for them out of the sacred grain, and a plentiful daily supply of goose-meat and beef, with wine in addition. Fish they are forbidden to touch; and as for beans, they cannot even bear to look at them, because they imagine they are unclean (in point of fact the Egyptians never sow beans, and even if any happen to grow wild, they will not eat them, either raw or boiled). They do not have a single priest for each god, but a number, of which one is chief-priest, and when a chief-priest dies his son is appointed to succeed him.

38 Bulls are considered the property of the god Epaphus – or Apis – and are therefore tested in the following way: a priest appointed for the purpose examines the animal, and if he finds even a single black hair upon him, pronounces him unclean; he goes over him with the greatest care, first making him stand up, then lie on his back, after which he pulls out his tongue to see if that, too, is 'clean' according to the recognized marks – what those are I will explain later.[25] He also inspects the tail to make sure the hair on it grows properly; then, if the animal passes all these tests successfully, the priest marks him by twisting round

his horns a band of papyrus, which he seals with wax and stamps with his signet ring. The bull is finally taken away, and the penalty is death for anybody who sacrifices an animal which has not been marked in this manner. The method of sacrifice is as follows: they take the beast (one of those marked with the seal) to the appropriate altar and light a fire; then, after pouring a libation of wine and invoking the god by name, they slaughter it, cut off its head, and flay the carcase. The head is loaded with curses and taken away – if there happen to be Greek traders in the market, it is sold to them; if not, it is thrown into the river. The curses they pronounce take the form of a prayer that any disaster which threatens either themselves or their country may be diverted and fall upon the severed head of the beast. Both the libation and the practice of cutting off the heads of sacrificial beasts are common to all Egyptians in all their sacrifices, and the latter explains why it is that no Egyptian will use the head of any sort of animal for food. The methods of disembowelling and burning are various, and I will describe the one which is followed in the worship of the goddess whom they consider the greatest and honour with the most important festival.[26] In this case, when they have flayed the bull, they first pray and then take its paunch out whole, leaving the intestines and fat inside the body; next they cut off the legs, shoulders, neck, and rump, and stuff the carcase with loaves of bread, honey, raisins, figs, frankincense, myrrh, and other aromatic substances; finally they pour a quantity of oil over the carcase and burn it. They always fast before a sacrifice, and while the fire is consuming it they beat their breasts. When they have finished that, they serve a meal out of the portions left over.

All Egyptians use bulls and bull-calves for sacrifice, if they have passed the test for 'cleanness'; but they are forbidden to sacrifice heifers, on the ground that they are sacred to Isis. The statues of Isis show a female figure with cow's horns, like the Greek representations of Io, and of all animals heifers are universally held by the Egyptians in the greatest reverence. This is the reason why no Egyptian, man or woman, will kiss a Greek, or use a Greek knife, spit, or cauldron, or even eat the flesh of a bull known to be clean, if it has been cut with a Greek knife.

They have a curious method of disposing of dead bulls and cows: cows are thrown into the river, but bulls are buried on the outskirts of towns, with one horn, or sometimes both, sticking out from the ground to mark the place. In due time, when the carcase has rotted, a barge comes from the island called Prosopitis to collect the bones. This island is part of the Delta and is nine *schoeni* in circumference; it contains a number of towns, the one from which the barges come being Atarbechis, where there is a temple of much sanctity dedicated to Aphrodite. From Atarbechis many people go round to the various towns to dig up the bones, which they take away and bury again all together in one spot. Other cattle which die a natural death are disposed of in the same way as bulls – for that is the law. None of them are slaughtered. The Egyptians who possess a temple dedicated to the Theban Zeus, or live in the province of Thebes, never sacrifice sheep but only goats; for not all Egyptians worship the same gods – the only two to be universally worshipped are Isis and Osiris, who, they say, is Dionysus. On the other hand, those who have a temple dedicated to Mendes, or live in the Mendesian province, never sacrifice goats but only sheep. The Thebans and those who follow them explain the origin of their custom of abstaining from the sacrifice of sheep by a story of Heracles,[27] who, they say, wished above all things to see Zeus. Zeus, however, was unwilling that his wish should be gratified. Heracles persisted, and Zeus had to devise a means of getting out of the difficulty. His plan was to skin a ram and cut off its head; then, holding the head before him and covering himself in the fleece, he showed himself to Heracles. This story explains why the Egyptians represent Zeus with a ram's head – a practice which has extended to the Ammonians, who are a joint colony of Egyptians and Ethiopians and speak a language which has points of resemblance to both.[28] So far as I can see, the Ammonians took their name too from this circumstance; for Amun is the Egyptian name for Zeus. So much, then, for the reason why the Thebans do not sacrifice rams but consider them to be sacred animals. Nevertheless on the festival of Zeus, which occurs once a year, they break this custom and do, in fact, slaughter a ram – but only one. They cut the animal in pieces, skin it, and put the fleece upon the statue of Zeus, just as Zeus once put it upon himself, and then lead towards the statue of Zeus a statue of Heracles. Then all who are engaged in the ceremony beat their breasts as if in mourning for the ram's death, and afterwards bury the carcase in a sacred sepulchre.

I was told that this Heracles was one of the twelve gods. Of the other Heracles, with whom the Greeks are familiar, I could get no information anywhere in Egypt.[29] Nevertheless it was not the Egyptians who took the name Heracles from the Greeks. The opposite is true: it was the Greeks who took it from the Egyptians – those Greeks, I mean, who gave the name to the son of Amphitryon. There is plenty of evidence to prove the truth of this, in particular the fact that both parents of Heracles – Amphitryon and Alcmene – were of Egyptian origin.[30] Again, the Egyptians say they do not know the names of Poseidon or the Dioscuri, or receive them as gods amongst the rest. But surely, if they had taken the name of any gods from the Greeks, it is precisely these they would have been most likely to notice – unless I am greatly mistaken in my belief that the Egyptians were already at that time a sea-faring nation, and that some of the Greeks, too, used the sea. Being sailors, the Egyptians would have learnt the name of Poseidon and the Dioscuri even before that of Heracles.[31]

Nevertheless the Egyptians have had a god named Heracles from time immemorial. They say that seventeen thousand years before the reign of Amasis the twelve gods were produced from the eight;[32] and of the twelve they hold Heracles to be one. To satisfy my wish to get the best information I possibly could on this subject, I made a voyage to Tyre in Phoenicia, because I had heard that there was a temple there, of great sanctity, dedicated to Heracles.[33] I visited the temple, and found that the offerings which adorned it were numerous and valuable, not the least remarkable being two pillars, one of pure gold, the other of emerald which gleamed in the dark with a strange radiance. In the course of conversation with the priests I asked how long ago the temple had been built, and found by their answer that they, too, did not share the Greek view; for they said that the temple

43

44

was as ancient as Tyre itself, and that Tyre had already stood for two thousand three hundred years. I also saw another temple there, dedicated to the Thasian Heracles; and I also went to Thasos, where I found a temple of Heracles built by the Phoenicians who settled there after they had sailed in search of Europa. Even this was five generations before Heracles the son of Amphitryon made his appearance in Greece. The result of these researches is a plain proof that the worship of Heracles is very ancient; and I think that the wisest course is taken by those Greeks who maintain a double cult of this deity, with two temples, in one of which they worship him as Olympian and

45 divine, and in the other pay him such honour as is due to a hero. The Greeks tell many stories with no thought. One of the silliest is the story of how Heracles came to Egypt and was taken away by the Egyptians to be sacrificed to Zeus,[34] with all due pomp and the sacrificial wreath upon his head; and how he quietly submitted until the moment came for the beginning of the actual ceremony at the altar, when he exerted his strength and killed them all. For me at least such a tale is proof enough that the Greeks know nothing whatever about Egyptian character and custom. The Egyptians are forbidden by their religion even to kill animals for sacrifice, except sheep and such bulls and bull-calves as have passed the test for 'cleanness' – and geese: is it likely, then, that they would sacrifice human beings? Besides, if Heracles was a mere man (as they say he was) and single-handed, how is it conceivable that he should have killed tens of thousands of people? And now I hope that both gods and heroes will forgive me for saying what I have said on these matters!

46 I mentioned the fact that certain Egyptians (the Mendesians) will not sacrifice goats, either male or female. The reason is this: they believe Pan to be one of the eight gods who existed before the subsequent twelve, and painters and sculptors represent him just as the Greeks do, with the face and legs of a goat.[35] Not that they think he is, in fact, like that – on the contrary they do not believe he differs in form from the rest of the gods. But that is how they paint him – why, I should prefer not to mention. The Mendesians hold all goats in veneration, especially male ones, whose keepers enjoy special honours. One of them is held

in particular reverence, and when he dies the whole province goes into mourning. Mendes is the Egyptian name both for Pan and for a goat. In this province in my lifetime a goat had intercourse with a woman, in full view of everybody – a most surprising incident, which became publicly known.

Pigs are considered unclean. If anyone touches a pig accident-ally in passing, he will at once plunge into the river, clothes and all, to wash himself; and swineherds, though of pure Egyptian blood, are the only people in the country who never enter a temple, nor is there any intermarriage between them and the rest of the community, swineherds marrying their daughters and taking their wives only from amongst themselves.

The only deities to whom the Egyptians consider it proper to sacrifice pigs are Dionysus and the Moon.[36] To both of these they offer pigs at the same time, at the same full moon, and afterwards eat the flesh. To explain the reason why they abhor the notion of sacrificing swine at any festival except this one, there is a legend current amongst them, which I know but think it seemly not to mention. The method of sacrificing a pig to the Moon is to slaughter the animal, put together the tip of the tail, the spleen, and the caul, cover them with all the fat found in the belly, and burn them; the rest of the meat is eaten on the same day as the sacrifice is offered – the day of the full moon; on no other day would they consent to taste it. People of slender means make models of pigs out of dough, which they bake and offer in sacrifice instead of real ones.

Everyone, on the eve of the festival of Dionysus, sacrifices a hog before the door of his house. When the animal is slaugh-tered, it is given back to the swineherd from whom it was procured. The swineherd then removes the carcase. In other ways the Egyptian method of celebrating the festival of Dionysus is much the same as the Greek, except that the Egyptians have no choric dance. Instead of the phallus they have puppets, about eighteen inches high; the genitals of these figures are made almost as big as the rest of their bodies, and they are pulled up and down by strings as the women carry them round the villages. Flutes lead the procession, and the women as they follow sing a hymn to Dionysus. There is a religious legend to account for the size of the genitals and the fact that they are the only part of the puppet's body which is made to move.

49   Now I have an idea that Melampus the son of Amythaon knew all about this ceremony; for it was he who introduced the name of Dionysus into Greece, together with the sacrifice in his honour and the phallic procession.[37] He did not, however, fully comprehend the doctrine, or communicate it in its entirety; its more perfect development was the work of later teachers. Nevertheless it was Melampus who introduced the phallic procession, and from Melampus the Greeks learned the rites which they now perform. Melampus, in my view, was an able man who acquired the art of divination and brought into Greece, with little change, a number of things which he had learned in Egypt, and amongst them the worship of Dionysus. I will never admit that the similar ceremonies performed in Greece and Egypt are the result of mere coincidence – had that been so, Greek rites would have been more Greek in character and less recent in origin. Nor will I allow that the Egyptians ever took over from Greece either this custom or any other. Probably Melampus got his knowledge of the worship of Dionysus through Cadmus of Tyre and the people who came with him from Phoenicia to the country now called Boeotia.[38] The names

50   of nearly all the gods came to Greece from Egypt. I know from the inquiries I have made that they came from abroad, and it seems most likely that it was from Egypt, for the names of all the gods have been known in Egypt from the beginning of time, with the exception (as I have already said) of Poseidon and the Dioscuri – and also of Hera, Hestia, Themis, the Graces, and the Nereids. I have the authority of the Egyptians themselves for this. I think that the gods of whom they profess no knowledge were named by the Pelasgians – with the exception of Poseidon, of whom they learned from the Libyans; for the Libyans are the only people who have always known Poseidon's name, and always worshipped him. Heroes have no place in the religion of Egypt.[39]

51   These practices, then, and others which I will speak of later, were borrowed by the Greeks from Egypt. This is not the case, however, with the Greek custom of making images of Hermes

with the phallus erect; it was the Athenians who first took this from the Pelasgians, and from the Athenians the custom spread to the rest of Greece.[40] For just at the time when the Athenians were assuming Hellenic nationality, the Pelasgians joined them, and thus first came to be regarded as Greeks. Anyone will know what I mean if he is familiar with the mysteries of the Cabiri – rites which the men of Samothrace learned from the Pelasgians, who lived in that island before they moved to Attica, and communicated the mysteries to the Athenians.[41] This will show that the Athenians were the first Greeks to make statues of Hermes with the erect phallus, and that they learned the practice from the Pelasgians – who explained it by a certain religious doctrine, the nature of which is made clear in the Samothracian mysteries.

In ancient times, as I know from what I was told at Dodona, the Pelasgians offered sacrifices of all kinds, and prayed to the gods, but without any distinction of name or title – for they had not yet heard of any such thing. They called the gods by the Greek word *theoi* – 'disposers' – because they had 'disposed' and arranged everything in due order, and assigned each thing to its proper division. Long afterwards the names of the gods were brought into Greece from Egypt and the Pelasgians learnt them – with the exception of Dionysus, about whom they knew nothing till much later; then, as time went on, they sent to the oracle at Dodona (the most ancient and, at that period, the only oracle in Greece) to ask advice about the propriety of adopting names which had come into the country from abroad. The oracle replied that they would be right to use them. From that time onward, therefore, the Pelasgians used the names of the gods in their sacrifices, and from the Pelasgians the names passed to Greece.

But it was only – if I may so put it – the day before yesterday that the Greeks came to know the origin and form of the various gods, and whether or not all of them had always existed; for Homer and Hesiod are the poets who composed theogonies and described the gods for the Greeks, giving them all their appropriate titles, offices, and powers, and they lived, as I believe, not more than four hundred years ago. The poets who are said to have preceded them were, I think, in point of fact

later. This is my personal opinion, but for the former part of my
statement on these matters I have the authority of the priestesses
of Dodona.[42]

54   About the oracles – that of Dodona in Greece and of Ammon
in Libya – the Egyptians have the following legend: according
to the priests of the Theban Zeus, two women connected with
the service of the temple were carried off by the Phoenicians and
sold, one in Libya and the other in Greece, and it was these
women who founded the oracles in the two countries. I asked
the priests at Thebes what grounds they had for being so sure
about this, and they told me that careful search had been made
for the women at the time, and that though it was unsuccessful,
they had afterwards learned that the facts were just as they had
reported them. At Dodona, however, the priestesses who deliver
55   the oracles have a different version of the story: two black doves,
they say, flew away from Thebes in Egypt, and one of them
alighted at Dodona, the other in Libya. The former, perched on
an oak, and speaking with a human voice, told them that there,
on that very spot, there should be an oracle of Zeus. Those who
heard her understood the words to be a command from heaven,
and at once obeyed. Similarly the dove which flew to Libya told
the Libyans to found the oracle of Ammon – which is also an
oracle of Zeus. The people who gave me this information were
the three priestesses at Dodona – Promeneia the eldest, Timarete
the next, and Nicandra the youngest – and their account is
confirmed by the other Dodonaeans connected with the temple.
56   Personally, however, I would suggest that if the Phoenicians
really carried off the women from the temple and sold them
respectively in Libya and Greece, the one who was brought to
Greece (or Pelasgia as it was then called) must have been sold
to the Thesprotians; and later, while she was working as a slave
in that part of the country, she built, under an oak that happened
to be growing there, a shrine to Zeus; for she would naturally
remember in her exile the god whom she had served in her native
Thebes. Subsequently, when she had learned to speak Greek,
she established an oracle there, and mentioned, in addition, that
the same Phoenicians who had sold her, also sold her sister in
57   Libya. The story which the people of Dodona tell about the

doves came, I should say, from the fact that the women were
foreigners, whose language sounded to them like the twittering
of birds; later on the dove spoke with a human voice, because
by that time the woman had stopped twittering and learned to
talk intelligibly. That, at least, is how I should explain the
obvious impossibility of a dove using the language of men. As
to the bird being black, they merely signify by this that the
woman was an Egyptian. It is certainly true that the oracles at
Thebes and Dodona are similar in character. Another form of
divination – by the inspection of sacrificial victims – also came
from Egypt.[43]

It was the Egyptians too who originated, and taught the   58
Greeks to use ceremonial meetings, processions, and pro-
cessional offerings: a fact which can be inferred from the obvious
antiquity of such ceremonies in Egypt, compared with Greece,
where they have been only recently introduced. The Egyptians   59
meet in solemn assembly not once a year only, but on a number
of occasions, the most important and best attended being the
festival of Artemis at Bubastis: second in importance is the
assembly at Busiris – a city in the middle of the Delta, containing
a vast temple dedicated to Isis, the Egyptian equivalent of
Demeter, in whose honour the meeting is held. Then there
are the assemblies in honour of Athene at Sais, of the Sun
at Heliopolis, of Leto at Buto, and of Ares at Papremis. The   60
procedure at Bubastis is this: they come in barges, men and
women together, a great number in each boat; on the way, some
of the women keep up a continual clatter with castanets and
some of the men play flutes, while the rest, both men and
women, sing and clap their hands. Whenever they pass a town
on the river-bank, they bring the barge close in-shore, some of
the women continuing to act as I have said, while others shout
abuse at the women of the place, or start dancing, or stand up
and pull up their skirts. When they reach Bubastis they celebrate
the festival with elaborate sacrifices, and more wine is consumed
than during all the rest of the year. The numbers that meet
there are, according to native report, as many as seven hundred
thousand men and women – excluding children. I have already   61
mentioned the festival of Isis at Busiris: it is here that everybody

– tens of thousands of men and women – when the sacrifice is over, beat their breasts: in whose honour, however, I do not feel it is proper for me to say.[44] Any Carians who happen to live in Egypt go even further and cut their foreheads with knives, thus proving that they are foreigners and not Egyptians. At Sais, on the night of the sacrifices, everybody burns a great number of lights in the open air round the houses; the lamps they use are flat dishes filled with oil and salt, with a floating wick which keeps burning throughout the night. The festival is called the Festival of Lamps, and even the Egyptians who cannot attend it mark the night of the sacrifice by lighting lamps, so that on that night lamps are burning not in Sais only but throughout the country. There is a sacred tradition which accounts both for the date and for the manner of these observances.

63   At Heliopolis and Buto the assemblies are for the purpose of sacrifice only; but at Papremis there is a special ceremony in addition to the ordinary rites and sacrifices as practised elsewhere. As the sun draws towards setting, only a few of the priests continue to employ themselves about the image of the god, while the majority, armed with wooden clubs, take their stand at the entrance of the temple; opposite these is another crowd of men, more than a thousand strong, also armed with clubs and consisting of men who have vows to perform. The image of the god, in a little wooden gold-plated shrine, is conveyed to another sacred building on the day before the ceremony. The few priests who are left to attend to it, put it, together with the shrine which contains it, in a four-wheeled cart which they drag along towards the temple. The others, waiting at the temple gate, try to prevent it from coming in, while the votaries take the god's side and set upon them with their clubs. The assault is resisted, and a vigorous tussle ensues in which heads are broken and not a few actually die of the wounds they receive. That, at least, is what I believe, though the Egyptians told me that nobody is ever killed. The origin of this festival is explained locally by the story that the mother of Ares once lived in the temple; Ares himself was brought up elsewhere, but when he grew to manhood he wished to get to know his mother and for that purpose came to the temple where she was.[45] Her attend-

ants, however, not knowing him by sight, refused him admission, and succeeded in keeping him out until he fetched help from another town and forced his way in by violence. This, they say, is why the battle with clubs is part of the ceremony at the festival of Ares.

It was the Egyptians who first made it an offence against piety to have intercourse with women in temples, or to enter temples after intercourse without having previously washed. Hardly any nation except the Egyptians and Greeks has any such scruple, but nearly all consider men and women to be, in this respect, no different from animals, which, whether they are beasts or birds, they constantly see coupling in temples and sacred places – and if the god concerned had any objection to this, he would not allow it to occur. Such is the theory, but, in spite of it, I must continue to disapprove the practice. The Egyptians are meticulous in their observance of this point, as indeed they are in everything else which concerns their religion.

There are not a great many wild animals in Egypt, in spite of the fact that it borders on Libya. Such as there are – both wild and tame – are without exception held to be sacred. To explain the reason for this, I should have to enter into a discussion of religious principles which is a subject I particularly wish to avoid – any slight mention I have already made of such matters having been forced upon me by the needs of my story. But, reasons apart, how they actually behave towards animals I will proceed to describe. The various sorts have guardians appointed for them, sometimes men, sometimes women, who are responsible for feeding them; and the office of guardian is handed down from father to child. Their manner, in the various cities, of performing vows is as follows: praying to the god to whom the particular creature, whichever it may be, is sacred, they shave the heads of their children – sometimes completely, sometimes only a half or a third part – and after weighing the hair in a pair of scales, give an equal weight of silver to the animals' keeper, who then cuts up fish (the animals' usual food) to an equivalent value and gives it to the animal to eat. Anyone who deliberately kills one of these animals, is punished with death; should one be killed accidentally, the penalty is whatever the priests choose to impose; but for killing an ibis or a hawk, whether deliberately or not, the penalty is inevitably death.

66   The number, already large, of domestic animals would have been greatly increased, were it not for an odd thing that happens to the cats. The females, when they have kittens, avoid the toms; but the toms, thus deprived of their satisfaction, get over the difficulty very ingeniously, for they either openly seize, or secretly steal, the kittens and kill them – but without eating them – and the result is that the females, deprived of their kittens and wanting more (for their maternal instinct is very strong), go off to look for mates again. What happens when a house catches fire is most extraordinary: nobody takes the least trouble to put it out, for it is only the cats that matter: everyone stands in a row, a little distance from his neighbour, trying to protect the cats, who nevertheless slip through the line, or jump over it, and hurl themselves into the flames. This causes the Egyptians deep distress. All the inmates of a house where a cat has died a natural death shave their eyebrows, and when a dog dies they
67   shave the whole body including the head. Cats which have died are taken to Bubastis, where they are embalmed and buried in sacred receptacles; dogs are buried, also in sacred burial-places, in the towns where they belong. Mongooses are buried in the same way as dogs; field-mice and hawks are taken to Buto, ibises to Hermopolis. Bears, which are scarce, and wolves (which in Egypt are not much bigger than foxes) are buried wherever they happen to be found lying dead.

68   The following is an account of the crocodile. During the four winter months it takes no food. It is a four-footed, amphibious creature, lays and hatches its eggs on land, where it spends the greater part of the day, and stays all night in the river, where the water is warmer than the night-air and the dew. The difference in size between the young and the full-grown crocodile is greater than in any other known creature; for a crocodile's egg is hardly bigger than a goose's, and the young when hatched is small in proportion, yet it grows to a size of some twenty-three feet long or even more. It has eyes like a pig's but great fang-like teeth in proportion to its body, and is the only animal to have no tongue and a stationary lower jaw; for when it eats it brings the upper

jaw down upon the under. It has powerful claws and a scaly hide, which on its back is impenetrable. It cannot see under water, though on land its sight is remarkably sharp. One result of its spending so much time in the water is that the inside of its mouth gets covered with leeches. Other animals avoid the crocodile, as do all birds too with one exception – the sandpiper, or Egyptian plover; this bird is of service to the crocodile and lives, in consequence, in the greatest amity with him; for when the crocodile comes ashore and lies with his mouth wide open (which he generally does facing towards the west), the bird hops in and swallows the leeches. The crocodile enjoys this, and never, in consequence, hurts the bird. Some Egyptians reverence **69** the crocodile as a sacred beast; others do not, but treat it as an enemy. The strongest belief in its sanctity is to be found in Thebes and round about Lake Moeris; in these places they keep one particular crocodile, which they tame, putting rings made of glass or gold into its ears and bracelets round its front feet, and giving it special food and ceremonial offerings. In fact, while these creatures are alive they treat them with every kindness, and, when they die, embalm them and bury them in sacred tombs. On the other hand, in the neighbourhood of Elephantine crocodiles are not considered sacred animals at all, but are eaten. In the Egyptian language these creatures are called *champsae*. The name crocodile – or 'lizard' – was given them by the Ionians, who saw they resembled the lizards commonly found on stone walls in their own country.[46]

Of the numerous different ways of catching crocodiles I will **70** describe the one which seems to me the most worthy to report. They bait a hook with a chine of pork and let it float out into midstream, and at the same time, standing on the bank, take a live pig and beat it. The crocodile, hearing its squeals, makes a rush towards it, encounters the bait, gulps it down, and is hauled out of the water. The first thing the huntsman does when he has got the beast on land is to plaster its eyes with mud; this done, it is dispatched easily enough – but without this precaution it will give a lot of trouble.

The hippopotamus is held sacred in the district of Papremis, **71** but not elsewhere. This animal has four legs, cloven hoofs like an ox, a snub nose, a horse's mane and tail, conspicuous tusks, a voice like a horse's neigh, and is about the size of a very large ox. Its hide is so thick and tough that when dried it can be made

72 into spear-shafts.[47] Otters, too, are found in the Nile; they, and the fish called lepidotus, and eels are all considered sacred to

73 the Nile, as is also the bird known as the foxgoose. Another sacred bird is the phoenix; I have not seen a phoenix myself, except in paintings, for it is very rare and visits the country (so they say at Heliopolis) only at intervals of 500 years, on the occasion of the death of the parent-bird. To judge by the paintings, its plumage is partly golden, partly red, and in shape and size it is exactly like an eagle. There is a story about the phoenix which I do not find credible; it brings its parent in a lump of myrrh all the way from Arabia and buries the body in the temple of the Sun. To perform this feat, the bird first shapes some myrrh into a sort of egg as big as it finds, by testing, that it can carry; then it hollows the lump out, puts its father inside and smears some more myrrh over the hole. The egg-shaped lump is then just of the same weight as it was originally. Finally it is carried by the bird to the temple of the Sun in Egypt. Such, at least, is the story.[48]

74 Near Thebes a species of snake is found said to be sacred to Zeus; these snakes are small and quite harmless, and have two horns growing from the top of their heads. Such as are found dead are buried in the temple of Zeus.

75 There is a place in Arabia more or less opposite the city of Buto, where I went to try to get information about the flying snakes. On my arrival I saw their skeletons in incalculable numbers; they were piled in heaps, some of which were big, others smaller, others smaller still, and there were many piles of them. The place where these bones lie is a narrow mountain pass leading to a broad plain which joins on to the plain of Egypt, and it is said that when the winged snakes fly to Egypt from Arabia in spring, the ibises meet them at the entrance to the pass and do not let them get through, but kill them.[49] According to the Arabians, this service is the reason for the great reverence with which the ibis is regarded in Egypt, and the

76 Egyptians themselves admit the truth of what they say. The ibis

is jet-black all over; it has legs like a crane's, a markedly hooked
beak, and is about the size of a crake. That, at any rate, is what
the black ibis is like – the kind namely that attacks the winged
snakes; there is, however, another sort, more commonly found
in inhabited districts; this has a bald head and neck and is white
except for the head, throat, wing-tips, and rump, which are
jet-black; its legs and beak are similar to those of the black ibis.
The winged snakes resemble watersnakes; their wings are not
feathered, but are like a bat's. I will now leave the subject of
sacred animals and say something of the people.

The Egyptians who live in the cultivated parts of the country,   77
by their practice of keeping records of the past, have made
themselves much the most learned of any nation of which I have
had experience. I will describe some of their habits: every month
for three successive days they purge themselves, for their health's
sake, with emetics and clysters, in the belief that all diseases
come from the food a man eats; and it is a fact – even apart from
this precaution – that next to the Libyans they are the healthiest
people in the world. I should put this down myself to the absence
of changes in the climate; for change, and especially change of
weather, is the prime cause of disease. They eat loaves made
from emmer – *cyllestes* is their word for them – and drink a
wine made from barley, as they have no vines in the country.
Some kinds of fish they eat raw, either dried in the sun, or salted;
quails, too, they eat raw, and ducks and various small birds,
after pickling them in brine; other sorts of birds and fish, apart
from those which they consider sacred, they either roast or boil.
When the rich give a party and the meal is finished, a man carries   78
round amongst the guests a wooden image of a corpse in a
coffin, carved and painted to look as much like the real thing as
possible, and anything from eighteen inches to three foot long;
he shows it to each guest in turn, and says: 'Look upon this
body as you drink and enjoy yourself; for you will be just like it
when you are dead.'

The Egyptians keep to their native customs and never adopt   79
any from abroad. Many of these customs are interesting, especially, perhaps, the 'Linus'[50] song. This person, under different
names, is celebrated in song not only in Egypt but in Phoenicia,

Cyprus, and other places, and appears to be the person whom the Greeks celebrate as Linus; if this is so, it is yet one more of the many surprises that Egypt has to offer; for where did the Egyptians get this song from? It is clearly very ancient; the Egyptian name for Linus is Maneros, and their story is that their first king had an only son, who died young, and that this dirge – their first and only melody – was invented to be sung in his honour.

80   There is another point in which the Egyptians resemble one section of the Greek people – the Lacedaemonians: I mean the custom of young men stepping aside to make room for their seniors when they meet them in the street, and of getting up from their seats when older men come in. But they are unlike any of the Greeks in that they do not greet one another by name in the streets, but make a low bow and drop one hand to the

81   knee. The clothes they wear consist of a linen tunic with a fringe hanging round the legs (called in their language *calasiris*), and a white woollen garment on top of it. It is, however, contrary to religious usage to be buried in a woollen garment, or to wear wool in a temple. This custom agrees with the rites known as Orphic and Bacchic (actually Egyptian and Pythagorean); for anyone initiated into these rites is similarly debarred from burial in a garment of wool. They have a sacred story which explains the reason for this.

82   The Egyptians were also the first to assign each month and each day to a particular deity, and to foretell by the date of a man's birth his character, his fortunes, and the day of his death – a discovery which Greek poets have turned to account.[51] The Egyptians, too, have made more use of omens and prognostics than any other nation; they keep written records of the observed results of any unusual phenomenon, so that they come to expect a similar consequence to follow a similar occurrence in the

83   future. The art of divination is not attributed by them to any man, but only to certain gods: for instance, Heracles, Apollo, Athena, Artemis, Ares, and Zeus all have an oracle in the country, while the oracle of Leto in Buto is held in greater repute than any of them. The method of delivering the responses varies in the different shrines.

The practice of medicine they split up into separate parts, 84
each doctor being responsible for the treatment of only one
disease. There are, in consequence, innumerable doctors, some
specializing in diseases of the eyes, others of the head, others of
the teeth, others of the stomach, and so on; while others, again,
deal with the sort of troubles which cannot be exactly
localized.[52] As regards mourning and funerals, when a distin- 85
guished man dies all the women of the household plaster their
heads and faces with mud, then, leaving the body indoors,
perambulate the town with the dead man's female relatives,
their dresses fastened with a girdle, and beat their bared breasts.
The men too, for their part, follow the same procedure, wearing
a girdle and beating themselves like the women. The ceremony
over, they take the body to be mummified.

Mummification is a distinct profession. The embalmers, when 86
a body is brought to them, produce specimen models in wood,
painted to resemble nature, and graded in quality; the best and
most expensive kind is said to represent a being whose name I
shrink from mentioning in this connexion; the next best is
somewhat inferior and cheaper, while the third sort is cheapest
of all. After pointing out these differences in quality, they ask
which of the three is required, and the kinsmen of the dead man,
having agreed upon a price, go away and leave the embalmers
to their work. The most perfect process is as follows: as much
as possible of the brain is extracted through the nostrils with an
iron hook, and what the hook cannot reach is rinsed out with
drugs; next the flank is laid open with a flint knife and the whole
contents of the abdomen removed; the cavity is then thoroughly
cleansed and washed out, first with palm wine and again with
an infusion of pounded spices. After that it is filled with pure
bruised myrrh, cassia, and every other aromatic substance with
the exception of frankincense, and sewn up again, after which
the body is placed in natrum, covered entirely over, for seventy
days – never longer. When this period, which must not be
exceeded, is over, the body is washed and then wrapped from
head to foot in linen cut into strips and smeared on the under
side with gum, which is commonly used by the Egyptians instead
of glue. In this condition the body is given back to the family,

who have a wooden case made, shaped like the human figure, into which it is put. The case is then sealed up and stored in a

87 sepulchral chamber, upright against the wall. When, for reasons of expense, the second quality is called for, the treatment is different: no incision is made and the intestines are not removed, but oil of cedar is injected with a syringe into the body through the anus which is afterwards stopped up to prevent the liquid from escaping. The body is then pickled in natrum for the prescribed number of days, on the last of which the oil is drained off. The effect of it is so powerful that as it leaves the body it brings with it the stomach and intestines in a liquid state, and as the flesh, too, is dissolved by the natrum, nothing of the body is left but the bones and skin. After this treatment it is returned to the family without further fuss.

88 The third method, used for embalming the bodies of the poor, is simply to clear out the intestines with a purge and keep the body seventy days in natrum. It is then given back to the family to be taken away.

89 When the wife of a distinguished man dies, or any woman who happens to be beautiful or well known, her body is not given to the embalmers immediately, but only after the lapse of three or four days. This is a precautionary measure to prevent the embalmers from violating the corpse, a thing which is said actually to have happened in the case of a woman who had just died. The culprit was given away by one of his fellow workmen.

90 If anyone, either an Egyptian or a foreigner, is found drowned in the river or killed by a crocodile, there is the strongest obligation upon the people of the nearest town to have the body embalmed in the most elaborate manner and buried in a consecrated burial-place; no one is allowed to touch it except the priests of the Nile – not even relatives or friends; the priests alone prepare it for burial with their own hands and place it in the tomb, as if it were something more sacred than the body of a man.

91 The Egyptians are unwilling to adopt Greek customs, or, to speak generally, those of any other country. There is, however, one exception to this almost universal rule in the case of Chemmis, a large town near Neapolis in the district of Thebes. In this place there is a square of enclosed ground sacred to

Perseus the son of Danae; palm trees grow round it, and there is a stone gateway of great size surmounted by two very large stone figures. Within the enclosure is a shrine containing a statue of Perseus. According to the people of Chemmis, Perseus is frequently to be seen in the neighbourhood, and also within the temple; sometimes a sandal which he has worn, three feet long, is found – a sign, they say, of the approach of a period of great prosperity for the whole of Egypt. In the worship of Perseus Greek ceremonies are used, athletic contests with all the usual events, and prizes of cattle, cloaks, and skins. When I asked why it was that Perseus revealed himself only to the people of Chemmis, and why they alone of the Egyptians celebrated games in his honour, the answer was that Perseus belonged by birth to their city; Danaus and Lynceus, they said, were Chemmites before they sailed to Greece, and from them they traced Perseus' descent. Further, when he came to Egypt from Libya with the Gorgon's head (which is the reason the Greeks also assign for his going there) he paid a visit to Chemmis, having previously learned the name of the place from his mother, and there acknowledged all his kinsmen. On his arrival he instructed them to celebrate games in his honour, and they accordingly did so.[53]

Up to this point I have described the life of the Egyptians who live south of the marsh-country; those who inhabit the marshes are in most things much the same as the rest; and they also practise monogamy, as the Greeks do; nevertheless they are peculiar in certain ways which they have discovered of living more cheaply: for instance, they gather the water-lilies (called lotus by the Egyptians), which grow in great abundance when the river is full and floods the neighbouring flats, and dry them in the sun; then from the centre of each blossom they pick out something which resembles a poppy-head, grind it, and make it into loaves which they bake. The root of this plant is also edible; it is round, about as big as an apple, and tastes fairly sweet. There is another kind of lily to be found in the river; this resembles a rose, and its fruit is formed on a separate stalk from that which bears the blossom, and has very much the look of a wasps' comb. The fruit contains a number of seeds, about the size of an olive-stone, which are good to eat either fresh or dried. They pull up the annual crop of papyrus-reed which grows in the marshes, cut the stalks in two, and eat the lower part, about eighteen inches in length, first baking it in a closed pan, heated red-hot, if they want to enjoy it to perfection. They also sell it. The upper section of the stalk is used for some other purpose. Some of these people, however, live upon nothing but fish, which they gut as soon as they catch them, and eat after drying them in the sun.

93   Gregarious fish are not found in large numbers in the rivers; they frequent the lakes, which they leave at the breeding season to swim in shoals to the sea. In front go the males, dropping their milt, which the females, following behind, gulp down. It is this that causes the females to conceive, and after a period in the sea, when they are about to spawn, the whole shoal returns to its former haunt in the inland lakes. This time, however, it is the females who lead the way, and as they swim along in their hundreds they do just what the males did on the way out, dropping their grains of spawn, a little here, a little there, while the males who follow behind swallow them up. Each of these grains of spawn is a fish in embryo; some of them escape and are not swallowed by the males, and it is these which afterwards grow to maturity. Fish which are caught on their way to the sea are found to have their heads bruised on the left side, while those taken as they return upstream have similar bruises on the right side. The reason is that as they swim down river to the sea they keep close to the bank on their left, and still stick to the same side of the river on their return, keeping as near the bank as they possibly can and continually brushing against it, for fear of being carried out of their course by the strength of the stream.

When the Nile begins to rise, the hollows and marshy ground close beside it are the first to fill, the water from the river seeping through the banks, and no sooner are these low-lying bits of ground formed into lakes than they are found to contain a multitude of small fish. I think I understand the probable reason for this: the fish, I should say, when the river is falling the previous year, lay their eggs in the mud just before they get away with the last of the water, so that when the flood comes round again in due course, the eggs at once hatch and produce the fish. These are the facts about the fish in the Nile.

The Egyptians who live in the marsh-country use an oil 94 extracted from the castor-oil plant. This plant, which grows wild in Greece, they call *Kiki*, and the Egyptian variety is very prolific and has a disagreeable smell. Their practice is to sow it along the banks of rivers and lakes, and when the fruit is gathered it is either cut and pressed, or else roasted and boiled down, and the liquid thus obtained is of an oily nature and quite as good as olive-oil for burning in lamps, though the smell is unpleasant.

The country is infested by swarms of mosquitoes, and the 95 people have invented various methods of dealing with them; south of the marshes they sleep at night on raised structures, which is a great benefit to them because the mosquitoes are prevented by the wind from flying high; in the marsh-country itself they do not have these towers, but everyone, instead, provides himself with a net, which during the day he uses for fishing, and at night fixes up round his bed, and creeps in under it before he goes to sleep. For anyone to sleep wrapped in a cloak or in linen would be useless, for the mosquitoes would bite through them; but they do not even attempt to get through the net.

The Nile boats used for carrying freight are built of acacia 96 wood – the acacia resembles in form the lotus of Cyrene, and exudes gum. They cut short planks, about three feet long, from this tree, and the method of construction is to lay them together like bricks and through-fasten them with dowels set close together, and then, when the hull is complete, to lay the benches across on top. The boats have no ribs and are caulked from inside with papyrus. They are given a single steering-oar, which is driven down through the keel; the masts are of acacia wood, the sails of papyrus. These vessels cannot sail up the river without a good leading wind, but have to be towed from the banks; and for dropping downstream with the current they are handled as follows: each vessel is equipped with a raft made of tamarisk wood, with a rush mat fastened on top of it, and a stone with a hole through it weighing some hundred pounds;

the raft and the stone are made fast to the vessel with ropes, fore and aft respectively, so that the raft is carried rapidly forward by the current and pulls the 'baris' (as these boats are called) after it, while the stone, dragging along the bottom astern, acts as a check and gives her steerage-way. There are a great many of these vessels on the Nile, some of them of many tons' carrying capacity.

97   When the Nile overflows, the whole country is converted into a sea, and the towns, which alone remain above water, look like the islands in the Aegean. At these times water transport is used all over the country, instead of merely along the course of the river, and anyone going from Naucratis to Memphis would pass right by the pyramids instead of following the usual course by Cercasorus and the tip of the Delta. If you go by boat from Canopus on the coast across the flats to Naucratis, you will pass Anthylla and Archandropolis, of which the former, a city of

98 some repute, has been made over ever since the Persian conquest of Egypt to the wife of the reigning monarch to keep her in shoes. The latter town, I fancy, took the name of Archandropolis from Archander the son of Phthius, grandson of Achaeus and son-in-law of Danaus. There may, of course, have been another Archander; but the name in any case is not Egyptian.

99   Up to this point I have confined what I have written to the results of my own direct observation and research, and the views I have formed from them; but from now on the basis of my story will be the accounts given to me by the Egyptians themselves – though here, too, I shall put in one or two things which I have seen with my own eyes.[54]

    The priests told me that it was Min, the first king of Egypt, who raised the dam which created Memphis. The river used to flow along the base of the sandy hills on the Libyan border, and this monarch, by damming it up at the bend about a hundred furlongs south of Memphis, drained the original channel and diverted it to a new one half-way between the two lines of hills. To this day the elbow which the Nile forms here, where it is forced into its new channel, is most carefully watched by the Persians, who strengthen the dam every year; for should the river burst it, Memphis might be completely overwhelmed. On the land which had been drained by the diversion of the river, King Min built the city which is now called Memphis – it lies in the narrow part of Egypt – and afterwards on the north and west sides of the town excavated a lake, communicating with the river, which itself protects it on the east. In addition to this the priests told me that he built there the large and very remarkable temple of Hephaestus.[55]

Next, the priests read to me from a written record the names [100] of three hundred and thirty monarchs, in the same number of generations, all of them Egyptians except eighteen, who were Ethiopians, and one other, who was an Egyptian woman. This last had the same name – Nitocris – as the queen of Babylon. The story was that she ensnared to their deaths hundreds of Egyptians in revenge for the king her brother, whom his subjects had murdered and forced her to succeed; this she did by constructing an immense underground chamber, in which, under the pretence of opening it by an inaugural ceremony, she invited to a banquet all the Egyptians whom she knew to be chiefly responsible for her brother's death; then, when the banquet was in full swing, she let the river in on them through a large concealed conduit-pipe. The only other thing I was told about her was that after this fearful revenge she flung herself into a room full of ashes, to escape her punishment. The other kings, [101] the priests told me, were in no way distinguished and left nothing to commemorate their reigns, with the exception of the last of them, Moeris, who is remembered by the northern gateway he built for the temple of Hephaestus and the lake with the pyramids in it, which were constructed by his orders. The extent of the lake and the size of the pyramids I will mention later on.[56] As none of the other kings on the priests' roll left any memorial [102] at all, I will pass on to say something of Sesostris, who succeeded them.[57] Sesostris, the priests said, sailed first with a fleet of warships from the Arabian gulf along the coast of the Indian Ocean, subduing the coastal tribes as he went, until he found that shoal water made further progress impossible; then on his return to Egypt (still according to the priests' account) he raised a powerful army and marched across the continent, reducing to subjection every nation in his path. Whenever he encountered a

courageous enemy who fought valiantly for freedom, he erected
pillars on the spot inscribed with his own name and country,
and a sentence to indicate that by the might of his armed forces
he had won the victory; if, however, a town fell easily into his
hands without a struggle, he made an addition to the inscription
on the pillar – for not only did he record upon it the same facts
as before, but added a picture of a woman's genitals, meaning
to show that the people of that town were no braver than
103   women.[58] Thus his victorious progress through Asia continued,
until he entered Europe and defeated the Scythians and Thracians; this, I think, was the furthest point the Egyptian army
reached for the memorial columns are to be seen in this part of
the country but not beyond. On his way back Sesostris came to
the river Phasis, and it is quite possible that he here detached a
body of troops from his army and left them behind to settle –
or, on the other hand, it may be that some of his men were sick
of their travels and deserted. I cannot say with certainty which
104   supposition is the right one. But it is undoubtedly a fact that the
Colchians are of Egyptian descent. I noticed this myself before
I heard anyone else mention it, and when it occurred to me I
asked some questions both in Colchis and in Egypt, and found
that the Colchians remembered the Egyptians more distinctly
than the Egyptians remembered them. The Egyptians did, however, say that they thought the original Colchians were men
from Sesostris' army. My own idea on the subject was based
first on the fact that they have black skins and woolly hair (not
that that amounts to much, as other nations have the same), and
secondly, and more especially, on the fact that the Colchians, the
Egyptians, and the Ethiopians are the only races which from
ancient times have practised circumcision.[59] The Phoenicians
and the Syrians of Palestine themselves admit that they learned
the practice from Egypt, and the Syrians who live near the rivers
Thermodon and Parthenius, as well as their neighbours the
Macronians, say that they learnt it only a short time ago from
the Colchians. No other nations use circumcision, and all these
are without doubt following the Egyptian lead. As between the
Egyptians and the Ethiopians, I cannot say which learned from
the other, for the custom is evidently a very ancient one; but I

have no doubt that the other nations adopted it as a result of their intercourse with Egypt, and in this belief I am strongly supported by the fact that Phoenicians who have contact with Greece drop the Egyptian usage, and allow their children to go uncircumcised.

And now I think of it, there is a further point of resemblance 105 between the Colchians and Egyptians: they share a method of weaving linen different from that of any other people; and there is also a similarity between them in language and way of living. The linen made in Colchis is known in Greece as Sardonian linen; that which comes from Egypt is called Egyptian.

Most of the memorial pillars which King Sesostris erected in 106 the conquered countries have disappeared, but I have seen some myself in Palestine, with the inscription I mentioned, and the drawing of a woman's genitals. In Ionia also there are two images of Sesostris cut on rock, one on the road from Ephesus to Phocaea, the other on the road between Sardis and Smyrna; in each case the carved figure is nearly seven feet high and represents a man with a spear in his right hand and a bow in his left, and the rest of his equipment to match – partly Egyptian, partly Ethiopian. Across the breast from shoulder to shoulder runs an inscription, cut in the Egyptian sacred script: *By the strength of my shoulders I won this land.* The name and country of the conqueror are not here recorded, and some who have seen the image suppose it to represent Memnon; however, they are wide of the mark, for Sesostris has made the truth plain enough elsewhere.[60]

The priests went on to tell me that Sesostris, on his return 107 home with a host of prisoners from the conquered countries, was met at Daphnae, near Pelusium, by his brother, whom he had left to govern Egypt during his absence, and invited with his sons to a banquet. While they were at dinner, his brother piled faggots round the building and set them on fire. Seeing what had happened, Sesostris at once asked his wife (for she too was a member of the party) what he should do about it, and was advised by her to take two of their sons – of whom there were six – and lay them out over the burning wood to make a bridge by which they might walk through the fire to safety. The king took her advice, with the result that two of his sons were burnt to death, while the others, together with their father, were saved.

108   Once home again in Egypt, Sesostris punished his brother and proceeded to employ his prisoners of war in various tasks. It was they who were forced to drag the enormous masses of stone which were brought during Sesostris' reign for the temple of Hephaestus, and to dig the dykes which one finds there today, thereby depriving Egypt – though it was far from their intention to do so – of the horses and carriages which were formerly in such common use throughout the country. All Egypt is flat; yet from that time onwards it has been unfit for horses or wheeled traffic because of the innumerable dykes, running in all directions, which cut the country up. The king's object was to supply water to the towns which lay inland at some distance from the river; for previously the people in these towns, when the level of the river fell, had to go short and to drink brackish water

109   from wells. It was this king, moreover, who divided the land into lots and gave everyone a square piece of equal size, from the produce of which he exacted an annual tax. Any man whose holding was damaged by the encroachment of the river would go and declare his loss before the king, who would send inspectors to measure the extent of the loss, in order that he might pay in future a fair proportion of the tax at which his property had been assessed. I think this was the way in which geometry was invented, and passed afterwards into Greece – for knowledge of the sundial and the gnomon and the twelve divisions of the day came into Greece from Babylon.

110   Sesostris was the only Egyptian king to rule Ethiopia. As memorials of his reign he left stone statues of himself and his wife, each forty-five feet high, and statues thirty feet high of each of his four sons. They were erected in front of the temple of Hephaestus.[61] Long afterwards the priest of Hephaestus would not allow Darius the king of Persia to erect a statue of himself in front of these, because (as he put it) his deeds had not been as great as the deeds of Sesostris the Egyptian; the conquests of Sesostris, no less extensive than those of Darius, included the Scythians, whom Darius had been unable to subdue; it was not

right, therefore, that he should put his statue in front of those dedicated by a monarch whose achievements he had failed to surpass. Darius, they say, admitted the truth of this.[62]

When Sesostris died, he was succeeded by his son Pheros,[63] a   111
prince who undertook no military adventures. He went blind, and the reason for it is explained in the following story: one year the Nile rose to an excessive height, as much as twenty-seven feet, and when all the fields were under water it began to blow hard, so that the river got very rough. The king in insensate rage seized a spear and hurled it into the swirling waters, and immediately thereafter he was attacked by a disease of the eyes, and became blind. He was blind for ten years, and in the eleventh he received an oracle from the city of Buto to the effect that the time of his punishment being now ended, he would recover his sight, if he washed his eyes with the urine of a woman who had never lain with any man except her husband. He tried his wife first, but without success; then he tried other women, a great many, one after another, until at last his sight was restored. Then he collected within the walls of a town, now called Red Clod, all the women except the one whose urine had proved efficacious, set the place on fire, and burnt them to death, town and all; afterwards he married the woman who had been the means of curing him. In gratitude for his recovery he dedicated a number of offerings in all the temples of repute; but the most remarkable of them were two stone obelisks which he set up in the precinct of the temple of the Sun. These are well worth seeing; they are twelve feet broad and a hundred and fifty feet high, each hewn from a single block of stone.

Pheros was succeeded by a native of Memphis, whose name   112
in the Greek language was Proteus. To this day there is a sacred precinct of his at Memphis, very fine and richly adorned, and situated south of the temple of Hephaestus. The whole district hereabouts is known as the Camp of the Tyrians, because the houses in the neighbourhood are occupied by Phoenicians from Tyre. Within the enclosure there is a temple dedicated to the foreign Aphrodite. I should guess, myself, that it was built in honour of Helen the daughter of Tyndareus, not only because I have heard it said that she passed some time at the court of

Proteus, but also, and more particularly, because of the description of Aphrodite as 'the foreigner', a title never given to this goddess in any of her other temples.[64] I questioned the priests about the story of Helen, and they told me in reply that Paris was on his way home from Sparta with his stolen bride, when, somewhere in the Aegean sea, he met foul weather, which drove his ship towards Egypt, until at last, the gale continuing as bad as ever, he found himself on the coast, and managed to get ashore at the Salt-pans, in the mouth of the Nile now called the Canopic. Here on the beach there was a temple, which still exists, dedicated to Heracles, and in connexion with it there is a very ancient custom, which has remained unaltered to my day. If a runaway slave takes refuge in this shrine and allows the sacred marks, which are the sign of his submission to the service of the god, to be set upon his body, his master, no matter who he is, cannot lay hands on him. Now some of Paris' servants found out about this and, wishing to get him into trouble, deserted, and fled as suppliants to the temple and told against him the whole story of his abduction of Helen and his wicked treatment of Menelaus. They brought these charges against their master not only before the temple priests, but also before the warden of that mouth of the Nile, a man named Thonis. Thonis at once sent a dispatch to Proteus at Memphis. 'A Trojan stranger (the message ran) has arrived here from Greece, where he has been guilty of an abominable crime: first he seduced the wife of his host, then carried her off together with a great deal of valuable property; and now stress of weather has forced him to land on this coast. Are we to let him sail away again in possession of his stolen goods, or should we confiscate them?' Proteus answered: 'No matter who it is that has committed this crime against his friend, arrest him and send him to me, that I may hear what he can say for himself.' Thonis accordingly arrested Paris, held his ships, and took both him and Helen to Memphis, together with the stolen property and the servants who had taken sanctuary in the temple. On their arrival Proteus asked Paris who he was and where he had come from, and Paris gave him his name and all the details of his family and a true account of his voyage; but when he was further asked how he had got possession of Helen, then, instead of telling the truth, he began to vacillate, until the runaway servants convicted him of lying and told the whole story of his crime. Finally Proteus gave his judgement: 'If,' he said, 'I did not consider it a matter of great importance that I have never yet put to death any stranger who has been forced upon my coasts by stress of weather, I should have punished you for the sake of your Greek host. To be welcomed as a guest, and to repay that kindness by so foul a deed! You are a villain. You seduced your friend's wife, and, as if that were not enough, persuaded her to escape with you on the wings of passion you roused. Even that did not content you – but you must bring with you besides the treasure you have stolen from your host's house. But though I cannot punish a stranger with death, I will not allow you to take away your ill-gotten gains: I will keep this woman and the treasure, until the Greek to whom they belong chooses to come and fetch them. As for you and the companions of your voyage, I give you three days in which to leave my country – and to find an anchorage elsewhere. If you are not gone by then, I shall treat you as enemies.'

This was the account I had from the priests about the arrival of Helen at Proteus' court. I think Homer[65] was familiar with the story; for though he rejected it as less suitable for epic poetry than the one he actually used, he left indications that it was not unknown to him. For instance, when he describes the wanderings of Paris in the *Iliad* (and he has not elsewhere contradicted his account), he says that in the course of them he brought Helen to Sidon in Phoenicia. The passage occurs in the section of the poem where Diomedes performs his great deeds and it runs like this:

> There were the bright robes woven by the women of Sidon,
> Whom the hero Paris, splendid as a god to look on,
> Brought from that city when he sailed the wide sea
> Voyaging with high-born Helen, when he took her home.

There is also a passage in the *Odyssey* alluding to the same fact:

These drugs of subtle virtue the daughter of Zeus was given
By an Egyptian woman, Polydamna, wife of Thon;
For the rich earth of Egypt bears many herbs
Mixed together, which have power to cure, or to kill.

and, again, Menelaus is made to say to Telemachus:

In Egypt the gods still stayed me, though I longed to return,
For I had not paid them their due of sacrifice.

Homer makes it quite clear in these passages that he knew
about Paris going out of his way to Egypt – the point of the
first I have quoted being that Syria borders on Egypt, and the
117   Phoenicians, to whom Sidon belongs, live in Syria. Another
thing which is proved by these passages, and especially by the
one about Sidon, is that Homer was not the author of the
Cypria; for in that poem it is stated that Paris reached Troy with
Helen three days after he left Sparta, having had a good voyage
with a fair wind and calm sea, whereas we learn from the *Iliad*
that he was forced to take her far out of his way – but I must
take my leave of Homer and the *Cypria*.

118   I asked the priests if the Greek story of what happened at
Troy had any truth in it, and they gave me in reply some
information which they claimed to have had direct from Menelaus himself. This was, that after the abduction of Helen, the
Greeks sent a strong force to the Troad in support of Menelaus'
cause, and as soon as the men had landed and established
themselves on Trojan soil, ambassadors, of whom Menelaus
was one, were dispatched to Troy. They were received within
the walls of the town, and demanded the restoration of Helen
together with the treasure which Paris had stolen, and also
satisfaction for the injuries they had received. The Trojans,
however, gave them the answer which they always stuck to
afterwards – sometimes even swearing to the truth of it: namely,
that neither Helen nor the treasure was in their possession, but
both were in Egypt, and there was no justice in trying to force
them to give satisfaction for property which was being detained
by the Egyptian king Proteus. The Greeks, supposing this to be

a merely frivolous answer, laid siege to the town, and persisted until it fell; but no Helen was found, and they were still told the same story, until at last they believed it and sent Menelaus to visit Proteus in Egypt. He sailed up the river to Memphis, and when he had given a true account of all that had happened, he was most hospitably entertained and Helen, having suffered no evils, was restored to him with all the rest of his property. Nevertheless, in spite of this generous treatment, Menelaus proved himself no friend to Egypt; for when he wished to leave, but was delayed for a long time by contrary winds, he took two Egyptian children and offered them in sacrifice. The discovery of this foul act turned the friendship of the Egyptians to hatred; he was pursued, but managed to escape with his ships to Libya. Where he went afterwards the Egyptians could not say. They told me that they had learned of some of these events by inquiry, but spoke with certain knowledge of those which had taken place in their own country.

This, then, is the version the Egyptian priests gave me of the story of Helen, and I am inclined to accept it for the following reason: had Helen really been in Troy, she would have been handed over to the Greeks with or without Paris' consent; for I cannot believe that either Priam or any other kinsman of his was mad enough to be willing to risk his own and his children's lives and the safety of the city, simply to let Paris continue to live with Helen. If, moreover, that had been their feeling when the troubles began, surely later on, when the Trojans had suffered heavy losses in every battle they fought, and there was never an engagement (if we may believe the epic poems) in which Priam himself did not lose two of his sons, or three, or even more: surely, I repeat, in such circumstances as these, there can be little doubt that, even if Helen had been the wife of Priam the king, he would have given her back to the Greeks, if to do so offered a chance of relief from the suffering which the war had caused. Again, Paris was not heir to the throne, and so could not have been acting as regent for his aged father; for it was Hector, his elder brother and a better man than he, who was to have succeeded on Priam's death, and it was not likely that Hector would put up with his brother's lawless behaviour, especially as it was the cause of much distress both to himself and to every other Trojan besides. The fact is, they did not give Helen up because they had not got her; what they told the Greeks was the truth, and I do not hesitate to declare that the refusal of the Greeks to believe it came of divine volition in order that their utter destruction might plainly prove to mankind that great offences meet with great punishments at the hands of God. This, then, is my own interpretation.

121   The next king after Proteus was Rhampsinitus, who is remembered by the entrance gates which he erected at the western end of the temple of Hephaestus, and by two statues which face them, each about thirty-eight feet high; the more northerly of the two is called by the Egyptians Summer; the more southerly, Winter. The former they honour and bow down before, but their behaviour towards the latter is quite the reverse.[66]

a   Rhampsinitus possessed a vast fortune in silver, so great that no subsequent king came anywhere near it – let alone surpassed it. In order to keep the treasure safe, he proposed to have a stone building put up, with one of its walls forming a part of the outer wall of his palace. The builder he employed had designs upon the treasure and ingeniously contrived to construct the wall in such a way that one of the stone blocks of which it was composed could easily be removed by a couple of men – or even by one. When the new treasury was ready, the king's money was stored away in it; and after the lapse of some years the builder, then on his death-bed, called his two sons and told them how clever he had been, saying that he had planned the device of the moveable stone entirely for their benefit, that they might live in affluence. Then he gave the precise measurements, and instructions for its removal, and told them that if only they kept the secret well, they would be the Royal Treasurers as long as they lived. So the father died and his sons lost no time in setting to work; they came by night to the palace, found the stone in the treasury wall, took it out easily enough and got away with a
b   good haul of silver. The king, on his next visit to the treasury, was surprised to see that some of the vessels in which the money was stored were no longer full, but as the seals were unbroken

and all the locks in perfect order, he was at a loss to find the culprit. When the same thing happened again, and yet again, and he found that each time he visited the chamber the level of the money in the jars had still further fallen (for the thieves persisted in their depredations), he ordered traps to be made and set near the money-jars. The thieves came as usual, and one of them made his way into the chamber; but, as soon as he approached the money-jar he was after, the trap got him. Realizing his plight, he at once called out to his brother to tell him what had happened, and begged him to come in as quickly as he could and cut off his head, lest the recognition of his dead body should involve both of them in ruin. The brother, seeing the sense of this request, acted upon it without delay; then, having fitted the stone back in its place, went home taking the severed head with him. Next morning the king visited his   c treasury, and what was his astonishment when he saw in the trap the headless body of the thief, and no sign of damage to the building, or any apparent means of entrance or exit! Much perplexed, he finally decided to have the thief's body hung up outside the wall, and a guard set with orders to arrest and bring before him anyone they might see thereabouts in tears, or showing signs of mourning. Now the young man's mother was deeply distressed by this treatment of her dead son's body, and begged the one who was still alive to do all he possibly could to think of some way of getting it back, and even threatened, if he refused to listen to her, to go to the king and denounce him as the thief. The young man made many excuses, but to no purpose; his mother continued to pester him, until at last he thought of a   d way out of the difficulty. He filled some skins with wine and loaded them on to donkeys, which he drove to the place where the soldiers were guarding his brother's corpse. Arrived there, he gave a pull on the necks of two or three of the skins, which undid the fastenings. The wine poured out, and he roared and banged his head, as if not knowing which donkey to deal with first, while the soldiers, seeing the wine streaming all over the road, seized their pots and ran to catch it, congratulating themselves on such a piece of luck. The young man swore at them in pretended rage, which the soldiers did their best to soothe, until finally he changed his tune, and, appearing to have recovered his temper, drove the donkeys out of the roadway and began to rearrange the wineskins on their backs. Meanwhile, as he chatted with the soldiers, one of them cracked a joke at his expense and made him laugh, whereupon he made them a present of a wineskin, and without more ado they all sat down to enjoy themselves, and urged their benefactor to join the party and share the drink. The young man let himself be persuaded, and soon, as cup succeeded cup and the soldiers treated him with increasing familiarity, he gave them another skin. Such a quantity of wine was too much for the guards; very drunk and drowsy, they stretched themselves out at full length and fell asleep on the spot. It was now well after dark, and the thief took down his brother's body and as an insult shaved the right cheek of each of the guards. Then he put the corpse on the donkeys' backs and returned home, having done successfully what his mother demanded.

e   The king was very angry when he learnt that the thief's body had been stolen, and determined at any cost to catch the man who had been clever enough to bring off such a coup. I find it hard to believe the priests' account of the means he employed to catch him – but here it is: he sent his own daughter to a brothel with orders to admit all comers, and to compel each applicant, before granting him her favours, to tell her what was the cleverest and wickedest thing that he had ever done; and if anyone told her the story of the thief, she was to get hold of him and not allow him to escape. The girl obeyed her father's orders, and the thief, when he came to know the reason for what she was doing, could not resist the temptation to go one better than the king in ingenuity. He cut the hand and arm from the body of a man who had just died, and, putting them under his cloak, went to visit the king's daughter in her brothel. When she asked him the question which she had asked all the others, he replied that his wickedest deed was to cut off his brother's head when he was caught in a trap in the king's treasury, and his cleverest was to make the soldiers drunk, so that he could take down his brother's body from the wall where it was hanging. The girl immediately clutched at him; but under cover of the darkness the thief pushed towards her the hand of the corpse, which she seized and held tight in the belief that it was his own. Then, leaving it in her grasp, he made his escape through the door.

The cleverness and audacity of this last exploit filled the king with astonishment and admiration; soon after the news of it reached him, he went to every town in Egypt with a promise to the thief, should he give himself up, not only of a free pardon but of a rich reward. The thief trusted him and presented himself, and Rhampsinitus gave him his daughter in marriage, on the grounds that the thief was the most intelligent of mankind: for the Egyptians surpass everyone else in knowledge, and this man surpassed all the Egyptians.

Another story I heard about Rhampsinitus was, that at a later period he descended alive into what the Greeks call Hades, and there played dice with Demeter, sometimes winning and sometimes losing, and returned to earth with a golden cloth which she had given him as a present. I was told that to mark his descent into the underworld and subsequent return, the Egyptians instituted a festival, which they certainly continued to celebrate in my own day – though I cannot state with confidence that the reason for it is what it was said to be. The priests weave a robe, taking one day only over the process; then they bandage the eyes of one of their number, put the robe into his hands, and lead him to the road which runs to the temple of Demeter. Here they leave him, and it is supposed that he is escorted to the temple, twenty furlongs from the city, by two wolves which afterwards bring him back to where they found him. Anyone may believe these Egyptian tales, if he is sufficiently credulous; as for myself, I keep to the general plan of this book, which is to record the traditions of the various nations just as I heard them related to me.

The Egyptians say that Demeter and Dionysus are the chief powers in the underworld; and they were also the first people to put forward the doctrine of the immortality of the soul, and to maintain that after death it enters another creature at the moment of that creature's birth. It then makes the round of all living things – animals, birds, and fish – until it finally passes once again, at birth, into the body of a man. The whole period of transmigration occupies three thousand years. This theory has been adopted by certain Greek writers, some earlier, some later, who have put it forward as their own. Their names are known to me, but I refrain from mentioning them.[67]

124   Up to the time of Rhampsinitus, Egypt was excellently governed and very prosperous; but his successor Cheops[68] (to continue the account which the priests gave me) brought the country into all sorts of misery. He closed all the temples, then, not content with excluding his subjects from the practice of their religion, compelled them without exception to labour as slaves for his own advantage. Some were forced to drag blocks of stone from the quarries in the Arabian hills to the Nile, where they were ferried across and taken over by others, who hauled them to the Libyan hills. The work went on in three-monthly shifts, a hundred thousand men in a shift. It took ten years of this oppressive slave-labour to build the track along which the blocks were hauled – a work, in my opinion, of hardly less magnitude than the pyramid itself, for it is five furlongs in length, sixty feet wide, forty-eight feet high at its highest point, and constructed of polished stone blocks decorated with carvings of animals. To build it took, as I said, ten years – including the underground sepulchral chambers on the hill where the pyramids stand; a cut was made from the Nile, so that the water from it turned the site of these into an island. To build the pyramid itself took twenty years; it is square at the base, its height (800 feet) equal to the length of each side; it is of polished stone blocks beautifully fitted, none of the blocks being less than

125   thirty feet long.[69] The method employed was to build it in steps, or, as some call them, *krossai* or platforms. When the base was complete, the blocks for the first tier above it were lifted from ground level by contrivances made of short timbers; on this first tier there was another, which raised the blocks a stage higher, then yet another which raised them higher still. Each tier, or storey, had its set of levers, or it may be that they used the same one, which, being easy to carry, they shifted up from stage to stage as soon as its load was dropped into place. Both methods are mentioned, so I give them both here.[70] The finishing-off of the pyramid was begun at the top and continued downwards,

ending with the lowest parts nearest the ground. An inscription
is cut upon it in Egyptian characters recording the amount spent
on radishes, onions, and leeks for the labourers, and I remember
distinctly that the interpreter who read me the inscription said
the sum was 1600 talents of silver. If this is true, how much
must have been spent in addition on tools, and bread and
clothing for the labourers during all those years the building
was going on – not to mention the time it took (not a little, I
should think) to quarry and haul the stone, and to construct the
underground chamber?[71]

But no crime was too great for Cheops: when he was short of   126
money, he sent his daughter to a brothel with instructions to
charge a certain sum – they did not say how much. This she
actually did, adding to it a further transaction of her own; for
with the intention of leaving something to be remembered by
after her death, she asked each of her customers to give her a
block of stone, and of these stones (the story goes) was built the
middle pyramid of the three which stand in front of the great
pyramid. It is a hundred and fifty feet square.

Cheops reigned for fifty years, according to the Egyptians'   127
account, and was succeeded after his death by his brother
Chephren. Chephren was no better than his predecessor; his rule
was equally oppressive, and, like Cheops, he built a pyramid, but
of a smaller size (I measured both of them myself).[72] It has no
underground chambers, and no channel was dug, as in the case
of Cheops' pyramid, to bring to it the water from the Nile. The
cutting of the canal, as I have already said, makes the site of the
pyramid of Cheops into an island, and there his body is supposed
to be. The pyramid of Chephren lies close to the great pyramid
of Cheops; it is forty feet lower than the latter, but otherwise of
the same dimensions; its lower course is of the coloured stone
of Ethiopia. Both these pyramids stand on the same hill, which
is about a hundred feet in height. Chephren reigned for fifty-six   128
years – so the Egyptians reckon a period of a hundred and six
years, all told, during which the temples were never opened for
worship and the country was reduced in every way to the
greatest misery. The Egyptians can hardly bring themselves to
mention the names of Cheops and Chephren, so great is their

hatred of them; they even call the pyramids after Philitis, a shepherd who at that time fed his flocks in the neighbourhood.

129   The next king of Egypt after Chephren was Mycerinus, the son of Cheops. Mycerinus, reversing his father's policy of which he did not approve, reopened the temples and allowed his subjects, who had been brought into such abject slavery, to resume the practice of their religion and their normal work. Of all kings who ruled in Egypt he had the greatest reputation for justice in the decision of legal causes, and for this the Egyptians give him higher praise than any other monarch; for apart from the general equity of his judgements, he used to compensate out of his own property any man who was dissatisfied with the result of his suit, and so leave him nothing to complain of.

Such were the generosity and mild rule of Mycerinus, when the first of his troubles fell upon him: his daughter, who was his only child, died. Wishing, in the excess of his grief at this calamity, to give his daughter a tomb which should be different from any other, he had a wooden cow made, hollow inside and plated on the outside with gold, to receive her body. The cow

130   was not buried, but was still to be seen in my day at Sais, standing in a richly decorated chamber of the royal palace; incense of all kinds is burnt before it every day, and at night a lamp is kept always lighted in the room. Close by in another chamber, the priests of Sais told me, are some statues, which represent the concubines of Mycerinus: there are, indeed, twenty or so naked wooden figures of great size in this chamber, but as to whom they represent I can only pass on such information as was given me.

131   There is another, and quite different, story about the cow and the statues; according to this, Mycerinus conceived a passion for his daughter and violated her, and distress at the outrage drove her to hang herself; she was entombed in the cow, and her mother cut off the hands of the servants who had allowed the king access to her. The statues represent the servants, and, like their living originals, they have no hands. Personally I think this story is nonsense, especially in its explanation of the statues' missing hands; I could see for myself that they had simply

dropped off through age. They are still there, plainly visible – lying on the ground near the statues' feet.[73]

The cow is covered with a purple cloth, all but the head and neck, which are bare and very thickly coated with gold. Between its horns there is a gold disc representing the sun. The figure is not erect but in a kneeling posture, and is of the size of a large live cow. Once a year, at the festival on which the Egyptians beat themselves in honour of that deity whom I must not name in this connexion, the cow is taken from the chamber into the sunlight; for it is said that the girl on her deathbed begged her father Mycerinus to be allowed once a year to see the sun. [132]

After the death of his daughter a second calamity fell upon Mycerinus: he received an oracle from Buto to the effect that he was destined to live only for six more years and to die within the seventh. He sent back an angry message to the shrine, and reproached the god with the injustice of allowing a man so pious as himself to die so soon, when his father and uncle, who had closed the temples, forgotten the gods, and afflicted their fellow men, had lived to a good old age. In answer to this there was another message from the oracle, which declared that his life was being shortened precisely because he had not done what he ought to have done: for it was fated that Egypt should suffer for a hundred and fifty years – a thing which his two predecessors, unlike himself, had understood very well. Mycerinus, convinced by this that his doom was sealed, had innumerable lamps made, by the light of which he set himself every evening to drink and be merry, and never ceased day or night from the pursuit of pleasure, travelling about from place to place amongst the pools and woodlands, wherever he heard of a particularly delightful spot. His object in this was by turning night into day to extend the six remaining years of his life to twelve, and so to convict the oracle of falsehood. He, too, left a pyramid, built square, with its lower half of Ethiopian stone; it is much smaller than his father's, each side at the base being only about 280 feet long.[74] [133] [134]

There are people in Greece who say that this pyramid was erected by the courtesan Rhodopis. They are quite wrong, and I do not think they even know who Rhodopis was; for if they did, they could never have attributed to her the erection of such a monument, which must have cost a sum of money vast beyond reckoning. Besides this, they show their ignorance of the fact that Rhodopis lived during the reign of Amasis, not in Mycerinus' time – much later than the period of the kings who built these pyramids. She was by birth a Thracian, the slave of Iadmon, son of Hephaestopolis of Samos, and fellow-slave of Aesop the fable-writer. The clearest proof that Aesop was the slave of Iadmon is the fact that when the Delphians, in obedience to the oracle's command, repeatedly advertised for someone to claim compensation for Aesop's murder, the only person to come forward was the grandson of Iadmon (a man of the same name).

135   She was brought to Egypt by Xanthus the Samian, to follow her trade, and Charaxus of Mytilene, son of Scamandronymus and brother of Sappho the poetess, paid a large sum to redeem her from slavery. Having in this way obtained her freedom, she remained in Egypt and succeeded by her great beauty in amassing a fortune which – for her – was a considerable one, but certainly not sufficient for building a pyramid. There is no sense in pretending she was excessively rich, for the tenth part of her property can be seen today by anyone who cares to go and look at it: for wishing to be remembered in Greece by some sort of temple-offering such as nobody had ever thought of before, she spent a tenth of her money on as many iron roasting-spits as it would buy, and sent them to Delphi. They still lie in a heap behind the altar which the Chians dedicated, opposite the actual shrine. The prostitutes of Naucratis are somehow particularly attractive; for not only did Rhodopis live there, and become so famous that every Greek was familiar with her name, but, at a later period, there was Archidice who, though less a subject of common gossip than Rhodopis, figured in poetry from one end of Greece to the other. When Charaxus returned to Mytilene after purchasing Rhodopis' freedom, he was ridiculed by Sappho in one of her poems. So much, then, for Rhodopis.

136   The successor of Mycerinus, the priests told me, was Asychis, and he it was who added to the temple of Hephaestus its eastern entrance-gate, much the finest and biggest of the four.[75] Like the

other gates, but to a much greater extent, it is decorated with carvings and an enormous quantity of other architectural adorn- ment. During the reign of Asychis money was so short, that a law was passed allowing a man to borrow on the security of his father's dead body, with the further provision, added later, that the lender should have power over the family vault of the borrower in its entirety, so that anyone who borrowed on this security and died before he could repay the loan, was excluded from burial either in his own family tomb, or anywhere else – nor was he allowed to bury in his own vault any of his relatives.

Wishing to go one better than his predecessors on the throne, Asychis built a pyramid of brick to commemorate his reign, and on it cut an inscription in stone to the following effect: 'Do not compare me to my disadvantage with the stone pyramids. I surpass them as far as Zeus the other gods. They pushed a pole to the bottom of a lake, and the mud which stuck on it they collected and made into bricks. That was how they built me.'

Having no further achievements of this monarch to recount, 137 I will pass to the next. This was Anysis, a blind man who came from a city of the same name. During his reign Egypt was invaded in great force by the Ethiopians under Sabacos, their king. The blind Anysis fled and took refuge in the marsh- country, leaving Egypt in the hands of the Ethiopian, who remained master of it for fifty years.[76] When an Egyptian com- mitted a crime, it was not the custom of Sabacos to punish him with death; but instead of the death-penalty he compelled the offender, according to the seriousness of the offence, to raise the level of the soil in the neighbourhood of his native town. In this way the cities came to stand even higher than they did before; for the level of the ground had already been raised once, in Sesostris' reign, when the canals were dug. This was the second time, and the result was that the cities came to stand very high indeed. None of the Egyptian cities, I think, was raised so much as Bubastis, where there is a temple of Bubastis (the Greek Artemis) which is well worth describing. Other temples may be larger, or have cost more to build, but none is a greater pleasure to look at. The site of the building is almost an island, 138 for two canals have been led from the Nile and sweep round it, one on each side, as far as the entrance, where they stop short without meeting; each canal is a hundred feet wide and shaded with trees. The gateway is sixty feet high and is decorated with remarkable carved figures some nine feet in height. The temple stands in the centre of the city, and, since the level of the buildings everywhere else has been raised, but the temple itself allowed to remain in its original position, the result is that one can look down and get a fine view of it from all round. It is surrounded by a low wall with carved figures, and within the enclosure stands a grove of very tall trees about the actual shrine, which is large and contains the statue of the goddess. The whole enclosure is a furlong square. The entrance to it is approached by a stone-paved road about four hundred feet wide and about two thousand feet long, running eastward through the market-place and joining the temple of Bubastis to the temple of Hermes. The road is lined on both sides with immense trees – so tall that they seem to touch the sky.

139   It was a dream which finally caused the departure, or, rather, the flight, of the Ethiopian Sabacos from Egypt. He dreamt that a man stood by his bed and advised him to assemble all the priests in Egypt and cut them in half, and he is supposed to have said that he believed the dream to have been sent by the gods, to provoke him to sacrilege and involve him in some disaster at the hands of either gods or men. He refused, therefore, to do what was advised; on the contrary, he preferred to leave Egypt, as the destined period of his rule there had now come to an end – for before he left Ethiopia, he had received a prophecy from the Ethiopian oracle that he was fated to govern Egypt for fifty years. The fifty years were now up; and that fact, added to the disquieting effect of his dream, caused him to leave Egypt of his own accord.

140   After the departure of the Ethiopian, the blind Anysis returned from the marsh-country, where for fifty years he had lived on an island which he had built up of earth and ashes, and resumed the government of Egypt. During those years of exile, he had instructed all the Egyptians whose duty it was to smuggle food to him without Sabacos knowing of it, to bring with them, as

an additional present, a certain quantity of ashes. Amyrtaeus was the first, in after days, to discover this island, the site of which was unknown for more than seven hundred years, in spite of attempts by previous kings to find it. It is called Elbo, and is about ten furlongs across in each direction.

Next on the throne after Anysis was Sethos,[77] the high priest 141 of Hephaestus. He is said to have neglected the warrior class of the Egyptians and to have treated them with contempt, as if he had been unlikely to need their services. He offended them in various ways, not least by depriving them of the twelve acres of land which each of them had held by special privilege under previous kings. As a result, when Egypt was invaded by Sennacherib, the king of Arabia and Assyria, with a great army, not one of them was willing to fight. The situation was grave; not knowing what else to do, the priest-king entered the shrine and, before the image of the god, complained bitterly of the peril which threatened him. In the midst of his lamentations he fell asleep, and dreamt that the god stood by him and urged him not to lose heart; for if he marched boldly out to meet the Arabian army, he would come to no harm, as the god himself would send him helpers.

By this dream the king's confidence was restored; and with such men as were willing to follow him – not a single one of the warrior class, but a mixed company of shopkeepers, artisans, and market-people – he marched to Pelusium, which guards the approaches to Egypt, and there took up his position. As he lay here facing the enemy, thousands of field-mice swarmed over the Assyrians during the night, and ate their quivers, their bowstrings, and the leather handles of their shields, so that on the following day, having no arms to fight with, they abandoned their position and suffered severe losses during their retreat. There is still a stone statue of Sethos in the temple of Hephaestus; the figure is represented with a mouse in its hand, and the inscription: 'Look upon me and learn reverence.'[78]

Up to this point I have relied on the accounts given me by the 142 Egyptians and their priests. They declare that three hundred and forty-one generations separate the first king of Egypt from the last I have mentioned – the priest of Hephaestus – and that there was a king and a high priest corresponding to each generation. Now to reckon three generations as a hundred years, three hundred generations make ten thousand years, and the remaining forty-one generations make 1340 years more; thus one gets a total of 11,340 years, during the whole of which time, they say, no god ever assumed mortal form; nothing of the sort occurred either under the former or under the later kings. They did say, however, that four times within this period the sun changed his usual position, twice rising where he normally sets, and twice setting where he normally rises. They assured me that Egypt was quite unaffected by this: the harvests, and the produce of the river, were the same as usual, and there was no change in the incidence of disease or death.

143   When the historian Hecataeus was in Thebes, the priests of Zeus, after listening to him trace his family back to a god in the sixteenth generation, did to him precisely what they did to me – though, unlike Hecataeus, I kept clear of personal genealogies.[79] They took me into the great hall of the temple, and showed me the wooden statues there, which they counted; and the number was just what I have said, for each high priest has a statue of himself erected there before he dies. As they showed them to me, and counted them up, beginning with the statue of the high priest who had last died, and going on from him right through the whole number, they assured me that each had been the son of the one who preceded him. When Hecataeus traced his genealogy and connected himself with a god sixteen generations back, the priests refused to believe him, and denied that any man had ever had a divine ancestor. They countered his claim by tracing the descent of their own high priests, pointing out that each of the statues represented a 'piromis' (a word which means something like 'gentleman') who was the son of another 'piromis', and made no attempt to connect them with either a god or a hero. Such, then, were the beings represented by the statues; they were far from being gods – they were men.

144   Nevertheless, before their time Egypt was, indeed, ruled by gods, who lived on earth amongst men, sometimes one of them, sometimes another being supreme above the rest. The last of them was Horus the son of Osiris – Horus is the Apollo, Osiris

the Dionysus, of the Greeks. It was Horus who vanquished Typhon and was the last god to sit upon the throne of Egypt.

In Greece, the youngest of the gods are thought to be Heracles, 145 Dionysus, and Pan; but in Egypt Pan is very ancient, and one of the 'eight gods' who existed before the rest; Heracles is one of the 'twelve' who appeared later, and Dionysus one of the third order who were descended from the twelve. I have already mentioned the length of time which by the Egyptian reckoning elapsed between the coming of Heracles and the reign of Amasis; Pan is said to be still more ancient, and even Dionysus, the youngest of the three, appeared, they say, 15,000 years before Amasis. They claim to be quite certain of these dates, for they have always kept a careful written record of the passage of time. But from the birth of Dionysus, the son of Semele, daughter of Cadmus, to the present day is a period of about 1000 years only; from Heracles the son of Alcmena, about 900 years; from Pan the son of Penelope – he is supposed by the Greeks to be the son of Penelope and Hermes – not more than about 800 years, a shorter time than has elapsed since the Trojan war.

It is open to anyone to believe whichever of these two tra- 146 ditions he prefers; I have already stated my own opinion. If indeed these gods had been publicly known and had grown old in Greece, like Heracles, the son of Amphitryon, and Dionysus, the son of Semele, and Pan, the son of Penelope, it might have been said that the two last-mentioned were men who bore the names of previously existing gods; but the Greek tradition is that Dionysus, as soon as he was born, was sewn up in Zeus' thigh and taken to Nysa, which is in Ethiopia above Egypt; and as to what happened after the birth of Pan, tradition is silent. It is clear to me, therefore, that the names of these gods became known in Greece later than the rest, and that the Greeks trace their genealogy from the time when they first acquired the knowledge of them.

So far the Egyptians themselves have been my authority; but 147 in what follows I shall relate what other people, too, are willing to accept in the history of this country, with a few points added from my own observation.[80] After the reign of Sethos, the priest of Hephaestus, the Egyptians for a time were freed from monarchical government. Unable, however, to do without a king for long, they divided Egypt into twelve regions and appointed a king for each of them. United by intermarriage, the twelve kings governed in mutual friendliness on the understanding that none of them should attempt to oust any of the others, or to increase his power at the expense of the rest. They came to the understanding, and ensured that the terms of it should be rigorously kept, because, at the time when the twelve kingdoms were first established, an oracle had declared that the one who should pour a libation from a bronze cup in the temple of Hephaestus would become master of all Egypt. They held their meetings in all the temples.[81]

148   To strengthen the bond between them, they decided to leave a common memorial of their reigns, and for this purpose constructed a labyrinth a little above Lake Moeris, near the place called the City of Crocodiles. I have seen this building, and it is beyond my power to describe; it must have cost more in labour and money than all the walls and public works of the Greeks put together – though no one would deny that the temples at Ephesus and Samos are remarkable buildings. The pyramids, too, are astonishing structures, each one of them equal to many of the most ambitious works of Greece; but the labyrinth surpasses them. It has twelve covered courts – six in a row facing north, six south – the gates of the one range exactly fronting the gates of the other, with a continuous wall round the outside of the whole. Inside, the building is of two storeys and contains three thousand rooms, of which half are underground, and the other half directly above them. I went through the rooms in the upper storey, so what I shall say of them is from my own observation, but the underground ones I can speak of only from report, because the Egyptians in charge refused to let me see them, as they contain the tombs of the kings who built the labyrinth, and also the tombs of the sacred crocodiles. The upper rooms, on the contrary, I did actually see, and it is hard to believe that they are the work of men; the baffling and intricate passages from room to room and from court to court were an endless wonder to me, as we passed from a courtyard into rooms, from rooms into galleries, from galleries into more

rooms, and thence into yet more courtyards. The roof of every chamber, courtyard, and gallery is, like the walls, of stone. The walls are covered with carved figures, and each court is exquisitely built of white marble and surrounded by a colonnade. Near the corner where the labyrinth ends there is a pyramid, two hundred and forty feet in height, with great carved figures of animals on it and an underground passage by which it can be entered. Marvellous as the labyrinth is, the so-called 149 Lake of Moeris beside which it stands is perhaps even more astonishing; the circumference of it is 3600 *stades*, or sixty *schoeni*: a distance, that is to say, of about 420 miles, equal to the length of the whole Egyptian coastline; in shape it is elongated, running north and south, and its greatest depth is fifty fathoms. Now this immense basin is obviously artificial, for nearly in the middle of it are two pyramids, standing three hundred feet out of the water (with their bases an equal depth below the surface), and each surmounted by the stone image of a man sitting on a throne.[82] The water in the lake is not supplied by natural springs (the country hereabouts being excessively dry), but has been brought from the Nile through an artificial duct, and flows in during six months of the year, and out again into the river during the other six. For the half-year that the water runs out, the lake pays the treasury a talent of silver for the fish that are caught; for the other half, only twenty *minae* – one-third of the amount.

The people who live here told me that there is a subterranean 150 passage, running westward into the interior along the hills above Memphis, by which the water of the lake reaches the Libyan Syrtis. I was anxious to know what had been done with the soil which had been removed when the lake was excavated; for I could see no sign of it; and when I asked the people who live nearest the lake to enlighten me about this, I had no difficulty in believing their answer – for I remembered the story of a similar thing that happened at Nineveh, the capital of Assyria. King Sardanapalus had a vast treasure, which he kept in a strong-room underground, and some thieves plotted to steal it. They tunnelled a passage to the strong-room from the house where they lived, making as good a guess as possible at the distance and direction, and every night dumped the soil they took out into the Tigris, which flows past the city, until their purpose was achieved. Just the same method, I was told, was adopted in the excavation of the lake – except, indeed, that there was no need to wait for darkness before dumping the soil: they dug it out, and flung it into the Nile, and knew well enough that the Nile would carry it away and get rid of it.

151   Now as time went on, the twelve kings, who had kept their compact not to molest one another, met to offer sacrifice in the temple of Hephaestus. It was the last day of the festival, and when the moment for pouring the libation had come, the high priest, in going to fetch the golden cups which were always used for the purpose, made a mistake in the number and brought one too few, so that Psammetichus, who was standing last in the row, did not get one. As their custom was, all the kings were wearing their bronze helmets, and Psammetichus, finding himself without a cup, quite innocently and without any ulterior motive took his helmet off, held it out to receive the wine, and so made his libation. The other kings at once connected this action with the oracle, which had declared that whichever of them poured his libation from a bronze cup, should become sole monarch of Egypt. They proceeded to question him, and when they were satisfied that he had acted with no thought of malice, they decided not to put him to death, but to strip him of the greater part of his power and banish him to the marsh-country, forbidding him to leave it or to have any communication with the rest of Egypt.

152   This was the second time that Psammetichus had been exiled; the first was when he fled the country to escape Sabacos, the Ethiopian, who had killed Necos his father; on that occasion he took refuge in Syria, and after the departure of Sabacos in consequence of his dream, he was brought back by the Egyptians of the province of Sais. And now it was his ill-luck to be driven again from his throne by the eleven kings, and exiled to the marshes – all because of what he did with his helmet. In bitter resentment at the treatment he had received, Psammetichus planned revenge. He sent for advice to the oracle at Buto (the most veracious in Egypt) and was told in reply that vengeance

would come from the sea, whence bronze men would appear. Psammetichus did not believe a word of this, and thought it most improbable that he would get any help from bronze men; but not long afterwards it so happened that a company of sea-raiders from Ionia and Caria were forced by bad weather to land on the Egyptian coast. They wore bronze armour, and an Egyptian, who had never seen such a thing before, hurried off to the marshes and told Psammetichus that bronze men had come from the sea and were plundering the country. Seeing in this the fulfilment of the oracle, Psammetichus made friends with the raiders, and by the promise of rich rewards persuaded them to enter his service, and by their help and the help of his supporters in Egypt defeated and deposed his eleven enemies.[83]

Having become sole master of Egypt, Psammetichus built the southern gateway of the temple of Hephaestus at Memphis, and opposite to it a court for Apis – or Epaphus, which is the Greek name. Apis is kept in this court whenever he appears; it has a colonnade round it, with statues eighteen feet high instead of pillars, and is richly carved with figures.

To the Ionians and Carians who helped him to gain the throne Psammetichus granted two pieces of land, opposite one another on each side of the Nile, which he named the Camps, and in addition to the grant of land kept all the other promises he had made them. He even went so far as to put some Egyptian boys into their charge, to be taught Greek; and their learning of the language was the origin of the class of Egyptian interpreters. The tracts of land where the Ionians and Carians settled, and where they lived for many years, lie a little distance seaward from Bubastis, on the Pelusian mouth of the Nile. Amasis subsequently turned them out and brought them to Memphis, to protect him from his own people. They were the first foreigners to live in Egypt, and after their original settlement there, the Greeks began regular intercourse with them, so that we have accurate knowledge of Egyptian history from the time of Psammetichus onward. The docks and ruined houses of their first home, where they lived before Amasis moved them to Memphis, were still to be seen in my day. This, then, is the story of how Psammetichus won the throne of Egypt.

153

154

155   I have already referred more than once to the Egyptian oracle,
but it is sufficiently interesting to warrant further notice. The
temple, which is dedicated to Leto, stands in a great city called
(as I have already mentioned) Buto, at the Sebennytic mouth of
the Nile, on the right-hand side as one enters the river from
seaward. The city also contains two other temples, one of
Apollo, the other of Artemis. The shrine of Leto, where the
oracle is, is a building of great size with a gateway sixty feet
high, but the most remarkable sight it has to offer is not the
temple itself, but a small shrine within the enclosure made out
of a single block of stone; it is cubical in shape, each side sixty
feet long and sixty high. The roof is formed of another single
block, which projects beyond the walls to a distance of six feet.

156   This was certainly the most marvellous thing I actually saw
here; after it, what impressed me most was the island called
Chemmis. This lies in a deep, broad lake by the temple, and the
Egyptians say that it floats. I never saw it move, and it did not
actually look as if it were floating, and I wondered very much,
when I heard about it, if there could be such a thing as a floating
island. There is a large temple of Apollo on it with three separate
altars, and numerous date-palms and other trees, some of them
fruit trees, some not. The Egyptians have a legend to explain
how the island came to float: in former times Leto, one of the
eight original deities, lived in Buto, where her oracle now is, and
having received Apollo, son of Osiris, as a sacred trust from
Isis, she saved him from Typhon when he came there in his
world-wide search, by hiding him in the island. The Egyptians say that Apollo and Artemis are the children of Isis and
Dionysus, and that Leto saved them and brought them up. In
Egyptian, Apollo is Horus, Demeter is Isis, Artemis is Bubastis.
It was from this tradition that Aeschylus, son of Euphorion,
borrowed the idea (not found in earlier poets) of making Artemis
the daughter of Demeter. This is why it was made to float, and
is today called the floating island.

157   The reign of Psammetichus lasted for fifty-four years, during
twenty-nine of which he was engaged in the siege of Azotus, a
large town in Syria, until he finally took it. Azotus held out
longest of any city in history known to us.

Psammetichus left a son, Necos, who succeeded him. It was 158
Necos who began the construction of the canal to the Arabian
gulf, a work afterwards completed by Darius the Persian. The
length of the canal is four days' journey by boat, and its breadth
sufficient to allow two triremes to be rowed abreast. The water
is supplied from the Nile, and the canal leaves the river at a
point a little south of Bubastis and runs past the Arabian town
of Patumus, and then on to the Arabian gulf. The first part of
its course is along the Arabian side of the Egyptian plain, a little
to the northward of the chain of hills by Memphis, where the
stone-quarries are; it skirts the base of these hills from west to
east, and then enters a narrow gorge, after which it trends in a
southerly direction until it enters the Arabian gulf. The shortest
distance from the Mediterranean, or Northern Sea, to the
Southern Sea – or Indian Ocean – namely, from Mt Casius
between Egypt and Syria to the Arabian gulf, is just a thousand
stades. This is the most direct route – by the canal, which does
not keep at all a straight course, the journey is much longer. The
construction of the canal in the time of King Necos cost the lives
of 120,000 Egyptians. Necos did not complete the work, but
broke it off in deference to an oracle, which warned him that
his labour was all for the advantage of the 'barbarian' – as the
Egyptians call anyone who does not speak their language. He 159
then turned his attention to war; he had triremes built, some on
the Mediterranean coast, others on the Arabian gulf, where the
docks are still to be seen, and made use of his new fleets as
occasion arose; and in addition he attacked the Syrians by land
and defeated them at Magdolus, afterwards taking Gaza, a large
town in Syria. The clothes he happened to wear on this occasion
he sent as an offering to Apollo at Branchidae in Milesia. Then,
after a reign of sixteen years, he died, and was succeeded by his
son Psammis.

After his accession to the throne, Psammis was visited by a 160
deputation from Elis. These men had come to boast of the
excellence of the organization of the Olympic games, which,
they thought, could not possibly be run better or more fairly,
even by the Egyptians themselves, who were the ablest people
in the world. When the Eleans had explained the reason for

their visit, the king summoned a meeting of the most learned of his subjects, who proceeded to ask questions of the Eleans, and received in reply a full account of their method of organizing the games. Having described in detail everything they did, the Eleans then said that they had come to find out if the Egyptians could think of anything fairer to suggest. The Egyptians, after considering the matter, asked if the Eleans allowed any people from their own city to compete in the games, and when they were informed that competition was free and open to members of all the Greek states, including Elis, they expressed the opinion that to organize the games on such a principle was not fair at all; for it was quite impossible, when men from one's own city took part in some event, not to favour them at the expense of the strangers. If they really wanted fair play at the games, and if that was indeed the purpose of their visit to Egypt, then (they said) they should open the various events to visitors only, and not allow anyone from Elis to compete.

161   During the six short years of his reign, Psammis attacked Ethiopia; but soon after the expedition he died and was succeeded by his son Apries. Except his great-grandfather Psammetichus, Apries was more prosperous than any of the former kings; his reign lasted for twenty-five years, and in the course of it he sent an army against Sidon and fought a naval battle with the Tyrians. He was not, however, to escape misfortune in the end; the occasion of it, when it came, I will describe more fully in my account of Libya, only touching upon it here.[84] The facts, to put them as briefly as I can, were these: an expedition which he sent against Cyrene failed disastrously, and he was held personally responsible for the defeat; the Egyptians believed that he had deliberately sent them to certain destruction, and desired their deaths in order to strengthen his grip on those of his subjects who were left alive. In their indignation at this, the survivors who got home and the friends of the men who had been killed

162   at once broke into rebellion. Apries sent Amasis to try to argue the rebels into submission, and while Amasis was doing his best to persuade them to return to their duty, a man who was standing behind him as he spoke put a helmet on his head and said that he was crowning him king. Amasis was not altogether

displeased by this, as he soon showed; for when the rebels had
actually offered him the throne, he prepared to lead them against
Apries, who, hearing of the danger which threatened him, sent
Patarbemis, a distinguished member of his court, with orders to
bring Amasis alive into his presence. Amasis, however, in answer
to Patarbemis' summons, rose in his saddle (he was on horseback
at the time), broke wind, and told him to take *that* back to his
master. Patarbemis persisted in his request that the rebel should
obey the king's command and go along with him, whereupon
Amasis replied that that was precisely what he had long been
intending to do: the king would have no cause of complaint
upon that score – he would come, sure enough, and bring others
with him. This answer, and the preparations he saw already
going on, were enough to convince Patarbemis of Amasis' intentions; he hurried back to the court, to inform the king with the
least possible delay of the turn events had taken. On his arrival
there without Amasis, Apries fell into a violent rage and, on the
spur of the moment, ordered his nose and ears to be cut off. The
Egyptians, who up to then had been loyal to the king, seeing a
fellow countryman of such distinction treated in this shameful
way, immediately went over to the rebels and put themselves at
the disposal of Amasis. At the news of their defection, Apries 163
armed his mercenaries (a body of 30,000 Carians and Ionians,
who were with him at Sais, where his palace was – a large and
noteworthy building), and advanced to the attack, the Egyptians
under Amasis marching to meet them. The two forces encountered one another at Momemphis, and prepared for the coming
battle.[85]

The Egyptians are divided into seven classes named after their 164
occupations: priests, warriors, cowherds, swineherds, tradesmen, interpreters, and pilots. The warrior-class, known as
Calasirians and Hermotybians, come from the following districts (all Egypt is divided into districts): the Hermotybians from 165
the districts of Busiris, Sais, Chemmis, Papremis, the island of
Prosopitis, and half of Natho. At their most numerous, they
numbered 160,000 men. None of them touch trade of any kind,
but all have a purely military education. The Calasirians are 166
from the districts of Thebes, Bubastis, Aphthis, Tanis, Mendes,

Sebennytus, Athribis, Pharbaethus, Thmuis, Onuphis, Anysis, and Myecphoris (this last is an island, opposite Bubastis). At their most numerous, the Calasirians numbered 250,000. They, like the Hermotybians, are forbidden to follow any trade or craft, and have an exclusively military training, son following

167   father. I could not say for certain whether the Greeks got their ideas about trade, like so much else, from Egypt or not; the feeling is common enough, and I have observed that Thracians, Scythians, Persians, Lydians – indeed, almost all foreigners – reckon craftsmen and their descendants as lower in the social scale than people who have no connexion with manual work: only the latter, and especially those who are trained for war, do they count amongst the 'nobility'. All the Greeks have adopted this attitude, especially the Spartans; the feeling against handicraft is least strong in Corinth.[86]

168   The Egyptian warrior-class had certain privileges, shared by no other class except the priests: each man had a grant of twelve *arurae* of land, free of tax (an *arura* is 100 Egyptian – or Samian – cubits square). Other privileges were enjoyed, not by the whole class together, but in rotation, no one man enjoying them twice: for instance, a thousand Calasirians and a thousand Hermotybians served each year in the king's bodyguard, and received during their service, in addition to the grant of land, a daily allowance of 5 lb of bread, 2 lb of beef, and 4 cupfuls of wine.

169   In the fight which ensued the foreign mercenaries gave a good account of themselves but were greatly outnumbered and defeated. Apries is said to have believed that his power was so firmly established, that not even a god could have brought him down; nevertheless, he had the worst of the engagement, was taken prisoner, and conveyed to his former royal palace at Sais – his no longer, but now the property of the victorious Amasis. Here he was kept for a time, and well treated by his conqueror, but in the end the Egyptians objected to the injustice of maintaining a man who was his – and their – worst enemy, and persuaded Amasis to surrender the prisoner. They strangled him, and buried his body in the family tomb in the temple of Athene, nearest the shrine, on the left-hand side as one goes in. The people of Sais buried all the kings who came from the

province inside this precinct – the tomb of Amasis, too, though further from the shrine than that of Apries and his ancestors, is in the temple court, a great cloistered building of stone, decorated with pillars carved in imitation of palm-trees, and other costly ornaments. Within the cloister is a chamber with double doors, and behind the doors stands the sepulchre. Here too, in 170 Athene's precinct at Sais, is the tomb of one whose name I prefer not to mention in such a connexion; it stands behind the shrine and occupies the whole length of the wall. Great stone obelisks stand in the enclosure, and there is a stone-bordered lake near by, circular in shape and about the size, I should say, of the lake called the Wheel on the island of Delos. It is on this lake that 171 the Egyptians act by night in what they call their Mysteries the Passion of that being whose name I will not speak.[87] All the details of these performances are known to me, but – I will say no more. Similarly I propose to hold my tongue about the mysterious rites of Demeter, which the Greeks call Thesmophoria, though in this case there are one or two points which may be mentioned without impiety. I may say, for instance, that it was the daughters of Danaus who brought this ceremony from Egypt and instructed the Pelasgian women in it, and that after the Dorian conquest of the Peloponnese it was lost; only the Arcadians, who were not driven from their homes by the invaders, continued the celebration of it.

When Apries had been deposed in the way I have described, 172 Amasis came to the throne. He belonged to the district of Sais and was a native of the town called Siuph. At first the Egyptians were inclined to be contemptuous, and did not think much of him because of his humble and undistinguished origin; but later on he cleverly brought them to heel, without having recourse to harsh measures. Amongst his innumerable treasures, he had a gold foot-bath, which he and his guests used on occasion to wash their feet in. This he broke up, and with the material had a statue made to one of the gods, which he then set up in what he thought the most suitable spot in the city. The Egyptians constantly coming upon the statue, treated it with profound reverence, and as soon as Amasis heard of the effect it had upon them, he called a meeting and revealed the fact that the deeply revered statue was once a foot-bath, which they washed their feet and pissed and vomited in. He went on to say that his own case was much the same, in that once he had been only an ordinary person and was now their king; so that just as they had come to revere the transformed foot-bath, so they had better pay honour and respect to him too. In this way the Egyptians were persuaded to accept him as their master.

173   He used to organize his working day on a regular principle: from dawn till the time when the markets filled up, at mid-morning, he gave all his attention to such business as was brought to him, after which he spent the rest of the day in frivolous amusements, drinking and joking with friends. His well-wishers were pained by this behaviour, and advised him to mend his ways; 'My lord,' they said, 'this excessive levity is not the thing to maintain your royal dignity. You ought rather to sit all day in state upon a stately throne, attending to your kingly affairs; for then the Egyptians would feel that a great man ruled them, and you would have a better name amongst them. Your present conduct, on the contrary, is not at all suitable for a king.'

'Archers,' Amasis replied, 'string their bows when they wish to shoot, and unstring them after use. A bow kept always strung would break, and so be useless when it was needed. It is the same with a man; anyone who was always serious, and never allowed himself a fair share of relaxation and amusement, would suddenly go off his head, or get a stroke. It is because I know this that I divide my time between duty and pleasure.'

174   It is said that Amasis in his private life, before he came to the throne, was just as fond of his joke and his glass, and was never inclined to serious pursuits; indeed, if ever he found himself short of means to continue his round of drinking and enjoyment, he would go out on the prowl and steal, and people who claimed that property of theirs was in his possession would, if he denied it, take him off to the nearest oracle. Sometimes the oracle would convict him, sometimes not. In consequence of this, when he came to the throne, he had a low opinion of the gods who had acquitted him of theft; he neglected their temples, contributed nothing to their adornment, and never frequented them for

sacrifice, on the ground that their oracles were false and they were worth nothing; those on the other hand who had convicted him, he held in the highest honour – for their oracles were true, and they were gods indeed.

His first work was the marvellous gateway for the temple of Athene in Sais. He left everyone else far behind him by the size and height of this building, and by the size and quality of the blocks of stone of which it was constructed. He then presented to the temple some large statues and immense men-sphinxes, and brought for its repair other enormous blocks of stone, some from the quarries near Memphis, and the biggest of all from Elephantine, which is twenty days' voyage by river from Sais. But what caused me more astonishment than anything else was a room hollowed from a single block of stone; this block also came from Elephantine, and took three years to bring to Sais, two thousand men, all of the pilot-class, having the task of conveying it. The outside measurements of this chamber are: length, 21 cubits; breadth, 14 cubits; height, 8 cubits. Inside, its length is $18\frac{5}{6}$ cubits, its breadth 12, and its height 5. It lies by the entrance to the temple, for the story goes that it was not dragged inside the enclosure, because, during the process of moving it, the man chiefly responsible for its construction groaned with vexation at the amount of time and labour which was being wasted, and Amasis took this for a bad omen and refused to have it brought any further. Another story is that it was left outside, because one of the workmen who were levering it along with crowbars got crushed to death underneath it.[88]

To all the temples of note Amasis presented a number of works remarkable for their size; I might mention particularly the recumbent image, seventy-five feet long, in front of the temple of Hephaestus at Memphis. On the same base stand two images in Ethiopian stone, one on each side, both twenty feet high. At Sais there is another recumbent image of the same size as the one at Memphis. It was also Amasis who built the spacious and very remarkable temple of Isis at Memphis.[89]

It is said that the reign of Amasis was a time of unexampled material prosperity for Egypt; the river gave its riches to the earth and the earth to the people. The total number of inhabited

175

176

177

towns, they say, was twenty thousand. Amasis established an admirable custom, which Solon borrowed and introduced at Athens where it is still preserved; this was that every man once a year should declare before the Nomarch, or provincial governor, the source of his livelihood; failure to do this, or inability to prove that the source was an honest one, was punishable by death.

178   Amasis favoured the Greeks and granted them a number of privileges, of which the chief was the gift of Naucratis as a commercial headquarters for any who wished to settle in the country. He also made grants of land upon which Greek traders, who did not want to live permanently in Egypt, might erect altars and temples. Of these latter the best known and most used – and also the largest – is the Hellenium; it was built by the joint efforts of the Ionians of Chios, Teos, Phocaea, and Clazomenae, of the Dorians of Rhodes, Cnidos, Halicarnassus, and Phaselis, and of the Aeolians of Mytilene. It is to these states that the temple belongs, and it is they who have the right of appointing the officers in charge of the port. Other cities which claim a share in the Hellenium do so without any justification; the Aeginetans, however, did build a temple of Zeus separately, the Samians one in honour of Hera, and the Milesians another in honour of Apollo.[90]

179   In old days Naucratis was the only trading post in Egypt, and anyone who brought a ship into any of the other mouths of the Nile was bound to state on oath that he did so of necessity and then proceed to the Canopic mouth; should contrary winds prevent him from doing so, he had to carry his freight to Naucratis in barges all round the Delta, which shows the exclusive

180   privilege the port enjoyed. And when the Amphictyons, after the accidental destruction by fire of the temple at Delphi, contracted to have it rebuilt at a cost of three hundred talents (a quarter of that sum to be furnished by the Delphians), and the Delphians went round from city to city asking for contributions, Egypt was by no means least in giving assistance. Amasis gave them a thousand talents of alum, and the Greeks who had settled in Egypt, twenty *minae*.[91]

181   After the conclusion of a pact of friendship and alliance with

Cyrene, Amasis, as a token of his goodwill – or perhaps merely because he wanted a Greek wife – decided to marry a woman from that city. The woman he chose was Ladice, daughter of either Battus, son of Arcesilaus, or (for accounts differ) of Critobulus, one of the leading citizens. For a time the marriage was not consummated; for whenever the king went to bed with her, he was unable to have intercourse, while with his other wives he did. This happened frequently, until at last Amasis told her that she must have bewitched him, and there was no escape for her, in consequence, from a most miserable death. Ladice denied the charge, but in vain; the king's anger was not softened, so she made a silent vow to Aphrodite that if that very night – the last which could save her from death – the marriage could be consummated, she would present a statue to the temple of the goddess in Cyrene. Her prayer was at once answered; Amasis lay with her successfully, and continued to do so on every occasion afterwards, and came to love her deeply. Ladice fulfilled her vow to Aphrodite; she had the statue made and sent it to Cyrene, where it still remained up to my own time, looking outward from the city. Ladice herself suffered no harm when Cambyses conquered Egypt; for when he learnt who she was, Cambyses sent her back safely to her native Cyrene.

Amasis further showed his goodwill to Greece by sending presents to be dedicated in Greek temples; to Cyrene he sent a gold-plated statue of Athene and a painting of himself; to the temple of Athene at Lindos, two statues in stone and a remarkable linen corslet; and to the goddess Hera in Samos two likenesses of himself, in wood, which until my own time stood behind the doors in the great temple. These last were a mark of his friendship with the ruler of Samos, Polycrates, son of Aeaces; but the gifts to Lindos in Rhodes were not the expression of any personal feeling, but were given because of the tradition that the temple of Athene there was founded by the daughters of Danaus, who touched at the island during their flight from the sons of Aegyptus.

Amasis was also the first man to take Cyprus and compel it to pay tribute.

BOOK THREE

1   It was against this Amasis, then, that Cyrus' son Cambyses
marched at the head of an army drawn from various subject
nations and including both Ionian and Aeolian Greeks.[1] His
pretext was as follows. Cyrus had sent to Amasis to ask for the
services of the best oculist in Egypt, and the one who was
selected, in resentment at being torn from his wife and family
and handed over to the Persians, suggested to Cambyses by way
of revenge that he should ask for Amasis' daughter in marriage,
knowing that consent would cause the Egyptian king personal
distress, and that refusal would embroil him with Cambyses.
Cambyses did as the man suggested, and sent a representative
to Egypt to make the request. Amasis, who dreaded the power
of Persia, and was well aware that Cambyses wanted his daughter not as a wife but as a concubine, found himself in an awkward
position, and unable to say either yes or no. Now there was a
daughter of the late King Apries, a tall and beautiful girl named
Nitetis, the last survivor of her family, and Amasis, after thinking the matter over, decided to dress her up like a princess in
fine clothes adorned with gold, and send her to Persia as his
own daughter. This he did; and some time later, when Cambyses
happened to address her by her father's name, she replied: 'My
lord, you do not know how Amasis has cheated you; he dressed
me in gorgeous clothes and sent me to you as his own daughter
– but indeed I am not; I am the daughter of Apries, his master,
whom he killed when he led the Egyptians to rebel against him.'
It was these words, and the cause of quarrel they disclosed,
which, according to the Persian account, brought down upon
2   Egypt the wrath of Cambyses, son of Cyrus. The Egyptians, on

the other hand, claim that Cambyses was the son of Nitetis, Apries' daughter, and was thus a native of their own country – for it was Cyrus, they say, not Cambyses, who sent to Amasis to demand his daughter. The claim, however, is not justified by facts; for knowing as they do – none better – the laws of Persia, they could not fail to be aware, first, that Persian usage bars a bastard from the succession so long as there is a legitimate heir, and, secondly, that Cambyses was the son of Cassandane, daughter of Pharnaspes, one of the Achaemenidae, and not of this Egyptian woman. The fact is, they wish to claim kinship with Cyrus, and pervert the truth to justify their claim. There is also another story current, but not, I think, a convincing one: namely, that a Persian woman paid a visit to Cyrus' wives, and greatly admired the fine tall sons which she saw standing by Cassandane's side. Hearing her praises, Cassandane, who was vexed with Nitetis, said: 'In spite of my beautiful children Cyrus treats me with contempt and gives all his attention to that woman he got from Egypt.' 'Well then, mother,' exclaimed Cambyses, the elder of her two sons, 'when I'm a man, I'll turn Egypt upside-down for you.' He was only about ten when he astonished the women by making this promise, but he never forgot it; for when he grew up and had ascended the throne, he did, indeed, invade Egypt.

There was another thing, quite different from all this, which helped to bring about the Egyptian expedition. One of the Greek mercenaries of Amasis, a Halicarnassian called Phanes, a brave and intelligent soldier, being dissatisfied for some reason or other with Amasis, escaped from Egypt by sea, with the object of getting an interview with Cambyses. As he was a person of consequence in the army and had very precise knowledge of the internal condition of Egypt, Amasis was anxious to catch him and sent the most trustworthy of his eunuchs to pursue him in a trireme. He was caught in Lycia but not brought back; for getting his guards to drink themselves stupid, he outwitted his captor and made good his escape to Persia. Cambyses was anxious to launch his attack on Egypt and was wondering how best he could cross the desert, when Phanes arrived, and not only revealed to him all the secrets of Amasis, but also advised him that the best way of getting his army through the desert would be to send to the Arabian king and ask for a safe-conduct.

5   The only entrance into Egypt is through this desert. From Phoenicia to the boundaries of Gaza the country belongs to the Syrians known as 'Palestinian': from Gaza, a town, I should say, not much smaller than Sardis, the trading ports as far as Ienysus belong to the king of Arabia; from there as far as Lake Serbonis, near which Mt Casius runs down to the sea, it is once more Syrian territory; and after Lake Serbonis (where Typhon is supposed to be hidden) Egypt begins.[2] The whole area between Ienysus on the one side, and Mt Casius and the Lake on the other – and it is of considerable extent, not less than three days' journey – is desert and completely without water.

6   I will now mention something of which few voyagers to Egypt are aware. Throughout the year, not only from all parts of Greece but from Phoenicia as well, wine is imported into Egypt in earthenware jars; yet one might say that not a single empty wine-jar is to be seen anywhere in the country. The obvious question is: what becomes of them? I will explain. The local official of each place has orders to collect all the jars from his town and send them to Memphis, and the people of Memphis have to fill them with water and send them to this tract of desert in Syria. In this way every fresh jar of wine imported into Egypt, and there emptied of its contents, finds its way into Syria to join

7   the previous ones. It was the Persians, immediately after their conquest of Egypt, who devised this means of storing water in the desert, and so making the passage into the country practicable; but at the time of which I am speaking there was no water at all, so Cambyses took the advice of his Halicarnassian friend Phanes, and sent to the Arabian king with a request for safe-conduct. The request was granted, and pledges were exchanged between the two parties.

8   No nation regards the sanctity of a pledge more seriously than the Arabs.[3] When two men wish to make a solemn compact, they get the service of a third, who stands between them and with a sharp stone cuts the palms of their hands near the base of the thumb; then he takes a little tuft of wool from their clothes, dips it in the blood and smears the blood on seven

stones which lie between them, invoking as he does so, the names of Dionysus and Urania; then the person who is giving the pledge, commends the stranger – or fellow citizen, as the case may be – to his friends, who in their turn consider themselves equally bound to honour it. The only gods the Arabs recognize are Dionysus and Urania; the way they cut their hair – all round in a circle, with the temples shaved – is, they say, in imitation of Dionysus. Dionysus in their language is Orotalt, and Urania Alilat.

When the Arabian king had made his vow of friendship with the messengers of Cambyses, the method he devised of helping the Egyptian army was to fill camel-skins with water, load them on to all his live camels, and so convey them to the desert, where he awaited the arrival of the troops. That, at any rate, is the more credible account of his procedure; there is also another, which I ought to mention since it too is told, though it is not so easy to believe. According to this, the Arabian king had cow-hides and other skins stitched together to form a pipe long enough to reach from the Corys – a large river in Arabia which runs into the Red Sea – all the way to the desert;[4] here he had large reservoirs constructed, filled them by means of the pipe, and so stored the water. The water was brought to three separate places, over a total distance – between river and desert – of a twelve days' journey.

Psammenitus, Amasis' son, took up a position on the Pelusian mouth of the Nile, to await the attack of Cambyses. Amasis had died before the invasion actually began, after a reign of forty-four years, during which he had suffered no serious disaster. His body was embalmed and buried in the sepulchre he had himself built in the temple of Athene in Sais. In the reign of his successor Psammenitus, an unparalleled event occurred – rain fell at Thebes, a thing which the men of that city say had never happened before, or has ever happened since till my day. Normally, in upper Egypt no rain falls at all; but on this occasion it did – a light shower.[5]

The Persians crossed the desert, took up a position near the Egyptian army, and prepared for an engagement. Before the battle the Greek and Carian mercenaries who were serving with the Egyptians contrived the following against Phanes in their anger at his bringing a foreign army against Egypt: they seized his sons, whom he had left behind, and brought them to the camp, where they made sure their father could see them; then, placing a bowl in the open ground between the two armies, they led the boys up to it one by one, and cut their throats over it. Not one was spared, and when the last was dead, they poured wine and water on to the blood in the bowl, and every man in the mercenary force drank. That done, the fight began; and after a hard struggle and heavy casualties on both sides, the Egyptians were routed.

12   At the place where this battle was fought I saw a great marvel which the natives had told me about. The bones still lay there, those of the Persian dead separate from those of the Egyptian, just as they were originally divided, and I noticed that the skulls of the Persians are so thin that the merest touch with a pebble will pierce them, but those of the Egyptians, on the other hand, are so tough that it is hardly possible to break them with a blow from a stone. I was told, very credibly, that the reason was that the Egyptians shave their heads from childhood, so that the bone of the skull is hardened by the action of the sun – this is also why they hardly ever go bald, baldness being rarer in Egypt than anywhere else. This, then, explains the thickness of their skulls; and the thinness of the Persians' skulls rests upon a similar principle: namely that they have always worn felt skull-caps, to guard their heads from the sun. I also observed the same thing at Papremis, where the Persians serving under Achaemenes, the son of Darius, were destroyed by Inarus the Libyan.[6]

13   After their defeat, the Egyptians fled in disorder and shut themselves up in Memphis. Cambyses called upon them to come to terms, sending a Persian herald up the river to the town in a Mytilenean vessel; but directly they saw the ship coming into the town, they rushed out from the walls in a body, smashed up the ship, tore everyone on board limb from limb, and carried the bits back inside the walls. They then stood a siege, but after a time surrendered. The neighbouring Libyans were alarmed by the fate of Egypt and gave themselves up without a battle, agreeing to pay tribute and sending presents. A similar fear

caused the people of Cyrene and Barca to follow their example. Cambyses graciously accepted what the Libyans sent him; the offering from Cyrene, on the contrary, he treated with contempt. I suppose he objected to the smallness of the amount – it was only 500 *minae* of silver; anyway, he snatched the money into his own hands and flung it to his men.

Ten days passed, and Cambyses, wishing to see what stuff the Egyptian king Psammenitus was made of – he had been but six months on the throne – forced him, with other Egyptians, to witness from a seat in the city outskirts a spectacle deliberately devised to humiliate him. First, he had his daughter dressed like a slave and sent out with a pitcher to fetch water, accompanied by other young girls similarly dressed and chosen from noble families. The girls cried bitterly as they passed the place where their fathers sat watching them, and the fathers, in their turn – all but Psammenitus himself – wept and lamented no less bitterly at the sight of such an insult to their children. Psammenitus, however, after a single glance of recognition, bent to the ground in silence. The girls with their pitchers passed on, and then came the king's son with two thousand others of the same age, their mouths bridled and a rope round their necks, on their way to execution for the murder of the Mytileneans at Memphis and the destruction of the ship – for the sentence of the royal judges had been that for each man ten Egyptian noblemen should die. Psammenitus watched them pass, and knew that his son was going to his death; but, though the other Egyptians who were sitting near him continued to weep and to show every sign of distress, he did just what he had done before at the sight of his daughter. So the young men, too, passed on; and then there chanced to walk by the place where Psammenitus, son of Amasis, sat with the others in the city outskirts, an old man who had once been the king's friend and had dined at his table, but had been stripped of his fortune and was now nothing more than a beggar trying to get what he could from the soldiers. At the sight of him Psammenitus burst into tears, and called him by name, and beat his head in distress. Guards were standing near, whose duty it was to report to Cambyses exactly how Psammenitus behaved as each of the processions went by, and

Cambyses was so much amazed at what he heard, that he sent a messenger to Psammenitus to ask how he could behave as he did. 'Your master Cambyses,' the messenger said, 'asks why it is, that you made no sound and shed no tear when you saw your daughter insulted and your son going to his death, yet honoured with those signs of grief a beggar who, he understands, is not even related to you.' 'Son of Cyrus,' was the answer, 'my own suffering was too great for tears, but I could not but weep for the trouble of a friend, who has fallen from great wealth and good fortune and been reduced to beggary on the threshold of old age.'[7]

When this answer was reported, it was recognized as just, and the Egyptians relate that Croesus – who, as it happened, had accompanied Cambyses in the expedition against Egypt – wept when he heard it, as did the Persians who were present, and that even Cambyses felt a touch of pity – for he at once gave orders that Psammenitus' son should be reprieved from the sentence of death, and that Psammenitus himself should be brought before him from the place where he sat in the city outskirts.

15   The messengers were too late to save the young man, for he had been the first to be killed; but they brought Psammenitus to Cambyses, at whose court he lived from that time onward. Here he was well treated; and indeed, if he had only had the sense to keep out of mischief, he might have recovered Egypt and ruled it as governor; for the Persians are in the habit of treating the sons of kings with honour, and even of restoring to their sons the thrones of those who have rebelled against them. There are many instances from which one may infer that this sort of generosity is usual in Persia: one obvious one is the case of Thannyras, the son of Inarus the Libyan, who was allowed to succeed his father. Pausiris, the son of Amyrtaeus, is another example: to him, too, his father's kingdom was restored – and all this in spite of the fact that nobody ever caused the Persians more trouble and loss than Inarus and Amyrtaeus. Psammenitus, however, did not refrain from stirring up trouble, and paid for it. He was caught trying to raise a revolt amongst the Egyptians, and as soon as his guilt was known by Cambyses, he

drank bull's blood and died on the spot. And that was the end
of Psammenitus.[8]

Cambyses now left Memphis and went on to Sais, fully 16
resolved on what he would do when he got there. This intention
he at once carried out, for no sooner had he entered the palace
of Amasis than he gave orders for his body to be taken from the
tomb where it lay. This done, he proceeded to have it treated
with every possible indignity, such as lashing with whips, prick-
ing with goads, and the plucking of its hairs. All this was done
till the executioners were weary, and at last, as the corpse had
been embalmed and would not fall to pieces under the blows,
Cambyses ordered it to be burnt. This was an unholy thing to
do, because the Persians believe that fire is a god, and never
burn their dead. Indeed, such a practice is unheard of either
amongst them or the Egyptians: in the former case for the reason
I mentioned, and because the Persians think it is wrong to give
a man's dead body to a god; in the latter, because the Egyptians
believe fire to be a living animal which devours whatever it gets,
and, when it has eaten enough, dies with the food it feeds on. It
is wholly contrary to Egyptian custom to allow dead bodies to
be eaten by animals: that is why they embalm them – to prevent
them from being eaten in the grave by worms. Cambyses, therefore, in giving this order, was running counter to the religious
belief of both nations. The Egyptians have a story that it was
not Amasis at all whose body received this treatment; it was
another man's, of about the same stature, but the Persians
thought it was the king's when they committed the outrage upon
it. For Amasis, according to this story, had learnt from an oracle
of the fate which threatened him after his death, and, in order
to avert it, buried close to the doors, just within his tomb, the
body of this man who was lashed with the Persian whips, but
his own body he instructed his son to place in the furthest
possible recess of the burial-chamber. I do not myself believe
that Amasis ever gave these orders at all – it is just a tale the
Egyptians tell to save face.

Cambyses next made plans for three separate military ven- 17
tures: one against the Carthaginians, another against the
Ammonians, and the third against the long-lived Ethiopians, on

the coast of the Indian Ocean, south of Libya.[9] He proposed to send his fleet against the Carthaginians and a part of his land forces against the Ammonians; to Ethiopia he decided first to send spies, ostensibly with presents to the king, but actually to collect what information they could; in particular he wanted them to find out if the so-called Table of the Sun really existed.

18   (The story about the Table of the Sun is that there is a meadow, situated in the outskirts of the city, where a plentiful supply of boiled meat of all kinds is kept; it is the duty of the magistrates to put the meat there at night, and during the day anybody who wishes may come and eat it. The natives say that the meat appears spontaneously and is the gift of the earth.)

19   Having decided that the spies should go, Cambyses sent to Elephantine for some men of the Fish-Eaters who were acquainted with the Ethiopian language, and, while they were being fetched, gave orders for the fleet to sail against Carthage. The Phoenicians, however, refused to go, because of the close bond which connected Phoenicia and Carthage, and the wickedness of making war against their own children.[10] In this way, with the Phoenicians out of it and the remainder of the naval force too weak to undertake the campaign alone, the Carthaginians escaped Persian domination. Cambyses did not think fit to bring pressure to bear, because the Phoenicians had taken service under him of their own free will, and his whole naval power was dependent on them. The Cyprians, too, had given their services to Persia and took part in the Egyptian campaign.

20   The Fish-Eaters who had been summoned from Elephantine were sent off to Ethiopia with instructions on what they were to say on their arrival: they took with them as presents for the king a scarlet robe, a gold chain-necklace and bracelets, an alabaster casket of myrrh, and a jar of palm-wine. The Ethiopians, who were the objects of all this attention, are said to be the tallest and best-looking people in the world. Their laws and customs are peculiar to themselves, and the strangest is the method they have of choosing for their king the man whom they judge to be the tallest, and strong in proportion to his height.

21   The Fish-Eaters duly arrived in the country and presented their

gifts to the king with the following words: 'Cambyses, King of Persia, wishing to be your friend and guest, has sent us here with orders to have speech with you, and these gifts he offers you are just the things which he himself takes most pleasure in using.'

But the Ethiopian king knew the men were spies, and answered: 'The king of Persia has not sent you with these presents because he puts a high value upon being my friend. You have come to get information about my kingdom; therefore, you are liars, and that king of yours is unjust. Had he any respect for what is right, he would not have coveted any other kingdom than his own, nor made slaves of a people who have done him no wrong. So take him this bow, and tell him that the king of Ethiopia has some advice to give him: when the Persians can draw a bow of this size thus easily, then let him raise an army of superior strength and invade the country of the long-lived Ethiopians.[11] Till then, let him thank the gods for not turning the thoughts of the children of Ethiopia to foreign conquest.' He then unstrung the bow, put it into the hands of the Fish-Eaters, and picked up the scarlet robe, asking what it was and how it was made. The men explained about the dye and how the material was dipped in it, whereupon the king replied that both the dyers and the garments they dyed were pretending to be what they were not, and were therefore cheats. Then he asked about the gold chain and the bracelets, and when the Fish-Eaters explained their use as ornaments he laughed and, supposing them to be fetters, remarked that they had stronger ones in their own country. Next he asked about the myrrh, and after hearing how it was prepared and how people rubbed it on their bodies for a perfume, he repeated the comment he had made about the scarlet robe. Finally he came to the wine and, having learnt the process of its manufacture, drank some and found it delicious; then, for a last question, he asked what the Persian king ate and what was the greatest age that Persians could attain. Getting in reply an account of the nature and cultivation of wheat, and hearing that the Persian king ate bread, and that people in Persia did not commonly live beyond eighty, he said he was not surprised that anyone who ate dung should die so soon, adding that Persians would doubtless die younger still, if they did not keep themselves going with that drink – and here he pointed to the wine, the one thing in which he admitted the superiority of the Persians.

23   The Fish-Eaters, in their turn, asked the king how long the Ethiopians lived and what they ate, and were told that most of them lived to be a hundred and twenty, and some even more, and that they ate boiled meat and drank milk. When they expressed amazement that anyone should live to such an advanced age, they were taken to a spring, the water from which smelt like violets and caused a man's skin, when he washed in it, to glisten as if he had washed in oil. They said the water of this spring lacked density to such a degree that nothing would float in it, neither wood nor any lighter substance – everything sank to the bottom. If this account is true, then their constant use of it must be the cause of the Ethiopians' longevity. After the visit to the spring the king conducted them to a prison in which all the prisoners were bound with gold chains – for in Ethiopia the rarest and most precious metal is bronze. Inspection of the prison was followed by inspection of the Table of the Sun, and last of all they were taken to see the coffins. These

24   coffins are said to be made of crystal, and the method the Ethiopians follow is first to dry the corpse, either by the Egyptian process or some other, then cover it all over with gypsum and paint it to resemble as closely as possible the living man; then they enclose it in a shaft of crystal which has been hollowed out, like a cylinder, to receive it. The stuff is easily worked and is mined in large quantities. The corpse is plainly visible inside the cylinder; there is no disagreeable smell, or any other cause of annoyance, and every detail can be as distinctly seen as if there were nothing between one's eyes and the body. The next-of-kin keep the cylinder in their houses for a year, offering it the first fruits and sacrificing to it; then they carry it out and set it up near the town.

25   Having now seen all they could, the spies returned to Egypt to make their report, which so angered Cambyses that he at once began his march against Ethiopia, without any orders for the provision of supplies, and without for a moment considering

the fact that he was to take his men to the ends of the earth. He lost his wits completely and, like the madman he was, the moment he heard what the Fish-Eaters had to say, off he went with his whole force of infantry, leaving behind the Greeks who were serving under him. Arrived at Thebes, he detached a body of 50,000 men with orders to attack the Ammonians, reduce them to slavery, and burn the oracle of Zeus; then with his remaining forces he continued his march towards Ethiopia.[12] They had not, however, covered a fifth of the distance, when everything in the nature of provisions gave out, and the men were forced to eat the pack-animals until they, too, were all gone. If Cambyses, when he saw what the situation was, had changed his mind and returned to his base, he would, in spite of his original error, have shown some sense; but as it was, he paid not the least attention to what was happening and continued his advance. The troops kept themselves alive by eating grass so long as there was any to be had in the country, but once they had reached the desert, some of them were reduced to the dreadful expedient of cannibalism. One man in ten was chosen by lot to be the victim. This was too much even for Cambyses; when it was reported to him, he abandoned the expedition, marched back, and arrived at Thebes with greatly reduced numbers. From Thebes he went down to Memphis and allowed the Greeks to sail home. So ended the expedition against Ethiopia.

26   The force which was sent against the Ammonians started from Thebes with guides, and can be traced as far as the town of Oasis, which belongs to Samians supposed to be of the Aeschrionian tribe, and is seven days' journey across the sand from Thebes. The place is known in Greek as the Islands of the Blessed. General report has it that the army got as far as this, but of its subsequent fate there is no news whatever. It never reached the Ammonians and it never returned to Egypt. There is, however, a story told by the Ammonians themselves and by others who heard it from them, that when the men had left Oasis, and in their march across the desert had reached a point about mid-way between the town and the Ammonian border, a southerly wind of extreme violence drove the sand over them in

heaps as they were taking their mid-day meal, so that they disappeared for ever.

27   After the arrival of Cambyses at Memphis, Apis – the Greek Epaphus – appeared to the Egyptians. Immediately the whole people put on their best clothes and went on holiday, and Cambyses, seeing the festivities and convinced that the Egyptians were rejoicing over recent disaster, summoned the officers in charge of Memphis and asked them why it was that the Egyptians had done nothing of the kind during his previous visit to the city, but had waited to celebrate their holiday until the present occasion, when he had returned after the loss of a large part of his army. They replied that a god had appeared amongst them; he was wont to reveal himself only at long intervals of time, and whenever he did so, all Egypt rejoiced and celebrated a festival. Cambyses' answer to this was, that the men were

28   liars, and as such he had them executed. Then he called the priests into his presence, and when they made precisely the same assertion, he replied that if some tame god or other had really revealed himself to the Egyptians he would find out about it soon enough; and without another word he ordered the priests to fetch Apis – which they did.

This Apis – or Epaphus – is the calf of a cow which is never afterwards able to have another.[13] The Egyptians say that a flash of light descends upon the cow from heaven, and this causes her to receive Apis. The Apis-calf has distinctive marks: it is black, with a white diamond on its forehead, the image of an eagle on its back, the hairs on its tail double, and a scarab under its

29   tongue. The priests brought the animal and Cambyses, half mad as he was, drew his dagger, aimed a blow at Apis' belly, but missed and struck his thigh. Then he laughed, and said to the priests: 'Do you call that a god, you poor creatures? Are your gods flesh and blood? Do they feel the prick of steel? No doubt a god like that is good enough for the Egyptians; but you won't get away with trying to make a fool of me.' He then ordered the priests to be whipped by the men whose business it was to carry out such punishments, and any Egyptian who was found still keeping holiday to be put to death. In this way the festival was broken up, the priests punished, and Apis, who lay in the temple

for a time wasting away from the wound in his thigh, finally died and was buried by the priests without the knowledge of Cambyses.

Even before this Cambyses had been far from sound in his mind; but the Egyptians are convinced that the complete loss of his reason was the direct result of this crime. Of the outrages he subsequently committed the first was the murder of his brother Smerdis (his father's son by the same mother as himself). He had already sent Smerdis back to Persia, because he was jealous of him for being the only Persian to succeed in drawing – though only a very little way, about two fingers' breadth – the bow which the Fish-Eaters brought from Ethiopia. After Smerdis had returned, Cambyses dreamt that a messenger came to him from Persia with the news that Smerdis was sitting on the royal throne and that his head touched the sky. In alarm lest the dream should mean that his brother would kill him and reign in his stead, Cambyses sent Prexaspes, the most trusted of his Persian friends, to make away with him. Prexaspes went up-country to Susa and did the deed – according to one account he took his victim out hunting, according to another he lured him down to the Persian Gulf and drowned him. This, they say, was the beginning; and the next crime Cambyses committed was the murder of his sister who had come with him to Egypt. This woman was his sister by both parents, and also his wife, though it had never before been a Persian custom for brothers and sisters to marry. Cambyses got over the difficulty in the following way: having fallen in love with one of his sisters and wishing afterwards to take the illegal step of making her his wife, he summoned the royal judges and asked them if there was any law in the country which allowed a man to marry his sister if he wished to do so. These royal judges are specially chosen men, who hold office either for life or until they are found guilty of some misconduct; their duties are to determine suits and to interpret the ancient laws of the land, and all points of dispute are referred to them. When, therefore, Cambyses put his question, they managed to find an answer which would neither violate the truth nor endanger their own necks: namely, that though they could discover no law which allowed brother to marry sister, there was undoubtedly a law which permitted the king of Persia to do what he pleased. In this way they avoided breaking any established law, in spite of their fear of Cambyses; and at the same time, by bringing in a particular law to help the king to realize his wish, they escaped the danger to themselves which a too rigid attention to ancestral usage would have involved. Cambyses accordingly married the sister he was in love with, and not long afterwards married another one as well – and this, the younger of the two, was the one who went with him to Egypt.

32   As in the case of Smerdis, there are two accounts of her death; the Greeks say that Cambyses set a puppy and a lion-cub to fight, and that his wife was amongst the spectators; the puppy was getting the worst of it, when another from the same litter broke its chain and came to its brother's help, and the two together proved too much for the cub. Cambyses enjoyed watching the fight, but his sister, who was sitting beside him, began to cry. Noticing her tears, Cambyses asked the reason for them, and she replied that it was the sight of the puppy coming to help its brother that had made her weep; for she could not but remember Smerdis, and think how there was nobody now to come to help her husband. It was this remark which, according to the Greek version, made Cambyses put her to death. The Egyptians, on the other hand, say that the two were sitting at table, when the woman took a lettuce and, after pulling off the leaves, asked her husband whether he thought it looked better with its leaves on or off. Cambyses said that he preferred it before it was stripped, whereupon his sister replied that he had treated the house of Cyrus just as she had treated the lettuce – he had stripped it bare. Cambyses, in a fury, kicked her; and, as she was pregnant at the time, she had a miscarriage and died.

33   These two crimes were committed against his own kin; both were the acts of a madman – whether or not his madness was due to his treatment of Apis. It may, indeed, have been the result of any one of the many maladies which afflict mankind, and there is, in fact, a story that he had suffered from birth from the serious complaint which some call 'the sacred sickness'.[14] There would then be nothing strange in the fact that a serious physical

malady should have affected his brain. But in addition to the   34
two crimes already mentioned, there were other Persians, too,
whom he treated with the savagery of a lunatic; for instance,
there was the case of Prexaspes, a man who was highly valued
by the king and used to bring him his dispatches, and whose son
was the king's cupbearer – also a position of no small honour.
On one occasion Cambyses said to this distinguished official:
'What sort of man do the Persians think I am, and what do they
say about me?' 'Master,' Prexaspes replied, 'you are highly
praised by them, and they have but one criticism to make: they
say you are too fond of wine.' This enraged Cambyses. 'So now,'
he said, 'the Persians say that excessive drinking has driven me
mad. They said something quite different before; but I see it was
a lie.' For on a former occasion, when a number of Persians
were sitting with him, and Croesus was also present, he had
asked what they thought of him compared with his father, and
they had answered that he was better than his father, because
he had kept all Cyrus' possessions and acquired Egypt and the
command of the sea into the bargain. Croesus, however, was
not satisfied with this opinion, and said: 'Son of Cyrus, I at least
do not think you are equal to your father; for you have not yet
a son like the son he left behind him in yourself.' Cambyses was   35
delighted with this, and praised Croesus' judgement, and it was
the memory of this incident which made him, on the present
occasion, say in a rage to Prexaspes: 'I'll soon show you if the
Persians speak the truth, or if what they say is not a sign of their
own madness rather than of mine. You see your son standing
there by the door? If I shoot him through the middle of the
heart, I shall have proved the Persians' words empty and meaningless; if I miss, then say, if you will, that the Persians are right,
and my wits are gone.'

Without another word he drew his bow and shot the boy,
and then ordered his body to be cut open and the wound
examined; and when the arrow was found to have pierced the
heart, he was delighted, and said with a laugh to the boy's
father: 'There's proof for you, Prexaspes, that I am sane and the
Persians mad. Now tell me if you ever saw anyone else shoot so
straight.'

Prexaspes knew well enough that the king's mind was un-balanced, so in fear for his own safety he answered: 'Master, I do not believe that God himself is a better marksman.' On another occasion he arrested twelve Persians of the highest rank on some trifling charge, and buried them alive, head downwards.

36 For this action Croesus the Lydian thought fit to give him some advice. 'My lord,' he said, 'do not always act on the passionate impulse of youth. Check and control yourself. There is wisdom in forethought, and a sensible man looks to the future. If you continue too long in your present course of killing your countrymen for no sufficient cause – and of killing children too – then beware lest the Persians rise in revolt. Again and again your father Cyrus urged me to give you whatever advice I might think would help you.'

In spite of the fact that Croesus spoke in all friendship, Cambyses answered: 'So even you dare tell me how I ought to behave! You – who governed your own country so finely, and gave such excellent advice to my father to cross the Araxes and attack the Massagetae, when all they wanted was to come over themselves and attack us! You – who ruined yourself by your own bad government, and ruined Cyrus simply because he took your advice! But now you are going to pay for it – I have long wanted an excuse to get even with you.' He was just reaching for his bow to shoot him down, when Croesus leapt from his seat and ran from the room. Robbed of his shot, Cambyses sent his servants to catch him and kill him; but they knew their master's moods and hid him instead, so that if Cambyses changed his mind and asked for Croesus, they would be able to produce him and get a reward for saving his life; for they knew they could kill him later, if the king kept to his purpose and showed no signs of regret. And it did in fact happen that quite soon afterwards Cambyses missed Croesus, and his servants, as soon as they noticed it, let him know that he was still alive. Cambyses said that he rejoiced to hear it, but the men who saved him would not get off so lightly: he would punish them with death – which he did.

37 All this may pass for a sample of the maniacal savagery with which Cambyses treated the Persians and his allies during his

stay in Memphis; amongst other things, he broke open ancient
tombs and examined the bodies, and even entered the temple of
Hephaestus and jeered at the god's statue. This statue closely
resembles the Pataici which the Phoenicians carry about on the
prows of their triremes – but I should make it clearer to anyone
who has never seen these, if I said it was like a pygmy. He also
entered the temple of the Cabiri, which no one but the priest is
allowed to do, made fun of the images there (they resemble
those of Hephaestus, and are supposed to be his sons), and
actually burnt them.[15]

In view of all this, I have no doubt whatever that Cambyses   38
was completely out of his mind; it is the only possible explanation of his assault upon, and mockery of, everything which
ancient law and custom have made sacred in Egypt. For if
anyone, no matter who, were given the opportunity of choosing
from amongst all the nations in the world the beliefs which he
thought best, he would inevitably, after careful consideration of
their relative merits, choose those of his own country. Everyone
without exception believes his own native customs, and the
religion he was brought up in, to be the best; and that being so,
it is unlikely that anyone but a madman would mock at such
things. There is abundant evidence that this is the universal
feeling about the ancient customs of one's country. One might
recall, in particular, an account told of Darius. When he was
king of Persia, he summoned the Greeks who happened to be
present at his court, and asked them what they would take to
eat the dead bodies of their fathers. They replied that they would
not do it for any money in the world. Later, in the presence of
the Greeks, and through an interpreter, so that they could
understand what was said, he asked some Indians, of the tribe
called Callatiae, who do in fact eat their parents' dead bodies,
what they would take to burn them. They uttered a cry of horror
and forbade him to mention such a dreadful thing. One can see
by this what custom can do, and Pindar, in my opinion, was
right when he called it 'king of all'.[16]

While Cambyses was occupied with the Egyptian expedition,   39
the Lacedaemonians made an expedition to Samos against

Polycrates, the son of Aeaces. Polycrates had seized power in
the island, and at the outset had divided his realm into three
and gone shares with his brothers, Pantagnotus and Syloson;
later, however, he killed the former, banished the latter (the
younger of the two) and held the whole island himself. Once
master of it, he concluded a pact of friendship with Amasis,
king of Egypt, sealing it by a mutual exchange of presents. It
was not long before the rapid increase of his power became the
talk of Ionia and the rest of Greece. All his campaigns were
victorious, his every venture a success. He had a fleet of a
hundred penteconters and a force of a thousand bowmen. His
plundering raids were widespread and indiscriminate – he used
to say that a friend would be more grateful if he gave him back
what he had taken, than if he had never taken it. He captured
many of the islands and a number of towns on the mainland as
well. Amongst other successes, he defeated at sea the Lesbians,
who had sent their whole fleet to the help of Miletus; the
prisoners he took were forced to dig, in chains, the whole moat
which surrounds the walls of Samos.[17]

40   Amasis was fully aware of the remarkable luck which Polycrates enjoyed, and it caused him some uneasiness; accordingly
when he heard of his ever-mounting tale of successes, he wrote
him the following letter, and sent it to Samos: 'Amasis to Polycrates: – It is a pleasure to hear of a friend and ally doing well,
but, as I know that the gods are jealous of success, I cannot
rejoice at your excessive prosperity. My own wish, both for
myself and for those I care for, would be to do well in some
things and badly in others, passing through life with alternate
success and failure; for I have never yet heard of a man who
after an unbroken run of luck was not finally brought to complete ruin. Now I suggest that you deal with the danger of your
continual successes in the following way: think of whatever it is
you value most – whatever you would most regret the loss of –
and throw it away: throw it right away, so that nobody can ever
see it again. If, after that, you do not find that success alternates
with failure, then go on using the remedy I have advised.'

41   Polycrates read the letter and approved of the advice which it
contained; so he began to look around amongst his treasures

for what he felt he would be most grieved to lose, and finally hit upon a ring. This was a signet-ring he used to wear, an emerald set in gold, the work of a Samian named Theodorus, the son of Telecles. Having decided that this was the thing to get rid of, he manned a penteconter, went aboard, and gave orders to put to sea. When the vessel was a long way off-shore, he took the ring from his finger, in full view of everyone on board, and threw it into the water. Then he rowed back to the island, returned to his house, and lamented his lost treasure.

Five or six days later it happened that a fisherman caught a 42 fine big fish and thought it would make a worthy present for Polycrates. He took it to the door and asked for an audience; this being granted, he offered the fish, and said: 'My King, I did not think it right to take this fish I caught to market, poor working man though I am; it is such a fine one that I thought it good enough for you and your greatness. So I have brought it here to give you.'

Polycrates, much pleased with what the fisherman said, replied: 'You have done very well, and I thank you twice over – once for your words, and again for your present. I invite you to take supper with me.'

The fisherman then went home, very proud of the honour done him. Meanwhile Polycrates' servants cut up the fish, and found the signet-ring in its belly. The moment they saw it, they picked it up, and taking it to Polycrates in triumph, told him how it had been found. Seeing in this the hand of divinity, Polycrates wrote a letter to Amasis in Egypt, and related to him everything he had done and what the result had been. Amasis 43 read the letter, and at once replied how impossible it is for one man to save another from his destiny, and how certain it was that Polycrates, whose luck held even to the point of finding again what he deliberately threw away, would not end well. He forthwith sent a messenger to Samos to say that the pact between Polycrates and himself was at an end. This he did in order that when the destined calamity fell upon Polycrates, he might avoid the distress he would have felt, had Polycrates still been his friend.[18]

This, then, was the man, still in the enjoyment of unbroken 44 success, with whom the Lacedaemonians were at war, having been called in by the Samians, who afterwards founded Cydonia in Crete. For Polycrates, at the time when Cambyses the son of Cyrus was raising the force for his Egyptian expedition, had secretly sent him a request to apply to Samos for a contingent of troops to join him, and Cambyses had gladly complied, sending to the island to ask Polycrates to contribute a naval force for the coming campaign against Egypt. Polycrates thereupon manned forty triremes with carefully selected crews, every man of which he had particular reason to suspect of disloyalty to himself, and sent them off, with instructions to Cambyses never

45 to allow them to return to Samos. According to one account, these people never arrived in Egypt, but having got as far as Carpathus, talked things over and decided not to continue their voyage; according to another, they did reach Egypt, where they were put under guard, and later escaped and sailed back to Samos. Off the island Polycrates met them with his own fleet, and a battle was fought in which they were victorious; after their success they landed on the island, but the fight which then ensued went against them, and they finally took to their ships again and sailed to Lacedaemon. There are some who maintain that these men who came back from Egypt actually defeated Polycrates; I think, however, that this is unlikely to be true, because if they were strong enough to have dealt with Polycrates unaided, there would have been no need for them to call on the Lacedaemonians for assistance; moreover, it is unreasonable to suppose that a man with so large a paid army and force of native bowmen could be defeated by the exiled Samians, who were but few in number. To prevent the Samians who were still subject to him from playing traitor and joining the returned exiles, Polycrates had their wives and children shut up in the boat-sheds, and was prepared to burn them, sheds and all, in case of need.

46   When those who had been forced to leave the island reached Sparta, they procured an audience with the magistrates and made a long speech to emphasize the urgency of their request. The Spartans, however, at this first sitting, answered the speech by saying that they had forgotten the beginning of it, and could

not understand the end; so the Samians had to try again. At the second sitting they brought a bag, and merely remarked that the bag needed flour – to which the Spartans replied that the world 'bag' was superfluous.[19] All the same, they decided to grant the request for assistance, and began their preparations for the expedition.

The Samians claim that the Spartans undertook the campaign in return for the service they had themselves rendered them in sending ships on a previous occasion to assist them against the Messenians;[20] the Spartans, however, deny that their motive was gratitude: it was not so much the wish to grant the request for help, as the determination to punish the Samians for the theft of the bowl which they had sent to Croesus,[21] and of the corslet, which the Egyptian king Amasis had sent them as a present. The Samians had carried off this corslet in a raid a year before they took the bowl; it was of linen, embroidered with gold thread and cotton, and had a number of figures of animals woven into the fabric. The most remarkable thing about it was that each fine thread of which the material was woven was made up of three hundred and sixty separate strands, all distinctly visible. Similar to it was the corslet which Amasis presented to the temple of Athene at Lindos.

The Corinthians, too, were very willing to lend help in the expedition against Samos, in revenge for an insult which they had suffered at the hands of the Samians a generation before, about the time of the seizure of the bowl. Periander, the son of Cypselus, had sent off to Alyattes at Sardis three hundred boys belonging to the leading families in Corcyra, to be made into eunuchs.[22] The Corinthians in charge touched at Samos on the way, and the people of the island, when they heard why the boys were being taken to Sardis, told them to take refuge in a temple of Artemis and refused to allow the Corinthians to drag them away from it. The Corinthians tried to starve them out, but the Samians were too clever for them: they improvised a festival (it is still celebrated in the original way) in which every night during the whole period that the boys remained as suppliants, they organized dances close to the temple, and the dancers – boys and young girls – carried cakes made of millet-seed and

47

48

honey, which they let the Corcyraean boys snatch as they passed, and so get enough to eat to keep them alive. This went on until the Corinthian guards got tired of it and left the island, leaving behind the boys, who were afterwards taken by the Samians back home to Corcyra.

49   If, after the death of Periander, relations between Corinth and Corcyra had been friendly, the Corinthians would never, on account of this incident, have taken part in the expedition against Samos; but the fact is that ever since the original settlement of the island the two peoples have been on bad terms; so the incident was remembered and the Corinthians bore the Samians a grudge for it. Periander had chosen the boys from amongst the leading families in Corcyra, and sent them to Sardis for eunuchs in revenge for a brutal crime by which the Corcyraeans had started the quarrel. Periander had murdered

50   his wife Melissa; and another misfortune was to follow. He had two sons by Melissa, one seventeen years old, the other eighteen, and these young men, after their mother's death, were sent for by Procles, who was their maternal grandfather and tyrant of Epidaurus. Procles treated them with all the kindness due to his daughter's children, and when the time came for them to say goodbye, he accompanied them a part of the way, and asked them if they knew who had killed their mother. The elder of the two took no notice of this question, but the younger, whose name was Lycophron, was profoundly disturbed – so much so, indeed, that when he was back in Corinth, convinced that his father was his mother's murderer, he refused to greet him, or answer his questions, or to have any talk with him whatever. This went on until Periander, in a rage, turned him out of the

51   house. Then he asked his other son, the elder, what it was that their grandfather had said to them. The young man described the kindly welcome they had received; but as to what Procles had said at the moment of bidding them goodbye, he had quite forgotten it – it had gone in at one ear and out of the other. Periander, however, was not satisfied; he continued to press his questions, saying it was quite impossible that this was all, and that Procles must have given them some hint or other, until at last the young man remembered what it was, and told him.

Periander thought this over, and, having no intention of relent-
ing his harshness, sent a message to the people with whom his
younger son was staying and forbade them to keep him in their
house. So once more Lycophron was turned out, and had to find
another refuge, when the same thing happened again, Periander
commanding his hosts, upon pain of his displeasure, to shut
their doors against him. In this way the boy was driven from
one friend's house to another's, and each family in turn, in spite
of their fear of the consequences, took him in on the strength
of his being Periander's son, until at last Periander made a   52
proclamation to the effect that anyone who gave the boy shelter,
or even spoke to him, should be fined a certain sum, the money
to be dedicated to the service of Apollo. This was enough to
make everyone refuse to talk to him or let him into the house,
and even Lycophron himself did not think that he ought to
attempt to break the prohibition, but made the best of a bad job
and found what shelter he could by lying on the ground under
the porticoes. Four days later Periander saw him; he was dirty
and hungry, and the father's heart melted at the sight. Going up
to him, he said: 'Which is better, my son – the wretched condition
you are now in, or the prospect of inheriting the wealth and
tyranny which I enjoy, merely on the condition of obeying me,
your father? You are my son and I am king of the rich city of
Corinth; but in spite of that you have chosen a beggar's life,
because you set yourself up in resistance and resentment against
the one person you least ought to treat in such a way. If anything
unfortunate has occurred to make you suspect me, remember
that I am a sufferer from it as well as you – indeed more than
you, because it was I who caused it. It is much more agreeable
to be the object of envy than of pity, and you now know the
consequence of being angry with one's parents and one's betters
– so go back home.' Lycophron's only answer to this attempt to
win him over was to tell his father that he owed the fine to
Apollo, for having spoken to him. Then, realizing that the boy's
trouble was desperate and incurable, Periander put him aboard
ship and sent him away out of his sight to Corcyra, which was
also a part of his dominions. Having got rid of Lycophron,
Periander made war against his father-in-law Procles, as the

chief cause of his present difficulties. He captured Epidaurus, and took Procles himself prisoner.

53   Time passed, and when Periander was an old man and no longer felt himself equal to the task of managing his affairs, he sent to Corcyra to invite Lycophron to return to Corinth and take over the tyranny, passing over his elder son, who seemed to him a dull-witted fellow without any sort of ability. Lycophron, however, did not deign even to answer the messenger: so Periander, who was now very anxious to be reconciled to him, sent his daughter, the boy's sister, to plead with him, in the belief that he would be more likely to listen to her than to anyone else. 'Brother,' she said, 'would you rather see our father's power pass into strange hands, and the family's fortune broken up than come back to Corinth and enjoy them yourself? Stop punishing yourself, and come home with me. Obstinacy never got a man anywhere. Do not try to cure one evil by another. Many think that mercy is a better thing than justice, and many a man, too, by pushing his mother's claims has thrown away his father's fortune. Tyranny is a slippery thing, and has never lacked lovers to woo it. Our father is an old man now and far past his prime. Take then what belongs to you, and keep it – do not abandon it to strangers.' Periander had told the girl to use these arguments, as most likely to influence her brother; but his only reply was that he would never return to Corinth while he knew that his father was still alive. Periander, when he heard of it, made a third and last effort: he sent a messenger to say that he was willing to come to Corcyra himself, if his son would return to Corinth and assume power in his place. To this Lycophron agreed, and each began his preparations for leaving – Periander for Corcyra, Lycophron for Corinth; but the Corcyraeans, when they got wind of what was happening, murdered the young man in order to keep Periander away. It was for this deed that Periander took his vengeance on them.

54   The Lacedaemonians arrived with a powerful force and laid siege to Samos. In an assault on the defences they fought their way forward to the tower near the sea, on the side of the town where the suburbs are, but Polycrates brought a strong party to meet the threat and drove them off. At the upper tower on the

ridge which joins on to the high ground, the mercenaries and many of the Samians sallied out, and for a short time held the attack; but they were soon forced to retreat, and the Lacedaemonians followed up their advantage and killed many of them. If all the Lacedaemonians that day had shown the spirit of Archias and Lycopes, Samos would have fallen; for these two men, unsupported by any of their companions, pressed forward upon the retreating Samians and entered the town with them, where they were cut off and killed. I myself once met at Pitana – his native village – the grandson of this Archias;[23] he bore the same name, and was the son of Samius and grandson of the original Archias, and professed a greater admiration for the Samians than for any other foreigners. He told me his father had been called Samius in memory of his grandfather's heroic death in Samos, and his respect for the Samians was due to the fact that they had honoured his grandfather with a public funeral.

After an unsuccessful siege of forty days the Lacedaemonians returned to the Peloponnese. A foolish story got about that Polycrates coined a large amount of the local money in lead, which he then gilded, and offered to buy them off with it; they took it – and that was the reason for their departure. This was the first military expedition to Asia undertaken by the Dorians of Lacedaemon.

The Samians who had fought against Polycrates, seeing that the Lacedaemonians were about to leave them in the lurch, also abandoned the campaign and sailed to Siphnos. They were in need of money, and the Siphnians at that time were at the height of their prosperity; they were richer than any other of the island peoples, having gold and silver mines so productive that a tenth part of their output was enough to furnish a treasury at Delphi not inferior in value to the most splendid to be found there. The remainder of the yield was shared out each year amongst the islanders themselves. When they began depositing money in their treasury at Delphi, they asked the oracle if it was possible that their present prosperity could last for any length of time, and the Priestess gave them the following answer:

When the council-chamber in Siphnos shines white,
And white too is the forehead of the market-place,
Then is there need of a man of foresight to beware.
Danger threatens from a wooden host and a scarlet messenger.

Now it was a fact that at that time the council-chamber and
market-place in Siphnos had recently been adorned with Parian
marble. The islanders could make nothing of the oracle, either
when it was given, or later when the Samians came; for as soon
as they arrived off the island, they sent one of their ships to the
city with a delegation on board. Here, then, was the explanation
of the oracle: all ships in the old days had their topsides painted
scarlet – so that was what the Priestess meant when she warned
the Siphnians to beware of a 'wooden host and a scarlet
messenger'.

On their arrival the Samian envoys asked the Siphnians to
lend them ten talents, and, the request being refused, set about
harrying the country. The Siphnians at once came out in force
to save their crops, but got the worst of it, and many of them
were cut off from the town. The Samians then exacted a hundred
talents. With this money the Samians bought from the Hermion-
ians the island of Hydrea, off the Peloponnese, and handed it
over in trust to the people of Troezen, while they themselves
went on to Crete where they founded the city of Cydonia. Their
object, when they sailed, was not to settle in Crete, but to drive
out the Zacynthians from their islands; settle, however, they
did, and enjoyed five years of great prosperity in the island. It
was they who built the temples, including the shrine of Dictyna,
which are still to be seen in Cydonia. But in the sixth year they
were attacked by the Aeginetans, who with the help of the
Cretans beat them in an engagement at sea and reduced them
to slavery. They sawed off the boars' heads which the Samian
ships carried on their prows, and laid them up in the temple of
Athene in Aegina. The attack was made to pay off an old score;
for some time previously, when Amphicrates was king of Samos,
the Samians had attacked Aegina and inflicted great damage on
the island – though not without suffering heavy loss themselves.

I have dwelt longer upon the history of the Samians than I

should otherwise have done, because they are responsible for three of the greatest building and engineering feats in the Greek world: the first is a tunnel nearly a mile long, eight feet wide and eight feet high, driven clean through the base of a hill nine hundred feet in height. The whole length of it carries a second cutting thirty feet deep and three broad, along which water from an abundant source is led through pipes into the town. This was the work of a Megarian named Eupalinus, son of Naustrophus. Secondly, there is the artificial harbour enclosed by a break-water, which runs out into twenty fathoms of water and has a total length of over a quarter of a mile; and, last, the island has the biggest of all Greek temples known. The first architect of it was Rhoecus, son of Phileus, a Samian. These three works seemed to me sufficiently important to justify a rather full account of the history of the island.[24]

Cambyses, son of Cyrus, after going out of his mind, still ling-   61
ered on in Egypt; and while he was there, two brothers, who belonged to the caste of the Magi, rose in rebellion against him at home.[25] One of them – Patizeithes – had been left by Cambyses as controller of his household during his absence, and this was the one who planned the revolt. Aware that Smerdis was dead, but that his death was concealed from all but a few of the Persians, most of whom believed that he was still alive, he took advantage of this state of affairs to make a bid for the throne. The brother, whom I have already mentioned as his confederate, bore a close resemblance to Cyrus' son Smerdis, the brother Cambyses had murdered. Besides the physical likeness, it also happened that he bore the same name. Patizeithes having per-suaded this brother of his that he would successfully carry the business through, made him take his seat upon the royal throne, and then sent out a proclamation to the troops, not only throughout Persia but also in Egypt, that they should take their orders in future not from Cambyses but from Smerdis.[26] The   62
proclamation was duly published; and the herald who was instructed to take it to Egypt happened to find Cambyses and his army at Ecbatana in Syria. Here he took his stand before the assembled troops and proclaimed the new order. When

Cambyses got to know of it, he at once supposed that what the herald said was true and that Prexaspes, whom he had sent to Persia to get rid of Smerdis, had failed to do so, and betrayed him. He looked at Prexaspes and said: 'So that is the way you carried out my orders!'

'Master,' Prexaspes replied, 'this is a lie. Your brother Smerdis has not rebelled against you, and you will never again have cause of quarrel with him, big or little. I did what you told me to do, and buried him with my own hands. If dead men rise from their graves, you may believe, if you will, that Astyages the Mede may return to fight against you; but if the course of nature continues unchanged, I can promise you that from Smerdis at least you will never have anything more to fear. My advice to you is, that we catch this herald and examine him, to find out who it was that sent him with this order to obey King Smerdis.'

63   Cambyses agreed, and a party was at once sent in pursuit of the herald. When he was brought in, Prexaspes said to him: 'You claim to have come with a message from Smerdis the son of Cyrus; now, my good fellow, if you want to get away safe, you had better tell us the truth – did Smerdis in person give you these orders, or was it one of his subordinates?'

'Since King Cambyses went with the army to Egypt,' the man replied, 'I have never set eyes upon Smerdis the son of Cyrus. It was the Magus, whom Cambyses made steward of his household, who gave me my instructions; but he said it was on the authority of Smerdis that I was to give the message which I have.' This statement was perfectly true. Cambyses then said: 'Prexaspes, you have carried out my orders like an honest man, and no blame attaches to you; but tell me – who can it be who has assumed Smerdis' name and risen in revolt against me?'

'I think, my lord,' he replied, 'that I understand what has happened: the rebels are the two Magi – Patizeithes, whom you left in control of your household, and his brother Smerdis.'

64   The moment Cambyses heard the name, he was struck with the truth of what Prexaspes had said, and realized that his dream of how somebody told him that Smerdis was sitting on the throne with his head touching the sky, had been fulfilled. It was

clear to him now that the murder of his brother had been all to
no purpose; he lamented his loss, and at last, in bitterness and
anger at the whole miserable set of circumstances, he leapt upon
his horse, meaning to march with all speed to Susa and attack
the Magus. But as he was springing into the saddle, the cap fell
off the sheath of his sword, exposing the blade, which pierced
his thigh – just in the spot where he had previously struck Apis
the sacred Egyptian bull. Believing the wound to be mortal,
Cambyses asked what the name of the town was, and was told
it was Ecbatana. There had been a prophecy from the oracle at
Buto that he would die at Ecbatana; and he had supposed that
to mean the Median Ecbatana, his capital city, where he would
die in old age. But, as it turned out, the oracle meant Ecbatana
in Syria. After the mention of the name, the double shock of his
wound and of Patizeithes' rebellion brought him back to his
senses. The meaning of the oracle became clear, and he said:
'Here it is fated that Cambyses, son of Cyrus, should die.' At   65
the moment he said nothing more; but some twenty days later
he sent for the leading Persians who were present with the army
and addressed them in the following words: 'Men of Persia,
circumstances compel me to reveal to you something which I
have done my utmost to conceal. When I was in Egypt I had a
dream – and would that I had never dreamt it! The dream was,
that a messenger from Persia came to tell me that Smerdis was
sitting on my throne and that his head touched the sky. Fearing
my brother would rob me of the crown, I acted with more haste
than judgement – for I now realize that it is not in human power
to avert what is destined to be. In my folly I sent Prexaspes to
Susa to kill Smerdis. The dreadful deed was done, and I lived
without fear, never imagining that when Smerdis was dead
another man would rise against me. Failing to grasp the true
nature of what was in store for me, I murdered my brother for
nothing, and have lost my kingdom just the same. It was Smerdis
the Magus, not my brother, of whose rebellion God warned me
in my dream. Well – I did the deed, and you may be sure you
will never see Smerdis the son of Cyrus again. You have the two
Magi to rule you now: Patizeithes, whom I left in control of my
household, and his brother Smerdis. The one man who of all

others should have helped me against the shameful plot of the two Magi, has come to a horrid end at the hands of those nearest and dearest to him. But since he is dead, I must do that next best thing and tell you with my last breath what I would wish you to do. In the name of the gods who watch over our royal house, the command I lay upon all of you, and especially upon those of the Achaemenidae who are here present, is this: do not allow the dominion to pass again into the hands of the Medes. If they have won it by treachery, with the same weapon take it from them; if by force, then play the man and by force recover it. If you do as I bid you, I pray that the earth may be fruitful for you, your wives bear you children, your flocks multiply and freedom be yours for ever: but if you fail to recover, or make no attempt to recover, the sovereign power, then my curse be upon you – may your fate be just the opposite, and, in addition to that, may every Persian perish as miserably as I.' Having said

66 this, Cambyses bitterly lamented the cruelty of his lot, and when the Persians saw the king in tears, they tore their clothes, and showed their sympathy by a great deal of crying and groaning. Shortly afterwards gangrene and mortification of the thigh set in, and Cambyses died, after a reign in all of seven years and five months. He had no children, either sons or daughters.

The Persians who were with Cambyses at his death found it difficult to believe that the Magi had seized power; it seemed to them much more likely that Cambyses' story about the death of Smerdis was a malicious invention designed to set the whole of

67 Persia against him. They were convinced that it was Smerdis the son of Cyrus who was on the throne – and all the more so because Prexaspes vehemently denied the murder, knowing, as he did, that it would be dangerous, now that Cambyses was gone, to admit that a son of Cyrus had died by his hand. The result was that the Magus, after assuming the name of Smerdis, son of Cyrus, found himself securely on the throne, and continued there for the seven months which were needed to make up the eighth year of Cambyses. During this time his subjects received great benefits from him, and he was regretted after his death by all the Asiatics under his rule, except by the Persians themselves, for to every nation within his dominion he pro-

claimed, directly he came to the throne, a three years' remission
of taxes and military service. But after seven months of power,   68
the following circumstances led to his exposure.

The first person to suspect that he was not the son of Cyrus,
but an impostor, was a certain Otanes, the son of Pharnaspes,
one of the wealthiest members of the Persian nobility, and his
suspicions were aroused by the fact that Smerdis never ventured
outside the central fortifications of the capital, and never summoned any eminent Persians to a private audience.

Now when the Magus usurped the throne, he took over all
Cambyses' wives, amongst whom there was a daughter of
Otanes called Phaidime. Otanes, to test the truth of his suspicions, sent a message to this daughter, and asked her who it
was she slept with – Smerdis the son of Cyrus, or some other
man. She replied that she did not know; she had never seen
Smerdis the son of Cyrus, and had no idea who her husband
was. Otanes sent a second message: 'If,' it ran, 'you do not
yourself know Smerdis the son of Cyrus, ask Atossa who it is
with whom you both live. She can hardly fail to know her own
brother.' Phaidime replied: 'I have no means of speaking to
Atossa, nor of seeing any other of the king's wives; for as soon
as this man, whoever he may be, came to the throne, he separated
us and gave us all different quarters.' This was a further indi-   69
cation of the truth of what Otanes suspected, so he sent a third
message to his daughter. 'Phaidime,' he wrote, 'you have noble
blood in your veins, and must not shrink from any danger your
father orders you to face. If your husband is the man I think he
is, and not the son of Cyrus, he must not get away with sharing
your bed and sitting on the throne of Persia. He must be punished. This, then, is what you must do: next time he spends the
night with you, wait till you are sure he is asleep and then feel
for his ears. If you find that he has got ears, consider yourself
the wife of Smerdis, son of Cyrus; but if he has none, then you
will know you are married to Smerdis the Magus.' Phaidime
answered that it would be an extremely risky thing to do; for if
her husband proved to have no ears, and she were caught feeling
for them, he would be certain to kill her. Nevertheless she was
willing to take the risk. Now when Cyrus was on the throne he

had punished Smerdis the Magus for some serious crime by having his ears cut off.[27]

Phaidime, then, kept the promise she had made to her father Otanes; when her turn came to sleep with the Magus (in Persia a man's wives share his bed in rotation), she entered the bedroom, lay down, and then, as soon as the Magus was soundly asleep, felt for his ears. She quickly satisfied herself that he had not got any; so next morning she lost no time in letting her father know the result of the experiment. Otanes took into his confidence Aspathines and Gobryas, two eminent Persians whom he had special reason to trust, and told them of his discovery. Both these men already had their suspicions of the truth, and were ready enough, in consequence, to accept what Otanes said, and it was then agreed that each of the three should choose his most trustworthy friend and bring him in as an accomplice. Otanes chose Intaphrenes, Gobryas Megabyzus, and Aspathines Hydarnes. The number of conspirators was thus raised to six, and on the arrival at Susa from Persia of Darius, whose father Hystaspes was governor there, it was decided to add him to the number.[28]

The seven conspirators now met to pledge loyalty to one another and discuss the measures they were to take. When it was Darius' turn to express his views, he said that he had supposed himself to be the only person who knew that Smerdis the son of Cyrus was dead, and that the present king was the Magus. 'And for that very reason,' he went on, 'I hurried to Susa in order to arrange to get rid of him. Now, as it turns out that I am not the only one in the secret, my opinion is that we should act promptly. There would be nothing but danger in delay.'

Otanes answered: 'You are the son of Hystaspes, Darius, and seem likely to prove as good a man as he; nevertheless I advise you not to be rash or in too much of a hurry. What we need is prudence – and we must add to our number before we strike the blow.'

'Listen, all of you,' Darius replied; 'if you take Otanes' advice, the result will be ruin for everyone. Somebody is sure to seek advantage for himself by betraying us to the Magus. You ought really to have done this thing entirely on your own; but as you have seen fit to let others in on it, and have communicated your intentions to me, I have only one thing to say – let us act immediately. If we let a single day slip by, I promise you one thing: nobody will have time to betray *me* – for I will myself denounce you all to the Magus.'

Otanes was alarmed by the passionate urgency of Darius. 'I see,' he said, 'that you are determined to compel us to rush, and will not allow us a moment's delay for deliberation. But can you tell us how to get into the palace to make our attack? Doubtless you know as well as we do that there are guards everywhere; even if you haven't seen them, you have surely heard of them. How are we to get past?' 72

'Otanes,' Darius answered, 'there are many occasions when words are useless, and only deeds will make a man's meaning plain; often enough, too, it is easy to talk – and only to talk, for no brave act follows. You know there will be no difficulty in passing the guards. Who will dare to refuse admission to men of our rank and distinction, if not from respect, then from fear of the consequences? Besides, I have a perfect excuse for getting us in: I will say I have just come from Persia and have a message from my father for the king. If a lie is necessary, why not speak it? We are all after the same thing, whether we lie or speak the truth: our own advantage. Men lie when they think to profit by deception, and tell the truth for the same reason – to get something they want, and to be the better trusted for their honesty. It is only two different roads to the same goal. Were there no question of advantage, the honest man would be as likely to lie as the liar is, and the liar would tell the truth as readily as the honest man. Any sentry who lets us through without question, will be rewarded later; anyone who tries to stop us must be treated instantly as an enemy. We must force our way past him and set to work at once.'

'Friends,' said Gobryas, 'will there ever be a better moment than now to save the throne – or, if we fail, to die in the attempt? Are Persians to be ruled by a Mede – a Magus – a fellow who has had his ears chopped off? Those of you who stood by the deathbed of Cambyses are not likely to forget his dying curse 73 upon the Persians who should make no effort to save the throne. We took it lightly then – thinking Cambyses was speaking slander. But now the situation has changed, and I propose that we follow Darius' advice, and break up the meeting for no other purpose than to march straight to the palace and attack the Magus.' All the conspirators agreed to this proposal.

74 While this discussion was in progress, events had been taking place elsewhere. The two Magi had been thinking things over and had decided to take Prexaspes into their confidence. There were several reasons for this decision: first, Prexaspes had been cruelly treated by Cambyses, who shot his son dead; then, as he had been directly responsible for the murder of Smerdis the son of Cyrus, he was the only person in the secret of his death; and, lastly, he was highly respected in Persian society. They summoned him therefore to their presence and began to bargain for his support; they tried to get from him a promise upon oath never to say a word to anybody about the hoax they had practised upon the Persians, and offered to pay him enormous sums as the price of his silence. Prexaspes agreed, whereupon the Magi made the further proposal that they should themselves call upon all the Persians to meet at the base of the palace wall, and that Prexaspes should proclaim, from the top of a tower, that the king was none other than Smerdis the son of Cyrus. In giving Prexaspes these instructions, the Magi relied on the fact that the Persians would be more likely to believe him than anyone else, seeing that he had frequently denied the murder and expressed the opinion that Smerdis was still alive. Again

75 Prexaspes agreed; so the Magi summoned the people to assemble, and told Prexaspes to climb to the top of the tower and make his declaration. But then Prexaspes, deliberately ignoring everything which the Magi had asked him to say, made a speech in which he traced the genealogy of Cyrus right back from Achaemenes, went on to describe the great services which Cyrus had rendered to his country, and finally revealed the true state of affairs, adding that he had concealed it hitherto out of regard to his own safety, but that the time had now come when it was no longer possible to hold his tongue. He kept back nothing; he himself, he said, had been forced by Cambyses to kill Smerdis

the son of Cyrus, and the country was now in the power of the two Magi. Finally, with a prayer that the Persians might suffer untold misery if they did not recover the throne and punish the usurpers, he threw himself headlong from the tower to the ground. Such was the end of Prexaspes, who throughout his life had been a man of high distinction.

Meanwhile the seven conspirators, having reached their 76 decision to attack the Magi without a moment's delay, had prayed for luck and were on their way to the palace. They knew nothing about the affair of Prexaspes, and were half-way there before they learnt the truth. The news pulled them up, for they thought it advisable to discuss this new element in the situation. The supporters of Otanes urged delay and the risk of making their attempt until things calmed down again; but Darius and his party were still for immediate action and opposed to any change of plan. The argument was growing hot, when they suddenly saw seven pairs of hawks chasing two pairs of vultures, which they tore at, as they flew, with both beak and claw. It was an omen; forthwith the plan of Darius was unanimously accepted, and with renewed confidence the seven men hurried on towards the palace. When they reached the gates, everything 77 turned out just as Darius had foreseen: the sentries, out of respect for their exalted rank and having no suspicion of the real purpose of their visit, allowed them to pass without question – almost as if they were under the special protection of heaven. In the great court, however, they were met by some of the eunuchs – the king's messengers – who stopped them and asked their business, at the same time threatening the guards for having let them through. The check was momentary; eager to press on, the seven, with a word of mutual encouragement, drew their daggers, stabbed the eunuchs who were trying to hold them up, and ran forward into the hall.

Both the Magi were at this time indoors, discussing the situ- 78 ation which had been brought about by Prexaspes' treachery. They heard the eunuchs crying out in evident alarm, and sprang up to see what the matter was; then, realizing their danger, they at once prepared to fight it out. One just had time to get his bow down, the other seized his spear. The one with the bow had no chance to use it – the fight was at much too close quarters; the other, however, used his spear to advantage, keeping off his attackers and wounding Aspathines in the leg, and Intaphrenes in the eye – Intaphrenes, as a result of the wound, lost his eye but survived. His companion, unable to use his bow and finding himself defenceless, ran into a bedroom, which opened out of the hall, and tried to shut the doors on his pursuers; but two of them, Darius and Gobryas, managed to force their way in with him, and Gobryas got his arms round the Magus. It was dark in the room, and Darius, standing over the two men locked together on the floor, hesitated to intervene; for he was afraid that, if he struck, he might kill the wrong man. But Gobryas, aware of his hesitation, cried out: 'What's your hand for – if you don't use it?'

'I dare not strike,' said Darius, 'for fear of killing you.'

'Fear nothing,' answered Gobryas; 'spit both of us at once – if need be.'

Darius then drove his dagger home – by luck into the body of the Magus.

79   When both the Magi had been killed, the confederates decapitated them, and ran out into the street, shouting and making a great noise, with the severed heads in their hands. The two wounded men had been left behind in the palace, being too weak to move – they were needed, moreover, to keep a watch upon the citadel. Once outside, the five who were unhurt appealed to their fellow citizens, told them what had happened, and showed them the heads – and then set about murdering every Magus they came across. The other Persians, once they had learnt of the exploit of the seven confederates, and understood the hoax which the two brothers had practised on them, were soon ready to follow their example: they, too, drew their daggers and killed every Magus they could find – so that if darkness had not put an end to the slaughter, the whole tribe would have been exterminated. The anniversary of this day has become a red-letter day in the Persian calendar, marked by an important festival known as the Magophonia, or Killing of the Magi, during which no Magus is allowed to show himself – every member of the tribe stays indoors till the day is over.

Five days later, when the excitement had died down, the 80
conspirators met to discuss the situation in detail. At the meeting
certain speeches were made – some of the Greeks refuse to
believe they were actually made at all; nevertheless they were.[29]
The first speaker was Otanes, and his theme was to recommend
the establishment in Persia of popular government. 'I think,' he
said, 'that the time has passed for any one man amongst us to
have absolute power. Monarchy is neither pleasant nor good.
You know to what lengths the pride of power carried Cambyses,
and you have personal experience of the effect of the same thing
in the conduct of the Magus. How can one fit monarchy into
any sound system of ethics, when it allows a man to do whatever
he likes without any responsibility or control? Even the best of
men raised to such a position would be bound to change for the
worse – he could not possibly see things as he used to do. The
typical vices of a monarch are envy and pride; envy, because it
is a natural human weakness, and pride, because excessive
wealth and power lead to the delusion that he is something more
than a man. These two vices are the root cause of all wickedness:
both lead to acts of savage and unnatural violence. Absolute
power ought, by rights, to preclude envy on the principle that
the man who possesses it has also at command everything he
could wish for; but in fact it is not so, as the behaviour of kings
to their subjects proves: they are jealous of the best of them
merely for continuing to live, and take pleasure in the worst;
and no one is readier than a king to listen to tale-bearers. A
king, again, is the most inconsistent of men; show him reasonable respect, and he is angry because you do not abase yourself
before his majesty; abase yourself, and he hates you for being a
toady. But the worst of all remains to be said – he breaks up the
structure of ancient tradition and law, forces women to serve
his pleasure, and puts men to death without trial. Contrast with
this the rule of the people: first, it has the finest of all names to
describe it – equality under law; and, secondly, the people
in power do none of the things that monarchs do. Under a
government of the people a magistrate is appointed by lot and
is held responsible for his conduct in office, and all questions
are put up for open debate. For these reasons I propose that we

do away with the monarchy, and raise the people to power; for the state and the people are synonymous terms.'

81   Otanes was followed by Megabyzus, who recommended the principle of oligarchy in the following words: 'Insofar as Otanes spoke in favour of abolishing monarchy, I agree with him; but he is wrong in asking us to transfer political power to the people. The masses are a feckless lot – nowhere will you find more ignorance or irresponsibility or violence. It would be an intolerable thing to escape the murderous caprice of a king, only to be caught by the equally wanton brutality of the rabble. A king does at least act consciously and deliberately; but the mob does not. Indeed how should it, when it has never been taught what is right and proper, and has no knowledge of its own about such things? The masses handle affairs without thought; all they can do is to rush blindly into politics like a river in flood. As for the people, then, let them govern Persia's enemies; but let us ourselves choose a certain number of the best men in the country, and give *them* political power. We personally shall be amongst them, and it is only natural to suppose that the best men will produce the best policy.'

82   Darius was the third to speak. 'I support,' he said, 'all Megabyzus' remarks about the masses but I do not agree with what he said of oligarchy. Take the three forms of government we are considering – democracy, oligarchy, and monarchy – and suppose each of them to be the best of its kind; I maintain that the third is greatly preferable to the other two. One ruler: it is impossible to improve upon that – provided he is the best. His judgement will be in keeping with his character; his control of the people will be beyond reproach; his measures against enemies and traitors will be kept secret more easily than under other forms of government. In an oligarchy, the fact that a number of men are competing for distinction in the public service cannot but lead to violent personal feuds; each of them wants to get to the top, and to see his own proposals carried; so they quarrel. Personal quarrels lead to civil wars, and then to bloodshed; and from that state of affairs the only way out is a return to monarchy – a clear proof that monarchy is best. Again, in a democracy, malpractices are bound to occur; in this case,

however, corrupt dealings in government services lead not to private feuds, but to close personal associations, the men responsible for them putting their heads together and mutually supporting one another. And so it goes on, until somebody or other comes forward as the people's champion and breaks up the cliques which are out for their own interests. This wins him the admiration of the mob, and as a result he soon finds himself entrusted with absolute power – all of which is another proof that the best form of government is monarchy. To sum up: where did we get our freedom from, and who gave it us? Is it the result of democracy, or of oligarchy, or of monarchy? We were set free by one man, and therefore I propose that we should preserve that form of government, and, further, that we should refrain from changing ancient ways, which have served us well in the past. To do so would not profit us.'

These were the three views set out in the three speeches, and the four men who had not spoken voted for the last. Otanes (who had urged equality before the law), finding the decision against him, then made another speech. 'My friends,' he said, 'it is clear that the king will have to be one of ourselves, whether we draw lots for it, or ask the people of Persia to make their choice between us, or use some other method. I will not compete with you for the crown, for I have no wish to rule – or to *be* ruled either. I withdraw, therefore, upon one condition: that neither I myself, nor any of my descendants, shall be forced to submit to the rule of that one of you, whoever he is, who becomes king.' The other six agreed to this condition, and Otanes stood down. To this day the family of Otanes continues to be the only free family in Persia, and submits to the king only so far as the members of it may choose, while not disobeying the laws of the Persians.

The other six then discussed the fairest way of deciding who should have the throne. They agreed that, if it fell to any of themselves, Otanes and his descendants should receive, every year, a suit of Median clothes and such other gifts as are held to be of most value by the Persians, as a mark of honour for the part he had played in the plot against the Magi, of which he was the prime mover and principal organizer. These privileges were

83

84

for Otanes only; they also agreed upon another to be shared by all: permission, namely, for any of the seven to enter the royal presence unannounced, except when the king was in bed with a woman. They further agreed that the king should not marry outside the families of the seven confederates. To choose which should be king, they proposed to mount their horses on the outskirts of the city, and he whose horse neighed first after the sun was up should have the throne.

85   Darius had a clever groom called Oebares. After the meeting had broken up, he went to see this fellow, and told him of the arrangement they had come to, whereby they should sit on their horses' backs and the throne should be given to the one whose horse neighed first as the sun rose. 'So if,' he added, 'you can think of some contrivance or other, do what you can to see that this prize falls to me, and to no one else.'

'Well, master,' Oebares answered, 'if your chance of winning the throne depends upon nothing but that, you may set your mind at rest; you may be perfectly confident – you, and nobody else, will be king. I know a charm which will just suit our purpose.'

'If,' said Darius, 'you really have got something which will do the trick, you had better hurry and get it all worked out, for tomorrow is the day.'

Oebares, accordingly, as soon as it was dark, took from the stables the mare which Darius' horse was particularly fond of, and tied her up on the outskirts of the city. Then he brought along the stallion and led him round and round the mare, getting closer and closer in narrowing circles, and finally allowed him

86   to mount her. Next morning just before dawn the six men, according to their agreement, came riding on their horses through the city suburb, and when they reached the spot where the mare had been tethered on the previous night, Darius' horse started forward and neighed. At the same instant, though the sky was clear, there was a flash of lightning and a clap of thunder, as if it were a sign from heaven; the election of Darius was assured, and the other five leapt from their saddles and bowed to the ground at his feet.

87   That is one account of how Oebares made the horse neigh.

The Persians also have another, namely that he rubbed the
mare's genitals and then kept his hand covered inside his
breeches. When the sun was rising and the horses were about to
be released, he drew his hand out and put it to the nostrils of
Darius' horse, which at the smell of the mare at once snorted
and neighed.

In this way Darius son of Hystaspes became king of Persia. 88
Following the conquests of Cyrus and Cambyses, his dominion
extended over the whole of Asia, with the exception of Arabia.
The Arabs had never been reduced to subjection by the Persians,
but friendly relations had continued between the two countries
ever since the Arabs let Cambyses pass through their territory
on his Egyptian campaign; for without this service the invasion
of Egypt would have been impracticable.

The first women Darius married were Cyrus' two daughters
Atossa and Artystone; the former had previously been the wife
of her brother Cambyses and also of the Magus; the latter was
a virgin. Subsequently he married Parmys, a daughter of Cyrus'
son Smerdis, and, in addition to these, the daughter of Otanes,
the man who had exposed the Magus.

Now that his power was felt in every corner of his dominions,
his first act was to erect a stone monument with a carving of a
man on horseback, and the following inscription: *Darius, son
of Hystaspes, by the virtue of his horse and of his groom
Oebares, won the throne of Persia.* The horse's name was
included.[30] This was in Persia; he then proceeded to set up 89
twenty provincial governorships, called satrapies. The several
governors were appointed and each nation assessed for taxes;
for administrative purposes neighbouring nations were joined
in a single unit; outlying peoples were considered to belong to
this nation or that, according to convenience.

Before I record the amount of the annual tribute paid by
the various provinces, I should mention that those who paid in
silver were instructed to use the Babylonian talent as the
measure of weight, while the Euboean talent was the standard for gold – the Babylonian being worth $1\frac{1}{6}$ of the Euboean.
During the reigns of Cyrus and Cambyses there was no fixed
tribute at all, the revenue coming from gifts only; and because

of his imposition of regular taxes, and other similar measures, the Persians have a saying that Darius was a tradesman, Cambyses a tyrant, and Cyrus a father – the first being out for profit wherever he could get it, the second harsh and careless of his subjects' interests, and the third, Cyrus, in the kindness of his heart always occupied with plans for their well-being.

90   Now for the account of the tribute paid by the twenty provinces:[31]

First: the Ionians, the Magnesians in Asia, the Aeolians, Carians, Lycians, Milyans, and Pamphylians contributed together a total sum of 400 talents of silver.

Second: the Mysians, Lydians, Lasonians, Cabalians, and Hytennians, 500 talents.

Third: the people on the southern shore of the Hellespont, the Phrygians, the Thracians of Asia, the Paphlagonians, Mari-andynians, and Syrians, 360 talents.

Fourth: the Cilicians paid 500 talents of silver, together with 360 white horses (one for each day in the year); of the money, 140 talents were used to maintain the cavalry force which guarded Cilicia, and the remaining 360 went to Darius.

91   *Fifth*: from the town of Posideiium, which was founded by Amphilochus, son of Amphiaraus, on the border between Cilicia and Syria, as far as Egypt – omitting Arabian territory, which was free of tax – came 350 talents. This province contains the whole of Phoenicia and that part of Syria which is called Palestine, and Cyprus.

Sixth: Egypt, together with the Libyans on the border and the towns of Cyrene and Barca (both included in the province of Egypt) paid 700 talents, in addition to the money from the fish in Lake Moeris, and the 120,000 bushels of corn allowed to the Persian troops and their auxiliaries who were stationed in the White Castle at Memphis.

Seventh: the Sattagydians, Gandarians, Dadicae, and Aparytae paid a joint tax of 170 talents.

Eighth: Susa, with the rest of Cissia – 300 talents.

92   *Ninth*: Babylon and the rest of Assyria – 1000 talents of silver and 500 eunuch boys.

Tenth: Ecbatana and the rest of Media, with the Paricanians and Orthocorybantes – 450 talents.

Eleventh: Caspians, Pausicae, Pantimathi, and Daritae – a joint sum of 200 talents.

Twelfth: the Bactrians and their neighbours as far as the Aegli – 360 talents.

Thirteenth: Pactyica, together with the Armenians and their neighbours as far as the Black Sea – 400 talents. 93

Fourteenth: the Sagartians, Sarangians, Thamanaeans, Utians, Myci, together with the inhabitants of the islands in the Persian gulf where the king sends those displaced from their homes in war – 600 talents.

Fifteenth: the Sacae and Caspians – 250 talents.

Sixteenth: the Parthians, Chorasmians, Sogdians, and Arians – 390 talents.

Seventeenth: the Paricanians and Asiatic Ethiopians – 400 talents. 94

Eighteenth: the Matienians, Saspires, and Alarodians – 200 talents.

Nineteenth: the Moschi, Tibareni, Macrones, Mosynoeci, and Mares – 300 talents.

Twentieth: the Indians, the most populous nation in the known world, paid the largest sum: 360 talents of gold-dust.

If the Babylonian talents here referred to are reduced to the Euboean scale, they will make a total of 9880; and if gold is reckoned at thirteen times the value of silver, the Indian gold-dust will be found to amount to 4680 talents. Thus the grand total of Darius' annual revenue comes to 14,560 Euboean talents – omitting the odd ones. 95

This was the revenue derived from Asia and a few parts of Libya; but as time went on, other tribute came in from the islands and from the peoples in Europe as far as Thessaly. The method adopted by the Persian kings of storing their treasure is to melt the metal and pour it into earthenware jars; the jar is then chipped off, leaving the solid metal. When the money is wanted, the necessary amount is coined for the occasion. 96

That completes the list of provinces, with the amounts they 97 had to contribute in taxation. The one country I have not mentioned as paying taxes is Persia herself – for she does not pay any. A few peoples upon whom no regular tax was imposed made a contribution in the form of gifts; the Ethiopians, for instance, on the Egyptian border; these people were subdued by Cambyses during his campaign against the 'long-lived' Ethiopians and occupy the country round about the sacred mountain of Nysa, and hold festivals in honour of Dionysus.[32] The grain which they and their next neighbours use is the same as that used by the Calantian Indians – and they live underground. Every second year these two nations brought – and still bring today – about two quarts of unrefined gold, two hundred logs of ebony, and twenty elephant tusks. Again, a voluntary contribution was undertaken by the Colchians and the neighbouring tribes between them and the Caucasus – the limit of the empire in this direction, everything to the northward being outside the range of Persian influence. In their case the contribution consisted (and still does) in the gift, every fourth year, of a hundred boys and a hundred girls. Lastly, the Arabians brought a thousand talents of frankincense every year. This, then, was the revenue which the king received over and above what was produced by regular taxation.

98   I will say something of the method by which the Indians get their large supplies of gold, which enable them to bring to Persia the gold-dust I have already mentioned. Eastward of India lies a desert of sand; indeed of all the inhabitants of Asia of whom we have any reliable information, the Indians are the most easterly – beyond them the country is uninhabitable desert. There are many tribes of Indians, speaking different languages, some pastoral and nomadic, others not. Some live in the marsh-country by the river and eat raw fish, which they catch from boats made of reeds – each boat made from a single joint. The people of this tribe make their clothes from a sort of rush which grows in the river, gathering it and beating it out, and then weaving it into a kind of matting which they wear to cover their

99   chests, like a breastplate. Another tribe further to the east is nomadic, known as the Padaei; they live on raw meat. Among their customs, it is said that when a man falls sick, his closest

companions kill him, because, as they put it, their meat would be spoilt if he were allowed to waste away with disease. The invalid, in these circumstances, protests that there is nothing the matter with him – but to no purpose. His friends refuse to accept his protestations, kill him and hold a banquet. Should the sufferer be a woman, her woman friends deal with her in the same way. If anyone is lucky enough to live to an advanced age, he is offered in sacrifice before the banquet – this, however, rarely happens, because most of them will have had some disease or other before they get old, and will consequently have been killed by their friends.

There is another tribe which behaves very differently: they will not take life in any form; they sow no seed, and have no houses and live on a vegetable diet. There is a plant which grows wild in their country, and has seeds in a pod about the size of millet seeds; they gather this, and boil and eat it, pod and all. In this tribe, a sick man will leave his friends and go away to some deserted spot to die – and nobody gives a thought either to his illness or death. 100

All the Indian tribes I have mentioned copulate in the open like cattle; their skins are all of the same colour, much like the Ethiopians'. Their semen is not white like other peoples', but black like their own skins; the same is to be found in the Ethiopians.[33] Their country is a long way from Persia towards the south, and they were never subject to Darius. 101

There are other Indians further north, round the city of Caspatyrus and in the country of Pactyica, who in their mode of life resemble the Bactrians. These are the most warlike of the Indian tribes, and it is they who go out to fetch the gold – for in this region there is a sandy desert. There is found in this desert a kind of ant of great size – bigger than a fox, though not so big as a dog. Some specimens, which were caught there, are kept at the palace of the Persian king. These creatures as they burrow underground throw up the sand in heaps, just as ants in Greece throw up the earth, and they are very similar in shape. The sand has a rich content of gold, and this it is that the Indians are after when they make their expeditions into the desert. Each man harnesses three camels abreast, a female, on which he rides, in 102 the middle, and a male on each side in a leading-rein, and takes care that the female is one who has as recently as possible dropped her young. Their camels are as fast as horses, and much more powerful carriers. There is no need for me to describe the camel, for the Greeks are familiar with what it looks like; one thing, however, I will mention, which will be news to them: the camel in its hind legs has four thighs and four knees, and its genitals point backwards towards its tail.[34] That, then, is how these Indians equip themselves for the expedition, and they plan their time-table so as actually to get their hands on the gold during the hottest part of the day, when the heat will have driven the ants underground. In this part of the world the sun is not, as it is elsewhere, hottest at noon, but in the morning: from dawn, that is, until closing-time in the market. During this part of the day the heat is much fiercer than it is at noon in Greece, and the natives are said to soak themselves in water to make it endurable. At midday the heat diminishes and is much the same here as elsewhere, and, as the afternoon goes on, it becomes about equal to what one finds in other countries in the early morning. Towards evening it grows cooler and cooler, until at sunset it is really cold.

When the Indians reach the place where the gold is, they fill the bags they have brought with them with sand, and start for home again as fast as they can go; for the ants (as is said in the Persians' story) smell them and at once give chase; nothing in the world can touch these ants for speed, so not one of the Indians would get home alive, if they did not make sure of a good start while the ants were mustering their forces. The male camels, who are slower movers than the females, soon begin to drag and are left behind, one after the other, while the females are kept going hard by the memory of their young, who were left at home.

According to the Persians, most of the gold is got in the way I have described; they also mine a certain quantity – but not so much – within their own territory.[35]

It would seem that the remotest parts of the world have the finest products, whereas Greece has far the best and most temperate climate. The most easterly country in the inhabited world is, as I said just now, India; and here both animals and birds are much bigger than elsewhere – if we except the Indian horse, which is inferior in size to the Median breed known as the Nisaean. Gold, too, is found here in immense quantity, either mined, or washed down by rivers, or stolen from the ants in the manner I have described; and there are trees growing wild which produce a kind of wool better than sheep's wool in beauty and quality, which the Indians use for making their clothes.[36]

Again, the most southerly country is Arabia; and Arabia is the 107 only place that produces frankincense, myrrh, cassia, cinnamon, and the gum called ledanon. All these, except the myrrh, cause the Arabians a lot of trouble to collect. When they gather frankincense, they burn storax (the gum which is brought into Greece by the Phoenicians) in order to raise a smoke to drive off the flying snakes; these snakes, the same which attempt to invade Egypt,[37] are small in size and of various colours, and great numbers of them keep guard over all the trees which bear the frankincense, and the only way to get rid of them is by smoking them out with storax. The Arabians say that the whole 108 world would swarm with these creatures were it not for a certain peculiar fact – the same thing, incidentally, as keeps down the spread of adders. And indeed it is hard to avoid the belief that divine providence, in the wisdom that one would expect of it, has made prolific every kind of creature which is timid and preyed upon by others, in order to ensure its continuance, while savage and noxious species are comparatively unproductive. Hares, for instance, which are the prey of all sorts of animals, not to mention birds and men, are excessively prolific; they are the only animals in which superfetation occurs, and you will find in a hare's womb young in all stages of development, some with fur on, others with none, others just beginning to form, and others, again, barely conceived. A lioness, on the contrary, the most bold and powerful of beasts, produces but a single cub, once in her life – for she expels from her body not only the cub, but her womb as well – or what is left of it. The reason for this is that when the unborn cub begins to stir, he scratches at the walls of the womb with his claws, which are sharper than any other animal's, and as he grows bigger scrabbles his way further

and further through them until, by the time he is about to be
109 born, the womb is almost wholly destroyed. In the same way,
if adders and the Arabian flying snakes were able to replace
themselves naturally, it would be impossible for men to live.
Fortunately, however, they are not; for when they couple, the
female seizes the male by the neck at the very moment of the
release of the sperm, and hangs on until she has bitten it through.
That finishes the male; and the female, too, has to pay for her
behaviour, for the young in her belly avenge their father by
gnawing at her insides, until they end by eating their way out.[38]
Other species of snakes, which are harmless to men, lay eggs
and hatch out their young in large numbers. The reason why
flying snakes seem so numerous in Arabia is that they are all
concentrated in that country – you will not find them anywhere
else, whereas adders are common all over the world.

110   When the Arabians go out to collect cassia, they cover their
bodies and faces, all but their eyes, with ox-hides and other
skins. The plant grows in a shallow lake which, together with
the ground round about it, is infested by winged creatures very
like bats, which screech alarmingly and are very pugnacious.
111 They have to be kept from attacking the men's eyes while they
are cutting the cassia. The process of collecting cinnamon is
still more remarkable. Where it comes from and what country
produces it, they do not know; the best some of them can do is
to make a fair guess that it grows somewhere in the region where
Dionysus was brought up. What they say is that the dry sticks,
which we have learnt from the Phoenicians to call cinnamon,
are brought by large birds, which carry them to their nests,
made of mud, on mountain precipices, which no man can climb,
and that the method the Arabians have invented for getting hold
of them is to cut up the bodies of dead oxen, or donkeys, or
other animals into very large joints, which they carry to the spot
in question and leave on the ground near the nests. They then
retire to a safe distance and the birds fly down and carry off the
joints of meat to their nests, which, not being strong enough to
bear the weight, break and fall to the ground. Then the men
come along and pick up the cinnamon, which is subsequently
112 exported to other countries. Still more surprising is the way of

getting ledanon – or ladanon, as the Arabians call it. Sweet-smelling substance though it is, it is found in a most malodorous place; sticking, namely, like glue in the beards of he-goats who have been browsing amongst the bushes. It is used as an ingredient in many kinds of perfume, and is what the Arabians chiefly burn as incense.

So much for the perfumes: let me only add that the whole country exhales a more than earthly fragrance. One other thing is remarkable enough to deserve a mention – the sheep. There are two kinds, such as are found nowhere else: one kind has such long tails – not less than $4\frac{1}{2}$ feet – that if they were allowed to trail on the ground, they would develop sores from the constant friction; so to obviate this, the shepherds have devised the art of making little carts of wood, and fix one of them under the tail of each sheep.[39] The other kind have flat tails, eighteen inches broad.

The furthest inhabited country towards the south-west is Ethiopia; here gold is found in great abundance, and huge elephants, and ebony, and all sorts of trees growing wild; the men, too, are the tallest in the world, the best-looking, and longest-lived.

So much for the countries at the furthest limits of Asia and Libya. About the far west of Europe I have no definite information, for I cannot accept the story of a river called by non-Greek peoples the Eridanus, which flows into the northern sea, where amber is supposed to come from; nor do I know anything of the existence of islands called the Tin Islands, whence we get our tin. In the first place, the name Eridanus is obviously not foreign but Greek, and was invented by some poet or other; and, secondly, in spite of my efforts to do so, I have never found anyone who could give me first-hand information of the existence of a sea beyond Europe to the north and west.[40] Yet it cannot be disputed that tin and amber do come to us from what one might call the ends of the earth. It is clear that it is the northern parts of Europe which are richest in gold, but how it is procured I cannot say exactly. The story goes that the one-eyed Arimaspians steal it from the griffins who guard it; personally, however, I refuse to believe in one-eyed men who in other

113

114

115

116

respects are like the rest of men. In any case it does seem to be true that the countries which lie on the circumference of the inhabited world produce the things which we believe to be most rare and beautiful.[41]

117   There is a plain in Asia surrounded by a ring of hills, which are broken by clefts in five separate places. This tract of land used to belong to the Chorasmians and lies on the boundaries of five different tribes: the Chorasmians themselves, the Hyrcanians, the Parthians, the Sarangians, and the Thamanaeans; but ever since the Persian rise to power it has been the property of the Persian king. In the ring of hills a considerable river rises – the Aces – which used to supply water to the five tribes I have mentioned, being split into five channels and flowing out to each of them through a different gorge; now, however, that the Persians are masters of the country, all these people find themselves in a serious difficulty, for the king has blocked up the gorges and constructed sluice-gates to contain the flow of water, so that what used to be a plain has now become a large lake, the river flowing in as before but no longer having any means of egress. The result of this for the people who depended upon the use of the water, but are now deprived of it, has been disastrous. In winter, to be sure, they get rain like anyone else, but they need the river water when they are sowing their millet and sesame in the summer. When therefore they find themselves waterless, they go in a body with their wives to the Persians, and stand howling in front of the gates of the king's palace, until the king gives orders to open the sluices and allow the water to flow to whichever tribe it may be that needs it most. Then, when the land has drunk all the water it wants, the sluices are shut, and the king orders others to be opened in turn, according to the needs of the remaining tribes. I know that he opens the sluices only upon receipt of a heavy payment over and above the regular tax.

118   Soon after the rising of the seven Persians against the Magus, one of their number, Intaphrenes, was executed for a failure to show proper respect to the king's authority. Having business to transact with Darius, he wished to enter the palace. Now it had

already been agreed that any of the conspirators might visit the
king unannounced, provided that he was not, at the moment,
in bed with a woman; and in view of this Intaphrenes refused to
have his name sent in by a messenger, and claimed it as his right,
as one of the seven, to walk straight in. He was, however,
stopped by the king's chamberlain and the sentry on duty at the
palace gate, who told him that Darius had, in fact, a woman
with him at the time. Thinking this was only a trumped-up
excuse to keep him out, Intaphrenes drew his scimitar and cut
off their ears and noses, strung them on his horse's bridle, tied
the bridle round their necks, and sent them packing. They
showed themselves to Darius and explained the reason for their
plight, which at once suggested to the king the alarming possibility of a fresh conspiracy. Thinking his six former confederates
might all be in this business together, he sent for each of them
in turn, and sounded them to see if they approved of what
Intaphrenes had done. None of them did; so as soon as he
was satisfied that Intaphrenes had acted entirely on his own
initiative, he had him arrested with his children and all his near
relations, in the strong suspicion that he and his family were
about to raise a revolt. All the prisoners were then chained, as
condemned criminals. After his arrest, Intaphrenes' wife came
to the palace and began to weep and lament outside the door,
and continued so long to do so that Darius, moved to pity by
her incessant tears, sent someone out to speak to her. 'Lady,'
the message ran, 'the king is willing to spare the life of one
member of your family – choose which of the prisoners you
wish to save.' Having thought this offer over, the woman
answered that, if the king granted her the life of one only of her
family, she would choose her brother. The answer amazed
Darius, and he sent again and asked why it was that she rejected
her husband and children, and preferred to save her brother,
who was neither so near to her as her children, nor so dear as
her husband. 'My lord,' she replied, 'God willing, I may get
another husband, and other children when these are gone. But
as my father and mother are both dead, I can never possibly
have another brother. That was the reason for what I said.'[42]
Darius appreciated the lady's good sense, and, to mark his

119

pleasure, granted her not only the life she asked, but also that of her eldest son. The rest of the family were all put to death. This, then, was the early end of one of the seven confederates.

120   About the time of Cambyses' last sickness the following events occurred. A Persian called Oroetes who had been appointed by Cyrus governor of Sardis, conceived a purpose of peculiar impiety – the murder of Polycrates of Samos. He was determined to capture and kill him, in spite of the fact that he had never received any injury at his hands, either by word or deed, and had never even met him in person. This outrage is generally supposed to have been the result of a quarrel between Oroetes and another Persian named Mitrobates, governor of the province of Dascyleium. The two men, the story goes, were sitting near the palace entrance, engaged in talk; their talk grew heated, and they were soon quarrelling over the question of which of them was the better man, when Mitrobates said with a sneer: 'What? You call yourself a man, when you have neglected to add Samos to the king's dominions, though it lies so near your province and is so easy to subdue? Why, one of the islanders with fifteen soldiers at his back raised a revolt and took it, and is now master there.' Oroetes was stung by this reproach; but instead of having his revenge upon the man who uttered it, he conceived the desire of removing the cause of it by destroying Polycrates.

121   According to another account, less generally accepted, Oroetes sent a messenger to Samos to make some request or other (what it was is not stated), and on his arrival Polycrates was at table in the hall with Anacreon, the poet of Teos. It so happened that Polycrates sat facing the wall of the room with his back to the man as he came forward to say what he had to say; and – either to show his contempt for Oroetes' power, or perhaps merely by chance – he not only omitted to give an answer, but did not even bother to turn round while the messen-

122   ger was speaking. Both stories are told to account for Polycrates' death and the reader may take his choice between them.[43]

However, when Oroetes was living at Magnesia on the Maeander, he had already got to know of the design which Polycrates had in mind – for Polycrates was the first Greek we know of to plan the dominion of the sea, unless we count Minos of Cnossus and any other who may possibly have ruled the sea at a still earlier date. In ordinary human history at any rate, Polycrates was the first; and he had high hopes of making himself master of Ionia and the islands. Knowing, then, of Polycrates' ambition, Oroetes sent a Lydian named Myrsus, the son of Gyges, to Samos with a message to the following effect: 'I understand, Polycrates, that you have an important enterprise in mind, but your resources are not equal to your designs. I have a proposal to make which, if you adopt it, will ensure your success – and my own safety, for it is clear from reports I have received that Cambyses is plotting my death. Come, then, and get me out of the country; I promise you a share in everything I possess, and that will give you money enough to get control of the whole of Greece. If you have any doubts about my wealth, send whoever it is you most trust, and I will show him what I have.' Polycrates, who was very fond of money, was delighted 123 by this proposal and did not hesitate to accept it. He sent his secretary, a Samian called Maeandrius, son of a father of the same name, to see if Oroetes' claim was true – it was Maeandrius who not long afterwards sent as an offering to the temple of Hera the magnificent furniture from Polycrates' hall. Oroetes, however, as soon as he knew that someone was actually on the way and must shortly be expected to come and view his treasure, filled eight chests with stones very nearly to the brim, topped them up with a thin layer of gold, fastened them securely and kept them ready for inspection. Maeandrius arrived, saw the gold, and returned with his report to Polycrates.[44]

In spite of many attempts by his friends and by professional 124 soothsayers to dissuade him, Polycrates now prepared to visit Oroetes in person. His daughter, too, did her best to stop him; for she had dreamt she saw her father hanging in the air, washed by Zeus and anointed by the sun-god Helios, and the dream had frightened her so much that she would have done anything in the world to prevent her father from going to Oroetes; and she did, in fact, follow him to the ship with words prophetic of disaster. Polycrates, however, in irritation, merely threatened that, if he got home safely, he would delay her marriage for many years – to which she answered that she prayed the threat might be fulfilled, for she would rather be a maiden all her life than lose her father. But all warnings were lost upon Polycrates; taking with him a number of friends, amongst whom was Democedes of Crotona, the son of Calliphon, and the most distinguished physician of his day, he sailed for Magnesia, where he met an end unworthy of his personal distinction and high ambition. For apart from those of Syracuse, no other tyrant in the Greek world can be compared with Polycrates for magnificence. In a manner not worthy to be recorded Oroetes had him murdered, and the dead body hung on a cross. Of the men who accompanied him, Oroetes let the Samians go, and told them they could be grateful to him for their freedom; the rest, who were either foreigners or slaves, he reckoned as prisoners of war and detained.

The dream of Polycrates' daughter was thus fulfilled by his impalement; when rain fell he was 'washed by Zeus', and he was 'anointed by Helios' when under the sun's heat the moisture was sweated out from his body. This, then, was the end of the long-continued prosperity of Polycrates: it was just as Amasis, king of Egypt, had previously foretold.

It was not long before Polycrates had his revenge. After the death of Cambyses, and throughout the period when Persia was controlled by the Magi, Oroetes had lived in Sardis and offered no help to his countrymen in resisting the Median usurpation. He had, moreover, during these unsettled times, procured the death of Mitrobates, the governor of Dascyleium, who had taunted him about Polycrates, and of Mitrobates' son Cranaspes, both distinguished Persians. Nor were these two murders by any means his only acts of violence; he also, for instance, made away with one of Darius' couriers; the man had come with a message which was not to Oroetes' taste, so he sent a party to waylay him on his return journey. He was killed, and neither his body, nor that of his horse, was ever discovered.

Darius, once his power was established, was anxious to punish Oroetes for his many crimes, and not least for the murder of Mitrobates and his son. He thought it would be unwise, things being as they were, to send an armed force openly against him;

for the country was still in an unsettled state; he himself had only recently come to the throne, and he knew that Oroetes was a powerful man, being governor of Phrygia, Lydia, and Ionia, with a thousand Persians in his bodyguard. Darius had recourse, in consequence, to subtler methods, and called a meeting of the leading men in the country, whom he addressed in the following words: 'It is my wish, gentlemen, that one of you should undertake on my behalf a matter which calls for craft rather than the combined force of numbers. Force is always beside the point when subtlety will serve. Which of you will kill Oroetes for me, or bring him to me alive? He is a man who has never yet lifted a finger to help his country: on the contrary, he has done us grave disservice. He has made away with two of our friends, Mitrobates and his son; and now he kills my own messengers whom I send to summon him. This is a defiance of authority which is not to be tolerated. Before he can do us further harm, he must be stopped, by death.'

Thirty of the company who were present competed so hotly for the privilege of undertaking this service, that Darius was forced to make them draw lots, to stop the argument. This they did, and the lucky man proved to be Bagaeus, the son of Artontes, who at once set about having a number of documents prepared on various subjects, which he sealed with the king's seal, and took with him to Sardis. Here he called upon Oroetes, and in his presence opened the papers one by one, handing them to the king's secretary (an officer who forms part of every governor's establishment), with instructions to read them aloud. His object in this was to test the loyalty of Oroetes' bodyguard in case they might be willing to act against their master. When, therefore, he noticed that they regarded the documents with respect – and, still more, the words they heard read from them – he passed one to the secretary which contained an order, purporting to come from Darius, to the effect that the guards were to refuse service to Oroetes. The order was read out, and the guards promptly laid their spears at Bagaeus' feet. Then Bagaeus, seeing the written order obeyed, ventured to hand to the secretary the paper he had reserved till last. This contained the words: 'King Darius commands the Persians in Sardis to kill

128

Oroetes.' The guards immediately drew their scimitars, and
dispatched him – and that was how Oroetes the Persian was
punished for his betrayal of Polycrates.

129   Soon after Oroetes' money had been confiscated and conveyed to Susa, Darius was out hunting and happened to twist
his foot as he dismounted from his horse. The injury was serious,
the ankle being actually dislocated. It had been his custom for
some time to keep in attendance certain Egyptian doctors, who
had a reputation for the highest eminence in their profession,
and these men he now consulted. But in their efforts to reduce
the joint, they wrenched the foot so clumsily that they only
made matters worse. For seven days and nights Darius was
unable to sleep for pain, and was very ill; on the eighth day,
however, being informed about the skill of Democedes of Croton by someone who had previously heard of him in Sardis, he
ordered him to be fetched immediately.[45] The man was found
in a neglected condition amongst Oroetes' slaves, and brought
to the palace just as he was, dressed in rags and dragging his
130   chains. When he came into the royal presence and Darius asked
him if he understood the art of medicine, he replied that he did
not, for he was afraid that if he declared himself he would never
be allowed to return home to Greece. Darius, however, was not
deceived; realizing that Democedes was concealing his knowledge, he told the men who had brought him to fetch the whips
and the iron spikes. This was enough to force an admission –
up to a point; for Democedes still maintained that he had
no thorough medical knowledge, but had merely acquired a
smattering of it by living with a doctor. All the same, Darius
put himself in his hands, and Democedes, by using Greek
methods and substituting milder remedies for the rough-and-
ready treatment of the Egyptian doctors, enabled the king to get
some sleep, and very soon cured him completely. Darius, who
had never expected to be able to use his foot again, presented
him with two sets of gold chains, a gift which caused Democedes
to ask if the king was determined to double his sufferings as a
reward for the cure he had effected. This amused Darius, who
thereupon sent him off to visit his wives, and when the eunuchs
who conducted him to their apartments told them that this was

the man who had saved the king's life, they each scooped a cupful of gold coins from a chest and gave them to Democedes. There was such a lot of the money that a servant called Sciton, by picking up the coins which spilt over the cups, managed to collect quite a fortune.

Democedes had left Croton and gone to live with Polycrates 131 in order to escape from his father, who was a man of savage temper. Unable to bear the treatment he received, he cleared out and went first to Aegina, where within a year he proved himself the best doctor in the island, in spite of the fact that he had no equipment or surgical instruments. In the second year of his residence the Aeginetans gave him a state appointment at a salary of a talent; a year later the Athenians employed him at a salary of 100 *minae*; and a year after that Polycrates offered him two talents; and that was how he came to Samos. It was chiefly because of Democedes' success that Crotoniate doctors came to have such a high reputation. Darius' accident happened during the period when the physicians of Croton were considered the best in Greece, and those of Cyrene the next best. During the same period the Argives were considered the best musicians.

After his successful treatment of Darius, Democedes lived in 132 a large house in Susa, took his meals at the king's table, and enjoyed every privilege but one – the liberty of returning to Greece. The Egyptian doctors who had tried to cure Darius in the first place were about to be impaled as a punishment for being outdone by a Greek; but so great was Democedes' influence with the king, that they were let off as a result of his intercession in their favour; and – another instance of his power – he procured the release of a professional soothsayer from Elis, who had gone with Polycrates and was lying neglected amongst his slaves. He stood very high with the king.

But the story of Democedes is not yet by any means finished. 133 Shortly after this Atossa, the daughter of Cyrus and wife of Darius, developed on her breast an abscess, which later burst and began to spread. Shame had induced her to conceal it, and to say nothing about it to anyone, while it was still small; but when it got worse and she found herself dangerously ill, she sent for Democedes and let him see it. He said he could cure her, but before he did so he made her swear to do him in return any service he might choose to ask, adding that he would not ask for anything she could blush to give. On these terms he treated the abscess, effected a cure, and told the queen what he wished her to do. Then when in bed with Darius she began the following conversation: 'My lord, with the immense resources at your command, the fact that you are making no further conquests to increase the power of Persia, must mean that you lack ambition. Surely a young man like you, who is master of great wealth, should be seen engaged in some active enterprise, to show the Persians that they have a man to rule them. Indeed, there are two reasons for ending this inactivity: for not only will the Persians know their leader to be a man, but, if you make war, you will wear down their strength and leave them no leisure to plot against you. Now is the time for action, while you are young; for as the body grows in strength, so does the mind; but as the years pass and the body weakens, the mind ages too and loses its edge.'

This, of course, was what Democedes had instructed Atossa to say; and Darius replied: 'What you have said is precisely what I intend to do. I have already decided to bridge the straits between Asia and Europe, and attack the Scythians. You will not have long to wait before it is done.'

'Never mind about the Scythians for the moment,' Atossa went on; 'they are yours for the asking at any moment you please. Look – what I want you to do is to invade Greece. I have heard people talk of the women there, and I should like to have Spartan girls, and girls from Argos and Attica and Corinth, to wait upon me. You have a man better fitted than anyone in the world to give you full information about Greece and to act as guide – I mean the doctor who cured your foot.'

'Lady,' Darius answered, 'as you think Greece should be my first objective, I had better begin by sending a party of Persians over to Greece to reconnoitre, together with the man you mentioned. They can then bring me back a full report of everything they see and hear. After that, when I have the information I need, I will begin the war.'

It was no sooner said than done. At dawn the next morning 135
he sent for fifteen Persians, all men of distinction, and gave them
instructions to cruise along the Greek coast, taking Democedes
with them to show them the way. He added a strict order that
Democedes should not be allowed to escape, but should be
brought back at all costs. He then summoned Democedes himself, and begged him to give the reconnoitring party such
guidance and information as they needed, and afterwards to
return to Persia. He told him to take all his household furniture
with him and make a present of it to his father and brothers,
promising to replace it at double its value when he came back,
and adding a further offer of a merchant vessel which should
sail in company with them, loaded with valuable goods.

I do not myself believe that Darius' motive, when he made
these promises, was anything but genuine and straightforward;
Democedes, however, was afraid he might be laying a trap to
make him reveal his true intentions, so instead of accepting with
open arms everything Darius offered, he said he would leave his
property where it was, to await his return to claim it; the ship,
however, and its cargo, which Darius wished to give as a present
to his brothers, he was willing to take.

Democedes and the Persians, having received their orders
from Darius, were now sent down to the coast. At Sidon in 136
Phoenicia they lost no time in fitting out two triremes, and a
merchant vessel which they loaded with a rich assortment of
goods; then, when all was ready for sea, they got under way for
Greece, made a written record of the results of a careful survey
of most of the notable features of the coast, and finally arrived
at Tarentum in Italy. Here Aristophilides, who was in control
of the town, showed himself a good friend to Democedes by
getting the steering-gear removed from the Persian ships, and
the Persians themselves arrested as spies, so that while they were
under restraint Democedes was able to get away to Croton.
Once he was safe home, Aristophilides released his prisoners
and restored the gear he had taken from the ships, whereupon
they put to sea in pursuit of Democedes, found him in the 137
market-place at Croton, and laid hands on him. Some of the
people in the town were prepared to give him up through fear

of Persia; but others took his part, and setting about his captors with their sticks, did their best to drag him away. The Persians tried to scare them by pointing out that the man they wanted to save was a runaway slave of Darius. 'Do you realize what you are doing?' they cried. 'Do you suppose the king will be content to submit to this high-handed treatment? What good will it do you, if you take this fellow from us? Won't your city be the first objective in the war which is bound to ensue – and the first we shall reduce to slavery?' Their threats, however, were of no avail; forced to abandon not only Democedes himself but also the merchant vessel which had accompanied them, they returned to Asia, making no further attempt, now that they had lost their guide, to pursue their survey of the Greek coasts. Just before they left, Democedes told them to let Darius know that he was engaged to be married to the daughter of Milo, the wrestler, whose name was in high esteem at the Persian court. I think myself that Democedes was determined to make this marriage, however much money it cost him, in order to show Darius that he was a man of mark in his own country as well as abroad.

138   After sailing from Crotona, the Persians were wrecked on the Iapygian coast and taken as slaves, but were afterwards ransomed and brought home to the court of Darius by a man named Gillus, a Tarentine exile. In gratitude for their recovery Darius was willing to grant any request that Gillus might make, and Gillus, after relating the story of his political misfortunes, declared that what he most wished for was to be enabled to return to Tarentum, and added that, to prevent setting Greece by the ears if a powerful armament sailed to Italy on his behalf, he would be quite content to be escorted home by the people of Cnidos only; their help, he thought, would be most likely to ensure the success of his enterprise, as Cnidos and Tarentum were on very friendly terms. Darius complied with his wishes and sent an order to Cnidos for the necessary steps to be taken. The order was obeyed, but the Cnidians failed to induce the people of Tarentum to agree to the exile's return, and were not strong enough to use force.

These Persians of whom I have just written were the first who ever came from Asia to Greece; their object was to collect information, for the reasons I have given.

These events were followed by the capture of Samos, which 139 was the first place, either inside or outside the Greek world, to fall to Darius, and this was why: during the campaign of Cambyses in Egypt, a great many Greeks visited that country for one reason or another: some, as was to be expected, for trade, some to serve in the army, others, no doubt, out of mere curiosity, to see what they could see. Amongst the sightseers was Aeaces' son Syloson, the exiled brother of Polycrates of Samos. While he was in Egypt, Syloson had an extraordinary stroke of luck: he was hanging about the streets of Memphis dressed in a flame-coloured cloak, when Darius, who at that time was a member of Cambyses' guard and not yet of any particular importance, happened to catch sight of him and, seized with a sudden longing to possess the cloak, came up to Syloson and made him an offer for it. His extreme anxiety to get it was obvious enough to Syloson, who was inspired to say: 'I am not selling this for any money, but if you must have it, I will give it to you free.' Darius thereupon thanked him warmly and took it. Syloson at the moment merely thought he had lost it by his foolish good-nature; then came the death of Cambyses and the 140 revolt of the seven against the Magus, and Darius ascended the throne. Syloson now had the news that the man, whose request for the flame-coloured cloak he had formerly gratified in Egypt, had become King of Persia. He hurried to Susa, sat down at the entrance of the royal palace, and claimed to be one of the king's benefactors. The sentry on guard reported his claim to Darius, who asked in amazement who the man might be. 'For surely,' he said, 'as I have so recently come to the throne, there cannot be any Greek to whom I am indebted for a service. Hardly any of them have been here yet, and I certainly cannot remember owing anything to a Greek. But bring him in all the same, that I may know what he means by this claim.'

The guard escorted Syloson into the royal presence, and when the interpreters asked him who he was and what he had done to justify the statement that he was the king's benefactor, he reminded Darius of the story of the cloak, and said that he was the man who had given it him. 'Sir,' exclaimed Darius, 'you are the most generous of men; for while I was still a person of no power or consequence you gave me a present – small indeed, but deserving then as much gratitude from me as would the most splendid of gifts today. I will give you in return more silver and gold than you can count, that you may never regret that you once did a favour to Darius the son of Hystaspes.' 'My lord,' replied Syloson, 'do not give me gold or silver, but recover Samos for me, my native island, which now since Oroetes killed my brother Polycrates is in the hands of one of our servants. Let Samos be your gift to me – but let no man in the island be killed or enslaved.'

141   Darius consented to Syloson's request, and dispatched a force under the command of Otanes, one of the seven, with orders to do everything that Syloson had asked; and Otanes, accordingly, went down to the coast to make his preparations.

142   In Samos power was in the hands of Maeandrius, the man whom Polycrates on leaving the island had appointed to attend to his affairs. When he learned of Polycrates' death, he would have liked, had he been allowed, to behave with exemplary regard for justice; but he was not given the chance. His first act was to erect an altar to Zeus the Liberator, and to enclose it in a piece of ground just outside the city, where it is still to be seen; then he called a meeting of all the citizens of Samos and addressed them in the following terms: 'You know as well as I do that the sceptre of Polycrates, and the power it represents, have passed into my hands, so that I may, if I wish, become your absolute master. So far as I am able, however, I shall refrain from doing myself what I should object to in another. I did not approve the conduct of Polycrates, nor should I that of any other man who sought irresponsible power over people as good as himself; therefore, now that Polycrates has met his end, I intend to surrender the power to which I am entitled, and to proclaim you equal before the law. All I claim as a special privilege for myself, is the sum of six talents from Polycrates' fortune, together with the right of keeping for myself and my posterity the priesthood of Zeus the Liberator to whom I built the shrine; I who now offer you your liberty.'

One of his audience, a man of repute named Telesarchus, at once sprang to his feet. 'What?' he cried; 'that's a fine speech to hear from a low-born rogue like you! Far from being fit to govern us, you ought rather to account for the money you have had your hands on.' This was enough to show Maeandrius that, if he surrendered the tyranny, somebody else would be sure to seize it; so he changed his mind and determined to hold on to what he had got. Withdrawing to the citadel, he sent for each one of the leading men in turn, making out that he intended to show them his accounts, arrested them all, and put them in irons.

Shortly after the arrests Maeandrius fell ill, and his brother Lycaretus thought he was going to die; so in order to facilitate his own seizure of power, he had all the prisoners put to death. So, it seems, the people of Samos did not want liberty.[46]

The result was that when the Persians arrived in Samos to restore the exiled Syloson, nobody lifted a finger against them. Maeandrius and his party professed themselves willing to leave the island upon certain terms, which were agreed to by Otanes; a truce was made, and the Persians of the highest rank then had chairs of state placed for them opposite the citadel, and took their seats upon them.

Now Maeandrius had a crazy brother called Charilaus, who for some fault or other had been shut up in a dungeon; this fellow, hearing what was going on, put his head out through the bars of his prison, and when he saw the Persian grandees peacefully sitting on their chairs of state, he shouted out that he had something which he wanted to say to Maeandrius. Maeandrius, on being told of this, sent word to have his brother taken out of gaol and brought to him. The moment he arrived he began with much violent and abusive language to urge Maeandrius to set upon the Persians. 'What a coward you are!' he exclaimed. 'Here am I, your own brother, who has never done you the least harm, whom you think fit to keep chained up in a dungeon, while you have not spirit enough to punish those foreigners who would throw you out of house and home! Why – you could crush them easily! If you're afraid of them, give me command of the soldiers and I will soon see they get what they

143

144

145

deserve for daring to come here. As for you, I am quite willing to see you safely out of the island.'

146   Maeandrius agreed to his brother's proposal, not, I imagine, because he was foolish enough to think himself able to get the better of the Persian force, but rather out of spite – for he did not relish the idea of Syloson recovering control of the city without any loss or damage, and without even striking a blow. What he wanted was to incense the Persians against Samos, so that he could hand it over to Syloson when things were in a state of the greatest possible weakness and confusion, knowing that the Persians would be savage for revenge if they were roughly handled. As for himself, he was sure of getting away safely at any time he wished, by means of a secret tunnel which he had made, leading from the citadel to the sea.

   Maeandrius then escaped from Samos on shipboard, and his brother Charilaus armed the soldiers, opened the city gates, and fell upon the unsuspecting Persians, who thought that everything had been peacefully settled. So the leading Persians were killed where they sat. But the rest of the Persian force now came to the rescue, and Charilaus' men, hard pressed, were driven

147 back into the citadel. When Otanes saw the serious loss which the Persians had suffered, he deliberately put out of his mind all memory of the instructions he had received from Darius before the expedition started – that is, not to kill or capture any Samian, but to hand the island over to Syloson intact – and commanded his troops to kill everyone they could catch, boy or man. The order was obeyed; and while some of the Persian force laid siege to the citadel, others began the massacre, killing all they fell in with, inside or outside sacred ground, without discrimination.

148   After his escape Maeandrius sailed to Lacedaemon, taking with him the various articles of value which he had brought out of the island. Arrived here, he angled for the help of Cleomenes, the son of Anaxandrides, the king of Sparta, in the following way: he would set out gold and silver drinking cups on his table and, while his servants were polishing them, would get into conversation with Cleomenes and induce him to come to the house. Every time Cleomenes, at the sight of the cups, was struck

with admiration and astonishment, and every time Maeandrius
would ask him to take away as many of them as he pleased.
Cleomenes, however, after being subjected two or three times to
this temptation, showed a quite extraordinary sense of propriety
and refused to accept the offered gift. Knowing, moreover, that
Maeandrius would be sure to get assistance if he made a similar
offer to other Spartans, he went to the magistrates and said that
it would be better for Sparta if the visitor from Samos left the
country, before he succeeded in persuading either him or some
other Spartan to disgrace himself. The suggestion was accepted,   149
and it was publicly proclaimed that Maeandrius must go. As for
Samos, the Persians took the entire population like fish in a
drag-net, and presented Syloson with an empty island. Some
years later, however, Otanes contracted some disease of the
genital organs and that, in conjunction with a dream he had,
induced him to repopulate the place.

While the Persian fleet sailed for Samos, Babylon revolted.   150
The revolt had been long and carefully planned; indeed, preparations for withstanding a siege had been going quietly on all
through the reign of the Magus and the disturbances which
followed the rising of the seven against him, and somehow or
other the secret never leaked out. When the moment finally
came to declare their purpose, the Babylonians, in order to
reduce the consumption of food, herded together and strangled
all the women in the city – each man exempting only his mother,
and one other woman whom he chose out of his household to
bake his bread for him. When the news reached Darius, he   151
marched against them with all the forces at his disposal, and laid
siege to the city.[47] The Babylonians, however, were unimpressed;
they climbed on to their battlements and danced and hurled
insulting jibes at Darius and his army, calling out: 'What are
you sitting there for, men of Persia? Why don't you go away?
Oh yes, you will capture our city – when mules have foals.'

Now whoever it was who made this last remark, naturally
supposed that no mule would ever have a foal.

A year and seven months went by, and Darius and his army   152
began to chafe at their inability to make any progress towards
taking the city. Every trick of strategy, every possible device,

had been tried; but to no purpose. The town could not be taken, not even when Darius, after all else had failed, attempted to repeat the method which Cyrus had previously used with success. The Babylonians were always on the watch with extraordinary vigilance, and gave the enemy no chance.

153   At last, in the twentieth month of the siege, a marvellous thing happened to Zopyrus, son of the Megabyzus who was one of the seven conspirators who killed the Magus: one of his sumpter-mules foaled. When Zopyrus was told of this, he refused to believe it till he had seen the foal with his own eyes; then, forbidding the others who had seen it to say a word to anyone of what had occurred, he began to think hard, and came to the conclusion that the time had come when Babylon could be taken – for had not that Babylonian, at the beginning of the siege, said that the city would fall when mules foaled? That the man should have used the phrase, and that the miracle should actually have happened – surely that meant that the hand of God was in it.

154   Convinced, therefore, that Babylon was now doomed to destruction, he went to Darius and asked him if the capture of the city was really of supreme importance to him, and, on being told that it was, set himself to devise a way of bringing it about by his own sole act and initiative; for in Persia any special service to the king is very highly valued. Accordingly he passed in review every scheme he could think of, and finally decided that there was one way only in which he could bring the place under, namely by maiming himself and then going over to the enemy as a deserter. Taking this dreadful expedient as a mere matter of course, he at once put it into practice, and there were no half-measures in the way he set about it: he cut off his nose and ears, shaved his hair like a criminal's, raised weals on his body with a whip, and in this condition presented himself to Darius.

155   Darius was shocked at the sight of a man of Zopyrus' eminence so fearfully mutilated, and springing from his chair with an exclamation of horror, asked who it was that inflicted this punishment upon him, and what Zopyrus had done to deserve it. 'My lord,' Zopyrus answered, 'there is no one but yourself who has power enough to reduce me to this condition. The

hands that disfigured me were none other than my own, for I could not bear to hear the Assyrians of Babylon laugh the Persians to scorn.'

'You speak like a madman,' said Darius; 'to say you did this horrible thing because of our enemies in the beleaguered city, is merely to cloak a shameful act in fine words. Are you fool enough to think that the mutilation of your body can hasten our victory? When you did that to yourself, you must have taken leave of your senses.'

'Had I told you of my intention,' Zopyrus answered, 'you would not have allowed me to proceed. So I acted upon my own initiative. And now – if you too will play your part – we will capture Babylon. I will go as I am to the city walls, pretending to be a deserter, and I will tell them that it was you who caused my misery. They will believe me readily enough – and they will put their troops under my command.[48] Now for your part: wait till the tenth day after I enter the town, and then station by the gates of Semiramis a detachment of a thousand men, whose loss will not worry you. Then, seven days later, send 2000 men to the Nineveh gates and, twenty days after that, another 4000 to the Chaldaean gates. None of these three detachments must be armed with anything but their daggers – let them carry daggers only. And then, after a further interval of twenty days, order a general assault upon the city walls from every direction, taking care that our own Persian troops have the sectors opposite the Belian and Cissian gates. It is my belief that the Babylonians, when they see that I have done them good service, will increase my responsibility – even to trusting me with the keys of the gates. And after that – I and the Persians will attend to what must be done.'

Having given these directions to the king, Zopyrus fled 156 towards the gates of Babylon, glancing over his shoulder as he ran, like a deserter in fear of pursuit. When the soldiers on watch saw him, they hurried down from the battlements, and opening one of the gates just a crack, asked him his name and business. Saying he was Zopyrus and had deserted from the Persian army, he was let in, and conducted by the sentries to the magistrates. Here he poured out his tale of woe, pretending that the injuries he had done to himself had been inflicted upon him by Darius, and all because he had advised him to abandon the siege, as there appeared to be no means of ever bringing it to a successful conclusion. 'And now,' he added, 'here I am, men of Babylon; and my coming will be gain to you, but loss – and that the severest – to Darius and his army. He little knows me if he thinks he can get away with the foul things he has done me – moreover, I know all the ins and outs of his plans.'

157   The Babylonians, seeing a Persian of high rank and distinction in such a state – his nose and ears cut off and his body a mess of blood from the lash of whips – were quick to believe that he spoke the truth and had really come to offer them his services, and in this belief were prepared to give him whatever he asked. At once he asked for the command of some troops, and, when the request was granted, proceeded to put into practice the plan he had arranged with Darius. The tenth day after his arrival he marched his force out of the city, and surrounded and killed the first detachment of a thousand men which he had instructed Darius to send. This was enough to show the Babylonians that his deeds were as good as his words; they were in high glee, and ready to put themselves under his orders in anything he might propose. After waiting, therefore, the agreed number of days, he picked another party from the troops in the city, marched out, and killed the two thousand Persians which Darius had posted by the Nineveh gates. As a result of this second service, the reputation of Zopyrus went up with a jump and his name was on everybody's lips. Then once more, after the agreed interval, he marched his men out through the Chaldaean gates, and surrounded the four thousand. After this achievement Zopyrus was the one and only soldier in Babylon, the city's hero, and was created General in Chief and Guardian of the Wall.

158   And now Darius, as had been agreed, ordered a general assault upon the walls from every direction – which was the signal for Zopyrus to reveal the full extent of his cunning. Waiting till the Babylonian forces had mounted the battlements to repel Darius' onslaught, he opened the Cissian and Belian gates and let the Persians in. Those of the Babylonians who were near enough to

see what had happened, fled to the temple of Bel; the rest remained at their posts until they, too, realized that they had been betrayed.

Thus Babylon was captured for the second time, and Darius after his victory – unlike Cyrus, its previous conqueror – destroyed its defences, pulled down all the city gates, and impaled the leading citizens to the number of about three thousand.[49] The rest he allowed to remain in their homes. I mentioned at the beginning of my account how the Babylonians strangled their women to save food, and it was in consequence of this that Darius, in order to prevent the race from dying out, compelled the neighbouring peoples each to send a certain stated number of women to Babylon. In all, as many as fifty thousand were collected there. It is from these that the present inhabitants are descended.

In the judgement of Darius no Persian surpassed Zopyrus, either before his time or after, as a benefactor of his country, except only Cyrus – with whom nobody in Persia has ever dreamt of comparing himself. We are told that Darius often said that he would rather have Zopyrus without his frightful wounds than twenty more Babylons. He rewarded him with the highest honours, giving him every year the sort of gifts which are most prized amongst the Persians, and, amongst much else, the governorship of Babylon, free from tax, for as long as he lived.

Megabyzus, who held the command in Egypt against the Athenians and their allies, was Zopyrus' son; and the son of this Megabyzus was Zopyrus, who deserted from the Persian army and came to Athens.[50]

BOOK FOUR

1   After the capture of Babylon Darius invaded Scythia.[1] The Scythians, having on a previous occasion invaded and conquered Media, had begun the wrongdoing and Darius, having an immense revenue in money and an unlimited number of men to draw upon in his Asiatic dominions, found himself anxious to have his revenge. There had been a period of twenty-eight years, as I mentioned, during which the Scythians were in control of upper Asia after destroying the power of the Medes, its previous masters.[2] They entered the country in pursuit of the Cimmerians, and, on their return home after the long gap of twenty-eight years, found trouble waiting for them hardly less serious than their struggle with the Medes. This was in the shape of a large hostile army, which opposed their entrance; for the Scythian women, wearied with their husbands' protracted absence, had intermarried with the slaves.

2   The Scythians blind their slaves, a practice in some way connected with the milk which they prepare for drinking in the following way: they insert a tube made of bone and shaped like a flute into the mare's anus, and blow; and while one blows, another milks. According to them, the object of this is to inflate the mare's veins with air and so cause the udder to be forced down. They make the blind men stand round in a circle, and then pour the milk into wooden casks and stir it; the part which rises to the top is skimmed off, and considered the best; what remains is not supposed to be so good. The reason why they blind their prisoners of war is connected with the fact that the Scythians are not an agricultural people, but nomadic.

3   From the union of these slaves with the women of Scythia a

new generation had grown to manhood, and when they learned the circumstances of their birth they resolved to oppose the return of the army from Media. As a preliminary measure of defence they dug a broad trench from the Tauric mountains to the widest part of Lake Maeotis; then, taking up defensive positions along it, resisted all attempts to force an entrance. Many engagements were fought, but the invading army could make no headway until one of their number thought of a new plan of attack. 'My friends,' he said, 'what we are doing is absurd. In this war with our own slaves we stand to lose both ways, by the casualties we inflict no less than by the casualties we suffer; for the more we kill of them, the fewer we shall have, when we are once again their masters. I propose, therefore, that we should stop using spears and bows, and go for them each one of us with a horsewhip. When they saw us armed, they naturally felt that they were as good as we are, and were meeting us on equal terms; but when they see us coming with whips instead, they will remember they are slaves. Once they admit that, they will never try to stand up to us.'

The Scythians put the plan into action with immediate suc- 4 cess; the opposing army was dumbfounded; every man forgot he was a soldier and fled. This, then, is the story of how the Scythians dominated Asia, were expelled by the Medes, and returned to Scythia; and it was to punish them for their original invasion that Darius was now raising an army against them.

The Scythians say that they are the youngest of all nations, 5 and the following is the account they give of their origin. The first man to live in their country, which before his birth was uninhabited, was a certain Targitaus, the son of Zeus and of a daughter of the river Borysthenes – I merely repeat the tradition, and do not myself believe it. Targitaus had three sons, Lipoxais, Arpoxais, and Colaxais, the youngest; and during their reign in Scythia there fell from the sky a golden plough, a golden yoke, a golden battle-axe, and a golden cup. The eldest of the three was the first to see these treasures, and as he went to pick them up the gold caught fire. At this he retired, and the second of the brothers approached; but the gold caught fire and blazed, just as before. Lastly, when the two elder brothers had been kept off by the flames, the youngest came along, and this time the fire went out, so that he was able to pick up the golden implements and carry them home. The elder brothers accepted this as a sign from heaven and made over the whole kingdom to Colaxais.

6 The descendants of Lipoxais were those Scythians now known as Auchatae; those of the second brother, Arpoxais, are the Catiari and Traspies; those of the youngest brother are the Royal Scythians, now called Paralatae. They are known indiscriminately under the general name of Scoloti, after one of their

7 kings, and the Greeks call them Scythians. Such is the Scythians' account of their origin, and they add that the period from Targitaus, their first king, to Darius' crossing of the Hellespont to attack them, is just a thousand years. The gold which fell from heaven is guarded by the kings with the utmost care, and every year they visit it and offer it magnificent sacrifices. There is a legend in the country that any guardian of the gold who falls asleep in the open air during the festival will die within the year, and because of this the person concerned is given as much land as he can ride round in a day. In view of the great size of Scythia, Colaxais split it up into three separate kingdoms for his sons, making the one where the gold was kept larger than the other two. It is said to be impossible to travel through the region which lies further north, or even to see it, because of falling feathers – both earth and air are thick with them and they shut out the view.

8   The Greeks of Pontus[3] give a different account of Scythia and the country beyond it. According to them, Heracles came into this part of the world, which was then uninhabited, with the oxen of Geryon. Geryon's home was far away, on an island which the Greeks call Erythea, near Gades, which lies on the Ocean beyond the Pillars of Heracles. Legend says that Ocean is a great river running from the east all round the world; but there is nothing to prove this. When Heracles reached the country which is now Scythia, the weather was bad and it was bitterly cold, so he drew his lion's skin over him and went to sleep. While he slept, the horses which he had unharnessed from his chariot and turned loose to graze mysteriously disappeared.

As soon as he awoke Heracles began to look for them, and 9
roamed all over the country until he came at last to a place
called Hylaea, or the Woodland, where in a cave he found a
viper-maiden – a creature which from the buttocks upwards
was a woman, but below them a snake. For a moment he looked
at her in astonishment; then asked if she had seen his mares
straying around. She replied that they were in her own keeping,
and promised to return them to him on condition that he lay
with her. Heracles complied. The viper-woman, however, did
not at once give him back the mares, but put off the fulfilment
of her bargain in order to keep Heracles as long as possible for
her lover, though all he wanted himself was to get the horses
and go. At last she let him have them, and said: 'I kept these
horses safe for you, when I found them here; and you have given
me my reward, for I have three sons by you. Now tell me what
I am to do with them: when they grow up, shall I settle them
here in this country, of which I am mistress, or send them to
you?' 'When the boys are grown to be men,' Heracles answered,
'you will not be far wrong if you do what I will now tell you.
Whichever of them you find can draw this bow as I do, and put
on this girdle in the way I will show you, should be settled here
in this country; but any of them who fail to do these two things
must be sent away. Do this, and you will not only show proper
obedience to me but find happiness for yourself as well.'

Heracles then strung one of his bows – up to that time he 10
always carried two – and showed her how to put on the girdle,
after which he put into her hands both bow and girdle, and
went away. The girdle had a little gold cup for the tongue of its
buckle. When the boys grew up, their mother named the eldest
Agathyrsus, the next Gelonus, and the youngest Scythes, and
carried out the instructions which she remembered Heracles had
given her. Two of the young men, Agathyrsus and Gelonus,
failed to accomplish the task assigned them and were therefore
banished from the country by their mother; but the youngest
brother, Scythes, succeeded and was allowed to remain. In this
way Scythes, the son of Heracles, became father of the line of
Scythian kings; and to this day the Scythians wear belts with
little cups attached, in memory of the belt of their ancestor

Heracles. This was the only thing the mother of Scythes did for him.

11   Besides the story which the Greeks of Pontus tell, there is another which I myself consider the most likely of the three. This relates how the nomadic tribes of Scythians who lived in Asia, being hard pressed by the Massagetae, were forced across the Araxes into Cimmeria (what is now Scythia is said to have been long ago inhabited by Cimmerians). The Cimmerians could not agree upon what line to take when they saw the hordes of Scythians flooding into their country, but split into two sharply opposed opinions, that of the princes (the better one) and that of the people. Each party urged its view with equal insistence, the people maintaining that the proper course was to clear out without risking an engagement against so powerful an invader, the princes – more courageously – calling upon everyone to make a stand and fight for their country. Neither party, however, could win the other's acceptance of its view, so the one decided to take to its heels and surrender the country to the invader without a blow, while the other, the princes, remembering the blessings they had enjoyed in the past, and imagining the misery they must expect to suffer if they left their homes, refused to accompany the fugitives and preferred to die where they were and be buried in the earth which belonged to them. Accordingly they divided themselves into two equal bodies, and fought until every man of them was dead. The people buried them by the river Hyras, where their tomb may still be seen, and then left the country, so that when the Scythians entered soon

12   afterwards to take possession they found it uninhabited. There are still traces of the Cimmerians in Scythia: one finds, for instance, remains of fortifications, a Cimmerian strait, a Cimmerian Bosphorus, and a tract of land called Cimmeria.[4]

It is clear that the Cimmerians entered Asia to escape the Scythians, and built settlements on the peninsula where the Greek town of Sinope now stands; and there is no doubt that the reason why the Scythians in the course of their pursuit entered Median territory was that they took the wrong route by mistake; for whereas the Cimmerians kept along the coast, the Scythians took the inland road, keeping the Caucasus on their right, until they found themselves in Media. These facts are admitted by Greeks and Asians alike.

More information about this part of the world is to be found in a poem by Aristeas, son of Caÿstrobius, a native of Proconnesus. He tells us that 'inspired by Phoebus' he journeyed to the country of the Issedones, and that beyond the Issedones live the one-eyed Arimaspians, and beyond them the griffins which guard the gold, and beyond the griffins the Hyperboreans, whose land comes down to the sea.[5] All these, except the Hyperboreans, were continually encroaching upon one another's territory, beginning with the Arimaspians, so that the Issedones were expelled by the Arimaspians, the Scythians by the Issedones, and the Cimmerians by the Scythians, who forced them from their homes along the shores of the Black Sea. Here, then, is further evidence against the Scythians' account of this region.

I have mentioned the birthplace of Aristeas, the author of this poem; now here is a story I heard about him in Proconnesus and Cyzicus. He belonged to one of the first families in his home town, and one day, upon entering a fuller's shop, he fell down dead. The fuller closed his shop and hurried out to inform his relatives of what had occurred, but no sooner had the news of Aristeas' death got about, than a person from Cyzicus, who had just arrived from the town of Artaca, contradicted the rumour and declared that he had met him going towards Cyzicus and had talked to him. He was absolutely certain of this and would take no denial. Meanwhile, Aristeas' relatives were on their way to the shop with what was necessary for the funeral, intending to take the body away; they opened the door, and the room was empty – Aristeas was not there, either dead or alive. Seven years later he reappeared in Proconnesus, wrote the poem the Greeks now call *The Tale of the Arimaspians*, and again vanished. I will add something which I know happened to the people of Metapontum in Italy two hundred and forty years (as I found by computation in Proconnesus and Metapontum) after the second disappearance of Aristeas. The Metapontines say that Aristeas appeared and told them to erect an altar to Apollo, with a statue beside it bearing the name of Aristeas of Proconnesus; then, after explaining that they were the only people in

Italy whom Apollo had visited, and that he himself on the occasion of his visit had accompanied the god in the form of a raven, he vanished. The Metapontines sent to Delphi to ask the oracle what the apparition signified, and were told to obey it and thus it would go better for them. This advice they took, with the result that in the market-square of the town a statue inscribed with the name of Aristeas stands today by the side of the image of Apollo, surrounded by myrtle bushes.

16   No one has any accurate information about what lies beyond the region I am now discussing, and I have never met anyone who claims to have actually seen it. Even Aristeas, whom I have just mentioned, does not pretend in his poem to have gone further than the country of the Issedones, and admits that his account of what lies beyond is hearsay, founded on tales which the Issedones told him. I will, nevertheless, put down everything which careful inquiry about these remote parts has brought to

17   my notice. West of the seaport at the mouth of the Borysthenes[6] – which lies in the middle of the Scythian coastline – the first people are the Graeco-Scythian tribe called Callipidae, and their neighbours are the Alizones. Both these people resemble the Scythians in their way of life, and also grow grain for food, as well as onions, leeks, lentils, and millet. North of the Alizones are agricultural Scythian tribes, growing grain not for food but for export; beyond these are the Neuri, and north of the Neuri the country, so far as we know, is uninhabited. So much for the

18   peoples along the Hypanis, west of the Borysthenes; east of the Borysthenes, starting from the sea one comes first to Hylaea – the Woodland – to the northward of which are Scythians who get their living from the land and are known to the Greeks on the river Hypanis as Borysthenites. They call themselves Olbiopolites. These Scythians extend eastward as far as a river named the Panticapes – the distance of a three days' journey – and northward as far up the Borysthenes as a boat can sail in eleven days. Further north is a great tract of uninhabited desert, beyond which live the Androphagi – the Maneaters – who have no connexion with the Scythians but are a quite distinct race. Northward again, so far as we can tell, there is utter desert

19   without trace of human life. Eastward of the Scythians who

lived off the land, and on the other side of the Panticapes, are
the nomadic Scythians, who know nothing of agriculture. All
this region with the exception of Hylaea is treeless. The nomadic
tribes are to be found over a stretch of country extending eastward fourteen days' journey as far as the river Gerrhus, on the   20
further side of which lies what is called the country of the
Kings, and the Royal Scythians, who are the most warlike and
numerous section of their race, and look upon the others as
their slaves. Their territory runs south as far as Taurica and east
to the trench which was dug by the sons of the blind slaves, and
to Cremni, the trading post on the shore of the Maeotic Lake.
Part of it reaches as far as the river Tanais. North of the Royal
Scythians is a non-Scythian race called Melanchlaeni, or Black-
Cloaks, and north of them, so far as one knows, is a region of
lakes and uninhabited country.

Once across the Tanais, one has left Scythia behind, and   21
comes first to the Sauromatae, who occupy a stretch of country
which runs northward fifteen days' journey from the northern
tip of the Sea of Azov, and is entirely bare of trees, wild or
cultivated. The next region beyond the Sauromatae belongs to
the Budini, and is plentifully supplied with timber of all sorts.
Northward again the country is uninhabited over the distance   22
of a seven days' journey, until by turning a little easterly one
comes to the Thyssagetae, a distinct and numerous race which
gets its living by hunting. These folk live alongside another tribe
called Iyrcae, who, like them, are hunters, and climb trees, of
which there are many in the country, to wait for their game.
Each man is provided with a dog and a horse, which has been
trained to crouch flat on its belly to keep out of view, and when,
from his hiding-place in the branches, the huntsman catches
sight of the game, he lets fly, jumps down on to his horse, and
gives chase, the dog following.

Further to the north and east lives another Scythian tribe,
which moved into these parts after revolting from the Royal
Scythians to which it originally belonged. As far as this, the   23
country I have been describing is a level plain with good deep
soil, but further on it becomes rugged and stony; beyond this
region, which is of great extent, one comes to the foothills of a

lofty mountain chain, and a nation of bald men. They are said to be bald from birth, women and men alike, and to have snub noses and long chins; they speak a peculiar language, dress in the Scythian fashion, and live on the fruit of a tree called ponticum – a kind of cherry – which is about the size of a fig-tree and produces a stoned fruit as large as a bean. They strain the ripe fruit through cloths and get from it a thick dark-coloured juice which they call *aschy*. They lap the juice up with their tongues, or mix it with milk for a drink, and make cakes out of the thick sediment which it leaves. They have but few sheep, as the grazing is poor. Every man lives under his ponticum-tree, which he protects in winter with bands of thick white felt, taking them off in the summer. These people are supposed to be protected by a mysterious sort of sanctity; they carry no arms and nobody offers them violence; they settle disputes amongst their neighbours, and anybody who seeks asylum amongst them is left in peace. They are called Argippaei.

24   As for the bald men, a great deal is known of the country and of the people to the south and west from the reports, which are easy enough to come by, of Scythians who visit them, and of Greeks who frequent the trading port on the Dnieper and other ports along the Black Sea coast. The Scythians who penetrate as far as this do their business through seven interpreters in seven

25 languages. Beyond the Argippaei, however, lies a region of which no one can give an accurate account, for further progress is barred by a lofty and impassable range of mountains. The bald men themselves tell the tale (which I do not believe) that the mountains are inhabited by a goat-footed race, beyond which, still further north, are men who sleep for six months in the year – which to my mind is utterly incredible.[7] East of the Argippaei, however, the country is definitely known to be inhabited by the Issedones; but the region north of those two nations is unknown, apart from the stories they themselves tell of it.

26   Some knowledge of the customs of the Issedones has come through to us: when a man's father dies, his kinsmen bring sheep to his house as a sacrificial offering; the sheep and the body of the dead man are cut into joints and sliced up, and the two sorts of meat, mixed together, are served and eaten. The dead man's

head, however, they gild, after stripping off the hair and cleaning out the inside, and then preserve it as a sort of sacred image, to which they offer sacrifice. Son does this to father, just as the Greeks observe ancestral commemoration.

In other respects the Issedones appear to have a sound sense of justice and among them men and women have equal authority. It is amongst the Issedones themselves that the strange tales of the distant north originate – tales of the one-eyed men and the griffins which guard the gold – and the Scythians have passed them on to the rest of us, which explains why we call the one-eyed men by the Scythian name of Arimaspians – *arima* being the Scythian word for 'one', and *spu* for 'eye'.

The whole region I have been describing has excessively hard winters; for eight months in the year the cold is intolerable; the ground is frozen iron-hard, so that to turn earth into mud requires not water but fire. The sea freezes over, and the whole of the Cimmerian Bosphorus; and the Scythians, who live outside the trench which I mentioned previously, make war upon the ice, and drive waggons across it to the country of the Sindi. Even apart from the eight months' winter, the remaining four months are cold; and a further point of difference between the winters here and in all other parts of the world is that here, in Scythia, no rain worth mentioning falls during the season when one would naturally expect it, whereas throughout the summer it never stops. There are no thunderstorms during what is the usual season for them elsewhere, but only in the summer, when they are very violent; a winter thunderstorm is looked upon as a prodigy, as are earthquakes whether in summer or winter. Horses stand the winter well, but mules and donkeys cannot stand it at all; this is unusual, for elsewhere mules and donkeys bear cold easily, but horses kept standing during hard weather, are subject to frostbite. I think the cold may explain the fact that the cattle in this part of the world have no horns: a verse in Homer's *Odyssey* supports this view, where the poet speaks of

Libya, where horns grow quickly on the foreheads of lambs,

a sensible remark, indicating that a hot climate favours the rapid growth of horns; whereas in severe cold cattle do not grow them at all, or hardly at all.[8]

30   A remarkable fact occurs to me (I need not apologize for the digression – it has been my habit throughout this work) that mules cannot be bred in Elis, though Elis is not a cold place, and there is apparently nothing else to account for it. The people there say it is the result of some curse or other. Their practice is to wait for the breeding season and drive their mares over the border, and put the donkeys to them in their neighbours' land; then, when they are pregnant, they drive them home again.

31   About the feathers which the Scythians say fill the air, and make it impossible to traverse, or even to see, the more northerly parts of the continent – I think myself that it must be always snowing in those northerly regions, though less, probably, in summer than in winter. Anyone who has seen heavy snow at close quarters will know what I mean – it is very like feathers; and it is because of the severity of these northern winters that the country is uninhabited. No doubt the Scythians and their neighbours when they talk of the feathers really mean snow – because of the likeness between the two. I have now related the utmost which can be gathered from report.

32   Of the Hyperboreans we get no information from the Scythians or anyone else in that part of the world, except, perhaps, from the Issedones. Not that the Issedones really tell us anything, in my opinion; for if they did, we should have it from the Scythians too, like the story of the one-eyed men. There is, however, a mention of the Hyperboreans in Hesiod, and in Homer's *Epigoni* – if, indeed, Homer was the author of that

33   poem.[9] But the people who tell us by far the most about them are the Delians; for, according to them, certain sacred offerings wrapped up in wheat-straw come from the Hyperboreans into Scythia, whence they are taken over by the neighbouring peoples in succession until they get as far west as the Adriatic; from there they are sent south, and the first Greeks to receive them are the Dodonaeans. Then, continuing southward, they reach the Malian gulf, cross to Euboea, and are passed on from town to town as far as Carystus. Then they skip Andros, the

Carystians take them to Tenos, and the Tenians to Delos. That
is how these things are said to reach Delos at the present time;
but on the first occasion they were sent in charge of two girls,
whose names the Delians say were Hyperoche and Laodice. To
protect the girls on the journey, the Hyperboreans sent five men
to accompany them – the people now known as 'Perpherees',
and greatly honoured in Delos. Later, however, when the Hyperboreans found that their messengers did not return, they
changed their plan, and, disliking the idea that they might always
lose whoever it was that they sent away on this long journey,
began the practice of wrapping the offerings in straw and taking
them to the border, with instructions to their neighbours to see
them conveyed to their destination by a process of relay, from
one nation to another. And that is how they arrive in Delos
today. I know of something similar to this in Thrace and
Paeonia: the women there, in their sacrifices to Artemis the
Queen, always bring wheat-straw with their offerings.

The two Hyperborean girls died in Delos, and the boys and   34
girls of the island still cut their hair as a sign of mourning for
them – the girls, before they marry, cutting off a lock, which
they twist round a spindle and lay upon the tomb (it stands on
the left, as one enters the temple of Artemis, and has an olive
growing on it); the boys twisting a strand of hair round a new
shoot from some plant which, like the girls, they too lay on the
tomb. There is also a Delphic story that before the time of   35
Hyperoche and Laodice, two other Hyperborean girls, Arge and
Opis, came to Delos by the same route. Hyperoche and Laodice
came to bring to Eileithyia, who presides over childbirth, the
thank-offering which they had promised for easy labour, but
Arge and Opis came to the island at the same time as Apollo
and Artemis, and are therefore honoured in a different way; for
the women of Delos make collections for them, and name them
in the hymn which Olen of Lycia wrote in their honour – a
ceremony which the other islanders, and the Ionians too, have
learned from the women of Delos; Olen of Lycia was also the
author of the other ancient hymns which are sung in Delos. The
ashes from the thigh-bones burnt upon the altar are all scattered
upon the tomb of Opis and Arge, where it stands behind the

temple of Artemis, facing east, close to the banqueting-hall of the Ceians.

36   So much, then, for the Hyperboreans; for I will not tell the tale of Abaris, who was supposed to have been a Hyperborean, and carried his arrow all round the world without eating a bite. Let me just add, however, that, if Hyperboreans exist 'beyond the north-wind' there must also be Hypernotians 'beyond the south'.

I cannot help laughing at the absurdity of all the map-makers – there are plenty of them – who show Ocean running like a river round a perfectly circular earth, with Asia and Europe of the same size.[10] Let me spend a few words in giving a proper

37   notion of the size and shape of these two continents. Persian territory extends southward to the Red Sea, as it is called; north of them are the Medes, then the Saspires, then the Colchians, who go as far as the northern sea, where the mouth of the Phasis is. These four nations fill the area between the Black Sea and

38   the Persian Gulf. Thence run westward two great continental promontories, one of which stretches from the Phasis on the north along the Black Sea and the Hellespont to the Mediterranean at Sigeum in the Troad, and again, in the south, along the Mediterranean coast from the Myriandic gulf, near Phoenicia, to Cape Triopium. This branch of the continent contains

39   thirty different nations. The other starts from Persia, and embraces successively Persia, Assyria, and Arabia, and ends – conventionally – at the Arabian gulf,[11] which Darius connected by canal with the Nile. Between Persia and Phoenicia lies a very large area of country; and from Phoenicia the branch I am speaking of runs along the Mediterranean coast through Palestine-Syria to Egypt, where it ends. It contains three nations

40   only. Such is Asia from Persia westward; eastward, beyond Media and the territories of the Saspires and Colchians, lies the Red Sea and, at the northern limit, the Caspian Sea and the river Araxes, which flows eastwards. Asia is inhabited as far as India; further east the country is uninhabited, and nobody knows what

41   it is like. Such, then, are the shape and size of Asia. Libya is a part of the second branch I mentioned, for it adjoins Egypt; Egypt itself forms a narrow neck, only about 120 miles across

from the Mediterranean to the Red Sea; but it soon broadens
out, and what is known as Libya covers a very large area.

In view of what I have said, I cannot but be surprised at   42
the method of mapping Libya, Asia, and Europe. The three
continents do, in fact, differ very greatly in size. Europe is as
long as the other two put together, and for breadth is not, in my
opinion, even to be compared with them. As for Libya, we know
that it is washed on all sides by the sea except where it joins
Asia, as was first demonstrated, so far as our knowledge goes,
by the Egyptian king Neco, who, after calling off the construction of the canal between the Nile and the Arabian gulf, sent
out a fleet manned by a Phoenician crew with orders to sail
round and return to Egypt and the Mediterranean by way of
the Pillars of Heracles. The Phoenicians sailed from the Red Sea
into the southern ocean, and every autumn put in where they
were on the Libyan coast, sowed a patch of ground, and waited
for next year's harvest. Then, having got in their grain, they put
to sea again, and after two full years rounded the Pillars of
Heracles in the course of the third, and returned to Egypt. These
men made a statement which I do not myself believe, though
others may, to the effect that as they sailed on a westerly course
round the southern end of Libya, they had the sun on their right
– to northward of them.[12] This is how Libya was first discovered   43
to be surrounded by sea, and the next people to make a similar
report were the Carthaginians; for Sataspes, son of Teaspes, the
Achaemenian, though sent out for the purpose, took fright at
the length and loneliness of the voyage and turned back. It was
Sataspes' mother who sent him upon this venture; he had raped
a daughter of Megabyzus' son Zopyrus, and was about to be
impaled as a punishment by Xerxes, when his mother, who was
a sister of Darius, begged him off by promising to inflict upon
him a punishment even more severe; this was to force him to
circumnavigate Libya, returning by way of the Arabian gulf.
Xerxes agreed; and Sataspes, on his arrival in Egypt, procured
a vessel and crew and sailed to the Straits of Gibraltar. Passing
through the Straits, he doubled Cape Soloeis in Libya and continued on a southerly course for many months; but when he
found that, far though he had sailed, there was always need to

sail further yet, he put about and returned to Egypt. From Egypt he went to Xerxes' court, where he reported that at the most southerly point they had reached they found the coast occupied by small men, who wore clothes made from palm leaves.[13] When they landed, the small men used to abandon their settlements and escape to the hills. Sataspes' men had done them no harm, beyond entering their villages and taking some of their cattle. As to his failure to complete the circumnavigation, Sataspes declared that the reason was that his ship was brought to a standstill and was unable to make headway. Xerxes, however, refused to pardon him, and, on the ground that he had failed to accomplish his set task, exacted the original penalty and had him impaled. A eunuch in Sataspes' service, when he learned of his master's death, escaped to Samos with a great deal of money. It was all seized, however, by a certain Samian, whose name I willingly forget – though I know it well.

44   The greater part of Asia was discovered by Darius. He wanted to find out where the Indus joins the sea – the Indus is the only river other than the Nile where crocodiles are found – and for this purpose sent off on an expedition down the river a number of men whose word he could trust. Led by a Caryandian named Scylax, the expedition sailed from Caspatyrus in the district of Pactyica, following the course of the river eastward until it reached the sea; then, turning westward, the ships followed the coast, and after a voyage of some thirty months reached the place from which the king of Egypt had sent out the Phoenicians, whom I have already mentioned, to circumnavigate Libya. After this voyage was completed, Darius subdued the Indians and made regular use of the southern ocean. In this way all Asia, with the exception of the easterly part, has been proved to be surrounded by sea, and so to have a general geographical resemblance to Libya.

45   With Europe, however, the case is different; for no one has ever determined whether or not there is sea either to the east or to the north of it; all we know is that in length it is equal to Asia and Libya combined. Another thing that puzzles me is why three distinct women's names should have been given to what is really a single land-mass; and why, too, the Nile and the Phasis – or,

according to some, the Maeotic Tanais and the Cimmerian Strait – should have been fixed upon for the boundaries. Nor have I been able to learn who it was that first marked the boundaries, or where they got the names from. Most Greeks assume that Libya was so called after a native woman and that Asia was named after the wife of Prometheus; the Lydians, however, claim the latter name for themselves, and say that Asia was named not after the wife of Prometheus, but after Asies, the son of Cotys and grandson of Manes, who passed it on besides to the tribe called Asias in Sardis. As for Europe, nobody knows if it is surrounded by sea, or where it got its name from, or who gave it, unless we are to say that it came from Europa, the Tyrian woman, and before that was nameless like the rest. This, however, is unlikely; for Europa was an Asiatic and never visited the country which we now call Europe, but only sailed from Phoenicia to Crete and from Crete to Lycia. But that is quite enough on this subject – and in any case I shall continue to use the names which custom has made familiar.

Round the Black Sea – the scene of Darius' campaign – are to 46 be found, if we except Scythia, the most unlearned nations in the world. For we can put forward no nation of those on the Black Sea renowned for wisdom, nor do we know any man of repute, except Scythes and Anacharsis. The Scythians, however, though in other respects I do not admire them, have managed one thing, and that the most important in human affairs, better than anyone else on the face of the earth: I mean their own preservation. For such is their manner of life that no one who invades their country can escape destruction, and if they wish to avoid engaging with an enemy, that enemy cannot by any possibility come to grips with them. A people without fortified towns, living, as the Scythians do, in waggons which they take with them wherever they go, accustomed, one and all, to fight on horseback with bows and arrows, and dependent for their food not upon agriculture but upon their cattle: how can such a people fail to defeat the attempt of an invader not only to subdue them, but even to make contact with them? They have 47 been helped in this by the nature of their country and by the rivers which it contains, the land consisting of a rich and well-

watered plain, with excellent pasture, and the rivers being
almost as numerous as canals are in Egypt. The best known of
the rivers, those, namely, which are navigable by sea-going
ships, I will mention: they are the Danube which has five mouths,
the Tyras, the Hypanis, the Borysthenes, the Panticapes, Hypa-
48 cyris, Gerrhus, and Tanais. The Danube, which is the mightiest
river of those we know, and never varies, summer or winter, in
the volume of its waters, is the most westerly of the Scythian
rivers, and owes its great size to the tributary streams which
join it. Of these tributaries, five are genuine Scythian rivers and
have their source in the country: namely, the Pyretus (or Porata,
as the Scythians call it), the Tiarantus, the Araros, the Naparis,
and the Ordessus. The first of these – a big river – is the most
easterly of the five; the second, the Tiarantus, is smaller and
further to the west, while the Araros, the Naparis, and the
Ordessus join the Danube somewhere between the two. In
addition to the tributaries which can properly be called Scythian,
there are also many others: the Maris, flowing from the country
49 of the Agathyrsi; three large rivers, the Atlas, the Auras, and the
Tibisis, which flow with a northerly course from the heights of
Haemus; the Athrys, the Noes, and the Artanes from Thrace
and the country of the tribe of Thracians called Crobyzi; the
Scios, flowing from Paeonia and Mt Rhodope through the
Haemus mountains; the Angrus, running northward from Illyria
through the Triballian plain, to join the Brongus, thus making
two more, both of considerable size; the Carpis and the Alpis,
flowing northward, too, from the country beyond the Umbri-
ans.[14] All these rivers discharge into the Danube, which, rising
amongst the Celts, the most westerly, after the Cynetes, of all
European nations, traverses the whole length of the continent
50 before it enters Scythia. No wonder that with all the tributaries
I have mentioned, and many others besides, the Danube is the
greatest of rivers – though if we discount the tributaries and
compare the single stream of the Danube with the single stream
of the Nile, the latter is the greater of the two; for no river, or
even rivulet, flows into the Nile to increase its volume. The fact
that the height of the Danube remains constant summer and
winter, I think I can explain in the following way: in winter the

volume of water is normal, or slightly above normal, for though there is much snow, the rainfall is negligible; but in summer the great mass of the previous winter's snow melts, and the water from it, pouring into the river, combined with frequent heavy rains – which at this season are common – increases its volume. So though there is more evaporation in summer than in winter, the effect of it is offset by the increased volume of the tributary streams; thus a balance is produced, and the level of water is kept constant, throughout the year.

The next river, the Tyras, runs southward from its source in 51 a large lake, which forms the boundary between Scythia and the country of the Neuri. Greeks called Tyritae have established a settlement at its mouth. The third river, the Hypanis, has its 52 source in Scythia, in another great lake, round the borders of which wild white horses graze. The lake is called – very properly – the Mother of Hypanis. Five days' sail from the lake the water continues fresh and shallow; but thence on towards the sea, a distance of four days' journey, it is excessively salt; the sudden change is caused by a spring which here joins the river and is so salt that, though it is quite small, it taints the entire volume of water – and the Hypanis is a pretty big stream. The spring, or rivulet, rises where the territory of the Scythian agricultural tribes borders on that of the Alizones; its name, and the name of the place in the immediate neighbourhood of its source, is in the Scythian language Exampaeus, which might be rendered in Greek as 'Sacred Ways'. The Tyras and the Hypanis draw close together in the country of the Alizones, but afterwards diverge, leaving a wider and wider space between them.

The Borysthenes, the second largest of the Scythian rivers, is, 53 in my opinion, the most valuable and productive not only of the rivers in this part of the world, but anywhere else, with the sole exception of the Nile – with which none can be compared. It provides the finest and most abundant pasture, by far the richest supply of the best sorts of fish, and the most excellent water for drinking – clear and bright, whereas that of other rivers in the vicinity is turbid; no better crops grow anywhere than along its banks, and where grain is not sown the grass is the most luxuri-ant in the world. An unlimited supply of salt is formed by natural processes at the mouth of the river, which also produces a very large spineless fish, good for pickling and known locally as *antacaeus*, and a number of other most remarkable things. The course of the river is southerly, and it is known as far as the place called Gerrhus, forty days' voyage up; beyond that, nobody can say through what countries it flows. We do know, however, that it enters the territory of the agricultural Scythians after crossing an uninhabited region; for these Scythians live along its banks as far as would take a boat ten days to cover. This river and the Nile are the only ones of which I do not know the source; nor, I think, does any other Greek. Not far from the sea the Borysthenes and Hypanis unite and flow through low-lying marsh-country, and the pointed spit of land between them is called Cape Hippolaus; there is a temple of Demeter upon it, and opposite the temple, on the Hypanis, is the settlement of the Borysthenites.

54   The fifth river, the Panticapes, also rises in a lake and flows in a southerly direction through Hylaea – the Woodland – to join the Borysthenes. The country between it and the Borysthenes is
55   occupied by the Scythian agricultural tribes. The Hypacyris, the sixth river, flows from a lake right through the territory of the Scythian nomads, and reaches the sea near Carcinitis, leaving Hylaea and the place called Achilles' Racecourse to the right.
56   The Gerrhus splits off from the Borysthenes, far to the north at a spot which goes by the same name and lies somewhere about the region where the Borysthenes begins to be known. It forms the boundary between the Nomad and the Royal Scythians, and
57   runs into the Hypacyris. The eighth river, the Tanais, has its source far up country in a large lake, and empties itself into a larger one still, Lake Maeotis. It divides the Royal Scythians from the Sauromatae, and is joined by yet another river, the
58   Hyrgis. These, then, are the most notable of the rivers with which Scythia is provided. The grass which grows hereabouts is more apt to cause bile in cattle than any other we know of, as can be seen plainly enough when the carcasses are cut open.

59   Having described the natural resources of the country, I will go on to give some account of the people's customs and beliefs. The only gods the Scythians worship are Hestia (their chief

deity), Zeus, and Earth (whom they believe to be the wife of Zeus), and, as deities of secondary importance, Apollo, Celestial Aphrodite, Heracles, and Ares. These are recognized by the entire nation; the Royal Scythians also offer sacrifice to Poseidon. In the Scythian language Hestia is *Tabiti*, Zeus (very properly, in my opinion) *Papaeus*,[15] Earth *Api*, Apollo *Oetosyrus*, Celestial Aphrodite *Argimpasa*, Poseidon *Thagimasadas*.

It is not their custom to make statues, or to build altars and temples, in honour of any god except Ares. The method of sacrifice is everywhere and in every case the same: the victim has its front feet tied together, and the person who is performing the ceremony gives a pull on the rope from behind and throws the animal down, calling, as he does so, upon the name of the appropriate god; then he slips a noose round the victim's neck, pushes a short stick under the cord and twists it until the creature is choked. No fire is lighted; there is no offering of first-fruits, and no libation. As soon as the animal is strangled, he is skinned, and then comes the boiling of the flesh. This has called for a little inventiveness, because there is no wood in Scythia to make a fire with; the method the natives adopt after skinning the animal is to strip the flesh from the bones and put it into a cauldron – if, that is, they happen to possess one: these cauldrons are made in the country, and resemble Lesbian mixing-bowls in shape, though they are much larger – and then make a fire of the bones underneath it. In the absence of a cauldron, they put all the flesh into the animal's paunch, mix water with it, and boil it like that over the bone-fire. The bones burn very well, and the paunch easily contains all the meat once it has been stripped off. In this way an ox, or any other sacrificial beast, is ingeniously made to boil itself. When the meat is cooked, the sacrificer offers a portion of both flesh and entrails by throwing it on the ground in front of him. All sorts of cattle are offered in sacrifice, but most commonly horses.

Ceremonies in honour of Ares are conducted differently. In every district, at the seat of government, Ares has his temple; it is of a peculiar kind, and consists of an immense heap of brushwood, three furlongs each way and somewhat less in height. On top the heap is levelled off square, like a platform,

60

61

62

accessible on one side but rising sheer on the other three. Every year a hundred and fifty waggon-loads of sticks are added to the pile, to make up for the constant settling caused by rains, and on the top of it is planted an ancient iron scimitar, which serves for the image of Ares. Annual sacrifices of horses and other cattle are made to this scimitar, which, indeed, claims a greater number of victims than any other of their gods. Prisoners of war are also sacrificed to Ares, but in their case the ceremony is different from that which is used in the sacrifice of animals: one man is chosen out of every hundred; wine is poured on his head, and his throat cut over a bowl; the bowl is then carried to the platform on top of the woodpile, and the blood in it poured out over the scimitar. While this goes on above, another ceremony is being enacted below, close against the pile: this consists in cutting off the right hands and arms of the prisoners who have been slaughtered, and tossing them into the air. This done, and the rest of the ceremony over, the worshippers go away. The victims' arms and hands are left to lie where they fall, separate from the trunks. They never use pigs for sacrifice and will not even breed them anywhere in the country.

63

64   As regards war, the Scythian custom is for every man to drink the blood of the first man he kills. The heads of all enemies killed in battle are taken to the king; if he brings a head, a soldier is admitted to his share of the loot; no head, no loot. He strips the skin off the head by making a circular cut round the ears and shaking out the skull; he then scrapes the flesh off the skin with the rib of an ox, and when it is clean works it in his fingers until it is supple, and fit to be used as a sort of handkerchief. He hangs these handkerchiefs on the bridle of his horse, and is very proud of them. The best man is the man who has the greatest number. Many Scythians sew a number of scalps together and make cloaks out of them, like the ones peasants wear, and often, too, they take the skin, nails and all, off the right hands and arms of dead enemies and use it to cover their quivers with – having discovered the fact that human skin is not only tough, but white, as white as almost any skin. Sometimes they flay a whole body, and stretch the skin on a wooden frame which they carry around with them when they ride. They have a special

65

way of dealing with the actual skulls – not with all of them, but only those of their worst enemies: they saw off the part below the eyebrows, and after cleaning out what remains stretch a piece of rawhide round it on the outside. If a man is poor, he is content with that, but a rich man goes further and gilds the inside of the skull as well. In either case the skull is then used to drink from. They treat the skulls of their kinsmen in the same way, in cases where quarrels have occurred and a man has been beaten in fight in the presence of the king. When important visitors arrive, these skulls are passed round and the host tells the story of them: how they were once his relatives and made war against him, and how he defeated them – all of which passes for a proof of courage. Once a year the governor of each district 66 mixes a bowl of wine, from which every Scythian who has killed his man in battle has the right to drink. Those who have no dead enemy to their credit are not allowed to touch the wine, but have to sit by themselves in disgrace – the worst, indeed, which they can suffer. Any man, on the contrary, who has killed a great many enemies, has two cups and drinks from both of them at once.

There are many soothsayers in Scythia, and their method is 67 to work with willow rods. They bring great bundles of them, which they put down on the ground; then they untie them, lay out each rod separately, and pronounce their prophecy. While they are speaking it, they collect the rods into a bundle again as before. This is the native mode of divination in Scythia; but the women-men, called 'Enarees', use a different method, which they say was taught them by Aphrodite: these people take a piece of the inner bark of the lime-tree and cut it into three pieces, which they keep twisting and untwisting round their fingers as they prophesy.[16]

When the king of Scythia falls sick, he sends for three of the 68 most reputable soothsayers, who proceed to practise their arts in the way I have described; more often than not they declare that such and such a person (whose name they mention) has sworn falsely by the king's hearth – it being customary in Scythia to use this form of oath for the most solemn purposes. The supposed culprit is at once arrested and brought into the king's presence, where he is charged by the soothsayers, who tell him that their powers of divination have revealed that he has sworn by the king's hearth and perjured himself, and that his perjury is the cause of the king's sickness. The man, of course, denies the charge, and makes a great fuss, whereupon the king sends for more soothsayers – six this time instead of three – who also bring their skill to bear. Should they convict the accused of perjury, he is beheaded without more ado, and his property is divided by lot amongst the first three soothsayers; if, however, the new six acquit him, more are brought in, and, if need be, still more again, and if, in the final result, the majority declare for the man's innocence, the law is that the three original ones

69   should be executed. The method of execution is this: a cart is filled with sticks and harnessed to oxen; the guilty men, gagged and bound hand and foot, are thrust down amongst the sticks, which are then set alight, and the oxen scared off at a run. Often the oxen are burnt to death together with the soothsayers; often, too, the pole of the cart is burnt through soon enough to allow them to escape with a scorching. Peccant soothsayers – 'lying prophets' as they are called – are burnt to death in this way for other crimes besides the one I have described. When the king orders an execution, he does not allow the soothsayer's sons to survive him: all males are put to death, but not the females, who are in no way harmed.

70   When Scythians swear an oath or make a solemn compact, they fill a large earthenware bowl with wine and drop into it a little of the blood of the two parties to the oath, having drawn it either by a prick with an awl or a slight cut with a knife; then they dip into the bowl a scimitar, some arrows, a battle-axe, and a javelin, and speak a number of prayers; lastly, the two contracting parties and their chief followers drink the mixture of wine and blood.

71   The burial-place of the Scythian kings is in the country of the Gerrhi, near the spot where the Borysthenes first becomes navigable.[17] When a king dies, they dig a great square pit, and when it is ready, they take up the corpse, which has been previously prepared in the following way: the belly is slit open, cleaned out, and filled with various aromatic substances,

crushed galingale, parsley-seed, and anise; it is then sewn up again and the whole body coated over with wax. In this condition it is carried in a waggon to a neighbouring tribe within the Scythian dominions, and then on to another, taking the various tribes in turn; and in the course of its progress, the people who success-ively receive it, follow the custom of the Royal Scythians and cut a piece from their ears, shave their hair, make circular incisions on their arms, gash their foreheads and noses, and thrust arrows through their left hands. On each stage of the journey those who have already been visited join the procession, until at last the funeral cortège, after passing through every part of the Scythian dominions, finds itself at the place of burial amongst the Gerrhi, the most northerly and remote of Scythian tribes. Here the corpse is laid in the tomb on a mattress, with spears fixed in the ground on either side to support a roof of withies laid on wooden poles, while in other parts of the great square pit various members of the king's household are buried beside him: one of his concubines, his butler, his cook, his groom, his steward, and his chamberlain – all of them strangled. Horses are buried too, and gold cups (the Scythians do not use silver or bronze), and a selection of his other treasures. This ceremony over, everybody with great enthusiasm sets about raising a mound of earth, each competing with his neighbour to make it as big as possible. At the end of a year another ceremony 72 takes place: they take fifty of the best of the king's remaining servants, strangle and gut them, stuff the bodies with chaff, and sew them up again – these servants are native Scythians, for the king has no bought slaves, but chooses people to serve him from amongst his subjects. Fifty of the finest horses are then subjected to the same treatment. The next step is to cut a number of wheels in half and to fix them in pairs, rim-downwards, to stakes driven into the ground, two stakes to each half-wheel; then stout poles are driven lengthwise through the horses from tail to neck, and by means of these the horses are mounted on the wheels, in such a way that the front pairs support the shoulders and the rear pairs the belly between the thighs. All four legs are left dangling clear of the ground. Each horse is bitted and bridled, the bridle being led forward and pegged down. The bodies of the men are dealt with in a similar way: straight poles are driven up through the neck, parallel with the spine, and the lower protruding ends fitted into sockets in the stakes which run through the horses; thus each horse is provided with one of the young servants to ride him. When horses and riders are all in place around the tomb, they are left there, and the mourners go away. When an ordinary person dies, the nearest relatives lay the corpse in a cart and take it round to visit their friends. The various families in turn entertain their guests to a meal, and serve the corpse with food just like the rest. The round of visits lasts forty days, and then the body is buried. After a burial the Scythians go through a process of cleaning themselves; they wash their heads with soap, and their bodies in a vapour-bath, the nature of which I will describe. On a framework of three sticks, meeting at the top, they stretch pieces of woollen cloth, taking care to get the joins as perfect as they can, and inside this little tent they put a dish with red-hot stones in it. Now, hemp grows in Scythia, a plant resembling flax, but much coarser and taller. It grows wild as well as under cultivation, and the Thracians make clothes from it very like linen ones – indeed, one must have much experience in these matters to be able to distinguish between the two, and anybody who has never seen a piece of cloth made from hemp, will suppose it to be of linen. They take some hemp seed, creep into the tent, and throw the seed on to the hot stones. At once it begins to smoke, giving off a vapour unsurpassed by any vapour-bath one could find in Greece. The Scythians enjoy it so much that they howl with pleasure.[18] This is their substitute for an ordinary bath in water, which they never use. The women grind up cypress, cedar, and frankincense on a rough stone, mix the powder into a thick paste with a little water, and plaster it all over their bodies and faces. They leave it on for a day, and then, when they remove it, their skin is clean, glossy, and fragrant.

Like the Egyptians, the Scythians are dead-set against foreign ways, especially against Greek ways. An illustration of this is what happened to Anacharsis – and, later, to Scylas.[19] The former was a great traveller, and a man of great and varied knowledge; he had given proof of this in many parts of the world, and was on his way home to Scythia when, as he was passing through the Hellespont, he broke his journey at Cyzicus. Finding the people of this town engaged in celebrating a magnificent festival in honour of the Mother of the Gods, Anacharsis made a vow that, if he got home safe and sound, he would himself celebrate a night-festival and offer sacrifice to this goddess in exactly the same way as he had seen it done at Cyzicus.[20] On his arrival in Scythia, he entered the Woodland – that forest of all sorts of trees, which lies near Achilles' Racecourse – and, according to his promise, went through the ceremony with all the proper rites and observances, drum in hand and the images fastened to his clothing. He happened to be noticed by some Scythian or other, who at once went and told Saulius, the king; Saulius then came in person, and, seeing Anacharsis occupied with these outlandish rites, drew his bow and shot him dead. Today, if anyone asks about Anacharsis, the Scythians say they never heard of him – all because he travelled abroad into Greece and adopted foreign practices. But as I was told by Tymnes, the agent of Ariapithes, Anacharsis was the uncle of the Scythian king Idanthyrsus, and son of Gnurus, grandson of Lycus, and great-grandson of Spargapithes. If he was really a member of this family, he must have been killed by his own brother; for Idanthyrsus was a son of Saulius, and it was Saulius who shot him. There is also a different story about Anacharsis which I 77 have heard in the Peloponnese; according to this, he was sent abroad by the king of Scythia to find out what he could about Greece, and told the king on his return that all the Greeks were too busy to study any branch of learning, with the sole exception of the Lacedaemonians, who were the only ones to be able to keep up a sensible conversation. This story, however, is only a frivolous Greek invention; the plain truth is that Anacharsis was killed in the way I have described, for associating with Greeks and adopting foreign ways.

Many years later Scylas came to grief in a similar manner. He 78 was one of the sons of the Scythian king Ariapithes, and his mother, who was not a native woman but came from Istria, taught him to speak and read Greek. As time went on, Ariapithes was treacherously murdered by Spargapithes, the king of the Agathyrsi, and Scylas succeeded to the throne and married Opoea, his father's wife. This woman was a native of Scythia, and Ariapithes had a son by her, named Oricus. During his reign, Scylas, as a result of the education his mother had given him, found himself discontented with the traditional way of life in Scythia, and powerfully attracted by Greek ideas. Whenever, therefore, he went with his army to the Greek settlement of the Borysthenites – these people claim to have come originally from Miletus – his custom was to leave his men outside the wall and enter the town himself. Then, when the gates were barred behind him, and the townspeople on the watch to prevent any of the Scythians seeing what he was up to, he would change into Greek clothes, stroll about the streets without any sort of bodyguard or personal attendant, take part in religious ceremonies and behave in every way just as if he were a Greek himself. Often a month or more would go by, before he would change back into his Scythian clothes and leave for home. He was constantly doing this, and even built himself a house there, and married a woman from the neighbourhood to look after it for him. He was destined, however, to come to a bad end, as the sequel will show. It happened one day that Scylas conceived the desire to be initiated into the mysteries of Dionysus, and just as he was on the point of beginning the ritual, a great portent occurred: the house I mentioned, which he had built in the city – it was a very large and expensive building, set about with marble sphinxes and griffins – was struck from heaven by a thunderbolt and burnt to the ground. In spite of this, however, Scylas carried through the ceremony of initiation.

Now the Greek custom of celebrating Dionysiac rites is, in Scythian eyes, a shameful thing; and no Scythian can see sense in imagining a god who drives people out of their wits. On this occasion, therefore, at the initiation of Scylas, one of the Borysthenites slipped away and told the Scythians, who were waiting outside the town, of what was going on. 'You laugh at us,' he said, 'for being possessed by the spirit of Dionysus when we celebrate his rites. Well, this same spirit has now taken hold of your own king; he is under its influence – Dionysus has driven him mad. If you don't believe it, come along and I will let you see for yourselves.' The chief Scythians present accepted the offer, and the man took them secretly to the top of a high building, from which they could get a good view of what was happening in the streets. Presently a party of revellers came by, with Scylas amongst them; and when the Scythians saw their king in the grip of the Bacchic frenzy, they were profoundly disturbed and, returning to the army, let every man know of the disgraceful spectacle they had witnessed. Later, when Scylas 80 was at home again, the Scythians put themselves under the protection of his brother Octamasades, the son of Teres' daughter, and rose in rebellion, and Scylas himself, when he learnt what was afoot and understood the reason for it, fled the country and took refuge in Thrace. Octamasades started in pursuit at the head of an army, and was opposed by the Thracian forces on the Ister; but before the battle could begin, Sitalces[21] sent a message in the following terms: 'There is really no need for us to begin hostilities. You are my sister's son, and my brother is with you' (this, I should mention, was the truth: Sitalces' brother had fled from Thrace and was living with Octamasades). 'Give me back my brother, and I will do the same with Scylas; then neither of us need risk his army in an engagement.' Octamasades agreed to the proposal and the exchange was effected, where-upon Sitalces went off with his brother, and Octamasades, there and then, had Scylas beheaded. These two stories will show the importance which the Scythians attach to their national traditions, and the severity of the punishments they inflict upon anyone who introduces alien customs.

I was never able to learn exactly what the population of 81 Scythia is. The reports I have heard are not consistent, some putting it very high, others comparatively low – considering, that is, the power and importance of Scythia. They did, however, actually show me something, which gave me a notion of their numbers: between the rivers Borysthenes and Hypanis there is a place called Exampaeus, which I mentioned a little further back in connexion with the salt spring which rises there and makes the water of the Hypanis undrinkable. In this place there stands a brazen bowl, six times as big as the one which was set up as a dedicatory offering at the entrance to the Black Sea by Pausanias, son of Cleombrotus.[22] Anyone who has not seen Pausanias' bowl will understand me better if I say that the Scythian bowl can easily hold 5000 gallons and is of metal about four inches thick. The people of the district told me that this huge vessel was made out of arrowheads; for one of their kings, named Ariantes, wishing to know how many men there were in Scythia, gave orders that each of them should bring him a single arrowhead, failure to do so being punishable by death. An enormous number were brought, and Ariantes decided to turn them into something which might serve as a permanent record. The result was the brazen bowl, which he set up at Exampaeus.[23]

82   Scythia has few really remarkable features, except its rivers, which are more numerous, and bigger, than anywhere else in the world. There is, however, one other interesting thing besides the rivers and the vast extent of the plains – a footprint left by Heracles. The natives show this to visitors on a rock by the river Tyras. It is like a man's footprint, but is three feet long. I must now leave this subject and get back to the story which I set out to tell.

83   While Darius was preparing his invasion of Scythia, and sending messengers to every part of his dominions with orders to raise troops here, ships there, and labourers somewhere else to work on the bridge over the Bosphorus, his brother Artabanus did his utmost to make him abandon the enterprise, on the ground that the Scythians were such difficult people to get at. Good though the advice was, it had no effect upon Darius; Artabanus, son of Hystaspes, stopped trying to persuade him, and Darius completed his preparations and marched from Susa

84   at the head of his army. A Persian named Oeobazus, who had three sons, all of them in the army, asked Darius to let one of them stay behind, and Darius, as if in answer to a modest request from a personal friend, said he would willingly leave all three. Oeobazus, supposing his sons to be excused service, was delighted, but the king ordered his officers to put the three young men to death. So they were indeed left behind – with their throats cut.

Darius continued his march from Susa to Chalcedon on the   85
Bosphorus, where the bridge was, and then took ship and sailed
to the Cyanean rocks – those rocks which according to the
Greek story used to be constantly changing their position.[24]
Here, seated in the temple which stands by the straits, he looked
out over the Black Sea – a sight indeed worth seeing. No sea is
as marvellous as the Black Sea; it is 1380 miles long, and 410
wide in its widest part. Its mouth is half a mile wide, and the
length of the Bosphorus, the narrow strait which leads into it
(and where the bridge was), is nearly fifteen miles. The Bosphorus joins the Propontis, which is about sixty miles wide and
a hundred and seventy long, and runs into the Hellespont, a
narrow strait nearly fifty miles long but less than one mile wide.
The Hellespont leads into the broad sea called the Aegean. The   86
foregoing measurements were arrived at in the following way:
in a summer day a ship can cover a distance of approximately
70,000 fathoms, and in a night 60,000. To sail from the entrance
of the Black Sea to Phasis – which represents a voyage along its
greatest length – takes nine days and eight nights; this would
make a distance of 1,110,000 fathoms, or 1380 miles.[25] Across
the broadest part, from Sindica to Themiscyra on the Thermodon, it is a voyage of three days and two nights; this comes to
330,000 fathoms, or 410 miles.

I have now given the measurements – and the method of
arriving at them – of the Black Sea, Bosphorus, and Hellespont;
it remains to add that the Black Sea is connected with a lake
nearly as big as itself, called Maeotis, or Mother of the Pontus.

When he had looked on the waters of the Black Sea, Darius   87
returned by ship to the bridge, which had been designed by a
Samian named Mandrocles. Then, after seeing what he could of
the Bosphorus, he had two marble columns erected, on one of
which was an inscription in Assyrian characters showing the
various nations which were serving on the campaign; the other
had a similar inscription in Greek. These nations were, in fact, all
over which he had dominion, and made a total force, including
cavalry but excluding the naval contingent, of 700,000 men.
There were 600 ships. Years afterwards the people of Byzantium
removed these columns and used them in their own city to build

the altar of Artemis the Protectress; a single plinth, however, covered with Assyrian characters, was left lying near the temple of Dionysus in Byzantium. I imagine, in my reckoning, that Darius' bridge was half-way between Byzantium and the temple which stands on the strait between the Bosphorus and the Black Sea.

88   Darius was so pleased with the bridge that he loaded its designer with presents, and Mandrocles spent a certain portion of what he received in having a picture painted, showing the whole process of the bridging of the strait, and Darius himself sitting on his throne, with the army crossing over. This picture he presented as a dedicatory offering to the temple of Hera, with the following verses inscribed upon it, to serve as a permanent record of his achievement:

> Goddess, accept this gift from Mandrocles,
> Who bridged the Bosphorus' fish-haunted seas.
> His labour, praised by King Darius, won
> Honour for Samos, for himself a crown.

89   Darius, having rewarded Mandrocles, then crossed over into Europe. Before he went, he gave orders to the Ionians – who, with other Greeks from Aeolia and the Hellespont, were in charge of the fleet – to sail into the Black Sea as far as the Danube, where they were to bridge the river and await his arrival. The orders were obeyed: the naval contingent, passing through the Cyanean Islands, carried right on to the Danube, sailed up the river for two days as far as the point where the main stream divides, and here built the bridge. Darius, after
90   passing over the Bosphorus bridge, marched through Thrace and stopped for three days at the source of the Tearus, a river which has the local reputation of being the best in the world for its curative properties, especially in cases of scab in both men and horses. It originates in thirty-eight separate springs, some hot, some cold, and all issuing from the same rock, which lies at a spot two days' journey both from Heraeum, near Perinthus, and from Apollonia on the Black Sea. The river is a tributary of the Contadesdus which, in its turn, joins the Agrianes, the two

streams subsequently uniting with the Hebrus, which falls into the sea near Aenus.

Darius was so greatly charmed with the Tearus, that he 91 erected another pillar close to its source with this inscription: 'The springs of the Tearus, whose water is the finest in action and noblest in appearance of all rivers, was visited in the course of his march against Scythia by Darius son of Hystaspes, finest in action and noblest in appearance of all men, King of Persia and the whole continent.'[26]

Continuing his march, Darius came to another river, the 92 Artescus, which flows through the country of the Odrysians. Here he indicated a certain spot where every man in the army was ordered to deposit a stone as he passed by. This was done, with the result that when Darius moved on he left great hills of stones behind him.

Before he reached the Danube, the first people he subdued 93 were the Getae, who believe that they never die. The Thracians of Salmydessus and those who live beyond Apollonia and Mesembria, known as the Scyrmiadae and Nipsaeans, surrendered without fighting; but the Getae, who are the most manly and law-abiding of the Thracian tribes, offered fierce resistance and were at once reduced to slavery. The belief of these people 94 in their immortality takes the following form: they never really die, but every man, when he takes leave of this present life, goes to join Salmoxis, a divine being who is also called by some of them Gebeleizis. Every five years they choose one of their number by lot and send him to Salmoxis as a messenger, with instructions to ask him for whatever they may happen to want. To effect the dispatch, some of them with three javelins in their hands arrange themselves in a suitable position, while others take hold of the messenger by his hands and feet, and swing him up into the air in such a way as to make him fall on the upturned points of the javelins. If the man is killed, they take it as a sign that Salmoxis is in a favourable mood; if he escapes, they put it down to his own bad character, tell him what they think of him, and send another messenger instead. The instructions are given to the messenger while he is still alive. This same tribe of Thracians will, during a thunderstorm, shoot arrows up into the sky, and utter threats against the lord of the lightning and the thunder, because they recognize no god but their own.

95   I myself have heard a very different account of Salmoxis from the Greeks who live on the Hellespont and the Black Sea. According to this, he was a man, and lived in Samos, where he was a slave in the household of Pythagoras, the son of Mnesarchus. He subsequently gained his freedom, amassed a fortune, and returned to his native country of Thrace, where he found the people in great poverty and ignorance. As he had gained, from living with Greeks and from his association with one of their more influential teachers, Pythagoras, an insight into Ionian ideas and a wiser way of living than was to be found in Thrace, he built himself a hall in which he used to entertain the leading men of the country with much liberality, and endeavour to teach them that neither he nor they, who were his guests, nor any of their descendants, would ever die, but would go to a place where they would live in perpetual enjoyment of every blessing. All the time that he was trying to promulgate this new doctrine, he was occupied in the construction of an underground chamber, and when it was ready he entered it and disappeared from sight. For three years he lived in this room underground, and his fellow countrymen missed him sadly, and mourned for him as if he were dead; then in the fourth year he reappeared, and in this way persuaded the Thracians that the doctrine he had taught was true. For my part I neither put entire faith in
96   this story of Salmoxis and his underground chamber, nor wholly disbelieve it; I think, however, that Salmoxis lived long before Pythagoras' time. In any case, whether there was once a man of that name, or whether he is a local god belonging to the Getae, that is enough of him.[27]

The Getae, whose practices I have described, were defeated
97   by the Persians and forced to accompany the army of Darius, who then continued his march with all his land forces to the Danube. When they had crossed the river, he ordered the Ionians to break up the bridge and join him in his march across country together with all the men from the ships. They were about to carry out this order and destroy the bridge, when Coes the son of Erxander, who was in command of the contingent from

Mytilene, obtained an interview with Darius, after first
satisfying himself that the king was willing to listen to other
people's suggestions. 'My lord,' he said, 'you are going to attack
a country without a single town in it, and no part of which is
under cultivation. Surely it would be wiser to leave this bridge
intact, and under the guard of the men who built it; for whether
we make contact with the Scythians and succeed in what we
hope to do, or not, we should then, in either case, have a safe
means of getting back by the same route. I have never been
afraid of direct defeat by the Scythians in battle; the danger, to
my mind, is rather that we should fail to find them, and that
endless and indeterminate marching in the attempt to do so
would get us into difficulty. Some may think that I make this
suggestion for my own advantage, in the hope of being left
behind to guard the bridge; but that is not true: I am merely
putting forward, my lord, what I believe to be the best plan for
you to follow, and as for myself, I have no intention of staying
here, but will accompany your army in its march.'

Darius was highly pleased with Coes' advice. 'When I am
safely home again, my Lesbian friend,' he answered, 'be sure to
come and see me, so that I may make some practical return for
your excellent counsel.' Soon after, he called a meeting of the   98
Ionian tyrants and showed them a long leather strap in which
he had tied sixty knots. 'Men of Ionia,' he said, 'my orders to
you about the bridge are now cancelled; I want you to take this
strap, and every day undo one of the knots, beginning with the
day on which you see me start my march against the Scythians.
Should I fail to return before all the knots have given out, you
are at liberty to sail home; meanwhile, in accordance with my
change of plans, guard the bridge with every possible care for
its safety. This will be the greatest service you can do me.'

After giving his new orders, Darius pressed on without further
delay.

Scythia is divided from us by Thrace, which comes down to   99
the sea. Then the coast sweeps round in a great bend where
Scythia begins and the Danube flows eastward into the sea.
I will now give some indication of the extent of the Scythian
coastline, starting from the Danube: across the Danube eastward,

ancient Scythia begins, and continues, with the Black Sea as its
southern boundary, as far as the town called Carcinitis. Then,
still on the Black Sea, the land runs out in a great mountainous
promontory and is inhabited by the Tauri, as far as what is
known as the Rugged Chersonese which comes down into the
eastern sea, Lake Maeotis. For Scythia is bounded on two sides
by two different seas, one to the south, the other to the east,
much as Attica is; and the position of the Tauri in Scythia is – if
I may compare small things with great – as if the promontory
of Sunium from Thoricus to Anaphlystus in Attica projected
rather further into the sea and were inhabited by some race
other than Athenians. Or, to give a different illustration for the
benefit of those who have not sailed along this bit of the Attic
coast, it is as if some race other than the present inhabitants were
to draw a line between the port of Brundisium and Tarentum in
Iapygia, and occupy the promontory to seaward of it.[28] These
two examples may suggest many others, where the shape of the
land resembles the Tauric peninsula. North of the Tauri, and
along the sea-coast to the eastward, is again Scythian territory,
as is also the country west of the Cimmerian Bosphorus and
Lake Maeotis as far as the river Tanais, which flows into the far
corner of the lake. On the landward side Scythia is bounded,
starting from the Danube, by the following tribes: first the
Agathyrsi, next the Neuri, then the Androphagi, and lastly the
Melanchlaeni.[29] In shape it is a square, of which the two sides
touch the sea; all four sides are equal, those on the sea and
those inland. It is a ten days' journey from the Danube to
the Borysthenes, and another ten on to Lake Maeotis, making
twenty; and it is also a twenty days' journey inland from the
Black Sea to the Melanchlaeni whose territory forms the northern boundary. I reckon a day's journey at 200 furlongs, so the
two sides of the square which run inland, and the two transverse
ones running east and west, are each 4000 furlongs in length.

The Scythians, after discussing the situation and concluding
that by themselves they were unequal to the task of coping with
Darius in a straight fight, sent off messengers to their neighbours,
whose chieftains had already met and were forming plans to
deal with what was evidently a threat to their safety on a very

large scale. The conference was attended by the chieftains of
the following tribes: the Tauri, Agathyrsi, Neuri, Androphagi,
Melanchlaeni, Geloni, Budini, and Sauromatae. It is the custom   103
of the Tauri to sacrifice to the Maiden Goddess all shipwrecked
sailors and such Greeks as they happen to capture upon their
coasts; their method of sacrifice is, after the preliminary ceremonies, to hit the victim on the head with a club. Some say that
they push the victim's body over the edge of the cliff on which
their temple stands, and fix the head on a stake; others, while
agreeing about the head, say the body is not pushed over the
cliff, but buried. The Tauri themselves claim that the goddess
to whom these offerings are made is Agamemnon's daughter,
Iphigenia. Any one of them who takes a prisoner in war, cuts
off his head and carries it home, where he sets it up high over
the house on a long pole, generally above the chimney. The
heads are supposed to act as guardians of the whole house over
which they hang. War and plunder are the sources of this
people's livelihood.

The Agathyrsi live in luxury and wear gold on their persons.   104
They have their women in common, so that they may all be
brothers and, as members of a single family, be able to live
together without jealousy or hatred. In other respects their way
of life resembles that of the Thracians.

The Neuri share the customs of Scythia. A generation before   105
the campaign of Darius they were forced to quit their country
by snakes, which appeared all over the place in great numbers,
while still more invaded them from the uninhabited region to
the north, until life became so unendurable that there was
nothing for it but to move out, and take up their quarters with
the Budini. It appears that these people practise magic; for there
is a story current amongst the Scythians and the Greeks in
Scythia that once a year every Neurian turns into a wolf for a
few days, and then turns back into a man again. I do not believe
this tale; but all the same, they tell it, and even swear to the
truth of it.[30] The Androphagi are the most savage of men, and   106
have no notion of either law or justice. They are herdsmen
without fixed dwellings; their dress is Scythian, their language
peculiar to themselves, and they are the only people in this part

107 of the world to eat human flesh. The Melanchlaeni all wear
black cloaks – hence their name. In all else they resemble the
108 Scythians. The Budini, a numerous and powerful nation, all
have markedly blue-grey eyes and red hair; there is a town in
their territory called Gelonus, all built of wood, both dwelling-
houses and temples, with a high wooden wall round it, thirty
furlongs each way. There are temples here in honour of Greek
gods, adorned after the Greek manner with statues, altars, and
shrines – though all constructed of wood; a triennial festival,
with the appropriate revelry, is held in honour of Dionysus.
This is to be accounted for by the fact that the Geloni were
originally Greeks, who, driven out of the trading ports along
the coast, settled amongst the Budini. Their language is still
109 half Scythian, half Greek. The language of the Budini is quite
different, as, indeed, is their culture generally: they are a pastoral
people who have always lived in this part of the country (a
peculiarity of theirs is eating lice), whereas the Geloni cultivate
the soil, eat grain, and keep gardens, and resemble them neither
in appearance nor complexion. In spite of these facts the Greeks
lump the Budini and Geloni together under the name of the
latter; but they are wrong to do so.

The country here is forest with trees of all sorts. In the most
densely wooded part there is a big lake surrounded by reedy
marshland; otters and beavers are caught in the lake, and
another sort of creature with a square face, whose skin they use
for making edgings for their jackets; its testicles are good for
curing diseases of the womb.

110 About the Sauromatae there is the following story. In the war
between the Greeks and the Amazons, the Greeks, after their
victory at the river Thermodon, sailed off in three ships with as
many Amazons on board as they had succeeded in taking alive.[31]
(The Scythians call the Amazons *Oeorpata*, the equivalent of
man-killers, oeor being the Scythian word for 'man', and *pata*
for 'kill'.) Once at sea, the women murdered their captors, but,
as they had no knowledge of boats and were unable to handle
either rudder or sail or oar, they soon found themselves, when
the men were done for, at the mercy of wind and wave, and
were blown to Cremni – the Cliffs – on Lake Maeotis, a place

within the territory of the free Scythians. Here they got ashore and made their way inland to an inhabited part of the country. The first thing they fell in with was a herd of horses grazing; these they seized, and, mounting on their backs, rode off in search of loot. The Scythians could not understand what was happening and were at a loss to know where the marauders had come from, as their dress, speech, and nationality were strange to them. Thinking, however, that they were young men, they fought in defence of their property, and discovered from the bodies which came into their possession after the battle that they were women. The discovery gave a new direction to their plans; they decided to make no further attempt to kill the invaders, but to send out a detachment of their youngest men, about equal in number to the Amazons, with orders to camp near them and take their cue from whatever it was that the Amazons then did: if they pursued them, they were not to fight, but to give ground; then, when the pursuit was abandoned, they were once again to encamp within easy range. The motive behind this policy was the Scythians' desire to get children by the Amazons. The detachment of young men obeyed their orders, and the Amazons, realizing that they meant no harm, ignored them, with the result that every day the two camps drew a little closer together. Neither party had anything but their weapons and their horses, and both lived the same sort of life, hunting and plundering.

Towards midday the Amazons used to scatter and go off to some little distance in ones and twos to ease themselves, and the Scythians, when they noticed this, followed suit; until one of them, coming upon an Amazon girl all by herself, began to make advances to her. She did not resist and let him have her, and then told him by signs (being unable to express her meaning in words, as neither understood the other's language) to return on the following day with a friend, making it clear that there must be two men, and that she herself would bring another girl. The young man then left her and told the others what had happened, and on the next day took a friend to the same spot, where he found his Amazon waiting for him and another one with her. Having learnt of their success, the rest of the young Scythians

soon succeeded in getting the Amazons to submit to their wishes.
114 The two camps were then united, and Amazons and Scythians
lived together, every man keeping as his wife the woman whose
favours he had first enjoyed. The men could not learn the
women's language, but the women succeeded in picking up
the men's; so when they could understand one another, the
Scythians made the following proposal: 'We,' they said, 'have
parents and property. Let us give up our present way of life and
return to live with our people. We will keep you as our wives
and not take any others.' The Amazons replied: 'We and the
women of your nation could never live together; our ways are
too much at variance. We are riders; our business is with the
bow and the spear, and we know nothing of women's work;
but in your country no woman has anything to do with such
things – your women stay at home in their waggons occupied
with feminine tasks, and never go out to hunt or for any other
purpose. We could not possibly agree. If, however, you wish to
keep us for your wives and to behave as honourable men, go
and get from your parents the share of property which is due to
115 you, and then let us go off and live by ourselves.' The young
men agreed to this, and when they came back, each with his
portion of the family possessions, the Amazons said: 'We dread
the prospect of settling down here, for we have done much
damage to the country by our raids, and we have robbed you of
your parents. Look now – if you think fit to keep us for your
wives, let us get out of the country altogether and settle some-
116 where on the other side of the Tanais.' Once again the Scythians
agreed, so they crossed the Tanais and travelled east for three
days, and then north, for another three, from Lake Maeotis,
until they reached the country where they are today, and settled
down there. Ever since then the women of the Sauromatae
have kept to their old ways, riding to the hunt on horseback
sometimes with, sometimes without, their men, taking part in
117 war and wearing the same sort of clothes as men.[32] The language
of these people is the Scythian, but it has always been a corrupt
form of it because the Amazons were never able to learn to
speak it properly. They have a marriage law which forbids a
girl to marry until she has killed an enemy in battle; some of

their women, unable to fulfil this condition, grow old and die unmarried.

These, then, were the nations whose chieftains had met 118 together to discuss the common danger; and to them the envoys from Scythia brought the news that the Persian king, having overrun the whole of the other continent, had bridged the Bosphorus and crossed into Europe, where he had already brought Thrace into subjection and was now engaged in throwing a bridge across the Danube, with the intention of making himself master of all Europe too. 'We beg you,' they said, 'not to remain neutral in this struggle; do not let us be destroyed without raising a hand to help us. Let us rather form a common plan of action, and meet the invader together. If you refuse, we shall be forced to yield to pressure and either abandon our country or make terms with the enemy. Without your help, what else could we do? What will become of us? Moreover, if you stand aside, you will not on that account get out of things any more lightly; for this invasion is aimed at you just as much as at us, and, once we have gone under, the Persians will never be content to leave you unmolested. There is plain proof of the truth of this: for had the Persian attack been directed against us alone in revenge for the old wrong we did them when we enslaved their country, they would have been bound to come straight for Scythia without touching any other nation on the way. By doing that they would have made it plain to everyone that the object of their attack was Scythia, and Scythia alone; but, as things are, they no sooner crossed into Europe than they have begun to bring under their heel in turn every nation through whose territory they pass. Not to mention the other Thracians, even our neighbours the Getae have been enslaved.'

The assembled chieftains deliberated upon what the Scythian 119 envoys had reported, but failed to reach a unanimous conclusion. Those of the Geloni, Budini, and Sauromatae agreed to stand by the Scythians, but the rest – the chieftains, namely, of the Agathyrsi, Neuri, Androphagi, Melanchlaeni, and Tauri – returned the following answer. 'Had you not yourselves been the aggressors in your trouble with Persia, we should have considered your request justified; we should have granted what you ask and been willing enough to fight at your side. But the fact is, you invaded Persia without consulting us, and remained in possession of it as long as God allowed you, and now the same God is urging the Persians to pay you back in your own coin. We did the Persians no injury on that former occasion, and we will not be the first to start trouble now. Of course, should they prove to be the aggressors and actually invade us, we shall do our best to keep them out; but until we see that happen, we shall stay where we are and do nothing. In our opinion, the invasion is directed not against us, but against you, who were the aggressors in the first place.'[33]

120   When this reply was reported to the Scythians, seeing that these nations refused to support them, they decided to avoid a straight fight, and to retire, blocking up all the wells and springs which they passed and trampling the pasture. They organized their forces in two divisions. One, under the command of Scopasis, was to be joined by the Sauromatae, and had orders if the Persians turned against them to withdraw along the coast of Lake Maeotis towards the river Tanais, and, should the Persians themselves retreat, to attack them in their turn. This was one division, and this was the route it was to take. Of the other, the two sections – the greater under Idanthyrsus and the second under Taxacis – were to unite forces and, after joining up with the Geloni and Budini, were, like the first division, to withdraw before the Persian advance at the distance of a day's march, and carry out as they went the same strategy. This division was to begin by retiring in the direction of those nations who had refused to join the alliance, with the idea of involving them in the war against their will, if they would not fight on their own initiative. Subsequently, this second force was to go back to their own country and launch an attack, if the situation seemed to justify it.

121   Having determined on this plan of action, the Scythians marched out to meet Darius, sending their best horsemen in advance. The waggons which served as houses for the women and children, and all the cattle, except what they needed for food, were ordered to move northward at once, in advance of

122   their future line of retreat. The advance-guard made contact

with the Persians about three days' march from the Danube, and at once encamped at a distance of a single day's march in front of them, devastating the land. The Persians, on the appearance of the Scythian cavalry, gave chase and continued to follow in their tracks as they withdrew before them. The Persian advance was now directed against the single division of the Scythian army under Scopasis, and was consequently eastward towards the Tanais. The Scythians crossed the river, and the Persians followed in pursuit, until they had passed through the territory of the Sauromatae and reached that of the Budini, where they came across the wooden fortified town of Gelonus, abandoned and empty of defenders, and burnt it. 123 Previously, so long as their route lay through the country of the Scythians and Sauromatae, they had done no damage, because the country was barren and there was nothing to destroy. After burning the town, they continued to press forward on the enemy's heels until they reached the great uninhabited region which lies beyond the territory of the Budini. This tract of land is seven days' journey across, and on the further side of it lies the country of the Thyssagetae, from which four great rivers, Lycus, Oarus, Tanais, and Syrgis, flow through the land of the Maeotae to empty themselves into Lake Maeotis.

When he reached this uninhabited area, Darius called a halt 124 on the banks of the Oarus, and began eight large forts, spaced at regular intervals of approximately eight miles. The remains of them were still to be seen in my day. While these forts were under construction, the Scythians whom he had been following changed the direction of their march, and by a broad sweep through the country to the northward returned to Scythia and completely disappeared. Unable to see any sign of them, Darius left his forts half finished and himself turned back towards the west, supposing that the Scythians he had been chasing were the whole nation, and that they were now trying to escape in that direction. He made the best speed he was capable of, and on 125 reaching Scythia fell in with the other two combined divisions of the Scythian army; at once he gave chase, and they, as before, withdrew a day's march in front of him. As Darius continued to press forward in hot pursuit, the Scythians now carried out

their plan of leading him into the territory of the people who
had refused, in the first instance, to support them in their resistance to Persia. The first were the Melanchlaeni, and the double
invasion of their country, first by the Scythians and then by the
Persians, caused great disturbance; the turn of the Androphagi
came next, and then the Neuri, with the same result. Finally,
still withdrawing before the Persian advance, the Scythians
approached the frontiers of the Agathyrsi. These people, unlike
their neighbours, of whose terrified attempt to escape they had
been witness, did not wait for the Scythians to invade them, but
sent a representative to forbid them to cross the frontier, adding
a warning that, if they attempted to do so, they would be resisted
by force of arms. This challenge they followed up by manning
their frontiers in arms. The other tribes – the Melanchlaeni,
Androphagi, and Neuri – offered no resistance to the successive
invasions of Scythians and Persians, but forgot their former
threats and in great confusion fled northwards into the waste.
The Scythians, finding the Agathyrsi prepared to keep them out,
then changed direction, and, from the land of the Neuri, drew
the Persians back into Scythia.

126   Finding no end of this, Darius at last dispatched a rider with
a message for Idanthyrsus, the Scythian king. 'Why on earth,
strange man,' the message ran, 'do you keep on running away?
You have, surely, a choice of two alternatives: if you think
yourself strong enough to oppose me, stand up and fight, instead
of wandering all over the world in your efforts to escape me; or,
if you admit that you are too weak, what is the good, even so,
of running away? You should rather send earth and water to
your master, as the sign of your submission, and come to a
conference.'

127   'Persian,' Idanthyrsus replied, 'I have never yet run from any
man in fear; and I am not doing so now from you. There is, for
me, nothing unusual in what I have been doing: it is precisely
the sort of life I always lead, even in times of peace. If you want
to know why I will not fight, I will tell you: in our country there
are no towns and no cultivated land; fear of losing which, or
seeing it ravaged, might indeed provoke us to hasty battle. If,
122   however, you are determined upon bloodshed with the least

possible delay, one thing there is for which we will fight – the tombs of our forefathers. Find those tombs, and try to wreck them, and you will soon know whether or not we are willing to stand up to you. Till then – unless for good reason – we shall continue to avoid a battle. This is my reply to your challenge; and as for your being my master, I acknowledge no masters but Zeus from whom I sprang, and Hestia the Scythian queen. I will send you no gifts of earth and water, but others more suitable; and your claim to be my master is easily answered – be damned to you!' This was the message which was carried back to Darius.   128

The mere suggestion of slavery filled the Scythian chieftains with rage, and they dispatched the division under Scopasis, which included the Sauromatae, with orders to seek a conference with the Ionians, who were guarding the bridge over the Danube. Those who remained decided to stop leading the Persians the usual dance, and to attack them whenever they found them foraging. This policy they carried out, waiting for the proper opportunities to present themselves. On every occasion the Scythian cavalry proved superior to the Persian, which would give ground and fall back on the infantry for support; this checked the attack, for the Scythians knew the Persian infantry would be too much for them, and regularly turned tail after driving in the cavalry. Similar raids were made at night.

I must mention one very surprising thing which helped the   129
Persians and hampered the Scythians in these skirmishes: I mean the unfamiliar appearance of the mules and the braying of the donkeys. As I have already pointed out, neither donkeys nor mules are bred in Scythia – indeed, there is not a single specimen of either in the whole country, because of the cold.[34] This being so, the donkeys' braying caused great confusion amongst the Scythian cavalry; often, in the course of an attack, the sound of it so much upset the horses, which had never heard such a noise before or seen such a creature as that from which it proceeded, that they would turn short round, ears pricked, in consternation. This gave the Persians some small advantage in the campaign.

Seeing the Persians disorganized by these continual raids, the   130
Scythians hit upon a stratagem to keep them longer in the

country and reduce them in the end to distress from lack of supplies. This was to slip away from time to time to some other position leaving behind a few cattle in the charge of shepherds; the Persians would come and take the animals, and be much

131 encouraged by the momentary success. This happened again and again, until at last Darius did not know where to turn, and the Scythians, seeing his acute embarrassment, sent him the promised presents – a bird, a mouse, a frog, and five arrows. The Persians asked the man who brought these things what they signified, but got no reply. The man's orders – so he said – were merely to deliver them, and to return home as quickly as he could: the Persians themselves, if they were clever, could find out what the presents meant. Thereupon the Persians put their

132 heads together, and Darius expressed the view that the Scythians were giving him earth and water and intended to surrender: mice, he reasoned, live on the ground and eat the same food as men; frogs live in water; birds are much like horses; and the arrows symbolized the Scythian power, which they were giving into his hands. Gobryas, however (one of the seven conspirators who put down the Magus), by no means agreed with him, but interpreted the gifts as saying: 'Unless you Persians turn into birds and fly up in the air, or into mice and burrow under ground, or into frogs and jump into the lakes, you will never get home again, but stay here in this country, only to be shot by the Scythian arrows.'[35]

133 While the Persians were thus interpreting the gifts, the division of the Scythian force which had previously had orders to keep watch along the shore of Lake Maeotis, and had now been sent to confer with the Ionians on the Danube, made its way to the bridge. 'Men of Ionia,' began the Scythian spokesman, 'we bring you freedom, if only you will do what we suggest. We understand that your orders from Darius were to guard the bridge for sixty days – no more; and after that if he failed to put in an appearance, to go home. Now, therefore, the obvious thing for you to do is to wait till the sixty days have passed and then clear out – neither Darius nor ourselves will have anything to reproach you for in that.' The Ionians agreed and the Scythians rode back without loss of time.

After the presents had been sent to Darius, the Scythians who 134
had not gone to the Danube drew up their cavalry and infantry
with the apparent intention of offering the Persians battle. But
as soon as their dispositions were made, a hare started up
between the two armies and began running. The Scythians were
after it in a moment – company after company of them, directly
they caught sight of it – while the army was reduced to a shouting
rabble. Darius inquired what all the noise and fuss were about,
and upon learning that the enemy was engaged in hunting a
hare, he turned to those of his officers he was in the habit of
talking with, and said: 'These fellows have a hearty contempt for
us, and I am now ready to believe that Gobryas' interpretation of
those things they sent me was the right one. Well then – as I
have come round to his opinion, it is time to think of the best
way of getting out of this country in safety.'

'My lord,' Gobryas answered. 'I already knew pretty well
from hearsay how difficult the Scythians were to deal with, and
now that I am on the spot and can see how they fool us with
their tricks, I know it all the better. As to our next move, my
proposal is this: as soon as it is dark, I suggest that we should
light the camp-fires as usual, and then, tethering the donkeys
and leaving behind on some pretext or other those of our men
who are least fit to face the hardship and privation, clear out
before the Scythians advance to the Danube and destroy the
bridge, and before the Ionians on guard can take any measures
which may lead to our destruction.'

Darius adopted this proposal, and as soon as night fell began 135
the homeward march, leaving behind the sick and such other of
his troops as he could most easily spare, as well as the donkeys
all tethered in their usual places. His object in leaving the donkeys was to let their braying disguise the fact of his withdrawal;
as for the men, they were incapacitated by sickness and he did
not want them – though he gave it out that they were to guard
the camp, while he, with his best troops, launched an attack on
the Scythians. Having thus explained his departure to the men
whom he was, in point of fact, deserting, Darius had the camp-
fires lighted and moved off at his best speed towards the Danube.
The donkeys made more noise than ever when they were aware

that the main body of the army had gone; and when the Scythians heard it they never suspected any change in the situation, but were confident that the whole Persian army was still there.

136 Dawn came; and the Persian remnant, realizing that Darius had betrayed them, held out their arms in sign of surrender, and told the Scythians of what had occurred. On hearing the news, the whole Scythian force – all the three divisions of it, joined by the Sauromatae, the Budini, and Geloni – without a moment's delay set off for the Danube in pursuit of the Persians. The greater part of the Persian army was travelling on foot, and, in the absence of regular roads, was uncertain of the way; and the consequence was that the Scythians, who were all mounted, and perfectly familiar with the most direct route, reached the bridge long before them. The two armies had missed each other on the way, and the Scythians, realizing that the Persians had not yet arrived, seized the opportunity of another word with the Ionians on the ships. 'Men of Ionia,' they said, 'your sixty days are now up, and you have no business to wait any longer. Hitherto you stayed at your post because you feared the consequences of desertion; but now things have changed – break up the bridge and be off. Good luck go with you, and thank the gods and the Scythians for your freedom. As for your former master, we will settle with him in such a way that his present campaign will prove his last.'

137 In the discussion which followed, Miltiades the Athenian, who was tyrant of the Chersonese on the Hellespont and in command of its contingent,[36] expressed the opinion that they should take the Scythians' advice, and so liberate Ionia; he was opposed, however, by Histiaeus of Miletus, who pointed out that each one of them owed his position as tyrant to Darius, and, in the event of Darius' fall, he himself would be unable to maintain his power at Miletus, nor would any of the rest of them. Each state would be sure to turn against tyranny, and choose democracy. The meeting had begun by supporting Miltiades; but no sooner had Histiaeus put forward this view than everyone present changed his mind and it was unanimously

138 adopted. The voters on this occasion were these: Daphnis of Abydos, Hippoclus of Lampsacus, Herophantus of Parium,

Metrodorus of Proconnesus, Aristagoras of Cyzicus, and Ariston of Byzantium – all men highly esteemed by Darius, and all tyrants of their states on the Hellespont; in addition to these there were, from Ionia, Strattis of Chios, Aeaces of Samos, Laodamas of Phocaea, and Histiaeus of Miletus – the same who opposed Miltiades. The only distinguished Aeolian present was Aristagoras of Cyme.

Once they had accepted the view put forward by Histiaeus, 139 they decided upon the next step to be taken, and how they would disguise its true purpose. The plan was to remove a portion of the bridge – about the length of a bowshot – on the Scythian side of the river, which would serve the double purpose of appearing to be doing something which they were not, and of preventing the Scythians from forcing a passage over, and to assure the Scythians, while the work of demolition was going on, that they would do all they were asked. This was how they intended to work out in practice the proposal of Histiaeus; and when the decision was made, Histiaeus himself was chosen to address the Scythians. 'Men of Scythia,' he said, 'you bring good news, and it is lucky you have got here so soon. Everything is going ahead well, and to our mutual benefit – your service to us, and ours to you. As you see, we are demolishing the bridge, and we shall spare no effort to recover our freedom. The best thing you can do, while we are busy with the demolition, is to go and look for the Persian army; then, when you have found it, you can punish the invaders as they deserve, both for your own sakes and for ours.' Once again the Scythians believed in 140 the good faith of the Ionians; they went back in search of the Persian army, but completely failed to make contact with it anywhere. The failure was their own fault, for they could easily have found the Persians if they had not blocked up the wells and destroyed everything which the horses could eat – precisely the move on which they most congratulated themselves. But as it turned out, it was the one thing that wrecked their chances; for in their search for the Persian army they followed a route through a part of the country where there was both pasture and water, thinking that the Persians, in their attempt to escape, would naturally do the same. The Persians, however, kept strictly to the route they had originally followed. They had great difficulty in reaching the crossing. It was dark when they arrived, and the discovery that the bridge was broken caused a panic, for they at once supposed that the Ionians had left them in the lurch. Darius, however, told an Egyptian he happened to have with him, a man with a tremendous voice, to stand on the river bank and shout for Histiaeus. The fellow obeyed, and Histiaeus, who heard him at the very first hail, set all the ships to the task of ferrying the army over, and made good the broken section of the bridge. In this way the Persians got safely out of the country, having twice avoided the Scythians' attempt to make contact with them. The Scythians have a low opinion of the men of Ionia in consequence of all this: to consider them as a free people, they are, they say, the most despicable and craven in the world; and, considered as slaves, the most subservient to their masters and the least likely to run away.[37]

Darius now marched through Thrace to Sestos in the Chersonese, where he took ship for Asia, leaving a distinguished Persian named Megabazus to command in Europe. Darius had once paid this man a high compliment: wishing to eat some pomegranates, he had just opened the first of them, when his brother Artabanus asked him which of his possessions he would like to be multiplied to a number as great as the seeds in a pomegranate. Darius' answer was 'Megabazus': he would rather, he said, have such a number of men like Megabazus than be master of Greece. It was in Persia that Darius paid him this compliment, and on the present occasion he left him in Europe with a corps of the army 80,000 strong. This same Megabazus once made a remark for which the people along the Hellespont have never forgotten him: he was in Byzantium, and on hearing that Chalcedon was settled seventeen years earlier than that city, he said the men of Chalcedon must have been blind at the time; for if they had had any eyes, they would never have chosen an inferior site, when a much finer one lay ready to hand. Megabazus, then, as I have said, being left behind in command on the Hellespont, began the reduction of such communities as did not submit to Persia.

While Megabazus was thus occupied, another powerful force   145
was on its way against Libya.[38] Before I explain the reason for
this, I have some preliminary matters to relate. The grandsons
of the crew of the ship *Argo* were expelled from Lemnos by
the Pelasgians who had kidnapped the Athenian women from
Brauron. Leaving Lemnos, they sailed to Lacedaemon, where
they encamped on Mt Taygetus. The Lacedaemonians, seeing
the fires that these men had kindled on the ridge, sent someone
to find out who they were and where they had come from. On
being questioned, they said they were Minyae, descendants of
the heroes who had sailed in the *Argo* and had put in at Lemnos,
where they started the families to which they belonged. When
the Lacedaemonians heard this account of their parentage, they
sent a second messenger to ask what their object was in coming
to Lacedaemon and lighting their fire. To this they replied that,
having been thrown out of Lemnos by the Pelasgians, they
had come to the land of their fathers – which was the most
honourable thing they could do; and that now they wanted to
settle down there, and have a share in the land and in the
privileges of government. The Lacedaemonians, moved in particular by the fact that the sons of Tyndareus had sailed in
the *Argo*, consented to receive the Minyae on the terms they
proposed, and gave them grants of land and divided them
amongst the various tribes. At once the Minyae married Spartan
wives, and gave the women they had brought from Lemnos to
Spartan husbands. It was not long, however, before the Minyae,   146
in the pride of their newly won privileges, began to go too far,
even claiming a share in the royal power, and doing other things
no less impious. The Lacedaemonians, therefore, decided to kill
them, and, with this purpose in view, arrested them and threw
them into prison. Now judicial killings at Sparta are always
carried out at night, never by day; so just before sentence could
be executed on the Minyae, their wives asked leave to be admitted into the prison, in order to have a word with their
husbands. These women were all natives of Sparta and daughters of leading Spartan citizens, so no one suspected treachery,
and they succeeded in getting their request granted. Once inside
the prison, however, they changed clothes with the men, who

were enabled by this disguise to pass themselves off as women and get out. Then, having made their escape, they once more established themselves on Taygetus.

147   While all this was going on, Theras the son of Autesion (Autesion's father Tisamenus was the son of Thersander and grandson of Polyneices) was preparing to leave Lacedaemon to found a settlement elsewhere. Theras was a Cadmeian by descent, and maternal uncle of Eurysthenes and Procles, the two sons of Aristodemus, and acted as regent in Sparta during his nephews' infancy; but when the boys grew up and took over the reins of government, he so deeply resented finding himself, after a taste of power, in a subordinate position, that he refused to stay in Lacedaemon and declared that he would sail away to join his kinsfolk in the island of Thera. This island used to be known as Callista, and certain descendants of Membliarus, son of the Phoenician Poiciles, were living in it. Cadmus, the son of Agenor, touched at it during his search for Europa and, whether because he liked the place or for some other reason, left there a number of Phoenicians with his own kinsman Membliarus amongst them. These men and their descendants lived in Callista for eight generations before Theras came from
148   Lacedaemon, and it was to join with them that Theras was now preparing to sail with a party of colonists chosen from the various tribes in Sparta. He had no intention of turning them out – he insisted strongly that he meant to settle down with them as a kinsman.

It was just at this time that the Minyae escaped from prison and sat themselves down on Taygetus; and the Lacedaemonians were planning their destruction, when Theras, wishing to prevent bloodshed, begged them off and undertook to carry them away out of the country. The Lacedaemonians agreed, so he set sail to join the descendants of Membliarus in three thirty-oared galleys, taking with him the Minyae – or, rather, some few of them; for the great number went off to the country of the Paroreatae and Caucones, whom they drove from their home, and afterwards built six towns of their own, to correspond to the six groups into which they had divided themselves. The towns were Lepreum, Macistus, Phrixae, Pyrgus, Epium, and

Nudium: most of them were destroyed within my own time by the people of Elis. Callista was renamed Thera after Theras, the founder.

Theras' son refused to accompany the expedition, and Theras said he would be leaving him behind like a sheep amongst wolves: the remark caught on, and led to the young man being known as Oeolycus – a name which stuck to him.[39] He was later the father of Aegeus, who gave his name to the Aegidae, a powerful Spartan clan – the men of this clan were advised by an oracle to build a shrine to the Furies of Oedipus and Laius, because their children never survived. The remedy was successful and the mortality ceased. The same thing happened to their descendants in Thera.

Up to this point the Lacedaemonians and the Theraeans tell the same story; what follows is on the authority of the latter only. Grinnus, the son of Aesanius, a descendant of Theras and king of the island, went to Delphi to offer a sacrifice of a hundred victims on behalf of the community. Amongst the people of the island who accompanied him was Battus, son of Polymnestus, a member of the Minyan family of the Euphemidae. During his stay at Delphi, Grinnus consulted the oracle on quite different matters, and received from the Priestess the apparently irrelevant answer that he must found a city in Libya.[40] 'Lord Apollo,' he replied, 'I am too old and inactive to start on such a journey; can you not tell one of these younger men to undertake it instead of me?' And as he spoke he pointed at Battus. For the moment, nothing further occurred; they left Delphi, put the oracle out of their minds, and did nothing about it – for they did not even know where Libya was, and shrank from sending out a party of settlers merely, as it were, into the blue. During the seven years that followed not a drop of rain fell in Thera, and every tree on the island, except one, withered and died. In this difficult situation the Theraeans sent to Delphi for advice, and were reminded about the colony which they had omitted to send to Libya. There was now nothing else to be done, so they sent some men to Crete to inquire if any native of that island, or any stranger living there, had ever been to Libya. In the course of their travels about Crete, the party from Thera came to Itanus,

149

150

151

where they met a certain Corobius, a purple-fisher, who told
them that he had once been blown out of his course and had
fetched up at the island of Platea, just off the Libyan coast.
This man they paid to return with them to Thera, and shortly
afterwards a small reconnoitring party, with Corobius as pilot,
set sail. They reached Platea and put Corobius ashore with
enough supplies for a stated number of months, and then made
sail again with all speed for home, to bring the news about the
152 island. They had agreed with Corobius to be away a definite
length of time; this period, however, was exceeded, and Corobius was in distress from lack of supplies, until a Samian vessel
bound for Egypt, under the command of a man called Colaeus,
was forced by the weather to run for Platea. The Samians
listened to Corobius' story, left him enough food to last a year,
and resumed their voyage to Egypt, which they were anxious to
reach. Easterly winds, however, prevented them from getting
there, and continued so long that they were driven away to the
westward right through the Pillars of Heracles until, by a piece
of more than human luck, they succeeded in making Tartessus.
This trading post had not at that period been exploited, and the
consequence was that the Samian merchants, on their return
home, made a greater profit on their cargo than any Greeks
of whom we have precise knowledge, with the exception of
Sostratus of Aegina, the son of Laodamas – with him, nobody
can compare. A tenth part of their profits, amounting to six
talents, they spent on the manufacture of a bronze vessel, shaped
like an Argive wine-bowl, with a continuous row of griffins'
heads round the rim; this bowl, supported upon three kneeling
figures in bronze, eleven and a half feet high, they placed as an
offering in the temple of Hera. The help given by the Samian
merchants to Corobius was the origin of the strong bond of
friendship between Samos on the one hand, and Cyrene and
Thera on the other.

153   The Theraeans who had left Corobius in Platea told their
compatriots, when they reached home, that they had established
a settlement on an island off the Libyan coast, and it was
thereupon decided to send a party to join the new colony; the
party was to represent all the seven villages in Thera, and

brothers were to draw lots to determine which should join it. It was to be under the sole authority of Battus. Two penteconters then got under way for Platea.

I have related the foregoing on the authority of the Theraeans only; for the sequel, the people of Cyrene are in agreement with them. Nevertheless, in what concerns Battus, they tell a different story. Etearchus, they say, the ruler of a city in Crete called Oaxus, had a daughter named Phronima, and, when the girl's mother died, married a second wife. This woman had no sooner entered the family than she thought fit to make herself a proper stepmother to Phronima, in deed as well as name, and thought of everything she possibly could to torment her. To crown all, she accused her of fornication and persuaded her husband that it was true. Etearchus planned, in consequence, to get rid of his daughter in a most unholy manner. He made guest-friendship with a man called Themison, a Theraean merchant living in Oaxus, and obtained from him a promise upon oath to perform whatever service should be asked of him. Then, as soon as he had got him to take the oath, he fetched his daughter, put her into Themison's charge, and told him to take her away and throw her into the sea. Themison was very angry at the way he had been caught, and broke off his friendship with Etearchus; then, in order to clear himself of the obligation under which his oath had laid him, he put to sea with the girl and, when they were clear of the land, lowered her into the water on the end of a rope, hauled her up again, and sailed home with her to Thera, where a distinguished Theraean named Polymnestus afterwards made her his mistress. In course of time she gave birth to a son, who lisped and stammered, and this child – according, at any rate, to what is said at Thera and Cyrene – was called Battus. My own view, however, is that he was never known as Battus until after he went to Libya, where he assumed the name in consequence of the words spoken by the Delphic oracle, and of the high position he held there – for 'battus' in the Libyan language means 'king', and that, I fancy, is why the Priestess at Delphi, when she spoke the prophecy, addressed him by the Libyan word, knowing, as she did, that he was to become a king in Libya. For after he had grown to manhood he went to Delphi

154

155

to consult the oracle about his defective speech,[41] and was answered by the lines:

> O Battus, for a voice you come; but the lord Apollo
> Sends you to Libya, nurse of flocks, to build a city –

which would have been the equivalent of saying in Greek, 'O King, for a voice you come'. Battus replied: 'Lord, I consulted your oracle about my speech, and you tell me, quite irrelevantly, to found a settlement in Libya! It is impossible. What resources have I? What men?' But his complaint was useless; he could get no other answer from the oracle, and when the same command was repeated, he left the temple before the Priestess had finished 156 speaking and returned to Thera. Subsequently, however, he had no better luck than before; indeed, everything began to go wrong both with Battus himself and the others on the island. What was the cause of their distress they could not understand, and, when they sent to Delphi for enlightenment, the old answer was yet again repeated: if, the Priestess said, they would join Battus in founding a settlement at Cyrene in Libya, their fortunes would mend. So then they sent Battus off, and he and a party of men sailed for Libya in two penteconters; they reached the coast, but, unable to decide what their next move should be, sailed home again to Thera. The islanders, however, refused to allow them to come ashore; they threw things at them as they were making up for the harbour, and shouted that they must put about and go back again; so, as they were compelled, they once more got under way for Libya. This time, they established themselves on Platea, the island off the coast which I mentioned before. It is said to be of the same size as the city of Cyrene is today.

157   The settlers stayed in Platea for two years; but they failed to prosper in their new home, and all made sail again for Delphi, leaving one man behind on the island. They went to the oracle, and declared that, in spite of the fact that they were living in Libya, they were no better off than before. To this the Priestess replied:

If you know sheep-breeding Libya better than I do,
Not having been there – I have – I marvel much at your cunning!

On this, Battus and his men sailed away once more for Platea,
for it was plain that Apollo would not let them off until they
established a settlement actually on the Libyan mainland. After
calling, therefore, at the island and taking off the man they had
left there, they crossed to the mainland and built a town on the
coast, just south of Platea, at a spot called Aziris – a charming
place with a river on one side and lovely valleys on both. Here   158
they lived for six years, but were then persuaded to leave by the
Libyans, who undertook to show them a better place. After
getting them to consent to the move, the Libyans took them
further west, and so timed the journey as to pass through the
finest bit of country – called Irasa – in the dark, in order to
prevent them from seeing it. Finally they reached the spring
called Apollo's Fountain and the Libyan guides said to the
Greeks: 'This is the place for you to settle in, for here there is a
hole in the sky.'[42]

During the lifetime of Battus, the founder of Cyrene, who   159
ruled there for forty years, and of his son Arcesilaus, who ruled
for sixteen, the number of people in the town remained equal
to that of the original settlers; but under the rule of its third king
– known as Battus the Fortunate – an oracle delivered at Delphi
was the cause of a great rush amongst the Greeks generally to
join the colony. For the people of Cyrene themselves were
offering land to new settlers, and the oracle declared that whoever came to delightful Libya after the land was parcelled out
should one day regret it.

In this way the population of the place greatly increased, and
it began to encroach upon the territory of its neighbours. Its
expansion continued, until the Libyans under their king,
Adicran, in resentment at their loss of territory and the domi-
neering attitude of Cyrene, dispatched an embassy to Egypt and
put themselves at the disposal of the Egyptian king Apries,
who collected a strong force and sent it against Cyrene. The
Cyrenaeans took the field and, marching to the Well of Thestis
in Irasa, engaged and defeated the Egyptian army. This severe

defeat – so severe that few of them returned home alive – was doubtless due to the fact that the Egyptians had had no previous experience of Greek fighting and were not prepared to treat it seriously. Apries' subjects blamed him personally for this disastrous campaign, and it was the reason for their rebellion against him.[43]

160   Battus the Fortunate had a son named Arcesilaus, who on coming to power quarrelled with his brothers, until they left him and went off to another part of the country, where they founded on their own initiative a second settlement – the town called, then as now, Barca. While the town was still building, they persuaded the Libyans to withdraw their allegiance from Cyrene, and Arcesilaus made war upon those of them who had consented to do so. Alarmed by the approach of the troops from Cyrene, the Libyans hastily withdrew to the eastward, and Arcesilaus gave chase as far as the place in Libya called Leucon, where the Libyans decided to attack him. In the fight which ensued the Cyrenaeans were soundly beaten, losing as many as 7000 hoplites. Following this severe blow, Arcesilaus fell ill and, after taking some drug, was strangled by his brother Learchus,

161   who, in his turn, was murdered by Eryxo, Arcesilaus' wife. The lordship of Cyrene then passed to Arcesilaus' son Battus – a lame man with a limp. These misfortunes prompted the Cyrenaeans to send to the oracle at Delphi for advice – how, they asked, should they order their affairs so as to secure the most satisfactory sort of government? In reply, the Priestess told them to call in a man from Mantinea in Arcadia to put things right for them; so they applied for a suitable person and were given the services of a certain Demonax, who enjoyed the highest reputation amongst the citizens of Mantinea. Demonax, accordingly, went to Cyrene and, after making himself familiar with all the facts of the situation there, took the following measures: he divided the population into three sections, or tribes, the first consisting of the emigrants from Thera and their neighbours, the second of men from the Peloponnese and Crete, and the third of men from the islands. Next, he appropriated to Battus, the ruler of the city, certain special lands and priestly offices, and threw open to the people in general all the other privileges which

had previously been enjoyed by the kings. These arrangements   162
remained unaltered during Battus' lifetime, but under his son
and successor Arcesilaus there was a great rumpus about the
various state offices and privileges, and Arcesilaus (the son, that
is, of Battus the lame and Pheretima) refused to put up with
the new order introduced by Demonax, and demanded the
restoration of his ancestral rights. In the civil struggles which
followed, he was defeated and fled to Samos, and his mother
sought refuge at Salamis in Cyprus – a town which was controlled at that period by Euelthon, who dedicated the remarkable censer in the Corinthian treasure-house at Delphi.
Pheretima went to Euelthon's court and asked for an army to
put the party she represented back in power at Cyrene; but an
army was the one thing Euelthon was unwilling to give her.
Other things he gave her generously enough, and each time she
accepted a present she said it was a fine one, but not so fine as
to give her what she really wanted – an army. As she continued
on every occasion to make the same remark, Euelthon ended
by sending her a golden spindle and distaff, with wool on it.
Pheretima repeated the same words as before, which drew from
Euelthon the reply that he had sent her a present which, unlike
an army, he thought suitable to her sex.

Arcesilaus, meanwhile, was in Samos, collecting all manner   163
of men, with promises of a general share-out of the land. When
he had got a large force together he set off for Delphi to ask the
oracle about the chances of his return to Cyrene. 'Apollo
Loxias,' the Priestess replied, 'grants you kingship in Cyrene
over a period of eight generations under four rulers named
Battus and four named Arcesilaus; but he advises you to make
no attempt to keep your power beyond that period. As for
yourself, when you return to your country, be gentle. If you find
the oven full of jars, do not bake them but send them away
down-wind. But if you do heat the oven, enter not the land
surrounded by water, for otherwise you will die, and the best
of the bulls with you.' Having heard this oracular utterance,   164
Arcesilaus went back to Cyrene with his Samian supporters and
recovered possession of supreme power. But once there, he
forgot the warning of the oracle and took proceedings against

his political opponents, who had driven him into exile. Some of them left the country for good; others fell into his hands and were sent to their death in Cyprus. These last, however, were forced by the weather to put in at Cnidus, and were rescued by the islanders and sent to Thera. Others shut themselves up in a high tower, the private stronghold of one Aglomachus, and Arcesilaus stacked wood round the place and burnt them alive. After this deed, realizing, too late, that this was what the oracle had meant when the Priestess warned him, if he should find the jars in the oven, not to bake them, he deliberately kept away from Cyrene, because he thought it might be the 'land surrounded by water' which the oracle had spoken of, and he was afraid the prophecy of his death might be fulfilled. He had a wife related to him by blood, the daughter of Alazir, the ruler of Barca; to this man he went, and the people of Barca, with some of the exiles from Cyrene, saw him in the market and killed him. They also killed his father-in-law Alazir. So Arcesilaus, whether he would or not, missed the meaning of the oracle and fulfilled his destiny.

165   While Arcesilaus was in Barca after doing the deed which was to bring him to ruin, his mother Pheretima represented him at Cyrene, enjoying his privileges, attending to the business of government, and taking her seat in the council; but on hearing of her son's death, she fled to Egypt on the strength of certain services which Arcesilaus had rendered to Cambyses, the son of Cyrus; for it was he who had put Cyrene under Cambyses' control and fixed a rate of tribute. On her arrival there she sat as a suppliant to Aryandes, justifying her request for help by the argument that it was Arcesilaus' friendship with Persia that had
166   caused his death. Aryandes had been made governor of Egypt by Cambyses: he subsequently lost his life as the result of an attempt to rival Darius. Aware by what he had seen and heard that Darius wished to perpetuate his memory by something no other king had previously done, Aryandes started to follow his example – but he soon got punished for his impudence. The facts were these: Darius had issued a gold coinage, of which the metal was of the greatest possible purity,[44] and Aryandes as governor of Egypt had followed suit by a similar issue of silver

– and indeed to this day the purest silver coinage is the Aryandic. Darius, when he came to know of this, disguised the real cause of his anger by bringing a charge of rebellion against Aryandes, and had him executed.

Now, however, Aryandes took pity on Pheretima and put 167 at her service all the forces in Egypt, both army and fleet, with Amasis, a man of the Maraphian tribe, to command the former, and Badres, of the Pasargadae, to command the latter; then, before giving the order to move, he sent a herald to Barca to inquire the name of the man who had murdered Arcesilaus. To this the people of the town replied that they were all equally responsible – for they had received many injuries at his hands. At that Aryandes ordered the troops to march with Pheretima. This, at any rate, was the cause which served as a pretext for the expedition; its real object, I fancy, was the subjugation of Libya. The races of men in Libya are many and various, and only a few of them were subject to the Persian king; the greater number never gave Darius a moment's thought.

The following is a description of the Libyan tribes in their 168 order: starting from Egypt, the first are the Adyrmachidae, whose way of living is more or less Egyptian in character. They dress like the rest of the Libyans. Their women wear a bronze ring on each leg, and grow their hair long; when they catch a bug on their persons, they give it bite for bite before throwing it away. They are the only Libyan tribe to follow this practice, as also that of taking girls who are about to be married to see the king. Any girl who catches his fancy, leaves him a maid no longer. This tribe extends from the Egyptian border as far as the port called Plynus.

Next come the Giligamae, whose territory runs westward as 169 far as the island of Aphrodisias. In between lies Platea, the island off the coast where the Cyrenaeans first settled, and on the mainland is the Harbour of Menelaus, and Aziris where the Cyrenaeans also lived for a time. It is in this part of the country that silphium begins to be found, and extends all the way from Platea to the mouth of the Syrtis. The Giligamae live in much the same sort of way as the other tribes. Next to the westward 170 are the Asbystae; their territory lies further inland than Cyrene, and does not extend to the coast, which is occupied by the Cyrenaeans. This tribe is conspicuous amongst the Libyans for its use of four-horse chariots, and in its general way of life does

171 its best to imitate that of Cyrene. Westward, again, are the Auschisae, who live south of Barca and touch the sea near Euesperides. Within their territory is the small tribe of the Bacales, who reach the coast near Tauchira, a town belonging to Barca; they live in the same sort of way as the people south

172 of Cyrene. Still proceeding in a westerly direction, one comes next to the Nasamones, a numerous tribe, who in the summer leave their cattle on the coast and go up country to a place called Augila for the date harvest. The date-palms here grow in large numbers and to a great size, and are all of the fruit-bearing kind. These people also catch locusts, which they dry in the sun and grind up fine; then they sprinkle the powder on milk and drink it. Each of them has a number of wives, which they use in common, like the Massagetae – when a man wants to lie with a woman, he puts up a pole to indicate his intention. It is the custom, at a man's first marriage, to give a party, at which the bride is enjoyed by each of the guests in turn; they take her one after another, and then give her a present – something or other they have brought with them from home. In the matter of oaths, their practice is to swear by those of their countrymen who had the best reputation for integrity and valour, laying their hands upon their tombs; and for purposes of divination they go to sleep, after praying, on the graves of their forebears, and take as significant any dream they may have. When two men make a solemn compact, each drinks from the other's hand, and if there is no liquid available, they take some dust from the ground and lick it up.

173   The neighbours of the Nasamones are the Psylli – but they no longer exist. There is a story which I repeat as the Libyans tell it: that the south wind dried up the water in their storage tanks, so that they were left with none whatever, as their territory lies wholly within the Syrtis. Upon this they held a council, and having unanimously decided to declare war on the south wind, they marched out to the desert, where the wind blew and buried

them in sand. The whole tribe was wiped out, and the Nasamones occupied their former domain.

Further inland to the southward, in the part of Libya where   174
wild beasts are found, live the Garamantes, who avoid all intercourse with men, possess no weapons of war, and do not know
how to defend themselves.[45] Along the coast to the westward   175
the neighbours of the Nasamones are the Macae. These people
wear their hair in the form of a crest, shaving it close on either
side of the head and letting it grow long in the middle; in war
they carry ostrich skins for shields. The river Cinyps, which rises
on a hill called the Hill of the Graces, runs through their territory
to the sea. The Hill of the Graces is about twenty-five miles
inland, and is densely wooded, unlike the rest of Libya so far
described, which is bare of trees.

Next come the Gindanes. The women of this tribe wear   176
leather bands round their ankles, which are supposed to indicate
the number of their lovers: each woman puts on one band for
every man she has gone to bed with, so that whoever has the
greatest number enjoys the greatest reputation because she has
been loved by the greatest number of men. Within the territory   177
of the Gindanes a headland runs into the sea, and it is here that
the Lotophagi live, a tribe which lives exclusively on the fruit of
the lotus. The lotus fruit is about as big as a mastic-berry, and
as sweet as a date. The Lotophagi also make wine from it.

Next along the coast are the Machlyes, who also make use of   178
the lotus, but to a lesser extent than the Lotophagi. Their territory reaches to a large river called Triton, which flows into the
great lagoon of Tritonis. In the lagoon there is an island named
Phla, and there is said to be an oracle to the effect that the
Lacedaemonians should send settlers there. The story is also   179
told of how Jason, when he had finished building the *Argo*
under Mt Pelion, put on board, in addition to the usual offerings,
a bronze tripod, and set sail to round the Peloponnese on his
way to Delphi. Off Cape Malea he was caught by a northerly
blow and carried to Libya, where, before he could get his bear-
ings, he found himself in the shoal water off the lagoon of
Tritonis. How to get clear was a problem; but at that moment
Triton appeared and told Jason to give him the tripod, in return

for which he would show him the channel and let them all get away in safety. Jason did as he was asked, whereupon Triton showed him the course to steer in order to clear the shallows. He then placed the tripod in his own temple, after uttering over it in full detail, for the benefit of Jason's crew, the prophecy that when a descendant of the *Argo*'s company should carry off the tripod, it was unavoidably decreed by fate that a hundred Grecian cities should then be built on the shores of Lake Tritonis. The Libyans in the neighbourhood got to know of this prophecy, and hid the tripod.

180   The people next to the Machlyes are the Auses; both these tribes live on the shores of the lagoon, and the river Triton forms the boundary between them. The Machlyes let the hair grow on the back of their heads, the Auses on the front. They hold an annual festival in honour of Athene, at which the girls divide themselves into two groups and fight each other with stones and sticks; they say this rite had come down to them from time immemorial, and by its performance they pay honour to their native deity – which is the same as our Greek Athene. If any girl, during the course of the battle, is fatally injured and dies, they say it is a proof that she is no maiden. Before setting them to fight, they pick out the best-looking girl and dress her up publicly in a full suit of Greek armour and a Corinthian helmet; then they put her in a chariot and drive her round the lagoon. How they dressed these girls before there were Greeks settled in the neighbourhood, I cannot say; presumably the armour they used was Egyptian – for I am prepared to maintain that both shields and helmets were introduced into Greece from Egypt.[46] There is a belief amongst these people that Athene is the daughter of Poseidon and the Triton lake, but that having some quarrel with her father she put herself at the disposal of Zeus, who made her his own daughter. The women of the tribe are common property; there are no married couples living together, and intercourse is casual, like that of animals. When a child is fully grown, the men hold a meeting every third month, and it is considered to belong to the one it most closely resembles.

181   I have now mentioned all the pastoral tribes along the Libyan coast. Up country further to the south lies the region where wild

beasts are found, and beyond that there is a great belt of sand, stretching from Thebes in Egypt to the Pillars of Heracles. Along this belt, separated from one another by about ten days' journey, are little hills formed of lumps of salt, and from the top of each gushes a spring of cold, sweet water.[47] Men live in the neighbourhood of these springs – beyond the wild beasts' region, they are the furthest south, towards the desert, of any human beings. The first of them, ten days' journey from Thebes, are the Ammonians, with their temple derived from that of the Theban Zeus – I have already pointed out how the image of Zeus in both temples has a ram's face. They have another spring there, of which the water is tepid in the early morning and cools down towards market time; by noon it is very cold, and that is the moment when they water their gardens; then, as the days draw towards evening, the chill gradually goes off it, until by sunset it is tepid again; after that it gets hotter and hotter as the night advances, and at midnight it boils furiously. Then, after midnight, the process is reversed, and it steadily cools off until dawn. The spring is known as the Fountain of the Sun.

Ten days' journey west of the Ammonians, along the belt of sand, there is another similar salt-hill and spring. This place, called Augila, is also inhabited, and it is here that the Nasamonians come for their date harvest. Again at the same distance to the west is a salt-hill and spring, just as before, with date-palms of the fruit-bearing kind, as in the other springs; and here live the Garamantes, a very numerous tribe of people, who spread soil over the salt to sow their seed in. From these people is the shortest route – thirty days' journey – to the Lotophagi; and it is amongst them that the cattle are found which walk backwards as they graze. The reason for this curious habit is provided by the formation of their horns, which bend forwards and downwards; this prevents them from moving forwards in the ordinary way, for, if they tried to do so, their horns would stick in the ground. In other respects they are just like ordinary cattle – except for the thickness and toughness of their hide. The Garamantes hunt the Ethiopian troglodytes, in four-horse chariots, for these troglodytes are exceedingly swift of foot – more so than any people of whom we have any information.

They eat snakes and lizards and other reptiles and speak a language like no other, but squeak like bats.[48]

184   Ten days' journey from the Garamantes is yet another hill and spring – this time the home of the Atarantes, the only people in the world, so far as our knowledge goes, to do without names. Atarantes is the collective name – but individually they have none. They curse the sun as it rises and call it by all sorts of opprobrious names, because it wastes and burns both themselves and their land. Once more at a distance of ten days' journey there is a salt-hill, a spring, and a tract of inhabited country, and adjoining it rises Mt Atlas. In shape the mountain is a slender cone, and it is so high that according to report the top cannot be seen, because summer and winter it is never free of cloud. The natives (who are known as the Atlantes, after the mountains) call it the Pillar of the Sky. They are said to eat no living creature, and never to dream.

185   Thus far I am able to give the names of the tribes who inhabit the sand-belt, but beyond this point my knowledge fails. I can affirm, however, that the belt continues to the Pillars of Heracles and beyond, and that at regular intervals of ten days' journey are salt-hills and springs, with people living in the neighbourhood. The houses are all built of salt-blocks – an indication that there is no rain in this part of Libya; for if there were, salt walls would collapse. The salt which is mined there is of two colours, white and purple. South of the sand-belt, in the interior, lies a waterless desert, without rain or trees or animal life, or a drop of moisture of any kind.[49]

186   The coast of Libya, then, between Egypt and Lake Tritonis is occupied by nomads living on meat and milk – though they do not breed pigs, and abstain from cows' meat for the same reason as the Egyptians. Even at Cyrene women think it is wrong to eat heifers' meat, out of respect for the Egyptian Isis, in whose honour they celebrate both fasts and festivals. At Barca the
187   women avoid eating pigs' flesh, as well as cows'. West of Tritonis, nomad tribes are no longer found; the people are quite different, not only in their general way of life, but in the treatment of their children. Many of the nomads – perhaps all, but I cannot be certain about this – when their children are four

years old, burn the veins on their heads, and sometimes on their temples, with a bit of greasy wool, as a permanent cure for catarrh. For this reason they are said to be the healthiest people in the world – indeed, it is true enough that they are healthier than any other race we know of, though I cannot be too certain that this is the reason.[50] Anyway, about the fact of their health there is no doubt. Should the cauterizing of the veins bring on convulsions, they have discovered that the effective remedy is to sprinkle goat's urine on the child – I repeat in all this what is said by the Libyans. When the nomad tribes sacrifice, the process 188 is to begin by cutting off the victim's ear, which they throw over the house as a preliminary offering, and then to wring the animal's neck. They sacrifice to the sun and moon, the worship of which is common to all the Libyans, though those who live round Lake Tritonis sacrifice chiefly to Athene, and, after her, to Triton and Poseidon. It is evident, I think, that the Greeks 189 took the clothing and 'aegis' with which they adorn statues of Athene from the dress of the Libyan women; for except that the latter is of leather and has fringes of leather thongs instead of snakes, there is no other point of difference.[51] Moreover, the word 'aegis' itself shows that the dress represented in statues of Athene is derived from Libya; for Libyan women wear goatskins with the hair stripped off, dyed red and fringed at the edges, and it was from these skins that the Greeks took their word 'aegis'. I think too that the crying of women at religious cere-monies also originated in Libya – for the Libyan women are much addicted to this practice, and they do it very beautifully. Another thing the Greeks learnt from Libya was to harness four horses to a chariot. The nomad Libyans – except the 190 Nasamonians – bury their dead just as in Greece; the Nasa-monians, however, bury them in a sitting position, and take care when anyone is dying to make him sit up, and not to let him die flat on his back. Their houses, which are portable, are made of the dry haulms of some plant, knit together with rush ropes.

West of the Triton, and beyond the Auses, Libya is inhabited 191 by tribes who live in ordinary houses and practise agriculture. First come the Maxyes, a people who grow their hair on the right side of their heads and shave it off on the left. They stain their bodies red and claim to be descended from the men of Troy. The country round here, and the rest of Libya to the westward, has more forest and a greater number of wild animals than the region which the nomads occupy. The latter – that is, eastern Libya – is low-lying and sandy as far as the river Triton, whereas the agricultural region to the west is very hilly, and abounds with forest and animal life. It is here that the huge snakes are found – and lions, elephants, bears, asps, and horned asses, not to mention dog-headed men, headless men with eyes in their breasts (I merely repeat what the Libyans say), wild men and wild women, and a great many other creatures by no means

192 of a fabulous kind.[52] In the nomads' country none of these occur; instead, one finds white-rump antelopes, gazelles, deer, asses – not the horned sort but a different species which can do without water; it is a fact that they do not drink – another kind of antelope, about as big as an ox, the horns of which are used for making the curved sides of lyres, foxes, hyaenas, hedgehogs, wild rams, jackals, panthers, and others, including land-crocodiles like huge lizards, four and a half feet long, ostriches, and small snakes with a single horn. All these are found, together with other animals common elsewhere, with the exception of the stag and the wild boar, of which there are none at all in Libya. There are, however, three kinds of mice, called respectively *dipodes, zegeries,* and *echines* – also weasels which are found amongst the silphium, and resemble those at Tartessus. So much, then, for the animal life in that part of Libya where the nomads are: I have made it as full and accurate as my extensive inquiries permit.

193   Continuing westward from the Maxyes, one comes next to the Zaueces: amongst this people the drivers of the war-chariots

194 are the women. Their neighbours are the Gyzantes, whose country is very well supplied with honey – much of it made by bees, but even more by confectioners. Everybody here paints himself red and eats monkeys, of which there is an abundant

195 supply in the hills. Off the coast, according to the Carthaginian account, is an island called Cyrauis, about twenty-five miles long, but narrow, which can be reached on foot from the main-

land and is full of olive-trees and vines.⁵³ In the island is a lake,
and the native girls dip feathers smeared with pitch into the mud
at the bottom of it, and bring up gold dust – again, I merely
record the current story, without guaranteeing the truth of it. It
may, however, be true enough; for I have myself seen something
similar in Zacynthus, where pitch is fetched up from the water
in a lake. There are a number of lakes – or ponds – in Zacynthus,
of which the largest measures seventy feet each way and has a
depth of two fathoms. The process is to tie a branch of myrtle
on to the end of a pole, which is then thrust down to the bottom
of this pond; the pitch sticks to the myrtle, and is thus brought
to the surface. It smells like bitumen, but in all other respects it
is better than the pitch of Pieria. It is then poured into a trench
near the pond, and when a good quantity has been collected, it
is removed from the trench and transferred to jars. Anything
that falls into this pond, passes underground and comes up
again in the sea, a good half mile distant. In view of all this, the
account of what happens in the island off Libya may quite
possibly be true.

The Carthaginians also say that they trade with a race of men 196
who live in a part of Libya beyond the Pillars of Heracles. On
reaching this country, they unload their goods, arrange them
tidily along the beach, and then, returning to their boats, raise
a smoke. Seeing the smoke, the natives come down to the beach,
place on the ground a certain quantity of gold in exchange for
the goods, and go off again to a distance. The Carthaginians
then come ashore and take a look at the gold; and if they think
it represents a fair price for their wares, they collect it and go
away; if, on the other hand, it seems too little, they go back
aboard and wait, and the natives come and add to the gold until
they are satisfied. There is perfect honesty on both sides; the
Carthaginians never touch the gold until it equals in value what
they have offered for sale, and the natives never touch the goods
until the gold has been taken away.

I have now mentioned all the Libyans whose names I am 197
acquainted with; most of them cared nothing for the king of
Persia, either then or now. One other thing I can add about this
country: so far as one knows, it is inhabited by four races,

and four only, of which two are indigenous and two not. The indigenous peoples are the Libyans and Ethiopians, the former occupying the northerly, the latter the more southerly, parts;

198   the immigrants are the Phoenicians and Greeks. I do not think the country can be compared for the fertility of its soil with either Asia or Europe, with the single exception of the region called Cinyps – so named after the river which waters it. This region, however, is quite different from the rest of Libya, and is as good for cereal crops as any land in the world. The soil here, unlike the soil elsewhere, is black and irrigated by springs; it has no fear of drought on the one hand, or of damage, on the other, from excessive rain (it does, by the way, rain in that part of Libya). The yield of the harvests is equal to the yield in Babylonia. There is also good soil at Euesperides – in the best years it will yield a hundred-fold – but the yield in Cinyps is three

199   times as great. The land of Cyrene, the highest of that part of Libya which is inhabited by nomads, has the remarkable peculiarity of three separate harvest-seasons: first, the crops near the coast ripen and are ready for cutting or picking; then, when these are in, the crops in what they call the hill-country – the middle region above the coastal belt – are ready for harvesting; and lastly, when this second harvest is over, the crops in the highest tract of country are ripe and ready, so that by the time the first harvest is all eaten or drunk, the last comes in – making, for the fortunate people of Cyrene, a continuous harvest of eight months on end. So much for this subject.

200   On their arrival at Barca, the troops sent from Egypt by Aryandes to assist Pheretima laid siege to the town and called upon the inhabitants to surrender the men who were responsible for the murder of Arcesilaus.[54] The Barcaeans, however, refused, on the ground that every one of them was equally responsible. The siege therefore continued for nine months, the Persians endeavouring to effect an entrance by digging underground tunnels to the wall as well as by direct assault. A metal-worker very ingeniously discovered the saps in the following way: he went all round the inner circuit of the town wall with a bronze shield, with which he kept tapping the ground, and getting a dull, dead sound in every place except over the saps, where

the bronze of the shield echoed and rang. In these places the
Barcaeans dug counter-mines and killed the Persian sappers;
and they also succeeded in beating off the direct attacks. When   201
the siege had dragged on for a long time with much misery and
loss on both sides, especially in the Persian army, Amasis, who
was in command of the infantry, decided on a change of tactics:
realizing that Barca could not be taken by force, but might
nevertheless fall to fraud, he waited for darkness and dug up a
broad trench, over which he laid thin planks, finally making up
the surface with earth to the level of the ground on either side.
At dawn next morning he invited the Barcaeans to a conference,
to which they gladly came; and the conference ended in an
agreement on the following terms: standing upon the concealed
trench, they entered into solemn covenant to the effect that the
Barcaeans should pay a fair sum to the Persian king, and that
the Persians, in their turn, should do no further harm to Barca
– and that this covenant should stand so long as the earth
beneath their feet remained firm. As soon as the oaths were
sworn, the Barcaeans, without any thought of treachery, came
out of the town and, throwing open all the gates, invited any
Persian to enter it at will. The Persians accepted the invitation
and hurried in – but not before they had broken up the hidden
trench; for they wished to keep the oath which they had sworn
to the people of Barca, that the covenant should stand as long
as the ground under their feet. Well – the ground had given way,
so the oath no longer held.

The men of Barca who were most deeply involved in the   202
murder of Arcesilaus were delivered up by the Persians to
Pheretima, who impaled them on stakes all round the city wall.
She also cut off their wives' breasts, and stuck those up, too, in
the same position. The rest of the people she gave over to the
Persian soldiery to pillage, with the exception of those who
belonged to the house of Battus and were not implicated in the
murder. To these last she gave control of the town. Everyone   203
else the Persians reduced to slavery, and then started on their
march for home.

The people of Cyrene, on the appearance of the Persian army
before the town, decided, in fulfilment of some oracle or other,

to let it through. As they marched along the streets Badres, the commander of the fleet, recommended the seizure of the place, but Amasis, the commander of the infantry, refused on the ground that the objective of the expedition had been the single Greek city of Barca. Nevertheless, when they had passed through the town and come to a halt on the hill of Lycaean Zeus, they regretted their missed opportunity, and attempted to get into Cyrene again. This time, however, the Cyrenaeans refused to admit them, whereupon, though there was no fighting of any kind, the Persians were seized with panic and hastily retreated a distance of some seven miles before they dared come to a halt. Here the army encamped, and a message from Aryandes arrived, ordering them home; they applied to Cyrene for supplies, succeeded in obtaining them, and set off on their return to Egypt. But the Libyans harried their march, cutting off stragglers for the sake of their clothes and equipment, all the way to the border.

204   The furthest point in Libya reached by this Persian army was Euesperides. The Barcaeans who were taken as slaves were sent from Egypt to the Persian King Darius, who gave them a village in Bactria to live in. They named the village Barca, and it was still inhabited in my time.

205   Pheretima's web of life was also not woven happily to the end. No sooner had she returned to Egypt after her revenge upon the people of Barca, than she died a horrible death, her body seething with worms while she was still alive. Thus this daughter of Battus, by the nature and severity of her punishment of the Barcaeans, showed how true it is that all excess in revenge draws down upon men the anger of the gods.

BOOK FIVE

The Persians whom Darius had left in Europe under Megabazus' command began hostilities against the Greeks on the Hellespont by subduing the Perinthians, who refused to accept Persian domination.[1] Before this time they had already been roughly handled by the Paeonians. An oracle had told the Paeonians from the river Strymon to march on Perinthus, and if the Perinthians, once the armies faced each other, called them on by name, then they were to go for them; otherwise, they should hold back. The Perinthians took up their position on the outskirts of their town, a challenge was issued, and three champions from each side – a man, a horse, and a dog – engaged respectively in single combat. Seeing that two of their three champions were getting the better of the tussle, the Perinthians in great delight shouted out *Io Paean*, the cry of victory, whereupon the Paeonians at once supposed that this was what the oracle had meant. 'Now,' they said to each other, 'the oracle is fulfilled – and it's up to us.' They attacked immediately, won a resounding victory, and left few of their enemies alive. This incident took place a long time before; on the present occasion, in spite of a brave attempt to secure their freedom, the force of numbers was too much for them and they were defeated by Megabazus and the Persians. After the subjection of Perinthus, Megabazus marched through Thrace, bringing every city and every people in that country under the control of the Persian king. All this was according to orders; for he had received instructions from Darius to conquer Thrace.[2]

The population of Thrace is greater than that of any country in the world except India. If the Thracians could be united under a single ruler, or combine their purpose, they would be the most powerful nation on earth, and no one could cope with them – that, at any rate, is my own opinion; but in point of fact such a thing is impossible – there is no way of its ever being realized, and the result is that they are weak. They go by various names in different parts of the country, but they all live in much the same way with the exception of the Getae, the Trausi, and the people north of Creston. The customs of the Getae, who believe themselves immortal, I have already described;[3] the Trausi follow the normal practices of Thracians in general, except in one particular – their behaviour, namely, on the occasion of a birth or a death. When a baby is born the family sits round and mourns at the thought of the sufferings the infant must endure now that it has entered the world, and goes through the whole catalogue of human sorrows; but when somebody dies, they bury him with merriment and rejoicing, and point out how happy he now is and how many miseries he has at last escaped.[4]

With the Thracians who live beyond Creston, it is customary for a man to have a number of wives; and when a husband dies, his wives enter into keen competition, in which his friends play a vigorous part on one side or the other, to decide which of them was most loved. The one on whom the honour of the verdict falls is first praised by both men and women, and then slaughtered over the grave by her next of kin and buried by her husband's side.[5] For the other wives, not to be chosen is the worst possible disgrace, and they grieve accordingly. The rest of the Thracians carry on an export trade in their own children; they exercise no control over young girls, allowing them to have intercourse with any man they please; their wives, on the other hand, whom they purchase at high prices from their parents, they watch very strictly. They consider branding a mark of high birth, the lack of it a mark of low birth; the best man, in their opinion, is the idle man, and the sort least worthy of consideration is the agricultural labourer. The most reputable sources of income are war and plunder.[6] So much for their most striking customs. The only deities they worship are Ares, Dionysus, and Artemis – though their kings, in contrast to the people generally, pay particular reverence to Hermes; they swear by no other deity but Hermes, and claim their own descent from him. When a rich Thracian is buried, the custom is to lay out the body for three days, during which, after a preliminary period of mourning, a feast is held of all sorts of animals slaughtered for the purpose; then the body is buried, with or without cremation, a mound is raised over it, and elaborate games set on foot. The most valuable prizes in the games are awarded for single combat.

Of the country north of Thrace, and of who lives in it, there is no precise information; but it would seem that beyond the Danube lies a boundless tract of uninhabited land. One people only have I been able to hear of on the other side of the Danube: these are the Sigynnae, who dress, it is said, in the Median fashion, and have little, snub-nosed, shaggy horses, with hair about four inches long all over their bodies. These horses cannot carry a man, but are very fast in harness, with the result that driving is here the rule.[7] The borders of this country reach almost to the Veneti on the Adriatic. The Sigynnae claim to be colonists from Media, but how that can be so I cannot myself imagine – though anything can happen in the course of time. The word 'Sigynna' is used by the Ligurians above Marseilles for 'tradesman': in Cyprus it means 'spear'. According to the Thracian account the country beyond the Danube is infested by bees, which make further progress impossible; to my mind, however, this is an improbable story, as bees are not creatures which can stand the cold. I prefer to believe that it is cold which prevents men from living under the Great Bear. Such are the facts I have heard reported about this part of the world, the coastal region of which Megabazus was now bringing under Persian control.

As soon as Darius had crossed the Hellespont and arrived at Sardis, the recollection of the service rendered him by Histiaeus of Miletus, and of the good advice of the Mytilenean Coes, prompted him to send for the two men, and to ask them what they would like him to do for them in return. Histiaeus was already tyrant of Miletus, and did not ask for power over any other state in addition; instead, he put in a request for Myrcinus in the country of the Edoni, because he wished to found a city there;[8] Coes, on the other hand, who was a private person

without any rule, asked for the tyranny of Mytilene. Both pet-
itions were granted, and the two men went off to the places of
their choice.

12   Meanwhile Darius happened to see something which
prompted him to order Megabazus to effect the transfer of the
whole Paeonian nation from Europe to Asia. Two Paeonians
called Pigres and Mastyes wanted to seize power in their
country; so when Darius had crossed into Asia, they went to
Sardis with a sister of theirs, a tall and beautiful girl. Awaiting
the moment when Darius should take his seat in state before the
Lydian capital, they dressed the girl as finely as they could and
sent her off with a jar on her head to fetch water, leading a horse
by a halter round her arm and spinning flax as she went. The
sight of her as she passed was sufficiently remarkable to catch
Darius' eye; for what she was doing was not what one would
expect of a Persian or a Lydian, or any other Asiatic woman.
Darius, indeed, did more than notice her: he sent some of his
bodyguard to see what she would do with the horse. The men
followed her, and the girl, on reaching the river, watered the
horse, filled her pitcher, and started back by the same way as
she had come, with the pitcher of water on her head, leading
13   the horse and turning her spindle. Darius, much amazed both
by what his men had witnessed and by what he saw with his
own eyes, gave orders for the girl to be brought into his presence.
Soon she came, and with her her two brothers, who had kept at
hand to watch: Darius asked what nation the girl belonged to,
and the young men replied that they were Paeonians and that
she was their sister. The king then wanted to know who the
Paeonians were, and where their country was, and why the two
brothers had come to Sardis, and was told in reply that the
Paeonians were Teucrian colonists from Troy, that their country
was on the Strymon, not far from the Hellespont, and that the
reason for their coming to Sardis was to put themselves under
his power. Darius then asked if all the women in Paeonia were
as hard-working as this one, and the young men eagerly asserted
– which was, of course, the whole point of their proceedings –
that they were.

14   The result of this was that Darius wrote to Megabazus, whom

he had left in command in Thrace, instructing him to turn the Paeonians, men, women, and children, out of their homes and bring them to him.⁹ A messenger rode off with all speed to the Hellespont, crossed the water, and delivered the letter to Megabazus, who the moment he had read it provided himself with Thracian guides and marched against Paeonia. On hearing the news of his approach the Paeonians took the field in a body on the coast road, under the impression that the Persians would try to force their way in from that direction. They were fully prepared to resist Megabazus had he done what they expected; but the Persians no sooner learned of their concentration to guard the seaward approaches to their country than they procured guides and, taking the inland route, gave the Paeonians the slip and launched an attack on their towns, which, being undefended, fell an easy prey. At the news that their towns were in enemy hands, the Paeonian army disintegrated; the men went off on their own and surrendered individually to the Persians. The result of the campaign was that a number of Paeonian tribes – the Siriopaeones, Paeoplae, and the others as far as Lake Prasias – were transferred bodily to Asia. The tribes in the neighbourhood of Mt Pangaeum and on the lake itself were not subjugated by Megabazus – though he did attempt the conquest of the latter. The houses of these lake-dwellers are actually in the water, and stand on platforms supported on long piles and approached from the land by a single narrow bridge. Originally the labour of driving the piles was presumably undertaken by the tribe as a whole, but later they adopted a different method; now the piles are brought from Mt Orbelus and every man drives in three for each wife he marries – and each has a great many wives. Each member of the tribe has his own hut on one of the platforms, with a trap-door opening on to the water underneath. To prevent their babies from tumbling in, they tie a string to their legs. Their horses and other pack-animals they feed on fish, which are so abundant in the lake that, when they open the trap-door and let down an empty basket on a rope, they have only a minute to wait before they pull it up again, full. The fish are of two kinds – they call them *papraces* and *tilones*.

17   The captured Paeonians were taken to Asia, and Megabazus,
after his successful campaign, sent to Amyntas of Macedonia a
demand for earth and water, as a sign of his submission to
Darius. The seven most distinguished Persians in the army, after
himself, were entrusted with the task of conveying the message.
It is a very short way from Lake Prasias to Macedonia; next to
the lake is the mine which later produced a talent of silver every
day for Alexander,[10] and then one has only to cross a mountain
18   named Dysorum to get there. On their arrival the seven Persian
envoys obtained an audience with Amyntas and made their
demands for earth and water. It was not refused; Amyntas,
moreover, invited them to a magnificent dinner which he had
prepared, and entertained them most hospitably. After dinner,
while the wine was still going round, one of the Persians said:
'At important dinners like this, my Macedonian friend, it is our
custom in Persia to get our wives and mistresses to come and sit
with us in the dining-room. You have welcomed us kindly,
provided us with an excellent dinner, and offered earth and
water to our King Darius; come then – won't you follow our
custom?'[11]

'Persians,' Amyntas replied, 'what you mention is by no means
the custom in Macedonia; with us, men and women are kept
separate. However, you are our masters, and, as you ask for this
favour, you shall not be refused.'

Amyntas sent for the women, and they came in and sat down
in a row opposite the Persians, who, finding them very charming,
remarked to Amyntas that such an arrangement was by no
means a good one: it would surely have been better for the
women not to have come at all if, instead of sitting beside them,
they merely intended to sit opposite. It was a painful thing only
to be allowed to look at them. Amyntas, of necessity, told the
women to move over and sit with the guests, and as soon as
they did so, the Persians, who were very drunk, began to touch
their breasts, and even, in some cases, to try to kiss them.
19   Amyntas saw what was going on, but his great fear of the
Persians helped him, in spite of his anger, to hold his tongue;
his son Alexander, however, who was also present and a witness
of the Persians' behaviour, was quite unable to restrain himself

– he was a young man, ignorant of the harsh ways of the world, and in his resentment he said to Amyntas: 'You are an old man, father, and should look after yourself. Don't try to sit out the drinking, but go and rest. I will stay at table, and give our guests all they need.' Amyntas, convinced that his son was about to do something rash, said he could tell by the way the boy spoke that he was all on fire, and wanted to get his father out of the way only to commit some violence. 'But,' he added, 'I beg you not to do these men any mischief; for if you do, you will ruin us all. Have the courage to endure the sight of their behaviour. As for myself, I will leave the room as you suggest.'

With this warning, Amyntas went out, and Alexander turned   20 to the Persians. 'My friends,' he said, 'these women are entirely at your service; you may go to bed with any of them you like – indeed, with all of them. You have but to say the word. Now, however, as it is nearly bedtime and you are, as I observe, agreeably primed with drink, perhaps you will allow me to send them away to take a bath – after which you may have them back again.' The Persians agreed, and Alexander, after telling the women to return to their quarters, dressed in their clothes an equal number of smooth-chinned young men, gave them a dagger each, took them back into the dining-room, and said to the Persians: 'Gentlemen, you have had, I think, a really perfect dinner. Everything we had, and everything we could get, has been yours; and now, to put the finishing touch to your entertainment, we make you a free and generous offer of our mothers and sisters, that you may know without any doubt that we honour you as you deserve, and that you may tell your king, who sent you, that a Greek, the lord of Macedonia, entertained you royally both with bed and board.' Alexander then put a Macedonian by the side of each Persian; and when the Persians, thinking they were women, tried to touch them, they were stabbed.

That was the end of the Persian envoys to Macedon – and of   21 their servants too; servants, and carriages, and a great deal of luggage of every kind – all disappeared together. Not long afterwards the Persians went to much trouble in an attempt to trace the lost envoys; but Alexander cleverly succeeded in

keeping the affair dark by giving Bubares, the Persian commander of the search-party, a large sum of money and his own
sister Gygaea. In this way the murder was hushed up and never
discovered.

22   I happen to know, and will demonstrate in a subsequent
chapter of this history,[12] that these descendants of Perdiccas
are, as they themselves claim, of Greek nationality. This was,
moreover, recognized by the managers of the Olympic games,
on the occasion when Alexander wished to compete and his
Greek competitors tried to exclude him on the ground that
foreigners were not allowed to take part. Alexander, however,
proved his Argive descent, and so was accepted as a Greek and
allowed to enter for the foot-race. He came in equal first.

23   Megabazus took the Paeonians to the Hellespont, crossed
over, and continued his march to Sardis. Histiaeus of Miletus
was already engaged in the fortification of Myrcinus, the place
which he had asked Darius to give him for his services in
guarding the bridge over the Danube. Myrcinus is on the
Strymon. His proceedings did not escape Megabazus' attention;
so as soon as he reached Sardis with the Paeonians, he said to
Darius: 'I am astonished, my lord, at your rashness in allowing
an accomplished and clever Greek like Histiaeus to found a
settlement in Thrace. The site, with its silver mines, and abundance of timber for building ships and making oars, is a very
valuable one. The neighbourhood is thickly populated both
with Greeks and barbarians, all of whom will accept him as
their master and do what he tells them, night and day. I beg you
to put a stop to what he is doing, or you will find yourself
involved in a war with your own subjects. Send for him, so that
he can't go on with it – and let your message be a tactful one;
but once you have him, see that he never has a chance to get
24   back to Greece.' Megabazus, who showed admirable foresight
in this, had no difficulty in persuading Darius to do as he asked,
and a courier was dispatched to Myrcinus with the following
message: 'Darius the King to Histiaeus: On thinking the matter
over, I find that I have no friend more loyal than yourself, or
more devoted to my prosperity; and the proof of it has been
deeds, not words. Therefore, as I have an important enterprise

in hand, I beg you to come to me without fail, in order that I may communicate it to you.'

Histiaeus took the message as genuine and was much flattered at being a King's Counsellor. He obeyed the summons, and on his arrival at Sardis, Darius said to him: 'I will tell you, Histiaeus, why I sent for you. Ever since I lost sight of you after my return from Scythia I have never desired anything so much as to see and talk to you again; for I am convinced that a man's most precious possession is a wise and loyal friend, and that you are both these things my own experience has shown me. Now, therefore, as you have been kind enough to come to Sardis, I have a proposal to make: forget about Miletus and this new settlement of yours in Thrace, and come with me to Susa. All I have will there be yours. You will eat at my table and be my counsellor.'[13]

Darius then left for Susa and made Histiaeus accompany him. 25 Before he went, he appointed Artaphernes, his brother by the same father, as governor of Sardis, and gave Otanes the command of the coast. Otanes' father Sisamnes had been put to death by Cambyses: he was one of the royal judges, and as a punishment for taking a bribe and perverting justice Cambyses had him flayed; all his skin was torn off and cut into strips, and the strips stretched across the seat of the chair which he used to sit on in Court. Cambyses then appointed his son to be judge in his place, and told him not to forget what his chair was made of, when he gave his judgements. This Otanes – the one who had 26 the remarkable chair – after taking over Megabazus' command, captured Byzantium and Chalcedon, and also Antandrus in the Troad, and Lamponium; then with Lesbian ships he captured Lemnos and Imbros, both of which islands were at that time still occupied by Pelasgians. The men of Lemnos put up a stiff 27 resistance, but were finally crushed, and the Persians appointed Lycaretus, the brother of Maeandrius the ruler of Samos, to take charge of those of them who were left alive. Lycaretus died as governor in Lemnos. The reason Otanes gave for subjugating and enslaving all these people was that some had shirked service in the Scythian expedition, while others had molested Darius' army on its way home.

28   Such were the exploits of Otanes after he took over the command. Then trouble ceased for a while, until it broke out again in Ionia.[14] This time it came from Naxos and Miletus. Naxos, just then, was the richest island in the Aegean, and Miletus during the same period had reached the peak of her prosperity and was the glory of Ionia. Previously Miletus had been terribly weakened by civil disorders, which lasted for two generations, until a commission from Paros was asked in to put her on her feet again. The Parians, whom the people of Miletus had chosen out of all the Greeks to settle their disputes, managed 29   the business in the following way: their best men visited the place, and when they saw the widespread ruin there they asked to be allowed to make a thorough inspection of all the land. This they did, and whenever in the desolated countryside they saw a bit of well-cultivated ground, they made a note of its owner's name. Of such farms, however, though they examined the whole Milesian territory, they found very few. After their inspection the commissioners returned to the city and lost no time in calling a general assembly, at which they announced their decision to entrust the government to the men whose land they had found in good order – for there was no doubt, in their opinion, that such men would manage public business as efficiently as they had managed their own. The other Milesians were told to take their orders from the new government.

30   But to return from this business of the Parians to the Ionian troubles I mentioned just now – to those, I mean, which originated in Naxos and Miletus. Certain substantial citizens of Naxos, forced by the commons to leave the island, took refuge in Miletus, which had been put under Aristagoras, son of Molpagoras, as deputy governor. He was nephew and son-in-law of Histiaeus, the son of Lysagoras, who was being detained by Darius at Susa. Power in Miletus actually belonged to Histiaeus – but, as I said, he was in Susa when the Naxian exiles, formerly his guest-friends, arrived. The first thing they did when they got there was to ask Aristagoras to lend them some troops, in the hope of recovering their position at home. This suggested to Aristagoras that if he helped the exiles to return he himself would be ruler of Naxos; so using their friendship with Histiaeus

to cloak his purpose, he made them an offer. 'Personally,' he said, 'I cannot engage to furnish enough troops to force your return to Naxos against the wishes of the party now in power. They have, I understand, eight thousand armoured men, and they have a powerful fleet. I will, however, do my very best to find a means of helping you. My idea is this: Artaphernes is a friend of mine – and Artaphernes, you must know, is the son of Hystaspes and the brother of Darius, and is in command of the whole coastal district of Asia, with a large army and navy. This, I think, is the man who will do our business for us.'

On this, the Naxians authorized Aristagoras to make the best arrangements he could, and told him to promise certain sums of money which they would themselves furnish, and pay for the troops; for they had great hopes that, when they appeared in Naxos, the people would submit to their orders, and then the other islands of the Cyclades, for none of these had yet been subdued by Darius.

Aristagoras then went to Sardis and told Artaphernes that Naxos, in spite of its small size, was a fine and fertile island, close to the Ionian coast, and rich both in treasure and slaves. 'Therefore,' he went on, 'I suggest that you attack it, and restore the exiles. If you do this, two advantages will accrue: first, I have a large sum of money for you, over and above the expenses of the expedition (which would naturally be met by us who undertake it), and, secondly, you will add to the king's dominions not only Naxos itself but the other islands of the Cyclades, such as Paros and Andros, which are dependent on it. Then with the Cyclades as your base you will have no difficulty in attacking Euboea, a large island – as large as Cyprus – and very prosperous and easy to take. For the whole enterprise you will need not more than a hundred ships.'

'The plan you propose,' Artaphernes replied, 'is likely to be of great benefit to our royal house, and I think your advice is excellent, except in one particular – the size of the fleet. Instead of a hundred, I shall have two hundred ready for you next spring. The only other thing we need is to get the king's approval.'

Aristagoras returned to Miletus much pleased with this answer, and Artaphernes at once communicated with Susa. He laid the proposal of Aristagoras before the king, obtained his consent, and set about his preparations, equipping two hundred triremes and a strong force of Persian and allied troops, the whole of which he put under the command of Megabates, one of the Achaemenidae, and a cousin both of Darius and himself. Megabates' daughter – if there is any truth in the story – was subsequently betrothed to Pausanias, son of Cleombrotus, when he had his heart set on making himself master of Greece.[15]

33   After the appointment of Megabates to the command, Artaphernes gave him instructions to proceed to Miletus, where he took Aristagoras on board together with the Ionian contingent and the Naxian exiles. He then made sail ostensibly for the Hellespont; but, on reaching Chios, he brought up at Caucasa, meaning to make a passage from there to Naxos as soon as he got a northerly wind. However, the Naxians were not destined to come to grief as a result of this expedition. What happened was this: Megabates, on making his rounds to inspect the watch, found a Myndian vessel on which no watch had been set. Angry at this neglect of duty, he ordered his guard to find the captain – a man named Scylax – and to put him in irons with his head sticking out through an oar-port in the ship's side. Somebody told Aristagoras about this ignominious punishment of his Myndian guest-friend, and Aristagoras went to Megabates and tried to get him released. Megabates refused, so Aristagoras released the man with his own hands. The Persian commander was furious – and said so with great vigour; to which Aristagoras answered: 'All this is none of your business. Didn't Artaphernes put you under my orders when he sent you out here? Didn't he tell you to sail wherever I thought fit? Why are you meddling?'

Megabates was angry at this; and as soon as it was dark he sent off a party of men in a boat to Naxos, to warn the people
34   of their danger; for they had no idea that it was against them that the expedition was directed. On receipt of the warning, however, they lost no time in preparing for a siege; all the stuff from the open country was brought inside the city walls, a stock of food and drink was laid in, and the defences strengthened. As a result of these preparations for imminent war, the enemy,

after making the passage from Chios, found the islanders in a strong position and quite ready to receive them. The siege began and continued for four months; by that time all the stores which the Persians had brought with them were exhausted; Aristagoras had spent a great deal of money from his private funds – and still more was needed, if the siege was to continue. The Persians, therefore, decided to give up. They built some forts for the exiles and withdrew to the mainland. The expedition had been a failure.

Aristagoras was now unable to keep his promise to Arta- 35 phernes. The call upon him to meet the expenses of the men's pay had landed him in difficulties and he was afraid that, owing to the failure of the attempt on Naxos and his quarrel with Megabates, he might lose his position in Miletus. These various causes of alarm were already making Aristagoras contemplate rebellion, when something else occurred to confirm his purpose: this was the arrival from Susa of a slave, sent by Histiaeus, the man with the tattooed scalp, urging him to do precisely what he was thinking of, namely, to revolt. Histiaeus had been wanting to make Aristagoras take this step, but was in difficulty about how to get a message safely through to him, as the roads from Susa were watched; so he shaved the head of his most trust-worthy slave, pricked the message on his scalp, and waited for hair to grow again. Then, as soon as it had grown, he sent the man to Miletus with instructions to do nothing when he arrived except to tell Aristagoras to shave his hair off and look at his head. The message found there was, as I have said, an order to revolt. What prompted Histiaeus to do this was his distress at being detained in Susa, and he hoped that, if a rebellion were started, he might be sent down to the coast to deal with it, whereas if nothing of the sort occurred he had little expectation of ever seeing Miletus again. With this purpose in mind he sent 36 off the messenger; and so Aristagoras found himself faced with a combination of circumstances, all of which urged him in the same direction. Accordingly, he called a council of his sup-porters, declared his views, and told them of Histiaeus' message. His friends were unanimous in their approval, and all recom-mended revolt – with a single exception: the writer Hecataeus.

Hecataeus was strongly opposed to war with Persia, enumerating the resources at Darius' command, and supporting his point with a long list of the nations under Persian dominion.[16] This argument, however, failed to convince the meeting, so, as second best, he advised them to work for control of the sea. He then went on to say that, in view of the weakness of Miletus, of which he was well aware, there was, in his opinion, only one way in which this could be done: namely, by taking from the temple at Branchidae the treasure which had been deposited there by the Lydian King Croesus. If that were done, he had good hope that they might succeed in gaining command of the sea – in any case they would themselves have the use of the money, and prevent it from falling into enemy hands. This treasure was of great value, as I have shown in the first part of my History.[17]

Hecateus' proposal was not adopted; but they did decide, none the less, to throw off the Persian yoke, and, as a first step, to send one of their number to Myus, where the army was which had returned from Naxos, and there to try to seize the fleet's 37 commanders. The man they sent was Iatragoras, and a number fell into the trap he laid – Oliatus, the son of Ibanolis of Mylasa, Histiaeus, son of Tymnes of Termera, Coes, son of Erxander (to whom Darius had given Mytilene), Aristagoras, son of Heracleides, of Cyme: all these and many more he managed to get into his hands. After that all disguise was thrown off, and Aristagoras, in open rebellion, set himself to damage Darius in every way he could think of. To induce the Milesians to support him, he began by professing to abdicate his tyranny in favour of a popular government, and then went on to do the same thing in the other Ionian states, where he got rid of the tyrants. Some of them he drove out; others, whom he had arrested on the ships which had joined his expedition to Naxos, he handed over to the cities to which they respectively belonged, hoping thereby 38 to get the goodwill of their former subjects. At Mytilene, Coes was taken out and stoned to death the moment the people got their hands on him; at Cyme, however, Aristagoras was allowed to go free, and most of the other cities showed a similar leniency.

Having thus put down the despots in the various states of

Ionia, Aristagoras of Miletus first ordered each state to establish a board of generals,[18] and then, as he needed to find some powerful ally, embarked in a trireme and set sail on a mission to Lacedaemon.

Anaxandrides, son of Leon, was no longer king of Sparta, for   39
he had died and his son Cleomenes had succeeded him – not, indeed, by right of merit but merely by right of birth.[19] Anaxandrides had married his sister's daughter, to whom he was devoted; but the marriage was childless, and in view of this fact he was summoned to appear before the Ephors, who declared that even if he chose to neglect his own interests, they, at least, could not allow the family of Eurysthenes to die out. 'As your wife bears no children,' they said, 'you had better get rid of her and marry someone else, if you wish to please the Spartans.' Anaxandrides answered that he had no intention of doing either; his wife had been guilty of no fault, and the magistrates' advice that he should send her away and marry another woman instead was most improper – he would do nothing of the kind. At this,   40
the Ephors and Elders began to think again, and finally made another proposal. 'It is clear,' they said, 'that you are much attached to your wife. You would be wise, therefore, to make no objection to what we are now about to suggest – to refuse again might make it necessary for the Spartans to take unpleasant measures against you.[20] As for your present wife, we do not ask you to divorce her; you may continue to give her all the privileges she now enjoys; but you must marry another woman as well, to bear you children.' Anaxandrides consented, and from that time had two wives and two separate households – an unheard-of thing in Sparta.

Not long after, his second wife gave birth to Cleomenes, and   41
no sooner had she presented the Spartans with an heir to the throne than, strangely enough, his first wife, who had formerly been childless, also happened to become pregnant. The relatives of the second wife made a great fuss when they heard the news, and maintained – what was quite untrue – that she was pretending to be pregnant for the sake of her reputation, and meant to pass off a supposititious baby as her own. So great

was the outcry they made that when her time came the Ephors, who were not convinced one way or the other, sat round her bed while the child was actually being born. The child was named Dorieus; and almost immediately after his birth she was again pregnant, this time with Leonidas, and yet again, after a very short interval, with Cleombrotus – though some have said that the two latter were twins. Anaxandrides' second wife, however, the mother of Cleomenes – she was a daughter of Prinetades, son of Demarmenus – never had another child.

42　　But to return to Cleomenes: he was, the story goes, not quite right in his head – even, indeed, on the verge of madness, whereas Dorieus was the finest young man of his generation and confident that his merits would assure his succession. As a result of this he was naturally indignant when, on the death of Anaxandrides, the Spartans followed their usual custom and put the eldest son, Cleomenes, on the throne. Unable to bear the prospect of being ruled by Cleomenes, he asked the Spartans for a body of men and took them off to found a settlement elsewhere, without previously consulting the Delphic oracle on a suitable site, or observing any of the usual formalities: he just went off, in a fit of temper, to Libya, with some men from Thera to act as guides. Arrived there, he settled by the river Cinyps, on a piece of excellent land belonging to the Libyans. Within three years, however, he was driven out by the Macae (a Libyan tribe)

43　　and the Carthaginians, and returned to the Peloponnese.[21] Here he was advised by a certain Antichares of Eleon, on the strength of the oracles given to Laius, to found the city of Heraclea in Sicily; for, according to this person, all the country of Eryx in Western Sicily belonged to the Heraclids, as Heracles himself was its original conqueror. Dorieus, accordingly, went to Delphi to consult the oracle on his chance of acquiring the land which he was after, and was told by the Priestess that it would certainly be his, whereupon he fetched the band of settlers whom he had taken to Libya and sailed with them along the Italian coast.

44　　The people of Sybaris say that just about this time they and their ruler Telys were contemplating war against Crotona; the Crotoniates in great alarm asked, and obtained, the assistance of Dorieus, who joined them in their campaign and helped them to capture Sybaris. This, as I said, is the account the Sybarites give; but the Crotoniates say that they had no foreign ally in their war with Sybaris, except the Elean soothsayer Callias, one of the Iamidae, who joined after deserting Telys, because he found, on offering sacrifice, that the omens were unfavourable for an attack on Croton. Both parties produce evidence to support their stories: the Sybarites, first, show a piece of consecrated ground, with a temple in it, near the dry bed of the Crathis, and declare that it was Dorieus who, after the capture of the town, dedicated it to Athene Crathias; and, secondly, adduce as the strongest proof of all the death of Dorieus, who, they maintain, lost his life because he transgressed the instructions of the oracle. Had he done only what he was sent to do, and not allowed himself to be led into incidental adventures, he would have taken and held the country of Eryx, and neither he nor his army would have perished. The Crotoniates, on the other hand, point to the extensive lands in their territory which were granted to Callias (they were still, within my own memory, in the possession of his family), whereas Dorieus and his descendants were granted none at all. Yet if – they argue – Dorieus really did help in the war, a great deal more would have been given to him than to Callias. In this conflict of evidence, you may agree with whichever party you think is telling the truth.

Other Spartans sailed with Dorieus to assist in founding the new settlement. These were Thessalus, Paraebates, Celeas, and Euryleon. They reached Sicily, but were defeated and killed, with all the men under their command, in a battle with the Phoenicians and the people of Egesta. The only one of them to escape was Euryleon, who collected the few survivors of the army and captured Minoa, a colony of Selinus, and helped the people of Selinus to free themselves from their ruler Peithagoras. Later, after the expulsion of Peithagoras, he attempted to seize power in Selinus himself, and did actually enjoy it for a while, until the people of the town organized a revolt and killed him, though he took sanctuary at the altar of Zeus of the Market-Place.

Another man who accompanied Dorieus, and shared his fate,

was Philippus, the son of Butacides and a native of Croton; he had been engaged to marry a daughter of Telys of Sybaris; but the marriage came to nothing, as he was banished from Croton. In his disappointment he sailed for Cyrene, and it was from there that he equipped a trireme, which he manned at his own expense, to join in Dorieus' expedition. This Philippus was an Olympic victor and the best-looking man of his day; and because of his good looks he received from the people of Egesta the unparalleled honour of a hero's shrine erected on his tomb, at which religious ceremonies are still held to win his favour.[22]

48   This, then, was the end of Dorieus, who might have been king of Sparta had he only stayed there and put up for a time with being a subject of Cleomenes; for Cleomenes' reign was a brief one,[23] and he died without a son to succeed him, leaving only a daughter, whose name was Gorgo.

49   Cleomenes, however, was on the throne when Aristagoras of Miletus came to Sparta. According to the Spartan account, Aristagoras brought to the interview a map of the world engraved on bronze, showing all the seas and rivers, and opened the conversation in the following way: 'I hope, Cleomenes, that you will not be too much surprised at my anxiety to visit you. The circumstances are these. That Ionians should have become slaves in place of free men is a bitter shame and grief not only to us, but to the rest of Greece, and especially to you, who are the leaders of the Greek world. We beg you, therefore, in the name of the gods of Greece, to save from slavery your Ionian kinsmen. It will be an easy task, for these foreigners have little taste for war, and you are the finest soldiers in the world. The Persian weapons are bows and short spears; they fight in trousers and turbans – that will show you how easy they are to beat! Moreover, the inhabitants of that continent are richer than all the rest of the world put together – they have everything, gold, silver, bronze, elaborately embroidered clothes and beasts of burden and slaves. All this you may have if you wish. I will show you the relative positions of the various nations.'

Here Aristagoras produced the map he had brought with him.[24] 'Look,' he continued, pointing to it, 'next to the Ionians here are the Lydians – theirs is a fine country, rich in money.

Then come the Phrygians, farther east, richest in cattle and crops
of all the nations we know. And here, adjoining them are the
Cappadocians – Syrians, we Greeks call them; and next to them
the Cilicians, with their territory extending to the coast – see,
here's the island of Cyprus – who pay annual tribute to the
Persian king of five hundred talents. Now, the Armenians –
they, too, have cattle in abundance; and next to them, here, the
Matieni. Again, farther east, lies Cissia: you can see the
Choaspes marked, with Susa on its banks, where the Great King
lives, and keeps his treasure. Why, if you take Susa, you need
not hesitate to compete with Zeus himself for riches. You should
suspend your wars over a scrap of land – and poor land at that
– with your rivals the Messenians and Arcadians and Argives,
who have nothing whatever in the nature of gold or silver which
is worth fighting and dying for, when you are offered the chance
of an easy conquest of the whole land of Asia. Is there really
any choice between the two?'[25]

'Milesian,' Cleomenes replied, 'I will wait two days before I
give you an answer.'

That was as far as they got at the moment; but when the day   50
came on which Cleomenes had agreed to give his decision and
they met at the appointed place, he asked Aristagoras how far
off Susa was, and how many days it took to reach it from the
Ionian coast. Up to this, Aristagoras had been clever, and had
led Cleomenes on with great success; but in answering this
question he made a bad mistake. If he wanted to induce the
Spartans to invade Asia, he never ought to have told the truth;
but he did, and said it took three months. Cleomenes stopped
Aristagoras from saying any more of the road to Susa. 'Milesian
stranger,' he cried, 'you must leave Sparta before sunset. Your
proposal to take Lacedaemonians a three months' journey from
the sea is a highly improper one.'

Cleomenes then went home, and Aristagoras followed him   51
with a branch of olive in his hand, like a suppliant, made his
way in, and besought Cleomenes to listen, and send away the
child – for his only daughter Gorgo, a little girl of eight or nine,
happened to be standing by her father's side. Cleomenes told
him to say what he wished and not to mind the child, and

Aristagoras, in answer, began with an offer of ten talents, to be paid to Cleomenes if he consented to do what he asked. Cleomenes shook his head, and Aristagoras gradually increased his offer. When he went as high as fifty talents the little girl suddenly exclaimed: 'Father, you had better go away, or the stranger will corrupt you.' Cleomenes appreciated his daughter's warning, and went into another room, and Aristagoras left Sparta for good, without succeeding in saying any more about the road to Susa.[26]

52 That information I will now supply myself. At intervals all along the road are recognized stations, with excellent inns, and the road itself is safe to travel by, as it never leaves inhabited country. In Lydia and Phrygia, over a distance of $94\frac{1}{2}$ parasangs – about 330 miles – there are 20 stations. On the far side of Phrygia one comes to the river Halys; there are gates here, which have to be passed before one crosses the river, and a strong guard-post. Once over the river and into Cappadocia, a distance of 104 parasangs, with 28 stations, brings one to the Cilician border, where the road passes through two sets of gates, both guarded. These left behind, the distance through Cilicia is $15\frac{1}{2}$ parasangs, with three stations. Separating Cilicia from Armenia is a river, the Euphrates, which has to be crossed in a boat, and the distance across Armenia itself is $56\frac{1}{2}$ parasangs, with 15 stations or stopping-places. Here, too, there is a guard. Through this part of the country four rivers run, all of which have to be crossed by a ferry: the first is the Tigris; the second and third both have the same names – Zabatus – though they are different rivers and flow from distinct sources, one rising in Armenia, the other in Matiene; and the fourth is the Gyndes – the river which Cyrus once split up into three hundred and sixty channels. Leaving Armenia and entering Matiene, one has 137 parasangs to go, with 34 stations, and, passing from thence into Cissia, another $42\frac{1}{2}$ with 11 stations, which bring one to the river Choaspes – another navigable stream – on which the city of Susa stands. Thus the total number of stations, or posthouses, 53 on the road from Sardis to Susa is 111. If the measurement of the Royal Road in parasangs is correct, and if a parasang is equal (as indeed it is) to 30 furlongs, then the distance from

Sardis to the Palace of Memnon (450 parasangs) will be 13,500 furlongs. Travelling, then, at the rate of 150 furlongs a day, a man will take just ninety days to make the journey. So one can see that Aristagoras of Miletus was quite right when he told the Spartan Cleomenes that it took three months to reach Susa from the sea. But, if anyone wants still greater accuracy, I would point out that the distance from Ephesus to Sardis should be added to the total, so that one gets, as a final measurement of the distance from the Aegean to Susa – the 'city of Memnon' – 14,040 furlongs, Ephesus to Sardis being 540 furlongs, which increase the three months' journey by three days.

Repulsed from Sparta, Aristagoras went on to Athens, which had been liberated from tyranny in the way which I will now describe.[27] Hipparchus, the son of Pisistratus and brother of the despot Hippias, in spite of a vivid dream which warned him of his danger, was murdered by Harmodius and Aristogeiton, two men belonging to the family of the Gephyraei; the murder, however, did the Athenians no good, for the oppression they suffered during the four succeeding years was worse than before.[28] Hipparchus had dreamt, on the night before the Panathenaic festival, that the tall and beautiful figure of a man stood over his bed and spoke to him these obscure and riddling words:

> O lion, endure the unendurable with enduring heart;
> No man does wrong and shall not pay the penalty.

At dawn next morning he was seen communicating his dream to the interpreters; but later he put it out of his mind and took part in the procession, during which he was killed.

The Gephyraei, to whom the two men who killed Hipparchus belonged, came, by their own account, originally from Eretria; but I have myself looked into the matter and find that they were really Phoenicians, descendants of those who came with Cadmus to what is now Boeotia, where they were allotted the district of Tanagra to make their homes in. After the expulsion of the Cadmeans by the Argives, the Gephyraei were expelled by the Boeotians and took refuge in Athens, where they were received into the community on certain stated terms, which excluded them from a few privileges not worth mentioning here.

58   The Phoenicians who came with Cadmus – amongst whom were the Gephyraei – introduced into Greece, after their settlement in the country, a number of accomplishments, of which the most important was writing, an art till then, I think, unknown to the Greeks.[29] At first they used the same characters as all the other Phoenicians, but as time went on, and they changed their language, they also changed the shape of their letters. At that period most of the Greeks in the neighbourhood were Ionians; they were taught these letters by the Phoenicians and adopted them, with a few alterations, for their own use, continuing to refer to them as the Phoenician characters – as was only right, as the Phoenicians had introduced them. The Ionians also call paper 'skins' – a survival from long ago when paper was hard to get, and they did actually use goat and sheep skins to write on. Indeed, even today many foreign peoples use this material. In

59   the temple of Ismenian Apollo at Thebes in Boeotia I have myself seen tripods with inscriptions cut on them in Cadmean characters – most of them not very different from the Ionian. There were three of these tripods; one was inscribed: 'Amphityron dedicated me from the spoils of the Teleboae', and would date from about the time of Laius, son of Labdacus, grandson of Polydorus and great-grandson of Cadmus. Another had an

60   inscription of two hexameter verses:

> Scaeus the boxer, victorious in the contest,
> Gave me to Apollo, the striker from afar, a lovely offering.

This might be Scaeus the son of Hippocoön; and the bowl, if it was dedicated by him and not by someone else of the same

61   name, would be contemporary with Laius' son Oedipus. The third was also inscribed in hexameters:

> Laodamas, while he reigned, dedicated this cauldron
> To the good archer Apollo – a lovely offering.

It was during the reign of this Laodamas, the son of Eteocles, that the Cadmeans were expelled by the Argives and took refuge with the Encheles. The Gephyraei remained in the country, but were later forced by the Boeotians to withdraw to Athens, where they have certain temples set apart for their own special use, which the other Athenians are forbidden to enter; one of them is the temple of Demeter Achaeia, in which secret rites are performed.

Having told the story of Hipparchus' dream, and traced the descent of the Gephyraei, the family to which the men who murdered him belonged, I must now get back to my original theme: the liberation of Athens from despotic rule, and how that liberation was brought about. Hippias was still tyrant and embittered against the Athenians because of the murder of his brother. The Alcmaeonidae, an Athenian family which had been driven into exile by the house of Pisistratus, attempted with the help of the other exiles to procure their return by force and liberate Athens. They seized and fortified Leipsydrium above Paeonia,[30] but the enterprise met with disaster. Resolved to attempt any device which might help them against the Pisistratidae, they got a contract from the Amphictyons to build the temple which stands today at Delphi, but at that time did not exist.[31] They were wealthy men, and came of a long and distinguished line; and the temple they built was better in various respects than the plan required; in particular, they gave it a façade of Parian marble, whereas the agreement had been to use freestone for the whole. The Athenians say that these men, during their stay at Delphi, bribed the Priestess to tell any Spartans that might happen to consult the oracle, either on state or private business, that it was their duty to liberate Athens; and the Spartans, as a result of the constant repetition of the same injunction, sent Anchimolius, the son of Aster, a distinguished citizen, at the head of an army to drive out the Pisistratidae.[32] The Pisistratidae were good friends of theirs: but no matter – the commands of God were more important to them than human ties. Anchimolius and his force were sent by sea, and landed at Phalerum; but the Pisistratidae, who already knew of their intentions, had sent for help to Thessaly, with which country they had an alliance. The Thessalians responded to the appeal, and dispatched a troop of cavalry, a thousand strong, under

62

63

their king, Cineas of Condia. The plan the Pisistratidae adopted, on the strength of this reinforcement, was to clear the ground round Phalerum of trees so as to give horses freedom of movement, and then to launch a cavalry attack. The attack succeeded; many Lacedaemonians were killed, Anchimolius amongst them, and the survivors driven back to their ships. That was the end of the first Spartan attempt; Anchimolius was buried at Alopecae in Attica, and his tomb can be seen near the temple of Heracles in Cynosarges. Later, however, they tried again; and this time the expedition was on a larger scale; it was commanded by their king, Cleomenes the son of Anaxandrides, and went by land instead of by sea. The army crossed the border into Attica, and was met by the Thessalian cavalry, which was routed after a short engagement, leaving more than forty dead; the remainder made their way straight back to Thessaly. Cleomenes then marched to Athens, and, together with those Athenians who wished for freedom, besieged Hippias and his party on the Acropolis. The Lacedaemonians had not intended to undertake a siege, and the Pisistratidae had ample supplies of food and drink; it is likely, therefore, that, but for an unexpected accident, Cleomenes would have kept up the siege for days and then retired to Sparta; but, luckily for the Spartans and unluckily for their enemies, the children of the Pisistratidae were caught as they were being smuggled out of the country for safety. This disaster upset all their plans; in order to recover the children, they were forced to accept the Athenians' terms, and agreed to leave Attica within five days. They afterwards withdrew to Sigeum on the Scamander. The family had enjoyed despotic power in Athens for thirty-six years.[33] The family was descended from Neleus of Pylos, as were Melanthus and Codrus, who in ancient times became kings of Athens, after settling in the country. It was in memory of this that Hippocrates named his son Pisistratus after the Pisistratus who was a son of Nestor.

This, then, is the story of how Athens was freed from tyrants. I will now proceed to relate whatever the Athenians did or suffered from the time of the liberation to the revolt of Ionia, and the arrival in Athens of Aristagoras of Miletus, with his request for aid against Persia.

Athens had been great before; now, her liberty won, she grew   66
greater still. The most powerful men in the city were two:
Cleisthenes, a member of the Alcmaeonid family – it was he, the
story goes, who bribed the priestess at Delphi – and Isagoras,
son of Tisander, a man of reputable family, though I do not
know the origin of it; however, members of his family offer
sacrifice to Carian Zeus. These two were rivals for power, and
Cleisthenes, who was getting the worst of it, took the people
into his party. He then changed the number of Athenian tribes
from four to ten, and abolished the old names – previously the
four tribes had been called after Geleon, Aegicores, Argades,
and Hoples, the four sons of Ion; but now he named the new
tribes after other heroes, all native Athenians except Ajax,
whom, though a foreigner, he admitted into the list as a neighbour and ally.[34] I think that in taking this step he was following   67
the example of his maternal grandfather, Cleisthenes the tyrant
of Sicyon; for he, after his war with Argos, stopped the rhap-
sodists' competitions in reciting from Homer's poems in Sicyon,
because they were full of praise for Argos and the Argives.
Again, he would have liked on similar grounds – because, that
is, Adrastus was an Argive – to abolish the influence of Adrastus
the son of Talaus, who had, and still has, a shrine dedicated to
him in the market-place at Sicyon. He did, in fact, visit Delphi
to ask the oracle if he might 'expel' him, but the prophetess
answered: 'Adrastus was King of Sicyon, but you are merely a
stone-thrower.' As the god would not allow this, Cleisthenes
went home and began to think out some means whereby
Adrastus might leave Sicyon of his own accord.[35] Presently he
hit on something which he thought would do. He sent to Thebes
in Boeotia and informed the Thebans that he wished to invite
the hero Melanippus, the son of Astacus, to Sicyon. The Thebans
allowed him to do this, so Cleisthenes then invited Melanippus,
and consecrated for him a sanctuary actually inside the government house, where he was established in the greatest possible
security. I must not omit to explain that Cleisthenes picked on
Melanippus as the person to introduce into Sicyon, because he
was a bitter enemy of Adrastus, having killed both Mecistes, his
brother, and Tydeus his son-in-law. After settling him in his

new shrine, he transferred to him the religious honours of sacrifice and festival which had previously been paid to Adrastus.

The people of Sicyon had always regarded Adrastus with
great reverence, because the country had once belonged to
Polybus, his maternal grandfather, who died without an heir
and bequeathed the kingdom to him. One of the most important of the tributes paid him was the tragic chorus, which the
Sicyonians celebrated in his honour; normally, the tragic chorus
belongs to the worship of Dionysus; but in Sicyon it was not so
– it was performed in honour of Adrastus, treating his life-story
and sufferings. Cleisthenes, however, changed this: he transferred the choruses to Dionysus, and the rest of the ceremonial
68   to Melanippus. In addition to all this, he changed the names of
the Dorian tribes, in order to make a distinction between the
Argive and the Sicyonian; moreover, the distinction was a highly
invidious one, and designed to make fools of the Sicyonians, for
the names he chose were derived from the words 'donkey' and
'pig' and 'swine', with only the endings changed. This applied
to all the tribes except his own, which he named the Archelai –
'rulers of the people' – after his own royal office; the others
he named Hyatae – 'pig-men', Oneatae – 'donkey-men', and
Choereatae – 'swine-men'. These names continued to be used in
Sicyon, not only during Cleisthenes' reign but for sixty years
after his death; then the matter was discussed, and the tribes
were renamed Hylles, Pamphyli, and Dymanatae, with the
addition of a fourth, the Aegiales, named after Adrastus' son
Aegialeus.[36]

69   Now Cleisthenes of Athens, following the lead of his grandfather and namesake Cleisthenes of Sicyon, decided, out of
contempt, I imagine, for the Ionians, that his tribes should not
be the same as theirs, so as soon as he had won the support of
the common people of Athens, previously held in contempt, he
renamed the tribes and increased their number, appointing ten
presidents – 'phylarchs' – instead of the original four, and
incorporating ten local subdivisions – 'demes' – in each tribe.[37]
Having once got the masses to support him, he found himself
much more powerful than his rivals. Isagoras, beaten in his turn,
70   then appealed to Cleomenes the Spartan, who had been his

guest-friend during the siege of the Pisistratidae (he was indeed rumoured to have had illicit relations with Isagoras' wife). Cleomenes then first sent an order to Athens for the expulsion of Cleisthenes, together with a large number of other Athenians, calling them the 'Accursed'. This was a suggestion of Isagoras; for the Alcmaeonidae and their allies were held to be involved in the blood-guilt it referred to, but Isagoras and his friends were not.

The Accursed had got their name as follows. There was an 71 Athenian called Cylon, who had been a victor at the Olympic games. This man began to plume himself on his chances of becoming tyrant of Athens, and, with that end in view, collected a band of friends and tried to seize the Acropolis. The attempt failed, and he took sanctuary as a suppliant at the feet of the statue there. The presiding officers of the naucraries of Attica, who at that period were in control of affairs, persuaded Cylon and the other fugitives to leave the statue and submit themselves to justice, promising, however, to spare their lives. Nevertheless, they were killed, and the Alcmaeonidae are said to have done the deed. This happened before the time of Pisistratus.[38]

On the arrival of Cleomenes' order for the expulsion of 72 Cleisthenes and the 'Accursed', Cleisthenes himself left Athens, but his departure did not prevent Cleomenes from coming to the city with a small force of men and banishing, as accursed, seven hundred Athenian families, whose names had been given him by Isagoras. Then he attempted to abolish the Council, and transfer power to a body of three hundred supporters of Isagoras. The Council resisted, and refused to obey his orders, whereupon he, together with Isagoras and his party, occupied the Acropolis. This united the rest of Athens against them; they were blockaded in the Acropolis for two days, but, on the day after, a truce was made, and all of them who were Lacedaemonians were allowed to leave the country. The end of this affair had already been foretold; for when Cleomenes climbed the hill to seize the Acropolis, he was just going into Athene's temple to say a prayer when the Priestess, before he could get through the door, rose from her chair and cried: 'Spartan stranger, go back. Do not enter the holy place. No Dorian is permitted to come in.' Answering that he was not a Dorian but an Achaean, Cleomenes paid no attention to the warning, and made his attempt upon the Acropolis, and, as I have said, he and his Spartans were flung out. The rest were put in prison by the Athenians and executed, amongst them Timesitheus of Delphi, a man of whose prowess and courage I could, if I would, tell great things.

73   After the execution of the prisoners, the Athenians recalled Cleisthenes and the seven hundred families which had been expelled by Cleomenes; they were well aware that they were now in a state of war with Cleomenes and Sparta, so to strengthen their position they sent representatives to Sardis, in the hope of concluding an alliance with Persia. When they got there and delivered their message, Artaphernes the son of Hystaspes, the governor, asked in reply who these Athenians were that sought an alliance with Persia, and in what part of the world they lived. Then, having been told, he put the Persian case in a nutshell by remarking that, if the Athenians would signify their submission by the usual gift of earth and water, then Darius would make a pact with them; otherwise they had better go home. Eager that the pact should be concluded, the envoys acted on their own initiative and accepted Artaphernes' terms – for which they were severely censured on their return to Athens.[39]

74   Meanwhile Cleomenes, who felt that he had been insulted by the Athenians both in word and deed, was busy collecting an army from every part of the Peloponnese. His purpose, though he kept it to himself and did not publish it, was to have his revenge upon Athens and to set up Isagoras, who had escaped with him from the Acropolis, as tyrant there. His preparations completed, he marched as far as Eleusis with a strong force, and at the same moment, by a previously concerted plan, the Boeotians seized the two outlying Attic demes of Oenoe and Hysiae, while the Chalcidians broke in from another direction and devastated part of Attica. Threatened though they were from two sides at once, the Athenians decided to oppose the Spartans at Eleusis, and to deal with the Boeotians and Chal-

75   cidians later. Just before the battle could begin, the Corinthian contingent, reflecting that they were acting wrongfully, changed

their minds and withdrew.[40] Then Demaratus, the son of Ariston, one of the two Spartan kings and joint commander of the
expedition, though he had had no previous difference with
Cleomenes, followed suit. This divergence in a matter of policy
gave rise to a new law in Sparta; previously both kings had gone
out with the army, but this was now made illegal, and it was
further provided that, as one had to remain in the capital, one
of the Tyndaridae as well should stay behind – both of whom
had hitherto accompanied the army as auxiliaries. Then the
other allied troops, when they saw the split between the Spartan
kings and the desertion of the Corinthians, also abandoned their
positions and left the field. This was the fourth time a Spartan 76
army had been seen on Attic soil: two of the occasions had been
acts of war; the other two, attempts to do service to the people
of Athens. The first invasion was when they founded Megara,
and is rightly assigned to the period when Codrus was King of
Athens; the second and third were the expeditions from Sparta
to drive out the Pisistratidae; the fourth and last was this present
one, when Cleomenes with a Peloponnesian army marched as
far as Eleusis.

Having witnessed this inglorious dispersal of the invading 77
army, the Athenians wanted revenge, and decided to march first
against the Chalcidians; but as the Boeotians were coming to
their aid, towards the Euripus strait, the Athenians decided to
tackle them first. In the fight which followed the Athenians won
an overwhelming victory, killing a great many and taking seven
hundred prisoners. The same day they crossed into Euboea,
engaged the Chalcidians, and beat them too. After the victory
they settled 4000 men, each with a piece of land assigned him,
on the estates of the 'hippobotae', or 'horse-owners', as the
wealthy Chalcidians were called. The prisoners taken in this
second engagement, together with the seven hundred Boeotians,
were kept under guard in chains, but afterwards ransomed at
200 drachmas apiece. The fetters they were bound with, the
Athenians hung up in the Acropolis; they were still there in my
day, hanging on the walls which the Persian fire had scorched,
opposite the shrine which faces westward.[41] With a tenth of the
ransom money they had a chariot-and-four made in bronze, and

consecrated it as an offering to Athene. It is the first thing you see on the left as you pass through the Propylaea on the Acropolis. The inscription on it is as follows:

> Athens with Chalcis and Boeotia fought,
> Bound them in chains and brought their pride to naught.
> Prison was grief, and ransom cost them dear –
> One tenth to Pallas raised this chariot here.

78   Thus Athens went from strength to strength, and proved, if proof were needed, how noble a thing equality before the law is, not in one respect only, but in all; for while they were oppressed under tyrants, they had no better success in war than any of their neighbours, yet, once the yoke was flung off, they proved the finest fighters in the world. This clearly shows that, so long as they were held down by authority, they deliberately shirked their duty in the field, as slaves shirk working for their masters; but when freedom was won, then every man amongst them was interested in his own cause.

79   Meanwhile the Thebans were anxious to pay off their score with Athens. They sent to Delphi for advice, and were told by the priestess of the oracle that they would be unable to get their revenge if they tried to act alone: they must, she said, bring the matter forward to be discussed by 'the many voices', and ask their 'nearest' to help them. When, therefore, the messengers returned, the Theban magistrates called a general assembly and announced what the oracle had advised. The people, hearing that this advice was to appeal for help to their 'nearest', and knowing that their nearest neighbours were the men of Tanagra, Coronea, and Thespia, wondered what could be meant by it. 'Surely,' they said to each other, 'these neighbours of ours need no asking; they have always been our allies and have fought at our side all through the war with the best will in the world.

80   Perhaps the oracle has some other meaning.' As they were debating the matter, one of them suddenly realized the truth. 'I believe,' he exclaimed, 'that I know what it means. Asopus, it is said, had two daughters, Thebe and Aegina. Thebe and Aegina – two sisters: *that* is what "nearest" signifies. The god has

advised us to ask the Aeginetans for aid.' No better solution
being offered, the Thebans at once sent a request for assistance
to Aegina, as being their 'nearest' according to the intention of
the oracle, and the Aeginetans met the request by agreeing to
send them their heroes, the sons of Aeacus. Relying upon this   81
powerful aid, the Thebans made their attempt, but were soundly
beaten by the Athenians. Thereupon they sent a second message
to Aegina, giving back the sons of Aeacus and asking for some
men instead. The Aeginetans at that period enjoyed very great
prosperity; this fact, together with the memory of their old
enmity with Athens, encouraged them to comply with the Thebans' request and to begin hostilities without a formal declaration
of war. While the Athenians were attending to the Boeotians,
they sent a squadron of triremes to Attica, wrecked the port of
Phalerum and a number of villages along the neighbouring
coast, and did considerable damage.[42]

The desire of the Aeginetans to pay off their old score against   82
Athens arose from the following circumstances. Once, long
before, the crops had failed in Epidaurus, and the Epidaurians
consulted the Delphic oracle upon what they should do to meet
their troubles. The Priestess replied that things would go better
for them if they set up statues of Damia and Auxesia. They then
asked if the statues should be made in bronze or in stone, and
were advised that neither of these materials should be used: the
statues should be made from the wood of the cultivated olive.
In consequence of this they asked the Athenians for permission
to fell some olive trees, in the belief that the olives of Attica were
of peculiar sanctity – or it is also said that in those days Athens
was the only place where olives grew. The Athenians gave them
permission to fell the trees, on condition that they offered an
annual sacrifice to Erechtheus and Athene Polias. The Epidaurians agreed, got what they wanted, and made the statues from
the olive-wood. The statues were erected, their harvests
improved, and the promise made to the Athenians was duly
kept.

Now at this period, as in the past, Aegina was subject to   83
Epidaurus: so much so, indeed, that the Aeginetans used to cross
to Epidaurus for the hearing of their own private law-suits. A

little later, however, the islanders built a fleet and, growing headstrong, rebelled against Epidaurus. Their superiority at sea enabled them, once the struggle had begun, to do much damage to the Epidaurians; amongst other things they carried off the statues of Damia and Auxesia and put them up at a place called Oea, in the interior of their island, about twenty furlongs from the town. Here they instituted in their honour certain cere-monies, consisting partly of sacrifices, partly of companies of female dancers and singers in the satirical and ribald mode, whose attacks were directed not against men, but against the women of the place. Ten 'choregi' were appointed to pay and train the dancers for each of the two deities. Similar modes of worship were in use also at Epidaurus, as well as other – secret – sorts.

84   After the theft of the statues the Epidaurians ceased to fulfil their undertaking to send an annual tribute to the gods of Athens. The Athenians remonstrated, but to no purpose, for the people of Epidaurus proved that they were in no way in the wrong. They had fulfilled their obligations so long as the statues were in their possession; but now they were gone, the obligation was at an end. Now, the Aeginetans had the statues; so the proper thing was to make the Aeginetans pay. At this, the Athenians sent a demand to Aegina for the return of the statues, but were told in reply that Aegina was not interested in Athens.

85   The Athenians claim that, after they had asked for the statues, they sent a party to Aegina in a single trireme, who attempted to bring the statues away, on the ground that, being made of Athenian wood, they were Athenian property. First they tried to wrench them off their pedestals; then, having failed to do so, they made ropes fast to them, and hauled. As they were heaving, there was a clap of thunder and an earthquake, and the ship's company suddenly went mad and began to kill each other, until

86   only one was left, who returned by himself to Phalerum. The Athenian story is, however, contradicted by the Aeginetans, who deny that it was a single trireme – they could easily have kept off a single ship, or several, for that matter, even if they had no navy themselves; on the contrary, the Athenians came with a large fleet, and they themselves made no attempt to

oppose them. They are not clear as to whether they avoided
battle because they acknowledged their inferiority at sea or
because they were planning what they then did. In any case, the
Athenians landed unopposed and made for the statues; then,
having failed to wrench them from their bases, they attached
their ropes and began heaving – and continued to heave until
an extraordinary thing happened. Personally I do not believe it,
though perhaps somebody may – but the story is that each statue
fell upon its knees, and in that attitude both have remained ever
since. The Aeginetans go on to affirm that as soon as they got
wind of the intended attack from Athens, they sought aid from
Argos, so that when the Athenians landed, Argive reinforcements were already on the spot to oppose them; they had slipped
across from Epidaurus, fell upon the Athenians before they
knew they were there, and cut off their retreat to their ships. It
was at that moment that the earthquake occurred, and the
thunderclap. The Argives and Aeginetans agree in this account, 87
and the Athenians, too, admit that only one of their men
returned to Attica alive: the only point of dispute is the occasion
of his escape, the Argives saying that he got away after they had
destroyed the rest of the Athenian force, the Athenians claiming
that the whole thing was an act of God. Even the sole survivor
soon came to a bad end; for when he reached Athens with a
report of the disaster, the wives of the other men who had gone
with him to Aegina, in grief and anger that he alone should have
escaped, crowded round him and thrust the brooches, which
they used for fastening their dresses, into his flesh, each one, as
she struck, asking him where her husband was. So he perished,
and the Athenians were more horrified at his fate than at the
defeat of their troops in Aegina. The only way they could punish
their women for the dreadful thing they had done was to make
them adopt Ionian dress; previously Athenian women had worn
Dorian dress, very similar to the fashion at Corinth; now they
were made to change to linen tunics, to prevent them from
wearing brooches. Actually this kind of dress is not originally 88
Ionian, but Carian; for in ancient times all women in Greece
wore the costume now known as Dorian. But the Argives and
Aeginetans passed a law that in both their countries brooch-pins

should be made half as long again as they used to be, and that brooches should be the principal things offered by women in the shrines of these two deities; also, nothing from Attica was to be taken to the temple, not even pottery, and thenceforward only drinking vessels made in the country should be used. From that time to the present day the women of Argos and Aegina have worn brooches with longer pins than in the past – and all because of their quarrel with Athens.

89   The origin, then, of the mutual hatred of Athens and Aegina was such as I have described. And now the Aeginetans, who had not forgotten the affair of the statues, eagerly responded to the Theban call for assistance, and began making raids on the Attic coast. The Athenians were about to start counter-measures when they were advised by an oracle from Delphi to hold their hand: they should wait, the oracle ran, for thirty years, and then, in the thirty-first year after the Aeginetans had started the trouble, they should consecrate a piece of ground to Aeacus, and declare war. If they followed this advice everything would go as they wished; if, on the other hand, they attacked Aegina forthwith they would, indeed, ultimately be victorious, but not without suffering in the meantime as much loss as they inflicted. On hearing this warning the Athenians did so far take it as to consecrate to Aeacus that precinct which is still to be seen by the market-place in Athens; but, in view of the intolerable injury they had received at the hands of the Aeginetans, they could not

90 bear to be told to wait thirty years for their revenge. They began their preparations accordingly, but were checked by new trouble from Sparta. This arose from the discovery by the Spartans that the Alcmaeonidae had corrupted the priestess at Delphi, and what she had done against Sparta and the Pisistratidae. The Spartans were doubly distressed; for they had driven their own friends into exile, and they now realized that by doing so they had not gained the goodwill of Athens. Moreover they were spurred to action by the discovery of certain prophecies of coming disasters at the hands of the Athenians – prophecies of which they had known nothing until Cleomenes brought them to Sparta. These prophecies had formerly been in the possession of the Pisistratidae, who left them in the temple on the Acropolis

when they were expelled from Athens. It was here that
Cleomenes found them and picked them up. When, therefore,   91
the Spartans got hold of them, and saw at the same time the
growth of Athenian power with the unlikelihood it brought of
Athens submitting to their authority, they realized that a free
Attica would be a match for them, and that the only way of
weakening their rivals and reducing them to obedience was to
establish a tyranny in Athens. On this realization they acted,
and sent to Sigeum on the Hellespont to recall Pisistratus' son
Hippias. Hippias responded to the summons; the Spartans then
sent for representatives from their other allied states, and the
assembly was addressed in the following words: 'We acknowledge to you, our comrades in arms, that we have made a mistake.
On the strength of certain oracles, which have proved to be a
swindle, we expelled from their country men who were our
friends, men who undertook to keep Athens dependent upon
us; these gone, we put power into the hands of an ungrateful
rabble, which had no sooner raised its head by our generous act
of liberation than it turned against us and flung us out, ourselves
and our king, with every mark of insult. Since then these people
have been growing in reputation and strength, as their neighbours the Boeotians and Chalcidians have learnt to their cost,
and as others perhaps will also discover, unless they mind their
step. This was the mistake we made; and now, with your help,
we will try to make up for it. Our object when we invited you
and Hippias, whom you see before you, to attend this meeting,
was to agree to unite our forces for his restoration. Together we
will take him to Athens and give him back the power of which
we formerly robbed him.'

Most of the allied representatives disapproved of the sub-   92
stance of this speech, but the only one to raise his voice in
protest was Sosicles of Corinth. 'Upon my word, gentlemen,' he   a
exclaimed, 'this is like turning the universe upside-down. Earth
and sky will soon be changing places – men will be living in the
sea and fish on land, now that you Spartans are proposing to
abolish political equality and restore despotism in the cities.
Believe me, there is nothing wickeder or bloodier in the world
than tyranny. If you think it is a good thing for other people,

why not give a lead by adopting it yourselves before trying to establish it elsewhere? Without any experience of it – indeed, you have taken the utmost care that it should never happen in Sparta – you are wronging your friends; if only you knew, as we know, what irresponsible government can be, your advice about it now would be better than it is.

b   'The government of Corinth was once an oligarchy: one clan – the Bacchiadae, who intermarried only amongst themselves – were in power there. Amphion, a member of this clan, had a lame daughter, Labda, whom none of the Bacchiadae was willing to marry, so she was taken by Eëtion, the son of Echecrates, a man from the village of Petra, but belonging by descent to the Lapithae and the family of Caeneus. Having no children either by Labda or any other wife, Eëtion went to Delphi to ask the oracle about his chance of an heir, and the moment he entered the shrine the Priestess addressed him in these words:

> Eëtion, worthy of honour, no man honours you.
> Labda is with child, and her child will be a millstone
> which will fall upon the rulers and will bring justice to Corinth.

The prophecy, though addressed to Eëtion, happened to reach the ears of the Bacchiadae, who till then had failed to grasp the meaning of an earlier prophecy about the future of Corinth. Now, however, it became apparent that both referred to the same event. The earlier one went like this:

> An eagle in the rocks[43] has conceived, and shall bring forth a lion,
> Mighty, ravening; and he will loose the knees of many.
> Give heed to these things, Corinthians, you who dwell
> About lovely Pirene and the rock-set town of Corinth.

c   This earlier prophecy, as I have said, had been unintelligible to the Bacchiadae; but as soon as they heard the second one, which was given to Eëtion, they saw the point of it and realized the similarity of the two. The meaning of both prophecies being now clear, they kept quiet, but resolved to make away with Eëtion's child as soon as it should be born. The moment, therefore, that Labda was brought to bed they sent ten of their number to the village where Eëtion lived, to kill the baby. Arrived at Petra, they entered the house, and asked to see the child; and Labda, who had no idea why they had come and supposed that they wished to see her baby out of affection for its father, gave it to one of them to hold. Now the plan they had made on the way to Petra was, that whoever first got hold of the baby should dash it to the ground; but chance – or providence – saved it, for as soon as Labda put it into the man's arms, it smiled at him, and he, seeing it smile, was touched, and could not bring himself to kill it, but passed it to his neighbour who, in his turn, passed it on again until all ten had had it in their arms, and not one could bring himself to kill it. So they gave the baby back to its mother and went out of the room. Close by the door they stopped and began to reproach one another, especially the man who had been the first to hold the baby, for not doing what they had decided to do, until at last, after a considerable time, they made up their minds to go back and all take a share in the killing. Fate, however, had decreed that Eëtion's child *d* should live and be a cause of misery to Corinth; for Labda, who had been standing close behind the door, heard everything that the men were saying, and, in fear lest the second time they got hold of her baby they might feel differently and actually destroy it, she hid it in a chest, which was the most unlikely place she could think of, knowing, as she did, that if the men came back they would be sure to make a thorough search. And this is just what happened: they entered the room, and after hunting everywhere without success, decided to go away and to tell the people who had sent them that their orders had been carried out. This they did; and Eëtion's son grew up, and was named *e* Cypselus after the chest, by means of which he had escaped the danger which threatened him.[44]

One day, after he had grown to maturity, Cypselus happened to consult the oracle, and on the strength of the answer he received – an answer which cut, as it were, both ways – set to work and made himself master of Corinth. The prophecy went like this:

Fortunate is he who steps down into my house,
Cypselus, son of Eëtion, lord of famous Corinth:
Fortunate he and his sons, but not the sons of his sons.

Such was the prophecy which induced Cypselus to seize power,
and I will now tell you what use he made of it when he got it:
many of the Corinthians he drove into exile, many he deprived
of their property, and still more, by a long way, of their lives.
_f_ He ruled in Corinth for thirty years, died in the height of
prosperity, and was succeeded by his son Periander. To begin
with, Periander was less violent than his father, but soon surpassed him in bloody-mindedness and savagery. This was the
result of a correspondence which he entered into with Thrasybulus, the tyrant of Miletus. He sent a representative to the court
of this despot, to ask his opinion on how best and most safely
to govern his city. Thrasybulus invited the man to walk with
him from the city to a field where corn was growing. As he passed
through this cornfield, continually asking questions about why
the messenger had come to him from Corinth, he kept cutting
off all the tallest ears of wheat which he could see, and throwing
them away, until the finest and best-grown part of the crop was
ruined. In this way he went right through the field, and then
sent the messenger away without a word. On his return to
Corinth, Periander was eager to hear what advice Thrasybulus
had given, and the man replied that he had not given any at all,
adding that he was surprised at being sent to visit such a person,
who was evidently mad and a wanton destroyer of his own
property – and then he described what he had seen Thrasybulus
_g_ do. Periander seized the point at once; it was perfectly plain to
him that Thrasybulus recommended the murder of all the people
in the city who were outstanding in influence or ability. Moreover, he took the advice, and from that time forward there was
no crime against the Corinthians that he did not commit; indeed,
anything that Cypselus had left undone in the way of killing or
banishing, Periander completed for him. Once, on a single day,
he stripped every woman in the town naked, on account of
his wife Melissa – but let me explain: Periander had mislaid
something which a friend had left in his charge, so he sent to

the oracle of the dead, amongst the Thesproti on the river Acheron, to ask where he had put it. The ghost of Melissa appeared and said that she would not tell, either by word or sign; for she was cold and naked, the clothes, which had been buried with her, having been of no use at all, since they had not been burnt. Then, as evidence for her husband that she spoke the truth, she added that Periander had put his loaves into a cold oven. The messengers reported what they had seen and heard, and Periander, convinced by the token of the cold oven and the loaves (because he had lain with her after she was dead), immediately issued a proclamation to the effect that every woman in Corinth should come to the temple of Hera. The women obeyed, crowding to the temple in their best clothes as if to a festival, and Periander, who had hidden some of his guards for the purpose, had them all stripped – every one of them, freeborn women and servants alike – and their clothes collected into a pit and burnt, while he prayed to the spirit of his wife Melissa. After this he sent to the oracle again, and Melissa's ghost told him where he had put whatever it was that his friend had left with him.

'Well, Lacedaemonians, now you can see what despotic government is, and the sort of things it can do. As for us in Corinth, we were astonished enough when we saw you were sending for Hippias; but our amazement is even greater now, at hearing you speak as you do. We implore you, in the name of the gods of Greece, not to saddle our cities with tyrants. If you refuse to desist from your purpose – if you still attempt to restore Hippias to power, contrary to all law and justice – you may at least be certain that you have no support from Corinth.'

When the Corinthian representative Sosicles had finished his speech, Hippias, who was more familiar than anyone else with the prophecies, swore by the same gods that the day would come when Corinth would find herself plagued by the Athenians, and that then the Corinthians would long for the Pisistratidae more than for anyone else in the world.[45] The representatives of the other allied states had made no comment until they heard Sosicles; then, however, every one of them held his tongue no longer, but spoke in Sosicles' support, and urged the Spartans

93

94   not to meddle with the affairs of any city in Greece. This settled the matter; the Spartans abandoned their purpose, and Hippias left the country. Before he went, Amyntas of Macedon offered him Anthemus, and the Thessalians Iolcus; but he returned to Sigeum without accepting either offer. This place Pisistratus had taken by force of arms from the Mytilenaeans, and had afterwards set up Hegesistratus as tyrant, a natural son of his by an Argive woman. Hegesistratus did not manage to enjoy his father's gift without a good deal of trouble; for there was constant war over a long period between the Athenians at Sigeum and the Mytilenaeans at Achilleum, the latter claiming the restoration of their lost territory, the former disputing the claim and endeavouring to prove that Aeolians had no more right to the country in the neighbourhood of Troy than they themselves had, or any other Greeks who helped Menelaus to avenge the

95   seizure of Helen. Amongst the various incidents of this war, one in particular is worth a mention: in the course of a battle in which the Athenians were victorious, the poet Alcaeus ran away, but left his arms in the hands of the victors, who hung them up in the temple of Athene at Sigeum. Alcaeus wrote some verses, describing his little accident to his friend Melanippus, and sent it to him at Mytilene. The war between Mytilene and Athens was brought to an end by Periander, who was invited by both parties to act as arbitrator; the condition he proposed was that each side should retain what it at the moment possessed. In this way Sigeum passed into the power of Athens.[46]

96   Hippias, on his return to Asia, moved heaven and earth to set Artaphernes against the Athenians, and to procure the subjection of Athens to himself and Darius; and the Athenians, when they learnt of the efforts he was making against them, sent to Sardis to urge the Persians not to listen to the exiles. Artaphernes replied that, if they valued their safety, they must take Hippias back. The Athenians refused, and made up their minds to accept the consequence – open hostility to Persia.

97   It was at this moment, when the Athenians had made their decision and were already on bad terms with Persia, that Aristagoras of Miletus, who had been turned out of Sparta by Cleomenes, arrived in Athens.[47] He knew that Athens at this

time was the next most powerful state in Greece; accordingly
he appeared before the people and made a speech, in which he
repeated the arguments he had previously used at Sparta, about
the good things to be found in Asia, and the Persian methods of
warfare – how they used neither shields nor spears and were
easy to beat. In addition to this he pointed out that Miletus had
been founded by Athenian settlers, so it was only natural that
the Athenians, powerful as they were, should help her in her
need. Indeed, so anxious was he to get Athenian aid, that he
promised everything that came into his head, until at last he
succeeded. Apparently it is easier to impose upon a crowd than
upon an individual, for Aristagoras, who had failed to impose
upon Cleomenes, succeeded with thirty thousand Athenians.
Once persuaded to accede to Aristagoras' appeal, the Athenians
passed a decree for the dispatch of twenty ships to Ionia, under
the command of Melanthius, a distinguished Athenian.

These ships were the beginning of evils for Greeks and barbarians.[48]

Aristagoras sailed in advance of the contingent, and, on reach-   98
ing Miletus, adopted a plan of action from which no advantage
could possibly accrue to the Ionians – indeed, he did not intend
that it should, his only object being to annoy Darius. He sent a
man to Phrygia, with a message to the Paeonians from the
Strymon, who had been taken prisoner by Megabazus and were
then living there with a tract of land and a village of their own.[49]
The man duly delivered the message, which ran as follows:
'Men of Paeonia, Aristagoras, tyrant of Miletus, has sent me to
propose a way by which you may save yourselves, if you will
adopt it. All Ionia is in revolt against the Persian king, and you
have the chance of getting back home. You must make your
own way to the sea; after that, we will look after you.' The
Paeonians were delighted, and taking their women and children
with them, made off for the coast – all but a few whose hearts
failed them, and who stayed behind. From the coast they crossed
to Chios, and while they were there, a large troop of Persian
cavalry, which had started in pursuit of them, arrived in their
track; having failed to overtake them, the Persians sent a message
across to the island and urged them to return. The Paeonians

refused, and were taken on to Lesbos by the Chians, and from there the Lesbians took them to Doriscus. Thence they made their own way on foot to Paeonia.

99   The Athenian squadron of twenty sail now reached Miletus. It was accompanied by five other triremes belonging to the Eretrians, who had joined the expedition not for the Athenians' sake, but to pay a debt of honour to the people of Miletus, who some time previously had fought at their side all through their war with the Chalcidians – who, in their turn, had the support of Samos.[50] On the arrival, therefore, of these two contingents, Aristagoras, as soon as the rest of his allies had assembled, proceeded to attack Sardis. He did not himself accompany the expedition, but stayed in Miletus, having appointed to the command of the Milesians his brother Charopinus and another Milesian named Hermophantus.

100   The fleet sailed for Ephesus, where the ships were left at Coressus in Ephesian territory; the troops, a strong force, then began their march up-country with Ephesian guides. They followed the course of the Cayster, crossed the ridge of Tmolus, and came down upon Sardis, which they took without opposition, except for the acropolis of the town, which was defended by

101   Artaphernes in person, with a considerable force. But they were prevented from sacking the place after its capture by the fact that most of the houses in Sardis were constructed of reeds, reed-thatch being used even on the few houses which were built of brick. One house was set alight by a soldier, and the flames rapidly spread until the whole town was ablaze. The outlying parts were all burning, so the native Lydians and such Persians as were there, caught in a ring of fire and unable to get clear of the town, poured into the market-square on either bank of the Pactolus, where they were forced to stand on their defence. The Pactolus is the river which brings the gold dust down from Tmolus. It flows through the market at Sardis, and then joins the Hermus, which, in its turn, flows into the sea. The Ionians, seeing some of the enemy defending themselves, and others approaching in large numbers, then became alarmed, and withdrew to Tmolus; and thence, just before nightfall, they marched

102   off to rejoin their ships. In the conflagration at Sardis a temple

of Cybebe, a goddess worshipped by the natives, was destroyed, and the Persians later made this a pretext for their burning of Greek temples.

All the Persians this side of the Halys, already alerted, were mustering to rescue the Lydians; finding the Ionians already gone from Sardis, they followed on their tracks and came up with them at Ephesus. The Ionians formed up to meet the attack, but were severely beaten. Amongst the large numbers of well-known men who were killed was Eualcides, the Eretrian commander, a man who more than once had been crowned as winner in the games, and had been highly praised in the poetry of Simonides of Ceos. The survivors scattered to their cities.

After this battle the Athenians would have nothing more to do with the Ionian rebellion, and in spite of frequent appeals from Aristagoras refused to help him.[51] But the Ionians, in view of the injury they had already done Darius, pressed on the war with no less vigour, even without Athenian aid. They sailed to the Hellespont and got control of Byzantium and all the other towns thereabouts, then, by an expedition outside those seas, they won over the greater part of Caria; even Caunus, which had previously held off, now, after the burning of Sardis, joined the rebel cause. With the exception of Amathus, all Cyprus, too, volunteered assistance and rebelled against Persia. The origin of the Cyprian revolt was this: a man named Onesilus, a younger brother of Gorgus the ruler of Salamis, and son of Chersis (whose father was Siromus, and grandfather Euelthon), had repeatedly urged Gorgus to throw off the Persian yoke, and then, on hearing the news of the revolt of the Ionians, had redoubled his appeals with the utmost importunity; but Gorgus refused to listen. Onesilus, therefore, with the help of his supporters, waited until he went out of town and then shut the gates on him. Having thus lost his city, Gorgus fled to the Persians, and Onesilus, becoming master of Salamis, tried to induce all the Cyprians to join in the revolt. His only failure was with Amathus; the men of this town refused to listen to him, so he laid siege to it.

While Onesilus was busy with the siege of Amathus, news was brought to Darius that Sardis had been taken and burnt by

103

104

105

the Athenians and Ionians, and that the prime mover in the joint enterprise was Aristagoras of Miletus. The story goes that when Darius learnt of the disaster, he did not give a thought to the Ionians, knowing perfectly well that the punishment for their revolt would come; but he asked who the Athenians were, and then, on being told, called for his bow. He took it, set an arrow on the string, shot it up into the air and cried: 'Grant, O God, that I may punish the Athenians.' Then he commanded one of his servants to repeat to him the words, 'Master, remember the Athenians', three times, whenever he sat down to dinner. After that he sent for Histiaeus the Milesian, whom he had already detained for a long time at his court, and said: 'I understand, Histiaeus, that your deputy, whom you put in charge of Miletus, has thrown off his allegiance to me. He has brought against me men from the continent across the sea, and has persuaded the Ionians – who shall assuredly pay for it – to join them in his service, and he has taken Sardis from me. Come now – was this well done? And could it have happened without your knowledge and advice? The time may come when you will blame yourself for this.'

'My lord,' Histiaeus replied, 'how can you say such a thing? Is it likely that I should plan to do anything which might injure you in any way whatever, small or great? I have all I want, so what motive could there be for such treachery? Is not what is yours, mine? And have I not the honour of sharing all your counsels? If my deputy at Miletus is indeed guilty of this thing, you may be very sure that he has acted entirely on his own initiative. Personally I find it impossible to believe that he and the Milesians are acting against your interests; if, however, they really are doing so – if you have really been told the truth – then, my lord, you can see how unwisely you acted when you forced me to leave the coast; for it appears that the Ionians have waited till I was out of sight to do what they have long passionately desired to do. If only I had still been there, not a single city would have stirred. Give me leave, therefore, at once to return to Ionia; I will put everything right for you, and deliver into your hands this deputy-governor of Miletus, who has caused all the trouble. Moreover, I will not only do this to your entire satisfaction, but I also swear by the gods of your royal house not to take off the clothes I am wearing on my arrival in Ionia, until I have forced Sardinia, the biggest island in the world, to pay tribute to you.'

The purpose of this was to deceive Darius – and it was 107 successful. The king believed Histiaeus and let him go, telling him to return to Susa when he had done what he promised.

Meantime – while, that is, the report on Sardis was on its 108 way to the king, and the king, after shooting the arrow, was conferring with Histiaeus, and Histiaeus by Darius' permission was on his way to the coast – the following events took place. During the siege of Amathus, Onesilus of Salamis got news that a Persian named Artybius was expected to arrive in Cyprus with a strong Persian force. Onesilus, therefore, dispatched messengers to all parts of Ionia with an appeal for help. The Ionians quickly made up their minds and came over to the island in strength. No sooner had they arrived than the Persians crossed from Cilicia and marched on Salamis, while the Phoenicians sailed round the promontory called the Keys of Cyprus. There- 109 upon the tyrants of Cyprus called a meeting of the Ionian commanders and addressed them in these words: 'Men of Ionia, we of Cyprus offer you the choice of engaging either the Persians or the Phoenicians. Should you prefer to try your strength on land against the Persians, now is the time to disembark and make your dispositions, while we, in our turn, go aboard your ships and fight the Phoenicians at sea. If, on the contrary, you would rather tackle the Phoenicians – by all means do so; but whichever you choose, take care to fight well. Let it not be your fault if Ionia and Cyprus fail to preserve their liberty.'

The Ionians replied: 'The common council of Ionia sent us here to guard the sea, not to hand over our ships to you and to fight the Persians on land. We will therefore keep the station assigned to us, and in that try to do our duty. And as for you – remember what you as slaves suffered from your masters the Persians, and be men.'

The Persian army arrived on the plain of Salamis, and the 110 Cyprian kings made their dispositions to meet them. Picked troops from Salamis and Soli they drew up to face the Persians,

leaving the remainder from other Cyprian towns to deal with
the other enemy groups. Onesilus volunteered in person to
111   oppose the Persian commander Artybius. Artybius rode a horse
which had been trained, when attacking a hoplite, to rear and
go for the man with his fore-hooves. Onesilus got to know of
this, and had a word about it with his armour-bearer, a Carian
by nationality and a very fine and courageous soldier. 'I am
told,' he said, 'that Artybius' horse rears, and savages with his
teeth and hooves anyone he comes on. Now think a moment,
and tell me which of the two – Artybius or his horse – you would
rather watch for a chance of striking.'

'My lord,' the attendant answered, 'I am quite ready to attack
both or either – indeed, I will do anything you bid me; but I will
tell you none the less what I think will be best for you. What I
say is, a ruler and a general should fight with another ruler, or
another general. If you kill a general, it will be a great thing for
you; and if he kills you – which God forbid – even death from a
worthy hand is only half as bad as it might otherwise have been.
You, then, must fight Artybius; we underlings will go for our
equals – and for the horse. Don't be afraid of his tricks: I promise
you, he will never rear up against anybody again.'

112   Shortly afterwards began the battle on land and at sea. In the
latter, the Ionians that day were in magnificent fettle – especially
the Samian contingent – and beat the Phoenicians; on land,
while the struggle was going on, Artybius on his horse came
charging down upon Onesilus, who, according to the arrangement with his armour-bearer, aimed a blow at the rider's body;
as Onesilus struck, the horse reared and brought his fore-feet
down upon his shield – and at that instant the Carian swung his
curved sword and sheared its feet clean off. The horse fell, and
113   Artybius, the Persian commander, with him. Elsewhere on the
field, Stesenor the tyrant of Curium (Curium is said to have been
a colony from Argos), with a considerable body of troops under
his command, played traitor; and his lead was immediately
followed by the war-chariots from Salamis. The result was a
victory for Persia, and in the rout of the Cyprian army many
were killed, including Onesilus, the son of Chersis and originator
of the Cyprian revolt, and Aristocyprus, the ruler of Soli. (Aristo-

cyprus was the son of Philocyprus, whom Solon the Athenian, when he visited Cyprus, praised in a poem more highly than any other ruler.)

The people of Amathus, in revenge for his having laid siege to their town, severed the head from the dead body of Onesilus and hung it up above their gates. In time it became hollow, and was occupied by a swarm of bees, who filled it with honeycomb. In consequence of this the townspeople consulted an oracle, and were advised to take the head down and bury it, and, if they wished to prosper, to regard Onesilus thenceforward as a hero, and to honour him with an annual sacrifice. This was done, and the ceremony was still observed in my own day. The Ionians who had won the action at sea, faced with the total failure of Onesilus' cause and the fact that all the towns in Cyprus were now under siege – with the one exception of Salamis, which the people of the town restored to their former ruler Gorgus – lost no time in returning home to Ionia. Of the Cyprian towns the one to hold out longest was Soli; the Persians took it after more than four months, by undermining the wall.

Thus after a year of freedom Cyprus was once more brought into subjection. Meanwhile Daurises, who had married a daughter of Darius, and two other Persian commanders, Hymaeës and Otanes, who had also married daughters of the king, pursued the Ionian force which had attacked Sardis, cut it up, and drove the survivors into their ships; the three commanders then divided their attentions between the various towns and proceeded to sack them. Daurises made for the settlements on the Hellespont, and took in as many days the five towns of Dardanus, Abydus, Percote, Lampsacus, and Paesus. Then, on his way from Paesus to Parium, hearing that the Carians had made common cause with the Ionians and thrown off the Persian yoke, he turned about, and marched against Caria. Somehow or other the Carians got wind of the movement before he arrived, and massed at a place called White Pillars on the Marsyas – a tributary of the Maeander, rising in Idrian territory. When the assembled Carians were debating how to deal with the danger which threatened them, what I think was the best suggestion came from Pixodarus, son of Mausolus, a man of Cindya, who had

114
115
116
117
118

married a daughter of the Cilician King Syennesis. The proposal was that the army should cross the Maeander and fight with the river in their rear; this would prevent them from running away, and every man, forced to remain at his post, would be even braver than nature made him. But this plan was not adopted: it was decided, instead, that the Persians, not the Carians, should have the Maeander at their backs – for if the Persians were defeated and compelled to retire, they would then fail to get away and be driven into the river. Soon the Persians arrived, crossed the Maeander, and were engaged by the Carians on the Marsyas. The struggle was long and violent, but the Carians were finally overwhelmed by weight of numbers. Some 2000 Persians were killed, and about 10,000 Carians. The Carian survivors shut themselves up at Labraunda, in the great grove of sacred plane-trees known as the precinct of Zeus of the Army. The Carians are the only people we know of who sacrifice to Zeus of the Army. While they were there, they discussed plans for saving themselves – not knowing if it would be better for them to surrender to the Persians or to leave Asia for good. However, during the course of their deliberations the Milesians and their allies came to offer assistance, and the Carians changed their minds entirely and prepared for fresh resistance. The Persians attacked, and there was a second battle; but the result of it was even more disastrous than before. The whole Carian and allied force suffered severe losses, but the Milesian contingent the worst of all. The Carians, however, recovered from this blow and later fought another action. Learning of the Persian intention to attack their towns, they laid a trap on the Pedasus road. The Persians fell into it during a night march and were cut to pieces. Three of their commanders, Daurises, Amorges, and Sisimaces, were killed – also Gyges' son Myrsus. The man who planned this ambush was Heracleides of Mylasa, a son of Ibanollis.

Meanwhile Hymaeës – another of the Persian officers who went in pursuit of the Ionians after their attack on Sardis – marched to the Propontis and captured Cius in Mysia. Hearing, after its capture, that Daurises had left the Hellespont and was on his way to Caria, he went to the Hellespont himself with the troops under his command, and crushed all the Aeolians in the neighbourhood of Troy, and also the Gergithes, a remnant of the ancient Teucrians. During these campaigns he died of disease in the Troad. Meanwhile Artaphernes, the governor of Sardis, 123 and Otanes, the third commander, attacked Ionia and the part of Aeolis which adjoins it, capturing Clazomenae in Ionia and Cyme in Aeolis.

It now plainly appeared that Aristagoras of Miletus was, after 124 all, but a poor-spirited creature: himself responsible for setting Ionia by the ears and all the subsequent trouble, nevertheless, when he saw these towns falling one after another, and realized that he had no chance against Darius, he began to look about for means of escape. He called a meeting of his supporters, and, saying they ought to have some place of refuge in the event of their being pushed out of Miletus, asked their advice on the most suitable place for a new settlement. The two alternatives he himself had in mind were Sardinia and Myrcinus, the Edonian town which Histiaeus had fortified when it was given him by Darius. Hecataeus the prose-writer, the son of Heges- 125 ander, objected to both, and proposed that Aristagoras should construct a fortress on the island of Leros and lie low there as long as necessary, if he should be driven from Miletus: then, with it as a base, he might return. Aristagoras, however, decided 126 that the best chance was to go for Myrcinus; accordingly, he turned over affairs at Miletus to Pythagoras, a man of distinc- tion, and himself sailed to Thrace with all who were willing to accompany him. There he gained control of the territory he was after, but on a subsequent venture, while he was besieging a neighbouring town, he was killed with all his men by the Thracians who had been willing to leave it under a truce.[52]

BOOK SIX

1 Thus died Aristagoras, the author of the Ionian rebellion. Meanwhile Histiaeus, the tyrant of Miletus, went to Sardis. He had obtained leave from Darius to quit Susa, and on his arrival at Sardis, Artaphernes, the governor, asked him what, in his opinion, had caused the Ionian revolt. Histiaeus pretended complete ignorance of the whole situation, and said he was astonished that such a thing should have occurred. Artaphernes, however, who knew that he was lying, and had, indeed, full knowledge of the history of the revolt, had his answer ready. 'I will tell you how it is, Histiaeus,' he said, 'you made the shoe
2 and Aristagoras put it on.' This remark, proving as it did that Artaphernes knew the truth, was alarming, and Histiaeus that very night made his escape to the coast. The promise he had made to Darius to bring Sardinia, the biggest island in the world, under Persian rule was thus broken; his real purpose was to take over command of the Ionians in their war against the king.

Crossing to Chios, Histiaeus was arrested by the islanders on suspicion of a plot against them in the Persian interest, but was subsequently released when the Chians had heard the whole
3 story and were convinced of his hostility to Darius. Then they asked him why he had been so anxious to urge Aristagoras to start the revolt which had caused Ionia so much distress, and Histiaeus, taking care to conceal the real reason, declared in reply that he had done so because Darius had been planning a transfer of population, intending to settle the Phoenicians in Ionia and Ionians in Phoenicia. This was quite untrue, but it was enough to alarm the Ionians.[1]

Histiaeus now sent letters to some Persians in Sardis, as 4
if they had previously discussed the rebellion with him. His
messenger was a certain Hermippus, a man from Atarneus.
Hermippus, however, instead of delivering the letters at the
proper addresses, gave them to Artaphernes, who, realizing
what was afoot, instructed Hermippus to take them on to the
people for whom they were intended and then bring back to
him the answers which each of them wrote to Histiaeus. When
he had seen them he executed many of the Persians, and Sardis
was in chaos.

After this disappointment, the Chians, at Histiaeus' request, 5
were prepared to take him back to Miletus; but the people there
had had a taste of liberty and were too well pleased to have got
rid of Aristagoras to be willing to welcome another ruler of the
same stamp. When Histiaeus attempted to force his way into
the town under cover of darkness, one of the Milesians wounded
him in the thigh. His next move, when he found himself excluded
from his own town, was to return to Chios, from which, having
failed to persuade the Chians to give him ships, he crossed to
Mytilene in Lesbos. Here he was successful; the Lesbians put
eight triremes into commission and sailed with him to Byzantium, which they made their base for the seizure of all ships
bound out from the Black Sea, except those whose crews
promised to obey his orders.[2]

While they were thus engaged, Miletus itself was in expec- 6
tation of a heavy combined attack by land and sea. The Persian
commanders had united their forces and were marching against
it, counting the lesser cities of secondary importance. Amongst
those who sailed with the fleet, it was the Phoenicians whose
heart was most in the business, though there were also contingents from Cyprus (which had recently been subjugated),
Cilicia, and Egypt.

The Ionians, learning of the Persians' intentions, sent their 7
representatives to the Panionium. In their deliberations it was
decided to raise no troops to oppose the Persians on land; the
actual defence of Miletus was to be left to its people, while they
themselves should man every available ship, and concentrate
them at the little island of Lade, just off the coast opposite

Miletus. Here they would fight a naval action in defence of the town.

8   Presently the Ionian fleet and the Lesbians from Aeolia began to arrive, and the ships took station in the following order: at the eastern end of the line were 80 vessels from Miletus; next to them came 12 from Priene and 3 from Myus, then 17 from Teos, and 100 from Chios. The contingents from Erythrae and Phocaea followed, consisting of 8 and 3 vessels respectively; and next to these lay the Lesbian contingent, 70 strong. Finally, on
9   the western end of the line were 60 vessels from Samos – making a grand total of 353 triremes, against the 600 which the Persians had at their disposal.

On the arrival of the combined Persian force, both ships and troops, the officers in command had something of a shock; the size of the Ionian fleet was greater than they had expected, and they were afraid they might be unable to defeat it. If they did not get command of the sea, they might fail to take Miletus and be punished by Darius for their failure. So they collected the tyrants of the various Ionian cities, who, after they were turned out by Aristagoras, had fled to the Persians; these men were now with the army before Miletus, and it was to them that the Persian commanders turned in their difficulty.[3] Having called them to a conference, they said: 'Men of Ionia, now is the time for you to show yourselves true servants of the king. Each of you must do his best to detach his own countrymen from the Ionian alliance. Make your proposals to them, and promise that, if they abandon their allies, there will be no disagreeable consequences for them; we will not set fire to their houses or their temples, or treat them with any greater harshness than before this trouble occurred. If, however, they refuse, and insist upon fighting, then you must resort to threats, and say exactly what we will do to them: tell them, that is, that when they are beaten they will be sold as slaves, their boys will be made eunuchs, their girls carried off to Bactria, and their land given to others.'

10   The exiled tyrants agreed to the Persian proposal, and each of them sent a message by night to the people of his town. The scheme, however, did not prosper; for in each town the

recipients of the letters thought that they were the only ones to be addressed, with the result that all of them firmly refused the invitation to treachery. This incident occurred immediately after the arrival of the Persian force at Miletus.

Soon afterwards meetings were held by the Ionians who had 11 assembled at Lade, and amongst the various speeches which were made, one of the most notable was that of the Phocaean commander, Dionysius. 'Fellow Ionians,' he said, 'our fate balances on a razor's edge between being free men or slaves – and runaway slaves at that. Come then: if you are willing to submit for a while to strict discipline and to spend a few laborious days, you will thereby be enabled to defeat the Persians and keep your liberty. If, on the other hand, you continue to live soft and to go as you please, then I see no hope whatever of your escaping punishment at the king's hands for your revolt. Now take my advice; put yourselves under my orders, and, if heaven gives us a fair deal, I promise you either that the enemy will refuse battle altogether, or, if he fights, that he will be soundly beaten.' The appeal succeeded; the Ionians agreed to take orders from 12 Dionysius, who at once got to work. Every day he had ships and crews out for training, making the fleet sail in line ahead, keeping the troops on board under arms, practising the oarsmen on the manoeuvre of 'breaking the line',[4] and insisting that all ships, for the remainder of the day, should lie to their anchors instead of being hauled ashore. Thus the men got no rest from morning to night. For seven days they continued to obey orders; but after that, being unaccustomed to such hard work and worn out with toiling away under the hot sun, they began to grumble. 'What god have we offended,' they said, 'to be punished like this? We must have taken leave of our senses, to have put ourselves into the hands of this swollen-headed Phocaean who provides no more than three ships for the fleet! Yet here he is, taking complete charge; the way he treats us is outrageous: we shall never recover from it – many of us are ill already, and many more expect to be. Anything would be preferable to the misery we now endure – if it's a choice between two sorts of slavery, then the one we are threatened with, however bad it turns out to be, could hardly be worse than what we are putting up with now. Now then – let us refuse to obey his orders.'[5]

It was no sooner said than done. Every seaman in the fleet refused duty. They pitched tents, like soldiers, in the island, lounged about in the shade, and refused to go aboard their vessels or to continue their training in any way whatever.

13   The commanders of the Samian contingent, when they realized how the Ionians were behaving and were aware of the complete lack of discipline amongst them, changed their minds about the proposal which had previously been made to them by Aeaces, the son of Syloson, at the request of the Persians. This proposal – to withdraw, namely, from the Ionian confederacy – they now decided to accept, convinced, as they were, that it would be impossible to get the better of the Persian fleet, and, even if they did, that Darius would soon send another fleet against them five times as great. The moment, therefore, that they saw the Ionians shirking their duty, they thought that the most profitable thing to do was to save their houses and temples, while they had the chance. Aeaces, who proposed the desertion, was the son of Syloson and grandson of Aeaces. He had been tyrant of Samos, and along with the other tyrants in the Ionian states was banished from power by Aristagoras of Miletus.[6]

14   Then the Phoenician fleet came forward, and the Ionians sailed in line ahead to meet them. They were soon at close quarters, and, once the fight had begun, I cannot relate for certain which of the Ionian contingents fought well and which fought ill; for the reports are confused, everybody blaming everybody else. As for the Samians, it is said that in accordance with their agreements with Aeaces they abandoned their place in the line, got sail on their vessels, and made for home – with the exception of eleven triremes, whose officers stayed and fought contrary to orders from their superiors. (To commemorate the courage of these men, the government at Samos had a column erected, with their names and parentage inscribed upon it. The column stands in the public square.)

The sight of the Samians under sail for home was too much for the Lesbians, who were next in the line; they soon followed

suit, as, indeed, did the majority of the Ionian fleet. Of those   15
who remained at their posts and fought it out, the most roughly
handled were the Chians who fought a brilliant and most valiant
action. As mentioned before, they contributed a hundred ships
to the combined fleet. Aboard each were forty picked men, of
citizen class, serving as marines. Though they saw the greater
number of the confederate fleet playing traitor, they scorned to
imitate such cowardly behaviour, but with the few friends still
fighting beside them again and again broke the enemy line and
continued the struggle, until, having captured a number of
enemy ships, they had lost nearly all their own; after which,
with the few that remained afloat, they made their escape to
Chios. Those of their ships which were crippled made for   16
Mycale, with the enemy in pursuit, and here they were run
ashore and abandoned, the crews continuing their journey overland on foot. On the way, they entered the territory of Ephesus.
It was after dark, and the women of the place were celebrating
the Thesmophoria, and the Ephesians, having had no news of
the Chians' predicament, and seeing that a company of armed
men had crossed their borders, at once supposed them to be
brigands who were after their women. They therefore hurried
to the rescue with every available man, and the Chians were
killed.

Such was their fate. Meanwhile the Phocaean commander   17
Dionysius, who had captured three enemy vessels in the course
of the engagement, also made good his escape once he realized
that all was lost. He did not, however, make for Phocaea,
because he knew his people would share the fate of all the other
Ionians and be reduced to slavery; instead he set his course,
without further preparation, straight for Phoenicia, where he
sank a number of cargo-vessels and took from them property of
considerable value; he then sailed for Sicily, which he made his
base for piratical raids against Carthaginian and Tyrrhenian
shipping – Greek ships he never molested.

After their victory over the Ionian fleet, the Persians invested   18
Miletus by land and sea. They dug saps under the walls, brought
up rams of all kinds, and, five years after the revolt of Aristagoras, overwhelmed it. So Miletus was reduced to slavery, and

19 the oracle's prediction was fulfilled. The prediction was as follows: the people of Argos had consulted the oracle at Delphi on a matter which concerned the safety of their own city, and had received an answer in which others were involved besides themselves; for while a part of it concerned Argos, there was an additional passage which referred to Miletus. The former I will mention when I reach the proper moment in my story;[7] the latter was in these words:

> You then, Miletus, contriver of wicked deeds,
> Shall be a feast for many, and a splendid prize;
> Your wives shall wash the feet of many a long-haired man,
> And others shall care for our shrine at Didyma.

This is just what happened to the Milesians; most of the men were killed by the Persians – and the Persians wear their hair long; the women and children were made slaves, and the temple at Didyma, both shrine and oracle, was plundered and burnt. The wealth of this temple I have frequently spoken of elsewhere

20 in my story.[8] The men in the city who were captured alive were sent as prisoners to Susa; Darius did them no harm, and settled them in Ampe on the Persian Gulf, near the mouth of the Tigris. The Persians themselves occupied the land in the immediate neighbourhood of the town, and the rest of the cultivated region which belonged to it, and made over the mountainous interior to the Carians of Pedasus.

21 The people of Sybaris who, after the loss of their city, lived in Laus and Scidrus, failed to show proper sympathy with the Milesians in their misfortune; for at the capture of Sybaris by the Crotoniates, the whole male population of Miletus, from the boys upwards, had shaved their heads and gone into deep mourning, as a mark of the friendly connexion between the two towns – and indeed I know of no two towns more closely bound together by mutual ties. The Athenians, on the contrary, showed their profound distress at the capture of Miletus in a number of ways, and in particular, when Phrynichus produced his play, *The Capture of Miletus*, the audience in the theatre burst into tears. The author was fined a thousand drachmas for reminding

them of their own evils, and they forbade anybody ever to put the play on the stage again.[9]

In this way Miletus was emptied of its inhabitants.   22

In Samos the wealthier citizens were by no means pleased by the way their officers had come to an understanding with the Persians. Immediately after the fight off Lade they met in conference, and decided not to wait for the arrival of Aeaces, but to abandon the island and settle elsewhere rather than to stay and be slaves to Aeaces and his Persian masters. It happened that at this same time the people of Zancle in Sicily had sent to Ionia to invite settlers to Kale-Acte, or Fair Shore, a place on the north coast of the island facing Tyrrhenia, and inhabited by Sicilian natives. Their purpose was to found an Ionian settlement on this spot. The people of Samos were the only Ionians to accept the invitation, and they set sail in company with such of the Milesians as had escaped. In the course of their voyage, they   23 reached Western Locri, in southern Italy, just at the moment when Scythes, the ruler of Zancle, was attempting, with all his men, to capture by siege a Sicel town.[10] Anaxilaus, tyrant of Rhegium, who was at that period on bad terms with Zancle, and knew what was going on, got into touch with the Samians and persuaded them to forget about the Fair Shore, their original objective, and seize Zancle itself instead, while it was undefended. The Samians agreed; the town was taken, and the Zanclaeans, as soon as the news reached them, hurried back to recover it and called upon Hippocrates, despot of Gela, as an ally of theirs, to support them. Hippocrates responded to the appeal, but when he arrived at Zancle with his army, he repaid Scythes for the loss of the town he ruled by flinging him into chains and sending him off with his brother Pythogenes to Inyx; he then entered into negotiation with the Samians and, after an exchange of guarantees, completed the betrayal of the people of Zancle. His reward for this treachery was to be half of all the movable property and slaves in the town, and all in the open country. The greater number of the townspeople he thus kept as slaves; the three hundred leading citizens he handed over to the Samians to have their throats cut. The Samians, however, did not do this.

24   Scythes escaped from Inyx to Himera, and from there made his way to Asia and up-country to the court of Darius, who came to consider him the most honourable man who had ever come to him from Greece; for having got leave from Darius to revisit Sicily, he returned to Persia of his own accord, where he died in old age and great prosperity.

   This, then, is the story of how the Samians who escaped from Persian domination acquired without effort the lovely town of Zancle.

25   After the sea fight off Miletus, the Phoenicians, on instructions from Persia, restored Aeaces, the son of Syloson, to his previous authority in Samos, as a reward for the great and valuable services which he had rendered. Samos itself was not burnt by the Persians, neither the town nor the temples; of all the Ionian rebels the Samians alone escaped, because of the desertion of their ships during the battle of Lade. After capturing Miletus the Persians quickly occupied Caria, some of the towns being taken by force, others without resistance.

26   Meanwhile news of events at Miletus reached Histiaeus, who was still around Byzantium seizing Ionian merchantmen outward bound from the Black Sea. Leaving his business in the Hellespont in the hands of Bisaltes of Abydos, the son of Apollophanes, he at once sailed for Chios with a number of Lesbians, and attacked a Chian garrison, which refused to admit him, at a place called the Hollows. A great many of the garrison were killed, and Histiaeus, basing himself on Polichne, soon, with the help of his Lesbians, got the better of the rest of the Chians, weakened, as they were, by the sea battle.

27   It seems that there is nearly always a warning sign of some kind, when disaster is about to overtake a city or a nation. Chios was no exception – for before this happened the warnings it received were far from negligible. The Chians had sent a choir of a hundred young men to Delphi; ninety-eight of them caught the plague and died, and only two returned. Again, in the capital city of the island, at about the same time, a little before the sea battle, the roof of a school fell in on some children who were learning their letters, and of a hundred and twenty children only one escaped. Both these events were acts of God to forewarn

the people of Chios; they were followed by the battle of Lade, which brought the community to its knees, and then by the arrival of Histiaeus with his Lesbians, who, in their weakened state, had easily conquered them.

Histiaeus' next act was a campaign against Thasos with a 28 considerable force of Ionians and Aeolians.[11] While he was engaged in the blockade, news came that the Phoenician fleet had left Miletus and was sailing to attack the other Ionian states. He promptly raised the blockade of Thasos and hurried to Lesbos with all his troops. From Lesbos, finding his men short of food, he crossed to the mainland with the intention of cutting the crops round about Atarneus, and in the Mysian territory along the valley of the Caicus. It happened, however, that the Persian general Harpagus, who was in the neighbourhood at the head of a large army, fell in with Histiaeus' party as they came ashore, took Histiaeus prisoner, and killed most of his men. The circumstances of his capture were these: the Greek and Persian forces were engaged at Malene, in Atarnean terri- 29 tory:[12] for a long time it was an even struggle, until at last the Persian cavalry, arriving late on the scene, fell upon the enemy; this victory was their work. The Greeks fled; and Histiaeus, who did not expect Darius to punish his fault with death, made a last bid to save himself. He was overtaken by a Persian as he ran, and, just as he was about to be speared, he cried out in Persian, 'I am Histiaeus, the Milesian.' Now if after his capture he had 30 been taken to Darius, he would not, in my opinion, have found himself in serious trouble, but Darius would have pardoned him; but as it was, for this very reason – to prevent him, that is, from rising once more to a position of influence in Darius' court – Artaphernes, the governor of Sardis, and Harpagus, his actual captor, resolved upon his death. As soon as he reached Sardis he was impaled; his head was cut off, mummified, and sent to Darius in Susa. Darius, when he learned what Artaphernes and Harpagus had done, was angry with them for not bringing Histiaeus to him alive; he gave orders for the head to be washed and tended, and buried with all the honour due to a man who had done good service to Persia and the king. So ends the story of Histiaeus.

31   The Persian fleet lay during the winter at Miletus. The following year it put to sea again, and took without difficulty the islands of Chios, Lesbos, and Tenedos off the Asiatic coast. Each island, as soon as it was occupied, was gone through with the drag-net – a process in which men join hands and make a chain right across the island from north to south, and then move from one end to the other, hunting everybody out.[13] The Persians also took the Ionian towns on the mainland – but without the
32 netting process, as it was not practicable. The threats which the Persian commanders had uttered against the Ionians when they found them resolved upon opposition were now carried into effect; once the towns were in their hands, the best-looking boys were chosen for castration and made into eunuchs; the most beautiful girls were dragged from their homes and sent to Darius' court, and the towns themselves, temples and all, were burnt to the ground. In this way the Ionians were reduced for the third time to slavery – first by the Lydians, and then, twice, by the Persians.[14]

33   Leaving Ionia, the fleet proceeded to take all the places on the left-hand coast of the Hellespont, as one enters the strait. The towns on the opposite side had already fallen to the Persians by assault from inland. The places on the European side of the Hellespont are the Chersonese, which contains a great many towns, Perinthus, the strongholds on the Thracian coast, Selymbria, and Byzantium. The people of Byzantium, and their opposite neighbours in Chalcedon, instead of awaiting the attack of the Phoenicians by sea, abandoned their homes and fled to the Black Sea coast, where they established themselves at Mesembria. The Phoenicians, after destroying by fire the places I have mentioned, turned their attention to Proconnesus and Artace; then, having burnt these too, they returned to the Chersonese to take such places as had escaped destruction on their previous visit. The one exception was Cyzicus; for before the Phoenicians entered the strait, the people of this town had made their submission to Darius by coming to terms with Oebares, the son of Megabazus, who was governor of Dascyleium. Thus all the towns of the Chersonese, except Cardia, were taken by the Phoenicians.

Up to this period, the man who had been tyrant over this part   34
of the world was Miltiades, the son of Cimon and grandson
of Stesagoras. He had inherited his position from Miltiades
the son of Cypselus, who had come into possession of it in the
following way. The Dolonci, a Thracian people to whom the
Chersonese then belonged, finding themselves in difficulties in
a war with the Apsinthians, sent their chiefs to Delphi, to ask
advice from the oracle. The Priestess replied by recommending
them to take home with them, in order to resettle their affairs,
the first man who, after they left the temple, should invite them
into his friendship. The chiefs of the Dolonci, travelling by the
Sacred Road, passed through Phocis and Boeotia, and then, as
nobody asked them in, turned off and made for Athens.

Supreme power in Athens was at this time in the hands of   35
Pisistratus, but a position of considerable importance was also
enjoyed by Cypselus' son, Miltiades. Miltiades belonged to a
family whose fortune was great enough to allow them to enter
a four-horse chariot for the games, and traced his descent back
to Aeacus of Aegina; but further down the line his ancestry was
Athenian, and Philaeus, the son of Ajax, was the first of the
family to be naturalized in Athens. Now it happened that as the
Dolonci passed his house, Miltiades, who was sitting in his
porch, caught sight of them, and noticing that they were dressed
like foreigners and carried spears, called out to them. The men
came up to where he was sitting, whereupon he invited them in
and offered them shelter and hospitality. The invitation was
accepted, and, while they were staying in the house, they told
Miltiades all about the oracle, and then begged him to act upon
the advice which God had given. Miltiades had no sooner heard
their story than he agreed to do as they wished – for he disliked
Pisistratus' government and was very willing to be out of the
way. He lost no time, therefore, in going to Delphi, where he
asked the oracle if he was right in acceding to the request
which the Dolonci had made him. The Priestess replied in the   36
affirmative, and the matter was settled: and so Miltiades, son of
Cypselus – who before this time had won the four-horse chariot
race at Olympia – collected everybody in Athens who was
willing to take part in the venture, and sailed with the Dolonci.

He took possession of the country, and the chieftains who had brought him over made him their ruler.[15]

Miltiades' first act was to build a wall across the neck of the peninsula from Cardia to Pactya, to stop the Apsinthians from breaking into the Chersonese on plundering raids. Here at the neck the peninsula is some $4\frac{1}{2}$ miles wide, its total length being about $52\frac{1}{2}$ miles. Having completed the wall and shut out the Apsinthians, Miltiades next attacked Lampsacus; but he was ambushed and taken prisoner.

37

The Lydian King Croesus had had Miltiades much in his thoughts, so when he learned of his capture, he sent a command to the people of Lampsacus to set him at liberty; if they refused, he was determined, he added, to 'cut them down like a pine-tree'. The people of the town were baffled by Croesus' threat, and at a loss to understand what being cut down like a pine-tree might mean, until at last the true significance of the phrase dawned upon a certain elderly man: the pine, he explained, was the only kind of tree which sent up no new shoots after being felled – cut down a pine and it will die off completely. The explanation made the Lampsacenes so frightened of Croesus that they let Miltiades go.

38

Miltiades thus escaped, thanks to Croesus; nevertheless he died childless, leaving his authority and possessions to Stesagoras, the son of his half-brother on his mother's side, Cimon. Ever since his death the people of the Chersonese have offered in his honour the sacrifices commonly due to the Founder of a state, with chariot-races and athletic contests, in which nobody from Lampsacus is allowed to compete.

During the war with Lampsacus it was the fate of Stesagoras, too, to die without an heir – he was hit on the head with an axe in the Council chamber by a man who pretended to be a deserter, but was actually an enemy of his, and a pretty angry one.

39

Stesagoras having thus met his end, Miltiades the son of Cimon and brother of the murdered Stesagoras was dispatched by the Pisistratidae in a trireme to the Chersonese, to assume the direction of affairs. The Pisistratidae had treated Miltiades well while he was in Athens, just as if they had not been guilty of his father's death – *that* incident, however, I will treat of later on.[16]

On his arrival in the Chersonese Miltiades kept within doors, on the pretence of showing respect for his dead brother, and the leading men from every town all over the country met together, when they heard of this, and came in a body to show their sympathy with him. Miltiades then had every one of them arrested. He then made himself master of the Chersonese, kept a body of 500 mercenaries, and married Hegesipyle, daughter of the Thracian King Olorus.

This Miltiades – that is, Cimon's son – had not been long in 40 the Chersonese before he was involved in more serious difficulties, for two years after his arrival he was obliged to take to his heels to escape from the Scythian nomads who, incensed by the attack of Darius, joined forces and marched as far as the Chersonese. Miltiades did not await their attack, but fled, and remained away until they withdrew, when the Dolonci sent and fetched him back. This had occurred two years previously;[17] and now, when he learned that the Phoenicians were at Tenedos, 41 he shipped his property on board five triremes and made sail for Athens, starting from Cardia. He sailed down the Black Gulf, and, just as he got clear of the peninsula, fell in with the Phoenician fleet. Miltiades himself got away to Imbros with four of his five triremes, but the fifth, commanded by his eldest son Metiochus (his mother was not the daughter of Olorus the Thracian, but another woman), was overtaken and captured. The Phoenicians thought that they had a prize indeed, when they found that, together with the ship, they had caught Miltiades' son; for it was Miltiades who, when the Scythians urged the Ionians to break the bridge over the Danube and sail home, had advised them to consent. Remembering this, the Phoenicians brought Metiochus to Darius, in confident expectation of the royal favour. The king, however, far from doing any harm to Metiochus, treated him with the greatest liberality: he presented him with a house and property, and a Persian wife by whom he had children, who lived as Persians.[18]

Miltiades himself sailed from Imbros and arrived safely at Athens.

During the course of this year no further hostile measures 42 were undertaken by the Persians against Ionia; on the contrary, something was done greatly to its advantage. Artaphernes, governor of Sardis, sent for representatives from all the Ionian states and forced them to bind themselves by oath to settle their differences by arbitration, instead of raiding. In addition to this, he had their territories surveyed and measured in parasangs (the Persian equivalent of 30 furlongs), and settled the tax which each state was to pay at a figure which has remained unaltered down to my time.[19] The amount was, moreover, much the same as it had previously been.

43   These measures were conducive to peace. Then, in the following spring, Darius superseded all his other generals and sent Mardonius, the son of Gobryas, down to the coast in command of a very large force, both military and naval. Mardonius was still a young man, and had recently married Darius' daughter Artozostra. Reaching Cilicia with his army, he took ship and continued along the coast in company with the fleet, leaving other officers to conduct the troops to the Hellespont. When in the course of his voyage along the Asiatic coast he reached Ionia, he did something which will come as a great marvel to those Greeks who cannot believe that Otanes declared to the seven conspirators that Persia should have a democratic government: he suppressed the tyrants in all the Ionian states and set up democratic institutions in their place.[20] He then hurried on towards the Hellespont. Having got together a formidable fleet and army, he ferried the troops across the strait and began his

44   march through Europe, with Eretria and Athens as his main objectives. At any rate, these two places were the professed object of the expedition, though in fact the Persians intended to subjugate as many Greek towns as they could. Their fleet subdued Thasos without resistance, and the troops on land added the Macedonians to the list of Darius' subjects. All the peoples on the hither side of Macedonia were subjects already.

From Thasos the fleet stood across to the mainland and proceeded along the coast to Acanthus, and from there attempted to double Athos; but before they were round this promontory, they were caught by a violent northerly gale, which proved too much for the ships to cope with. A great many of them were driven ashore and wrecked on Athos – indeed, report

says that something like three hundred were lost with over
twenty thousand men. The sea in the neighbourhood of Athos
is full of monsters, so that those of the ships' companies who
were not dashed to pieces on the rocks, were seized and
devoured. Others, unable to swim, were drowned; others, again,
died of cold.

While this disaster was overtaking the fleet, on land Mardon- 45
ius and his army in Macedonia were attacked in camp one night
by the Brygi, a Thracian tribe. The Persian losses were heavy,
and Mardonius himself was wounded. But even so the Brygi did
not escape subjection; for Mardonius did not leave their country
until he had subdued them.

However, the casualties his army had suffered by the attack
of the Brygi, and the fearful losses of the fleet at Athos, now
induced Mardonius to begin his retreat. The whole force, therefore, returned to Asia in disgrace.

Next year Darius, on the strength of a tale put about by their 46
neighbours that the people of Thasos were planning a revolt,
sent them an order to dismantle their defences and bring their
fleet across to Abdera. The islanders of Thasos after they had
been blockaded by Histiaeus of Miletus had determined to
apply their ample resources to building warships and stronger
fortifications. The island's revenue was derived partly from
property on the mainland and partly from mines: the gold mines
at Scapte Hyle yielded in all eighty talents a year, those in the
island itself rather less, but a good sum all the same, so that
the islanders, without raising any tax on their own produce,
enjoyed, from the mines and the mainland, a revenue of two
hundred talents – and, in a particularly good year, of as much
as three hundred. I have seen these mines myself; much the most 47
remarkable are those discovered by the Phoenicians who came
with Thasus the son of Phoenix to colonize the island, which
has since borne his name. These Phoenician mines lie between
Coenyra and a place called Aenyra, on the south-eastern side of
Thasos, facing Samothrace. A whole mountain has been turned
upside down in the search for gold. In spite of all this, however, 48
the islanders obeyed Darius' order, pulled down their fortifications and sent their whole fleet over to Abdera.

Darius now began to test the attitude of the Greeks, and to find out whether they were likely to resist or surrender. He sent heralds to the various Greek states to demand earth and water for the king, and at the same time he sent orders to the Asiatic coast towns, which were already tributary, for the provision of
49 warships and transport vessels to carry cavalry. While these were being prepared, the heralds in Greece obtained what they asked from many of the towns on the mainland and from all the islanders whom they visited with their request. Amongst the islanders, moreover, who gave the sign of submission, were the Aeginetans.

This act on the part of Aegina produced an immediate reaction from the Athenians, who supposed that the Aeginetans had submitted out of enmity to themselves and intended to join the Persian attack upon them; at once, therefore (and they were not sorry to have the excuse), they entered into correspondence with Sparta and accused the Aeginetans of being traitors to Greece.
50 Having heard the accusation, Cleomenes, the son of Anaxandrides and one of the Spartan kings, crossed to Aegina with the intention of arresting the men chiefly responsible; but when he attempted the arrest, he found a number of other people in the island hotly opposed to him. Conspicuous amongst these was a son of Polycritus – a man called Crius (that is, Ram) – who declared that Cleomenes would never get away with the arrest of a single man on the island – for what he was doing had not the authority of the Spartan government behind it. He had been bribed, the man added, by Athens – otherwise both kings would have come together to make the arrest.[21] He did this on the instigation of Demaratus. As Cleomenes was leaving the island, he asked the man his name. 'Ram,' came the answer. 'Very well, Master Ram,' said Cleomenes, 'you had better get your horns sheathed in metal. There's trouble coming for you.'
51 Meanwhile Demaratus, the son of Ariston, who had stayed behind in Sparta, was talking against Cleomenes. Demaratus was the other of the two Spartan kings, but he belonged to the less honoured of the two houses: his family was not, indeed, actually of lower origin than the other, for both have a common ancestor; but the house of Eurysthenes, being the elder branch,

is held in higher respect. The Spartans maintain (contradicting 52
all the poets) that when they originally settled in their present
territory, Aristodemus – son of Aristomachus, grandson of Cleodaeus, and great-grandson of Hyllus – was himself their king,
and not Aristodemus' sons. Shortly afterwards, his wife Argeia
(who is said to have been the daughter of Autesion, the son
of Tisamenos, grandson of Thersander and great-grandson of
Polyneices) gave birth to twins. Aristodemus lived to see the
children, but immediately afterwards fell ill and died. The Spartans of that time determined, as the custom is, to make the elder
of the two children king, but as they were both the same size
and each exactly like the other, it was impossible to tell which
to choose. Thus baffled, or perhaps even before trying, they
asked the mother; but she said that she was no more able to tell
them apart herself. Actually, of course, she knew perfectly well
which was which, and only pretended not to, in the hope that
both of them might somehow be made kings. At a loss what to
do next, the Spartans sent to the Delphic oracle for advice, and
the Priestess replied that they must let both the children be kings,
but give the elder one the greater honour. The answer of the
oracle by no means solved the puzzle, for the Spartans were no
better able than before to determine which baby had been born
first. At last, however, a suggestion was made by a man from
Messenia called Panites: this was, that they should watch the
mother and see which she fed and washed first. If she always
kept to the same order, that fact alone would tell them all they
wanted to know; if, on the contrary, she varied it, and attended
sometimes to one child first and sometimes to the other, then it
would be clear that she knew no more than they did and they
would have to try some other plan.

The Spartans did as the man from Messenia advised. Keeping
a watch on the mother, who was quite unaware of their reason
for doing so, they found that she invariably fed and washed the
two children in the same order; so they took the one which was
singled out for preference as the elder, and had it brought up at
the public expense. The child was named Eurysthenes, and its
brother Procles. When the children grew up, the story goes that
they quarrelled as long as they lived, in spite of the fact that

they were brothers; and their descendants continued the family feud.[22]

53   This version of the story is found only in Sparta. The common Greek tradition is, that the Dorian kings as far back as Perseus, the son of Danae (thus not including the god), are as they stand in the accepted Greek lists, and are rightly considered as of Greek nationality, because even at this early date they ranked as such. I am justified in saying 'as far back as Perseus', and no farther, because Perseus has no human father by whose name he can be called, as Heracles, for instance, has Amphitryon. If, on the other hand, we trace the ancestry of Danae, the daughter of Acrisius, we find that the Dorian chieftains are genuine Egyp-

54 tians. This is the accepted Greek version of the genealogy of the Spartan royal house; the Persians, however, maintain that Perseus was an Assyrian who adopted Greek nationality; his ancestry, therefore, was not Greek; and the forebears of Acrisius were not related to Perseus at all, but were Egyptian – which

55 accords with the Greek version of the story. But there is no need to pursue this subject further. How it happened that Egyptians came to the Peloponnese, and what they did to make themselves kings in that part of Greece, has been chronicled by other writers;[23] I will add nothing, therefore, but proceed to mention some points which no one else has yet touched upon.

56   The prerogatives of the Spartan kings are these: two priest-hoods, of Zeus Lacedaemon and of Zeus Uranius, and the power of declaring war on whom they please. In this, no Spartan may attempt to oppose their decision, under pain of sacrilege. On service, the kings go first and return last; they have a bodyguard of a hundred picked men, and are allowed for their own use as many cattle as they wish. To them personally are allotted the

57 skins and chines of all animals offered for sacrifice. In peace-time their privileges are as follows: at all public religious celebrations they are the first to sit down at the dinner which follows the sacrifice; they are served first, each getting twice as much of every dish as anybody else. Theirs is the right to make the first ceremonial libation, and to them belong the hides of all animals offered in sacrifice. On the first and seventh days of every month each king is given a full-grown animal to offer in sacrifice in the

temple of Apollo, also a bushel of barley-meal and a Laconian quart of wine. At all public games seats of honour are reserved for them. It is their duty to select and appoint the officials who see to the entertainment of foreign visitors, and each of them nominates two 'Pythians' – officials, that is, whose duty it is to visit Delphi when occasion arises, and who take their meals with the kings at the public expense.

If the kings happen not to attend the usual state dinner, two quarts of meal and half a pint of wine are sent to each of them at his house; when they do attend, they are served with double quantities of everything, a privilege they also enjoy when they are invited to dinner at a private house.

They are responsible for the safe-keeping of all oracles (the 'Pythians' also have knowledge of them), and certain definite legal matters are left to their sole decision. These are as follows: first, if a girl inherits her father's estate and has not been betrothed by him to anybody, the kings decide who has the right to marry her; secondly, all matters connected with the public roads are in their hands; and, thirdly, anyone who wishes to adopt a child must do it in the king's presence.

They sit with the twenty-eight Elders in the Council chamber, and, in the event of their absence from a meeting, those of the Elders who are nearest of kin to them take over their privilege and cast two votes, in addition to their own.[24]

Besides these public marks of distinction during his lifetime,   58 special ceremonies are also observed upon a king's death. News of the death is carried by riders all over the country, and women go the rounds of the capital beating cauldrons. This is the signal for two people, one man and one woman, from every citizen's household to put on mourning – which they are compelled to do under penalty of a heavy fine. One custom is observed on the occasion of a king's death, which is the same in Sparta as in Asia: this is, that when a death occurs, not only Spartans but a certain number of the country people from all over Lacedaemon are forced to attend the funeral. A huge crowd assembles, consisting of many thousands of people – Spartan citizens, country folk, and helots[25] – and men and women together strike their foreheads with every sign of grief, wailing as if they could never stop and continually declaring that the king who has just died was the best they ever had.[26]

If a king is killed in war, they make a statue of him, and carry it to burial on a richly draped bier. After a king's funeral there are no public meetings or elections for ten days, all of which are 59 spent in mourning. When a new king comes to the throne on the death of his predecessor, he follows a custom which obtains in Persia on similar occasions: he remits, that is, all debts owed by Spartan citizens either to the king or to the treasury. This corresponds with the Persian custom whereby a king, on his accession, remits arrears of tribute from all his subject states.

60   The Spartans resemble the Egyptians in that they make certain callings hereditary: town-criers, flute-players, and cooks are all, respectively, sons of fathers who followed the same profession.[27] A man cannot, for instance, merely because he has a loud voice, adopt the profession of town-crier, or herald, to the exclusion of a competitor; he can be a herald only if his progenitors have been heralds.

61   At this time, then, when Cleomenes was in Aegina working for the common good of Greece, Demaratus continued to spread malicious stories about him – not because he felt any kindness towards Aegina, but simply out of envy and spite. Accordingly, on his return to Sparta Cleomenes began to consider ways of depriving Demaratus of his office, and he soon found something upon which he could base his attack. When Ariston was king of Sparta, although he married twice, he had no children. Unwilling to admit that this might be his own fault, he married a third time – and in the following circumstances: he had a friend, a Spartan citizen, with whom he was particularly intimate, and this friend's wife was much the most beautiful woman in Sparta. Oddly enough, she had been as a child extremely plain, and owed the transformation to her nurse, who, seeing that she was ugly, and that her parents, who were people of substance, were distressed about it, conceived the idea of carrying her every day to the shrine of Helen. (This is at Therapne, above the temple of Apollo.)[28] She would then take the baby in, lay it down in front of Helen's statue, and pray the goddess to take away its ugliness. One day as the nurse left the shrine, it is said that a

woman appeared and asked her what it was that she had in her arms. The nurse replied that it was a baby. The woman asked to see it, but the nurse refused, for the child's parents had forbidden her to show it to anybody. The woman, however, persisted, and at last the nurse, seeing how extremely anxious she was to have a look at the baby, showed it to her; and she stroked the baby's head and declared that it would grow to be the most beautiful woman in Sparta.

From that very day there was a change in its appearance. The child grew up, and, as soon as she was old enough, was married to Agetus, the son of Alcides – Ariston's friend, whom I mentioned before.

Now Ariston fell in love with Agetus' wife, and, as his desire   62
for her gave him no peace, he hit upon the following plan: going to his friend, the woman's husband, he offered to let him choose anything he possessed, and promised to make him a present of it, provided that his friend would do the like for him. Agetus agreed – for, as Ariston had a wife already, it never occurred to him that his own might be in danger. The compact was confirmed by oath, and Ariston handed over whatever it was that Agetus chose. Then, when his turn came to say what he wanted in exchange, he tried to take his friend's wife. Agetus protested that he had consented to anything else, but not that. However, he had sworn an oath; and that, together with Ariston's trick, forced him to let his wife go.

Thus Ariston married his third wife, after divorcing his   63
second; and quite shortly thereafter this woman, before her ten months were up, gave birth to a son – Demaratus. Ariston was with the Ephors, sitting on his state chair, when a servant brought him the news. Counting on his fingers the number of months since his marriage – the date of which he had not forgotten – he exclaimed with an oath: 'The child can't be mine.' The Ephors heard what he said, but, at the moment, paid little attention to it. Later on, when Demaratus grew older, Ariston regretted the remark he had made, for he had come to believe that the boy really was his son. Some time before all this happened, the whole Spartan people had joined in prayer that Ariston, whom they considered to be the most distinguished of

the kings who had ever reigned in Sparta, might have a son: this was why, when the son was born, he was named Demaratus.[29]

64   In course of time Ariston died and Demaratus succeeded to the throne. Apparently, however, it was fated that the whole story should come to light and lead to the deposition of Demaratus, through the quarrel between him and Cleomenes – first on the occasion when Demaratus brought the army back from Eleusis, and again when Cleomenes crossed to Aegina to deal with the islanders who had taken sides with Persia.

65   Eager to have his revenge, Cleomenes entered into an agreement with Demaratus' kinsman Leotychides, the son of Menares and grandson of Agis, whereby he undertook to make Leotychides king in place of Demaratus, on condition of getting his support in the attack upon Aegina.

Now Leotychides was a bitter enemy of Demaratus; and this was why. Leotychides had been engaged to marry Percalus, a daughter of Chilon, the son of Demarmenus, but Demaratus by a bold stroke had got in first, carried off the girl by force, and married her himself. This was the origin of the quarrel between the two men, and now Leotychides, at Cleomenes' urgent request, declared upon oath that Demaratus was not Ariston's son, and had no right to the throne. He followed this up by reminding people of what Ariston had said when the servant told him of the child's birth – how he had counted the months, and sworn that he could not be its father. This was the ground on which Leotychides tried to prove that Demaratus, not being Ariston's son, had therefore no right to the throne, and he produced as witnesses the Ephors who had been present on the

66   occasion and had heard what Ariston said. The case caused violent disputes, until finally the Spartans determined to settle the question of Demaratus' parentage by consulting the Delphic oracle. Upon the decision to refer the matter to Delphi, Cleomenes, who was mainly responsible for getting the Spartans to take this step, secured the support of Cobon, who was a very influential person in Delphi; and he persuaded Perialla the prophetess to give the answer which Cleomenes wanted. She replied, accordingly, to the messengers' question that Demaratus was not the son of Ariston. Afterwards, the facts of this

transaction became known. Cobon was exiled, and Perialla deprived of her office.

These were the events which led to the deposition of Demar- 67 atus; but his leaving the country for Persia was the result of a later humiliation. After his deposition, Demaratus had been elected to some other office in the state, and once when he was sitting amongst the spectators at the festival of the Naked Boys,[30] Leotychides, who was now king in his place, sent his servant to ask him what it felt like to be a magistrate after being a king. Stung by this question, the only point of which was to jeer at and humiliate him, Demaratus replied that, though he himself had had experience of both offices, Leotychides had not. 'Never-theless,' he added, 'this question will be the beginning of great things for Sparta – either for good or evil.' Then, wrapping his head in his cloak, he left the theatre and went home, where he prepared an ox for sacrifice and offered it to Zeus. That done, 68 he sent for his mother and, putting into her hand a portion of the beast's entrails, said to her with great earnestness: 'Mother, I beseech you by all the gods, and especially by Zeus the guardian of this home of ours, to tell me the truth; who was really my father? Leotychides, in the dispute we had, said that when you married Ariston you were already pregnant by your previous husband – and there is an even worse story told by some, that you became the lover of a servant – a stableman, who looked after the asses – and that I am his son. For God's sake, do not lie to me. Even if you have done what you are said to have done, you are not the only one – many women have done the same. Besides, there are many here in Sparta who say that Ariston was impotent; had the seed been in him, he would have had children by his other wives.'

'My son,' his mother answered, 'since you beg me so earnestly 69 to tell you the truth, nothing shall be hidden from you. On the third night after Ariston brought me to his house, I was visited by a phantom exactly resembling him. The phantom came to my bed, and afterwards took the wreath it was wearing and put it on me. Then it vanished, and when Ariston came in later, he asked who had given me the wreath. I said he had given it me himself, but he denied it; then I solemnly swore that it was so, and reproached him for his denial, since so short a time before he had had me in his arms and given me the wreath. Hearing me take my oath, Ariston was convinced, and realized that the hand of God was in this; moreover, the wreath proved to have come from the shrine of the hero Astrabacus, by the courtyard gate, and when we questioned the diviners, their answer was that the phantom who had visited me was Astrabacus himself. There, my son; now you know everything which you wish to know. Either the hero Astrabacus is your father, or Ariston; for that was the night when you were conceived.[31] As for the particular ground of your enemies' attack – I mean the fact that Ariston himself, when he was told of your birth, denied in the presence of witnesses that you could be his son, because the ten months were not up – it was merely ignorance of such things which made him say what he did say. A woman does not always carry her child till the tenth month; sometimes only seven – you yourself, my son, were a seven-months child. Ariston, too, realized soon afterwards that he had spoken in ignorance. There now: what I have told you is the truth – so listen to no other story about your parentage. As for stable-boys, may their children be born to Leotychides' wife, and the wives of all who say such things.'

70   Now that he had learned from his mother all that he wanted to know, Demaratus made provision for a journey and went to Elis, giving out that he was going to Delphi to consult the oracle. The Spartans, who suspected that he meant to flee the country, started in pursuit of him. But Demaratus was too quick for them, and got across from Elis to Zacynthus. The Spartans followed, laid hands on him, and took away his servants; but, as the people of Zacynthus refused to give him up, he afterwards crossed to Asia and presented himself at the court of Darius, who welcomed him with a magnificent gift of land and cities. Such, then, were the chances which brought Demaratus to Asia; he had been a man of the highest distinction in Sparta, both in action and in counsel – he had, moreover, given his country a victory at Olympia in the four-horse chariot race, and was the only king of Sparta ever to achieve this honour.

71   Leotychides, the son of Menares, succeeded Demaratus after

his deposition. He had a son, Zeuxidamus, who was known to some of the Spartans by the nickname 'Puppy'; he did not succeed to the throne, as he died before his father, leaving a son, Archidamus. After Zeuxidamus' death Leotychides married again; his second wife, who was Eurydame, sister of Menius and daughter of Diactorides, brought him no male issue, but only a daughter, Lampito, whom he gave in marriage to Archidamus, Zeuxidamus' son.

Leotychides himself did not end his days in Sparta; Demaratus 72 was to be avenged as follows.[32] While in command of the army in an expedition against Thessaly, just as complete success was within his grasp, he allowed himself to be heavily bribed. He was caught red-handed, sitting in his tent on a glove stuffed full of coins, whereupon he was brought to trial and banished, and his house was demolished. He took refuge in Tegea, where he afterwards died. All this, however, took place some time later, and I must now return to Cleomenes.

After the success of his scheme against Demaratus, Cleo- 73 menes, with Leotychides' support, went promptly to Aegina, embittered by the affront which had been put upon him. Now that both kings had come the Aeginetans thought it best to offer no further resistance. Cleomenes and his colleague chose ten of their wealthiest and most distinguished citizens, brought them over into Attica, and put them in charge of their bitterest enemies, the Athenians. Amongst the ten were the two most powerful men in the island: Crius the son of Polycritus, and Casambus the son of Aristocrates.

Later on, when his machinations against Demaratus became 74 known in Sparta, Cleomenes took fright and slipped away into Thessaly. From there he passed into Arcadia, where he began to stir up trouble and tried to win the support of the Arcadians for an attack on Sparta. He made them swear oaths to follow him wherever he might choose to take them, and even did his utmost to get the leading men to Nonacris, in order to make them swear by the water of Styx – for it is here at Nonacris that the Arcadians believe the waters of the Infernal River to be visible. It is, indeed, a fact that one can see a little water trickling out of a rock into a basin surrounded by a circular wall.

Nonacris, where this spring is to be found, is an Arcadian town near Pheneus.

75   The Spartans, alarmed by the news of Cleomenes' proceedings in Arcadia, brought him home and restored him to the same power as he had before possessed. He had always been a little strange in the head, but no sooner had he returned to Sparta than he went quite mad, and began poking his staff into the face of every Spartiate he met. As a result of this lunatic behaviour his relatives put him in the stocks. As he was lying there, fast bound, he asked his jailer, when no one else was there, to give him a knife. At first the man, who was a helot, refused, but Cleomenes, by threats of what he would do to him when he recovered his liberty, so frightened him that he at last consented. As soon as the knife was in his hands, Cleomenes began to mutilate himself, beginning on his shins. He sliced his flesh into strips, working upwards to his thighs, and from them to his hips and sides, until he reached his belly, and while he was cutting that into strips he died. Most people in Greece say that that was a punishment for having corrupted the Priestess at Delphi and inducing her to say what she did say about Demaratus; the Athenians, however, put it down to his devastating the sacred land of Demeter and Persephone, when he marched to Eleusis; while the Argives maintain that it was a punishment for his sacrilege when, after a battle, he fetched the Argive fugitives from the holy ground of Argos, and cut them to pieces, and then showed such contempt for the grove itself that he burned it down.

76   The story of this incident is as follows. Cleomenes had been told by the Delphic oracle that he would take Argos.[33] Thereupon at the head of a Spartan army he marched to the river Erasinus – a stream which is said to flow from Lake Stymphalis, whose waters drain into an unseen chasm and reappear in Argos, where they are known locally as the Erasinus. Arrived at the bank of this stream, Cleomenes offered sacrifice to it before venturing to cross. The appearance of the omens was not favourable. 'Very well,' said Cleomenes; 'I admire the god of the river for refusing to betray his countrymen. All the same, the Argives will not get away with it so lightly.'

He then withdrew his troops and marched to Thyrea, and after sacrificing a bull to the sea went on in boats to the territory of Tiryns and Nauplia. The Argives, learning of his movements, marched to the coast to defend their country, and on reaching the place called Sepia, near Tiryns, took up a position within easy range of the Spartan army. They were not now afraid of a pitched battle, though a certain oracle they had received made them apprehensive of treachery. The oracle was the one which was pronounced by the Priestess for the joint benefit of the Argives and Milesians, and ran as follows:

77

> But when the female subdues the male and drives him out,
> And wins thereby great glory amongst the Argives,
> Then shall she cause many Argive women to tear their cheeks;
> And thus shall they speak in the generations yet to come:
> 'The fearful thrice-coiled snake was tamed by the spear and slain.'

Alarmed by this conjunction of circumstances, the Argives decided to adopt the following plan. This was to conform to the orders called out to the Spartan army by its herald. Every time, therefore, that the Spartan herald repeated an order, the Argives did the same. Cleomenes, however, soon observed what was going on, and issued a command to his men, the next time his herald should pass the word for the midday meal, not to obey it, but to take up arms and attack the enemy instead. The plan succeeded perfectly; the Argives, having heard the Spartan army's call to the meal, were sitting quietly at their own when they were suddenly assaulted; many were killed, and many more escaped to the little wood which was held sacred to the hero Argos. Here they were surrounded and closely watched.

78

Next Cleomenes, having learnt from Argive deserters some names of men who had found sanctuary in the wood, sent a herald to tell individuals, by name, that he had received their ransom money, and to invite them, on the strength of that, to come out. (The regular Peloponnesian ransom is 2 minae for each prisoner.) In this way Cleomenes got about fifty of them to come out, one at a time, and had them all butchered. The

79

men who were still inside had no idea of what was taking place, because the wood was so thick that they could not see the fate of their comrades outside it. At last, however, one of them climbed a tree – and saw. After that, the invitation to come out

80 was no longer accepted. Cleomenes then ordered all the helots to pile faggots round the wood, set fire to them, and burn it to the ground. The order was obeyed, and while the fire was raging, Cleomenes asked one of the Argive deserters to what god the wood was held sacred. 'To Argos,' was the reply. Cleomenes groaned when he heard the name. 'Apollo,' he cried, 'O God of prophecy, you did indeed deceive me when you said I should take Argos, for now I believe that your prophecy to me is fulfilled.'[34]

81 After this Cleomenes sent the greater part of his army home, and with a thousand of his best troops went to the temple of Hera, to offer sacrifice. But the priest of the temple refused to allow him to do so, on the ground that to sacrifice in that temple was forbidden to strangers. Cleomenes thereupon made the helots drag the priest away from the altar and thrash him, and then performed the sacrifice himself and marched back to Sparta.

82 On his return to Sparta he was brought by his enemies before the Ephors; the charge against him was that he had accepted a bribe not to take Argos, when he might easily have done so. His answer – whether true or false I cannot be sure – was that when he had destroyed the shrine of the hero Argos, he supposed that the prophecy was already fulfilled, and on that account he did not think it proper to make an attempt on the *town* of Argos, until he had further consulted the god's wishes, and found out, by means of a sacrifice, whether he would grant him this further success or not. When, however, he attempted to get a favourable sign by offering a sacrifice in the temple of Hera, a flame shot out from the breast of the goddess' statue, and he knew from this with absolute certainty that he was not to capture Argos. Had the flame flashed from the statue's head, it would have meant that he was to capture the city completely; but the flash that came from the breast signified that he had already done all that God intended him to do. The Spartans accepted this as

a credible and reasonable defence, and Cleomenes was fully acquitted.

Argos, in consequence of these events, was left so short of 83 men that the management of the town's affairs fell into the hands of the slaves, who filled all the government posts until the sons of those who had been killed grew up and ejected them. These now resumed control, and the slaves, when driven out by force, occupied Tiryns. For a time Tiryns and Argos lived on friendly terms; but a certain Cleander, a seer from Phigalea in Arcadia, joined the slaves in Tiryns and persuaded them to attack their former masters. The result was a protracted struggle, and it was with much difficulty that the Argives finally got the upper hand.

Cleomenes' behaviour in this episode was, according to the 84 Argives, the cause of his subsequent madness and miserable death. His own countrymen, however, deny that his madness was a punishment from heaven; they are convinced, on the contrary, that he lost his wits because, in his association with the Scythians, he had acquired the habit of drinking his wine neat. These nomads, anxious for revenge upon Darius for his invasion of their country, had sent proposals to Sparta for a combined effort against him; the suggestion was that they themselves should try to invade Persia by way of the river Phasis, and that the Spartans should march inland from Ephesus and effect a junction with them. The story is, that when the Scythian representatives came to discuss this scheme, Cleomenes spent much time with them and from too close association with them acquired the habit of taking wine without water – and went off his head in consequence. The Spartans say that ever since then they have used the phrase 'Scythian fashion' when they want a stronger drink than usual.

There, then, is the Spartan story; my own opinion is that Cleomenes came to grief as retribution for what he did to Demaratus.

When the Aeginetans heard that Cleomenes was dead, they 85 sent envoys to Sparta to decry Leotychides about their friends who were being held as hostages in Athens. The Spartans submitted the matter to a court of law, and the verdict was that the people of Aegina had been monstrously abused by Leotychides. They condemned him, therefore, to be given up and taken away to Aegina in exchange for the Aeginetans who were held in Athens. The envoys were on the point of marching him off when a well-known Spartan, Theasides, son of Leoprepes, intervened. 'Men of Aegina,' he cried, 'what is this you are proposing to do? Will you dare to carry off the king of Sparta? True – he has been put into your hands by his own countrymen, because at the moment they are angry with him and have condemned him to this indignity; but I warn you – the time may come when, if you do this, they will destroy you utterly in revenge.' The warning words made the Aeginetans change their minds; instead of taking Leotychides along with them as a prisoner, they entered into an agreement with him, to the effect that he should accompany them to Athens and bring about the surrender of 86 the hostages. But when, on his arrival there, he asked for the men whom he had left in trust to be given back to him, the Athenians were unwilling to comply; they temporized and made excuses, and said that as two kings had put the men in their keeping, they could not feel it was right to give them up to only one. In fact, they refused; and their refusal drew from a Leotychides the following story. 'Athenians,' he said, 'you must act as you see fit. Surrender your charge like honourable men; or refuse to surrender it – *not* like honourable men. In either case, I should like to tell you what happened in Sparta once in connexion with some property left in trust. According to our belief, there lived in Sparta three generations ago a man named Glaucus, the son of Epicydes; he was in every respect an admirable person, and had, in particular, a reputation for honest dealing beyond any other Spartan of his day. Time, however, had something in store for him – you shall hear the story as we tell it. One day a man from Miletus came to Sparta and expressed a wish to talk to Glaucus. "I am a Milesian," he said, "and I have come to you because I should like to profit by your honesty. People all over Greece – yes, and in Ionia too – are always talking of your honesty, and that set me thinking. Ionia, I told myself, is never safe from sudden change – and property never stays long in the same hands; but the Peloponnese, on the contrary, is stable. This led me to make a decision, namely, to realize one-half of my property and to put the money in your hands, in full confidence that it will be safe there. I ask you, therefore, to take the money and with it these tallies, which you must please keep carefully. Then you can return the money to whoever brings you the corresponding halves." Glaucus listened *b* to what the stranger from Miletus said, and accepted the trust on the terms he proposed. Years went by, and one day there came to Sparta the sons of the Milesian who had made Glaucus his trustee. They sought an interview with him, produced their halves of the tallies, and asked for the money. "But," said Glaucus, trying to put them off, "I don't remember this transaction, and nothing you say has any effect in awakening my memory. Of course, when I *do* recollect it, I will act as an honest man should: I will pay the money back properly, if I received it, and, if I did not, I will prosecute you according to the law of the Hellenes. I promise to settle the matter, one way or the other, in three months' time."

'When the Milesians, supposing their money lost to them, *c* had gone home in great disappointment, Glaucus visited Delphi to ask the oracle's advice; and his question, whether or not he should perjure himself and so rob the Milesians of their property, was met by the Priestess with a rebuke, in the following words:

> Today, indeed, Glaucus, son of Epicydes, it is more profitable
> To prevail by false-swearing and rob them of their money.
> Swear if you will; for death awaits even the true-swearer.
> Yet an oath has a son, nameless, without hands or feet,
> But swift to pursue until he has seized and destroyed
> Utterly the race and house of the perjured one.
> The children of him who keeps his oath are happier hereafter

'Glaucus on hearing this answer begged the god to forgive him for this question; but the Priestess told him that to seek God's approval of a sin came to the same thing as committing it. So Glaucus sent for the Milesians and gave them back their *d* money.

'And now, gentlemen, I come to the real point of my story. Today Glaucus has not a single living descendant; not a family in Sparta bears his name; it has been totally rooted out. That will show you how wise a thing it is, where covenants are concerned, not to hesitate, even in thought, to make proper restitution.'

However, the Athenians would not listen even to this; so Leotychides went home.

87   The Aeginetans had never yet been punished for the unprovoked attack which they had previously made upon the Athenians at the request of Thebes.[35] Now, however, on the ground that it was Athens which was in the wrong, and they themselves the injured party, they made their preparations for revenge. The Athenians held a festival every four years at Sunium; on this occasion, therefore, the Aeginetans set a trap for their state vessel, and captured her with a number of leading
88   Athenians on board, whom they seized and imprisoned. The outrage stirred the Athenians to immediate action, and they prepared to use every resource they possessed against Aegina.

There was in Aegina a well-known man called Nicodromus, the son of Cnoethus, who had previously been banished from the island and still nursed resentment against his compatriots. When this person got to know that the Athenians were preparing to attack Aegina, he agreed to betray the island, and fixed the day upon which he would strike his blow and expect the arrival of Athenian troops to support him. In due course he carried out his part of the bargain by occupying what is called the Old Town; but the Athenians failed to keep their appointment.
89   Finding their fleet was not a match for the Aeginetans, they had asked the Corinthians to lend them ships; but this took time, and meanwhile the whole undertaking was ruined. The Corinthians were on the best of terms with Athens at this period, and when the Athenians asked them for ships they had put twenty at their disposal, charging five drachmae apiece (for it was illegal to make a free gift of them); and with these and what they already possessed the Athenians manned seventy vessels, and sailed for Aegina. They were one day too late.
90   Nicodromus, as soon as he found that the Athenians had not

appeared at the time agreed upon, escaped from the island in a boat together with a number of other Aeginetans. Later on, these people were allowed by the Athenians to settle at Sunium, which they made their base for raids upon their compatriots in Aegina.

In this way, then, the property-owning class in Aegina 91 defeated the revolt of the commons under Nicodromus, arrested a number of the revolutionaries and led them out to execution; but in the process of doing so they committed an act of sacrilege, which stuck to them in spite of all efforts to remove it by propitiatory sacrifices. Before they could regain the favour of the outraged goddess, they were driven from their island.[36] What happened was this: seven hundred prisoners were about to be executed when one of them broke loose. He ran for sanctuary into the doorway of the shrine of Demeter the Lawgiver and held on to the door-handle with both hands. His pursuers tried to drag him away, and, when they failed to detach his grip, cut his hands off. Then they led him away; and those hands stayed there, still clutching the handle.

That was how the Aeginetans dealt with each other. When 92 the Athenians arrived, seventy Aeginetan ships engaged them, but were defeated, whereupon a call for help was sent to Aegina's old ally, Argos. But this time the Argives refused to send assistance, on the ground that some Aeginetan ships which had been seized by Cleomenes had put in at ports in the Argolid, and helped the Spartan invasion. In this descent upon Argos the Spartans had also been joined by men from Sicyonian ships, and the Argives had imposed a joint fine of a thousand talents – five hundred upon each guilty party. The people of Sicyon acknowledged that they were in the wrong and agreed to pay a hundred talents to clear themselves, but not so the Aeginetans: they refused to humiliate themselves by any sort of admission. This was why, on the present occasion, the Argives refused the call for help; officially, not a single man was sent, though about a thousand volunteered, and went to Aegina under the command of Eurybates, a man who had trained for the pentathlon. Most of these volunteers were killed by the Athenians in Aegina and never returned; and their commander Eurybates, in a series of single combats, killed his man in the first three, but in the fourth was himself killed by a man from Decelea, named Sophanes.[37]

93   Later, the Aeginetans caught the Athenian fleet off its guard and beat it, capturing four ships with their crews.

94   While Athens and Aegina were at each other's throats, the king of Persia continued to mature his plans. His servant never failed to repeat to him the words 'Remember Athens'; the Pisistratidae, with their slanderous attacks upon the Athenians, were still with him, and besides, he himself was anxious to have an excuse to conquer all the Greek communities which refused to give earth and water. In consequence of the ill success of his previous expedition, he relieved Mardonius of his command, and appointed other generals, whom he proposed to send against Eretria and Athens, Datis, a Mede, and his own nephew, Artaphernes, son of the other Artaphernes, and their orders were to reduce Athens and Eretria to slavery and to bring the slaves before the king.

95   The new commanders left the court and with a powerful and well-equipped force made for the Aleian plain in Cilicia. Here they halted and were joined by the naval contingent – all the ships and men which the various subject communities had been ordered to supply – including the horse-transports which Darius had requisitioned from his tributary states the year before. The horses were embarked in the transports, the troops in the ships of war, and, six hundred triremes strong, they sailed to Ionia. From there they did not follow the coast to the Hellespont and Thrace, but started from Samos and sailed across the Icarian sea and through the islands, presumably because the commanders dreaded the passage round Athos, which in the previous year had been the cause of so terrible a disaster. Another reason which constrained them to take this course was their previous failure to capture Naxos, which was now their first objective in

96   the war.[38] On their arrival at the island from the sea of Icaria, the Naxians offered no resistance, but fled to the hills. The Persians caught some of them, carried them off to slavery, and burnt the city, temples and all. They then put to sea again, to attack the other islands.

97   While the Persians were thus employed, the inhabitants of

Delos left their island and fled to Tenos; and as the Persian fleet was coming in from seaward, Datis sailed on in advance and issued an order to the ships to come to anchor not at Delos, but at Rhenaea, opposite. He then ascertained where the Delians were, and sent them a message in the following words: 'Reverend sirs, what strange opinion have you conceived of me, thus to disappear? I surely have sense enough – even without the king's orders – to spare the island in which Apollo and Artemis were born, and to do no harm either to its soil or to its people. I beg you, therefore, to return to your homes, in the island which belongs to you.'[39] Datis followed the message by piling three hundred talents-weight of frankincense upon the altar, and burning it as an offering. He then left Delos and sailed with his army for Eretria, taking with him both Ionians and Aeolians. 98

The Delians declared that after his departure the island was shaken by an earthquake – the first and the last shock ever experienced there up to my time. It may well be that the shock was an act of God to warn men of the troubles that were on the way; for indeed, during the three generations comprising the reigns of Darius the son of Hystaspes, and of his son Xerxes and his grandson Artaxerxes, Greece suffered more evils than in the twenty generations before Darius was born – partly from the Persian wars, partly from her own internal struggles for supremacy. In view of this, it is not surprising that there should have been an earthquake in Delos, where there had never been an earthquake before.[40] Besides, there was an oracle, which contained the words,

Delos too I will shake, though it has never been shaken.

Darius is equivalent to 'Worker' in Greek; Xerxes means 'War- 99 rior', and Artaxerxes means 'Great Warrior'.

Sailing from Delos the Persians proceeded to make the rounds of the other islands, touching at each, pressing troops for service, and taking the islanders' children as hostages. They also visited Carystus and, when the people of the place refused to give hostages or supply men to fight against neighbours – by which they meant Athens and Eretria – they laid siege to the town and destroyed the crops in the surrounding country, until the Carystians were forced to do what the Persians demanded.

100   In Eretria at the news of the Persian approach the people at once called to Athens for help and the call was not refused, for the Athenians sent to their assistance the four thousand men whom they had previously settled on the estates of the wealthier Chalcideans.[41] Nevertheless, in spite of the appeals to Athens, things at Eretria were not in a healthy state; there was no firm resolve, and counsels were divided; one party proposed abandoning the town and taking refuge in the Euboean hills, another – having an eye to some gain from the Persians – was preparing to betray the city. When Aeschines the son of Nothon, one of the leading men of Eretria, came to know of what was afoot, he at once proceeded to act: he disclosed the whole situation to those of the Athenians who had already arrived, and urged them to go home again before they were involved in

101   the catastrophe which was bound to come. They took Aeschines' advice, and got safe away by crossing to Oropus.

Meanwhile the Persian fleet brought up at Tamynae, Choereae, and Aegilia – all three places in Eretrian territory. The horses were immediately put ashore, and preparations for an assault began. The Eretrians had no intention of leaving their defences to meet the coming attack in the open; their one concern (the proposal not to abandon the town having been carried) was to defend their walls – if they could.

The assault soon came, and there was weight behind it. For six days fighting continued with many killed on both sides; then, on the seventh, two well-known Eretrians, Euphorbus the son of Alcimachus and Philagrus the son of Cyneas, betrayed the town to the enemy. The Persians entered, and stripped the temples bare and burnt them in revenge for the burnt temples of Sardis, and, in accordance with Darius' orders, carried off all the inhabitants as slaves.

102   Having mastered Eretria the Persians waited a few days and then sailed for Attica, flushed with victory and confident that they would treat Athens in the same way.

The part of Attic territory nearest Eretria – and also the best ground for cavalry to manoeuvre in – was at Marathon. To

Marathon, therefore, Hippias the son of Pisistratus directed the   103
invading army, and the Athenians, as soon as the news arrived,
hurried to meet it.[42]

The Athenian troops were commanded by ten generals, of
whom the tenth was Miltiades. Miltiades' father, Cimon the
son of Stesagoras, had been banished from Athens by Pisistratus,
the son of Hippocrates. While in exile he had the good fortune
to win the chariot race at Olympia, thereby gaining the same
distinction as his half-brother Miltiades. At the next games he
won the prize again with the same team of mares, but this time
waived his victory in favour of Pisistratus, and for allowing the
latter to be proclaimed the winner was given leave to return to
Athens. At a later Olympic festival he won a third time, still
with the same four mares. Soon after, Pisistratus having died,
he was murdered by Pisistratus' sons, who sent some men to
waylay him one night near the Council House. He was buried
outside Athens, beyond what is called the Sunk Road, and
opposite his grave were buried the mares which had thrice
won the chariot race. This triple victory had once before been
achieved by a single team, that of Euagoras the Laconian; but
there are no other instances of it. At the time of Cimon's death,
Stesagoras, the elder of his two sons, was living in the Chersonese with Miltiades his uncle, and the younger son, who was
called Miltiades after the founder of the settlement in the
Chersonese, was with his father in Athens.[43]

It was this Miltiades who was now an Athenian general. He   104
had recently escaped from the Chersonese and twice nearly lost
his life – once when the Phoenicians chased him as far as Imbros
in their anxiety to catch him and take him to Darius, and again
when, after escaping that danger and getting home to what
looked like safety, he found his enemies waiting for him and
was prosecuted in the courts for his tyranny in the Chersonese.
But he escaped this too, and after the trial was elected a general
by the people.[44]

Before they left the city, the Athenian generals sent off a   105
message to Sparta. The messenger was an Athenian named
Pheidippides, a professional long-distance runner. According to
the account he gave the Athenians on his return, Pheidippides

met the god Pan on Mt Parthenium, above Tegea. Pan, he said, called him by name and told him to ask the Athenians why they paid him no attention, in spite of his friendliness towards them and the fact that he had often been useful to them in the past, and would be so again in the future. The Athenians believed Pheidippides' story, and when their affairs were once more in a prosperous state, they built a shrine to Pan under the Acropolis, and from the time his message was received they have held an annual ceremony, with a torch-race and sacrifices, to court his protection.

106   On the occasion of which I speak – when Pheidippides, that is, was sent on his mission by the Athenian commanders and said that he saw Pan – he reached Sparta the day after he left Athens and delivered his message to the Spartan government.[45] 'Men of Sparta' (the message ran), 'the Athenians ask you to help them, and not to stand by while the most ancient city of Greece is crushed and enslaved by a foreign invader; for even now Eretria has been enslaved, and Greece is the weaker by the loss of one fine city.' The Spartans, though moved by the appeal, and willing to send help to Athens, were unable to send it promptly because they did not wish to break their law. It was the ninth day of the month, and they said they could not take 107   the field until the moon was full.[46] So they waited for the full moon, and meanwhile Hippias, the son of Pisistratus, guided the Persians to Marathon.

The previous night Hippias had dreamed that he was sleeping with his mother, and he supposed that the dream meant that he would return to Athens, recover his power, and die peacefully at home in old age. So much for his interpretation. On the following day when he was acting as guide to the invaders, he put the prisoners from Eretria ashore on Aegilia, an island belonging to the town of Styra, led the fleet to its anchorage at Marathon, and got the troops into position when they had disembarked. While he was busy with all this, he happened to be seized by an unusually violent fit of sneezing and coughing, and, as he was an oldish man, and most of his teeth were loose, he coughed one of them right out of his mouth. It fell somewhere in the sand, and though he searched and searched in his efforts to find it, it was nowhere to be seen. Hippias then turned to his companions, and said with a deep groan: 'This land is not ours; we shall never be able to conquer it. The only part I ever had in it my tooth possesses.' So the meaning of the dream was now 108 clear to him.

The Athenian troops were drawn up on a piece of ground sacred to Heracles, when they were joined by the Plataeans, who came to support them with every available man. Some time before this the Plataeans had surrendered their independence to the Athenians, who had, in their turn, already rendered service to Plataea on many occasions and in difficult circumstances. The way it happened was this: Plataea was being hard pressed by Thebes, and as Cleomenes the son of Anaxandrides happened to be in the neighbourhood with a Spartan army, the Plataeans first thought of putting themselves into Spartan hands. The Spartans, however, refused the offer: 'We live too far apart and an alliance with us would be but cold comfort to you; you might be carried off into slavery several times over before any of us even heard of it. Our advice is that you make your surrender to Athens – Athens is your neighbour, and Athenian help is by no means to be despised.' The advice did not proceed from goodwill towards Plataea, but merely from the Spartans' desire to embroil Athens in quarrels with the Boeotians. Nevertheless the advice was taken: representatives from Plataea, while the Athenians were engaged in offering sacrifice to the Twelve Gods, came and sat by the altar, to make their solemn request, and the act of surrender was completed.

When the Thebans heard what the Plataeans had done, they at once sent an army against them. The Athenians hurried to their defence, and a fight was on the point of beginning when the Corinthians intervened. They came up, and as both sides submitted the dispute to their arbitration, they fixed the boundary between the two countries, with the condition that there should be no interference from Thebes with any Boeotians who might not wish to belong to the Boeotian state. The Corinthians after making this decision left for home, and the Athenians had also started on their return march, when they were set upon by the Boeotians. In the fight which ensued the Athenians were victorious, and they followed up their victory by crossing the borderline which the Corinthians had fixed for Plataea, and making the river Asopus the frontier between the territory of Thebes on the one side, and of Plataea and Hysiae on the other. These were the circumstances under which the people of Plataea put themselves into Athenian hands, and which led to their coming to the support of Athens at Marathon.[47]

109   Amongst the Athenian commanders opinion was divided: some were against risking a battle, on the ground that the Athenian force was too small to stand a chance of success; others – and amongst them Miltiades – urged it. It seemed for a time as if the more faint-hearted policy would be adopted – and so it would have been but for the action of Miltiades. In addition to the ten generals, there was another person entitled to a vote, namely the polemarch, or War Archon, appointed by lot. This office (which formerly carried an equal vote in military decisions with the generals) was held at this time by Callimachus of the deme Aphidnae.[48] To Callimachus, therefore, Miltiades turned. 'It is now in your hands, Callimachus,' he said, 'either to enslave Athens, or to make her free and to leave behind you for all future generations a memory more glorious than even Harmodius and Aristogeiton left. Never in our history have we Athenians been in such peril as now. If we submit to the Persians, Hippias will be restored to power – and there is little doubt what misery must then ensue: but if we fight and win, then this city of ours may well grow to pre-eminence amongst all the cities of Greece. If you ask me how this can be, and how the decision rests with you, I will tell you: we commanders are ten in number, and we are not agreed upon what action to take; half of us are for a battle, half against it. If we refuse to fight, I have little doubt that the result will be bitter dissension; our purpose will be shaken, and we shall submit to Persia. But if we fight before the rot can show itself in any of us, then, if God gives us fair play, we can not only fight but win. Yours is the decision; all hangs upon you; vote on my side, and our country will be free – yes, and the first city of Greece. But if you support those who have voted against fighting, that happiness will be denied you – you will get the opposite.'

Miltiades' words prevailed, and by the vote of Callimachus   110
the War Archon the decision to fight was made.

The generals held the presiding position in succession, each
for a day; and those of them who had voted with Miltiades,
offered, when their turn for duty came, to surrender it to him.
Miltiades accepted the offer, but would not fight until the day
came when he would in any case have presided.[49] When it did   111
come, the Athenian army moved into position for the coming
struggle. The right wing was commanded by Callimachus – for
it was the regular practice at that time in Athens that the War
Archon should lead the right wing; then followed the tribes, in
their regular order; and, finally, on the left wing, were the
Plataeans. Ever since the battle of Marathon, when the
Athenians offer sacrifice at their quadrennial festival, the herald
links the names of Athens and Plataea in the prayer for God's
blessing.

One result of the disposition of Athenian troops before the
battle was the weakening of their centre by the effort to extend
the line sufficiently to cover the whole Persian front; the two
wings were strong, but the line in the centre was only a few
ranks deep. The dispositions made, and the preliminary sacrifice   112
promising success, the word was given to move, and the
Athenians advanced at a run towards the enemy, not less than
a mile away.[50] The Persians, seeing the attack developing at the
double, prepared to meet it, thinking it suicidal madness for the
Athenians to risk an assault with so small a force – rushing in
with no support from either cavalry or archers. Well, that was
what they imagined; nevertheless, the Athenians came on, closed
with the enemy all along the line, and fought in a way not to be
forgotten; they were the first Greeks, so far as we know, to
charge at a run, and the first who dared to look without flinching
at Persian dress and the men who wore it; for until that day
came, no Greek could hear even the word Persian without terror.

The struggle at Marathon was long drawn out. In the centre,   113
held by the Persians themselves and the Sacae, the advantage
was with the foreigners, who were so far successful as to break
the Greek line and pursue the fugitives inland from the sea; but
the Athenians on one wing and the Plataeans on the other

were both victorious. Having got the upper hand, they left the defeated enemy to make their escape, and then, drawing the two wings together into a single unit, they turned their attention to the Persians who had broken through in the centre. Here again they were triumphant, chasing the routed enemy, and cutting them down until they came to the sea, and men were calling for

114 fire and taking hold of the ships. It was in this phase of the struggle that the War Archon Callimachus was killed, fighting bravely, and also Stesilaus, the son of Thrasylaus, one of the generals; Cynegirus, too, the son of Euphorion,[51] had his hand cut off with an axe as he was getting hold of a ship's stern, and so lost his life, together with many other well-known Athenians.

115 The Athenians secured in this way seven ships; but the rest got off, and the Persians aboard them, after picking up the Eretrian prisoners whom they had left on Aegilia, laid a course round Sunium for Athens, which they hoped to reach in advance of the Athenian army. In Athens the Alcmaeonidae were accused of suggesting this move; they had, it was said, an understanding with the Persians, and raised a shield as a signal to them when they were already on board.

116   While the Persian fleet was on its way round Sunium, the Athenians hurried back with all possible speed to save their city, and succeeded in reaching it before the arrival of the Persians.[52] Just as at Marathon the Athenian camp had been a plot of ground sacred to Heracles, so now they fixed their camp on another, also sacred to the same god, at Cynosarges. When the Persian fleet appeared, it lay at anchor for a while off Phalerum (at that time the chief harbour of Athens) and then sailed back to Asia.

117   In the battle of Marathon some 6400 Persians were killed; the losses of the Athenians were 192.[53] During the action a marvellous thing happened: Epizelus, the son of Cuphagoras, an Athenian soldier, was fighting bravely when he suddenly lost the sight of both eyes, though nothing had touched him anywhere – neither sword, spear, nor missile. From that moment he continued blind as long as he lived. I have heard that in speaking about what happened to him he used to say that he thought he was opposed by a man of great stature in heavy

armour, whose beard overshadowed his shield; but the phantom passed him by, and killed the man at his side.[54]

When Datis was on his way back to Asia with his army, he stopped at Myconos, where he had a dream. What the dream was is not recorded; but at the first light of dawn next morning he ordered the ships to be searched, and discovered, in a Phoenician vessel, a statue of Apollo, overlaid with gold. He made inquiries about where it had been stolen from, and as soon as he learned to which temple it belonged, he sailed in his own ship to Delos. The Delians by that time had returned to the island, so he had the statue placed in their temple for safe keeping, and instructed the islanders to take it back to Delium, a place in Theban territory, on the sea opposite Chalcis. Datis then left the island; but the Delians did not restore the statue. It was brought back to Delium by the Thebans themselves twenty years later, on the advice of an oracle.

Datis and Artaphernes, on their arrival in Asia, conveyed the prisoners taken in Eretria up-country to Susa. Before their capture Darius had nursed bitter resentment against the Eretrians, because they had injured him without provocation; now, however, when he saw them brought before him in defeat and knew that they were in his power, his anger vanished. He did them no further harm, but settled them on some land of his, called Ardericca, in Cissia, about twenty-six miles from Susa. Some five miles from Ardericca is the well which produces three different substances – bitumen, salt, and oil. They draw the liquid with a swipe; instead of a bucket, half a wineskin is attached to the rope at one end, and they dip with this, draw up the stuff, and pour it into a tank; from the tank it is drained off into another receptacle, and the three substances become separated: the bitumen and salt solidify at once. The Persian word for the oil is *rhadinace*; it is very dark in colour, and has a strong smell. Here, then, in Ardericca, the Eretrians were given their new home; they have continued to live there to my own day, and still speak their original language.

After the full moon, two thousand Spartans set off for Athens. They were so anxious not to be late that they were in Attica on the third day after leaving Sparta.[55] They had, of course, missed the battle; but such was their passion to see the Persians, that they went to Marathon to have a look at the bodies. That done, they praised the Athenians on their good work, and returned home.

121   The tale of the Alcmaeonidae treacherously signalling to the Persians with a shield is, to me, quite extraordinary, and I cannot accept it. Is it likely that these men, who were obviously greater tyrant-haters even than Callias the son of Phaenippus and father of Hipponicus, should have wished to see Athens ruled by Hippias under foreign control? Callias was the only man in Athens who at the expulsion of Pisistratus dared to buy any of his property when it was put up for public sale, besides showing

123   the most violent hostility to him in other ways.[56] Not even Callias, I repeat, could surpass the Alcmaeonidae in hatred of absolute government, so the charge that they could have been guilty of the treacherous signal is mere slander, and I confess it surprises me. They were men who remained in exile throughout the period of absolute government in Athens[57] – and it was they who thought of the plan which deprived the Pisistratidae of their power. Indeed, in my judgement it was the Alcmaeonidae much more than Harmodius and Aristogeiton who liberated Athens; for the two latter by their murder of Hipparchus merely exasperated the remaining members of the clan, without in any way checking their despotism, while the Alcmaeonidae did, in plain fact, actually bring about the liberation – provided that what I said further back is true, namely that it was the Alcmaeonidae who bribed the Delphic priestess to keep on

124   telling the Spartans that they must set Athens free.[58] Perhaps it might be argued that they betrayed their country because of some grudge they bore the Athenian commons; but they were better thought of and more respected than anybody else in Athens. It is unreasonable, therefore, to suppose that they gave the signal for any reason of that sort. A shield *was* held up: that is a fact and cannot be denied; but as to who did it, I can add nothing to what I have already said.

125   Even in very early days the Alcmaeonidae were a distinguished family in Athens, and from the time of Alcmaeon, and afterwards of Megacles, they became very distinguished indeed.[59]

Alcmaeon, the son of Megacles, gave all the assistance in his power to the Lydians who came from Croesus at Sardis to consult the oracle at Delphi; and Croesus, when the Lydians told him of the good service he had rendered, invited him to Sardis and offered him, as a reward, as much gold as he could carry on his person at one time. Alcmaeon thought of a fine way of taking advantage of this unusual offer: he put on a large tunic, very loose and baggy in front, and a pair of the widest top-boots that he could find, and, thus clad, entered the treasury to which the king's servants conducted him. Here he attacked a heap of gold dust; he crammed into his boots, all up his legs, as much as they would hold, filled the baggy front of his tunic full, sprinkled the dust all over his hair, stuffed some more into his mouth, and then staggered out, scarcely able to drag one foot after another and looking, with his bulging cheeks and swollen figure, like anything rather than a man. When Croesus saw him he burst out laughing, and gave him all the gold he was carrying, and as much again in addition. In this way Alcmaeon's family suddenly found itself rich, and Alcmaeon was able to keep race-horses, with which he won the chariot race at Olympia.

In the next generation the family became much more 126 famous than before through the distinction conferred upon it by Cleisthenes the tyrant of Sicyon. Cleisthenes, the son of Aristonymus, grandson of Myron, and great-grandson of Andreas, had a daughter, Agarista, whom he wished to marry to the best man in all Greece.[60] So during the Olympic games, in which he had himself won the chariot race, he had a public announcement made, to the effect that any Greek who thought himself good enough to become Cleisthenes' son-in-law should present himself in Sicyon within sixty days – or sooner if he wished – because he intended, within the year following the sixtieth day, to betroth his daughter to her future husband. Cleisthenes had had a race-track and a wrestling-ring specially made for his purpose, and presently the suitors began to arrive – every man of Greek nationality who had something to be proud of either in his country or in himself. From Sybaris in 127 Italy, then at the height of its prosperity, came Smindyrides the son of Hippocrates, a man noted above all others for delicate

and luxurious living, and from Siris, also in Italy, came Damasus
the son of Amyris who was nicknamed the Wise. Then there
was Amphimnestus, the son of Epistrophus, from Epidamnus
on the Ionian Gulf, and Males from Aetolia – Males, the brother
of Titormus who was the strongest man in Greece and went to
live in the remotest part of Aetolia to avoid living with other
human beings. From the Peloponnese came Leocedes the son of
Pheidon, who was tyrant of Argos and the man who brought in
the system of weights and measures for the Peloponnese – and
also turned out the Eleans whose duty it was to manage the
Olympic games and proceeded to manage them himself – the
wickedest and most arrogant thing ever done by a Greek. Next
there was Amiantus, the son of Lycurgus, from Trapezus in
Arcadia, and Laphanes, an Azanian from Paeus, whose father
Euphorion, the story goes, received Castor and Pollux under his
own roof and afterwards kept open house for all comers; and
then Onomastus of Elis, the son of Agaeus. From Athens there
were two: Megacles, whose father Alcmaeon visited the court
of Croesus, and Tisander's son Hippocleides, the wealthiest and
best-looking man in Athens. Euboea provided but a single suitor,
Lysanias from Eretria, which at that time was at the height of
its prosperity; then there was a Thessalian, Diactorides, one of
the Scopadae, from Crannon, and, lastly, Alcon from Molossia.
This was the list of suitors.

128   Cleisthenes began by asking each in turn to name his country
and parentage; then he kept them in his house for a year, to
get to know them well, entering into conversation with them
sometimes singly, sometimes all together, and testing each of
them for his manly qualities and temper, education and
manners. Those who were young he would take to the gymnasia
– but the most important test of all was their behaviour at the
dinner-table. All this went on throughout their stay in Sicyon,
and all the time he entertained them handsomely.

For one reason or another it was the two Athenians who
impressed Cleisthenes most favourably, and of the two Tisander's son Hippocleides came to be preferred, not only for his
manly virtues but also because he was related some generations
back to the family of Cypselus of Corinth.

At last the day came which had been fixed for the betrothal,   129
and Cleisthenes had to declare his choice. He marked the day
by the sacrifice of a hundred oxen, and then gave a great banquet,
to which not only the suitors but everyone of note in Sicyon was
invited. When dinner was over, the suitors began to compete
with each other in music and in talking in company. In both
these accomplishments it was Hippocleides who easily proved
his superiority to the rest, until at last, as more and more wine
was drunk, he asked the flute-player to play him a tune and
began to dance to it. Now it may well be that he danced to his
own satisfaction; Cleisthenes, however, who was watching the
performance, began to have serious doubts about the whole
business. Presently, after a brief pause, Hippocleides sent for a
table; the table was brought, and Hippocleides, climbing on to
it, danced first some Laconian dances, next some Attic ones,
and ended by standing on his head and beating time with his
legs in the air. The Laconian and Attic dances were bad enough;
but Cleisthenes, though he already loathed the thought of having
a son-in-law like that, nevertheless restrained himself and managed to avoid an outburst; but when he saw Hippocleides beating time with his legs, he could bear it no longer. 'Son of
Tisander,' he cried, 'you have danced away your marriage.'
'Hippocleides doesn't care,' was the reply. Hence the common   130
saying, 'Hippocleides doesn't care.'

Cleisthenes now called for silence and addressed the company. 'Gentlemen,' he said, 'you are here as suitors for my
daughter's hand. I have the highest opinion of you all; to distinguish one and reject the rest is not an agreeable task, and I
would gladly, were it possible, show my favour to every one of
you. Unfortunately, it is not possible; I have only one girl to
give, so how can I please you all? To each man, therefore, who
has failed to win the bride I propose to give a talent of silver, to
mark my appreciation of the honour he has done me by wishing
to marry into my family, and to compensate him for his long
absence from home; and my daughter Agarista I betroth, according to the Athenian law, to Megacles the son of Alcmaeon.'
Megacles declared that he accepted her, and the formalities of
the betrothal were completed.

131   Such is the story of the Trial of the Suitors, and this was the way in which the Alcmaeonidae came to be talked of throughout Greece. The issue of the marriage was that Cleisthenes (named after his grandfather, Cleisthenes of Sicyon) who reorganized the Athenian tribes and instituted the democracy in Athens. A second son of Megacles was Hippocrates, who became the father of another Megacles and another Agarista – the namesake of Cleisthenes' daughter – who married Xanthippus the son of Ariphron. This second Agarista dreamt during her pregnancy that she gave birth to a lion, and a few days later became the mother of Pericles.

132   After the slaughter at Marathon, the already high reputation of Miltiades in Athens was greatly increased. Consequently, when he asked for a fleet of seventy ships together with troops and money, without even telling the Athenians the object of the expedition he had in mind, but merely saying he would enrich them if they followed him, because it was a place where they could easily get as much money as they wanted, they were so carried away by excitement that they made no objections whatever. They let him have the ships and the men, whereupon

133   he set sail for Paros. Ostensibly the reason for the attack was the fact that the Parians had been the aggressors in that they had sent a trireme to Marathon with the Persian fleet; this, however, was only a pretext for his real purpose; for the truth of the matter was that he was angry with the Parians because Lysagoras the son of Teisias, a Parian by birth, had slandered him to Hydarnes the Persian.

        Arrived at the island, Miltiades drove the Parians within their defences and began the siege, at the same time sending in a demand for a hundred talents with the threat that, if they refused to pay, he would persist in the blockade until the town fell. The Parians, however, had not the least intention of giving Miltiades any money; instead, they began to exercise their ingenuity for the defence of the town. In this they were full of resource – they raised the wall by night to twice its original height in any section where it was assailable.

134   So far I have told the story of this episode as it is commonly accepted by everyone; for the sequel, the Parians themselves are

my only authority. Miltiades was making no progress in the siege of the town, and while he was puzzling himself about his next move, a prisoner – a Parian woman named Timo, who had been a Priestess of subordinate rank of the Earth Goddesses – sought an interview with him. This she obtained and suggested to Miltiades that, if he really wanted to capture Paros, he had better do as she advised. She proceeded to make her proposal, and Miltiades, in accordance with it, made his way to the hill in front of the town, where the shrine of Demeter the Lawgiver stood. Unable to open the door in the fence which surrounded the precinct, he jumped over and made straight for the shrine, intending perhaps to meddle with some of the things which it is sacrilege to touch or to do something else – but, whatever it was, when he reached the doors of the shrine, he was seized with a sudden fit of trembling, ran back the way he had come, and, in jumping down from the top of the fence, fell and twisted his thigh – or, as some say, smashed his knee. So when he returned to Athens he was in a poor way, and all he had achieved after twenty-six days' siege was to destroy the crops in the countryside; he had failed to annex the island, and he did not bring home a single penny.

135

When the Parians found out that the Priestess Timo had made her treacherous suggestion to Miltiades, they wanted to punish her; so as soon as the siege was raised they sent to Delphi to inquire if they would be right in putting her to death for giving to the enemy information which might have led to the ruin of her country, and for revealing to Miltiades the mysteries which no one of the male sex was allowed to know. The Priestess at Delphi told them in reply that Timo was not guilty of these crimes; on the contrary, Miltiades was destined to come to a bad end, and she had merely put in an appearance to lead him into trouble.

Miltiades on his return to Athens became the talk of the town; many were loud in their censure of him, and especially Xanthippus, the son of Ariphron, who brought him before the people to be tried for his life on the charge of defrauding the public.[61] Miltiades, though present in court, was unable to speak in his own defence because his leg was gangrened; he lay on a

136

couch and his friends spoke for him, basing their defence upon his past services to his country. They had much to say about the battle of Marathon and the capture of Lemnos, recalling how he had punished the Pelasgians and brought the island under Athenian control. The popular verdict was to spare his life, but to fine him fifty talents for his offence. Shortly afterwards the gangrene in his thigh grew worse; mortification set in and he died. The fifty talents were paid by his son Cimon.

137   The events which led to Miltiades' capture of Lemnos were as follows. The Athenians had forced certain Pelasgians to leave Attica.[62] Whether or not they were justified in doing this is not clear; all I can offer are two contradictory accounts, that of the Athenians themselves, on the one side, and of Hecataeus the son of Hegesander on the other. Hecataeus in his History maintains that the Athenians were in the wrong. According to him, they had given the Pelasgians in payment for building the wall round the Acropolis a tract of land, of poor quality and in bad condition, at the foot of Mt Hymettus; the Pelasgians had improved the land, and when the Athenians saw it changed out of recognition and in first-rate order, they grudged the gift and longed to take it back, until without any further justification they forcibly ejected the occupants. The Athenians, on the contrary, claim that right was on their side; their account is that the Pelasgians used to leave their settlement under Hymettus and come after the Athenian girls when they went to fetch water from the Nine Springs. Neither the Athenians nor any other Greeks had house-slaves in those days, so their own daughters used to go for the water; and whenever they did so, the Pelasgians, regardless of decency or respect, used to rape them. Nor was even this the end of it, for they were finally caught in the act of plotting an attempt upon Athens. In this situation the Athenians go on to point out the superiority of their own behaviour; they might easily have killed the Pelasgians when they discovered their plot, but all they did was to tell them to go. The Pelasgians accordingly left Attica and settled, amongst other places, in Lemnos. There, then, are the two accounts: that of the Athenians on the one side, and of Hecataeus on the other.

138   When the Pelasgians had been settled for some time in

Lemnos, they began to wish to have their revenge on the Athenians. Familiar as they were with the Athenian festivals, they fitted out some galleys and sailed to Brauron, where the Athenian women were celebrating the festival of Artemis; they surprised and seized a number of them, and sailed off with them to Lemnos, where they kept them as concubines. In time these women had numerous children, whom they brought up to behave like Athenians and to speak Attic Greek. The boys as they grew older would not mix with the children of the Pelasgian women, and all supported one another when it came to blows and a Pelasgian boy hit a Greek one. Indeed the children of the Greek mothers fancied themselves lords and masters of the rest and completely dominated them. The situation gave the Pelasgians something to think about; if these bastard children were already determined to support one another and to lord it over their legitimate children, what would they do when they were grown up? They decided in consequence to kill the Attic women's children; then, having done so, they murdered their mothers as well. This crime – together with the former one when the women of Lemnos murdered their husbands (and Thoas too) – is the origin of the Greek custom of referring to any specially horrible crime as a 'Lemnian deed'.

As a result of these murders the crops in Lemnos failed, the 139 birthrate declined, and the cattle no longer increased as rapidly as before, so that the islanders began to suffer severely from lack of food and dwindling population. In these circumstances they sent to Delphi to ask for advice on the best way of escaping from their troubles, and were told by the Priestess to submit to whatever punishment the Athenians might choose to impose upon them. So they went to Athens and declared their readiness to give full satisfaction for their offence. The Athenians spread the richest coverings they possessed on a couch in the Council House and, placing a table beside it loaded with good things, told the Pelasgians to surrender their land to them in a similar condition. 'We will do so,' the Pelasgians answered, 'when a ship sails from Attica to Lemnos with a northerly wind in a single day.' This, of course, they knew was impossible, because Attica is a long way south of Lemnos. Nothing further happened 140 at the time; but many years later, when the Chersonese was under Athenian control, Miltiades the son of Cimon during the period of the northerly winds sailed in a day from Elaeus in the Chersonese to Lemnos. On his arrival he ordered the Pelasgians out of the island, reminding them of the prophetic words which they had been so confident could never come true. The people of Hephaestia obeyed; in Myrina no one would admit that the Chersonese was part of Attica, so the town was besieged until it, too, was forced to yield. Thus it was that the Athenians, with the help of Miltiades, got possession of Lemnos.

BOOK SEVEN

When the news of the battle of Marathon reached Darius, son of Hystaspes and king of Persia, his anger against Athens, already great enough on account of the assault on Sardis, was even greater, and he was more than ever determined to make war on Greece. Without loss of time he dispatched couriers to the various states under his dominion with orders to raise an army much larger than before; and also warships, transports, horses, and grain. So the royal command went round; and all Asia was in an uproar for three years, with the best men being enrolled in the army for the invasion of Greece, and with the preparations. In the year after that, a rebellion in Egypt, which had been conquered by Cambyses, served only to harden Darius' resolve to go to war, not only against Greece but against Egypt too.[1]

Both expeditions were ready to start when a violent quarrel broke out between Darius' sons on the question of priority and succession; for according to Persian law the king may not march with his army until he has named his successor. Darius before his accession had three sons by his former wife, Gobryas' daughter, and four more after his accession by Atossa the daughter of Cyrus. The eldest of the first three was Artabazanes, and of the last four Xerxes. It was between these two, therefore, being sons of different mothers, that the dispute arose, Artabazanes basing his claim to the succession on the argument that he was the eldest of all Darius' sons and therefore, by universal custom, entitled to inherit his father's position, Xerxes urging in reply that he was the son of Atossa the daughter of Cyrus, who won the Persians their freedom.

3   Darius had not yet declared his mind, when Demaratus the son of Ariston arrived in Susa, after being deposed as king of Sparta and having gone into voluntary exile;[2] and the story goes that when he heard about the dispute between Darius' sons, he went to see Xerxes and advised him to point out, in addition to the arguments he was already using, that Darius was already on the throne of Persia when he was born, whereas Artabazanes was born before his father held any public office at all. It was therefore neither reasonable nor fair that the crown should pass to anyone but Xerxes. Even in Sparta, he went on to suggest, the custom was that if sons were born before the father came to the throne, and another was born afterwards when he was king, the latter should succeed him. Xerxes adopted the suggestion and Darius, recognizing the justice of the argument, proclaimed him heir to the throne. Personally, I believe that even without this advice from Demaratus, Xerxes would have become king, because of the immense power of Atossa.

4   Xerxes, then, was publicly proclaimed as next in succession to the crown, and Darius was free to turn his attention to the war. Death, however, cut him off before his preparations were complete; he died in the year following this incident and the Egyptian rebellion, after a reign of thirty-six years, and so was robbed of his chance to punish either Egypt or the Athenians. After his death the crown passed to his son Xerxes.

5   Xerxes at first was not at all interested in invading Greece but began his reign by building up an army for a campaign in Egypt. But Mardonius – the son of Gobryas and Darius' sister and thus cousin to the king – who was present in court and had more influence with Xerxes than anyone else in the country, used constantly to talk to him on the subject. 'Master,' he would say, 'the Athenians have done us great injury, and it is only right that they should be punished for their crimes. By all means finish the task you already have in hand; but when you have tamed the arrogance of Egypt, then lead an army against Athens. Do that, and your name will be held in honour all over the world, and people will think twice in future before they invade your country.' And to the argument for revenge he would add that Europe was a very beautiful place; it produced every kind of

garden tree; the land there was everything that land should be – it was, in short, too good for any mortal except the Persian king.[3] Mardonius' motive for urging the campaign was love of 6 mischief and adventure and the hope of becoming governor of Greece himself; and after much persistence he persuaded Xerxes to make the attempt. Certain other occurrences came to his aid. In the first place, messengers arrived from the Aleuadae in Thessaly (the Aleuadae were the Thessalian reigning family) with an invitation to Xerxes, promising zealous assistance; at the same time the Pisistratidae in Susa spoke to the same purpose and worked upon him even more strongly through the agency of an Athenian named Onomacritus, a collector of oracles, who had arranged and edited the oracles of Musaeus. The Pisistratidae had made up their quarrel with him before coming to Susa. He had been expelled from Athens by Hipparchus for inserting in the verses of Musaeus a prophecy that the islands off Lemnos would disappear under water – Lasus of Hermione had caught him in the very act of the forgery. Before his banishment he had been a close friend of Hipparchus. Anyway, he went to Susa; and now, whenever he found himself in the king's presence, the Pisistratidae would talk big about his wonderful powers and he would recite selections from his oracles. Any prophecy which implied a setback to the Persian cause he would carefully omit, choosing for quotation only those which promised the brightest triumphs, describing to Xerxes how it was fore-ordained that the Hellespont should be bridged by a Persian, and how the army would march from Asia into Greece. Subjected, therefore, to this double pressure, from Onomacritus' oracles on the one side, and the advice of the Pisistratidae and Aleuadae on the other, Xerxes gave in and allowed himself to 7 be persuaded to undertake the invasion of Greece.

First, however, in the year after Darius' death, he sent an army against the Egyptian rebels and decisively crushed them; then, having reduced the country to a condition of worse servitude than it had ever been in in the previous reign, he turned it over to his brother Achaemenes, who long afterwards, while he was still Governor, was killed by Inarus, the son of Psammetichus, a Libyan.

8   After the conquest of Egypt, when he was on the point of
     taking in hand the expedition against Athens, Xerxes called a
     conference of the leading men in the country, to find out their
     attitude towards the war and explain to them his own wishes.
a   When they met, he addressed them as follows: 'Do not suppose,
     men of Persia, that I am departing from precedent in the course
     of action I intend to undertake. We Persians have a way of
     living, which I have inherited from my predecessors and propose
     to follow. I have learned from my elders that ever since Cyrus
     deposed Astyages and we took over from the Medes the sover-
     eign power we now possess, we have never yet remained
     inactive. This is God's guidance, and it is by following it that
     we have gained our great prosperity. Of our past history you
     need no reminder; for you know well enough the famous deeds
     of Cyrus, Cambyses, and my father Darius, and their additions
     to our empire. Now I myself, ever since my accession, have been
     thinking how not to fall short of the kings who have sat upon
     this throne before me, and how to add as much power as they
     did to the Persian empire.[4] And now at last I have found a way
     to win for Persia not glory only but a country as large and as
     rich as our own – indeed richer than our own – and at the same
     time to get satisfaction and revenge. That, then, is the object of
     this meeting – that I may disclose to you what it is that I intend
b   to do. I will bridge the Hellespont and march an army through
     Europe into Greece, and punish the Athenians for the outrage
     they committed upon my father and upon us. As you saw,
     Darius himself was making his preparations for war against
     these men; but death prevented him from carrying out his pur-
     pose. I therefore on his behalf, and for the benefit of all my
     subjects, will not rest until I have taken Athens and burnt it to the
     ground, in revenge for the injury which the Athenians without
     provocation once did to me and my father. These men, you
     remember, came to Sardis with Aristagoras the Milesian, a slave
     of ours, and burnt the temples and sacred groves; and you
     know all too well how they treated our troops under Datis
c   and Artaphernes, when they landed upon Greek soil. For these
     reasons I have now prepared to make war upon them, and,
     when I consider the matter, I find several advantages in the

venture; if we crush the Athenians and their neighbours who dwell in the land of Pelops the Phrygian, we shall so extend the empire of Persia that its boundaries will be God's own sky, so that the sun will not look down upon any land beyond the boundaries of what is ours. With your help I shall pass through Europe from end to end and make it all one country. For if what I am told is true, there is not a city or nation in the world which will be able to withstand us, once these are out of the way. Thus the guilty and the innocent alike shall bear the yoke of servitude.

'If, then, you wish to gain my favour, each one of you must *d* present himself willingly and in good heart on the day which I shall name; whoever brings with him the best equipped body of troops I will reward with those marks of distinction held in greatest value by our countrymen. That is what you must do; but so that I shall not appear to consult only my own whim, I will throw the whole matter into open debate, and ask any of you who may wish to do so, to express his views.'

The first to speak after the king was Mardonius. 'Of all *9* Persians who have ever lived,' he began, 'and of all who are yet to be born, you, my lord, are the greatest. Every word you have spoken is true and excellent, and you will not allow the wretched Ionians in Europe to make fools of us. It would indeed be a fearsome thing if we who have defeated and enslaved the Sacae, Indians, Ethiopians, Assyrians, and many other great nations who did us no injury, but merely to extend the boundaries of our empire, should fail now to punish the Greeks who have been guilty of injuring us without provocation. Have we anything to fear from them? The size of their army? Their wealth? The *a* question is absurd; we know how they fight; we know how slender their resources are. People of their race we have already reduced to subjection – I mean the Greeks of Asia, Ionians, Aeolians, and Dorians. I myself before now have had some experience of these men, when under orders from your father I invaded their country; and I got as far as Macedonia – indeed almost to Athens itself – without a single soldier daring to oppose me.[5] Yet, from what I hear, the Greeks are pugnacious *b* enough, and start fights on the spur of the moment without sense or judgement to justify them. When they declare war on each other, they go off together to the smoothest and levellest bit of ground they can find, and have their battle on it – with the result that even the victors never get off without heavy losses, and as for the losers – well, they're wiped out. Now surely, as they all talk the same language, they ought to be able to find a better way of settling their differences: by negotiation, for instance, or an interchange of views – indeed by anything rather than fighting. Or if it is really impossible to avoid coming to blows, they might at least employ the elements of strategy and look for a strong position to fight from. In any case, the Greeks, with their absurd notions of warfare, never even thought of opposing me when I led my army to Macedonia.

c   'Well then, my lord, who is likely to resist you when you march against them with the millions of Asia at your back, and the whole Persian fleet? Believe me, it is not in the Greek character to take so desperate a risk. But should I be wrong and they be so foolish as to do battle with us, then they will learn that we are the best soldiers in the world. Nevertheless, let us take this business seriously and spare no pains; success is never automatic in this world – nothing is achieved without trying.'

10   Xerxes' proposals were made to seem plausible by these words of Mardonius, and when he stopped speaking there was a silence. For a while nobody dared to put forward the opposite view, until Artabanus, taking courage from the fact of his relationship to the king – he was a son of Hystaspes and therefore
a   Xerxes' uncle – rose to speak.[6] 'My lord,' he said, 'without a debate in which both sides of a question are expressed, it is not possible to choose the better course. All one can do is to accept whatever it is that has been proposed. But grant a debate, and there is a fair choice to be made. We cannot assess the purity of gold merely by looking at it: we test it by rubbing it on other gold – then we can tell which is the purer. I warned your father – Darius my own brother – not to attack the Scythians, those wanderers who live in a cityless land. But he would not listen to me. Confident in his power to subdue them he invaded their country, and before he came home again many fine soldiers who marched with him were dead. But you, my lord, mean to attack a nation greatly superior to the Scythians: a nation with the

highest reputation for valour both on land and at sea. It is my
duty to tell you what you have to fear from them: you have said   *b*
you mean to bridge the Hellespont and march through Europe
to Greece. Now suppose – and it is not impossible – that you
were to suffer a reverse by sea or land, or even both. These
Greeks are said to be great fighters – and indeed one might well
judge as much from the fact that the Athenians alone destroyed
the great army we sent to attack them under Datis and
Artaphernes. Or, if you will, suppose they were to succeed upon
one element only – suppose they fell upon our fleet and defeated
it, and then sailed to the Hellespont and destroyed the bridge:
then, my lord, you would indeed be in peril. It is no special   *c*
wisdom of my own that makes me argue as I do; but just such
a disaster as I have suggested did, in fact, very nearly overtake
us when your father bridged the Thracian Bosphorus and the
Danube to take his army into Scythia. You will remember how
on that occasion the Scythians went to all lengths in their efforts
to induce the Ionian guard to break the Danube bridge, and
how Histiaeus, the tyrant of Miletus, merely by following the
advice of the other Ionian tyrants instead of rejecting it, as he
did, had it in his power to ruin Persia. Surely it is a dreadful
thing even to hear said, that the fortunes of the king once wholly
depended upon a single man.[7]

'I urge you, therefore, to abandon this plan; take my advice   *d*
and do not run any such terrible risk when there is no necessity
to do so. Break up this conference; turn the matter over quietly
by yourself, and then, when you think fit, announce your
decision. Nothing is more valuable to a man than to lay his
plans carefully and well; even if things go against him, and
forces he cannot control bring his enterprise to nothing, he still
has the satisfaction of knowing that he was defeated by chance
– the plans were all laid; if, on the other hand, he leaps headlong
into danger and succeeds by luck – well, that's a bit of luck
indeed, but he still has the shame of knowing that he was ill
prepared.

'You know, my lord, that amongst living creatures it is the   *e*
great ones that God smites with his thunder, nor does he allow
them to show off. The little ones do not vex him. It is always the

great buildings and the tall trees which are struck by lightning. It is God's way to bring the lofty low. Often a great army is destroyed by a little one, when God in his envy puts fear into the men's hearts, or sends a thunderstorm, and they are cut to pieces in a way they do not deserve. For God tolerates pride in
f none but Himself. Haste is the mother of failure – and for failure we always pay a heavy price; it is in delay our profit lies – perhaps it may not immediately be apparent, but we shall find it, sure enough, as time goes on.

g   'This, my lord, is the advice I offer you. And as for you, Mardonius son of Gobryas, I warn you that the Greeks in no way deserve disparagement; so say no more silly things about them. By slandering the Greeks you increase the king's eagerness to make war on them, and, as far as I can see, this is the very thing you yourself most passionately desire. Heaven forbid it should happen! Slander is a wicked thing: in a case of slander two parties do wrong and one suffers by it. The slanderer is guilty in that he speaks ill of a man behind his back; and the man who listens to him is guilty in that he takes his word without troubling to find out the truth. The slandered person suffers doubly – from the disparaging words of the one and from the belief of the other that he deserves the disparagement.

h   'Nevertheless, if there is no avoiding this campaign in Greece, I have one final proposal to make. Let the king stay here in Persia; and you and I will then stake our children on the issue, and you can start the venture with the men you want and as big an army as you please. And if the king prospers, as you say he will, then I consent that my sons should be killed, and myself with them; if my own prediction is fulfilled, let *your* sons forfeit their lives – and you too – if you ever get home.

'Maybe you will refuse this wager, and still persist in leading an army into Greece. In that case I venture a prophecy: the day will come when many a man left at home will hear the news that Mardonius has brought disaster upon Persia, and that his body lies a prey to dogs and birds somewhere in the country of the Athenians or the Spartans – if not upon the road thither.[8] For that is the way you will find out the quality of the people against whom you are urging the king to make war.'

Xerxes was exceedingly angry. 'Artabanus,' he replied, 'you 11
are my father's brother, and that alone saves you from paying
the price your empty and ridiculous speech deserves. But your
cowardice and lack of spirit shall not escape disgrace: I forbid
you to accompany me on my march to Greece – you shall stay
at home with the women, and everything I spoke of I shall
accomplish without help from you. If I fail to punish the
Athenians, let me be no child of Darius, the son of Hystaspes,
the son of Arsames, the son of Ariaramnes, the son of Teispes,
the son of Cyrus, the son of Cambyses, the son of Teispes, the
son of Achaemenes!⁹ I know too well that if we make no move,
the Athenians will – they will be sure to invade our country.
One has but to make the inference from what they did before;
for it was they who marched into Asia and burnt Sardis. Retreat
is no longer possible for either of us: if we do not inflict the
wound, we shall assuredly receive it. All we possess will pass to
the Greeks, or all they possess will pass to the Persians. That is
the choice before us; for in the enmity between us there is no
middle course. It is right, therefore, that we should now revenge
ourselves for the injury we once received; and no doubt in doing
so I shall learn the nature of this terrible thing which is to happen
to me, if I march against men whom Pelops the Phrygian, a mere
slave of the Persian kings, once beat so soundly that to this very
day both people and country bear the conqueror's name.'

So ended the speeches at the conference. Later on that evening 12
Xerxes began to be worried by what Artabanus had said, and
during the night, as he turned it over in his mind, he came to the
conclusion that the invasion of Greece would not, after all, be a
good thing. Having reached this decision he fell asleep; and the
Persians say that before the night was over he dreamed that the
figure of a man, tall and of noble aspect, stood by his bed.
'Persian,' the phantom said, 'have you changed your mind and
decided not to lead an army against Greece, in spite of your
proclamation to your subjects that troops should be raised? You
are wrong to change; and there is one here who will not forgive
you for doing so. Continue to tread the path which you chose
yesterday.' The visionary figure then flew away, and next morning Xerxes put the dream out of his mind and summoned a 13

meeting of the same people as before. 'Gentlemen,' he said to them, 'I ask your forbearance for changing my mind so quickly. My understanding has hardly yet grown to its full strength, and those who would force me into this war do not leave me alone for a moment. When I heard what Artabanus said, my youth seethed for the moment, and I flung some words at him such as a young man ought not to address to his senior. But now I acknowledge the justice of what he said, and I will take his advice. I have changed my mind; there will be no war against Greece. Peace is to continue.'

14   The Persians were delighted at this, and bowed low before their master; but the following night Xerxes dreamed that the same figure as before stood by his bed and spoke to him. 'Son of Darius,' it said, 'so you have openly, in the presence of your subjects, renounced the campaign and made light of what I said to you, as if it had never been said at all. Now let me tell you what the result will be, if you do not at once undertake this war: just as in a moment you rose to greatness and power, so in a moment will you be brought low again.'

15   Terrified by the dream Xerxes leapt out of bed and sent for Artabanus. 'Artabanus,' he said, 'when you first gave me your good advice, I lost control of myself and answered wildly and foolishly. But I soon thought better of it and realized that I ought to do as you suggested. Now, however, I cannot do so, much as I should like it; for since I changed my mind I have been haunted by a dream which will not allow me to act as you advised. The last time I saw the vision, it left me with threats of disaster. Now if God sent the dream, and it is God's pleasure that we should invade Greece, the same vision will appear to you and will give you the same commands as it gave to me. And this, I think, is most likely to happen if you put on my clothes, take your seat on my throne, and then go to sleep in my bed.'

16   Artabanus, who thought it was improper for him to sit on the royal throne, did not at once do as Xerxes bade; but at last he was forced to yield – though not until he had addressed Xerxes
a   in the following words: 'In my belief, my lord, readiness to listen to good advice comes to much the same thing as being wise

oneself. You of course have both virtues; but you are led astray
by the companionship of bad men. Their advice to you is like
the gales of wind which do not allow the sea to be what it is
meant to be – the thing, namely, in all the world most useful to
us. As for myself, I was not so much hurt by your abuse of me
as by the fact that when we were offered a choice between two
courses, of which one tended to flatter our arrogance and the
other to check it by pointing out how wrong it is to teach
the heart always to seek for more than it possesses, you chose
the one which is the more likely to lead both yourself and your
country to disaster. Now you lean towards the better course; *b*
but you tell me that since you gave up your intention of attacking
Greece, you have been haunted by a dream which will not let
you lay your purpose aside. You imagine, my son, that your
dream was sent by some god or other; but dreams do not come
from God. I, who am older than you by many years, will tell
you what these visions are that float before our eyes in sleep:
nearly always these drifting phantoms are the shadows of what
we have been thinking about during the day; and during the
days before your dream we were, you know, very much occupied
with this campaign. Nevertheless it is possible that your dream *c*
cannot be explained as I have explained it: perhaps there is,
indeed, something divine in it – in which case what you have
said sums the matter up completely: let it appear to me as well
as to you, with its commands.

'All the same, if it means to come at all, it should not be more
likely to come if I wear your clothes than if I wear my own, or
if I sleep in your bed than if I sleep in mine. For surely this
phantom of your dreams, whatever it may be, is not so foolish
as to think that I am you simply because I wear your clothes.
But, apart altogether from the question of clothes, should the
phantom ignore me and not think fit to appear, but should
nevertheless come again to you – well, that indeed is something
we shall learn! For if it visits you often, even I shall admit that
it is sent by God.

'As for the rest, if your mind is made up and I cannot turn
you from your purpose: if I really must sleep in your bed – so
be it. I will do what you command – and then let us see if the

phantom comes. But until it does, I shall keep my own opinion
on the matter.'

17   Then Artabanus, hoping to prove that Xerxes was mistaken,
did as he had been bidden. He dressed himself in the king's
clothes and took his seat upon the royal throne; and afterwards
when he had gone to bed and fallen asleep, he dreamt that the
very same figure which had twice visited the king stood over
him. 'Are you the man,' said the phantom, 'who in would-be
concern for the king is trying to dissuade him from making war
on Greece? You will not escape unpunished, either now or
hereafter, for seeking to turn aside that which must happen; and
as for Xerxes, he has been told already what will happen to him
18   if he disobeys me.' The phantom after uttering these threats was
on the point of burning out Artabanus' eyes with hot irons,
when he leapt up with a shriek, and ran to find Xerxes. Then,
sitting beside him, he recounted the dream in detail and went
on to speak in the following words: 'Sire, like other men I have
seen in my time powerful kingdoms struck down by weaker
ones, and it was for that reason I tried to prevent you from
giving way to your youth. There is danger in insatiable desire,
and I could not but remember the fate of Cyrus' campaign
against the Massagetae and Cambyses' invasion of Ethiopia.
Yes, and did I not march with Darius, too, against the Scythians?
My memory of those disasters forced me to believe that the
world would call you happy only if you lived in peace. But now
I know that God is at work in this matter; and since apparently
heaven itself is about to send ruin upon Greece, I admit that I
was mistaken. Tell the Persians about the vision which God has
sent us; make them prepare for war according to the orders
which you previously gave them, and, as God is offering you
this great opportunity, play your own part to the full in realizing
it.'

       Both Artabanus and Xerxes now placed the fullest confidence
in the dream. The king, at the first light of dawn, laid the whole
matter before the Persians, and Artabanus who had been the
only one openly to oppose the project of war, now no less openly
supported it.[10]

19   After Xerxes had made his decision to fight, he had a third

dream. The Magi were consulted about its significance and expressed the opinion that it portended the conquest of the world and its total subjection to Persia. In the dream, Xerxes had imagined himself crowned with olive, of which the branches spread all over the earth; then the crown had suddenly vanished from his head. After the Magi's favourable interpretation, all the Persian nobles who had attended the conference hurried home to their respective provinces; and as every one of them hoped to win the reward which Xerxes had offered, no pains were spared in the subsequent preparations, and Xerxes, in the process of assembling his armies, had every corner of the continent ransacked. For the four years following the conquest 20 of Egypt the mustering of troops and the provision of stores and equipment continued, and towards the close of the fifth Xerxes, at the head of his enormous force, began his march.[11]

The army was indeed far greater than any other of which we know. It dwarfed the army Darius commanded on his Scythian campaign, and the great host of Scythians who burst into Media on the heels of the Cimmerians and brought nearly all upper Asia under their control. (It was this inroad which Darius' invasion was designed to avenge.) It was incomparably larger than the armies which the stories tell us Agamemnon and Mene-laus led to Troy, or than those of the Mysians and Teucrians who before the Trojan War crossed the Bosphorus into Europe, overwhelmed Thrace, and, coming down to the Adriatic coast, drove as far south as the river Peneus. All these armies together, 21 with others like them, would not have equalled the army of Xerxes. Was there a nation in Asia that he did not take with him against Greece? Save for the great rivers, was there a stream his army drank from that was not drunk dry? Some nations provided ships, others formed infantry units; from some cavalry was requisitioned, from others horse-transports and crews; from others, again, triremes for floating bridges, or provisions and naval craft of various kinds.[12]

In view of the previous disaster to the fleet off Mt Athos, 22 preparations had been going on in that area for the past three years. A fleet of triremes lay at Elaeus in the Chersonese, and from this base men of the various nations of which the army was composed were sent over in shifts to Athos, where they were put to the work of cutting a canal under the lash. The natives of Athos also took part. Bubares the son of Megabazus and Artachaees the son of Artaeus were the Persian officers in charge.[13]

Mt Athos is a high and famous mountain running out into the sea. People live on it, and where the high land ends on the landward side it forms a sort of isthmus with a neck about a mile and a half wide, all of which is level ground or low hillocks, across from the sea by Acanthus to the sea facing Torone. On this isthmus where Athos peters out stands the Greek town of 23   Sane, and south of it, on Athos itself, are Dium, Olophyxus, Acrothoon, Thyssus, and Cleonae – the inhabitants of which Xerxes now proposed to turn into islanders.

I will now describe how the canal was cut. The ground was divided into sections for the men of the various nations, on a line taped across the isthmus from Sane. When the trench reached a certain depth, the labourers at the bottom carried on with the digging and passed the soil up to others above them, who stood on terraces and passed it on to another lot, still higher up, until it reached the men at the top, who carried it away and dumped it. All the nations except the Phoenicians had their work doubled by the sides falling in, as they naturally would, since they made the cutting the same width at the top as it was intended to be at the bottom. But the Phoenicians, in this as in Xerxes' other works, gave a signal example of their skill. They, in the section allotted to them, took out a trench double the width prescribed for the actual finished canal, and by digging at a slope contracted it as they got further down, until at the bottom their section was the same width as the rest.

In a meadow near by the workmen had their meeting-place and market, and grain ready ground was brought over in great quantity from Asia.

24   Thinking it over I cannot but conclude that it was mere ostentation that made Xerxes have the canal dug – he wanted to show his power and to leave something to be remembered by. There would have been no difficulty at all in getting the ships hauled across the isthmus on land; yet he ordered the

construction of a channel for the sea broad enough for two triremes to be rowed abreast.[14] The same people who had to cut the canal also had orders to bridge the river Strymon. At the same time other work too was in progress: cables, some of papyrus, some of white flax, were being prepared for the bridges – a task which Xerxes entrusted to the Phoenicians and Egyptians; and provision dumps were being formed for the troops, lest either men or animals should go hungry on the march to Greece. For these dumps the most convenient sites were chosen after a careful survey, the provisions being brought from many different parts of Asia in merchantmen or transport vessels. The greatest quantity was collected at a place called the White Cape in Thrace; other dumps were at Tyrodiza in Perinthian territory, Doriscus, Eion on the Strymon, and in Macedonia.

So the work went on, and meanwhile the great army – all the troops from the continent which were to take part in the expedition – had assembled according to orders at Critalla in Cappadocia, and from there began to move forward with Xerxes to Sardis. Which of the Persian provincial governors received the king's prize for the best-equipped contingent, I am not able to say; nor do I even know if the matter was ever decided.

After crossing the Halys the army passed through Phrygia to Celaenae. In this place the springs of the river Maeander rise – and another river, too, of equal size, called (as its proper name) the Cataract. This latter stream rises in the actual market-square of Celaenae and joins the Maeander. Here, too, the skin of Marsyas the Silenus is exhibited; according to the Phrygian legend Apollo flayed Marsyas and hung the skin up here in the market-place. Here at Celaenae a Lydian named Pythius, the son of Atys, was awaiting Xerxes, and on his arrival entertained him and the whole army with most lavish hospitality, and promised besides to furnish money for the expenses of the war. The mention of money caused Xerxes to ask the Persians present who Pythius was and if he was really rich enough to make such an offer. 'My lord,' was the answer, 'it was this man who gave your father Darius the golden plane-tree and the golden vine; and still, so far as we know, he is the wealthiest man in the world, after yourself.'

28   Xerxes was amazed by this latter statement, and repeated his
question, this time asking Pythius himself how much money he
possessed. 'Sire,' said Pythius, 'I will be open with you and not
pretend that I do not know the amount of my fortune. I do
know it, and I will tell you exactly what it is. When I learned
that you were on your way to the Aegean coast, my immediate
wish was to make a contribution towards the expenses of the
war; so I went into the matter of my finances and found upon
calculation that I possessed 2000 talents of silver, and 3,993,000
gold Darics. This it is my intention to give you; I can live quite
comfortably myself on my slaves and the produce of my estates.'

29   Xerxes was much pleased. 'My Lydian friend,' he replied,
'you are the only man I have met since I left Persian territory
who has been willing to entertain my army, and nobody but
you has come into my presence with an offer to contribute
money for the war of his own free will. But you have done both,
and on a magnificent scale. Therefore, as a reward for your
generosity, I make you my guest-friend and, in addition, I will
give you from my own coffers 7000 gold Darics which are
needed to make your fortune up to the round sum of 4,000,000.
Continue, then, to possess what you have acquired; and have
the wisdom to remain always the man you have proved yourself
today. You will never regret it, now or hereafter.'[15]

30   Having carried out this promise, Xerxes moved on. Passing
the Phrygian town of Anaua, and a lake from which salt is
extracted, Xerxes now arrived at the large city of Colossae,
where the river Lycus disappears underground to reappear
about half a mile further on, where it, too, joins the Maeander.
Leaving Colossae the army made for the Lydian border and
arrived next at Cydrara, where a column with an inscription
upon it set up by Croesus defines the boundary between Phrygia

31   and Lydia. The road as it enters Lydia divides, one track leading
left towards Caria, the other to the right towards Sardis. A
traveller by the latter road has to cross the Maeander and pass
Callatebus, a town where the manufacture of honey out of
tamarisk-syrup and wheat flour is carried on. This was the road
which Xerxes took, and it was hereabouts that he came across
a plane-tree of such beauty that he was moved to decorate it

with golden ornaments and to appoint a guardian for it in perpetuity. The following day he reached the Lydian capital.

In Sardis Xerxes' first act was to send representatives to every 32 place in Greece except Athens and Sparta with a demand for earth and water and a further order to prepare entertainment for him against his coming. This renewed demand for submission was due to his confident belief that the Greeks who had previously refused to comply with the demand of Darius would now be frightened into complying with his own. It was to prove whether or not he was right that he took this step.

He then prepared to move forward to Abydos, where a bridge 33 had already been constructed across the Hellespont from Asia to Europe. Between Sestos and Madytus in the Chersonese there is a rocky headland running out into the water opposite Abydos. It was here not long afterwards that the Athenians under Xanthippus the son of Ariphron took Artaÿctes the Persian governor of Sestos, and nailed him alive to a plank – he was the man who collected women in the temple of Protesilaus at Elaeus and committed various acts of sacrilege.[16] This headland was 34 the point to which Xerxes' engineers carried their two bridges from Abydos – a distance of seven furlongs. One was constructed by the Phoenicians using flax cables, the other by the Egyptians with papyrus cables. The work was successfully completed, but a subsequent storm of great violence smashed it up and carried everything away. Xerxes was very angry when he 35 learned of the disaster, and gave orders that the Hellespont should receive three hundred lashes and have a pair of fetters thrown into it. I have heard before now that he also sent people to brand it with hot irons. He certainly instructed the men with the whips to utter, as they wielded them, the barbarous and presumptuous words: 'You salt and bitter stream, your master lays this punishment upon you for injuring him, who never injured you. But Xerxes the King will cross you, with or without your permission. No man sacrifices to you, and you deserve the neglect by your acid and muddy waters.' In addition to punishing the Hellespont Xerxes gave orders that the men responsible for building the bridges should have their heads cut off.[17] The men who received these invidious orders duly carried them 36 out, and other engineers completed the work. The method employed was as follows: penteconters and triremes were lashed together to support the bridges – 360 vessels for the one on the Black Sea side, and 314 for the other. They were moored slantwise to the Black Sea and at right angles to the Hellespont, in order to lessen the strain on the cables. Specially heavy anchors were laid out both upstream and downstream – those to the eastward to hold the vessels against winds blowing down the straits from the direction of the Black Sea, those on the other side, to the westward and towards the Aegean, to take the strain when it blew from the west and south. Gaps were left in three places to allow any boats that might wish to do so to pass in or out of the Black Sea.

Once the vessels were in position, the cables were hauled taut by wooden winches ashore. This time the two sorts of cable were not used separately for each bridge, but both bridges had two flax cables and four papyrus ones. The flax and papyrus cables were of the same thickness and quality, but the flax was the heavier – half a fathom of it weighed 114 lb. The next operation was to cut planks equal in length to the width of the floats, lay them edge to edge over the taut cables, and then bind them together on their upper surface. That done, brushwood was put on top and spread evenly, with a layer of soil, trodden hard, over all. Finally a paling was constructed along each side, high enough to prevent horses and mules from seeing over and taking fright at the water.[18]

37   The bridges were now ready; and when news came from Athos that work on the canal was finished, including the break-waters at its two ends, which had been built to prevent the surf from silting up the entrances, the army, after wintering at Sardis and completing its preparations, started the following spring on its march to Abydos.

No sooner had the troops begun to move than the sun vanished from his place in the sky and it grew dark as night, though the weather was perfectly clear and cloudless. Xerxes, deeply troubled, asked the Magi to interpret the significance of this strange phenomenon, and was given to understand that God meant to foretell to the Greeks the eclipse of their cities – for it was the sun which gave warning of the future to Greece, just as the moon did to Persia. Having heard this Xerxes continued the march in high spirits.

The army, however, had not gone far when Pythius the 38 Lydian, in alarm at the sign from heaven, was emboldened by the presents he had received to come to Xerxes with a request. 'Master,' he said, 'there is a favour I should like you to grant me – a small thing, indeed, for you to perform, but to me of great importance, should you consent to do so.' Xerxes, who thought the request would be almost anything but what it actually turned out to be, agreed to grant it and told Pythius to say what it was he wanted. This generous answer raised Pythius' hopes, and he said, 'My lord, I have five sons, and it happens that every one of them is serving in your army in the campaign against Greece. I am an old man, Sire, and I beg you in pity to release from service one of my sons – the eldest – to take care of me and my property. Take the other four – and may you return with your purpose accomplished.'

Xerxes was furiously angry. 'You miserable fellow,' he cried, 39 'have you the face to mention your son, when I, in person, am marching to the war against Greece with my sons and brothers and kinsmen and friends – *you*, my slave, whose duty it was to come with me with every member of your house, including your wife? Mark my words: it is through the ears you can touch a man to pleasure or rage – let the spirit which dwells there hear good things, and it will fill the body with delight; let it hear bad, and it will swell with fury. When you did me good service, and offered more, you cannot boast that you were more generous than I; and now your punishment will be less than your impudence deserves. Yourself and four of your sons are saved by the entertainment you gave me; but you shall pay with the life of the fifth, whom you cling to most.'

Having answered Pythius in these words Xerxes at once gave orders that the men to whom such duties fell should find Pythius' eldest son and cut him in half and put the two halves one on each side of the road, for the army to march out between them. The order was performed.

And now between the halves of the young man's body the 40

advance of the army began: first came the men with the gear and equipment, driving the pack-animals, and behind these a host of troops of all nationalities indiscriminately mixed. When more than half the army had passed, a gap was left in the marching column to keep these troops from contact with the king, who was immediately preceded by a thousand horsemen, picked out of all Persia, followed by a thousand similarly picked spearmen with spears reversed. Then came ten of the sacred horses, known as Nisaean, in magnificent harness. (The horses are so called because they come from the great Nisaean plain in Media, where horses of unusual size are bred.) They were followed by the holy chariot of Zeus drawn by eight white horses, with a charioteer on foot behind them holding the reins – for no mortal man may mount into that chariot's seat. Then came the king himself, riding in a chariot drawn by Nisaean horses, his charioteer, Patiramphes, son of Otanes the Persian, standing by his side.

41   That was how Xerxes rode from Sardis – and, when the fancy took him, he would leave his chariot and take his seat in a covered carriage instead. Behind him marched a thousand spearmen, their weapons pointing upwards in the usual way – all men of the best and noblest Persian blood; then a thousand picked Persian cavalry, then – again chosen for quality out of all that remained – a body of Persian infantry ten thousand strong. Of these a thousand had golden pomegranates instead of spikes on the butt-end of their spears, and were arrayed surrounding the other nine thousand, whose spears had silver pomegranates. The troops mentioned who marched with spears reversed also had golden pomegranates on the butt-end of their weapons, while those immediately behind Xerxes had golden apples. The ten thousand infantry were followed by a squadron of ten thousand Persian horse, after which there was a gap of two furlongs, and then came the remainder of the army, in a miscellaneous mass.

42   From Lydia the army made for the river Caicus and Mysia and thence proceeded through Atarneus to Carene, keeping Mt Cane on its left; then crossing the level country near Thebe it passed Atramyttium and the Pelasgian town of Antandrus, and

with Mt Ida on its left entered Trojan territory. During a night in camp at the foot of Mt Ida a heavy storm of thunder and lightning caused the death of a considerable number of men. When the army reached the Scamander, the first river since the march from Sardis began which failed to provide enough water for men and beasts, Xerxes had a strong desire to see Troy, the ancient city of Priam.[19] Accordingly he went up into the citadel, and when he had seen what he wanted to see and heard the story of the place from the people there, he sacrificed a thousand oxen to the Trojan Athene, and the Magi made libations of wine to the heroes. During the night which followed there was panic in the camp. At dawn the march continued; and the army after leaving on the left Rhoeteum, Ophryneum, and Dardanus which is next to Abydos, and the Teucrians of Gergithos on the right, arrived at Abydos.

Xerxes now decided to hold a review of his army. On a rise of ground near by, a throne of white marble had already been specially prepared for his use by the people of Abydos; so the king took his seat upon it and, looking down over the shore, was able to see the whole of his army and navy at a single view. As he watched them he was seized with the desire to witness a rowing-match. The match took place and was won by the Phoenicians of Sidon, to the great delight of Xerxes who was as pleased with the race as with his army. And when he saw the whole Hellespont hidden by ships, and all the beaches and plains of Abydos filled with men, he called himself happy – and the moment after burst into tears. Artabanus his uncle, the man who in the first instance had spoken his mind so freely in trying to dissuade Xerxes from undertaking the campaign, was by his side; and when he saw how Xerxes wept, he said to him: 'My lord, surely there is a strange contradiction in what you do now and what you did a moment ago. Then you called yourself a happy man – and now you weep.'

'I was thinking,' Xerxes replied; 'and it came into my mind how pitifully short human life is – for of all these thousands of men not one will be alive in a hundred years' time.'

'Yet,' said Artabanus, 'we suffer sadder things in life even than that. Short as it is, there is not a man in the world, either

43

44

45

46

here or elsewhere, who is happy enough not to wish – not once only but again and again – to be dead rather than alive. Troubles come, diseases afflict us; and this makes life, despite its brevity, seem all too long. So heavy is the burden of it that death is a refuge which we all desire, and it is common proof amongst us that God who gave us a taste of this world's sweetness has been jealous in his giving.'[20]

47 'Artabanus,' Xerxes replied, 'the lot of men here upon earth is indeed as you have described it; but let us put aside these gloomy reflections, for we have pleasant things in hand. Now tell me – if that figure had not appeared to you so vividly in your dream, would you have clung to your original opinion and tried to prevent me from making war on Greece, or would you have changed your mind? Answer me truly.'

'Sire,' said Artabanus, 'I pray that the dream we had may not disappoint either my hopes or your own. But ever since that night I have been beside myself with dread; many things contribute to the cause of it, but nothing so much as my knowledge that the two mightiest powers in the world are against you.'

48 'What a strange man you are,' said Xerxes; 'tell me, what powers do you mean? Have you any fault to find with my army? Isn't it big enough? Do you think the Greek army will be several times as large, or our navy smaller than theirs? Which are you afraid of? Both perhaps! But if you feel that our force is inadequate, another army could easily be mustered with little delay.'

49 'No man of sense, my lord,' Artabanus answered, 'could find any fault with the size of your army or the number of your ships. If you increase your forces, the two powers I have in mind will be even worse enemies to you than they are now. I will tell you what they are – the land and the sea. So far as I know there is not a harbour anywhere big enough to receive this fleet of ours and give it protection in the event of storms: and indeed there would have to be not merely one such harbour, but many – all along the coast by which you will sail. But there is not a single one; so I would have you realize, my lord, that men are at the mercy of circumstance, and not their master.

'Now let me tell you of your other great enemy, the land. If you meet with no opposition, the land itself will become more and more hostile to you the further you advance, drawn on and on; for men are never satisfied by success. What I mean is this – if nobody stops your advance, the land itself – the mere distance growing greater and greater as the days go by – will ultimately starve you.[21] No: the best man, in my belief, is he who lays his plans warily, with an eye for every disaster which might occur, and then, when the time comes, acts boldly.'

'There is good sense,' Xerxes answered, 'in everything you have said; nevertheless you ought not to be so timid always, or to think of every accident which might possibly overtake us. If upon the proposal of a plan you were always to weigh equally all possible chances, you would never do anything. I would much rather take a risk and run into trouble half the time than keep out of any trouble through being afraid of everything. 50

'If you dispute whatever is said to you, but can never prove your objections, you are as likely to be wrong as the other man – indeed there is nothing to choose between you. And as for proof – how can a man ever be certain? Certainty, surely, is beyond human grasp. But however that may be, the usual thing is that profit comes to those who are willing to act, not to the overcautious and hesitant. Just think how the power of Persia has grown: if my predecessors had felt as you do – or even if they had not, but had taken the advice of men who did – you would never have seen our country in its present glory. No indeed: it was by taking risks that my ancestors brought us to where we stand today. Only by great risks can great results be achieved. We, therefore, are following in the footsteps of our fathers; we are marching to war at the best season of the year; we shall conquer all Europe, and – without being starved to death anywhere or having any other unpleasant experience – we shall return home in triumph. For one thing, we are carrying ample stores with us; for another, we will have the grain belonging to any country we may enter, no matter who lives there. Our enemies, remember, are not nomad tribes[22] – they are agricultural peoples.'

'Sire,' said Artabanus, 'though you will not listen to my fears, take, at least, one piece of advice from me – for when there is 51 much to talk of, many words are needed. Cyrus, the son of Cambyses, conquered and made tributary to Persia all Ionia except Athens; I urge you therefore on no account to take these Ionians to attack men of their own blood. We are well able to defeat our enemy without their help. If the Ionians come with us, they will have two courses open to them: either to prove themselves dishonourable by helping to enslave their mother country, or to prove themselves honest men by helping to keep her free. By choosing the former course they will do us little good; by choosing the latter they will be able to cause serious injury to your army. Put away in your heart the truth of the old saying, that the end is not always to be seen in the beginning.'

52   Xerxes answered: 'Artabanus, of all the views you have put forward you are most mistaken in your fear that the Ionians will desert our cause. We have the best possible proof of their reliability, and you yourself like everybody else who took part in Darius' Scythian campaign can bear witness to it. On that occasion, when the Ionians had it in their power to save or destroy the whole Persian army, they did us no harm but acted with loyalty and honour. Besides, there is another reason for trusting them: for is it conceivable that they will try to wreck our cause, when they have left their wives, children, and property in our country? You may, therefore, dismiss this fear from your mind.[23] Doubt nothing, and keep safe for me my house and dominions; for to you, and you alone, I give my sovereignty in trust.'

53   After this conversation Xerxes sent Artabanus back to Susa and then summoned a meeting of the leading Persians. 'Gentlemen,' he said to them, 'I have brought you here because I wished to ask you to show courage in what lies before us; you must not disgrace our countrymen, who in former days did so much that was great and admirable. Let each and all of us exert ourselves to the utmost; for the noble aim we are striving to achieve concerns every one of us alike. Fight this war with all your might – and for this reason: our enemies, if what I hear is true, are brave men, and if we defeat them, there is no other army in the world which will ever stand up to us again. And now let us pray

to the gods who have our country in their keeping – and cross the bridge.'

All that day the preparations for the crossing continued; and on the following day, while they waited for the sun which they wished to see as it rose, they burned all sorts of spices on the bridges and laid boughs of myrtle along the way. Then sunrise came, and Xerxes poured wine into the sea out of a golden goblet and, with his face turned to the sun, prayed that no chance might prevent him from conquering Europe or turn him back before he reached its utmost limits. His prayer ended, he flung the cup into the Hellespont and with it a golden bowl and a Persian *acinaces*, or short sword. I cannot say for certain if he intended the things which he threw into the water to be an offering to the Sun-god; perhaps they were – or it may be that they were a gift to the Hellespont itself, to show he was sorry for having caused it to be lashed with whips.

This ceremony over, the crossing began. The infantry and cavalry went over by the upper bridge – the one nearer the Black Sea; the pack-animals and underlings by the lower one towards the Aegean. The first to cross were the Ten Thousand, all with wreaths on their heads, and these were followed by the mass of troops of all the nations. Their crossing occupied the whole of the first day. On the next day the first over were the thousand horsemen, and the contingent which marched with spears reversed – these, too, all wearing wreaths. Then came the sacred horses and the sacred chariot, and after them Xerxes himself with his spearmen and his thousand horsemen. The remainder of the army brought up the rear, and at the same time the ships moved over to the opposite shore. According to another account I have heard, the king crossed last.

From the European shore Xerxes watched his troops coming over under the whips. The crossing occupied seven days and nights without a break. There is a story that some time after Xerxes had passed the bridge, a native of the country thereabouts exclaimed: 'Why, O Zeus, have you assumed the shape of a man of Persia, and changed your name to Xerxes, in order to lead everyone in the world to the conquest and devastation of Greece? You could have destroyed Greece without going to that trouble.'

57   After the whole army had reached the European shore and the forward march had begun, a great portent occurred – a mare gave birth to a hare. Xerxes paid no attention to this omen, though the significance of it was easy enough to understand. Clearly it meant that he was to lead an army against Greece with the greatest pomp and circumstance, and then to come running for his life back to the place he started from. There had previously been another portent in Sardis, when a mule dropped a foal with a double set of sexual organs, male and female – the

58   former uppermost. Xerxes, however, ignored both omens and continued his march at the head of the army. The fleet followed the coast in a westerly direction down the Hellespont and then on to Cape Sarpedon, where it had orders to wait, and thus started in the opposite direction to the army, which marched eastwards through the Chersonese, keeping on its right the tomb of Helle, the daughter of Athamas, and on its left the town of Cardia. After passing through a place called The Market, it skirted the Black Gulf and crossed the river which gives the gulf its name – and which failed on that occasion to supply enough water for the army's needs. From that point it turned west, past the Aeolian settlement of Aenus and Lake Stentoris, to Doriscus.

59   Doriscus is the name given to a strip of coast in Thrace backed by a large plain through which flows the large river Hebrus. A fortress – also called Doriscus – had been built here, and a Persian garrison left in it by Darius ever since his invasion of Scythia. It occurred to Xerxes, therefore, that it would be a convenient place for organizing and numbering his troops, and this he proceeded to do.

The naval captains had orders from Xerxes to move all the ships from Doriscus to the adjoining beach where Zone stands, and the Samothracian town of Sale – the beach, that is, which runs out to the well-known headland of Serreum. In ancient times this whole district belonged to the Cicones. Here the ships were all hauled ashore and allowed to dry out.

Meanwhile Xerxes at Doriscus was occupied in numbering
60   his troops. As nobody has left a record, I cannot state the precise

number of men provided by each separate nation, but the grand total, excluding the naval contingent, turned out to be 1,700,000. The counting was done by first packing ten thousand men as close together as they could stand and drawing a circle round them on the ground; they were then dismissed, and a fence, about navel-high, was constructed round the circle; finally other troops were marched into the area thus enclosed and dismissed in their turn, until the whole army had been counted.[24] After the counting, the army was reorganized in divisions according to nationality.

The nations of which the army was composed were as 61 follows.[25] First the Persians themselves: the dress of these troops consisted of the tiara, or soft felt cap, embroidered tunic with sleeves, a coat of mail looking like the scales of a fish, and trousers; for arms they carried large wicker shields, quivers slung below them, short spears, powerful bows with cane arrows, and daggers swinging from belts beside the right thigh. They were commanded by Otanes, the father of Xerxes' wife Amestris. In ancient times the Greek name for the Persians was Cephenes, though they were known to themselves and their neighbours as Artaei. It was not till Perseus, the son of Zeus and Danae, on a visit to Cepheus, the son of Belus, married his daughter Androm-eda and had by her a son whom he named Perses (and left behind in that country because Cepheus had no male heir) that the Persians took, from this Perses, their present name.

The Median contingent, commanded by Tigranes the 62 Achaemenid, was equipped in the same way as the Persian – in point of fact this mode of dress was originally Median and not Persian at all. The Medes were once universally known as Arians, but they, too, changed their name. In their case the change, according to their own account, followed the visit of Medea the Colchian, who went to their country from Athens.

The dress of the Cissian contingent was like the Persian, except that instead of caps they wore turbans. They were com-manded by Anaphes, the son of Otanes. The Hyrcanians were armed in the same way as the Persians, and their commander was Megapanus, who afterwards became governor of Babylon. The Assyrians were equipped with bronze helmets made in a 63 complicated barbarian way which is hard to describe, shields, spears, daggers (like the Egyptian ones), wooden clubs studded with iron, and linen corslets. These people used to be called Syrians by the Greeks, Assyrians being the name for them elsewhere. With them were the Chaldeans. Their commander was Otaspes, the son of Artachaees.

64   The Bactrians had caps almost exactly like those worn by the Medes, and were armed with their native cane bows and short spears. The Sacae (a Scythian people) wore trousers and tall pointed hats set upright on their heads, and were armed with the bows of their country, daggers, and the *sagaris*, or battle-axe. 'Sacae' is the name the Persians give to all Scythian tribes: these were the Amyrgian Scythians. They, together with the Bactrians, were under the command of Hystaspes, the son of Darius and of Cyrus' daughter Atossa.

65   The Indians were dressed in cotton; they carried cane bows and cane arrows tipped with iron, and marched under the
66   command of Pharnazathres, the son of Artabates. The Arians, under Hydarnes' son Sisamnes, were armed with Median bows, the rest of their equipment being the same as the Bactrians'; also in Bactrian equipment were the Parthians and Chorasmians under Artabazus son of Pharnaces, the Sogdians under Azanes son of Artaeus, the Gandarians and Dadicae under Artyphius
67   son of Artabanus. Then there were the Caspians and the Sarangians, the former commanded by Ariomardus, the brother of Artyphius, dressed in leather jackets and armed with the *acinaces* and the cane bow of their country; the latter, under Megabazus' son Pherendates, armed with bows and Median spears, and conspicuous for their brightly coloured clothes and high boots reaching to the knee. They were equipped with leather jackets, bows, and daggers. The Pactyan commander was
68   Artaÿntes, the son of Ithamitres. The Utians and Myci under the command of Arsamenes son of Darius, and the Paricanians under Oeobazus' son Siromitres were equipped like the Pactyans.

69   The Arabians wore the *zeira*, caught in with a belt; their weapon was the bow, carried at the right side – a long bow, which assumed a reverse curve when unstrung. The Ethiopians,

in their leopard skins and lion skins, carried long bows made of palm-wood – as much as six feet long – which were used to shoot small cane arrows tipped not with iron but with stone worked to a fine point, like the stone they use for engraving seals. They also had spears with spearheads of antelope horn, and knotted clubs. When going to battle they smeared half their bodies with chalk and half with vermilion. The Arabians and the Ethiopians from the country south of Egypt were commanded by Arsames, the son of Darius – his mother was Cyrus' daughter Artystone, the favourite wife of Darius, who had a statue made of her in beaten gold.

The eastern Ethiopians – for there were two sorts of Ethiopians in the army – served with the Indians. These were just like the southern Ethiopians, except for their language and their hair: their hair is straight, while that of the Ethiopians in Libya is the crispest and curliest in the world. The equipment of the Ethiopians from Asia was in most respects like the Indian, except that they wore headdresses consisting of horses' scalps, stripped off with the ears and mane attached – the ears were made to stand erect and the mane served as a crest. For shields they used the skins of cranes.

The Libyans were clothed in leather and carried javelins hardened with fire. Their commander was Massages, the son of Oarizus. The Paphlagonians wore wicker helmets, small shields, fairly short spears, javelins, and daggers. They wore the native high boot reaching half-way to the knee. Similarly equipped were the Ligyans, Matieni, Mariandynians, and Syrians (or Cappadocians, as the Persians call them). In command of the Paphlagonians and Matieni was Dotus, the son of Megasidrus, and in command of the Mariandynians, Ligyans, and Syrians was Gobryas, the son of Darius and Artystone.

The dress of the Phrygians was, with a few small differences, like the Paphlagonian. This people, according to the Macedonian account, were known as Briges during the period when they were Europeans and lived in Macedonia, and changed their name at the same time as, by migrating to Asia, they changed their country. The Armenians, who are Phrygian colonists, were armed in the Phrygian fashion and both contingents were commanded by Artochmes, the husband of one of Darius' daughters.

74   The Lydian equipment closely resembled the Greek. These people were known anciently as Maeonians, and took their present name from Lydus, the son of Atys. The Mysians wore the native helmet and were armed with small shields and javelins made of wood hardened in fire. They are Lydian colonists, and are known as Olympieni after Mt Olympus. The two latter contingents were led by Artaphernes, son of the same Artaphernes who landed with Datis at Marathon.

75   The Thracian troops wore fox skins as a headdress, tunics with the *zeira*, or long cloak, in this case brightly coloured, thrown over them, and high fawnskin boots; their weapons were the javelin, light shield, and small dagger. The Thracians after their migration to Asia became known as Bithynians; previously, according to their own account, they were called Strymonians, after the river Strymon upon which they lived, and from which they were driven by the Teucrians and Mysians. The commander of these Asiatic Thracians was Bassaces, the son of Artabanus.

76   The Pisidians[26] carried little ox-hide shields and a pair of hunting-spears of Lycian workmanship, and wore bronze helmets, crested, and decorated with the ears and horns of an ox, also in bronze. Their legs were bound with strips of crimson cloth. In the country where these people live there is an oracle of Ares.

77   The Cabalians (who are really Maeonians but are known as Lasonians) had the same kind of equipment as the Cilicians – I will describe it when I come to the Cilicians in the course of this catalogue. The Milyans carried short spears and had their clothes fastened with brooches; some of them were also armed with Lycian bows and wore leather casques. All these troops were led by Badres, the son of Hystanes.

78   The Moschians had wooden helmets and were armed with shields and short spears with long heads. Similarly equipped were the Tibareni, Macrones, and Mossynoeci; the officers who organized and commanded these troops were, for the two former, Ariomardus, the son of Darius and Parmys (who was daughter of Smerdis and granddaughter of Cyrus), and, for the

two latter, Artaÿctes, the son of Cherasmis, governor of Sestos on the Hellespont.

The Marians wore the peculiar plaited helmets of their 79 country and were armed with little leather shields and javelins; the Colchians had wooden helmets, small shields made of raw-hide, short spears, and swords. These two contingents were under the command of Pharandates, the son of Teaspis. Similarly armed were the Alarodians and Saspires, under Masistius, the son of Siromitras. The troops from the islands in the Persian 80 Gulf (the islands, that is, where the Persian king settles people he has expelled from their homes) were dressed and armed very much in the Median fashion, and were commanded by Bagaeus' son Mardontes, who in the following year held a command at Mycale and was killed in the battle.

Such, then, were the troops of the various nations which made 81 up the infantry. The names of their chief commanders I have already recorded; it was they who organized and numbered the troops, and appointed the commanders of thousands and myriads of men. The latter were responsible for appointing men to take charge of small units – squads of ten or a hundred. There were also other officers commanding contingents and nations, but those whom I mentioned above were the commanders.

Over them, and in general command of the infantry, were 82 Mardonius, the son of Gobryas, Tritantaechmes, the son of Artabanus (the man who voted against the campaign), Smerdomenes, the son of Otanes (both nephews of Darius and Xerxes' cousins), Masistes, the son of Darius and Atossa, Gergis, the son of Ariazus, and Megabyzus, the son of Zopyrus. These six 83 commanded all the infantry except the Ten Thousand – a body of picked Persian troops under the leadership of Hydarnes, the son of Hydarnes. This corps was known as the Immortals, because it was invariably kept up to strength; if a man was killed or fell sick, the vacancy he left was at once filled, so that its strength was never more nor less than 10,000.

Of all the troops in the army the native Persians were not only the best but also the most magnificently equipped; their dress and armour I have mentioned already, but should add that every man glittered with the gold which he carried about his person in unlimited quantity. They were accompanied, moreover, by covered carriages containing their women and servants, all elaborately fitted out. Special food, separate from that of the rest of the army, was brought along for them on camels and mules.

84   The nations above mentioned use cavalry, but for this expedition only the following provided it: first the Persians – armed in the same way as their infantry, except that some of them wore devices of hammered bronze or iron on their heads.

85   Secondly, a nomad tribe called Sagartians, a people who speak Persian and dress in a manner half Persian, half Pactyan: these furnished a contingent 8000 strong. Their custom is to carry no weapons of bronze or iron except daggers; the special weapon upon which they chiefly rely is the lasso made of plaited strips of hide. In action, the moment they are in contact with the enemy, they throw their lassos, which have a noose at the end, and haul towards them whatever they catch, horse or man. The victim, tied up and helpless, is then dispatched. The Sagartian

86   contingent was attached to the Persian. The Medes and Cissians were equipped like their infantry. The Indians, also armed like the Indian foot, rode, some on horseback, some in chariots drawn by either horses or wild asses. The Bactrians and Caspians were equipped like their infantry. The Libyans were like their infantry in equipment, but all riding in chariots. The Caspeirians and Paricanians again had the same arms as their infantry. The Arabians, equipped like their infantry, rode camels, which in speed are not inferior to horses.

87   These were the only nations which provided cavalry, and the total strength, not counting camels and chariots, was 80,000. The cavalry was drawn up in squadrons, and the Arabian contingent brought up the rear to avoid spreading panic amongst the horses, who cannot endure the presence of camels.

88   In command of the cavalry were Datis' two sons, Harmamithras and Tithaeus. The third general of cavalry, Pharnuches, had been sick and left behind in Sardis. When the army was leaving Sardis, he met with an unhappy accident: a dog ran under his horse's feet, and the horse, taken by surprise, reared and threw its rider. As a result of the fall Pharnuches began to spit blood; and his sickness finally turned to consumption. His

servants at once dealt with the horse according to his orders – bringing him to the spot where he had thrown his master, and cutting his legs off at the knees. So Pharnuches was relieved of his command.

The fleet, apart from transport vessels, consisted of 1207 89 triremes.[27] They were furnished as follows:

The Phoenicians, with the Syrians of Palestine, contributed 300. The crews wore helmets very like the Greek ones, and linen corslets; they were armed with rimless shields and javelins. These people have a tradition that in ancient times they lived on the Persian Gulf, but migrated to the Syrian coast, where they are found today. This part of Syria, together with the country which extends southward to Egypt, is all known as Palestine.

The Egyptians contributed 200. They wore reticulated helmets and were armed with concave, broad-rimmed shields, boarding-spears, and heavy axes. Most of the crews wore corslets and carried long knives.

The Cyprians contributed 150. Their princes wore turbans, 90 the common sailors peaked hats. The rest of their equipment resembled the Greek. According to the Cyprians' own account, some of them came originally from Salamis and Athens, some from Arcadia, some from Cythnus, some from Phoenicia and Ethiopia.

The Cilicians contributed 100. The crews wore the native 91 helmet and woollen corslets and carried light rawhide shields. Each man was armed with two javelins and a sword which closely resembled the Egyptian long knife.

The ancient name of the Cilicians was Hypachaei; their present name they took from Cilix, the son of Agenor, a Phoenician.

The Pamphylians contributed 30. Their armour was Greek. These people are descended from the Greeks who followed Amphilochus and Calchas when the army was dispersed after the capture of Troy.

The Lycians contributed 50. They wore greaves and corslets; 92 they carried bows of cornel wood, cane arrows without feathers, and javelins. They had goatskins slung round their shoulders, and hats stuck round with feathers. They also carried daggers and riphooks. The Lycians are of Cretan origin; their

old name was Termilae, and they took their present one from
Lycus son of Pandion, an Athenian.

93   The Asiatic Dorians contributed 30. Coming originally from
the Peloponnese, they were armed in the Greek fashion.

The Carians contributed 70. Their equipment was similar to
the Greek, except that they carried riphooks and daggers. Their
old name I have already mentioned in an early chapter of this
history.

94   The Ionians contributed 100. Their equipment was Greek.
These people, according to the Greek account, as long as they
lived in what is now known as Achaea in the Peloponnese,
before the coming of Danaus and Xuthus, were called Pelasgians
of the Coast. They took their present name from Xuthus' son
Ion.

95   The islanders – also wearing Greek armour – contributed 17.
They, too, are a Pelasgian people; they were later known as
Ionians for the same reason as those who inhabited the twelve
cities founded from Athens.

The Aeolians (also, as the Greeks suppose, originally a Pelasgian people) contributed 60. Their equipment was Greek.

The towns on the Hellespont and Bosphorus (the people in
these places are Ionian and Dorian colonists) contributed 100
– all furnished with Greek equipment and armour. Abydos,
however, was not included: the men of this town had orders
from Xerxes to stay at home and guard the bridges.

96   All the ships also carried Persians, Medes, or Sacae as marines.
The fastest ships were the Phoenician – and of these the Sidonian
were the best. The men who served with the fleet like those who
served with the army had their own native officers; but, as my
story does not require it, I do not propose to mention their
names. Some of them were far from distinguished, and every
nation had as many officers as it had towns. In any case, these
native officers were not really commanders; like the rest of the
troops, they merely served as slaves. The names of the Persian
generals who had the real command and were at the head of the
contingents sent by the various nations, I have already recorded.

97   The naval commanders were as follows: Ariabignes son
of Darius; Prexaspes son of Aspathines; Megabazus son of

Megabates; Achaemenes son of Darius. Ariabignes, who was Darius' son by a daughter of Gobryas, commanded the Ionian and Carian contingent, Achaemenes, who was Xerxes' brother by both parents, the Egyptian. The rest of the fleet was under the other two. Galleys of thirty and fifty oars, horse-transports, and boats made the total number of the fleet up to 3000.

Next to the commanders the following were the best known 98 of those who sailed with the fleet: Tetramnestus son of Anysus, from Sidon; Matten son of Siromus, from Tyre; Merbalus son of Agbalus, from Aradus; Syennesis son of Oromedon, from Cilicia; Cyberniscus son of Sicas, from Lycia; Gorgus son of Chersis and Timonax son of Timagoras, from Cyprus; and Histiaeus son of Tymnes, Pigres son of Hysseldomus, and Damasithymus son of Candaules, from Caria.

There is no need for me to mention all the other subordinate 99 officers, but there is one name which I cannot omit – that of Artemisia. It seems to me a marvel that she – a woman – should have taken part in the campaign against Greece.[28] On the death of her husband the tyranny had passed into her hands, and she sailed with the fleet in spite of the fact that she had a grown-up son and that there was consequently no necessity for her to do so. Her own spirit of adventure and manly courage were her only incentives. She was the daughter of Lygdamis, a Halicarnassian; on her mother's side she was Cretan. She sailed in command of the men of Halicarnassus, Cos, Nisyra, and Calydna, and furnished five ships of war. They were the most famous in the fleet, after the contingent from Sidon, and not one of the confederate commanders gave Xerxes sounder advice than she did. The places I mentioned as being under her rule are all Dorian – the Halicarnassians being colonists from Troezen, and the rest from Epidaurus.

I have now finished what I had to say about the fleet. 100

When the counting and marshalling of the troops had been completed, Xerxes thought he would like to hold a general review. Accordingly he drove in his chariot past the contingents of all the various nations, asking questions, the answers to which were taken down by his secretaries, until he had gone from one end of the army to the other, both horse and foot. Next the

ships were launched, and Xerxes dismounting from his chariot
went aboard a Sidonian vessel, where he took his seat under a
canopy of gold and sailed along the line of the anchored fleet,
asking questions about each ship and having the answers
recorded, just as he had done with the army. The ships' masters
had taken their vessels some four hundred feet from the beach,
and brought up there in a single line with the bows turned
shoreward and the fighting men drawn up on deck fully armed
as for war. To hold his review, Xerxes passed along between
the line and the shore.

101   Having sailed from one end to the other of the line of anchored
ships, Xerxes went ashore again and sent for Demaratus, the
son of Ariston, who was accompanying him in the march to
Greece. 'Demaratus,' he said, 'it would give me pleasure at this
point to put to you a few questions. You are a Greek, and a
native, moreover, of by no means the meanest or weakest city
in that country – as I learn not only from yourself but from the
other Greeks I have spoken with. Tell me, then – will the Greeks
dare to lift a hand against me? My own belief is that all the
Greeks and all the other western peoples gathered together
would be insufficient to withstand the attack of my army – and
still more so if they are not united. But it is your opinion upon
this subject that I should like to hear.'

'King,' Demaratus replied, 'is it a true answer you would like,
or a pleasant one?'

'Tell me the truth,' said the king: 'and I promise that you will
102   not suffer by it.' Encouraged by this Demaratus continued: 'My
lord, you bid me speak nothing but the truth, to say nothing
which might later be proved a lie. Very well then; this is my
answer: poverty is Greece's inheritance from of old, but valour
she won for herself by wisdom and the strength of law. By her
valour Greece now keeps both poverty and despotism at bay.

'I think highly of all Greeks of the Dorian lands, but what I
am about to say will apply not to all Dorians, but to the Spartans
only. First then, they will not under any circumstances accept
terms from you which would mean slavery for Greece; secondly,
they will fight you even if the rest of Greece submits. Moreover,
there is no use in asking if their numbers are adequate to enable

them to do this; suppose a thousand of them take the field –
then that thousand will fight you; and so will any number,
greater than this or less.'

Xerxes laughed. 'Demaratus,' he exclaimed, 'what an extra- 103
ordinary thing to say! Do you really suppose a thousand men
would fight an army like mine? Now tell me, would *you* who
were once, as you say, king of these people, be willing at this
moment to fight ten men single-handed? And yet, if things in
Sparta are really as you have described them, then, according to
your laws, you as king ought to take on a double share – so that
if every Spartan is a match for ten men of mine, I should expect
you to be a match for twenty. Only in that way can you prove
the truth of your claim. But if you Greeks, who think so much
of yourselves, are all of the size and quality of those I have
spoken with when they have visited my court – and of yourself,
Demaratus – there is some danger of your words being nothing
but an empty boast. But let me put my point as reasonably as I
can – how is it possible that a thousand men, or ten thousand,
or fifty thousand, should stand up to an army as big as mine,
especially if they were not under a single master, but all perfectly
free to do as they pleased? Suppose them to have five thousand
men: in that case we should be more than a thousand to one! If,
like ours, their troops were subject to the control of a single
man, then possibly for fear of him, in spite of the disparity in
numbers, they might show some sort of factitious courage, or
let themselves be whipped into battle; but, as every man is free
to follow his fancy, it is not conceivable that they should do
either. Indeed, my own opinion is that even on equal terms the
Greeks could hardly face the Persians alone. We, too, have this
thing that you were speaking of – I do not say it is common, but
it does exist; for instance, amongst the Persians in my bodyguard
there are men who would willingly fight with three Greeks
together. But you know nothing of such things, or you could
not talk such nonsense.'

'King,' Demaratus answered, 'I knew before I began that if I 104
spoke the truth you would not like it. But, as you demanded the
plain truth and nothing less, I told you how things are with the
Spartans. Yet you are well aware that I now feel but little

affection for my countrymen, who robbed me of my hereditary power and privileges and made me a fugitive without a home – whereas your father welcomed me at his court and gave me the means of livelihood and somewhere to live. Surely it is unreasonable to reject kindness; any sensible man will cherish it. Personally I do not claim to be able to fight ten men – or two; indeed I should prefer not even to fight with one. But should it be necessary – should there be some great cause to urge me on – then nothing would give me more pleasure than to stand up to one of those men of yours who claim to be a match for three Greeks. So it is with the Spartans; fighting singly, they are as good as any, but fighting together they are the best soldiers in the world. They are free – yes – but not entirely free; for they have a master, and that master is Law, which they fear much more than your subjects fear you. Whatever this master commands, they do; and his command never varies: it is never to retreat in battle, however great the odds, but always to remain in formation, and to conquer or die. If, my lord, you think that what I have said is nonsense – very well; I am willing henceforward to hold my tongue. This time I spoke because you forced me to speak. In any case, I pray that all may turn out as you desire.'

105   Xerxes burst out laughing at Demaratus' answer, and good-humouredly let him go.[29]

After the conversation, Xerxes appointed Mascames, son of Megadostes, to the governorship of Doriscus in place of the man who had been given that post by Darius, and then continued
106   his march through Thrace towards Greece. Mascames was later to prove himself a very remarkable person; so much so, in fact, that Xerxes used to send a special present every year in recognition of his superiority to all the governors appointed either by himself or by Darius; moreover his son Artaxerxes showed the same favour to Mascames' descendants. Persian governors had held posts in Thrace and on the Hellespont before Xerxes' expedition, but in the years which succeeded it all of them except the governor of Doriscus were driven out by the Greeks – Mascames no one was able to expel, though many tried to do so.[30] This is the reason for the annual present from

the Persian king. Of the governors who were expelled by the   107
Greeks the only one whom Xerxes considered as a man of any
worth was Boges, governor of Eion. Boges he was never tired of
praising, and those of his sons who were left in Persia and
survived him he treated with marked respect. This man did,
indeed, deserve the highest praise; for when he was besieged by
the Athenians under Cimon, son of Miltiades, and the chance
was offered him of leaving the town under treaty and returning
to Asia, he refused to do so, because he was afraid the king
might think that he had shirked his duty to save his skin; so,
rather than surrender, he held out to the last extremity. When
all supplies were consumed, he made a huge pile of timber, set
it on fire, and then, cutting the throats of his children, wife,
concubines, and servants, flung their bodies into the flames;
then he collected all the gold and silver in the town, scattered it
broadcast from the walls into the Strymon, and ended by leaping
into the fire himself. For this behaviour his name is still mentioned in Persia with respect; and it is right that it should be.

From Doriscus Xerxes marched on towards Greece, pressing   108
into his service the men of every nation which lay in his path;
for, as I have already recorded, the whole country as far as
Thessaly had been forced into subjection and made tributary
to Persia by the conquests, first, of Megabazus and, later, of
Mardonius. After leaving Doriscus the army passed first by the
Samothracian forts, the most westerly of which is Mesembria;
the next place is Stryme, a town belonging to the Thasians.
Between the two runs the Lisus, a stream which on that occasion
failed to provide sufficient water for Xerxes' army. It was drunk
dry. This part of the country was once called Gallaica instead
of its present name of Briantica; strictly, however, it too belongs
to the Cicones. Having crossed the dried-up channel of the   109
Lisus, Xerxes moved on past the Greek towns of Maronia,
Dicaea, and Abdera, passing also some well-known lakes in that
neighbourhood, namely Ismaris, between Maronia and Stryme,
and Bistonis near Dicaea, a lake into which flow the rivers
Trauos and Compsatus. At Abdera there was not, to be sure,
any well-known lake for him to pass, but he crossed the river
Nestus, which there enters the sea. Next he reached the

settlements owned by the Thasians upon the continent, in one of which there is a lake about four miles in circumference, full of fish and very salt. It was drunk dry by the pack-animals alone. The town by this lake is called Pistyrus. All these Greek coastal settlements Xerxes kept on his left as he marched westward.

110 The Thracian tribes lying along his route were the Paeti, Cicones, Bistones, Sapaei, Dersaei, Edoni, and Satrae; some of these lived on the coast and furnished ships for the king's fleet, but others lived inland, and of these all the tribes I have mentioned except

111 the Satrae were forced to serve in the army. The Satrae, so far as we know, have never yet been reduced to subjection, and are the only Thracian people to have kept their independence right down to my day. The reason for this is the nature of their country, which consists of high mountains, thickly wooded with timber of all sorts and covered with snow. They are also first-rate fighters. It is in the territory of this people that there is the oracle of Dionysus, situated on the loftiest mountain range. The service of the temple belongs to the Bessi, a branch of the Satrae; and there is a Priestess, as at Delphi, to deliver the oracles – which, by the way, are not more complicated than the Delphic.[31]

112 Once through the region mentioned above, Xerxes next passed the Pierian forts, one of which is called Phagres and another Pergamus. His route led him close by the walls, as he kept on his right the great range of Pangaeum, where there are gold and silver mines worked partly by the Pierians and

113 Odomanti but mostly by the Satrae. Then he passed through the country of the Doberes and Paeoplae (Paeonian tribes living north of Pangaeum), and continued in a westerly direction as far as the Strymon and the town of Eion, where Boges, whom I mentioned just now, was governor during his lifetime. The country in the neighbourhood of Mt Pangaeum is known as Phyllis; it extends westward to the Angites, a stream which flows into the Strymon, and southward as far as the Strymon itself. This latter river the Magi tried to propitiate by a sacrifice of

114 white horses, and after performing many other magical tricks in the hope of winning the river's favour, they crossed it by the bridges which they found at Nine Ways, a place in the territory of the Edoni; and when they learnt that Nine Ways was the

name of the place, they took nine native boys and nine girls and buried them alive there.[32] Burying people alive is a Persian custom; I understand that Xerxes' wife Amestris in her old age did it to fourteen Persian boys of distinguished family, by way of a present which she hoped the supposed god of the underworld would accept instead of herself.

From the Strymon the army came to a strip of coast running westward, on which stands the Greek town of Argilus. The country here, and for some distance inland, is called Bisaltia. Thence, keeping the Gulf of Posidium on his left, Xerxes marched through the plain of Syleus, past the Greek town of Stagirus, until he arrived at Acanthus. Like the others whom I mentioned before, the inhabitants of these places and of the country round Mt Pangaeum were pressed into his service, those on the coast being forced to sail with the fleet, those inland to march with the army. The road which King Xerxes took remains untouched to my day; the Thracians hold it in profound reverence and never plough it up or sow crops on it.

At Acanthus Xerxes issued a proclamation of friendship to the people and made them a present of a suit of Median clothes, with many expressions of approval for their enthusiastic support of the war and for the work they had done on the canal. It was while Xerxes was here that Artachaees fell sick and died. He was a man of the Achaemenid family, much respected by Xerxes, and had been in charge of the construction of the canal. He was the biggest man in Persia – about 8 ft 2 ins. high – and had the loudest voice in the world, so that Xerxes was greatly distressed at his death and had him carried out and buried with all pomp and ceremony. The whole army helped to raise a mound over his grave. The people of Acanthus, in obedience to an oracle, offer sacrifice to Artachaees, as to a hero, and call upon his name in prayer.

The death of Artachaees was, as I said, very distressing for Xerxes; but things were even worse for the Greeks who had to entertain the Persian army and provide a dinner for the king. They were utterly ruined, and were obliged to leave house and home. For instance, when the Thasians, on behalf of their towns on the mainland, billeted and fed the army, Antipater, the

115

116

117

118

son of Orgeus, a citizen of the highest repute, to whom the
arrangements had been entrusted, proved that the meal cost 400
119   talents of silver. And similar accounts were returned by the
officers in the other towns. A great deal of fuss had been made
about the meal, and orders for its preparation had been issued
a long time in advance; accordingly, the moment that word
came from the officers who carried the king's commands, people
in every town distributed their stores of grain and employed
themselves for months on end in making barley and wheat flour,
in buying up and fattening the best cattle they could find, and
feeding poultry in coops and waterfowl in ponds, to be ready
for the army when it came. In addition to this they ordered the
manufacture of drinking cups and mixing-bowls of gold and
silver, and of everything else that is needed to adorn the table.
All this, of course, was for the king himself and those who
dined with him; for the troops in general the preparations were
confined to food. On the arrival of the army, there was always
a tent ready for Xerxes to take his rest in, while the men
bivouacked in the open; but it was when dinner-time came that
the real trouble for the unfortunate hosts began. The guests ate
their fill and, after spending the night in the place, pulled up the
tent next morning, seized the cups and table-gear and everything
else it contained, and marched off without leaving a single thing
120   behind. A man of Abdera called Megacreon spoke to the point
on this subject, when he advised all the people of the town to
take their wives to the temples and pray heaven to continue to
spare them one half of their troubles, with proper gratitude for
the blessing already received, that King Xerxes was not in the
habit of taking *two* dinners a day. It was clear enough that if
the orders had been to prepare a morning meal as well as an
evening one, the people of Abdera would have had to clear out
altogether before Xerxes arrived, or else be hopelessly crushed
121   by the burden of the expense. Nevertheless the various places
along the route did manage to carry out their orders, though
not without severe suffering.

At Acanthus Xerxes sent the fleet on separately, and ordered
the commanders to wait for him at Therma – the town on the
gulf to which it has given its name. It was through Therma that

he had ascertained his shortest route to lie. From Doriscus to
Acanthus the army had been marching in three divisions, of
which one under Mardonius and Masistes took the coast road
and kept in close touch with the fleet, another under Tritantaechmes and Gergis a parallel route some distance inland, and
the third under Smerdomenes and Megabyzus a route between
the two. This third division Xerxes himself accompanied.

Having received from Xerxes its orders to proceed, the fleet [122]
passed through the Athos canal, which led to the deep bight on
which stand the towns of Assa, Pilorus, Singus, and Sarte; from
all these places reinforcements were taken on board, and a
course was set for the Gulf of Therma. Rounding Ampelus, the
promontory in Torone, they sailed past the Greek towns of
Torone, Galepsus, Sermyle, Mecyberna, and Olynthus (the
country round here is known as Sithonia), levying more ships
and men; but the main body of the fleet sailed direct from Cape [123]
Ampelus to Canastraeum (the southernmost point of Pallene),
and then took over more reinforcements in both ships and men
from Potidaea, Aphytis, Nea, Aege, Therambos, Scione, Mende,
and Sane – all towns in what is now called Pallene, but used to
be called Phlegra. From here they continued to follow the coast
towards the rendezvous at Therma, taking over on the way
more men from the towns near Pallene and the Thermaic Gulf
– namely Lipaxus, Combreia, Lisae, Gigonus, Campsa, Smila,
and Aeneia. All this region is still known as Crossaea. After
passing the last of these towns – Aeneia – the fleet found itself
off Mygdonia and actually within the gulf, and proceeded to
the rendezvous at Therma. The ships also called at Sindus and
Chalestra on the river Axius, which forms the boundary between
Mygdonia and Bottiaeis. This latter district has a small strip of
coastline occupied by the towns of Ichanae and Pella.

While the fleet waited near Therma and the Axius and the [124]
intervening towns, Xerxes with the army was on his way from
Acanthus by the inland road to the rendezvous. He passed
through Paeonia and Crestonia to the river Echeidorus, which
rises in the latter country and flows through Mygdonia, to reach
the sea by way of the marshland at the mouth of the Axius. It [125]
was during this march that his pack-camels were attacked by

lions, which came down from their haunts at night and never attacked either the men or any of the other animals, but only the camels. I marvel at what it could have been that made the lions ignore every other living creature and set only upon the camels – beasts which they had never seen, or had any experience

126 of, before. This part of the country – namely the region between the river Nestus which runs through Abdera and the Achelous which runs through Acarnania – abounds with lions, and also with wild oxen, which have those enormous horns that are imported into Greece.[33] One would see no lions anywhere in Europe east of the Nestus, or in the continent west of the Achelous; they exist only in the country between those rivers.

127 At Therma[34] Xerxes halted his army, and the troops went into camp. They occupied the whole seaboard from Therma in Mygdonia to the Lydias and Haliacmon – two rivers which unite and form the boundary between Bottiaeis and Macedonia. While they were encamped here, all the rivers I have mentioned supplied enough water for their needs except the Echeidorus, which failed.

128 Xerxes could see from Therma the Thessalian mountains – the towering peaks of Olympus and Ossa – and on being informed that between the two mountains there was a narrow gorge through which the river Peneus ran, and also a road leading into Thessaly, he suddenly felt that he would like to go by sea and inspect the mouth of the river. His intention was to take the army by the upper road through the inland parts of Macedonia into Perrhaebia, past the town of Gonnus; for that, he heard, was the safest route. No sooner, therefore, had the fancy taken him than he acted upon it; and going aboard the Sidonian vessel which he always used for any such occasion, he gave the signal to the rest of the fleet to put to sea, leaving the army behind in its encampments. The appearance of the river-mouth, on his arrival there, was a great marvel to him, so that he called the guides and asked them if it was possible to turn the course of the river so as to bring it to the sea at some

129 other point. Now it is said that in the remote past Thessaly was a lake – a not unreasonable supposition, as the whole country is enclosed by lofty hills. To the eastward is the great barrier of

Pelion and Ossa, two mountains whose bases form a continuous chain; then there is the range of Olympus on the north, Pindus on the west, and Othrys on the south. In the centre of this ring of mountains lies the low plain of Thessaly. A number of rivers pour their waters into it, the best known being the Peneus, Apidanus, Onochonus, Enipeus, and Pamisus; all these flow down from the surrounding mountains, unite into a single stream, and find their way to the sea through one narrow gorge. After the junction the other names are all dropped and the river is known simply as the Peneus. The story then is that, ages ago, before the gorge existed and while there was as yet no outlet for the water, these rivers, though, like Lake Boebeis, they had yet no names, poured down from the hills as much water as they do today, and so made Thessaly an inland sea. The natives of Thessaly have a tradition that the gorge which forms the outlet for the river was made by Poseidon, and the story is a reasonable one; for if one believes that it is Poseidon who shakes the earth and that chasms caused by earthquake are attributable to him, then the mere sight of this place would be enough to make one say that it is Poseidon's handiwork. It certainly appeared to me that the cleft in the mountains had been caused by an earthquake.

So when Xerxes asked if there was any other outlet by which the Peneus could reach the sea, the guides, who were perfectly familiar with the facts, replied, 'No, my lord; there is no other outlet but this, because the whole of Thessaly is surrounded with a ring of mountains, like a crown.' At this Xerxes is said to have remarked: 'The Thessalians are wise men; it was with this very danger in view that they made their submission to me in good time – they realized, amongst other things, that their country is easy to take and very vulnerable. Nothing more would have been needed than to flood the country by damming the gorge, and so forcing the river from its present channel; that would have put all Thessaly except the mountains under water.' In saying this he had, of course, the Aleuadae in mind – the Thessalian family who were the first Greeks to submit to the Persian king. Doubtless he thought that they had made the offer of friendship in the name of the people generally.

Then, having seen the place, and having made this comment, Xerxes returned by sea to Therma.

131   His stay in Pieria lasted a number of days, during which one third of his army was felling the forest through the mountains of Macedonia, making a route for his troops to follow into Perrhaebia. Meanwhile the representatives who had been sent to Greece to demand submission rejoined the army – some
132   empty-handed, others bringing the earth and water. Those who gave the tokens of submission were the following: the Thessalians, Dolopes, Aenianes, Perrhaebi, Locrians, Magnetes, Malians, Achaeans of Phthiotis, Thebans, and all the other Boeotians except the people of Plataea and Thespiae. Against these the Greeks who determined to resist the invader swore an oath to the effect that, once the war was fought to a successful conclusion, they would punish all men of Greek blood, who without compulsion yielded to the Persians, and dedicate a tenth part of their property to the god at Delphi.

133   To Athens and Sparta Xerxes sent no demand for submission because of what happened to the messengers whom Darius had sent on a previous occasion: at Athens they were thrown into the pit like criminals, at Sparta they were pushed into a well – and told that if they wanted earth and water for the king, to get them from there. This time, therefore, Xerxes refrained from sending a request. Just what disagreeable consequences were suffered by the Athenians for this treatment of the king's messengers, I am unable to say; perhaps it was the destruction of their city and the countryside around it – though I do not myself
134   believe that this happened as a direct result of their crime.[35] The case is clear, however, with respect to the Spartans: upon them fell the anger of Agamemnon's herald Talthybius. There is in Sparta a temple dedicated to Talthybius, and a family – the Talthybiadae – descended from him, which enjoys the sole privilege of holding the office of herald. Now there was a long period after the incident I have mentioned above, during which the Spartans were unable to obtain favourable signs from their sacrifices; this caused them deep concern, and they held frequent assemblies at which the question 'Is there any Spartan who is willing to die for his country?' was put by the public crier.

Thereupon two Spartans, Sperchias, the son of Aneristus, and Bulis, the son of Nicoles, both men of good family and great wealth, volunteered to offer their lives to Xerxes in atonement for Darius' messengers who had been killed in Sparta. They were dispatched accordingly to Persia to meet their doom. The 135 courage of these two men is indeed admirable, and what they said is no less so. On their way to Susa they visited Hydarnes, a Persian by birth who was in command of the whole Asiatic seaboard; and by him they were given a hospitable welcome and invited to dinner. During the meal Hydarnes said: 'Why is it, Lacedaemonians, that you refuse to be friends with the king? You have only to look at me and the position I enjoy to see that he knows how to reward merit. Now Xerxes believes that you, too, are men of merit; and both of you, if only you would submit, might find yourselves in authority over lands in Greece which he would give you.'

'Hydarnes,' came the answer, 'the advice you give us does not spring from a full knowledge of the situation. You know one half of what is involved, but not the other half. You understand well enough what slavery is, but freedom you have never experienced, so you do not know if it tastes sweet or bitter. If you ever did come to experience it, you would advise us to fight for it not with spears only, but with axes too.'

After this they continued their journey to Susa, and the first 136 thing that happened when they entered the presence of the king was that the men of the royal bodyguard ordered – and, indeed, attempted to compel – them to bow down to the ground in the act of worship.[36] The two Spartans, however, declared that they would never do such a thing, even though the guards should push their heads down on to the floor. It was not, they said, the custom in Sparta to worship a mere man like themselves, and it was not for that purpose that they had come to Persia. So they persisted in their refusal, adding words to the following effect: 'King of the Medes, the Spartans sent us here to suffer punishment in reparation for the murder of the Persian messengers in Sparta'; to which Xerxes with truly noble generosity replied that he would not behave like the Spartans, who by murdering the ambassadors of a foreign power had broken the law which all the world holds sacred. He had no intention of doing the very thing for which he blamed them, or, by taking reprisals, of freeing the Spartans from the burden of their crime.

137   This conduct on the part of the Spartans succeeded for a time in allaying the anger of Talthybius, in spite of the fact that Sperchias and Bulis returned home alive; long afterwards, however, during the war between Athens and the Peloponnese, the Spartans believe that it was aroused again – and in this, I think, the hand of God was clearly to be seen. That Talthybius' anger should have fallen upon *ambassadors*, and should not have ceased until it was fully satisfied, was only just; but that it should have struck the sons of the very men who visited the Persian king because of it – that the objects of it should have been Bulis' son Nicolaus and Sperchias' son Aneristus, the same man who took Halieis, a Tirynthian colony, with a merchant ship and an armed crew – this, to me at least, is clear evidence of divine intervention. What happened was that these two men were sent by the Spartans on a mission to Asia and were betrayed by Sitalces son of Teres, the king of Thrace, and by Nymphodorus son of Pythes, a native of Abdera; they were made prisoners at Bisanthe on the Hellespont and taken to Attica, where they were put to death by the Athenians in company with Aristeas son of Adeimantus, of Corinth.[37] This, however, took place long after Xerxes' invasion of Greece, and I must get back to my story.

138   The purpose of Xerxes' expedition, which was directed nominally against Athens, was in fact the conquest of the whole of Greece. The various Greek communities had long been aware of this, but they viewed the coming danger with very different eyes. Some had already made their submission, and were consequently in good spirits, because they were sure of getting off lightly at the invaders' hands; others, who had refused to submit, were thrown into panic partly because there were not enough ships in Greece to meet the Persians with any chance of success, and partly because most of the Greeks were unwilling to fight

139   and all too ready to accept Persian dominion. At this point I find myself compelled to express an opinion which I know most people will object to; nevertheless, as I believe it to be true, I

will not suppress it.[38] If the Athenians, through fear of the approaching danger, had abandoned their country, or if they had stayed there and submitted to Xerxes, there would have been no attempt to resist the Persians by sea; and, in the absence of a Greek fleet, it is easy to see what would have been the course of events on land. However many lines of fortification the Spartans had built across the Isthmus, they would have been deserted by their confederates; not that their allies would have willingly deserted them, but they could not have helped doing so, because one by one they would have fallen victims to the Persian naval power. Thus the Spartans would have been left alone – to perform great deeds and to die nobly. Or, on the other hand, it is possible that before things came to the ultimate test, the sight of the rest of Greece submitting to Persia might have driven them to make terms with Xerxes. In either case the Persian conquest of Greece would have been assured; for I cannot myself see what possible use there could have been in fortifying the Isthmus, if the Persians had command of the sea. In view of this, therefore, one is surely right in saying that Greece was saved by the Athenians. It was the Athenians who held the balance: whichever side they joined was sure to prevail. It was the Athenians, too, who, having chosen that Greece should live and preserve her freedom, roused to battle the other Greek states which had not yet submitted. It was the Athenians who – after the gods – drove back the Persian king. Not even the terrifying warnings of the oracle at Delphi could persuade them to abandon Greece; they stood firm and had the courage to meet the invader.[39]

The Athenians had sent their envoys to Delphi to consult the oracle, and as soon as the customary rites were performed and they had entered the shrine and taken their seats, the Priestess Aristonice uttered the following prophecy: 140

Why sit you, doomed ones? Fly to the world's end, leaving
Home and the heights your city circles like a wheel.
The head shall not remain in its place, nor the body,
Nor the feet beneath, nor the hands, nor the parts between;
But all is ruined, for fire and the headlong god of war

Speeding in a Syrian chariot shall bring you low.
Many a tower shall he destroy, not yours alone,
And give to pitiless fire many shrines of gods,
Which even now stand sweating, with fear quivering,
While over the roof-tops black blood runs streaming
In prophecy of woe that needs must come. But rise,
Haste from the sanctuary and bow your hearts to grief.

141   The Athenian envoys heard these words with dismay; indeed
they were about to abandon themselves to despair at the dreadful fate which was prophesied, when Timon, the son of Androb-
ulus and one of the most distinguished men in Delphi, suggested
that they should take branches of olive in their hands and, in
the guise of suppliants, approach the oracle a second time. The
Athenians acted upon this suggestion. 'Lord Apollo,' they said,
'can you not, in consideration of these olive boughs which we
have brought you, give us some better prophecy about our
country? Otherwise we will never leave the holy place but stay
here till we die.'

Thereupon the Prophetess uttered a second prophecy, which
ran as follows:

Not wholly can Pallas win the heart of Olympian Zeus,
Though she prays him with many prayers and all her subtlety;
Yet will I speak to you this other word, as firm as adamant:
Though all else shall be taken within the bound of Cecrops
And the fastness of the holy mountain of Cithaeron,
Yet Zeus the all-seeing grants to Athene's prayer
That the wooden wall only shall not fall, but help you and
    your children.
But await not the host of horse and foot coming from Asia,
Nor be still, but turn your back and withdraw from the foe.
Truly a day will come when you will meet him face to face.
Divine Salamis, you will bring death to women's sons
When the corn is scattered, or the harvest gathered in.

142   This second answer seemed to be, as indeed it was, less
menacing than the first; so the envoys wrote it down and

returned to Athens. When it was made public upon their arrival in the city, and the attempt to explain it began, amongst the various opinions which were expressed there were two mutually exclusive interpretations. Some of the older men supposed that the prophecy meant that the Acropolis would escape destruction, on the grounds that the Acropolis was fenced in the old days with a thorn-hedge, and that this was the 'wooden wall' of the oracle; but others thought that by this expression the god indicated the ships, and they urged in consequence that everything should be abandoned in favour of the immediate preparation of a fleet. There was, however, for those who believed 'wooden wall' to mean ships, one disturbing thing – namely, the last two lines of the Priestess' prophecy:

> Divine Salamis, you will bring death to women's sons
> When the corn is scattered, or the harvest gathered in.

This was a very awkward statement and caused profound disturbance amongst all who took the wooden wall to signify ships; for the professional interpreters understood the lines to mean that they would be beaten at Salamis in a fight at sea. There was, however, a man in Athens who had recently come into prominence – Themistocles called Neocles' son; he now came forward and declared that there was an important point in which the professional interpreters were mistaken.[40] If, he maintained, the disaster referred to was to strike the Athenians, it would not have been expressed in such mild language. 'Hateful Salamis' would surely have been a more likely phrase than 'divine Salamis', if the inhabitants of the country were doomed to destruction there. On the contrary, the true interpretation was that the oracle referred not to the Athenians but to their enemies. The 'wooden wall' did, indeed, mean the ships; so he advised his countrymen to prepare at once to meet the invader at sea.

The Athenians found Themistocles' explanation of the oracle preferable to that of the professional interpreters, who had not only tried to dissuade them from preparing to fight at sea but had been against offering opposition of any sort. The only thing to do was, according to them, to abandon Attica altogether and seek a home elsewhere.

144   Once on a previous occasion Themistocles had succeeded in getting his views accepted, to the great benefit of his country. The Athenians had amassed a large sum of money from the produce of the mines at Laurium, which they proposed to share out amongst themselves at the rate of ten drachmas a man; Themistocles, however, persuaded them to give up this idea and, instead of distributing the money, to spend it on the construction of two hundred warships for use in the war with Aegina.[41] The outbreak of this war at that moment saved Greece by forcing Athens to become a maritime power. In point of fact the two hundred ships were not employed for the purpose for which they were built, but were available for Greece in her hour of need. The Athenians also found it necessary to expand this existing fleet by laying down new ships, and they determined in debate after the discussion on the oracle, to take the god's advice and meet the invader at sea with all the force they possessed, and with any other Greeks who were willing to join them.

145   At a conference of the Greek states who were loyal to the general cause guarantees were exchanged, and the decision was reached that the first thing to be done was to patch up their own quarrels and stop any fighting which happened to be going on amongst members of the confederacy.[42] There were a number of such disputes at the time, the most serious being the quarrel between Athens and Aegina. Having learnt that Xerxes and his army had reached Sardis, they next resolved to send spies into Asia to get information about the Persian forces; at the same time, in the hope of uniting, if it were possible, the whole Greek world and of bringing all the various communities to undertake joint action in face of the common danger, they decided to send an embassy to Argos to conclude an alliance, another to Gelon, the son of Deinomenes, in Sicily, and others, again, to Corcyra and Crete. Gelon was said to be very powerful – far more powerful than anyone else of Greek nationality.

146   These decisions were put into force at once. The private quarrels were settled, and three men sent off to Asia to collect information. They arrived in Sardis and found out all they could

about the king's army, but were caught in the process, tortured
by the Persian army commanders, and condemned to death. But
when Xerxes was told that they were about to be executed, he
disapproved of his generals' decision and sent men from his
bodyguard with orders, if the three spies were still alive, to bring
them before him. As the sentence had not yet been carried out,
the spies were brought to the king, who, having satisfied himself
about the reason for their presence in Sardis, instructed his
guards to take them round and let them see the whole army,
infantry and cavalry, and then, when they were satisfied that
they had seen everything, to let them go without molestation
to whatever country they pleased. After giving this order he
explained the purpose of it by pointing out that, if the spies had   147
been executed, the Greeks would not have been able to learn in
good time how incalculably great the Persian strength was –
and the killing of three men would not have done the enemy
much harm; but if, on the other hand, the spies returned home,
he was confident that their report on the magnitude of the
Persian power would induce the Greeks to surrender their liberty
before the actual invasion took place, so that there would be no
need to go to the trouble of fighting a war at all. Xerxes had
expressed a similar opinion on another occasion, when he was
at Abydos and saw boats sailing down the Hellespont with
cargoes of food from the Black Sea for Aegina and the Peloponnese. His counsellors, learning that they were enemy vessels,
were prepared to seize them, and looked to the king for orders
to do so. 'Where are they bound for?' Xerxes asked. 'To Persia's
enemies, my lord,' came the answer, 'with a cargo of grain.'
'Well,' said the king, 'are we not bound ourselves for the same
destination? And does not our equipment include grain amongst
other things? I do not see that the men in those ships are doing
us any harm in carrying our grain for us.' The three spies, then,   148
after their tour of inspection, were allowed to return to Europe.

The Greeks who had united for resistance to Persia next
dispatched their representatives to Argos.[43] The Argives themselves explain their subsequent behaviour as follows: they were
aware from the beginning of the Persian preparations against
Greece, and knew very well that the Greeks would try to enlist

their support in meeting the invasion; so they sent to Delphi for advice upon what action would, under the circumstances, be best for them to take. The reason for this step was the fact that six thousand of their men had recently been killed by the Spartans under Cleomenes, the son of Anaxandrides. The Priestess' answer to their question was this:

> Loathed by your neighbours, dear to the immortal gods,
> Hold your javelin within and sit upon your guard.
> Guard the head well, and the head will save the body.

This oracle had already been delivered, when the envoys arrived in Argos, and entered the council-chamber to deliver their message. The Argive answer was, that they were willing to do what they were asked upon two conditions: first they must obtain a thirty years' truce with Sparta, and, secondly, share with Sparta, on equal terms, the command of the confederate forces. By right Argos was entitled to the sole command; nevertheless they would be content with an equal division.

149   Such, according to them, was their Council's answer, in spite of the fact that the oracle had forbidden them to join the confederacy. Moreover, though they shrank from disobeying the oracle, it was important to them to secure the thirty years' truce, to give their sons the chance of growing up during the period of peace; and if they failed to secure it, and were unlucky enough to suffer another defeat – this time at the hands of the Persians – it seemed only too likely that they would find themselves permanently subject to Sparta. The Spartan envoys replied to the demands of the Argive government by saying that they would refer the question of the truce to their people; on the other matter, however, namely the army command, they already had their instructions, and their answer was that Sparta had two kings and Argos only one, and it was not possible to deprive either of the Spartan kings of his command; on the other hand, there was nothing to prevent the Argive ruler from having one vote like each of the two Spartans.

The Argives add that they found the Spartan attitude intolerably grasping, and, rather than give way to it, they preferred to submit to foreign domination; accordingly they gave notice to the envoys that they must be out of the country before sunset, or be treated as enemies.

So much for the Argive account of this transaction; there is, however, another story current throughout Greece, to the effect that Xerxes sent a man to Argos before his army started on its march. 'Men of Argos,' this person is supposed to have said upon his arrival, 'King Xerxes has a message for you. We Persians believe that we are descended from Perses, whose father was Danae's son Perseus, and whose mother was Andromeda the daughter of Cepheus. Thus we are of the same blood as yourselves, and it would not be right for us to make war upon the people from whom we have sprung, any more than it would be right for you to help others by opposing us. Rather you should hold aloof from the coming struggle and take no part in it. If things turn out as I hope they will, there is no people I shall hold in greater esteem than you.'

The story goes on to say that the Argives were much impressed by Xerxes' message; they made no promises for the moment, and put forward no demand for a share in the command of the army; later, however, when the Greeks were trying to obtain their support, they did make the claim, because they knew that the Spartans would refuse to grant it, and that they would thus have an excuse for taking no part in the war. There are people in Greece who say that this account is borne out by a remark made long afterwards by Artaxerxes. Callias, the son of Hipponicus, and a number of other Athenians were in Susa, the city of Memnon, on different business,[44] and it so happened that their visit coincided with that of some representatives from Argos, who had been sent to ask Xerxes' son Artaxerxes if the friendly relations, which the Argives had established with his father, still held good, or if they were now considered by Persia as enemies. 'They do indeed hold good,' Artaxerxes is said to have replied; 'there is no city which I believe to be a better friend to me than Argos.'

For my own part I cannot positively state that Xerxes either did, or did not, send the messenger to Argos; nor can I guarantee the story of the Argives going to Susa and asking Artaxerxes

150

151

152

about their relationship with Persia. I express no opinion on this matter other than that of the Argives themselves. One thing, however, I am very sure of: and that is, that if all mankind agreed to meet, and everyone brought his own sufferings along with him for the purpose of exchanging them for somebody else's, there is not a man who, after taking a good look at his neighbour's sufferings, would not be only too happy to return home with his own. So the Argives were not the worst offenders. My business is to record what people say, but I am by no means bound to believe it – and that may be taken to apply to this book as a whole. There is yet another story about the Argives: it was they, according to some, who invited the Persians to invade Greece, because their war with Sparta was going badly and they felt that anything would be better than their present plight.

153   Another embassy was sent by the confederates to Sicily, to confer with Gelon.[45] One of the allied representatives was the Spartan Syagrus.

Gelon's ancestor, who first settled at Gela, came from the island of Telos, off Triopium, and when the settlement at Gela was made by Antiphemus and the Lindians of Rhodes, he took part in the expedition. In course of time his descendants became priests of the Earth Goddesses, an office which they have continued to hold ever since Telines came into possession of it. How Telines got it makes a remarkable story: as a result of civil strife in Gela, a number of men had been compelled to leave the town and to seek refuge in Mactorium on the neighbouring hills. These people were reinstated by Telines, who accomplished the feat, not by armed force, but simply by virtue of the sacred symbols of the Earth Goddesses. How or whence he came by these things I do not know; but it was upon them, and them only, that he relied; and he brought back the exiles on condition that he and his descendants after him should hold the office of Priest. In view of what I have heard, it is a marvel that Telines should have been capable of such a feat. I have always imagined that it is by no means everybody who is equal to things like that, which usually call for both strength and courage; yet people in Sicily maintain that Telines was neither strong nor brave, but, on the contrary, a rather soft and effeminate person. In any case, that was how he obtained his office.

After the death of Cleander, the son of Pantares – he was 154 murdered by Sabyllus of Gela after ruling Gela for seven years – power passed to his brother Hippocrates; and Gelon, the descendant of the priest Telines, was, with many others including Aenesidemus and Pataecus, a member of his bodyguard. Gelon was soon to be General of Cavalry, for he had served with very great distinction under Hippocrates in various battles and sieges against Callipolis, Naxos, Zancle, Leontini, Syracuse, and a number of native peoples besides. Of the towns here mentioned not one escaped subjection except Syracuse, which, after a defeat on the river Elorus, was saved by the intervention of Corinth and Corcyra, who negotiated a peace on the condition that Syracuse should cede Camarina, a town that in old days belonged to it, to Hippocrates.

Hippocrates was tyrant at Gela for the same length of time 155 as his brother Cleander, and died attacking Hybla during a campaign against the Sicels. His death gave Gelon his opportunity: masking his real purpose under the pretence of supporting Hippocrates' sons, Eucleides and Cleander, in their struggle against the people of Gela, who were now eager to throw off the yoke, he crushed the insurgents by force of arms, and then, robbing the two young men of the fruits of victory, seized power himself. He followed this successful stroke by making himself master of Syracuse. The Syracusan landowners had been expelled by the commons with the help of their slaves (known as Cyllyrii), and had fled for refuge to Casmene. Gelon brought them back to Syracuse and got possession of the town; for the commons made no resistance, but surrendered as soon as they saw him coming.

The acquisition of Syracuse made Gelon much less interested 156 than before in Gela. He handed it over to his brother Hieron, and himself proceeded to strengthen Syracuse, which had now become the apple of his eye. At once Syracuse shot up and budded like a young tree; Gelon brought to it all the people of Camarina, which he had razed to the ground, and gave them citizen rights, and he did the same for more than half the population of Gela. The Sicilian Megara, too, had to make its contribution – the town had been at war with Gelon and had surrendered on terms; the men of substance, who had started the war, naturally expected death at Gelon's hands, but they were transferred instead to Syracuse and given citizen rights like the rest. The Megarian commons, who imagined they would be well treated because they had had no share of responsibility for the war, were also brought to Syracuse and then sold as slaves abroad. The Sicilian Euboea suffered similar treatment, the same distinction being made between the men of property and the commons. In both cases Gelon's motive was his belief that the masses are very disagreeable to live with. In these ways Gelon rose to tyrant and wielded very great influence.

157   And now the envoys from Greece arrived in Syracuse, approached Gelon, and spoke to the following effect: 'We have been sent by the Spartans and their allies to obtain your help against the foreigner. You are, of course, aware of what is coming to Greece; that a Persian is about to bridge the Hellespont and to march against us out of Asia with all the armies of the east at his back, and that his true purpose, which he veils under the pretence of an attack on Athens, is the subjugation of the whole of Greece. Your power is great; as lord of Sicily you possess no inconsiderable portion of the Greek world; we ask you, therefore, to help us, and to add your strength to ours in our struggle to maintain our country's liberty. Greece united will be strong and a match for the invader; but if some of us betray and others stand aside, and only a minority is sound, then there is reason to fear that all Greece may fall. Do not imagine that if the Persians defeat us in battle they will not afterwards visit *you*. They will – so be on your guard in time. By supporting us you will be defending yourself. It usually happens that well-laid plans have a prosperous issue.'

158   Gelon's answer to this speech was made with passionate vehemence. 'Men of Greece,' he cried, 'have you the face to come here and urge me with your selfish arguments to help you resist a foreign invader? Have you forgotten that I, too, was once at war with a foreign power – the Carthaginians – and that I applied to you for help? Yes, and I begged you to avenge

upon the men of Egesta their murder of Dorieus the son of Anaxandrides, and offered to help free the trading posts which have been the source of such profit and advantage to you. But what was your answer? You refused to come either to help me or to avenge Dorieus' death – and for all you cared, this whole country might now be subject to foreign rule. But my affairs are now in good order. And now the war has come down upon you – so you remember Gelon! Nevertheless, though you treated me with contempt, I will not imitate your conduct. I am willing to help you by a contribution of 200 triremes, 20,000 hoplites, 2000 cavalry, 2000 archers, 2000 slingers, and 2000 light horse-men; and I undertake to provision the entire Greek army for as long as the war may last. My offer, however, is subject to one condition – that the supreme command of the Greek forces against the Persians shall be mine. On any other terms I will neither come myself nor send troops.'

This was too much for Syagrus, and he burst out: 'Agamem- 159 non, son of Pelops, would groan in his grave if he heard that Sparta had been robbed of her command by Gelon and his Syracusans! Let us hear no more of our giving you command. If you wish to help Greece, you must understand that it will be under Spartan leadership. If you dislike the idea of a subordinate position, then you need not help.'

Gelon, seeing from what Syagrus said that he was unlikely to 160 accept his terms, made his last proposal. 'My Spartan friend,' he said, 'reproaches have a way of making a man angry; never-theless in spite of your insults I will answer you with courtesy. Surely, if you maintain so eagerly your right to the command, it is only reasonable that I should urge my own claim more strongly still, as I have a much bigger fleet and an army many times the size of yours. However, since my proposal is so painful to you, I will make some concession: suppose you command the army, and I the navy. Or, if you prefer to command at sea, I am willing to take over the land forces. You must either be content with this, or do without the powerful support I am able to give you.'

The Athenian envoy gave Syagrus no time to reply to this, but 161 as soon as Gelon had made his offer, 'King of Syracuse,' he

cried, 'Greece did not send us to ask for a commander but for
an army. But clearly you are unwilling to send troops unless you
have command – the one thing you are set upon getting. Now
when you asked for the supreme command of all the Greek
forces, we Athenians were content to hold our tongues, because
we knew that our colleague from Sparta would be quite capable
of answering for us both; but things are different now that,
having failed in your original claim, you ask to command at sea.
Even if Sparta allowed this, we should not. Command of the
fleet, provided Sparta herself does not want it, belongs to us.
We do not object to Sparta having it if she wishes, but we refuse
to give it up to anybody else. What would be the use of our
having built up the finest navy in Greece if we surrendered the
command of it to the Syracusans? Are we not Athenians – the
most ancient of all Greek peoples, the only nation never to have
left the soil from which it sprang? Did not the poet Homer say
that we sent to Troy the best man for ordering and marshalling
an army?[46] Surely, then, we need not be ashamed of speaking as
we do.'

162   'My friend,' Gelon replied, 'it looks as if you have the commanders – but will not have any men for them to command.
Since, therefore, you claim everything and yield nothing, you
had better go home as quickly as you can and tell Greece that
the spring of the year is lost to her.'[47]

163   That was the end of the Greek negotiations with Gelon, and
the envoys set out for home.

Gelon himself was afraid that Greece would be unable to
survive the Persian invasion; at the same time, as tyrant of Sicily,
he could not bring himself to go to the Peloponnese and submit
to taking orders from Spartans. Accordingly he chose a different
course. As soon as news came that Xerxes was over the Hellespont, he sent three penteconters under the charge of Cadmus,
the son of Scythes, a native of Cos, with instructions to go to
Delphi, where, equipped with a large sum of money and plenty
of friendly words, he was to wait and see how the war would
go; then, if the Persians won, he was to give the money to Xerxes
together with earth and water of Gelon's dominions. If the
Greeks won, he was to bring the money back again.

Some time before this Cadmus had inherited the position of   164
absolute master of Cos from his father, who had established his
power there on firm foundations; yet of his own free will,
without threat of violence from any quarter, he had, simply
from his sense of justice, abdicated his power and handed it
over to the people. He then left home for Sicily, where he took
the town of Zancle with[48] the Samians – or Messene, as it was
afterwards called – and lived there. This was how Cadmus came
to Sicily, and was the reason why Gelon, having had evidence
already of his sense of honour, chose him for the mission to
Delphi. And now yet another honest action, perhaps the most
remarkable of all, was to be added to the former ones: having
in his hands the large sum of money which Gelon had entrusted
to him, with every opportunity of keeping it, he preferred not
to; and after the Greek victory, and the departure of Xerxes, he
returned to Sicily with the money intact.

There is a story in Sicily that Gelon would have sent help   165
to Greece in spite of the necessity of serving under Spartan
commanders had it not been for the action of Terillus, the son
of Crinippus and tyrant of Himera. Driven from his home by
Aenesidemus' son Theron, the sole ruler of Agrigentum, he
brought into Sicily just about this time an army 300,000 strong,
from Carthage, Libya, Iberia, Liguria, Helisycia, Sardinia, and
Corsica – under the command of Hamilcar, the son of Hanno
and king of Carthage. Terillus had induced Hamilcar to bring
over this force partly by the friendship which existed between
them, but more particularly through the warm support of Anaxilaus, the tyrant of Rhegium, the son of Cretines; for Anaxilaus,
who was married to Terillus' daughter Cydippe, and wished to
be of service to his father-in-law, gave Hamilcar his own children
as hostages in order to persuade him to undertake the
expedition. Under these circumstances, as it was impossible for
Gelon to give military aid to Greece, he sent the money to
Delphi. The Sicilians also maintain that the victory of Gelon   166
and Theron over Hamilcar of Carthage took place on the same
day as the Greek victory over Persia at Salamis.[49] Hamilcar was
Carthaginian on his father's side only, for his mother came from
Syracuse; he won the throne of Carthage by right of merit, and

I have heard that during the battle, when things were beginning to go against him, he vanished. Gelon afterwards searched for him everywhere, but there was no trace of him, alive or dead.

167 The tradition in Carthage – and it is probable – is that all the time the battle lasted, which was from dawn to late in the evening, Hamilcar remained in camp trying to obtain a favourable omen from sacrifices, burning whole carcasses on an immense fire; and at last, seeing, as he poured the wine upon the sacrificed victims, that his army was giving way, he leapt into the flames, was burnt to nothing, and in this way disappeared. But whatever explanation we adopt of his disappearance, the fact remains that the Carthaginians offer sacrifice to him, and monuments were erected to him in all their colonies in addition to the one – the most splendid of all – in Carthage itself. So ended the campaign in Sicily.

168 The envoys who went to Sicily called also at Corcyra and put their request for help in the same words as they used to Gelon.[50] The immediate result was a promise from the Corcyraeans to send a fleet in support of the alliance. It was impossible, they said, to stand aside and see Greece overwhelmed; they must help her to the utmost of their power, because if she fell not a day would pass before they themselves were reduced to slavery. This answer sounded promising enough, but when the time came to act upon it, the Corcyraeans changed their minds; and having put into commission a fleet of sixty warships, they dawdled about before getting to sea, and then sailed only as far as the Peloponnese, where they hung round in the neighbourhood of Pylos and Taenarum, waiting, like Gelon, to see the result of the fighting. They thought it most unlikely that the Greeks would win; the Persians, in their opinion, would gain a complete victory and make themselves masters of all Greece. Their conduct was deliberately designed to enable them to say, in this event, to Xerxes that, though they might have answered the Greek appeal for aid by sending a fleet second in strength only to that of Athens, they had refused to do so, not wishing to oppose him or to take any action which he would not like. They hoped, no doubt, that this would get them better treatment than the other Greek states – and so, indeed, it would have done, I

admit. They also had an excuse ready to offer to the Greeks –
and used it when the time came and they were reproached for
their failure to send assistance. The excuse was that they had
fitted out sixty triremes, but had been prevented by prevailing
north-easters from getting round Cape Malea: this explained
their absence from the battle of Salamis – an absence in no way
due to disloyalty or cowardice.

The Cretans, on the arrival of the Greek envoys with their   169
appeal, sent to Delphi to inquire jointly whether or not it would
be to their advantage to make common cause with Greece.
'Foolish men,' the oracle replied, 'do you not still resent all the
tears which Minos in his anger caused you to weep after you
helped Menelaus? Was he not angry because the Greeks did not
help you to avenge his death at Camicus, whereas you did help
them to avenge the rape by a foreign prince of a woman from
Sparta?' When the Cretans heard that answer, they refrained
from joining the alliance.

The story goes that Minos went to Sicania – or Sicily, as it is   170
now called – in search of Daedalus, and there met a violent
death. In course of time all the Cretans except the people of
Polichna and Praesus, encouraged by the god, went with a large
fleet to Sicania, where for five years they besieged Camicus – a
town which in my day belonged to Agrigentum. Unable to take
the place, or to continue the siege because of lack of provisions,
they finally gave up and went away. In the course of their voyage
they were caught by a violent storm off Iapygia and driven
ashore, and, as their vessels were smashed up and they had no
apparent means of getting back to Crete, they built for themselves the town of Hyria. Here they stayed, and instead of
Cretans, became the mainland Iapygians of Messapia. From
Hyria they founded the other towns which the people of Tarentum, long after, suffered such severe loss in attempting to over-
throw; indeed, on that occasion there was, of all those we know,
the worst slaughter of Greeks; not only the Tarentines were
involved but the people of Rhegium as well, for they were
compelled by Micythus the son of Choerus to support Tarentum
and lost three thousand men.[51] The losses of Tarentum were too
many to count. Micythus had been a household servant of

Anaxilaus and was left by him in charge of Rhegium. It was he who settled in Tegea in Arcadia after his expulsion from Rhegium and made the offering of all those well-known statues at Olympia. However, I must leave this digression about Rhegium and Tarentum and get back to my story.

171

According to the tradition in Praesus, men of various nationality, but especially Greeks, came to settle in Crete after it was depopulated by the expedition to Sicily; then in the third generation after the death of Minos came the Trojan war, in which the Cretans proved themselves by no means the most despicable champions of Menelaus; their reward for this service on their return home was famine and plague for both men and cattle, so that for the second time Crete was denuded of its population. Thus it happens that the present Cretans, together with the remnant of the former population, are the third people to live in the island. It was these events of which the Delphic Priestess reminded the Cretans in her answer to their question, and thereby prevented them from joining the Greek confederacy in spite of their readiness to do so.

172

The Thessalians did not submit to Persia until they were compelled, for they showed plainly enough that the intrigues of the Aleuadae were not to their liking.[52] No sooner had the news reached them of the imminent crossing of the Persian army into Europe than they sent representatives to the Isthmus, where delegates from all Greek towns loyal to the common cause were assembled. On their arrival the Thessalian delegates addressed the assembly in these terms: 'Fellow countrymen, in order to save Thessaly and the whole of Greece, it is necessary to defend the passage past Mt Olympus. We are ready to assist you in the defence of this vital pass, and you, for your part, must send a strong force. If you fail to do so, we give you fair warning that we shall come to terms with Persia. We are in an exposed position, and cannot be expected, alone and unassisted, to give our lives merely to save the rest of you. If you are unwilling to send us aid, you cannot compel us to fight your battle for you; for sheer inability is stronger than any compulsion. We shall try to devise some means of saving ourselves.'

The Greek answer was to determine to send an army by sea 173
to Thessaly, to defend the pass. The troops assembled and, after
passing through the Euripus, came to Alus in Achaea, where
they left the ships and proceeded to Thessaly on foot. Here they
occupied Tempe, the pass which leads from lower Macedonia
into Thessaly along the Peneus river, between Mt Olympus
and Mt Ossa. It was here that some 10,000 Greek hoplites,
reinforced by the Thessalian cavalry, took up their position.
The Spartans were commanded by Euanetus son of Carenus,
who had been chosen for the post from the Polemarchs, though
he was not of the royal blood;[53] the Athenians were commanded
by Themistocles, son of Neocles. But the army had not been in
Tempe many days when a message arrived from Alexander, the
son of Amyntas, in Macedonia advising the Greek troops to
withdraw, and not stay in the pass to be trampled underfoot,
adding an indication of the strength of the Persian army and
fleet.[54] The advice seemed to be sound, and was clearly offered
by the Macedonian in a friendly spirit, so the Greeks took it. I
think myself that what persuaded them to go was the alarm they
felt upon learning that there was another way into Thessaly
through upper Macedonia and Perrhaebia, near the town of
Gonnus – the pass, in fact, by which Xerxes' army actually did
come in.[55]

The Greeks, then, re-embarked and returned to the Isthmus. 174
Such were the circumstances of the expedition to Thessaly – it
took place while Xerxes was at Abydos, just before he crossed
the strait from Asia into Europe. The result of it was that
the Thessalians, finding themselves without support, no longer
hesitated but whole-heartedly worked in the Persian interest, so
that in the course of the war they proved of the greatest use to
Xerxes.

The Greeks on their return to the Isthmus then discussed, in 175
consideration of the warning they had received from Alexander,
where they should make a stand. The proposal which found
most favour was to guard the pass of Thermopylae, on the
grounds that it was narrower than the pass into Thessaly and at
the same time nearer home. They knew nothing as yet about

the mountain track by means of which the men who fell at Thermopylae were taken in the rear, and only learnt of its existence from the people of Trachis after their arrival.[56]

The decision, then, was to hold the pass in order to prevent the Persians from entering Greece, and at the same time to send the fleet to Artemisium on the coast of Histiaea; for these two places being close together, communication would be easy. The
176 topography is as follows. Artemisium is where the sea south of Thrace contracts into a narrow channel between the island of Sciathus and the mainland of Magnesia; pass through this channel and you come to the strip of coast called Artemisium. It is a part of Euboea, and contains a temple of Artemis.[57] The pass through Trachis into Greece is, at Thermopylae, fifty feet wide; elsewhere, both east and west of Thermopylae, it is still narrower; at Alpeni to the eastward, it is only a single waggon track, and to the westward near Anthela on the river Phoenix it is about the same. To the south-west – inland – there is no way through, passage being barred by a lofty and precipitous ascent, running up to Mt Oeta, while on the other side of the roadway is the sea, full of banks and shoals. There are hot springs in the pass – known locally as the Basins – with an altar over them dedicated to Heracles. A wall was once built across this passage, and there used long ago to be a gateway in it; both were constructed by the Phocians in fear of an invasion from Thessaly, at the period when the Thessalians came from Thesprotia to settle in the country of Aeolis, which they still occupy. The new settlers tried to overrun Phocis, and the Phocians raised the wall as a protective measure, and at the same time turned the water from the hot springs over the pass, to cut up the ground into gullies, resorting to every device to keep the Thessalians out. The wall had been built a very long time ago and most of it had fallen into ruin through age; now, however, it was decided to rebuild it, and to use it to help stop the Persians from getting through into Greece. Quite close to the road is a village called Alpeni, from which the Greeks counted upon drawing supplies.

177 These, then, were the places which the Greeks thought would best suit their purpose; careful consideration of all the circumstances, and the realization that the Persians would be unable,

in the narrow pass, to use their cavalry or take advantage of their numbers, determined them to make their stand at this point against the invader; so when news came that the enemy was in Pieria, they broke up from the Isthmus and proceeded to their new positions, some on foot to Thermopylae, others by sea to Artemisium.

Meanwhile, as the Greek troops hurried to their stations, the   178 people of Delphi, in great alarm for their own safety and for Greece, applied to their oracle for advice. 'Pray to the winds,' was the answer; 'for they will be good allies to Greece.' The first thing the Delphians did upon receiving this oracular counsel was to report it to all the Greek states who were determined to fight for their freedom; and, by thus communicating the divine message at a time when Greece was in the grip of fear at the prospect of invasion, they earned everlasting gratitude. Subsequently they consecrated an altar to the winds at Thyia – a place named after Cephisus' daughter, who has a shrine there – and offered sacrifice upon it to the winds in supplication. In memory of this oracle the Delphians still, to this day, pray to the winds for favour.

Xerxes' fleet now left Therma, and ten of the fastest ships set   179 a course direct for Sciathus, where three Greek vessels, one from Troezen, one from Aegina, and one from Attica, were on the look-out. At the first glimpse of the enemy all three fled. The   180 Persians gave chase; the ship from Troezen, under the command of Prexinus, fell into their hands at once, and her captors, picking out the best-looking of the fighting men on board, took him up forward and cut his throat, thinking, no doubt, that the sacrifice of their first handsome Greek prisoner would benefit their cause. The man's name was Leon – and possibly his name had something to do with his fate.[58] The trireme from Aegina,   181 commanded by Asonides, gave the Persians some trouble. One of the soldiers on board – Pytheas, the son of Ischenous – distinguished himself that day; for after the ship was taken, he continued to resist until he was nearly cut to pieces. At last he fell, but, as there was still breath in his body, the Persian troops, anxious to do all they could to save the life of so brave a man, dressed his wounds with myrrh and bound them up with linen bandages. On returning to their base, they exhibited their prisoner admiringly to everybody there, and treated him with much kindness. The other prisoners from this ship they treated merely as slaves.

182   Two of the three Greek vessels thus fell into Persian hands; the third, commanded by the Athenian Phormus, went ashore, while trying to escape, at the mouth of the Peneus. Here she was taken, though the men in her got away; for the instant the vessel grounded the Athenians aboard leapt out and made their way back to Athens through Thessaly.

183   News of what had happened was flashed to the Greeks at Artemisium by fire-signal from Sciathus. In the panic which ensued they left their station and moved to Chalcis, intending to guard the Euripus, and leaving look-outs on the high ground of Euboea. Three of the ten Persian ships ran aground on the Ant, a sunken reef between Sciathus and Magnesia; in consequence of this the Persians marked the reef with a stone beacon, after which, the danger being removed, the whole fleet set sail from Therma, eleven days after Xerxes had marched from the town with his army. The Ant lies right in the fairway; Pammon, a native of Scyros, took the Persians to it when they erected their beacon. A day's voyage brought the Persian fleet to Sepias in Magnesia and the strip of coast between Cape Sepias and the town of Casthanea.

184   The Persian fleet got as far as Sepias, and the army as far as Thermopylae, without loss. I find by calculation that their numbers up to this stage were as follows: first there was the fleet of 1207 ships belonging to the various nations which sailed from Asia, with its original complement of 241,400 men – allowing 200 to each ship. Each of these vessels carried, apart from native soldiers – or marines – and in addition to the crew, thirty fighting men who were either Persians, Medes, or Sacae, making an additional 36,210. Add to these the crews of the penteconters, carrying roughly 80 men apiece; there were, as I have already said, 3000 penteconters, so this will make another 240,000. This was the naval force brought by Xerxes from Asia, and the total number of men aboard comes to 517,610.

As to the army, the infantry was 1,700,000 strong and the

cavalry 80,000. Then there were the Arabian camel corps and the Libyan charioteers, which I reckon as a further 20,000. The grand total, therefore, of land and sea forces brought over from Asia was 2,317,610, excluding army servants and the men in the food transports. To this, moreover, must be added the troops which were collected as Xerxes passed through Europe. Here I must be content with a rough estimate. The Greeks of Thrace and of the islands off the coast furnished, I should say, 120 ships: this would make 24,000 men. The strength of the infantry furnished by the Thracians, Paeonians, Eordi, Bottiaei, Chalcidians, Brygi, Pierians, Macedonians, Perrhaebians, Enionians, Dolopes, Magnetes, Achaeans, and the coastal settlements of Thrace, I would put at 300,000. So by adding these to the original force from Asia we get a total of 2,641,610 fighting men. Lastly, it is my belief that the army servants and camp followers, the crews of the provision boats and of other craft which sailed with the expedition were not less, but more, numerous than the actual fighting troops; however I will reckon them as neither more nor fewer, but as equal, and thus arrive at my final estimate, which is, that Xerxes, the son of Darius, reached Sepias and Thermopylae at the head of an army consisting, in all, of 5,283,220 men.[59]

So much for the actual army and its attendants; as for eunuchs, female cooks, and concubines, no one could attempt an estimate of their number, any more than of the various pack-animals and Indian dogs which followed the army. They were far too numerous to count. I am not surprised that with so many people and so many beasts the rivers sometimes failed to provide enough water; what does amaze me is that the food never gave out, for I reckon that if no more than a quart of meal was the daily ration for one man, the total daily consumption would have amounted to 110,340 bushels – and this without counting what was consumed by the women, eunuchs, pack-animals, and dogs. Amongst all these immense numbers there was not a man who, for stature and noble bearing, was more worthy than Xerxes to wield so vast a power.

The Persian fleet, as I have mentioned, made the Magnesian coast between the town of Casthanea and Cape Sepias, and on its arrival the leading ships made fast to the land, while the remainder, as there was not much room on the short stretch of beach, came to anchor and lay offshore in lines, eight deep. In this position they remained during the night; but at dawn next day the weather, which was clear and calm, suddenly changed, and the fleet was caught in a heavy blow from the east – a 'Hellespontian', as the people there call it – which raised a confused sea like a pot on the boil. Those who realized in time that the blow was coming, and all who happened to be lying in a convenient position, managed to beach their vessels and to get them clear of the water before they were damaged, and thus saved their own lives as well; but the ships which were caught offshore were driven some on to the place called the Ovens at the foot of Mt Pelion, others on to the beach itself; a number were driven on to Sepias, and others, again, were forced ashore off the towns of Meliboea and Casthanea. The storm was very violent and there was no chance of riding it out.

189   There is a story that the Athenians had called upon Boreas to help them, in consequence of another oracle, by which they were advised to 'ask the assistance of their son-in-law'. Boreas, according to the Greek account, married a woman of Attica, Erechtheus' daughter Orithyia, and in consequence of this marriage the Athenians (so the tale goes) supposed Boreas to be their son-in-law; so when they observed from their station at Chalcis in Euboea that a storm was coming – or possibly even sooner – they offered sacrifice to Boreas and Orithyia and begged them to come to their aid and to repeat the former disaster at Athos by once again destroying the Persian fleet. I cannot say if this was really the reason why the fleet was caught at anchor by the north-easter, but the Athenians are quite positive about it: Boreas, they maintain, had helped them before, and it was Boreas who was responsible for what occurred on this occasion too. On their return home they built him a shrine by the river Ilissus.

190   Four hundred ships, at the lowest estimate, are said to have been lost in this disaster, and the loss of life and of treasure was beyond reckoning. It proved, however, to be a very good thing indeed for a certain Magnesian named Ameinocles, the son of

Cretines, who owned land in the neighbourhood of Sepias; for he subsequently picked up a large number of gold and silver drinking-cups which were washed ashore, and found Persian treasure-chests containing more gold, beyond counting. This made him a very rich man, though in other respects he proved less fortunate; for he met with the distressing disaster of having killed his son.

The number of merchant vessels and other craft lost in the 191 storm was too great to reckon. Indeed, such was the magnitude of the disaster that the Persian naval commanders, fearing that the Thessalians might take advantage of their desperate plight to attack them, protected themselves by building a high barricade out of the wreckage. The storm lasted three days, after which the Magi brought it to an end by sacrificial offerings, and by putting spells on the wind, and by further offerings to Thetis and the sea-nymphs – or, of course, it may be that the wind just dropped naturally. The reason why the Magi sacrificed to Thetis was that they had learnt from the Ionians that she was supposed to have been carried off from here by Peleus, and that all the headland of Sepias was sacred to her and the other daughters of Nereus. In any case, on the fourth day the weather was fine 192 again.

On the second day of the storm the look-out men on the Euboean hills came hurrying to the Greeks and described in detail the destruction of the Persian ships. On hearing the news, they offered prayers of thanksgiving and libations of wine to Poseidon the saviour, and made all speed to return to their station at Artemisium, in the expectation that only a few ships would be left to oppose them. For the second time, therefore, they lay off Artemisium. From that day to this they have always addressed Poseidon by the title of Saviour.

Meanwhile, after the wind had dropped and the sea had gone 193 down, the Persians got the ships they had hauled ashore into the water again, and proceeded along the coast round the southern point of Magnesia straight into the bay which leads to Pagasae. There is a place in this bay where it is said that Heracles, at the start of the voyage of the *Argo* to fetch the Golden Fleece from Aea in Colchis, was put ashore by Jason and his companions to get water, and was left behind. The place got the name of Aphetae – 'putting forth' – because it was the intention of the Argonauts to make it their point of departure after watering the ship. It was here that Xerxes' fleet brought up.

194   Fifteen of the Persian ships were far behind in getting under way, and the men aboard, happening to catch sight of the Greek ships at Artemisium, mistook them for their own, and on making towards them fell into the enemies' hands. These vessels were under the command of Sandoces, the son of Thamasius and governor of Cyme in Aeolis. Sandoces, who was one of the royal judges, had been arrested by Darius some time before and crucified, on a charge of perverting justice for money. But while he was actually on the cross, Darius came to the conclusion that his services to the royal house outweighed his offences, and realizing in consequence that he had acted with more promptitude than wisdom, caused him to be taken down.[60] Thus he escaped with his life from King Darius, but this time, when he fell foul of the Greek navy, he was not destined to escape again; for as soon as the Greeks saw his squadron approaching they realized his mistake, put to sea, and captured

195   it without difficulty. Amongst the prisoners in one of the ships was Aridolis, the tyrant of Alabanda in Caria; in another was Penthylus, the son of Demonous, the Paphian commander, who had brought twelve ships from Paphos. Eleven of them were lost at Sepias in the storm, and he was taken as he sailed to Artemisium in the only one which survived. The Greeks questioned these two prisoners on all they wished to know about Xerxes' forces, and then sent them away in chains to the Isthmus of Corinth.

196   Meanwhile the Persian fleet, with the exception of the fifteen ships under Sandoces' command, arrived safely at Aphetae. Two days previously Xerxes with the army had passed through Thessaly and Achaea and entered the country of the Malians. While he was in Thessaly he had held races between the native horses and his own, because he had heard that the horses of Thessaly were the best in Greece. The Greek mares were, however, soundly beaten. Of the Thessalian rivers, the only one which failed to supply enough water for the troops was the

Onochonus; but in Achaea even the biggest – the Apidanus –
scarcely sufficed.

At Halos in Achaea Xerxes' guides, wishing to give him all   197
the information they could, told him the local account about
the Laphystian Zeus. The story is that Athamas, the son of
Aeolus, plotted with Ino the death of Phrixus; subsequently
the Achaeans in obedience to an oracle laid a penalty upon the
descendants of Phrixus and his son Cytissorus: this was that the
eldest of the family should be forbidden to enter the Council
Chamber – or People's House, as the Achaeans call it – and that
they themselves should keep watch to see that the ban was
observed. If one of them does enter the Chamber, he can never
get out again except to be offered as a sacrifice. They went on
to relate that many of them, when recognized entering the
Chamber and threatened with death in this way, escape in terror
to some other country, and perhaps return long afterwards.
They further described to Xerxes the ritual of the sacrifice, how
the man was always made to wear a wreath, and was led to his
death in a solemn procession. The reason why the descendants
of Cytissorus and Phrixus are forced to endure this treatment is
that when the Achaeans were about to kill Aeolus' son Athamas
as a sin-offering, or scapegoat, on behalf of their country,
Cytissorus came from Aea in Colchis and rescued him, thus
calling down the wrath of God upon his descendants.

In consequence of this story Xerxes kept clear of the sacred
ground and issued orders to his army to do the same; he showed
respect also to the house and precinct of the family of Athamas.

From Thessaly and Achaea Xerxes went on into Malis, fol-   198
lowing the coast of a bay in which there is a daily rise and fall
of tide. The country round this bay is flat – broad in one part,
very narrow in another; all round is a chain of lofty and trackless
mountains, called the Cliffs of Trachis, which enclose the whole
territory of Malis. As one comes from Achaea, the first town on
the bay is Anticyra, near to which is the mouth of the Spercheius,
a river which comes down from the country of the Enianes.
Some three and a half miles further on there is another river, the
Dyras, which, according to the legend, burst from the ground
to help Heracles when he was burning;[61] then, at about the same   199

distance, is a third stream, the Melas, and rather more than half a mile beyond that is the town of Trachis. At Trachis the space between the hills and the sea is more extensive than anywhere else, the area of the plain being over 5000 acres.[62] South of Trachis there is a cleft in the ring of hills; through it the river
200   Asopus issues, and comes down to the foot of the hills. Further south another small stream, the Phoenix, runs down from the hills and joins the Asopus. It is at the Phoenix that the plain is narrowest, there being room here only for a single cart-track. From the Phoenix to Thermopylae is about two miles, and between them lies the village of Anthela, which the Asopus passes just before it reaches the sea. Round Anthela the ground is more open; there is a temple there dedicated to Demeter of the Amphictyons, as well as seats for the deputies of the Amphictyonic league, and a shrine of Amphictyon himself.[63]
201   The position, then, was that Xerxes was lying with his force at Trachis in Malian territory, while the Greeks occupied the pass known locally as Pylae – though Thermopylae is the common Greek name. Such were the respective positions of the two armies, one being in control of all the country from Trachis
202   northward, the other of the whole mainland to the south. The Greek force which here awaited the coming of Xerxes was made up of the following contingents: 300 hoplites from Sparta, 500 from Tegea, 500 from Mantinea, 120 from Orchomenus in Arcadia, 1000 from the rest of Arcadia; from Corinth there were 400, from Phlius 200, and from Mycenae 80. In addition to these troops from the Peloponnese, there were the Boeotian
203   contingents of 700 from Thespiae and 400 from Thebes. The Locrians of Opus and the Phocians had also obeyed the call to arms, the former sending all the men they had, the latter one thousand. The other Greeks had induced these two towns to send troops by a message to the effect that they themselves were merely an advance force, and that the main body of the allies was daily expected; the sea, moreover, was strongly held by the fleet of Athens and Aegina and the other naval forces. Thus there was no cause for alarm – for, after all, it was not a god who threatened Greece, but a man, and there neither was nor ever would be a man who was not born with a good chance of

misfortune – and the greater the man, the greater the misfortune. The present enemy was no exception; he too was human, and was sure to be disappointed of his great expectations.

The appeal succeeded, and Opus and Phocis sent their troops to Trachis. The contingents of the various states were under their own officers, but the most respected was Leonidas the Spartan, who was in command of the whole army. Leonidas traced his descent directly back to Heracles, through Anaxandrides and Leon (his father and grandfather), Eurycratides, Anaxander, Eurycrates, Polydorus, Alcamenes, Telechles, Archelaus, Agesilaus, Doryssus, Leobotas, Echestratus, Agis, Eurysthenes, Aristodemus, Aristomachus, Cleodaeus – and so to Hyllus, who was Heracles' son. He had come to be king of Sparta quite unexpectedly, for as he had two elder brothers, Cleomenes and Dorieus, he had no thought of himself succeeding to the throne. Dorieus, however, was killed in Sicily, and when Cleomenes also died without an heir, Leonidas found himself next in the succession. He was older than Cleombrotus, Anaxandrides' youngest son, and was, moreover, married to Cleomenes' daughter. The three hundred men whom he brought on this occasion to Thermopylae were chosen by himself, all fathers of living sons. He also took with him the Thebans I mentioned, under the command of Leontiades, the son of Eurymachus. The reason why he made a special point of taking troops from Thebes, and from Thebes only, was that the Thebans were strongly suspected of Persian sympathies, so he called upon them to play their part in the war in order to see if they would answer the call, or openly refuse to join the confederacy. They did send troops, but their sympathy was nevertheless with the enemy. Leonidas and his three hundred were sent by Sparta in advance of the main army, in order that the sight of them might encourage the other confederates to fight and prevent them from going over to the enemy, as they were quite capable of doing if they knew that Sparta was hanging back; the intention was, when the Carneia was over (for it was that festival which prevented the Spartans from taking the field in the ordinary way), to leave a garrison in the city and march with all the troops at their disposal. The other allied states proposed to act similarly;

204

205

206

for the Olympic festival happened to fall just at this same period. None of them ever expected the battle at Thermopylae to be decided so soon – which was the reason why they sent only advance parties there.

207   The Persian army was now close to the pass, and the Greeks, suddenly doubting their power to resist, held a conference to consider the advisability of retreat. It was proposed by the Peloponnesians generally that the army should fall back upon the Peloponnese and hold the Isthmus; but when the Phocians and Locrians expressed their indignation at this suggestion, Leonidas gave his vote for staying where they were and sending, at the same time, an appeal for reinforcements to the various states of the confederacy, as their numbers were inadequate to cope with the Persians.[64]

208   During the conference Xerxes sent a man on horseback to ascertain the strength of the Greek force and to observe what the troops were doing. He had heard before he left Thessaly that a small force was concentrated here, led by the Lacedaemonians under Leonidas of the house of Heracles. The Persian rider approached the camp and took a thorough survey of all he could see – which was not, however, the whole Greek army; for the men on the further side of the wall which, after its reconstruction, was now guarded, were out of sight. He did, none the less, carefully observe the troops who were stationed on the outside of the wall. At that moment these happened to be the Spartans, and some of them were stripped for exercise, while others were combing their hair. The Persian spy watched them in astonishment; nevertheless he made sure of their numbers, and of everything else he needed to know, as accurately as he could, and then rode quietly off. No one attempted to catch him, or took the least notice of him.

209   Back in his own camp he told Xerxes what he had seen. Xerxes was bewildered; the truth, namely that the Spartans were preparing themselves to die and deal death with all their strength, was beyond his comprehension, and what they were doing seemed to him merely absurd. Accordingly he sent for Demaratus, the son of Ariston, who had come with the army, and questioned him about the spy's report, in the hope of finding

out what the behaviour of the Spartans might mean. 'Once before,' Demaratus said, 'when we began our march against Greece, you heard me speak of these men. I told you then how I saw this enterprise would turn out, and you laughed at me. I strive for nothing, my lord, more earnestly than to observe the truth in your presence; so hear me once more. These men have come to fight us for possession of the pass, and for that struggle they are preparing. It is the custom of the Spartans to pay careful attention to their hair when they are about to risk their lives.[65] But I assure you that if you can defeat these men and the rest of the Spartans who are still at home, there is no other people in the world who will dare to stand firm or lift a hand against you. You have now to deal with the finest kingdom in Greece, and with the bravest men.'

Xerxes, unable to believe what Demaratus said, asked further how it was possible that so small a force could fight with his army. 'My lord,' Demaratus replied, 'treat me as a liar, if what I have foretold does not take place.' But still Xerxes was unconvinced.

For four days Xerxes waited, in constant expectation that the Greeks would make good their escape; then, on the fifth, when still they had made no move and their continued presence seemed mere impudent and reckless folly, he was seized with rage and sent forward the Medes and Cissians with orders to take them alive and bring them into his presence. The Medes charged, and in the struggle which ensued many fell; but others took their places, and in spite of terrible losses refused to be beaten off. They made it plain enough to anyone, and not least to the king himself, that he had in his army many men, indeed, but few soldiers. All day the battle continued; the Medes, after their rough handling, were at length withdrawn and their place was taken by Hydarnes and his picked Persian troops – the King's Immortals – who advanced to the attack in full confidence of bringing the business to a quick and easy end. But, once engaged, they were no more successful than the Medes had been; all went as before, the two armies fighting in a confined space, the Persians using shorter spears than the Greeks and having no advantage from their numbers.

On the Spartan side it was a memorable fight; they were men who understood war pitted against an inexperienced enemy, and amongst the feints they employed was to turn their backs in a body and pretend to be retreating in confusion, whereupon the enemy would pursue them with a great clatter and roar; but the Spartans, just as the Persians were on them, would wheel and face them and inflict in the new struggle innumerable casualties. The Spartans had their losses too, but not many. At last the Persians, finding that their assaults upon the pass, whether by divisions or by any other way they could think of, were all 212 useless, broke off the engagement and withdrew. Xerxes was watching the battle from where he sat; and it is said that in the course of the attacks three times, in terror for his army, he leapt to his feet.

Next day the fighting began again, but with no better success for the Persians, who renewed their onslaught in the hope that the Greeks, being so few in number, might be badly enough disabled by wounds to prevent further resistance. But the Greeks never slackened; their troops were ordered in divisions corresponding to the states from which they came, and each division took its turn in the line except the Phocian, which had been posted to guard the track over the mountains. So when the Persians found that things were no better for them than on the previous day, they once more withdrew.

213   How to deal with the situation Xerxes had no idea; but just then, a man from Malis, Ephialtes, the son of Eurydemus, came, in hope of a rich reward, to tell the king about the track which led over the hills to Thermopylae – and thus he was to prove the death of the Greeks who held the pass.

Later on, Ephialtes, in fear of the Spartans, fled to Thessaly, and in his absence a price was put upon his head by the Amphictyons assembled at Pylae. Some time afterwards he returned to Anticyra, where he was killed by Athenades of Trachis. Athenades killed him not for his treachery but for another reason, which I will explain further on;[66] but the Spartans 214 honoured him none the less on that account. According to another story, it was Onetes, the son of Phanagoras of Carystus, and Corydallus of Anticyra who spoke to Xerxes and showed the Persians the way round by the mountain track. This is entirely unconvincing, my first criterion being the fact that the Amphictyons, presumably after careful inquiry, set a price not upon Onetes and Corydallus but upon Ephialtes of Trachis, and my second, that there is no doubt that the accusation of treachery was the reason for Ephialtes' flight. Certainly Onetes, even though he was not a native of Malis, might have known about the track, if he had spent much time in the neighbourhood – but it was Ephialtes, and no one else, who showed the Persians the way, and I put his name on record as the guilty one.

Xerxes found Ephialtes' offer most satisfactory. He was 215 delighted with it, and promptly sent off Hydarnes with the troops under his command. They left camp about the time the lamps are lit.

The track was originally discovered by the Malians of the neighbourhood; they afterwards used it to help the Thessalians, taking them over it to attack Phocis at the time when the Phocians were protected from invasion by the wall which they had built across the pass. So long, then, have its sinister uses been known to the Malians! The track begins at the Asopus, the 216 stream which flows through the narrow gorge, and, running along the ridge of the mountain – which, like the track itself, is called Anopaea – ends at Alpenos, the first Locrian settlement as one comes from Malis, near the rock known as Black–Buttocks' Stone and the seats of the Cercopes. Just here is the narrowest part of the pass.

This, then, was the mountain track which the Persians took, 217 after crossing the Asopus. They marched throughout the night, with the mountains of Oeta on their right hand and those of Trachis on their left. By early dawn they were at the summit of the ridge, near the spot where the Phocians, as I mentioned before, stood on guard with a thousand men, to watch the track and protect their country. The Phocians had volunteered for this service to Leonidas, the lower road being held as already described.

The ascent of the Persians had been concealed by the oak-218 woods which cover all these hills, and it was only when they were up that the Phocians became aware of their approach; for there was no wind, and the marching feet made a loud swishing and rustling in the fallen leaves. Leaping to their feet, the Phocians were in the act of arming themselves when the enemy was upon them. The Persians were surprised at the sight of troops preparing to resist; they had expected no opposition – yet here was a body of men barring their way. Hydarnes asked Ephialtes who they were, for his first fearful thought was that they might be Spartans; but on learning the truth he prepared to engage them. The Persian arrows flew thick and fast, and the Phocians, supposing themselves to be the main object of the attack, hurriedly withdrew to the highest point of the mountain, where they made ready to face destruction. But the Persians with Ephialtes and Hydarnes paid no further attention to them, but passed on along the descending track with all possible speed.

219   The Greeks at Thermopylae had their first warning of the death that was coming with the dawn from the seer Megistias, who read their doom in the victims of sacrifice; deserters, too, came in during the night with news of the Persian flank movement, and lastly, just as day was breaking, the look-out men came running from the hills. In council of war their opinions were divided, some urging that they must not abandon their post, others the opposite. The result was that the army split: some dispersed, contingents returning to their various cities, while others made ready to stand by Leonidas. It is said that Leonidas himself dismissed them, to spare their lives, but thought it unbecoming for the Spartans under his command to desert the post which they had originally come to guard.[67] I myself am inclined to think that he dismissed them when he realized that they had no heart for the fight and were unwilling to take their share of the danger; at the same time honour forbade that he himself should go. And indeed by remaining at his post he left great glory behind him, and Sparta did not lose her prosperity, as might otherwise have happened; for right at the outset of the war the Spartans had been told by the Delphic oracle that either their city must be laid waste by the foreigner or a Spartan king be killed. The prophecy was in hexameter verse and ran as follows:

Hear your fate, O dwellers in Sparta of the wide spaces;
Either your famed, great town must be sacked by Perseus' sons,
Or, if that be not, the whole land of Lacedaemon
Shall mourn the death of a king of the house of Heracles,
For not the strength of lions or of bulls shall hold him,
Strength against strength; for he has the power of Zeus,
And will not be checked till one of these two he has consumed.

I believe it was the thought of this oracle, combined with his wish to lay up for the Spartans a treasure of fame in which no other city should share, that made Leonidas dismiss those troops; I do not think that they deserted, or went off without orders, because of a difference of opinion. Moreover, I am **221** strongly supported in this view by the case of the seer Megistias, who was with the army – an Acarnanian, said to be of the clan of Melampus – who foretold the coming doom from his inspection of the sacrificial victims. He quite plainly received orders from Leonidas to quit Thermopylae, to save him from sharing the army's fate. He refused to go, but he sent his only son, who was serving with the forces.

Thus it was that the confederate troops, by Leonidas' orders, **222** abandoned their posts and left the pass, all except the Thespians and the Thebans who remained with the Spartans. The Thebans were detained by Leonidas as hostages very much against their will; but the Thespians of their own accord refused to desert Leonidas and his men, and stayed, and died with them. They were under the command of Demophilus the son of Diadromes.[68]

In the morning Xerxes poured a libation to the rising sun, **223** and then waited until the time when the market-place is filled before he began to move forward. This was according to Ephialtes' instructions, for the way down from the ridge is much shorter and more direct than the long and circuitous ascent. As the Persian army advanced to the assault, the Greeks under Leonidas, knowing that they were going to their deaths, went out into the wider part of the pass much further than they had done before; in the previous days' fighting they had been holding the wall and making sorties from behind it into the narrow neck, but now they fought outside the narrows. Many of the barbarians fell; behind them the company commanders plied their whips indiscriminately, driving the men on. Many fell into the sea and were drowned, and still more were trampled to death by one another. No one could count the number of the dead. The Greeks, who knew that the enemy were on their way round by the mountain track and that death was inevitable, put forth all their strength and fought with fury and desperation.

224 By this time most of their spears were broken, and they were killing Persians with their swords.

In the course of that fight Leonidas fell, having fought most gallantly, and many distinguished Spartans with him – their names I have learned, as those of men who deserve to be remembered; indeed, I have learned the names of all the three hundred. Amongst the Persian dead, too, were many men of high distinction, including two brothers of Xerxes, Habrocomes and Hyperanthes, sons of Darius by Artanes' daughter Phratagune. Artanes, the son of Hystaspes and grandson of Arsames, was Darius' brother; as Phratagune was his only child, his giving her to Darius was equivalent to giving him his entire estate.

225 There was a bitter struggle over the body of Leonidas; four times the Greeks drove the enemy off, and at last by their valour rescued it.[69] So it went on, until the troops with Ephialtes were close at hand; and then, when the Greeks knew that they had come, the character of the fighting changed. They withdrew again into the narrow neck of the pass, behind the wall, and took up a position in a single compact body – all except the Thebans – on the little hill at the entrance to the pass, where the stone lion in memory of Leonidas stands today. Here they resisted to the last, with their swords, if they had them, and, if not, with their hands and teeth, until the Persians, coming on from the front over the ruins of the wall and closing in from behind, finally overwhelmed them with missile weapons.

226 Of all the Spartans and Thespians who fought so valiantly the most signal proof of courage was given by the Spartan Dieneces. It is said that before the battle he was told by a native of Trachis that, when the Persians shot their arrows, there were so many of them that they hid the sun. Dieneces, however, quite

unmoved by the thought of the strength of the Persian army, merely remarked: 'This is pleasant news that the stranger from Trachis brings us: if the Persians hide the sun, we shall have our battle in the shade.' He is said to have left on record other sayings, too, of a similar kind, by which he will be remembered. After Dieneces the greatest distinction was won by two Spartan brothers, Alpheus and Maron, the sons of Orsiphantus; and of the Thespians the man to gain the highest glory was a certain Dithyrambus, the son of Harmatides.

The dead were buried where they fell, and with them the men who had been killed before those dismissed by Leonidas left the pass. Over them is this inscription, in honour of the whole force:

> Four thousand here from Pelops' land
> Against three million once did stand.[70]

The Spartans have a special epitaph; it runs:

> Go tell the Spartans, you who read:
> We took their orders, and here lie dead.

For the seer Megistias there is the following:

> Here lies Megistias, who died
> When the Mede passed Spercheius' tide.
> A prophet; yet he scorned to save
> Himself, but shared the Spartans' grave.

The columns with the epitaphs inscribed on them were erected in honour of the dead by the Amphictyons – though the epitaph upon the seer Megistias was the work of Simonides, the son of Leoprepes, who put it there for friendship's sake.

Two of the three hundred Spartans, Eurytus and Aristodemus, are said to have been suffering from acute inflammation of the eyes, on account of which they were dismissed by Leonidas before the battle and went to Alpeni to recuperate. These two men might have agreed together to return in safety to Sparta; or, if they did not wish to do so, they might have shared the fate of their friends. But, unable to agree which course to take, they quarrelled, and Eurytus had no sooner heard that the Persians had made their way round by the mountain track than he called for his armour, put it on, and ordered his helot to lead him to the scene of the battle. The helot obeyed, and then took to his heels, and Eurytus, plunging into the thick of things, was killed. Aristodemus, on the other hand, finding that his heart failed him, stayed behind at Alpeni. Now if only Aristodemus had been involved – if he alone had returned sick to Sparta – or if they had both gone back together, I do not think that the Spartans would have been angry; but as one was killed and the other took advantage of the excuse, which was open to both of them, to save his skin, they could hardly help being very angry indeed with Aristodemus.

230   There is another explanation of how Aristodemus got back alive to Sparta: according to this, he was sent from camp with a message, and though he might have returned in time to take part in the fighting, he deliberately loitered on the way and so saved himself, while the man who accompanied him on the errand joined in the battle and was killed. In any case, he was

231   met upon his return with reproach and disgrace; no Spartan would give him a light to kindle his fire, or speak to him, and he was called a Trembler. However, he afterwards made amends for everything at the battle of Plataea.[71]

232   There is also a story that one more of the three hundred – Pantites – survived. He had been sent with a message into Thessaly, and on his return to Sparta found himself in such disgrace that he hanged himself.

233   The Thebans under Leontiades remained for a time with the army and were compelled to make some show of resistance to the enemy; but as soon as they saw that things were going in favour of Persia, they took the opportunity of Leonidas' hurried retreat to the little hill, where his last stand was made, to detach themselves from his force; they then approached the enemy with outstretched hands, crying out that in their zeal for the Persian interest they had been amongst the first to give earth and water to the king, and had no share in the responsibility for the injury done him, because they had come to Thermopylae against their

will. And when it was backed up by the evidence of the Thessalians, it saved their lives. Nevertheless, their luck did not hold
in every respect; for a few were killed by the Persians on their
first approach, and all the rest were branded by Xerxes' orders
with the royal mark, beginning with Leontiades their commander. Leontiades' son Eurymachus was afterwards killed by
the Plataeans when he was leading a force of four hundred
Theban troops at the capture of Plataea.[72]

Such, then, is the story of the Greeks' struggle at Thermopylae.   234
Xerxes, when the battle was over, summoned Demaratus to ask
him some questions. 'Demaratus,' he began, 'you are a good
man – the truth of your words proves it. Everything has turned
out as you said it would. Now tell me – how many more
Lacedaemonians are there? And how many of them are as good
soldiers as these were? Or are they all as good?' 'Sire,' Demaratus
answered, 'there are a great many men and many towns in
Lacedaemon; but what you really want to know I will now tell
you: there is in that country a town called Sparta, which contains
about eight thousand men. All these are the equals of those who
fought in this battle. The other men in Lacedaemon are not their
equals – but good soldiers none the less.'

'Demaratus,' said Xerxes, 'tell me what you think would be
the easiest way of defeating these people. You were once their
king, so you must be well acquainted with all the ins and outs
of their policy.'

'Sire,' replied Demaratus, 'if you are really serious in asking   235
my advice, I am bound to tell you what I consider the best
plan. Suppose you send three hundred ships from the fleet to
Lacedaemon. Off the coast there is an island called Cythera –
Chilon, the wisest man who ever lived amongst us, once said
that it would be better for the Spartans if it were sunk beneath
the sea, for he always expected that it would provide just such
an opportunity for a hostile force as what I am now suggesting.
It was not, of course, your attack that he foresaw – it was the
prospect of any attack from any quarter that alarmed him. This,
then, is my proposal: let your ships make Cythera their base,
and from it spread terror over Lacedaemon. With a war of their
own, on their own doorstep, as it were, you need not fear that

they will help the other Greeks while your army is engaged in conquering them.[73] Thus the rest of Greece will be enslaved first and Lacedaemon will be left alone and helpless. On the other hand, if you decide against this plan, you may expect more trouble; for there is a narrow isthmus in the Peloponnese, and in it you will find all the troops from that part of Greece who have formed a league to resist you, and you will have to face bloodier battles than any you have yet witnessed. But if you take my advice, the Isthmus and the Peloponnesian towns will fall into your hands without a blow.'

236   Achaemenes, Xerxes' brother and commander of the fleet, who happened to be present and was afraid Xerxes might be persuaded to adopt Demaratus' proposal, spoke in answer: 'My lord,' he said, 'I see that you are allowing yourself to be influenced by a man who envies your success, and is probably a traitor to you. He is a typical Greek, and this is just how they love to behave – envying anyone else's good fortune and hating any power greater than their own. In our present circumstances, when we have already had four hundred ships wrecked, if you detach another three hundred from the fleet for a voyage round the Peloponnese, the enemy will be a match for us. Keep the fleet together, and they will never dare risk an engagement – the disparity in numbers will see to that; moreover, if fleet and army keep in touch and advance together, each can support the other; separate them, and you will be no more use to the fleet than the fleet to you. Only lay your own plans soundly, and you can afford not to worry about the enemy, or to keep wondering what they will do, how many they are, or where they will elect to make a stand. They are quite capable of managing their own affairs, just as we are of managing ours. If the Spartans risk another battle with us, they will certainly not repair the injury they have already received.'

237   'Achaemenes,' Xerxes replied, 'I think you are right, and I will take your advice. Nevertheless, though Demaratus' judgement is not so good as yours, he told me in good faith what he thought best for me. I will not accept your suggestion that he is secretly hostile to my cause; I have evidence of his loyalty in what he has said on previous occasions, and, apart from that, there is the

well-known fact that a man often hates his next-door neighbour and is jealous of his success, and when asked for advice will not tell him what he really thinks will help him most – unless, indeed, he is a man of exceptional virtue, such as one seldom finds. But the relationship between men of different countries is very different from that between men of the same town; a man is full of sympathy for the good fortune of a foreign friend, and will always give him the best advice he can. Demaratus is a foreigner and my guest; I should be obliged, therefore, if everyone would refrain from maligning him in future.'

After this conversation Xerxes went over the battlefield to see the bodies, and having been told that Leonidas was king of Sparta and commander of the Spartan force, ordered his head to be cut off and fixed on a stake. This is in my opinion the strongest evidence – though there is plenty more – that King Xerxes, while Leonidas was still alive, felt fiercer anger against him than against any other man; had that not been so, he would never have committed this outrage upon his body; for normally the Persians, more than any other nation I know of, honour men who distinguish themselves in war.[74] However, Xerxes' order was carried out. 238

I will now return to a point in my story where I omitted to mention something.[75] The Spartans were the first to get the news that Xerxes was preparing an expedition against Greece; thereupon they sent to the Delphic oracle and received the answer of which I spoke a little while ago. The way they received the news was very remarkable: Demaratus, the son of Ariston, who was an exile in Persia, was not, I imagine – and as is only natural to suppose – well disposed towards the Spartans; so it is open to question whether what he did was inspired by benevolence or by malicious pleasure. Anyway, as soon as news reached him at Susa that Xerxes had decided upon the invasion of Greece, he felt that he must pass on the information to Sparta. As the danger of discovery was great, there was only one way in which he could contrive to get the message through: this was by scraping the wax off a pair of wooden folding tablets, writing on the wood underneath what Xerxes intended to do, and then covering the message over with wax again. In this way the 239 tablets, being apparently blank, would cause no trouble with the guards along the road. When the message reached its destination, no one was able to guess the secret until, as I understand, Cleomenes' daughter Gorgo, who was the wife of Leonidas, divined it and told the others that, if they scraped the wax off, they would find something written on the wood underneath. This was done; the message was revealed and read, and afterwards passed on to the other Greeks. That, at any rate, is the story of what happened.

BOOK EIGHT

The following is the roll of the Greek naval force: 127 ships ₁
from Athens – partly manned by the Plataeans, whose courage
and patriotism led them to undertake this service in spite of
their ignorance of nautical matters; 40 from Corinth, 20 from
Megara, 20 more from Athens manned by crews from Chalcis,
18 from Aegina, 12 from Sicyon, 10 from Sparta, 8 from Epidaurus, 7 from Eretria, 5 from Troezen, 2 from Styra, and 2 –
together with two penteconters – from Ceos. Lastly, the Locrians
of Opus joined with seven penteconters.

These, then, were the states which sent ships to Artemisium, ₂
and I have given the number which each contributed. The total
strength of the fleet, excluding the penteconters, was thus 271
ships of war. The general officer in command, Eurybiades,
the son of Eurycleides, was provided by Sparta; for the other
members of the confederacy had stipulated for a Lacedaemonian
commander, declaring that rather than serve under an Athenian
they would break up the intended expedition altogether. From ₃
the first, even before Sicily was asked to join the alliance, there
had been talk of the advisability of giving Athens command of
the fleet; but the proposal had not been well received by the
allied states, and the Athenians waived their claim in the interest
of national survival, knowing that a quarrel about the command
would certainly mean the destruction of Greece.[1] They were,
indeed, perfectly right; for the evil of internal strife is worse than
united war in the same proportion as war itself is worse than
peace. It was their realization of the danger attendant upon lack
of unity which made them waive their claim, and they continued
to do so as long as Greece desperately needed their help. This

was made plain enough by their subsequent action; for when the Persians had been driven from Greece and the war had been carried to Persian territory, the Athenians made the insufferable behaviour of Pausanias their excuse for depriving the Lacedaemonians of the command.[2]

4   When the Greeks on their arrival at Artemisium found a large Persian fleet lying at Aphetae and all the neighbourhood full of troops, it was evident to them that things had gone very differently with the Persians from what they had expected. They were seized by panic, and began to consider abandoning Artemisium and making their escape into the inner parts of Greece. This greatly alarmed the Euboeans, who no sooner realized what they had in mind than they begged Eurybiades to stay at any rate long enough to allow them to move their children and servants to a place of safety. Eurybiades refused, whereupon they went to Themistocles, the Athenian commander, and by a bribe of thirty talents induced him so to arrange matters that the Greek fleet should stay and fight on the coast of Euboea.

5   The method Themistocles adopted to attain this object was to pass on to Eurybiades, as if it were a personal present from himself, a sixth part of the sum he had received from the Euboeans. This was enough to secure Eurybiades' consent; of the other commanders, however, there was still one who hesitated – Adeimantus son of Ocytus, the Corinthian, who declared that he would withdraw his ships from Artemisium. To him, therefore, Themistocles now addressed himself. 'Never,' he cried with an oath, 'shall you leave us in the lurch! I will give you more for staying with us than the Persian king would ever send you if you deserted us'; and without further delay he sent aboard Adeimantus' ship three talents of silver. So Adeimantus and Eurybiades yielded to bribery and the Euboeans' wishes were gratified; Themistocles, too, made something out of the transaction, for he kept the rest of the money himself. Nobody knew he had it, and the two men who had received their share imagined that it came from Athens especially for the purpose.

6   These were the circumstances which led to the Greeks engaging the Persians on the Euboean coast, and I will now describe the battle itself.[3]

The Persians reached Aphetae early in the afternoon, and saw for themselves what they had previously heard reported – namely that a small Greek force was concentrated at Artemisium. At once they were eager to engage, in the hope of capturing the Greek ships. It did not, however, seem advisable to advance, in the first instance, openly to the attack; for the Greeks, seeing them coming, might try to escape, and then, when darkness overtook them, they would be sure to get clear away. This would not do, as the Persians were determined that not even a fire-signaller (as they put it) must be allowed to escape alive. Laying their plans accordingly, they detached a squadron 7 of 200 ships with orders to sail outside Sciathus, in order to escape enemy observation, and then to turn southward round Euboea and into the Euripus by way of Caphareus and Geraestus; in this way they hoped to catch the Greeks in a trap, one squadron taking them in the rear and blocking their retreat, the rest of the fleet pressing upon them from in front. With this purpose in view the two hundred ships were dispatched, while the main body waited – for they did not intend to attack on that day, or until they knew by signal that the squadron coming up the Euripus had arrived. Meanwhile a review of the main fleet 8 was held at Aphetae, and while it was going on the following event occurred. Serving with the Persian force there was a man named Scyllias, a native of Scione and the most accomplished diver of his day, who after the wreck of the Persian ships at Pelion had saved a great deal of valuable property for his masters – besides getting a good deal for himself. This man had apparently been thinking for some time past of deserting to the Greeks, but no opportunity had occurred until then. I cannot say for certain how it was that he managed to reach the Greeks, and I am amazed if what is said is true; for, according to this, he dived under water at Aphetae and did not come up until he reached Artemisium – a distance of about ten miles. There are other somewhat tall stories, besides this, told about Scyllias – and also a few true ones; as to the one I have just related, my personal opinion is that he came to Artemisium in a boat. In any case, come he did; and on his arrival he lost no time in giving an account to the Greek commanders of all the circumstances of the disaster to the Persian fleet in the storm, and also told them about the squadron which was on its way round Euboea.[4]

9 The Greek commanders at once proceeded to discuss the situation which this piece of intelligence produced; and after a long debate it was decided to stay where they were until after midnight, and then put to sea to meet the Persians who were coming up the Euripus. However, as time went on and they met with no opposition, they waited till the evening of the following day and then attacked the main enemy fleet, with the intention of testing Persian seamanship and tactics.

10 When the officers and men of Xerxes' fleet saw the Greeks moving to the attack with such a small force, they thought they were mad and at once got under way themselves, in confident expectation of making an easy capture; nor, indeed, was the expectation unreasonable, in view of the disparity in numbers – the Greek ships being few, and their own many times as numerous, as well as faster. Thus assured of their superiority, they developed a movement to surround the enemy. Those of the Ionians who had been forced to serve with the Persian fleet in spite of their real sympathy with the Greek cause, were much distressed at the sight of the gradual encirclement of the Greeks, and convinced, in view of their apparent weakness, that not a man amongst them would escape alive; those, on the other hand, who welcomed the situation, entered into competition with each other to be the first to win a reward from Xerxes for the capture of an Athenian ship – for throughout the Persian fleet it was the Athenians who were most talked of.

11 At the first signal for action the Greek squadron formed into a close circle – bows outward, sterns to the centre;[5] then, at the second signal, with little room to manoeuvre and lying, as they were, bows-on to the enemy, they set to work, and succeeded in capturing thirty Persian ships. Amongst the prisoners was Philaon, the son of Chersis and brother of Gorgus the king of Salamis, and a person of repute in the enemy force. The first Greek to take a prize was the Athenian Lycomedes son of Aeschraeus. He was decorated for valour after the battle.

After this success, when darkness put an end to the fighting, the Greeks returned to Artemisium, and the Persians – who had

had a considerable shock – to Aphetae. The only Greek in the Persian force to desert and join his countrymen during the action was Antidorus, the Lemnian; the Athenians afterwards showed their appreciation by giving him a grant of land in Salamis.

After dark – the season was midsummer – there was a very 12 violent rainstorm, which lasted all night, accompanied by much thunder from the direction of Pelion. Dead bodies and bits of wreckage, drifting up to Aphetae, fell athwart the bows of the ships which lay there, and fouled the oar-blades of any that were under way; this, and the noise of the thunderstorm, caused a panic amongst the Persian troops, who began to think their last hour was come: they had, indeed, had much to put up with – for almost before they could draw breath again after the storm at Pelion, which wrecked so many of their ships, they were faced with a hard fight at sea, and now, on top of that, they were exposed to floods of rain, the rushing of swollen streams into the sea, and a tremendous thunderstorm.

For the Persians at Aphetae it was a bad enough night, but it 13 was far worse for the squadron which had been ordered to sail round Euboea, for they were at sea when the storm caught them. Their fate was miserable: just as they were off the Hollows of Euboea the wind and rain began, and every ship, overpowered and forced to run blind before it, piled up on the rocks. God was indeed doing everything possible to reduce the superiority of the Persian fleet and bring it down to the size of the Greek.[6] So much for the disaster off the Hollows. 14

The Persians at Aphetae were very glad to see the dawn next morning, and did not feel like taking any further risks; it was enough for them, badly shaken as they were, to let the ships lie and attempt nothing for the present. Meanwhile the Greeks received a reinforcement of fifty-three ships from Athens; the arrival of this fresh squadron, together with the news of the loss in the storm of the whole Persian force which was sailing round Euboea, was a great encouragement, and the Greeks, on the strength of it, waiting till the same time as on the previous day, once again put to sea and attacked some Cilician vessels; these they destroyed and then, at the approach of darkness, they returned to Artemisium.

15   The Persian commanders were humiliated at receiving such
rough treatment from so small a fleet; they were beginning,
moreover, to be alarmed at the thought of what Xerxes might
do to them; so on the third day they took the initiative, and,
without waiting for the Greeks to move, made their preparations
and put to sea round about midday. It so happened that these
battles at sea took place on the same days as the battles at
Thermopylae, and in each case the object was similar – to defend
the passage into the heart of Greece: the fleet was fighting for
the Euripus just as the army with Leonidas was fighting for the
pass. So the Greek cry was to stop the enemy from getting
through, while the Persians aimed at destroying the defending
forces in order to clear the passage.

16   Xerxes' fleet now moved forward in good order to the attack,
while the Greeks at Artemisium quietly awaited their approach.
Then the Persians adopted a crescent formation and came on
with the intention of surrounding their enemy, whereupon the
Greeks advanced to meet them, and the fight began. In this
engagement the two fleets were evenly matched – the Persian,
by its mere size, proving its own greatest enemy, as constant
confusion was caused by the ships fouling one another. None
the less they made a brave fight of it, to avoid the disgrace of
defeat by so small an enemy force. The Greek losses both in
ships and men were heavy, those of the Persians much heavier.
Finally the action was broken off with such results as I have
17   described. On the Persian side it was the Egyptians who came
out of it with the best record, their most notable achievement
being the capture of five Greek ships together with their crews;
of the Greeks the most conspicuous were the Athenians – and
in particular Cleinias, the son of Alcibiades, who was serving in
his own ship manned by two hundred men, all at his own
personal expense.[7]

18   Both sides were glad when they parted and made all speed
back to their moorings. The Greeks, once they were clear of
the fighting, did, indeed, manage to possess themselves of the
floating bodies and to salve the wreckage; nevertheless they had
been so roughly handled – especially the Athenians, half of
whose ships were damaged – that they determined to quit their

station and withdraw further south.[8] At this point it occurred 19
to Themistocles that if the Ionian and Carian contingents could
be detached from the Persian force, the Greeks would be able
to deal successfully with the rest; accordingly he called his
officers to a conference on the beach, to which the people of
Euboea were already driving their herds. Here he told them that
he thought he had a plan, which might succeed in depriving
Xerxes' fleet of its finest units. For the moment he gave no
further details of what the plan was, but merely advised them, in
view of the circumstances, to slaughter as many of the Euboean
herds as they pleased, as it was better that their own troops
should have them than the enemy. He further suggested that
every officer should order his men to light fires as usual; as for
the withdrawal from Artemisium, he made himself responsible
for choosing the proper moment and for seeing that they got
home safely. These proposals proved acceptable; so the commanders at once had fires lighted, and the men set to on the
herds.

I should add here that the Euboeans had paid no attention to 20
the oracle of Bacis, supposing it to have no significance; they
had taken no precautions against the threat of war, either by
removing property from the island or by getting in stores, and
consequently found themselves in a highly dangerous position.
The oracle was as follows:

> When one of foreign speech casts a papyrus yoke upon the sea,
> Bethink you to keep the bleating goats far from Euboea.

This warning they ignored; and the result was great suffering,
both then and later, in the troubles which were daily expected.

While the Greeks were thus occupied, their observer arrived 21
from Trachis. The Greeks had employed two, to keep communication between the fleet and the army: at Artemisium Polyas, a
native of Anticyra, kept a boat ready to report to the army at
Thermopylae any reverse which might be suffered by the fleet,
while the Athenian Abronichus, the son of Lysicles, did similar
duty with Leonidas, and had a thirty-oared galley always available to report to Artemisium, if the army got into any trouble.

It was this Abronichus who now arrived with the news of the fate of Leonidas and his men. The effect was immediate; the Greeks put off their withdrawal not a minute longer, but got under way at once, one after another, the Corinthians leading, the Athenians bringing up the rear.

22   Themistocles took the fastest ships and called on the way at all the places where drinking water was to be found, and cut notices on the rocks near by for the Ionians to read – as they did when they moved up on the following day. 'Men of Ionia' – his message ran – 'it is wrong that you should make war upon your fathers and help to bring Greeks into subjection. The best thing you can do is to join our side; if this is impossible, you might at least remain neutral, and ask the Carians to do the same. If you are unable to do either, but are held by a compulsion so strong that it puts desertion out of the question, there is still another course open to you: in the next battle, remember that you and we are of the same blood, that our quarrel with Persia arose originally on your account – and fight badly.'9

In leaving this message Themistocles probably had two possibilities in mind: in the first place, it might, if the kings did not get to know of it, induce the Ionians to come over to the Greeks, and, secondly, if it were reported to Xerxes and made the ground of an accusation against the Ionians, they would be distrusted and not allowed, in consequence, to take part in engagements at sea.

23   Immediately after this a native of Histiaea sailed to Aphetae with the news of the Greek withdrawal from Artemisium. The Persians refused to believe it; they put the man under guard and sent off a party of some fast ships to see for themselves. Then, assured that the news was true, they moved at sunrise with the whole fleet to Artemisium, where they stayed until midday, before going on to Histiaea. They took this town, and overran all the coastal villages of Ellopia, a district belonging to Histiaea.

24   While they were here, a messenger arrived from the king. Before sending him, Xerxes had arranged that of the twenty thousand men in the Persian army who had been killed at Thermopylae, all except about a thousand should be buried in trenches and covered over with earth and leaves, to prevent their being seen

by anyone from the fleet. The remaining thousand were left exposed.[10] On reaching Histiaea the messenger had the whole force assembled and delivered his message. 'Fellow-soldiers,' he said, 'the king grants leave for anyone who wants it, to go and see with his own eyes how he fights against the madmen who thought they could beat him.' The announcement was no sooner made than so many people wanted to avail themselves of the king's offer that the supply of boats ran out. All who could, crossed the water and toured the battlefield to see the bodies; some of the corpses were, of course, those of helots, but the sightseers imagined that they were all Spartans and Thespians; however, Xerxes' ludicrous attempt to conceal the number of his own dead deceived nobody. For on one side a thousand corpses lay scattered, and on the other side were the four thousand all lying together in the same spot. 25

On the day after this, which had been spent in sight-seeing, the seamen rejoined their ships at Histiaea and the army with Xerxes set forward on its march. A few Arcadian deserters came in – men who had nothing to live on and wanted employment; they were taken to Xerxes and questioned about what the Greeks were doing. One Persian conducted the interrogation on behalf of them all, and he was told in reply that the Greeks were celebrating the Olympic festival, where they were watching athletic contests and chariot-races. When he asked what the prize was for which they contended, the Arcadians mentioned the wreath of olive-leaves. This drew from Tritantaechmes, the son of Artabanus, a very sound remark – though it made Xerxes call him a coward; for when he learned that the prize was not money but a wreath, he could not help crying out in front of everybody, 'Good heavens, Mardonius, what kind of men are these that you have brought us to fight against – men who compete with one another for no material reward, but only for honour!' 26

Meanwhile, immediately after the disaster at Thermopylae, the Thessalians sent a representative to Phocis. They had always been on bad terms with the Phocians, but especially so since the last blow they had received from them. Not many years before the Persian invasion the Thessalians and their allies in full force 27 had invaded Phocis and been defeated with serious losses.[11] The Phocians were blocked up in Parnassus, and their subsequent success was due to a clever piece of work by an Elean named Tellias, who was serving with the Phocians as their diviner; what he did was to pick six hundred good men, cover their bodies and weapons all over with whitewash, and send them on a night attack against the enemy, with instructions to kill everyone they saw who was not whitened like themselves. The Thessalian sentries were the first to see them, and took them for some sort of appalling apparition; then the panic spread to the rest of the troops, who were so badly scared that the Phocians killed four thousand of them, and got possession of their bodies and shields. Half the shields were sent as an offering to the temple at Abae, the other half to Delphi, while from a tenth part of the plunder were made the great statues which stand around the tripod in front of the temple at Delphi, and also the similar figures at Abae.

28   In addition to breaking out from Parnassus and inflicting this signal defeat on the Thessalian infantry, the Phocians also did irreparable damage to the Thessalian cavalry during an attempted raid. They dug a deep trench across the pass near Hyampolis, put a number of big empty jars in it, and covered them over lightly with soil; then, making the surface smooth and level to conceal the trap, they awaited the attack. The Thessalians galloped up, expecting to sweep all before them, when their horses fell through into the jars and broke their legs.

29   Thus the Thessalians had two reasons for resentment when they sent their representative to Phocis. Their message ran as follows: 'Men of Phocis, now at last you must admit your error, and own that you are not our equals. In the past, while it suited us to be one with the Greeks, we were always considered more important than you; and now our influence with the Persians is so great that a word from us would get you turned out of your country, and sold as slaves into the bargain. All the same, though we have you completely in our power, we are willing to let bygones be bygones: just pay us off with fifty talents, and we undertake to divert the danger which is threatening your country.'

Now the Phocians were the only people in this part of Greece 30
who had not gone over to the Persians, and in my opinion
their motive was simply and solely their hatred of Thessaly. If
Thessaly had remained loyal, no doubt the Phocians would
have deserted to Persia. As it was, when they heard what the
Thessalian representative had to say, they refused to pay a penny
and declared that they could join Persia just as easily as the
Thessalians did, had they been inclined that way; nevertheless
they would never willingly prove traitors to Greece. This reply 31
to their message made the Thessalians very angry, and they
forthwith offered to act as guides to the Persian army.

From Trachis the army entered the narrow strip of Dorian
territory, barely four miles wide, which lies between Malis and
Phocis. In old days this region was called Dryopis, and was the
mother city of the Peloponnesian Dorians. The Persians did no
damage to this part of Doris on their way through; the people
in any case were friendly, and the Thessalians wished them to
be spared. Passing from Doris into Phocis, they failed to catch 32
the Phocians because they had already cleared out: some of
them had gone up into the mountains – the height of Parnassus,
called Tithorea, not far from the city of Neon, has plenty of
room for a large body of men, and a number of them had
climbed up on to it and taken with them all they could move –
while the majority had sought shelter with the Locrians of
Ozolae and taken their property to Amphissa, the town which
stands above the plain of Crisa. All Phocis was overrun; the
Thessalians did not let the Persian army miss a bit of it, and
everywhere they went there was devastation by fire and sword,
and towns and temples were burnt. Along the valley of the 33
Cephisus nothing was spared; Drymus, Charadra, Erochus,
Tethronium, Amphicaea, Neon, Pedies, Trites, Elateia, Hyampolis, Parapotamii – all these places were burnt to the ground,
including Abae, where there was a temple of Apollo richly
furnished with treasure and offerings of all kinds. There was an
oracle there, as indeed there is today; the shrine belonging to it
was plundered and burnt.[12] A few Phocians were chased and
caught near the mountains, and some women were raped successively by so many Persian soldiers that they died.

34   At Panopes, which they reached by way of Parapotamii, the
army divided and one division, the stronger and more numerous,
proceeded with Xerxes towards Athens, entering Boeotia at
Orchomenus. All the Boeotians had gone over to the enemy,
and their towns were protected by Macedonians, sent by Alexander, to make it clear to Xerxes that the people of Boeotia were
35   friendly to him. The other division of the army made with their
guides for the temple at Delphi, keeping Parnassus on their
right. They, too, devastated all the parts of Phocis through
which they passed, and burnt the towns of Panopes, Daulis, and
Aeolidae. This division was detached from the main body of the
army for the special purpose of plundering the temple at Delphi,
and bringing its treasures to Xerxes; I have been told that he
was better acquainted, from descriptions continually coming to
his notice, with everything of importance there than with his
own property at home, and especially with the precious objects
which had been presented to the shrine by Croesus, the son of
Alyattes.

36   The news of the approach of the Persians caused consternation at Delphi; and in their terror the people asked the god's
advice as to whether they should bury the sacred treasures or
get them out of the country. The god replied that they were not
to be disturbed, for he was well able to guard his own. This
being decided, the Delphians began to think about saving themselves; they sent their women and children across the water into
Achaea, and most of the men took to the mountains in the
summits of Parnassus, and stored their movable property in
the Corycian cave, while a few of them made their escape to
Amphissa in Locris. All abandoned the town except sixty men
and the Priest of the oracle.

37   The Persians were now close at hand and within sight of the
temple, when suddenly the Priest, whose name was Aceratus,
saw weapons lying on the ground in front of the shrine – they
were the sacred weapons which no human hand may touch, and
they had been brought out from their place within. He hastened
to report this portent to the other Delphians who were still in
the town. Meanwhile the enemy were drawing quickly nearer,
and when they reached the temple of Athene Pronaea even

greater portents happened to them than what I have just recorded. It is marvellous enough that weapons of war should move of their own accord and appear upon the ground outside the shrine; but what occurred next is surely one of the most amazing things ever known – for just as the Persians came to the shrine of Athene Pronaea, thunderbolts fell on them from the sky, and two pinnacles of rock, torn from Parnassus, came crashing and rumbling down amongst them, killing a large number, while at the same time there was a battle-cry from inside the shrine. All these things happening together caused 38 a panic amongst the Persian troops. They fled; and the Delphians, seeing them on the run, came down upon them and attacked them with great slaughter. All who escaped with their lives made straight for Boeotia. There is a story, I have learned, amongst those who got away, that there was yet another miraculous occurrence: they saw, so they said, two gigantic hoplites – taller than ever a man was – pursuing them and cutting them down. According to the Delphians, these were Phylacus and 39 Autonous, local heroes who have enclosed plots of ground near the temple, which are held sacred to them – that of Phylacus lies along the road above the temple of Pronaea, and that of Autonous is near the spring of Castalia under the peak called Hyampia.[13]

The rocks which fell from Parnassus were still there in my time; they lay in the enclosure round the shrine of Pronaea, where they embedded themselves after crashing through the Persian troops. So that was how these people took their departure from the Holy Place at Delphi.

The Greek fleet, having sailed from Artemisium, brought up, at 40 the Athenians' request, at Salamis. The Athenians' object in urging the commanders to take up this position was to give themselves an opportunity of getting their women and children out of Attica, and also of discussing their next move – as their present circumstances, and the frustration of their hopes, most evidently demanded. They had expected that the full strength of the Peloponnesian army would concentrate in Boeotia to hold up the Persian advance, but now they found nothing of the sort;

on the contrary, they learned that the Peloponnesians were concerned only with their own safety and were fortifying the Isthmus in order to protect the Peloponnese, while the rest of Greece, so far as they cared, might take its chance. It was this news which led to the request to the fleet to put in at Salamis.[14]

41   While, therefore, the rest of the fleet lay at Salamis, the Athenians returned to their own harbours, and at once issued a proclamation that every one in the city and countryside should get his children and all the members of his household to safety as best he could. Most of them were sent to Troezen, but some to Aegina and some to Salamis. The removal of their families was pressed on with all possible speed, partly because they wished to heed the warning which had been given them by the oracle, but more especially for an even stronger reason. The Athenians say that the Acropolis is guarded by a great snake, which lives in the temple; indeed they believed so literally in its existence that they put out monthly offerings for it to eat in the form of a honey-cake. Now in the past the honey-cake used always to be consumed, but on this occasion it was untouched. The temple Priestess told them of this, and in consequence, believing that the goddess herself had abandoned the Acropolis, they were all the more ready to evacuate the town. As soon as everything was removed, they rejoined the fleet on its station.

42   There were some other Greek ships which had been ordered to assemble at Pogon, the harbour of Troezen, and these, when news came through that the fleet from Artemisium had put into Salamis, left Troezen and joined it. Thus the fleet was larger than it had been at the battle of Artemisium,[15] and made up of ships from more towns. It was still under the same commander, Eurybiades, the son of Eurycleides – a Spartan but not of the royal blood; but the city which furnished by far the greatest 43   number of ships, and the fastest, was Athens. The composition of the fleet was as follows: 16 ships from Lacedaemon, the same number from Corinth as at Artemisium, 15 from Sicyon, 10 from Epidaurus, 5 from Troezen, 3 from Hermione. The people of all these places except Hermione are of Dorian and Macedonian blood, and had last emigrated from Erineus, Pindus, and Dryopis. The people of Hermione are Dryopes, and were driven

out by Heracles and the Malians from the country now called
Doris.

The contingents mentioned above were from the Peloponnese; 44
from outside the Peloponnese there were, first, the Athenians
with 180 ships, half the whole fleet. These were manned by
Athenians only, for the Plataeans did not serve with them at the
battle of Salamis, because during the withdrawal from
Artemisium, when the fleet was off Chalcis, they landed in
Boeotia on the opposite shore and set about conveying their
property and households to a place of safety, and were consequently left behind. When what is now called Greece was occupied by the Pelasgians, the Athenians, a Pelasgian people, were
called Cranai. In the reign of Cecrops they acquired the name
of Cecropidae. At the succession of Erechtheus they changed
their name to Athenians; and when Ion, the son of Xuthus,
became general of their armies, they took from him the title of
Ionians.

From Megara there was the same number of ships as at 45
Artemisium; then there were 7 from Ambracia, and 3 from
Leucas. The Ambraciots and Leucadians are Dorians from
Corinth. Of the island states Aegina contributed 30 ships. The 46
Aeginetans had others in commission, but these were employed
in guarding their own island; their best thirty were the ones
which fought at Salamis. The Aeginetans are Dorians from
Epidaurus; the island used to be known as Oenone. Next was
the squadron from Chalcis; this consisted of the same twenty
ships which served at Artemisium; from Eretria there were the
original 7. These two peoples are Ionians. Ceos (the Ceans are
Ionians from Athens) sent the same number as before, and
Naxos 4. The Naxian contingent, like those from the other
islands, had been sent to join the Persians, but disobeyed orders
and joined the Greeks at the instigation of Democritus, a man
of distinction who was then in command of a trireme. The
Naxians are Ionians of Athenian blood. Styra provided the
same ships as at Artemisium, and Cythnus one trireme and a
penteconter. The Styreans and Cythnians are Dryopes. Seriphus,
Siphnus, and Melos also took part – they were the only islands
not to make their submission to Persia. All these states are 47

situated on this side of the river Acheron and the country of the
Thesprotians, who are neighbours of the people of Ambracia
and Leucas – the two most distant places to contribute to the
fleet. Beyond them, there was only one community – Croton –
which helped Greece in her hour of danger; the Crotoniats sent
one ship, under the command of Phayllus, a man who had won
three victories at the Pythian games. The Crotoniats are of

48 Achaean blood. All the contingents consisted of triremes, except
the Melian, Siphnian, and Seriphian, which were penteconters.
The Melians, who are of Lacedaemonian blood, sent two, the
Siphnians and Seriphians, who are Ionians from Athens, one
each. The total number of warships (excluding the penteconters)
was 378.

49 When the commanders of the various contingents I have
mentioned met at Salamis, a council of war was held, and
Eurybiades called for suggestions, from anyone who wished to
speak, on the most suitable place for engaging the enemy fleet
in the territory still under their control – Attica was excluded,
as it had already been given up. The general feeling of the council
was in favour of sailing to the Isthmus and fighting in defence
of the Peloponnese, on the grounds that if they were beaten at
Salamis they would find themselves blocked up in an island,
where no help could reach them, whereas if disaster overtook
them at the Isthmus, they could find refuge amongst their own

50 people. This was the view of the Peloponnesian officers. While
the discussion was still going on, a man arrived from Athens
with the news that the Persians had entered Attica and were
firing the whole country. This was the work of the division of
the army under Xerxes which had taken the route through
Boeotia; they had burnt Thespia after the inhabitants had
escaped to the Peloponnese, and Plataea too, and then entered
Attica, where they were causing wholesale devastation. The
Thebans had told them that Thespia and Plataea had refused to

51 submit to Persian domination: hence their destruction. The
march of the Persian army from the Hellespont to Attica had
taken three months – and the actual crossing of the strait an
additional one; it reached Attica during the archonship of Cal-
liades.[16]

The Persians found Athens itself abandoned except for a few people in the temple of Athene Polias – temple stewards and needy folk, who had barricaded the Acropolis against the invaders with planks and timbers. It was partly their poverty which prevented them from seeking shelter in Salamis with the rest, and partly their belief that they had discovered the real meaning of the Priestess' oracle – that 'the wooden wall would not be taken'. The wooden wall, in their minds, was not the ships but the barricade, and that would save them.[17]

The Persians occupied the hill which the Athenians call the Areopagus, opposite the Acropolis, and began the siege. The method they used was to shoot into the barricade arrows with burning tow attached to them. Their wooden wall had betrayed them, but still the Athenians, though in imminent and deadly peril, refused to give in or even to listen to the proposals which the Pisistratidae made to them for a truce. All their ingenuity was employed in the struggle to defend themselves; amongst other things, they rolled boulders down the slope upon the enemy as he tried to approach the gates, and for a long time Xerxes was baffled and unable to take them. But in the end the Persians solved their problem: a way of access to the Acropolis was found – for it was prophesied that all Athenian territory upon the continent of Greece must be overrun by the Persians. There is a place in front of the Acropolis, behind the way up to the gates, where the ascent is so steep that no guard was set, because it was not thought possible that any man would be able to climb it; here, by the shrine of Cecrops' daughter Aglaurus, some soldiers managed to scramble up the precipitous face of the cliff. When the Athenians saw them on the summit, some leapt from the wall to their death, others sought sanctuary in the inner shrine of the temple; but the Persians who had got up first made straight for the gates, flung them open and slaughtered those in sanctuary. Having left not one of them alive, they stripped the temple of its treasures and burnt everything on the Acropolis. Xerxes, now absolute master of Athens, dispatched a rider to Susa with news for Artabanus of his success.

On the following day he summoned to his presence the Athenian exiles who were serving with the Persian forces, and ordered them to go up into the Acropolis and offer sacrifice there according to Athenian usage; possibly some dream or other had suggested this course to him, or perhaps his conscience was uneasy for the burning of the temple. The Athenian exiles did as they were bidden. I mention these details for a particular reason: on the Acropolis there is a spot which is sacred to Erechtheus who is called the 'earth-born', and within it is an olive-tree and a spring of salt water. According to the Athenians, they were put there by Poseidon and Athene, when they contended for possession of the land, as tokens of their claims to it. Now this olive was destroyed by fire together with the rest of the sanctuary; nevertheless on the very next day, when the Athenians, who were ordered by the king to offer the sacrifice, went up to that sacred place, they saw that a new shoot eighteen inches long had sprung from the stump. They told the king of this.

56   Meanwhile at Salamis the effect of the news of what had happened to the Acropolis at Athens was so disturbing, that some of the naval commanders did not even wait for the subject under discussion to be decided, but hurried on board and began hoisting sail for immediate flight. Some, however, stayed; and by these a resolution was passed to fight in defence of the Isthmus.

57   During the night, when the various commanders had returned to their ships after the break-up of the conference, an Athenian named Mnesiphilus made his way to Themistocles' ship and asked him what plan it had been decided to adopt.[18] On learning that they had resolved to sail to the Isthmus and to fight there in defence of the Peloponnese, 'No, no,' he exclaimed; 'once the fleet leaves Salamis, it will no longer be one country that you'll be fighting for. Everyone will go home, and neither Eurybiades nor anybody else will be able to prevent the total dissolution of our forces. The plan is absurd and will be the ruin of Greece. Now listen to me: try, if you possibly can, to upset the decision of the conference – it may be that you will be able to persuade Eurybiades to change his mind and remain at Salamis.'

58   Themistocles highly approved of this suggestion, and without saying a word he went to the ship of the commander-in-chief

and told him that he had something of public importance to discuss. Eurybiades invited him aboard and gave him permission to speak his mind, whereupon Themistocles, taking a seat beside him, repeated Mnesiphilus' arguments as if they were his own, with plenty of new ones added, until he convinced him, by the sheer urgency of his appeal, that the only thing to do was to go ashore and call the officers to another conference. The conference met, and then, before Eurybiades even had time to announce its purpose, Themistocles, unable to restrain his eagerness, broke into a passionate speech. He was interrupted by Adeimantus, the son of Ocytus, commander of the Corinthian contingent. 'Themistocles,' he observed, 'in the races, the man who starts before the signal is whipped.' 'Yes,' was Themistocles' retort, 'but those who start too late win no prizes.' It was a mild retort – for the moment. To Eurybiades he used none of his previous arguments about the danger of the force breaking up if they left Salamis; for it would have been unbecoming to accuse any of the confederates actually to their faces. The line he took this time was quite different. 'It is now in your power', he said, 'to save Greece, if you take my advice and engage the enemy's fleet here in Salamis, instead of withdrawing to the Isthmus as these other people suggest. Let me put the two plans before you, and you can weigh them up and see which is the better. Take the Isthmus first: if you fight there, it will have to be in the open sea, and that will be greatly to our disadvantage, with our smaller numbers and slower ships. Moreover, even if everything else goes well, you will lose Salamis, Megara, and Aegina. Again, if the enemy fleet comes south, the army will follow it; so you will yourself be responsible for drawing it to the Peloponnese, thus putting the whole of Greece in peril.

'Now for my plan: it will bring, if you adopt it, the following advantages: first, we shall be fighting in narrow waters, and there, with our inferior numbers, we shall win, provided things go as we may reasonably expect. Fighting in a confined space favours us but the open sea favours the enemy. Secondly, Salamis, where we have put our women and children, will be preserved; and thirdly – for you the most important point of all – you will be fighting in defence of the Peloponnese by remaining here just as much as by withdrawing to the Isthmus – nor, if you have the sense to follow my advice, will you draw the Persian army to the Peloponnese. If we beat them at sea, as I expect we shall, they will not advance to attack you on the Isthmus, or come any further than Attica; they will retreat in disorder, and we shall gain by the preservation of Megara, Aegina, and Salamis – where an oracle has already foretold our victory. Let a man lay his plans with due regard to common sense, and he will usually succeed; otherwise he will find that God is unlikely to favour human designs.'

61   During his speech Themistocles was again attacked by the Corinthian Adeimantus, who told him to hold his tongue because he was a man without a country, and tried to prevent Eurybiades from putting any question to the vote at the instance of a mere refugee. Let Themistocles, he cried, provide himself with a country before he offered his advice. The point of the jibe was, of course, the fact that Athens had fallen and was in Persian hands. This time Themistocles' retort was by no means mild; he heartily abused both Adeimantus and the Corinthians, and made it quite plain that so long as Athens had two hundred warships in commission, she had both a city and a country much stronger than theirs – for there was not a single Greek state capable of repelling them, should they choose to attack.

62   With this he turned to Eurybiades again, and, speaking more vehemently than ever, 'As for you,' he cried, 'if you stay here and play the man – well and good; go, and you'll be the ruin of Greece. In this war everything depends upon the fleet. I beg you to take my advice; if you refuse, we will immediately put our families aboard and sail for Siris in Italy – it has long been ours, and the oracles have foretold that Athenians must live there some day. Where will you be without the Athenian fleet? When you have lost it you will remember my words.'[19]

63   This was enough to make Eurybiades change his mind; and I think that his chief motive was apprehension of losing Athenian support, if he withdrew to the Isthmus; for without the Athenian contingent his strength would not have been adequate to offer battle. So he took the decision to stay where they were and fight it out at Salamis.

After these verbal skirmishes, when Eurybiades had made up   64
his mind, they prepared to fight where they were. Day broke;
just as the sun rose the shock of an earthquake was felt both on
land and at sea, and the Greeks resolved to offer prayers to the
gods and to call upon the Sons of Aeacus to fight at their side.
As they resolved, so they did: they prayed to all the gods, and
called upon Ajax and Telamon there in Salamis, and sent a ship
to Aegina for Aeacus himself and his other Sons.[20]

There is a story which used to be told by Dicaeus, the son of   65
Theocydes, an Athenian exile who had some repute among the
Persians. After the evacuation of Attica, when the Persian troops
were devastating the countryside, he happened to be in the plain
of Thria with Demaratus the Spartan. They saw a cloud of dust,
such as might have been raised by an army of thirty thousand
men on the march, coming from the direction of Eleusis, and
were wondering what troops they could be, when they suddenly
heard the sound of voices. Dicaeus thought he recognized the
Iacchus song, which is sung at the Dionysiac mysteries, but
Demaratus, who was unfamiliar with the religious ceremonial
of Eleusis, asked his companion whose voices they were. 'Sir,'
Dicaeus answered, 'without any doubt some dreadful disaster
is about to happen to the king's army. There is not a man left in
Attica; so the voice we heard must clearly be a divine voice,
coming from Eleusis to bring help to the Athenians and their
friends. If it descends upon the Peloponnese, there will be danger
for the king and for his army; if it moves towards the ships at
Salamis, Xerxes may well lose his fleet. Every year the Athenians
celebrate a festival in honour of the Mother and the Maid, and
anyone who wishes, from Athens or elsewhere, may be initiated
in the mysteries; the sound you heard was the *Iacchus* song
which is always sung at that festival.'[21]

'Do not breathe a word of this to anybody,' said Demaratus.
'If it should reach the ears of the king, you would lose your
head, and neither I nor anyone else in the world could save you.
So hold your tongue – the gods will see to the king's army.'

While Demaratus was speaking, the cloud of dust, from which
the mysterious voice had issued, rose high into the air and drifted
away towards Salamis, where the Greek fleet was stationed. By

this the two men knew that the naval power of Xerxes was destined to be destroyed. Such was Dicaeus' story, and he used to appeal to Demaratus and others to witness the truth of it.

66   Meanwhile the Persian sailors had returned from Trachis to Histiaea after their sight-seeing tour of the battlefield, and three days later the fleet set sail. The ships passed through the Euripus, and in another three days arrived off Phaleron. In my judgement the Persian forces both by land and sea were just as strong at the time of their entry into Attica as they had been at Sepias and Thermopylae; for as an offset to the losses suffered in the storm, at Thermopylae, and at Artemisium, I reckon the reinforcements which had subsequently joined them. These were the Malians, Dorians, and Locrians; the Boeotians in full force except the Thespians and Plataeans; and in addition to these the Carystians, Andrians, Tenians, and all the other island peoples except the five whom I mentioned above. The further Xerxes advanced into Greece, the more peoples followed him.

67   All these troops came as far as Attica except the Parians, who stayed behind in Cythnus to watch the course of the war; and the rest of the fleet arrived, as I have said, at Phaleron. Here Xerxes paid it a personal visit, because he wished to talk to the commanding officers and hear their opinions; so when he had seated himself, the tyrants of states and commanders of squadrons were summoned to appear before him, and took their seats according to the precedence which the king had assigned them – the lord of Sidon first, the lord of Tyre second, and so on in their order. Then, as they sat there in order of rank, Xerxes sent Mardonius to ask the opinion of each one about giving battle at

68   sea. Mardonius accordingly went around putting his question, beginning with the lord of Sidon. The answers, with a single exception, were unanimously in favour of engaging the Greek

a   fleet: the exception was Artemisia.[22] 'Mardonius,' she said, 'tell the king for me that this is the answer I give – I, whose courage and achievements in the battles at Euboea were surpassed by none: say to him, "Master, my past services give me the right to advise you now upon the course which I believe to be most to your advantage. It is this: spare your ships and do not fight at sea, for the Greeks are as far superior to your men in naval matters as men are to women. In any case, what pressing need have you to risk further actions at sea? Have you not taken Athens, the main objective of the war? Is not the rest of Greece in your power? There is no one now to resist you – those who did resist have fared as they deserved. Let me tell you how I *b* think things will now go with the enemy; if only you are not in too great a hurry to fight at sea – if you keep the fleet on the coast where it now is – then, whether you stay here or advance into the Peloponnese, you will easily accomplish your purpose. The Greeks will not be able to hold out against you for long; you will soon cause their forces to disperse – they will soon break up and go home. I hear they have no supplies in the island where they now are; and the Peloponnesian contingents, at least, are not likely to be very easy in their minds if you march with the army towards their country – they will hardly care to fight in defence of Athens.

'"If, on the other hand, you rush into a naval action, my fear *c* is that the defeat of your fleet may involve the army too. And put away in your heart one other point, my lord, to be considered: good masters, remember, usually have bad servants, and bad masters good ones. You, then, being the best master in the world, are ill served: these people who are supposed to be your allies – these Egyptians, Cyprians, Cilicians, Pamphylians – are a useless lot!"'

Artemisia's friends were dismayed when they heard this *69* speech, and thought that Xerxes would punish her for trying to dissuade him from battle; but those who were jealous of her standing among the most influential persons in the forces were delighted at the prospect of her ruin. However, when the several answers to his question were reported to the king, he was highly pleased with Artemisia's; he had always considered her an admirable person, but now he esteemed her more than ever. Nevertheless his orders were that the advice of the majority should be followed, for he believed that in the battles off Euboea his men had shirked their duty because he was not himself present – whereas this time he had made arrangements to watch the fight with his own eyes.

The command was now given to put to sea, and the ships *70*

proceeded towards Salamis, where they took up their respective stations at leisure. It was late in the evening, with not enough light left to attack at once; so they prepared to go into action next day.

The Greeks were in a state of acute alarm, especially those from the Peloponnese: for there they were, waiting at Salamis to fight for Athenian territory, and certain, in the event of defeat, to be caught and blocked up in an island, while their own
71   country was left without defence, and the Persian army that very night was on the march for the Peloponnese.

Nevertheless everything that ingenuity could contrive had been done to prevent the Persian army from forcing the Isthmus. On the news of the destruction of Leonidas' force at Thermopylae, troops from all the states hurried to the Isthmus, where they took up their position under Cleombrotus, the son of Anaxandrides and brother of Leonidas. Their first act was to break up and block the Scironian Way; then, in accordance with a decision taken in council, they began work on a wall across the Isthmus. As there were many thousands there and every man turned to, the work went fast. Stones, bricks, timbers, sand-baskets – all were used in the building, and the labour
72   went on continuously night and day. The peoples which joined in this work in full force were the following: Sparta, all the Arcadians, Elis, Corinth, Sicyon, Epidaurus, Phlius, Troezen, and Hermione: all these, in their overriding fear for the safety of Greece, helped in the work; but the other Peloponnesian communities (though the Olympic and Carneian festivals were now over) remained indifferent.

73   In the Peloponnese there are seven distinct peoples: two of them, the Arcadians and Cynurians, are indigenous; one, the Achaeans, have always been in the Peloponnese, though they moved from their original territory; the four others – Dorians, Aetolians, Dryopes, and Lemnians – are immigrants. The Dorian communities are numerous and well known; the Aetolians have only one, Elis; Hermione and Asine, near Cardamyle in Laconia, belong to the Dryopes, and all the Paroreatae are Lemnian. The indigenous Cynurians appear to be the only Ionians in this part of Greece, though they too have become

Dorianized during the long time that they have been subject to Argos.[23] Of these seven peoples all the communities except the ones I mentioned remained neutral in the war – which, to put it bluntly, is as good as saying that they were on the Persian side.

The Greeks at the Isthmus, convinced that all they possessed   74
was now at stake and not expecting any notable success at sea, continued to grapple with their task of fortification. The news of how they were employed nevertheless caused great concern at Salamis; for it brought home to everyone there not so much his own peril as the imminent threat to the Peloponnese. At first there was whispered criticism of the incredible folly of Eurybiades; then the smothered feeling broke out into open resentment, and another meeting was held. All the old ground was gone over again, one side urging that it was useless to stay and fight for a country which was already in enemy hands, and that the fleet should sail and risk an action in defence of the Peloponnese, while the Athenians, Aeginetans, and Megarians still maintained that they should stay and fight at Salamis.

At this point Themistocles, feeling that he would be outvoted   75
by the Peloponnesians, slipped quietly away from the meeting and sent a man over in a boat to the Persian fleet, with instructions upon what to say when he got there. The man – Sicinnus – was one of Themistocles' slaves and used to attend upon his sons; afterwards, when the Thespians were enrolling new citizens, Themistocles established him at Thespia and made him a rich man. Following his instructions, then, Sicinnus made his way to the Persian commanders and said: 'I am the bearer of a secret communication from the Athenian commander, who is a well-wisher to your king and hopes for a Persian victory. He has told me to report to you that the Greeks are afraid and are planning to slip away. Only prevent them from slipping through your fingers, and you have at this moment an opportunity of unparalleled success. They are at daggers drawn with each other, and will offer no opposition – on the contrary, you will see the pro-Persians amongst them fighting the rest.'[24]

His message delivered, Sicinnus lost no time in getting away.   76
The Persians believed what he had told them, and proceeded to put ashore a large force on the islet of Psyttaleia, between

Salamis and the coast; then, about midnight, they moved their western wing in an encircling movement upon Salamis, while at the same time the ships off Ceos and Cynosura also advanced and blocked the whole channel as far as Munychia. The object of these movements was – ironically – that the Greeks might be cut off in Salamis and there give the Persians their revenge for the battles of Artemisium. The troops were landed on Psyttaleia because it lay right in the path of the impending action, and once the fighting began, many men and damaged vessels would be carried on to it, and could be saved or destroyed according as they were friends or enemies. These tactical moves were carried out in silence, to prevent the enemy from being aware of what was going on; they occupied the whole night, so that none of the men had time for sleep.[25]

77   Now I cannot deny that there is truth in prophecies, and I have no wish to discredit them when they are expressed in unambiguous language. Consider the following:

When they shall span the sea with ships from Cynosura
To the holy shore of Artemis of the golden sword,
Wild with hope at the ruin of shining Athens,
Then shall bright Justice quench Excess, the child of Pride,
Dreadful and furious, thinking to swallow up all things.
Bronze shall mingle with bronze, and Ares with blood
Incarnadine the sea; and all-seeing Zeus
And gracious Victory shall bring to Greece the day of freedom.

With that utterance of Bacis in mind, absolutely clear as it is, I do not venture to say anything against prophecies, nor will I listen to criticism from others.[26]

78   The Greek commanders at Salamis were still at loggerheads. They did not yet know that the enemy ships had blocked their escape at both ends of the channel, but supposed them to occupy the same position as they had seen them in during the day.

79   However, while the dispute was still at its height, Aristides came over in a boat from Aegina. This man, an Athenian and the son of Lysimachus, had been ostracized by the Athenians, but the more I have learned of his character, the more I have come to

believe that he was the best and most just man that Athens ever produced.[27] Arrived at Salamis, Aristides went to where the conference was being held and, standing outside, called for Themistocles. Themistocles was no friend of his; indeed he was his most determined enemy; but Aristides was willing, in view of the magnitude of the danger which threatened them, to forget old quarrels in his desire to communicate with him. He was already aware of the anxiety of the Peloponnesian commanders to withdraw to the Isthmus; as soon, therefore, as Themistocles came out of the conference in answer to his call, he said: 'At this moment, more than ever before, you and I should be rivals, to see which of us can do most good to our country. First, let me tell you that the Peloponnesians may talk as much or as little as they please about withdrawing from Salamis – it will make not the least difference. What I tell you, I have seen with my own eyes: they *cannot* now get out of here, however much the Corinthians or Eurybiades himself may wish to do so, because our fleet is surrounded. So go in and tell them that!'

'Good news and good advice,' Themistocles answered; 'what 80 I most wanted has happened – and you bring me the evidence of your own eyes that it is true. It was I who was responsible for this move of the enemy; for as our men would not fight here of their own free will, it was necessary to make them, whether they wanted to do so or not. But take them the good news yourself; if I tell them, they will think I have invented it and will not believe me. Please, then, go in and make the report yourself. If they believe you, well and good; if they do not, it's all the same; for if we are surrounded, as you say we are, escape is no longer possible.'

Aristides accordingly went in and made his report, saying he 81 had come from Aegina and had been hard put to it to slip through the blockading enemy fleet, as the entire Greek force was surrounded. He advised them, therefore, to prepare at once to repel an attack. That said, he left the conference, whereupon another dispute broke out, because most of the commanders still refused to believe in the report. But while they still doubted, 82 a Tenian warship, commanded by Panaetius, the son of Sosimenes, deserted from the Persians and came in with a full account. For this service the name of the Tenians was afterwards inscribed on the tripod at Delphi amongst the other states who helped to defeat the invader.[28] With this ship which came over to them at Salamis, and the Lemian one which previously joined them at Artemisium, the Greek fleet was brought up to the round number of 380. Up till then it had fallen short of that figure by two.

83   Persuaded by the Tenians' report, the Greeks now at last prepared for action. At dawn the fighting men were assembled and Themistocles gave the finest speech there. The whole burden of what he said was a comparison of all that was best and worst in human nature and fortune, and an exhortation to the men to choose the better. Then, having rounded off his speech, he ordered the men to embark onto the ships. The order was obeyed and, just as the men were going aboard, the ship which had been sent to Aegina to fetch the Sons of Aeacus, rejoined the fleet.

       The whole fleet now got under way, and in a moment the
84   Persians were on them. The Greeks checked their way and began to back astern; and they were on the point of running aground when Ameinias of Pallene, in command of an Athenian ship, drove ahead and rammed an enemy vessel. Seeing the two ships foul of one another and locked together, the rest of the Greek fleet hurried to Ameinias' assistance, and the general action began. Such is the Athenian account of how the battle started; the Aeginetans claim that the first to go into action was the ship which fetched the Sons of Aeacus from Aegina. There is also a popular belief that the phantom shape of a woman appeared and, in a voice which could be heard by every man in the fleet, contemptuously cried out: 'Strange men, how much further do you propose to go astern?'[29]

85   The Athenian squadron found itself facing the Phoenicians, who formed the Persian left wing on the western, Eleusis, end of the line; the Lacedaemonians faced the ships of Ionia, which were stationed on the Piraeus, or eastern, end. A few of the Ionians remembered Themistocles' appeal and deliberately held back in the course of the fighting but most did not. I could if I wished give a long list of officers in the enemy fleet who captured

Greek ships, but the only ones I will mention are Theomestor, the son of Androdamas, and Phylacus, the son of Histiaeus, both of them Samians. My reason for naming these two is that Theomestor in reward for this service was invested by the Persians with the tyranny of Samos, and Phylacus was enrolled in the catalogue of the King's Benefactors and presented with a large estate. The Persian word for King's Benefactors is *orosangae*.

These two officers, as I say, had some success; but the greater 86 part of the Persian fleet suffered severely in the battle, the Athenians and Aeginetans accounting for a great many of their ships. Since the Greek fleet worked together as a whole, while the Persians had lost formation and were no longer fighting on any plan, that was what was bound to happen. None the less they fought well that day – far better than in the actions off Euboea. Every man of them did his best for fear of Xerxes, feeling that the king's eye was on him.[30]

I cannot give precise details of the part played in this battle 87 by the various Greek or foreign contingents in the Persian fleet; I must, however, mention Artemisia, on account of an exploit which still further increased her reputation with Xerxes. After the Persian fleet had lost all semblance of order, Artemisia was chased by an Athenian trireme. As her ship happened to be closest to the enemy and there were other friendly ships just ahead of her, escape was impossible. In this awkward situation she hit on a plan which turned out greatly to her advantage: with the Athenian close on her tail she drove ahead with all possible speed and rammed one of her friends – a ship of Calynda, with Damasithymus, the Calyndian king, on board. I cannot say if she did this deliberately because of some quarrel she had had with this man while the fleet was in the Hellespont, or if it was just chance that that particular vessel was in her way; but in any case she rammed and sank her, and was lucky enough, as a result, to reap a double benefit. For the captain of the Athenian trireme, on seeing her ram an enemy, naturally supposed that her ship was a Greek one, or else a deserter which was fighting on the Greek side; so he abandoned the chase and turned to attack elsewhere. That, then, was one piece of luck – 88 that she escaped with her life; the other was that, by this very act which harmed the king she raised herself higher than ever in Xerxes' esteem. For the story goes that Xerxes, who was watching the battle, observed the incident, and that one of the bystanders remarked: 'Do you see, my lord, how well Artemisia is fighting? She has sunk an enemy ship.' Xerxes asked if they were sure it was really Artemisia, and was told that there was no doubt whatever – they knew her ensign well, and of course supposed that it was an enemy ship that had been sunk. She was, indeed, lucky in every way – not least in the fact that there were no survivors from the Calyndian ship to accuse her. Xerxes' comment on what was told him is said to have been: 'My men have turned into women, my women into men.'

89   Amongst the killed in this struggle was Ariabignes, the son of Darius and Xerxes' brother, and many other well-known men from Persia, Media, and the confederate nations. There were also Greek casualties, but not many; for most of the Greeks could swim, and those who lost their ships, provided they were not killed in the actual fighting, swam over to Salamis. Most of the enemy, on the other hand, being unable to swim, were drowned. The greatest destruction took place when the ships which had been first engaged turned tail; for those stationed behind fell foul of them in their attempt to press forward and
90   do some service before the eyes of the king. In the confusion which resulted, some Phoenicians who had lost their ships came to Xerxes and tried to make out that the loss was due to the treachery of the Ionians. But the upshot was that it was they themselves, and not the Ionian captains, who were executed for misbehaviour. While they were speaking, a ship of Samothrace rammed an Athenian; the Athenian was going down, when an Aeginetan vessel bore down upon the Samothracian and sank her, but the Samothracian crew, who were armed with javelins, cleared the deck of the attacking vessel, leapt aboard, and captured her. This exploit saved the Ionians; for when Xerxes saw an Ionian ship do such a fine piece of work, he turned to the Phoenicians and, ready as he was in his extreme vexation to find fault with anyone, ordered their heads to be cut off, to stop them from casting cowardly aspersions upon their betters.

Xerxes watched the course of the battle from the base of Mt Aegaleos, across the strait from Salamis;[31] whenever he saw one of his officers behaving with distinction, he would find out his name, and his secretaries wrote it down, together with his city and parentage.

The Persian Ariaramnes, who was a friend of the Ionians and was present during the battle, also had a share in bringing about the punishment of the Phoenicians.

When the Persian rout began and they were trying to get back 91 to Phalerum, the Aeginetan squadron, which was waiting to catch them in the narrows, did memorable service. The enemy was in hopeless confusion; such ships as offered resistance or tried to escape were cut to pieces by the Athenians, while the Aeginetans caught those which attempted to get clear, so that any ship which escaped the one enemy promptly fell amongst the other. It happened at this stage that Themistocles, chasing 92 an enemy vessel, ran close by the ship which was commanded by Polycritus, the son of Crius, the Aeginetan. Polycritus had just rammed a Sidonian, the very ship which captured the Aeginetan guard-vessel off Sciathus – the one, it will be remembered, which had Pytheas on board, the man the Persians kept with them out of admiration for his gallantry in refusing to surrender in spite of his appalling wounds.[32] When the ship was taken with him and the Persian crew on board, he got safe home to Aegina. When Polycritus noticed the Athenian ship, and recognized the admiral's flag, he shouted to Themistocles and asked him in a tone of ironic reproach if he still thought that the people of Aegina were Persia's friends.

Such of the Persian ships as escaped destruction made their way back to Phalerum and brought up there under the protection of the army.

The most distinguished service at Salamis is admitted to have 93 been that of Aegina; and next after Aegina was Athens. The greatest individual distinction was won by Polycritus of Aegina, and the two Athenians, Eumenes of Anagyrus and Ameinias of Pallene. It was Ameinias who gave chase to Artemisia, and if he had known that Artemisia was on board, he would never have abandoned the chase until he had either taken her or been taken himself; for the Athenians resented the fact that a woman should appear in arms against them, and the ships' captains had received special orders about her, with the offer of a reward of 10,000 drachmae for anyone who captured her alive. However, as I said, she escaped; some others, too, got away with their ships, and these now lay at Phalerum.

94   The Athenians say that right at the beginning of the action the Corinthian commander Adeimantus got sail on his ship and fled in panic. Seeing the commander making off, the rest of the squadron followed; but when they were off that part of the coast of Salamis where the temple of Athene Sciras stands, they were met by a strange boat. It was all very mysterious, because nobody, apparently, had sent it, and the Corinthians, when it met them, knew nothing of how things were going with the rest of the fleet. From what happened next they were forced to the conclusion that the hand of God was in the matter; for when the boat was close to them, the people on board called out: 'Adeimantus, while you are playing the traitor by running away with your squadron, the prayers of Greece are being answered, and she is victorious over her enemies.' Adeimantus would not believe what they said, so they told him that he might take them with him as hostages, and kill them if the Greeks were not found to have won the battle. On this, he and the rest of the squadron put about, and rejoined the fleet after the action was over. This, as I said, is an Athenian story, and the Corinthians do not admit the truth of it: on the contrary, they believe that their ships played a most distinguished part in the battle – and the rest of Greece gives evidence in their favour.[33]

95   During the confused struggle a valuable service was performed by the Athenian Aristides, son of Lysimachus, whose high character I remarked upon a little while back. He took a number of the Athenian hoplites, who were posted along the coast of Salamis, across to Psyttaleia, where they killed every one of the Persian soldiers who had been landed there.

96   After the battle the Greeks towed over to Salamis all the disabled vessels which were adrift in the neighbourhood, and then prepared for a renewal of the fight, fully expecting that Xerxes would use his remaining ships to make another attack.

Many of the disabled vessels and other wreckage were carried by the westerly wind to a part of the Attic coast called Colias, and in this way it came about that not only the prophecies of Bacis and Musaeus about this battle were fulfilled, but also another prophecy which had been uttered many years previously by an Athenian soothsayer named Lysistratus: the words of this one were, 'The Colian women shall cook their food with oars.' The Greeks had forgotten about it at the time, but it was to happen, all the same, after Xerxes was gone.

Xerxes, when he realized the extent of the disaster, was afraid 97 that the Greeks, either on their own initiative or at the suggestion of the Ionians, might sail to the Hellespont and break the bridges there. If this happened, he would be cut off in Europe and in danger of destruction. Accordingly, he laid his plans for escape; but at the same time, in order to conceal his purpose both from the Greeks and from his own troops, he began to construct a causeway across the water towards Salamis, lashing together a number of Phoenician merchantmen to serve at once for bridge and breakwater. He also made other preparations, as if he intended to fight again at sea. The sight of this activity made everybody confident that he was prepared to remain in Greece and carry on the war with all possible vigour; there was, however, one exception – Mardonius, who thoroughly understood how his master's mind worked and was in no way deceived. At 98 the same time Xerxes dispatched a courier to Persia with the news of his defeat.

No mortal thing travels faster than these Persian couriers. The whole idea is a Persian invention, and works like this: riders are stationed along the road, equal in number to the number of days the journey takes – a man and a horse for each day. Nothing stops these couriers from covering their allotted stage in the quickest possible time – neither snow, rain, heat, nor darkness. The first, at the end of his stage, passes the dispatch to the second, the second to the third, and so on along the line, as in the Greek torch-race which is held in honour of Hephaestus. The Persian word for this form of post is *aggareïon*.

Xerxes' first dispatch telling of the capture of Athens caused 99 such rejoicing in Susa amongst the Persians who had not accompanied the expedition, that they strewed the roads with myrtle-boughs, burned incense, and gave themselves up to every sort of pleasure and merrymaking; the second, however, coming on top of it, soon put a stop to all this, and such was the distress in the city that there was not a man who did not tear his clothes and weep and wail in unappeasable grief, laying the blame for the disaster upon Mardonius. Nor was it distress for the loss of the ships which caused these demonstrations; it was fear for the personal safety of the king. The demonstrations, moreover, continued without a break until Xerxes himself came home.[34]

Mardonius could see that Xerxes took the defeat at Salamis very hard, and guessed that he had determined to get out of Athens. In these circumstances, reckoning that he was sure to be punished for having persuaded the king to undertake the expedition, he felt it would be better to renew the struggle in order either to bring Greece into subjection or, failing that, to die nobly in a great cause – though he expected the former alternative. Accordingly, he approached Xerxes with a proposal. 'My lord,' he said, 'I beg you not to take recent events too deeply to heart. What are a few planks and timbers? The decisive struggle will not depend upon them, but upon men and horses. Not one of all these people who now imagine that their work is done, will dare leave his ship in order to oppose you, nor will the mainland Greeks – those who have done so already have paid the price. I suggest, therefore, an immediate attack upon the Peloponnese. Or wait a while, if you prefer. In any case do not lose heart; for the Greeks cannot possibly escape ultimate subjection. They will be brought to account for the injuries they have done you, now and in the past. That is your best policy; nevertheless I have another plan to offer, should you be determined to withdraw the army from Greece. My lord, do not give the Greeks the chance to laugh at us. None of the reverses we have suffered have been due to us – you cannot say that we Persians have on any occasion fought like cowards. Why should we care if the Egyptians and Phoenicians and Cyprians and Cilicians have disgraced themselves? Persia is not involved in their disgrace. No; it is not we who are responsible for what has occurred. Listen, then, to what I have to propose;

if you have made up your mind not to stay here, then go home together with the greater part of the army, and I will make it my duty, with 300,000 picked troops, to deliver Greece to you in chains.'

The proposal was welcome to Xerxes in his dejection; he was highly delighted, and told Mardonius that he would consider the two alternatives and let him know which he preferred to adopt. Accordingly he summoned a conference, and during the debate it occurred to him that it would be just as well to send for Artemisia to take part in the discussion, as she on a previous occasion had been the only one to give him sound advice. When she presented herself, Xerxes dismissed his Persian advisers, and all the guards, and addressed her in these words: 101

'Mardonius urges me to stay in Greece and attack the Peloponnese. According to him, my army and my Persian troops, who have not been responsible for any of our recent disasters, are anxious to prove their worth. His advice, therefore, is, either that I should undertake this campaign, or allow him to choose 300,000 men from the army and lead the expedition himself, while I return home with the remainder of my troops. With that force he promises to deliver Greece into my hands. You gave me good advice when you tried to dissuade me from risking the battle we have just fought at sea; so I would ask you to advise me now. Which of these two courses should I be wise to follow?'

'My lord,' Artemisia answered, 'it is not easy to give you the best advice; nevertheless, circumstances being as they are, I think that you should yourself quit this country and leave Mardonius behind with the force he asks for, if that is what he wants, and if he has really undertaken to do as he has said. If his design prospers and success attends his arms, it will be *your* work, master – for your slaves performed it. And even if things go wrong with him, it will be no great matter, so long as you yourself are safe and no danger threatens anything that concerns your house. While you and yours survive, the Greeks will have to run many a painful race for their lives and land; but who cares if Mardonius comes to grief? He is only your slave, and the Greeks will have but a poor triumph if they kill him. As 102 for yourself, you will be going home with the object of your campaign accomplished – for you have burnt Athens.'

103   Artemisia's advice was most agreeable to Xerxes, for it was the expression of his own thoughts. Personally, I do not think he would have stayed in Greece, had all his counsellors, men and women alike, urged him to do so – he was much too badly frightened. As it was, he complimented Artemisia and sent her off to Ephesus with his sons – some of his bastards which had accompanied him on the expedition.

104   To look after these children he also sent Hermotimus, his chief eunuch. Hermotimus came originally from Pedasus, and we know of no case where a man has taken a more fearful

105   revenge for an injury than he did. He was put up for sale as a prisoner of war and bought by a Chian called Panionius, a man who made his living by the unholy trade of castrating any good-looking boys he could get hold of, and taking them to Sardis or Ephesus, where he sold them at a high price – for it is a fact that among the barbarians eunuchs are valued as being specially trustworthy in every way. Amongst the many boys whom Panionius, in the course of his trade, had treated in this way, was Hermotimus. Nevertheless, he was not without his share of luck; for he was taken from Sardis and sent with a number of other things as a present to the king, and in the course of time came to be valued by Xerxes more highly than any other

106   of his eunuchs. At the time when Xerxes was at Sardis at the start of his march to Athens, Hermotimus had gone on business to Atarneus, a port of Mysia which belongs to Chios. Here he happened to meet Panionius. He at once recognized him, and in a long and apparently friendly conversation told him of all the happy results of their previous relationship, and promised to do as much for him in return, if only he would bring his family to Sardis and settle there. Panionius was delighted, and brought his wife and children accordingly. Then, having got him and his whole household into his power, Hermotimus said: 'No man ever earned his living by an unholier trade than you. What harm had I, or anyone connected with me, ever done to you or yours, that you should have made me a nothing instead of a man? Doubtless you hoped to hide your beastly practices from the

eyes of the gods; but they are just, and for your vile crime have delivered you into my power, so that you cannot now complain of the vengeance I am about to take.'

Then, having told him what he thought of him, he sent for Panionius' sons – four in number – and forced him to castrate them with his own hand. That done, the boys were compelled to do the same to their father. In this way, retribution and Hermotimus overtook Panionius.

Xerxes, having entrusted Artemisia with the duty of con- 107 ducting his bastard sons to Ephesus, sent for Mardonius and told him to pick the troops he wanted, and to take care to make his deeds answer to his words. That day nothing further was done; but the same night the king gave his orders, and the fleet slipped away from Phalerum, the commander of every vessel making the best speed he could across to the Hellespont, in order to guard the bridges for Xerxes' use on his return. Off Zoster, where some little rocky headlands run out from the coast, the Persians mistook the rocks for enemy ships and gave them a very wide berth; however, they realized their mistake after a time, and continued the voyage in company.

At dawn the following day the Greeks, seeing that the Persian 108 army had not moved, thought that the fleet would still be lying at Phalerum; so they prepared to defend themselves in expectation of another attack by sea. But the moment they learnt that the fleet was gone, they resolved to give chase, and did actually sail in pursuit as far as Andros, but without getting a sight of any enemy ships. At Andros they brought up and held a conference, at which Themistocles proposed that they should carry on through the islands direct for the Hellespont, and break the bridges. Eurybiades, however, objected, on the ground that to destroy the bridges would be to do Greece the worst possible service. If, he argued, Xerxes were cut off from home and forced to stay in Greece, he would hardly be likely to remain inactive. Inactivity would ruin all his chances of success and rob him of any opportunity of getting home again, and his troops would starve; whereas if he took the offensive and acted with vigour, the whole of Europe might gradually go over to him; for the various towns and peoples would, one by one, either be beaten in the field or agree to submit; moreover, the annual harvests would allow his troops to live off the country. Therefore, as Xerxes evidently intended, in consequence of his defeat at Salamis, not to remain in Greece, he should be allowed to make his escape back to his own country; and then, Eurybiades concluded, the war could be transferred to Asia.

109 Eurybiades was supported in his view by the other Peloponnesian commanders, whereupon Themistocles, finding the majority against him, suddenly shifted his ground and addressed himself to the Athenians – who of all the confederates were the most vexed at the enemy's escape, and were anxious to go on to the Hellespont alone, if the others refused to accompany them. 'From my own experience,' Themistocles began, 'and still more from what others have told me, I know very well that people who are beaten and cornered will often hit out again and make amends for their previous failure to play the man. Now we've had the luck to save ourselves and our country by the repulse of this great force, which seemed, like a cloud, to darken the sea. That force is now in flight – let it go. Indeed it was not we who performed this exploit; it was the gods and the heroes, who were jealous that one man in his godless pride should be king of Asia and of Europe too – a man who does not know the difference between sacred and profane, who burns and destroys the statues of the gods, and dared to lash the sea with whips and bind it with fetters. At the moment, all is well with us; so let us stay where we are, in our own country, and look after ourselves and our families. The Persians are gone – flung out, once for all; so repair your houses, every one of you, and attend to the sowing of your land. Let us sail for the Hellespont and Ionia next spring.'

Themistocles' idea in saying this was to lay the foundation for a future claim upon Xerxes, in order to have somewhere to turn to in the event – which did in fact occur – of his getting
110 into trouble with the Athenians. But whatever his ulterior motives, the Athenians were ready to take his advice; they had always thought him clever, and now that he had proved beyond a doubt both clever and successful, they were willing to follow his lead in everything.

Once he had persuaded them to accept his proposal, Themistocles lost no time in getting a message through to Xerxes. The men he chose for this purpose were all people he could trust to keep his instructions secret, even under torture. One of them, as on a previous occasion, was his servant Sicinnus. The party crossed to Attica, and then, while the others waited by the boat, Sicinnus went to find Xerxes, and deliver his message. 'I have come,' he said, 'on behalf of Themistocles, son of Neocles and commander of the Athenian fleet, the most brilliant leader of the confederacy. I am to inform you that Themistocles of Athens, in his desire to serve your interests, has stopped the Greeks from pursuing your navy and destroying the bridges on the Hellespont, which is what they wished to do. You may now, therefore, march your army home without danger of interference.'[35]

The message delivered, the men returned to Andros; and the 111 Greeks, now that it was decided neither to continue the chase nor to sail to the Hellespont to break the bridges, invested the city with the intention of taking it. The Andrians were the first of the islanders to refuse Themistocles' demand for money; he had put it to them that they would be unable to avoid paying, because the Athenians had the support of two powerful deities, one called Persuasion and the other Compulsion, and the Andrians had replied that Athens was lucky to have two such useful gods, who were obviously responsible for her wealth and greatness; unfortunately, however, they themselves, in their small and inadequate land, had two utterly useless deities, who refused to leave the island and insisted on staying; and their names were Poverty and Inability. With the support of these, no money would be forthcoming; for however strong Athens was, she could never turn Andros' 'can't' into 'can'. This answer, and the refusal to pay, were the reasons for the siege.

Meanwhile Themistocles, always greedy for money, sent 112 demands to the other islands; he employed the same messengers as he had sent to Xerxes, and backed his demand by the threat that, if they did not pay what he asked, he would bring the Greek fleet and blockade them into surrender. By these means he succeeded in collecting large sums from the people of

Carystus and Paros, who took fright and paid up when they heard that Andros was already invested because of her support of Persia, and that Themistocles had the highest reputation of the Greek commanders. I cannot say whether or not any of the other islanders gave Themistocles money – though they probably did. The Carystians got no benefit from their compliance; the Parians, however, having thus propitiated Themistocles, escaped a visit from the fleet. Thus it was that Themistocles extorted money from the islanders, while he lay at Andros. The other commanders knew nothing of these proceedings.[36]

113   A few days after the battle of Salamis, Xerxes' army began its withdrawal, marching into Boeotia by the same route as it had taken during its advance. Mardonius wished to accompany the king for part of his way home, and, as it was not then the campaigning season, he judged that it would be better to winter in Thessaly and make his attempt upon the Peloponnese the following spring. On his arrival there he chose the troops which were to serve under his command: these were, first, the Persian regiment of Immortals, all except their commander, Hydarnes, who said that he was unwilling to leave the king; next, the Persian spearmen and the picked cavalry squadron, a thousand strong; and, lastly, the Medes, Sacae, Bactrians, and Indians, both horse and foot. These contingents he took over complete; from the other nationalities he picked a few men here and there, being guided in his choice either by their appearance or by his knowledge that they had distinguished themselves, until he had a total number, including the cavalry, of 300,000 men.[37] The Persians with their necklaces and armlets provided the largest contingent; next were the Medes – though the Medes were not actually inferior in number, but only in valour.

114   While Xerxes was in Thessaly and Mardonius was selecting the troops for his army, the Lacedaemonians received a message from the oracle at Delphi, urging them to demand reparation from Xerxes for the killing of Leonidas, and to accept whatever he offered them. The Spartans at once sent a representative, who was in time to catch the Persian army before it left Thessaly.

The man obtained an interview with Xerxes, and said: 'King of
the Medes, the Lacedaemonians and the house of Heracles in
Sparta demand satisfaction for blood, because you killed their
king while he was fighting in defence of Greece.' Xerxes laughed,
and for a time did not answer; then, pointing to Mardonius who
happened to be standing by him, 'They will get', he said, 'all the
satisfaction they deserve from Mardonius here.'[38] The messen-   115
ger accepted this for an answer and went home.

Xerxes now left Mardonius in Thessaly and made his way
with all speed to the Hellespont. He reached the crossing in
forty-five days, but with hardly a fraction of his army intact.
During the march the troops lived off the country as best they
could, eating grass where they found no grain, and stripping the
bark and leaves off trees of all sorts, cultivated or wild, to stay
their hunger. They left nothing anywhere, so hard were they put
to it for supplies. Plague and dysentery attacked them; many
died, and others who fell sick were left behind in the various
towns along the route, with instructions for their care and
keep – some in Thessaly, others at Siris in Paeonia, others in
Macedon.[39] It was at Siris that Xerxes, during the march to
Greece, had left the sacred chariot of Zeus, and now he failed
to recover it because the Paeonians had given it to the Thracians
and, when Xerxes demanded it, pretended that the mares had
been stolen at pasture by the up-country Thracians, who live
near the source of the Strymon. Here, too, a Thracian chieftain,   116
the king of Crestonia and the Bisaltae, did a peculiarly horrible
deed: he refused to submit to Xerxes and fled inland into the
hills of Mt Rhodope, and had also forbidden his sons to serve
in the expedition against Greece. They, however, all joined up
in the Persian army – either because they cared little about their
father's orders, or simply from a desire to see the war. All six of
them came back safe, and their father, to punish their dis-
obedience, gouged their eyes out. So that was the pay *they* got.   117

The Persians having passed through Thrace reached the passage over the Hellespont and lost no time in getting across to
Abydos. They crossed, however, in ships, as they found the
bridges no longer in position, but shattered by storms. Food
was more plentiful at Abydos than what they had had on the

march, with the result that the men over-ate themselves, and this, combined with the change of water, caused many deaths in what remained of the army. The remnant proceeded with Xerxes to Sardis.

118   There is another account, different from the preceding, according to which Xerxes, on his retreat from Athens, travelled by land only as far as Eion on the Strymon; here he turned the army over to Hydarnes for the march to the Hellespont, and himself crossed to Asia in a Phoenician ship. During the passage, they were caught by a strong wind, blowing from the mouth of the Strymon, accompanied by a heavy sea; in the worsening weather the ship, her deck covered with a crowd of Persians who were accompanying the king, was in considerable danger; and Xerxes in sudden fright called out to the ship's master to ask if there was any way of getting out of it alive. 'None whatever, my lord,' the man replied, 'unless we can rid ourselves of this crowd on deck.' Upon this Xerxes is supposed to have said: 'Men of Persia, now is the moment for each one of you to prove his concern for the king; for my safety, it seems, is in your hands.' The Persian noblemen bowed low, and then, without more ado, jumped overboard; and the ship, lightened of her load, came safely to her port on the Asian coast. The moment Xerxes had gone ashore he presented the master with a gold crown as a reward for saving the king's life, and then, to punish him for causing the death of a number of Persians, cut off his

119   head. Personally, I do not find this second account of Xerxes' return at all convincing – especially as regards what happened to the Persians. If the ship's master had really said to Xerxes what he is supposed to have said, surely not one in ten thousand would doubt that Xerxes would have made the people on deck go down below – after all, they were Persian noblemen – and would then have flung overboard an equivalent number of rowers – who were mere Phoenicians. No; the truth is, as I said before, that he returned to Asia by road with the army.

120   Moreover, this is corroborated by the fact that Xerxes is known to have passed through Abdera on his journey back, and to have made a pact of friendship with the people there, and to have given them a golden scimitar and a gold-embroidered headband.

The men of Abdera also say (though I do not believe them) that during Xerxes' retreat from Athens their town was the first place where he felt safe enough to undo his girdle. Now Abdera is nearer the Hellespont than Eion is, or the Strymon, where according to the other account Xerxes boarded a ship.

The Greeks, meanwhile, failed to take Andros and turned their attention to Carystus. They devastated its land, and then returned to Salamis. Their first act on reaching Salamis was to choose from the plunder taken in the battle the 'first fruits' to be offered in token of gratitude to the gods; these consisted of various objects, but most notably of three Phoenician triremes, one to be dedicated at the Isthmus (where it was still to be seen in my own day), another at Sunium, and another, as an offering to Ajax, in Salamis itself. They then turned to the division of the plunder, and sent to Delphi the 'first fruits' set apart for the purpose; from these was made the statue, eighteen feet high, which has the beak of a ship in its hand, and stands beside the gold statue of Alexander of Macedon.[40] 121

After the dispatch of the thank-offerings to Delphi, the Greeks asked the god, in the name of the country generally, if he felt he had received his full share and was satisfied. His answer was that he was satisfied with what everyone had given, except the Aeginetans: from them he demanded his due from their prize of valour won at Salamis. In consequence of this the Aeginetans dedicated the three gold stars on a bronze mast – now to be seen in the corner near the bowl which was dedicated by Croesus. 122

When the plunder had been distributed, the Greeks sailed to the Isthmus, where a prize of valour was to be awarded to the man who was judged best to deserve it by his conduct throughout the campaign. The commanders met at the altar of Poseidon to cast their votes for first and second place; and, as they all thought that they had fought more bravely than anybody else, every one of them put his own name at the top – though the majority agreed in putting Themistocles second. Consequently nobody got more than one vote for first place, while Themistocles easily headed the poll for the second. Mutual jealousy thus prevented a decision, and the various commanders sailed 123

124

off home without making an award; in spite of this, however, Themistocles' name was on everyone's lips, and he acquired the reputation of being by far the most able man throughout Greece.

Immediately after this, having failed to win from the men who fought at Salamis the mark of honour to which he was entitled, he went to Lacedaemon hoping for honour there. He was given a splendid welcome, and treated with the highest respect. The actual prize of valour – a wreath of olive – was, indeed, given to Eurybiades, but a similar wreath was granted to Themistocles as well, for his wisdom and cleverness. He was also presented with a chariot, the finest in Sparta, and received high praise. On his departure he was escorted as far as the borders of Tegea by the picked troop of three hundred Spartans called the Knights. Themistocles was the only person we know of who ever received the honour of an escort from the Spartans.

125   Back in Athens he came in for a deal of abuse from a certain Timodemus of Aphidna, whose hatred of Themistocles was his only claim to distinction. Mad with jealousy, he reviled him for going to Sparta, and maintained that he had earned his honours there not by his own merit but merely by the fame of Athens. The continual repetition of this taunt at last drew from Themistocles a reply: 'I'll tell you what,' he said; 'I should never have been honoured as I was if I had been born a Belbinite – and you wouldn't, Athenian though you are!'[41]

126   Artabazus, the son of Pharnaces, who was already a famous man in the Persian army and was further to increase his reputation as a result of the battle of Plataea, acted as escort to Xerxes, with 60,000 of Mardonius' picked troops, as far as the crossing over the Hellespont. Once the king was in Asia, Artabazus set out on his march back; realizing on his arrival in the neighbourhood of Pallene that Mardonius was wintering in Thessaly and Macedonia, and being as yet in no hurry to rejoin the rest of the army, he considered it his duty, as he found Potidaea in a state of revolt, to bring the town into subjection. The people of Potidaea, like the other inhabitants of the Pallene peninsula, had openly thrown off the Persian yoke as soon as Xerxes passed them on

his march to the eastward and they knew of the flight of the Persian fleet from Salamis.

Artabazus, therefore, began the siege, and at the same time invested Olynthus in expectations of a similar revolt – Olynthus was at that time occupied by the Bottiaei, who had been expelled by the Macedonians from the country round the gulf of Therma. The town soon fell; Artabazus butchered the inhabitants and threw their bodies into a lake, turning over the town itself to the control of Critobulus of Torone and the Chalcidians – which was how these people got possession of Olynthus. Artabazus then turned all his attention to Potidaea. While he was vigorously pressing the siege, Timoxenus, commander of the troops from Scione, agreed with him to betray the town. How the thing began, I cannot say, for no account has reached us; but the final stage of the plot was as follows. Whenever Timoxenus and Artabazus wished to communicate with one another, they wrote the message on a strip of paper, which they rolled round the grooved end of an arrow; the feathers were then put on over the paper, and the arrow was shot to some predetermined place. Timoxenus' treachery was finally discovered when Artabazus, on one occasion, missed his aim, and the arrow, instead of falling in the spot agreed upon, struck a Potidaean in the shoulder. As usually happens in war, a crowd collected round the wounded man; the arrow was pulled out, the paper discovered and taken to the commanding officers – those of Potidaea itself and of the other peninsular towns which were supporting her. The letter was read, and the officers, finding who the culprit was, nevertheless resolved to bring no charge of treachery against him, in order to spare the people of Scione from being branded for ever afterwards with the name of traitors.

Three months later, while the siege was still in progress, there was an exceptionally low tide which lasted a long time. The sight of the shallow water suggested to the Persians the possibility of getting through it and across into Pallene. But when they were two-fifths of the way over, they were caught by the succeeding flood, which was of corresponding height – indeed, according to the people thereabouts, higher than it had been before, though big tides are not uncommon there. All the men who could not swim were drowned, and those who could were killed by the Potidaeans, who went out after them in boats. This excessive tide and the consequent disaster to the Persians are put down by the people of Potidaea to the fact that the men who met their deaths were the same ones as had previously desecrated the shrine of Poseidon, and the statue of him which stands just outside the town. Personally, I think their explanation is the true one. After this incident Artabazus withdrew with the remainder of his men and rejoined Mardonius in Thessaly.

130   The surviving ships of Xerxes' fleet, having made good their escape from Salamis to Asia, had ferried the king and the army across the strait from the Chersonese to Abydos, and then laid up for the winter at Cyme. At the first gleam of spring the following year the fleet mustered at Samos – where, indeed, some of the ships had wintered. Most of the fighting troops serving on board were Persians or Medes; and the command was taken over by Mardontes, the son of Bagaeus, and Artaÿntes, the son of Artachaees, together with one other – Ithamitres, Artaÿntes' nephew, who had been chosen for the position by his uncle. In view of the serious blow they had suffered, they went no further west, nor did anyone attempt to force them to do so – but remained in Samos to guard against a possible Ionian revolt. Their fleet, including the Ionian contingent, numbered 300 ships of war. It never entered their thoughts that the Greeks would undertake an expedition to Ionia; it was much more likely, in the Persian view, that they would be content to defend their own country, especially as they had not pursued the Persian fleet during its flight from Salamis but had so readily given up the chase. The fact is that, so far as naval operations were concerned, the Persians had completely lost heart, though they still believed that Mardonius and his army were sure of an easy victory. Accordingly they kept the fleet at Samos, laying plans for any possible means of harassing the enemy, and at the same time waiting for news of Mardonius.

131   The coming of spring and the presence of Mardonius in Thessaly roused the Greeks to action again. Before the army mustered, the fleet, 110 strong, proceeded to Aegina under the

supreme command of Leotychides. Leotychides belonged to the younger branch of the Spartan royal house, and traced his descent back to Heracles through Menares, Agesilaus, Hippocratides, Leotychides, Anaxilaus, Archidamus, Anaxandrides, Theopompus, Nicander, Charilaus, Eunomus, Polydectes, Prytanis, Euryphon, Procles, Aristodemus, Aristomachus, Cleodaeus, and Hyllus – who was Heracles' son. All these except the two[42] first named had been kings of Sparta. The Athenian squadron was commanded by Xanthippus, the son of Ariphron.[43]

After the arrival of the fleet at Aegina, representatives from 132 Ionia – amongst them Herodotus, the son of Basileides – came to the Greek headquarters with a request for aid.[44] They were the same men as had visited Sparta not long before to ask the Spartans to liberate Ionia. Originally there were seven of them, and they had formed a conspiracy to murder Strattis, the tyrant of Chios; but the plot was betrayed by one of their number, and the remaining six left the island and went to Sparta; and after that, as I have said, they came on to Aegina with a request to the Greeks to undertake an expedition to Ionia. However, it was only with great difficulty that they persuaded them to advance as far as Delos, for the Greeks had little experience of what lay beyond, and imagined it to be full of Persian troops and of every sort of danger. As for Samos, it seemed to them as far away as the Pillars of Heracles. The result was that while the Persians were too badly scared to risk sailing west of Samos, the Greeks, in spite of the earnest solicitation of the Chians, did not dare to sail east of Delos. Their mutual fears stood sentry over the intervening area.[45]

While Mardonius was wintering in Thessaly, he instructed a 133 man named Mys, a Carian from the town of Europus, to make the round of all the oracles which it was possible for him to consult. What precisely he hoped to learn from the oracles when he gave this order, I cannot say, for there is no record; but presumably he sent for information and advice on the business he had at the moment in hand, and not for any other purpose.

It is known that Mys visited Lebadeia, where he paid a man 134 to enter the cave of Trophonius, and the oracle at Abae in

Phocis; he also visited Thebes, where he consulted the oracle of Apollo Ismenius (in whose temple oracles are sought by sacrifices, as at Olympia), and also paid somebody to pass the night in the temple of Amphiaraus. The person he persuaded to do this was not a Theban; for Thebans are forbidden to consult this oracle, because Amphiaraus, through the mouth of the Priestess, once gave them the exclusive choice of two alternatives – whether, that is, they would prefer to have him as a prophet to foretell the future, or as a friend to help them in war: and they chose the latter. And that is why no Theban may pass the night in his shrine.

135   One thing which the Thebans say happened at this time seems to me very remarkable: Mys, the man from Europus, visited during his tour of the oracles the precinct of Apollo Ptoiüs; the temple, which is called Ptoiüm, belongs to Thebes and is situated very near Acraephia, on the hill overlooking Lake Copais.[46] Mys entered the shrine accompanied by three men from Thebes, who had been officially appointed to take down whatever answer the god might give. The prophet through whom the god spoke at once delivered his oracles – in a foreign language. The three Thebans were astonished at hearing a strange tongue instead of Greek, and did not know what to do about it; Mys, however, snatched the tablet they had brought to write the oracle on, and, declaring that the god's response had been delivered in Carian,

136   wrote it down himself and hurried back to Thessaly. Mardonius read whatever it was the oracle said, and then sent Alexander, the son of Amyntas, to Athens with a message. He chose Alexander, who was a Macedonian, for two reasons: first, because he was connected with the Persians by marriage – Bubares, a Persian, had married Alexander's sister Gygaea;[47] they had a son who stayed in Asia, named Amyntas after his maternal grandfather, who enjoyed by the king's gift the revenues of the important Phrygian town of Alabanda; secondly, because he was well aware that Alexander's friendship with Athens was an official relationship, and was backed by deeds. Mardonius therefore thought that by sending him he would be most likely to bring Athens over to the Persian interest; he knew that the Athenians were a numerous and gallant people, and had been

chiefly responsible for the defeat of the Persian navy, and expected that if only he could form an alliance with them, he would have no difficulty in getting the mastery of the sea – an expectation which was perfectly justified – while he was already confident of his superiority on land. In this way he reckoned that the defeat of Greece would be within his grasp. Perhaps the Athenian alliance had been what the oracles advised, and it was in obedience to them that he sent Alexander on his mission.

This Alexander was descended, in the seventh generation, 137 from Perdiccas, who won the lordship of the Macedonians in the following way. Three brothers, Gauanes, Aeropus, and Perdiccas, descendants of Temenus, had been expelled from Argos and had taken refuge in Illyria. Thence they crossed into upper Macedonia and went to the town of Lebaea, where they hired themselves out to do menial work for the king, one tending the horses, another the oxen, and the youngest, Perdiccas, the sheep and goats. In the old days it was not only the common folk who were poor; even the reigning houses were of slender means, and in Lebaea the king's wife cooked the food. Now it happened that every time she baked, the loaf intended for the boy Perdiccas swelled to double its proper size. She said nothing for a while, but when it went on happening every time, she told her husband. At once it occurred to the king that it was a portent from heaven of some important event, so he sent for the three servants and ordered them to leave the country. The young men, in reply, said they had a right to their wages, and would go as soon as they were paid. The sun was shining through the smoke-hole in the roof of the house, and the king, when he heard wages mentioned, was inspired to his ruin, crying out: 'I give you the wages you deserve – there they are!' – and pointed to the sun. The two elder brothers, Gauanes and Aeropus, were struck dumb; but the boy, who had a knife in his hand, scratched a line with the point of it round the patch of sunlight on the floor, and said: 'King, we accept what you offer us.' Then three times he gathered the sunlight into the folds of his tunic, and left the town together with his brothers.

When they were gone, somebody who was in attendance 138 upon the king mentioned what a significant thing the boy had done; and suggested that the youngest of the three knew what he was doing in accepting the offered wage. The king was angry and ordered men to ride in pursuit of the brothers and kill them.

In this part of the country there is a river to which the descendants of these three men offer sacrifice as their saviour – for when the sons of Temenus had crossed it, it suddenly rose so high that their pursuers were unable to get over. Once safe on the other side, the brothers went on to another part of Macedonia and settled near the place called the Gardens of Midas, the son of Gordias, where roses grow wild – wonderful blooms, with sixty petals apiece, and sweeter smelling than any others in the world. According to the Macedonians it was in these gardens that Silenus was caught. Above them rises Mt Bermium, the heights of which are so cold that none can climb them, and it was from the slopes of these mountains that the brothers conquered, first, the land in the immediate neighbourhood, and afterwards the rest of Macedonia.[48]

139   From the Perdiccas of this story Alexander was descended: he was the son of Amyntas, Amyntas of Alcetas; the father of Alcetas was Aeropus; of Aeropus, Philippus; of Philippus, Argaeus; and of Argaeus, Perdiccas – who first won the sovereign power.

140 a   On his arrival at Athens as Mardonius' ambassador, Alexander spoke in the following terms: 'Men of Athens, this is from Mardonius: I have received a message from the king, which says: "I am willing to forget all the injuries which Athens has done me. So, Mardonius, first give the Athenians back their land; and secondly, let them take whatever other territory they wish, and have self-government. If they are willing to come to terms with me, you are also to rebuild the temples which I burnt." Those are the king's orders which I have to carry out, unless you yourselves put obstacles in the way. Why then – I ask you – are you so mad as to take arms against the king? You can never defeat him, and you cannot hold out for ever. You have seen his army, its size, and what it can do; you know, too, how powerful a force I have under me now. Even should you beat us – and, if you have any sense, you cannot hope to do so – another force many times as powerful will come against you.

So stop trying to be a match for the king, at the cost of the loss
of your country and continual peril of your lives. Come to terms
with him instead – you have the finest possible opportunity of
doing so, now that Xerxes is inclined that way. Make an alliance
with us, without craft and deceit, and so keep your freedom.'

'So much for what Mardonius instructed me to say to you.   *b*
Now let me speak for myself. There is no need to mention my
goodwill towards you – that you already know well enough; I
merely add my earnest entreaties that you will do as Mardonius
asks. It is clear to me that you will not be able to maintain your
struggle with Xerxes for ever – had I thought you could, I should
never have come to Athens on this mission. But the fact is,
Xerxes' power is superhuman, and his arm is long. If, then, you
do not at once conclude a peace, now that such excellent terms
are offered, I tremble for your future, when I think how of all
the confederate states you lie most directly in the path of danger.
You alone will continue to suffer, since your country will be a
sort of no-man's-land. Do, therefore, agree; for surely it is no
small thing that the Great King should single you out from all
the people of Greece, and be willing to forgive the past and to
become your friend.'

In Sparta the news of Alexander's visit to try to bring about   141
an alliance between Persia and Athens caused consternation.
The Spartans, remembering the prophecy that the Dorians
would one day be expelled from the Peloponnese by the Persians
and Athenians, and greatly fearing that the alliance might be
concluded, at once decided to send representatives to Athens. It
so happened that Alexander and the Spartan envoys had their
audience at the same time; for the Athenians had dragged out
their business with Alexander, realizing that the Spartans would
hear that someone had arrived in Athens to represent Persia in
peace negotiations, and would then send representatives of their
own without delay. So they did this on purpose, so that the
Spartans might be present when they declared their views.

Accordingly, when Alexander had finished his speech, the   142
Spartan envoys spoke in their turn: 'The Spartans have sent us
here to beg you not to endanger Greece by a departure from
your previous policy, and to listen to no proposals from Persia.

For any of the Greeks to do such a thing would be inconsistent with decency and honour; for you it would be far worse, for many reasons. It was you, in the first place, who started this war – our wishes were not considered.[49] It began by being a war for your territories only – now all Greece is involved. Again, it would be an intolerable thing that the Athenians, who in the past have been known so often as liberators, should now be the cause of bringing slavery upon Greece. We do, however, sympathize with you in your hardships – the loss of two successive harvests and the ruin of your homes and property over so long a time; and in compensation we offer, in the name of Sparta and her allies, to provide support for all the women and other non-combatant members of your households, for as long as the war lasts.

'Do not let Alexander's smooth-sounding version of Mardonius' proposals seduce you; he does only what one might expect of him – a despot himself, of course he collaborates with a despot. But such conduct is not for you – at least, not if you are wise; for surely you know that in foreigners there is neither truth nor trust.'

143   The Athenians then gave Alexander their answer. 'We know', it ran, 'as well as you do that the Persian strength is many times greater than our own: that, at least, is a fact which you need not rub in. Nevertheless, such is our love of freedom, that we will defend ourselves in whatever way we can. As for making terms with Persia, it is useless to try to persuade us; for we shall never consent. And now tell Mardonius, that so long as the sun keeps his present course in the sky, we Athenians will never make peace with Xerxes. On the contrary, we shall oppose him unremittingly, putting our trust in the help of the gods and heroes whom he despised, whose temples and statues he destroyed with fire. Never come to us again with a proposal like this, and never think you are doing us good service when you urge us to a course which is outrageous – for it would be a pity if you were to suffer some hurt at the hands of the Athenians, when you are our friend and benefactor.'

144   So much for the Athenians' answer to Alexander. To the Spartan envoys they said: 'No doubt it was natural that the

Lacedaemonians should dread the possibility of our making terms with Persia; none the less it shows a poor estimate of the spirit of Athens. There is not so much gold in the world nor land so fair that we would take it for pay to join the common enemy and bring Greece into subjection. There are many compelling reasons against our doing so, even if we wished: the first and greatest is the burning of the temples and images of our gods – now ashes and rubble. It is our bounden duty to avenge this desecration with all our might – not to clasp the hand that wrought it. Again, there is the Greek nation – the community of blood and language, temples and ritual, and our common customs; if Athens were to betray all this, it would not be well done. We would have you know, therefore, if you did not know it already, that so long as a single Athenian remains alive we will make no peace with Xerxes. We are deeply moved, however, by your kindness and thoughtfulness, and the offer you made to provide for our families in this time of distress. Nothing could be more generous; nevertheless we prefer to carry on as best we can, without being a burden to you. That being our resolve, get your army into the field with the least possible delay; for unless we are much mistaken, it will not be long before the enemy invades Attica – he will do it the instant he gets the news that we refuse his requests. Now, therefore, before he can appear in Attica, it is time for us to meet him in Boeotia.'[50]

Athens had given her answer; and the Spartan envoys left for home.

BOOK NINE

1   When Alexander returned with the Athenians' answer, Mardonius left Thessaly and marched with all speed for Athens, levying troops on the way from all the places through which he passed. The leading families of Thessaly continued to maintain their previous attitude; indeed they urged the Persians to the attack more vigorously than ever. Thorax of Larissa even escorted Xerxes in his retreat, and now openly encouraged Mardonius in his assault upon Greece.

2   In Boeotia an attempt was made by the Thebans to persuade him to halt. There was no better place, they said, to encamp, and their advice was that he should proceed no further, but, with Boeotia as his base, take measures for the conquest of Greece without striking a blow. If the former confederacy of Greek states continued to hold together, the whole world would have a hard task to defeat them; 'But if', the Thebans added, 'you do as we suggest, you will put an end to all their schemes with no trouble at all. Send money to the leading men in the various towns – by doing that you will destroy the unity of the country, after which you will easily be able, with the help of those who take your part, to crush those who still oppose you.'

3   Mardonius did not act upon this suggestion. His whole heart was set upon taking Athens again – partly, no doubt, through mere obstinacy, and partly because he wished to signal his capture of the town to the king in Sardis by a chain of beacons through the islands. When he reached Attica, once again there were no Athenians to be found; for nearly all of them, as he learnt, were either with the fleet or at Salamis. So he captured a deserted town – ten months after its previous capture by Xerxes.[1]

From Athens Mardonius sent Murychides, a Hellespontine 4
Greek, to Salamis with instructions to repeat to the Athenians
the proposals already made to them by Alexander. Not that he
was unaware of their feelings towards him; he knew well enough
that they were far from friendly; but he made his second
approach in the hope that the occupation of the whole of Attica
by his troops might have gone some way towards breaking
their spirit. So Murychides was dispatched on his errand, 5
and delivered Mardonius' message to the Athenian council
in Salamis. One of the councillors, a man named Lycidas,
expressed the opinion that the best course would be to admit
the proposals which Murychides brought, and to submit them
for approval to the general assembly of the people. This was his
expressed opinion – whether he had been bribed by Mardonius
to express it or really thought so. In any case the Athenians,
both those in the council and those outside, were so enraged
when they heard it that they surrounded Lycidas and stoned
him to death. Murychides they allowed to depart unharmed.
With all the uproar in Salamis over Lycidas, the Athenian
women soon found out what had happened; whereupon, without a word from the men, they got together, and, each one
urging on her neighbour and taking her along with the crowd,
flocked to Lycidas' house and stoned his wife and children.[2]

The circumstances in which the Athenians had crossed into
Salamis were these: so long as they expected an army from the 6
Peloponnese to come to their assistance, they remained in Attica;
but when they found that their Peloponnesian allies kept hanging about and were unwilling to move, and word came that the
Persians were advancing and had actually got as far as Boeotia,
they waited no longer, but crossed to Salamis with all their
movable property, and at the same time sent a message to
Lacedaemon to reproach the Spartans for allowing the enemy
to invade Attica instead of marching with them to meet him in
Boeotia, and to remind them, besides, of the offers they had
received from Persia in the event of their deserting the Greek
confederacy – not to mention the obvious fact that, if they got
no help from Sparta, they would have to find some means of
helping themselves.[3]

7 Just then it was the time of the Hyacinthia in Sparta; the people thought it most important to give the god his due.[4] It also happened that the wall they were building across the Isthmus was almost finished and about to have the battlements put on.

The Athenian messengers, accompanied by representatives from Megara and Plataea, reached Sparta and came before the a Ephors. This is what they said: 'The Athenians have sent us to tell you that the Persian king has offered both to restore our country to us, and at the same time, not only to make an alliance with us on fair and equal terms, openly and honestly, but also to give us any other territory we like to annex. We, however, from our reverence of Zeus whom all Greece worships, and our revulsion from the very thought of treachery, peremptorily refused the offer, in spite of the fact that we ourselves have been treated unjustly and basely betrayed by our own confederates, and are well aware that we should gain more by an agreement with Persia than by prolonging the war. None the less, we shall never willingly make terms with the enemy. Thus we, at any b rate, pay our debts to Greece with no counterfeit coin; but you, who were in terror lest we should make peace with Persia – now that you know our spirit without doubt, and that we shall never be traitors to Greece – and now, too, that your fortification of the Isthmus is almost complete – take no account of Athens. You agreed with us to oppose the invader in Boeotia, but you broke your word and allowed him to invade Attica. This conduct on your part has roused the anger of Athens; it was unworthy of the hour and of yourselves. However, your immediate duty is to accede to our present request: put your army in the field, that you and we together may meet Mardonius in Attica. Now that Boeotia is lost to us, the best place to engage him, within our own territory, is the plain of Thria.'

8 The Ephors undertook to give their answer on the following day; but when it came, they made a further postponement till the day after, and then till the day after that; in fact they kept putting it off from one day to the next for nearly a fortnight. Meanwhile the Peloponnesians in a body were working hard at the wall across the Isthmus, which was now nearing completion.

Why was it that, when Alexander visited Athens, the Spartans were desperately anxious lest the Athenians should go over to Persia, whereas now they did not seem to care a jot? The only explanation I can give is, that the fortifications of the Isthmus were now complete, and they therefore felt that Athenian help was no longer necessary. At the time of Alexander's visit, the wall was not complete – they were still working at it, in great fear of the Persians.

At last, however, the Spartans did give their answer, and did 9 put their army in the field. This was how it happened: on the eve of the day fixed for the final audience of the Athenian delegation, a Tegean named Chileus, a man with more influence in Sparta than anyone else who was not a native, asked the Ephors exactly what the Athenians had said, and having heard, he said: 'As I see it, gentlemen, if the Athenians desert us and make an alliance with Persia, then, however strongly the Isthmus is fortified, the gates are wide open for the Persian invasion of the Peloponnese. So you had better listen to them before they change their minds and adopt a policy which will ruin Greece.'

The Ephors took the warning to heart, and without a word 10 to the delegates, immediately, before daybreak, dispatched a force of 5000 Spartan troops, each man attended by seven helots, with Pausanias, son of Cleombrotus, in command.[5]

The chief power in Sparta belonged by right at this time to Leonidas' son Pleistarchus; but he was still a minor, and Pausanias was his guardian and cousin. Cleombrotus, Pausanias' father and son of Anaxandrides, was no longer alive, but had died soon after he brought back the troops who had been building the fortifications at the Isthmus – he had brought them home because the sun was darkened in the sky during the course of a sacrifice he was offering, in the hope of favourable omens for a battle.[6] Pausanias appointed Euryanax, son of Dorieus and a member of the same family as himself, to share the command.

Next day the ambassadors, quite unaware that Pausanias and 11 his troops were on the march, presented themselves before the Ephors for the last time, fully determined to leave Sparta and return to their respective homes. 'Then stay here if you want to,' they exclaimed; 'keep your Hyacinthia and amuse yourselves –

and betray your friends. But we warn you: the Athenians will resent this injustice and, for lack of other allies, will make such an arrangement with the Persians as they can. That being done, it is plain that we shall be Xerxes' friends and shall fight, in consequence, against whatever country the Persians choose to lead us. The effect of that upon yourselves you will then be able to appreciate.'

At this the Ephors replied that they would take their oath that the army was already at Orestheium, on its march against the 'strangers'. ('Strangers' was the word they used for foreigners.) The delegates, at a loss, asked what they meant, and were told the truth. They were surprised, and hurried off after them. With them went 5000 picked Lacedaemonian troops drawn from the outlying towns.[7]

12   The Argives, who had previously agreed with Mardonius to prevent Spartan troops from taking the field, no sooner learned that Pausanias' army had left Sparta than they dispatched the best runner they could find with a message to Attica. There he presented himself to Mardonius, and said: 'I have been sent by the Argives to tell you that the fighting force of Lacedaemon is on the march, and that the Argives have been powerless to stop it. You must take measures accordingly.' The runner then left

13   for home, and Mardonius, having heard his report, no longer felt inclined to remain in Attica. Up till then he had held on there because he wanted to find out which way the Athenians would go, and in the hope that they would come to terms he had refrained throughout his stay from doing damage of any kind to crops or property. Now, however, that he had failed to win them over, and the whole position was clear, he withdrew from the district before Pausanias' force reached the Isthmus. Before he went, he burnt Athens and reduced to complete ruin anything that remained standing – walls, houses, temples, and all. His reason for abandoning Attica was that it was bad country for cavalry; moreover, had he been beaten in an engagement, his only way of retreat would have been by a narrow defile, which could be held by a very small force. His plan, therefore, was to retire on Thebes, where he could fight in good cavalry country and near a friendly town.

He was already on the road when news reached him that 14
another Spartan force, 1000 strong, had arrived at Megara in
advance of Pausanias. Considering this news, and wishing, if
possible, to destroy them first, he wheeled about and made for
Megara, while his cavalry, pushing on ahead, overran all the
surrounding country. This was the most westerly point in
Europe that was reached by this Persian army.

More news now came that the Greek forces had concentrated 15
in strength at the Isthmus, and Mardonius, in consequence,
began his withdrawal by way of Decelea. The chief magistrates
of the Boeotians had sent for men from the valley of the Asopus,
and they acted as guides to the army, bringing it first to Sphen-
dale and then on to Tanagra, where it halted for a night. Next
day Mardonius made for Scolus, and so found himself in Theban
territory. In spite of the fact that the Thebans were on his side,
he cut down all the trees in the neighbourhood – not as an act
of hostility to Thebes, but simply for his own military needs, for
he wished to construct a palisade to protect his troops and to
have somewhere to retreat to in the event of the battle going
against him. The position he occupied was along the Asopus,
from Erythrae, past Hysiae, to the territory of Plataea; the
palisade did not cover all this ground, but was approximately
ten furlongs square.[8]

While the Persian troops were working on the palisade, a
Theban named Attaginus, the son of Phrynon, invited Mardonius and fifty other distinguished Persians to a banquet, for
which he had made elaborate preparations. The invitation was
accepted and the banquet was held in Thebes. What I am about 16
to relate, I heard from Thersander, a man greatly respected in
his native town Orchomenus. Thersander told me that he himself had an invitation from Attaginus, and that there were,
besides the Persians, fifty Thebans. At table, the two nationalities, Greek and Persian, were not kept separate, but on each
couch there sat a Persian and a Theban, side by side. During the
drinking which followed the banquet, the Persian who shared
Thersander's couch asked him, in Greek, what town he came
from. 'Orchomenus,' was the answer. 'Since you and I', the
Persian said, 'have eaten together at the same table and poured

a libation from the same cup, I should like to leave you something by which you may remember the soundness of my judgement; thus you will be forewarned and be able to take proper
measures for your own safety. You see these Persians at their
dinner – and the army we left in camp over there by the river?
In a short time from now you will see but a few of all these
men left alive.' The Persian, as he spoke, wept copiously, and
Thersander, greatly marvelling at what he had said, answered:
'Are not Mardonius and the other high Persian officers under
him the proper people to be told a thing like that?' 'My friend,'
rejoined the other, 'what God has ordained no man can by any
means prevent. Many of us know that what I have said is true;
yet, because we are constrained by necessity, we continue to
take orders from our commander. No one would believe us,
however true our warning. This is the worst pain a man can
have: to know much and have no power to act.'

This tale, as I have said, I heard from Thersander of Orchomenus; he also told me that he repeated it soon after to various
people before the battle of Plataea.[9]

17   While Mardonius was in Boeotia, all the Greeks in that part
of the country who had gone over to Persia sent troops to join
his army, and also took part in his attack on Athens – all, that
is, except the Phocians. The Phocians had, indeed, warmly
embraced the Persian interest, but under compulsion and not of
their free choice.[10] A few days after Mardonius' arrival at
Thebes, he was joined by a force of Phocian infantry, a thousand
strong, under the command of Harmocydes, one of their most
distinguished men. On their arrival, Mardonius sent them an
order to take up a position in open ground, apart from the rest
of the army. The order was no sooner obeyed than the Persian
cavalry made their appearance in full force. On this, a rumour
went round the Greek contingents serving with the Persians that
Mardonius meant to attack the Phocians and shoot them down.
The same idea ran through the Phocians, too. Their commander
Harmocydes then urged them to fight. 'Fellow-countrymen,' he
cried, 'you can't fail to see that these fellows have deliberately
planned to murder us – I suppose because of some lie the
Thessalians have told about us. Come then; show what you are

made of, every one of you. It is better to die actively defending ourselves than just to give up and be butchered – that disgrace, at least, we can avoid. Let us show them that the men they have plotted to murder are Greeks – and they themselves are barbarians.'

The Persian cavalry then surrounded them, and began to close in with weapons poised, as though to make an end of them. A few spears were actually let fly; but the Phocians stood firm, drawing close together and packing their ranks tight, whereupon the Persians wheeled about and retired. Possibly the Thessalians had asked them to commit this crime, but, on seeing their victims prepared to defend themselves, they were afraid of being roughly handled and withdrew, according to Mardonius' orders; it may be, on the other hand, that Mardonius merely wanted to test their courage. I cannot say for certain which explanation is the true one. In any case, after the cavalry had retired, Mardonius sent a message to the Phocians, telling them not to be alarmed: 'You have proved yourselves brave men,' he said, 'quite contrary to the report I had of you. Your duty now is to play a zealous part in the war. As for benefits, you will not outdo either me or the king.' That was the end of this incident.

The Lacedaemonians halted at the Isthmus on their arrival there, and the other Peloponnesians who chose to do their duty – some of them only when they saw the Spartans on the march – felt ashamed to stay behind and take no part in the expedition. Accordingly, after getting favourable omens from the sacrifice, the combined forces of the Peloponnese left the Isthmus and advanced to Eleusis. Here they again offered sacrifice, and again getting good omens continued their advance, having now been joined by the Athenians, who had crossed to the mainland from Salamis. At Erythrae in Boeotia they learnt that the enemy had taken up his position on the Asopus, and, in view of this, themselves occupied the lower slopes of Cithaeron.[11]

When the Greek forces showed no intention of leaving the high ground, Mardonius sent his cavalry to attack them in force, under command of the distinguished Persian officer Masistius – or Macistius, as the Greeks call him – who rode a Nisaean horse with a bridle of gold and other splendid trappings. The cavalry

advanced to the attack in successive squadrons, and at each
assault inflicted heavy losses on the Greeks, taunting them and
21 calling them women. It so happened that the point in the Greek
line which was most open and vulnerable to a cavalry charge
was held by the Megarians, who found themselves hard pressed
by the repeated attacks. Accordingly they sent a message to the
allied commanders. 'Fellow-soldiers,' the message ran, 'without
assistance we are unable to hold the Persian cavalry or to maintain our original position. Up to the present, in spite of severe
losses, we have continued to resist with firmness and courage;
but now, unless you send other troops to relieve us, we warn
you that we shall have to quit our post.'

Pausanias, on receipt of the message, called for volunteers to
relieve the Megarians, but nobody was willing to go except the
Athenians – three hundred of them, picked men, commanded
22 by Olympiodorus, the son of Lampon. This, then, was the force
which consented to act as relief; taking the archers to accompany
them, they marched to their post at the point of danger on behalf
of all the other Greek troops present at Erythrae. For some time
the battle continued, until, during the successive attacks of the
Persian squadrons, Masistius' horse, which was in advance of
the rest, was shot in the flank, and the pain of the wound made
him rear and throw his rider. No sooner was Masistius down
than the Athenians were upon him. They seized his horse and
finally – though not without difficulty – killed Masistius himself,
who fought hard for his life. The reason why they could not kill
him at once was the armour he wore – a corslet of golden scales
under his scarlet tunic. No blow upon the corslet had any effect,
until at last a soldier saw how it was and struck him in the eye,
and he fell dead. This occurred without the knowledge of the rest
of the squadron, who had not observed either their commander's
fall or his death; for he fell just as they had wheeled about and
retired for another charge. It was only when they drew rein
again that they missed him – for there was no one to give the
commands. Without a moment's delay, now that they realized
what had happened, word was passed from man to man, and
the entire force rode in again in the hope, at least, of recovering
23 the body. Seeing a mass attack now coming, the Athenians

called out to the rest of the army for support, and while the
infantry was on the way to their assistance, a sharp struggle
took place round Masistius' body. Before the reinforcements
arrived, the three hundred Athenians, fighting alone, had much
the worst of it and were forced to surrender the body; but once
they were joined by the other troops in full force, the enemy
cavalry were no longer able to hold their ground. They failed to
keep possession of the body, and lost, in the attempt, a number
of their men besides. They then retired a quarter of a mile or so,
to take stock of their situation, and finally decided, having lost
their commander, to report to Mardonius. On their arrival at   24
headquarters with the news, Mardonius and the whole army
showed the deepest distress at Masistius' death – a man more
highly thought of, both by the king and by his subjects, than
anyone else in the Persian army except Mardonius himself; they
shaved their heads, cut the manes of their horses and mules, and
abandoned themselves to such cries of grief that the whole of
Boeotia was loud with the noise of them.[12]

While the Persians, in this typical fashion, were paying their
respects to the dead Masistius, the Greeks, having both held   25
and repulsed the cavalry charge, were much encouraged. They
put Masistius' body on a cart and paraded it along the lines. It
was certainly worth looking at, for Masistius was a tall and
splendidly handsome man – this was why they did it – and men
broke their ranks to get a sight of Masistius.[13]

The Greeks now determined to leave the high ground and
move down to Plataea, a much more convenient position than
the country round Erythrae, especially as it was better supplied
with water. The best thing, therefore, seemed to be to shift camp
and take up a new position, in their proper detachments, near
the spring called Gargaphia in Plataean territory. The march
began, and, proceeding along the lower slopes of Cithaeron,
past Hysiae, the army reached the territory of Plataea, and the
contingents of the several confederated towns halted close to
the spring and the sacred enclosure of the hero Androcrates, in
flat country rising here and there in low hills. Here, in the process 26
of assigning to each contingent its position in the line, a hot
dispute arose between the troops from Tegea and those from

Athens. Both claimed the right to hold one of the wings, and both supported the claim by adducing instances of distinguished service either in their previous history or during recent events. 'Hitherto,' the Tegeans urged, 'we have always by universal consent been given the privilege of holding this position in every campaign undertaken jointly by the Peloponnesians both in recent and in former times – ever since, indeed, the Heracleidae made their attempt to force their way back into the Peloponnese after the death of Eurystheus. Let us remind you how, on that occasion, we won the privilege: the story goes that when, in company with the Achaeans and Ionians who then occupied the Peloponnese, we marched to the Isthmus to take our stand against the invaders, Hyllus made a proclamation to the effect that there was no need for the two armies to risk their lives in a general engagement; it would suffice, he suggested, if a champion chosen from the Peloponnesian army met him in single combat upon agreed conditions. The Peloponnesians accepted the proposal and engaged upon oath that, if Hyllus were victorious, the Heracleidae should be allowed to resume the ancient rights of their family, and that if he were vanquished, they should withdraw their army and make no further attempt upon the Peloponnese for a hundred years.

'The man chosen to represent the confederate armies was our own commander and king, Echemus, the son of Eëropus, and grandson of Phegeus. He volunteered for the service, engaged Hyllus in single combat, and killed him; and it was in recognition of this act that we were granted important privileges amongst the Peloponnesians of that time; we enjoy them still, and the greatest of them is the privilege of leading one of the wings in any campaign undertaken jointly by Peloponnesian troops. Naturally, we do not set ourselves up against you, the Spartan contingent; we willingly grant you the right of choosing whichever wing you prefer; but we do claim the privilege of commanding the other one, according to precedent.

'Even apart from the greatest exploit we have mentioned, our title to the position of honour is better than that of the Athenians – witness, for instance, the many glorious fights we have fought against Sparta herself, not to mention other towns. To us, therefore, belongs this privilege, not to them. They can point to no exploits of their own, either in modern or in ancient times, comparable to ours.'

The Athenian answer was as follows. 'We are well aware that we are assembled here to fight the invader, not to make speeches. Nevertheless, as the Tegeans have started a competition in talking of the brave actions we have respectively performed during the long course of our history, we can hardly refrain from indicating the grounds upon which we, as a people who have always distinguished themselves, claim precedence over the Arcadians as our proper heritage. In the first place, when the Heracleidae, whose chieftain the Tegeans claim to have killed at the Isthmus, were refused shelter by all the Greeks to whom they applied in the hope of escaping slavery under the Mycenaeans, we alone received them, and with their help brought down the tyrannical rule of Eurystheus by a victorious campaign against the masters of the Peloponnese. Again, when the dead Argives were left unburied after their attack upon Thebes with Polyneices, we marched against the Cadmeans, recovered the bodies, and gave them burial within our own territory at Eleusis. Another memorable exploit of ours was against the Amazons from the river Thermodon, on the occasion of their inroad into Attica; and in the troubles at Troy our men were by no means the least distinguished.[14] However, there is not much point in recalling all this ancient history; for people who were brave once might easily have deteriorated today, just as people who in old times were nothing to speak of might by now have improved. So let us leave ancient history out of it, and come to the present. Suppose, then, that we had never done anything but fight at Marathon – in point of fact we have done much besides: more than any other people of Greece – but just suppose; then Marathon alone would be enough to qualify us not only for the privilege we are claiming but for others too; for in that fight we stood alone against Persia – we dared a mighty enterprise and came out of it alive – we defeated forty-six nations![15] Do we not, for this act alone, deserve the place of honour on the wing?

'Nevertheless, at a time like this, it is unseemly to quarrel

27

about who shall hold which place in the line; we are ready to take our orders from you Spartans, and to hold whatever part of the line, against whatever enemy contingent, you consider most useful. Whatever that position may be, we shall endeavour to fight like men. Give us our orders; we shall obey.'

28   At this answer there was a shout from every man in the Lacedaemonian army that the Athenians were the better men and better deserved the position of honour than the Arcadians. So the Athenians got it – at the Tegeans' expense.

In addition to the Greek troops who had first arrived in the neighbourhood of Plataea, other reinforcements had subsequently joined; and after the incident mentioned above the various contingents moved into line. The order was as follows: on the right wing were 10,000 Lacedaemonians, of whom the 5000 from Sparta were attended by 35,000 light-armed helots – seven to a man.[16] Next to themselves the Spartans stationed the Tegeans – 1500 hoplites – as a tribute of respect to their worth. Next came the 5000 Corinthians – who had obtained leave from Pausanias to have the 300 men from Potidaea in Pallene at their side. Then there were 600 from Orchomenus in Arcadia, 3000 from Sicyon, and 800 from Epidaurus; after these, 1000 from Troezen, 200 from Lepreum, 400 from Mycenae and Tiryns, 1000 from Phlius, and 300 from Hermion; next, 600 from Eretria and Styra, 400 from Chalcis, 500 from Ambracia, 800 from Leucas and Anactorium, and 200 Paleans from Cephallenia; then 500 from Aegina, 3000 from Megara, and 600 from Plataea. Last or first came the Athenians, 8000

29   strong, on the left wing of the army, with Aristides, the son of Lysimachus, in command. All these troops, except the seven helots who attended each of the Spartans, were hoplites, and their total strength amounted to 38,700 men. In addition to the heavy infantry there were light-armed auxiliaries: the 35,000 helots in attendance, as already mentioned, upon the Spartans, all of them fighting men, and 34,500 others, belonging to the other towns both in Lacedaemon and elsewhere – at the rate,

30   that is, of one auxiliary to every man-at-arms. The total number of auxiliaries was thus 69,500, making the aggregate strength of the Greek army at Plataea 110,000 – all but 1800, a deficiency

which was made up by the Thespians, whose surviving men (1800 precisely) had joined the Greek force. They were not, however, fully armed.

So much for the strength and organization of the Greek army 31 when it took up its position on the Asopus. Mardonius' men, when they had finished mourning for Masistius, also moved up to the river upon learning that the Greeks were at Plataea, and were posted in the following order. Facing the Lacedaemonians Mardonius stationed his Persians, who, as they greatly out-numbered the Lacedaemonians, were drawn up in greater depth than usual and extended far enough to cover the Tegeans as well. Mardonius saw to it that the best of them faced the Lacedaemonians, the weaker ones being on their flank to cover the Tegeans. This precaution was taken at the suggestion, and by the advice, of the Thebans. On the right of the Persians were the Medes, covering the Greek contingents from Corinth, Potidaea, Orchomenus, and Sicyon; then the Bactrians, covering the Greeks from Epidaurus, Troezen, Lepreum, Tiryns, Mycenae, and Phlius; then the Indians, covering the men from Hermion, Eretria, Styra, and Chalcis; then the Sacae, covering the Ambraciots, Anactorians, Leucadians, Paleans, and Aeginet-ans; and, finally, on the right of the Sacae, and facing the Athenians, Plataeans, and Megarians, were posted the contin-gents from Boeotia, Locris, Malis, and Thessaly, together with the Phocians, 1000 strong. Not all the Phocians had gone over to Persia; a certain number of them, from their base amongst the hills of Parnassus, did good service to the Greek cause by raiding and harrying Mardonius' army and the Greeks who were serving with it. Mardonius also posted on his right wing, facing the troops from Athens, the Macedonians and certain contingents from Thessaly.

I have named here the most efficient and important of the 32 various national contingents which Mardonius put into the line on this occasion; his army also contained a sprinkling of troops of other nationalities – Phrygians, Mysians, Thracians, Paeoni-ans, and so on, as well as Ethiopians and Egyptians. These last belonged to the caste called Hermotybians and Calasirians – the only fighting men in Egypt. Their weapon is the sword. They had previously served with the fleet, but Mardonius brought them ashore before leaving Phalerum; there were no Egyptian troops in the land force which Xerxes brought to Athens.[17]

The foreign troops in Mardonius' army numbered, as I have already shown, 300,000; the number of Greeks who were serving under him nobody knows, for they were never counted. My own guess is that there were about 50,000 of them. All the above-mentioned troops which were put into the line were infantrymen; the cavalry formed a separate unit.

33   When Mardonius' dispositions were complete, with the national contingents all in their respective places in the line, both armies, on the following day, proceeded to offer sacrifice. The man who officiated for the Greeks was Tisamenus, the son of Antiochus, who was serving with the army in the capacity of diviner. He came originally from Elis and belonged to the Clytiad family of the Iamidae, but the Lacedaemonians had adopted him as one of themselves, under the following circumstances. Having no children, he had gone to Delphi to consult the oracle on the subject, and the Priestess, in her reply, told him that he was destined to win the 'five greatest contests'. Failing to understand the meaning of this prophecy, he went into training for athletics under the impression that that was the kind of 'contest' he was to win, and actually came within a single event of winning the Olympic pentathlon against Hieronymus of Andros. The Lacedaemonians, however, realized that the word 'contests' in the oracle referred not to athletics but to war, and attempted to induce him, by the offer of a wage, to become joint leader with their Heraclid kings in the conduct of their wars. Tisamenus saw that the Spartans were extremely anxious to get his support, and consequently raised his price, indicating that he would do as they asked only if they made him a Spartan citizen with full civic rights. Otherwise he would have nothing to do with the proposal. The first effect upon the Spartans of Tisamenus' demand was indignation, and they stopped asking for his services; but later on, under the terrible threat of the Persian invasion, they again sought him out and agreed to his terms. Tisamenus, however, seeing that they had come round, declared that he was no longer satisfied with the original con-

ditions, but must have his brother Hagias, too, made a citizen
of Sparta with the same rights as himself. In making this demand 34
Tisamenus was following the example of Melampus – if one can
compare a demand for citizenship with a demand for a throne.
For Melampus, it will be remembered, when he was fetched by
the Argives from Pylos and offered a fee to restore their women,
who had all gone mad, to sanity, claimed half the kingdom as
payment for the service.[18] The Argives thought the demand a
monstrous one, and left him; but later, when more of their
women caught the disease, they brought themselves to consent,
and went back to Melampus to promise what he asked. Thereupon Melampus, seeing they had come round to his terms,
reached out for a bit more, and refused to perform the service
they wanted unless they gave, in addition, one-third of the
kingdom to his brother Bias. The Argives, who were in dire
straits, had to consent to this too. It was just the same with 35
the Spartans – they needed Tisamenus badly, and consequently
gave him everything he asked for. The result was that this
man from Elis, having become a citizen of Sparta, helped the
Spartans, in his capacity as diviner, to win five 'contests' of the
greatest importance. (Tisamenus and his brother were the only
two foreigners ever to be made Spartan citizens.) They were the
following: first, the battle of Plataea, which I am about to
describe; second, the fight at Tegea against the Tegeans and
Argives; third, at Dipaees against the combined forces of
Arcadia, excluding Mantinea; fourth, against the Messenians at
Ithome; and, last, against the Athenians and Argives at
Tanagra.[19]

This Tisamenus, then, brought by the Spartans, was acting as 36
diviner for the Greek forces at Plataea. The omens turned out
to be favourable to the Greeks, provided that they fought a
defensive action, but unfavourable should they cross the Asopus
and attack. For Mardonius the omens were similar – good for 37
defence, bad if he yielded to his eagerness to attack. Mardonius
too made use of the Greek ritual to get his omens; his diviner
was Hegesistratus of Elis, the best-known member of the clan
of the Telliadae. He had once been arrested by the Spartans on
a charge of doing them a number of injuries of a very serious

nature. Flung into prison and condemned to death, Hegesistratus, realizing, in his desperate situation, not only that his life
was at stake but also that he would be tortured before his
execution, dared a deed which one cannot find words adequate
to tell. He was lying with one foot in the stocks – which were
made of wood reinforced with iron – and somehow managed to
get hold of a knife, which was smuggled into the prison. No
sooner was the knife in his hand than he contrived the means to
escape – and how he did it was the bravest action of all those
we know: he cut a bit off his foot, having nicely judged how
much to leave in order to pull it free. Then, as the prison was
guarded, he worked a hole through the wall and escaped to
Tegea, travelling at night and lying up during the day in the
woods. The Lacedaemonians went out in force to try to find
him, but he got clear and reached Tegea on the third night. They
were astonished at the man's daring when they saw half his foot
lying by the stocks and were unable to find him.

In this way Hegesistratus escaped his captors and made his
way successfully to Tegea, which was not at that time on good
terms with Sparta. When his wound healed he got himself a
wooden foot made, and openly avowed his enmity to the Spartans. This, however, was destined ultimately to bring him into
trouble; for at a later period – after Plataea – while he was
performing his duties as diviner in Zacynthus, the Spartans
38 caught him and put him to death.[20] On the occasion of which I
am speaking, he was with Mardonius on the Asopus; he was by
no means poorly paid, and he performed his duties with great
zest – partly out of hatred for the Spartans, partly for the sake
of the money.

All this time the Greek forces were increasing by a continual
influx of men; and in view of this, added to the fact that both
for the Persians and for their Greek allies (who were served by
their own diviner Hippomachus of Leucas) the omens were
unfavourable for attack, a Theban named Timagenides, the son
of Herpys, advised Mardonius to watch the passes of Cithaeron,
as he would be able to cut off a great many of the men who
every day were streaming through them to join the Greek army.
39 The proposal was made when the two armies had already been

eight days in position, facing one another. Mardonius saw that
it was a good one, and that evening sent his cavalry to the pass
over Cithaeron which leads to Plataea – the pass, that is, which
the Boeotians call Three Heads, though the Athenians call it
Oak Heads. The movement was not without success; a train of
five hundred mules bringing food from the Peloponnese for the
army was caught, together with the men in charge, just as it was
coming down from the hills. The Persian cavalrymen showed
no mercy; they killed beasts and men indiscriminately, and
drove the remnant, when they were sick of slaughter, back to
Mardonius within their own lines.

Two more days went by, and no further action took place. 40
Neither side was willing to begin the general engagement. The
Persians provoked the Greek forces to attack by advancing right
up to the river, but neither of them ventured actually to cross.
Nevertheless Mardonius' cavalry harassed the Greeks continually: this was due to the Thebans – Persia's firm friends;
their hearts were in the war, and again and again they led the
cavalry to within striking distance, when the Persians and Medes
took over, and proceeded to show what stuff they were made
of.

During those ten days nothing happened beyond what I have 41
mentioned. The armies faced one another and no move was
made, and all the time the Greek forces were rapidly increasing.
At last, on the eleventh day, Mardonius, irked by the protracted
inactivity, entered into conference with Artabazus, the son of
Pharnaces – a Persian of the very highest reputation with Xerxes.
In the discussion which followed Artabazus urged that the best
thing to do would be to abandon their present position at once,
and to withdraw the entire army within the fortifications of
Thebes, where they had stored abundant supplies, including
fodder for the animals. They had with them a great deal of gold,
both coined and uncoined, besides plenty of silver and drinking
vessels; and they could easily achieve their purpose, without
making any active move, simply by sending lavish presents out
of this treasure to the Greeks – especially to those of them who
were most influential in the various towns. This would very
soon bring them to give up their liberty. It would be a mistake,

on the other hand, to risk another battle. This opinion coincided with that of the Thebans – for they reckoned that Artabazus was a man of more than average foresight.

Mardonius expressed himself in much more uncompromising terms, and did not agree at all. In his view, the right policy, as the Persian army was far stronger than the Greek, was to force an engagement at once, and not allow the enemy forces to increase any further; as for Hegesistratus and his sacrifices, it would be best to ignore them – certainly not to try to force their meaning – and to engage in battle in the good old Persian
42 way. The proposal was carried without opposition – for it was Mardonius, not Artabazus, who held from Xerxes the command of the army.[21] He then sent for his divisional commanders and the Greek officers who were serving under him, and asked if they knew of any prophecy which foretold the destruction of Persian troops in Greece. Nobody said a word: some of them were unaware of the prophecies, while others, who knew them well enough, felt it was safer not to mention them. Mardonius accordingly said: 'Either you know of no such prophecy, or are afraid to speak of it. Well, I *do* know of one, and I will tell it to you. It says that the Persians will come to Greece, sack the temple at Delphi, and then perish to a man. Very well then: knowing that, we will keep away from the temple and make no attempt to plunder it – and thus avoid destruction.[22] All of you, therefore, who wish your country well, may rejoice at this, and be very sure that we shall defeat the Greeks.' Thereupon he issued his orders to prepare for battle on the following day.

43   I happen to know that the oracle, which Mardonius applied to the Persians, actually referred to the Illyrians and the army of the Encheles; there are, however, some verses of Bacis which did, in fact, refer to this battle:

> By Thermodon and Asopus, where the grass grows soft,
> Shall be gathering of Greeks and the sound of strange tongues;
> And there beyond lot and portion many Medes shall fall,
> Armed with the bow, when the day of doom comes.

These verses, and other similar ones of Musaeus, I know referred to the Persians. The Thermodon flows between Tanagra and Glisas.

After Mardonius had asked his question about the oracles 44 and spoken the words of encouragement which I mentioned, darkness fell and the watches were set. Some hours passed; and as soon as silence had descended on the two armies and the men all seemed to be asleep, Alexander, the son of Amyntas, the king and commander of the Macedonians, rode up to the Athenian guard-posts and asked permission to have a word with the officers in command. Most of the pickets stayed at their posts, but a few of them hurried off and informed their officers that a man on horseback had arrived from the Persian army: he would say nothing, except that he wanted to speak to the officers in charge, whose names he mentioned. The Athenians at once 45 accompanied the guards back to their post, and Alexander delivered his message. 'Men of Athens,' he said, 'I trust to your honour for what I am about to tell you: keep it a secret from everybody except Pausanias or you will ruin me. I should not be here at all if I had not at heart the common welfare of Greece – I am myself a Greek by descent, and have no wish to see Greece exchange her freedom for slavery. Listen, then: Mardonius and his army cannot get satisfactory omens from their sacrifices – but for this, you would have been fighting long before now. Mardonius has decided, however, to ignore the omens and to attack at dawn – in anxiety to prevent still further reinforcements from reaching you, as I guess. Be ready for him, therefore. If, on the contrary, he should postpone his attack, my advice to you is to hold on where you are: for he has only a few days' supplies left.

'In the event of your bringing this war to a successful conclusion, you must remember me, and do something for my freedom: for the sake of Greece I have taken a great risk, in my desire to acquaint you with what Mardonius intends, and thus to save you from a surprise attack. I am Alexander of Macedon.'

This said, Alexander rode back to the camp and resumed the position assigned to him, while the Athenian commanders 46 hurried to Pausanias, on the right wing of the Greek army, and told him what they had just heard. Pausanias was much alarmed. 'As we are to be in action at dawn,' he said, 'you Athenians had better take position opposite the Persians, while we deal with the Boeotians and the other Greeks now opposite you. Marathon gave you experience of Persian tactics – unlike us, who know nothing about them whatever. No Spartan here has ever been in action against Persian troops – but we are all familiar enough with the soldiers of Boeotia and Thessaly. So get moving at once, and come and take over the right wing. We will take your place on the left.'[23]

'It occurred to us,' the Athenians replied, 'long ago – ever since we saw that your section would have to face the Persian thrust – to make the very suggestion which you have now been the first to put forward; but we were afraid of offending you. Now, however, that you have mentioned it yourselves, we willingly accept, and will do what you ask.'

47   The matter being settled to the satisfaction of both parties, at the first signs of dawn the Athenian and Spartan contingents changed places. But the Boeotians detected the movement and reported to Mardonius, who immediately shifted his Persian troops to the other wing, so as still to face the Spartans. Pausanias, seeing that his own movement had not escaped observation, then marched his men back again to the right wing – and, as

48   before, Mardonius followed suit, so that Persians and Spartans were once again facing one another in their original positions. Mardonius then sent a herald to the Spartan lines. 'Men of Lacedaemon,' the message ran, 'everybody about here seems to think you are very brave. Everyone admires you for never retreating in battle and for never quitting your post: you stick to it, so they say, until death – either your enemy's or your own. But it turns out that all this is untrue: for here you are, running away and deserting your post before the battle has even begun or a single blow been struck, and giving the place of danger to the Athenians, while you yourselves face men who are merely our slaves. This is by no means what brave men would do; indeed, we have been greatly deceived about you. Your reputation led us to expect that you would send us a challenge, in your eagerness to match yourselves with none but Persian

troops. We should have accepted the challenge, had you sent it; but you did not. We find you, instead, slinking away from us. Well, as you have sent no challenge, we will send one ourselves: why should we not fight with equal numbers on both sides, with you (who are supposed to be the most valiant) as the champions of Greece, and ourselves as the champions of Asia? Then, if it seems a good thing that the rest should fight too, they can do so after we have finished; otherwise let us settle it between us, and let the victor be considered to have won the battle for the whole army.'

The herald waited for a time after delivering this challenge; then, as nobody gave him an answer, he returned to Mardonius and told him what had happened. Mardonius was overjoyed and, in all the excitement of his empty victory, ordered his cavalry to attack. The Persian cavalry, being armed with the bow, were not easy to come to grips with; so when they moved forward, they harried all the Greek line with their arrows and javelins; they also choked up and spoilt the spring of Gargaphia, from which all the Greek troops got their water. Actually, only the Lacedaemonians were near the spring, the rest of the army being some distance away, in their various positions, but all close to the river Asopus; nevertheless they, too, had been forced to resort to the spring for water, because the enemy cavalry, with their missile weapons, prevented them getting it from the river. In these circumstances, their men being continually harassed by the Persian cavalry and cut off from their water, the commanders of the various Greek contingents went in a body to Pausanias on the right wing, to discuss these and other difficulties with him. Lack of water, though bad enough, was by no means the only cause of distress; food, too, had run short, and the servants who had been sent to bring supplies from the Peloponnese had been stopped by parties of Persian cavalry and had failed to rejoin. In the course of the discussion it was agreed that, if the Persians let the day pass without bringing on a general engagement, they should shift their position to the Island – a tract of ground in front of Plataea, rather more than a mile from the Asopus and Gargaphia, where they then were. This place is a sort of 'island on land': there is a river which splits

49

50

51

into two channels near its source on Cithaeron, and in the plain below the channels are about three furlongs apart, before they unite again further on. The name of the river is Oeroe, and it is known locally as 'daughter of Asopus'. Two reasons led them to choose the Island for their new position: first, they would have an abundant supply of water; and, secondly, the enemy cavalry would be unable to hurt them. The plan was to make the move during the night, at the second watch, to prevent the enemy from observing them as they marched out, and thus to escape trouble from his cavalry on the way. It was further agreed that upon reaching the tract of land 'islanded' by the two channels of the Oeroe as it flows down from Cithaeron, they should detach, during the same night, one half of the army and send it as far as the hills of Cithaeron, to relieve the food convoys which were cut off there.

52   Having made these decisions, they continued throughout the day, without a moment's respite, to suffer harassment from the enemy cavalry; but towards evening the attacks ceased, and after dark, at the time agreed upon for departure, the greater part of the Greek forces moved off. However, they had no intention of making for the Island, according to plan: on the contrary, once they were on the move, they fled to Plataea, only too thankful to escape the Persian cavalry. Here they came to a halt in front of the temple of Hera, which stands outside the town, at a distance of about two and a half miles from Gargaphia.

53   When Pausanias saw the troops moving from their original position, he gave orders to the Lacedaemonians to strike camp and follow them, in the belief that those who had already started were making for the agreed position. Pausanias' officers were ready to obey the order, with one exception – Amompharetus, the son of Poliades and commander of the Pitanate regiment.[24] This officer refused to run away from the 'strangers' and thus deliberately to dishonour his country, and (as he had not been present at the conference) expressed his astonishment at the sight of this unexpected move. Pausanias and Euryanax were highly indignant at this refusal to obey orders; none the less they felt it would be even worse, just because of Amompharetus'

obstinacy, to leave the Pitanate regiment to its fate; for both he and his men would almost certainly be killed, if the rest of the army carried out their agreement and abandoned them. Accordingly the order to move was countermanded, and Pausanias and Euryanax made every endeavour to convince Amompharetus that he was mistaken. The Athenians, meanwhile, being well aware of the Spartan habit of saying one thing and meaning something else, did not move from the position they occupied, until the withdrawal began; then they sent a man on horseback to find out if the Spartans themselves had any intention of going, or not, and to ask Pausanias for instructions. The messenger found the Lacedaemonians still in their old position, and their officers at loggerheads; for Euryanax and Pausanias had failed in their efforts to persuade Amompharetus not to endanger the lives of his men by staying behind while the others withdrew, and they had begun to quarrel just at the moment when the Athenian messenger arrived. Still arguing violently, Amompharetus picked up a rock in both hands, and, laying it at Pausanias' feet, cried: 'Here's my voting-pebble – and I cast my vote against running away from the strangers!'[25] Pausanias said he was a fool and had taken leave of his senses; then, when the Athenian messenger put his question, he told him to report the state of affairs in the Spartan lines, adding a request that the Athenians should move over in their direction and, in the movement, conform to the Spartan lead. So the messenger returned, and the Spartans continued to wrangle until dawn next morning.

With the coming of daylight Pausanias, thinking – quite rightly, as the event proved – that Amompharetus would not stay behind if all the other Lacedaemonian troops withdrew, at last gave the order for retreat, and marched off all his men, except the Pitanates, along the line of the hills, the Tegean contingent accompanying them. The Athenians followed in good order, but by a different route; for while the Spartans kept to the higher ground and the foothills of Cithaeron for fear of attack by the Persian cavalry, the Athenians took the lower road across level country.

Amompharetus did not at first believe that Pausanias would

54

55

56

57

actually go so far as to leave him behind, and for that reason urged the necessity of holding their position; but when Pausanias' men had already got some distance on their way, he could no longer have any doubt about it: he was left behind in good earnest. Accordingly, he gave his regiment orders to march, and followed, at a leisurely pace, the rest of the Spartan troops, who halted about half a mile off to wait for him, near the river Moloïs and a place called Argiopium, where there is a temple dedicated to Demeter of Eleusis. Their reason for waiting was to give them a chance of going back to the assistance of Amompharetus and his men in the event of his deciding, after all, not to abandon his position. No sooner had Amompharetus rejoined the main body than the cavalry attacks began again: the Persian horse, meaning to continue their old harassing tactics, had found the enemy gone from the position they had occupied during the last few days, and had ridden in pursuit. Now, having overtaken the retreating columns, they renewed their attacks with vigour.

58 　　When Mardonius learned that the Greeks had slipped away under cover of darkness, and saw with his own eyes that not a man remained in the position they had previously held, he sent for Thorax of Larissa and his two brothers, Eurypylus and Thrasidaeus. 'Well, sons of Aleuas,' he exclaimed, 'what will you say, now that you see that place deserted? You, who are neighbours of the Lacedaemonians, used to tell me that they were grand fighters, and never ran away! Only yesterday you saw them try to get out of their place in the line, and now it is plain to all of us that last night they simply took to their heels and fled. Once they found it necessary to fight against troops which are, in actual fact, first-rate, they showed clearly enough that there's nothing in them, and that their reputation was gained merely amongst Greeks – who have nothing in them either. Now *you* I can excuse for praising these men: you know nothing about the Persians – and you did know one or two things the Spartans have done; but I was much more surprised at Artabazus, that *he* should be frightened of the Lacedaemonians, and allow his fear to suggest to him the shameful policy of a general retreat within the fortifications of Thebes, where we should stand a siege. I shall take care that the king is informed

of that proposal of his – but that can wait; our immediate task is not to let the Greeks escape us by what they have done: they must be pursued till they are caught and punished for all the injuries they have inflicted upon us.'

So saying, Mardonius gave the order to advance. His men 59 crossed the Asopus and followed at the double in the track of the Greek forces who, it was supposed, were in full flight. Actually, it was the Spartans and Tegeans only that Mardonius was after, for the Athenians, who had marched by a different route across the level ground, were hidden from sight by the intervening hills.

When the officers of the other divisions of Mardonius' army saw the Persian contingent start in pursuit, they immediately ordered the standards to be raised, and all the troops under their command joined in the chase as fast as their legs would carry them. Without any attempt to maintain formation they swept forward, yelling and shouting, never doubting that they would make short work of the fugitives. Pausanias, when the enemy 60 cavalry fell upon him, sent a rider to the Athenians with an appeal for help. 'Men of Athens,' the message ran, 'the great struggle is now upon us – the struggle which will determine the liberty or enslavement of Greece; but our friends fled last night from the field of battle and have betrayed us both. Now, therefore, our duty is plain: we must defend ourselves and protect each other as best we can. Had it been you who were first attacked by the Persian horse, we should have been bound to come to your assistance, together with the Tegeans who are, like us, loyal to the cause of Greece; but as we, not you, are bearing the whole weight of the attack, it is your duty to support those who are hardest pressed. If you are in any difficulty which prevents you from coming to our aid, then send us your archers, and we shall be grateful. We acknowledge that throughout this war your zeal has been equalled by none; you will not, then, refuse this request.'

On receipt of this message the Athenians started to the relief 61 of the Spartans, to whom they were anxious to give all the help they could; but they were no sooner on the move than they were attacked by the Greek troops under Persian command, who held the position facing them. The attack was a heavy one, and made it impossible for them to carry out their purpose, so that the Lacedaemonians and Tegeans, whom nothing could induce to leave their side, were left to fight alone – the former 50,000 strong, including the light-armed auxiliaries, the latter 3000.

Once more, as they were about to engage with Mardonius and his men, they performed the ritual of sacrifice. The omens were not favourable; and meanwhile many of their men were killed, and many more wounded, for the Persians had made a barricade of their wicker shields and from the protection of it were shooting arrows in such numbers that the Spartan troops were in serious distress; this, added to the unfavourable results of the sacrifice, at last caused Pausanias to turn his eyes to the temple of Hera and to call upon the goddess for her aid, praying her not to allow the Greeks to be robbed of their hope of victory.

62 Then, while the words were still upon his lips, the Tegeans sprang forward to lead the attack, and a moment later the sacrificial victims promised success. At this, the Spartans, too, at last moved forward against the enemy, who stopped shooting their arrows and prepared to meet them face to face.[26]

First there was a struggle at the barricade of shields; then, the barricade down, there was a bitter and protracted fight, hand to hand, close by the temple of Demeter, for the Persians would lay hold of the Spartan spears and break them; in courage and strength they were as good as their adversaries, but they were deficient in armour, untrained, and greatly inferior in skill. Sometimes singly, sometimes in groups of ten men – perhaps fewer, perhaps more – they fell upon the Spartan line and were

63 cut down. They pressed hardest at the point where Mardonius fought in person – riding his white charger, and surrounded by his thousand Persian troops, the flower of the army. While Mardonius was alive, they continued to resist and to defend themselves, and struck down many of the Lacedaemonians; but after his death, and the destruction of his personal guard – the finest of the Persian troops – the remainder yielded to the Lacedaemonians and took to flight. The chief cause of their discomfiture was their lack of armour, fighting without it against hoplites.

Thus the prophecy of the oracle was fulfilled,[27] and Mardon- 64
ius rendered satisfaction to the Spartans for the killing of
Leonidas; and thus, too, Pausanias, son of Cleombrotus and
grandson of Anaxandrides, won the most splendid victory of
all those we know. (I have given Pausanias' ancestors before
Anaxandrides where I gave the genealogy of Leonidas.) Mardonius was killed by Aeimnestus, a distinguished Spartan, who
some time after the Persian wars met his own death, together
with the three hundred men under his command, at Stenyclerus
fighting against the entire forces of the Messenians.[28]

Once their resistance was broken by the Lacedaemonians, the 65
Persian troops fled in disorder and took refuge in the wooden
fort which they had erected in Theban territory. It is a wonder
to me how it should have happened that, though the battle was
fought close to the holy precinct of Demeter, not a single Persian
soldier was found dead upon the sacred soil, or ever appears
to have set foot upon it, while round about the temple, on
unconsecrated ground, the greatest number were killed. My
own view is – if one may have views at all about divine matters
– that the Goddess herself would not let them in, because they
had burnt her sanctuary at Eleusis.[29]

Artabazus, the son of Pharnaces, had disapproved from the 66
first of Xerxes' action in leaving Mardonius behind in Greece,
and had done his best, though without success, to dissuade
Mardonius from an engagement; consequently having from the
first disliked Mardonius' strategy, this is what he did. He had
under his command a considerable force of some 40,000 men;
well aware, as he was, of what the issue was likely to be, he gave
orders to this force, as soon as the fighting began, to advance in
good order and to follow his lead at whatever pace he might set
them. At first he made as if to lead his men into battle; but he
had not advanced very far before he saw the Persians already in
flight, whereupon he no longer kept to his order of march, but
suddenly wheeled about and beat a retreat – not to the barricade,
or to Thebes, but direct to Phocis, in his desire to reach the
Hellespont with the least possible delay.

Most of the Greek troops on the king's side made little or no 67
attempt to distinguish themselves. This, however, was not true

of the Boeotians, who had a long struggle with the Athenians; for the Thebans who had gone over to the enemy, far from deliberately shirking duty, fought so hard that three hundred of their best and bravest men were killed. When they, too, were overpowered, they fled to Thebes, but not with the defeated Persians or the mixed crowd of confederate troops, who made their escape without striking a blow or doing any service what-

68   ever. It is perfectly obvious that everything depended upon the Persians: the rest of Mardonius' army took to their heels simply because they saw the Persians in retreat, and before they had even come to grips with the enemy. The only section of Mardonius' army which was not hopelessly routed was the cavalry – especially the Boeotian cavalry: this force did good service to the fugitives, keeping all the time in close contact with the enemy and acting as a screen between their friends and the pursuing Greeks.

69   During the panic rout of the enemy, while the victors were still pursuing the fugitives with great slaughter, news of the battle and of Pausanias' success reached the Greeks who were stationed near the temple of Hera and had taken no part in the fighting. The moment they heard the turn events had taken, they rushed forward in a mob, the Corinthians and their division by the upper routes across the foothills of Cithaeron, straight for the temple of Demeter, the Megarians, Phliasians and others by the level route through the plain. These last had nearly got into touch with the enemy when they were seen by the Theban cavalry under Asopodorus son of Timander, who, taking advantage of their complete lack of order and discipline, promptly attacked, killing six hundred of them and driving the remainder

70   in headlong flight into the hills – an inglorious end.[30] Mardonius' men – Persians and all – who took refuge behind their wooden palisade, managed to get up into the bastions before the Lacedaemonians were on them, and at once did what they could to strengthen their defences. When the Lacedaemonians arrived, a struggle of some vigour began, but, as they have never mastered the art of attacking defensive works, the Persians kept them out and had much the better of it, until the Athenians reached the scene of action. Then, with the arrival of the Athenians, the fight

for the palisade was long and violent, until at last, by courage and perseverance, they forced their way up and made a breach, through which the rest of the army poured. First in were the Tegeans; and it was they who plundered Mardonius' tent, taking from it, amongst much else, the manger used by his horses – a remarkable piece of work, all in bronze. They placed this manger as an offering in the temple of Athene Alea, whereas everything else they took was brought into the common stock of plunder taken by the Greeks generally. Once the palisade was down, the Persians no longer kept together as an organized force; soldierly virtues were all forgotten; chaos prevailed and, huddled in thousands within that confined space, all of them were half dead with fright. To the Greeks they were such an easy prey that of the 300,000 men (excluding the 40,000 who fled with Artabazus) not 3000 survived. The Spartan losses in the battle amounted to 91 killed; the Tegeans lost 16, the Athenians 52.

Of the enemy's infantry, the Persian contingent fought best; 71 of the cavalry, the Sacae; and of individuals Mardonius himself is said to have been as good as any. On the Greek side, the troops from Tegea and Athens were conspicuous in the fighting, but both were surpassed by the Lacedaemonians: the only evidence I can offer to support this statement (for all three were victorious in their own section of the line) is the fact that the Lacedaemonians had the hardest task. They were matched against the best troops of the enemy – and beat them. Much the greatest courage was shown, in my opinion, by Aristodemus – the man who had suffered the disgrace of being the sole survivor of the Three Hundred at Thermopylae. After him, the greatest personal distinction was won by the three Spartans, Posidonius, Philocyon, and Amompharetus. However, when, after the battle, the question of who had most distinguished himself was discussed, the Spartans present decided that Aristodemus had, indeed, performed great deeds, but that he had done so merely to retrieve his lost honour, rushing forward with the fury of a madman in his desire to be killed before his comrades' eyes; Posidonius, on the contrary, without any wish to be killed, had fought bravely, and was on that account the better man. It may, of course, have been envy which made them say this; in any case, the men I mentioned all received public honours except Aristodemus – Aristodemus got nothing, because he deliberately

72 courted death for the reason already explained.[31] These, then, were the men who beyond others made names for themselves at Plataea; Callicrates, on the other hand, was killed before the real action began – Callicrates, the handsomest man in the Greek army, Lacedaemonians and everyone else included. He was sitting in his place, while Pausanias was offering sacrifice, and was hit in the side by an arrow. As the two armies engaged, he was carried out of the line, and died hard. 'It is no sorrow to me', he said to Arimnestus the Plataean, 'to die for my country; what grieves me is, that I have not used my arm or done anything worthy of myself, such as I longed to do.'

73   The Athenian who is said most to have distinguished himself was Sophanes, the son of Eutychides, from the deme of Decelea – once upon a time the scene of an action which, the Athenians say, has been useful to them ever since. Long ago, when the sons of Tyndareus invaded Attica with a large army to recover Helen, and, unable to find her hiding-place, were laying the village in ruin, the men of Decelea (or some say Decelus himself), in resentment at Theseus' high-handed conduct, and alarm for the safety of the whole Athenian territory, revealed the whole thing to the invaders and guided them to Aphidnae, which Titacus, a native of the place, betrayed into their hands. In return for this service, Sparta has ever since given the Deceleans the freedom of their city and special seats at public functions – so that during the war, many years after these events between Athens and Sparta, the Spartans in their raids on Attica always left Decelea

74 unharmed.[32] This, then, was the village to which Sophanes belonged. Of his prowess at Plataea two accounts are given: according to one, he carried an iron anchor made fast to the belt of his corslet with a bronze chain; with this he would anchor himself whenever he got near the enemy, to prevent their attacks from shifting him; then, when the enemy retreated, he would up-anchor and chase them. According to the other account, which differs from the former one, he did not have an actual iron anchor attached to his corslet, but merely bore the device

of an anchor on his shield, which he kept continually spinning
round and round. Another famous exploit of Sophanes was   75
during the Athenian siege of Aegina, when he killed Eurybates
the Argive, a winner of the pentathlon, in single combat.[33] His
ultimate fate was to meet his death in a battle with the Edoni
for the gold mines at Datum, where he did good service as joint
commander of the Athenians with Leagrus, the son of Glaucon.

After the rout at Plataea, a woman, who had made her escape   76
from the Persians, came into the Greek lines. She was a concubine of the Persian Pharandates, the son of Teaspis; and when
she realized that the Persian army was done for and that the
Greeks were winning the day, she dressed herself and her maids
in the finest things she possessed, loaded herself with gold ornaments, and, getting down from her covered waggon, made her
way to the Spartans while the work of slaughter was still in
progress. She soon recognized Pausanias; for not only was she
already acquainted, from what she had often heard, with his
name and country, but she could also see for herself that he
was directing all the operations. 'O King of Sparta,' she cried,
clasping his knees in supplication, 'save me, I beg you, from the
slavery which awaits the prisoner of war! For one service I am
already in your debt – the killing of these men, who reverence
neither gods nor divinities. I am a native of Cos, and the daughter
of Hegetorides and granddaughter of Antagoras. That Persian
took me by force and kept me against my will.'

'You need not be afraid,' Pausanias replied; 'as a suppliant
you are safe – and still more so, if you are indeed the daughter
of Hegetorides of Cos, for he is bound to me by closer ties of
friendship than anyone else in those parts.' With these words he
put her in the charge of the Spartan magistrates who happened
to be on the spot, and afterwards sent her, at her own wish, to
Aegina.

Immediately after this woman's visit, the troops from Man-   77
tinea arrived upon the scene – too late. Such was their indignation and distress when they found that all was over, that they
declared they deserved to be punished. Somebody told them
about the Persian force which had made its escape with Artabazus, and they were all for going in pursuit of it to Thessaly;

but the Spartans refused to allow them, so they returned home and passed sentence of exile upon their army leaders. Next the troops from Elis arrived – and they, too, had to go home again in disappointment, which they marked in the same way as the Mantineans, by banishing their officers.

78   Serving with the Aeginetans at Plataea there was a man named Lampon. His father was Pytheas, and he was a person of the highest distinction in his native town. This man went to see Pausanias, and urged upon him an unholy proposal. 'Son of Cleombrotus,' he said, 'the service you have already rendered is noble beyond all expectation. God has granted you the privilege of saving Greece and of winning for yourself the greatest glory of all Greeks of whom we know. Now, to crown all, there is one thing more that you should do, both to increase your own reputation and to make foreigners think twice in future before they offer insult and injury to the Greeks. When Leonidas was killed at Thermopylae, Xerxes and Mardonius had his head cut off and stuck on a pike: have your revenge, then; render like for like, and you will win the praise not only of every man in Sparta, but of every man in Greece. Impale Mardonius' body, and Leonidas, your father's brother, will be avenged.'

Lampon really thought that this would be an acceptable
79   suggestion; Pausanias, however, replied: ' I thank you, my Aeginetan friend, for your goodwill and concern for me; but, in regard to your judgement, you have failed to hit the mark. First, you exalt me and my country to the skies by your praise of my success; and then you would bring it all to nothing by advising me to insult a dead body, and by saying that my good name would be increased if I were to do an improper thing fitter for barbarians than Greeks – and even then we think it repulsive. No, indeed; in this matter I hope I shall never please the Aeginetans, or anyone else who approves such beastliness. It is enough for me to please the Spartans, by reverence and decency in both word and deed. As for Leonidas, whom you wish me to avenge, he is, I maintain, abundantly avenged already – surely the countless lives here taken are a sufficient price not for Leonidas only, but for all the others, too, who fell at Thermopylae. Never come to me with such a proposal again, and be grateful that you

are allowed to go unpunished.' When he heard that, Lampon 80
retired.[34]

Pausanias now issued an order that everything of value which
had fallen into their hands as a result of the battle should be
collected by the helots, and that nobody else should touch it.
The helots accordingly went through the whole camp. Treasure
was there in plenty – tents full of gold and silver furniture;
couches overlaid with the same precious metals; bowls, goblets,
and cups, all of gold; and waggons loaded with sacks full of
gold and silver basins. From the bodies of the dead they stripped
anklets and chains and golden-hilted scimitars, not to mention
richly embroidered clothes which, amongst so much of greater
value, seemed of no account. Everything which the helots could
not conceal – and that was a great deal – they declared to their
superiors; but there was a great deal, too, which they stole and
sold afterwards to the Aeginetans, who, by buying the gold at
the price of brass (which the helots supposed it to be), laid the
foundation of their future wealth.

When all the stuff had been collected, a tenth was set apart 81
for the god at Delphi, and from this was made the gold tripod
which stands next the altar on the three-headed bronze snake;[35]
portions were also assigned to the gods at Olympia and the
Isthmus, and from these were made, in the first case, a bronze
Zeus, fifteen feet high,[36] and, in the second, a bronze Poseidon,
nine and a half feet high. The rest of the booty – the Persians'
women, pack-animals, gold, silver, and so on – was divided
amongst the troops, every man receiving his due. There is no
record of any special awards for distinguished service in the
battle, but I imagine that they must have been made. Pausanias
himself was granted ten of everything – women, horses, talents,
camels, and everything else.

It is said that Xerxes on his retreat from Greece left his tent 82
with Mardonius. When Pausanias saw it, with its embroidered
hangings and gorgeous decorations in silver and gold, he summoned Mardonius' bakers and cooks and told them to prepare
a meal of the same sort as they were accustomed to prepare for
their former master. The order was obeyed; and when Pausanias
saw gold and silver couches all beautifully draped, and gold and

silver tables, and everything prepared for the feast with great magnificence, he could hardly believe his eyes for the good things set before him, and, just for a joke, ordered his own servants to get ready an ordinary Spartan dinner. The difference between the two meals was indeed remarkable, and, when both were ready, Pausanias laughed and sent for the Greek commanding officers. When they arrived, he invited them to take a look at the two tables, saying, 'Men of Greece, I asked you here in order to show you the folly of the Persians, who, living in this style, came to Greece to rob us of our poverty.'

83   Long after these events many people in Plataea found coffers full of gold, silver, and other valuables. Another interesting thing also came to light: when the flesh had fallen away from the bodies of the Persian dead, and the Plataeans were collecting the skeletons, a skull was found with no join in it – the bone being seamless and continuous; a jaw, too, was picked up, which had all the teeth, front and back, joined together in a continuous line of bone; also the skeleton of a man of seven and a half feet high.[37]

84   The body of Mardonius disappeared the day after the battle; but I cannot say with certainty who it was that took it away. I have heard of many people of all sorts who are said to have buried him, and I know that many received substantial rewards from his son Artontes for doing so; none the less, I am unable to satisfy myself which of them it really was that removed the body and buried it. One story has it that it was a man from Ephesus named Dionysophanes. In any case it appears that he *was* buried somehow.

85   After the distribution of the booty the Greeks proceeded to bury their own dead, those from each contingent in a separate grave. The Lacedaemonians made three graves – one for the priests, amongst whom were Posidonius, Amompharetus, Philocyon, and Callicrates; another for the rest of the Spartans; and a third for the helots.[38] The Tegeans buried all their dead in a common grave; so did the Athenians, and the Megarians and Phliasians buried together those who had been killed by the cavalry.

Unlike these tombs, which were real ones containing the

bodies of the dead, all the other funeral mounds which are to be seen at Plataea were, so far as my information goes, erected merely for show: they are empty, and were put up to impress posterity by the various states who were ashamed of having taken no part in the battle. There is one tomb there, bearing the name of the Aeginetans, which I am told was constructed at their request ten years after the battle by Cleades, the son of Autodicus, and representative of Aeginetan interests in Plataea.[39]

After the burial of the dead, a conference was held at which 86 it was decided to attack Thebes and demand the surrender of all those who had gone over to the Persians, especially the chief leaders, Timagenides and Attaginus. In the event of a refusal, it was determined to continue the siege of the town until it fell. Accordingly, on the eleventh day after the battle, the siege of Thebes was begun, and the demand for the surrender of the traitors sent in. The demand was refused, and the besieging forces proceeded to assault the walls and devastate the surrounding country. For twenty days the devastation continued, 87 and then Timagenides made a proposal to his fellow-townsmen. 'The Greeks,' he said, 'are determined not to raise the siege until either the town is taken or you hand us over. Very well, then: Boeotia must not suffer any longer just because of us. If what they really want is money, and the demand for the surrender of our persons is only a pretext, then let us give them money out of the public funds – for it was with public approval that we joined the Persians; if, on the contrary, it is we whom they want, we will give ourselves up to answer their charges.' The suggestion seemed to meet the case admirably, so the Thebans at once sent a message to Pausanias to the effect that they were willing to hand the men over. The terms were no sooner 88 agreed upon than Attaginus made his escape from the town; his sons, however, were seized and taken to Pausanias, who refused to condemn them, on the ground that mere boys could not be held responsible for treachery. The other men whom the Thebans surrendered expected to get a chance to defend themselves and hoped, in that case, to secure acquittal by bribery; but Pausanias, who had a pretty good idea of what was in their

minds, had no sooner laid hands on them than he dismissed
the whole confederate army, and took the men to Corinth,
where he had them executed. So much for events at Plataea and
Thebes.

89   Artabazus, the son of Pharnaces, who had made his escape
from Plataea, was already some distance on his way. In Thessaly
he was hospitably received, and questions were asked him about
the rest of the Persian army, for no news of Plataea had yet
come in. Artabazus was well aware that, if he told the truth,
both he and his men would be in imminent danger, as everyone
who learned of the course events had taken would be sure to
attack them. Accordingly, as he had already done in the case
of the Phocians, he gave nothing away in his answer to the
Thessalians' question. 'As you can see,' he said, 'I am on my
way, in a great hurry, to Thrace, whither I have orders to take
this detachment on a special mission. Mardonius and his men
are close on my heels, and may be expected at any moment; when
he comes, mind you entertain him with the same friendliness as
you have shown to me – you will never have cause to regret it.'
He then continued his march straight for Thrace, by the inland
route through Thessaly and Macedonia – for he was, in point
of fact, in a very great hurry indeed. He reached Byzantium, but
not without severe losses; for many of his men were cut down
on the way by the Thracians, and many succumbed to hunger
and exhaustion. From Byzantium he crossed the water by boat,
and so reached Asia.

90   It so happened that the Persians suffered a further defeat at
Mycale in Ionia on the same day as their defeat at Plataea.[40]
While the Greek fleet under Leotychides the Spartan was lying
at Delos, three men arrived from Samos with a message; they
were Lampon, the son of Thrasycles, Athenagoras, the son of
Archestratides, and Hegesistratus, the son of Aristagoras, and
had been sent by the Samians without the knowledge either of
the Persians or of Theomestor, the son of Androdamas, whom
the Persians had set up as tyrant. They came to the commanders,
and Hegesistratus appealed to them with all sorts of arguments,
declaring that the mere sight of a Greek naval force would be

enough to make the Ionians revolt, and that the Persians would
offer no resistance to it – or, if they did, that they would provide
the Greeks with as rich a prize as they were ever likely to get.
Then, in the name of all the gods that Greece held sacred, he
urged them to save the Ionians, men of the same blood as
themselves, from slavery, and expel the foreigner. 'It will be easy
enough,' he said. 'The Persian ships are unhandy and no match
for yours. Moreover, if you suspect us of treachery, we are
willing to offer ourselves as hostages and to sail with you.' As   91
the stranger from Samos continued to press his appeal with the
greatest importunity, Leotychides – either by chance, or because
he really hoped that the answer might prove an omen of success
– asked what his name was. 'Hegesistratus,' the man replied;
whereupon Leotychides cut short anything else he might have
had in mind to say, and cried: 'My Samian friend, I accept the
omen!'[41] And now, before you and your two companions sail
away, give us a pledge that the people of Samos will grant us
their whole-hearted support.' No sooner were the words spoken   92
than the oath was administered; the Samians took it at once,
and a spoken compact of mutual support was made. Two of the
strangers then left; the third, Hegesistratus, was ordered to sail
with the Greek fleet, as Leotychides thought that his name
would be a good omen.

The Greeks stayed where they were for the rest of that day,
and on the following offered the usual sacrifice, with good
results. Their diviner was Deiphonus, the son of Euenius of
Apollonia in the Ionian gulf. Euenius' story I will here relate. In   93
Apollonia[42] there is a flock of sheep sacred to the sun; during
the daytime these sheep graze along the banks of the river which
rises on Mt Lacmon, and, after running through Apollonian
territory, joins the sea by the harbour of Oricus; at night, however, they are looked after by men specially chosen from the
wealthiest and most distinguished families – each man having
one year's spell of duty. The people of Apollonia value these
sheep very highly because of an oracle they once received concerning them. The place where they are penned for the night is
a cave, a long way from the town, and here it was that Euenius,
who had been chosen for the task, was keeping watch. One

night he fell asleep on duty, and some wolves got in and killed about sixty of the sheep. When, on waking, he saw what had happened, Euenius kept silent and told nobody about it, intending to buy some more to make good the losses; but the people of the town got to know of the disaster, and at once brought the culprit to trial and condemned him to have his eyes put out for sleeping at his post. The sentence was carried out, and immediately afterwards the sacred ewes had no more lambs, and the land ceased to produce the normal harvests. The oracles both at Dodona and Delphi were consulted upon the reason for this calamity, and the answer in each case was that it was due to the fact that Euenius, the guardian of the sacred sheep, had been unjustly deprived of his sight: it was the gods themselves who had set the wolves on the sheep, and they would continue to punish the people of Apollonia for the wrong they had done Euenius, until they made him such amends as he himself might choose; and when this was done, they, too, would give him something, for the possession of which many men would call

94   him blessed. The people of the town did not make this oracle generally known, but instructed certain men to carry out the arrangements with Euenius, which they did in the following way. They went up to him as he was sitting on a bench, and, taking their seats beside him, entered into conversation on various topics, leading up to an expression of sympathy for his misfortune. Having thus drawn him on, they asked him what he would choose by way of reparation, should the townspeople undertake to offer it. Euenius, who knew nothing of the oracle, replied that if he were given So-and-so's land (naming the men whom he knew to possess the two best estates in the community), and a certain house, which he also knew was the finest in the town, he would consider that adequate reparation had been made, and would bear no further resentment. 'Euenius,' came the answer, 'the citizens of Apollonia will grant what you ask, in compensation for the loss of your eyes, according to the advice of the oracle.' On learning the whole story, Euenius was angry at what he considered to be the deception which had been practised on him. The townspeople, however, bought the house and the two estates from their owners, and gave them to him;

and immediately afterwards he received the power of divination, so that he became a famous man.

The son of this Euenius was Deiphonus, who was brought by the Corinthians to act as diviner for the fleet. I have also heard a different story, according to which Deiphonus was not Euenius' son at all, but merely assumed the name and got work in various parts of Greece on the strength of it. 95

Once the ritual of sacrifice seemed to portend success, the Greek fleet got under way from Delos and sailed for Samos. Here the ships brought up near Calami, off the temple of Hera which stands there, and preparations were made for action. The Persians, however, learning of their approach, dismissed their Phoenician contingent and themselves made off towards the Asiatic coast; for they had decided after discussing the matter that, as they were no match for the Greek fleet, they had better not risk an engagement. Accordingly they sailed to Mycale on the mainland, where they could have the protection of their own troops which, at Xerxes' orders, had been detached from the main army to guard Ionia. This force was 60,000 strong, and commanded by Tigranes, the tallest and best-looking man in the Persian army. Their plan was to beach their vessels under the protection of these troops, and to construct a defensive rampart round them, within which they could themselves take refuge, should occasion arise. 96

With this purpose in mind they set sail, and after passing the temple of the Eumenides arrived at Gaeson and Scolopoeis in Mycale, where there is a temple sacred to Demeter of Eleusis; the temple was built by Philistus, the son of Pasicles, when he accompanied Neileus, the son of Codrus, on the expedition for the founding of Miletus. Here they beached the ships and threw up a wall of stone and timber round them, cutting down fruit-trees in the neighbourhood and adding an outer ring of sharpened stakes, so that all was ready to stand a siege. 97

The Greeks were much vexed when they discovered that the Persians had given them the slip and cleared out for the mainland, and could not at once decide whether to return home or sail for the Hellespont. Finally, however, they decided to do neither, but to make for the Asiatic coast. All gear – boarding- 98 gangways and so on – necessary for a naval engagement was put in readiness, and the fleet sailed for Mycale. No enemy vessel was to be seen coming out to meet them as they approached the Persian position; on the contrary, they saw that all his ships had been hauled ashore within the protection of the palisade, and that a strong infantry force was drawn up along the beach. In these circumstances Leotychides took his ship as close in-shore as he could, and, as he passed along, got a crier to shout the following appeal to the Ionians who were serving with the enemy: 'Men of Ionia, listen, if you can hear me, to what I have to say. The Persians, in any case, won't understand a word of it. When the battle begins, let each man of you first remember Freedom – and secondly our password, *Hebe*. Anyone who can't hear me should be told what I say by those who can.' In this he had the same intention as Themistocles had at Artemisium. Either the Persians would not know what he had said and the Ionians would be persuaded to leave them, or if his words were reported to the Persians they would mistrust their Greek subjects.[43]

99   Immediately after this appeal the Greeks ran their ships ashore and the troops took up positions on the beach. The first act of the Persians, when they saw the Greeks preparing to fight, was to disarm the Samians, whom they suspected of sympathy with the Greek cause; for it was a fact that when certain Athenians, caught in Attica by Xerxes' men, had been brought over in Persian ships as prisoners, the Samians had released them and sent them back to Athens with provision for their journey. This – the fact of their having rescued five hundred of Xerxes' enemies – was the chief cause of their being suspect. Next, the Persian command ordered the Milesians to guard the passes which lead up to the heights of Mycale – ostensibly because the Milesians were familiar with that part of the country, but actually to get them well out of the way.[44] Then, having taken these precautions against the Ionians who they thought might cause trouble if they got the chance, they proceeded to make their own dispositions – a defensive line protected by a barrier of interlocking shields.

100   The Greeks, on their side, moved forward against the enemy as soon as their preparations were complete. During the

advance, a herald's staff was found on the edge of the beach, close to the water, and at the same time a rumour flew through the ranks that the Greeks had beaten Mardonius in Boeotia.[45] Many things make it plain to me that the hand of God is active in human affairs – for how else could it be, when the Persian defeat at Mycale was about to take place on the same day as his defeat at Plataea, that a rumour of that kind should reach the Greek army, giving every man greater courage for the coming battle and a fiercer determination to risk his life for his country? It was another odd coincidence that both battles should have been fought near a precinct of Demeter of Eleusis – for, as I have already mentioned, the fighting at Plataea was in the immediate neighbourhood of Demeter's temple; and the same thing was to happen at Mycale. Moreover, the rumour that Pausanias' men had already been victorious at Plataea was perfectly correct; for Plataea was fought early in the day, but the action at Mycale did not take place until evening: and the fact of this concurrence of dates – the same day of the same month – was proved when they reckoned back a short time afterwards. Before the report of Plataea reached them, there was profound misgiving amongst the troops, not so much on their own account as for the fate of Greece at the hands of Mardonius; but once the good news came, they moved to the assault with better heart and quicker pace. And so it was that both sides were eager to come to grips, knowing that the stake for which they were fighting was control of the Hellespont and the Aegean islands.

Now the Athenians, with the troops next to them, approximately as far as the centre, had to advance along the beach and across flat ground, but the route of the Lacedaemonians and those next to them lay up a watercourse and over high hills. Consequently the Athenians were already engaged, while the Lacedaemonians were still on their way round. The Persians, so long as their line of shields remained intact, successfully repelled all attacks and had by no means the worst of things; soon, however, the Athenians and their neighbours in line, wanting the credit for the day's work for themselves rather than for the Spartans, passed along the word and made great effort – and from that moment it was a very different matter. They burst

101

102

through the line of shields and fell upon the enemy in a mass assault. For a time, indeed, the assault was held, but in the end the Persians were forced to retreat within the protection of their barricade. The Athenians (this was their order in line) and men of Corinth, Sicyon, and Troezen, forced their way inside on the heels of the enemy. That was the end; for once the barricade had fallen, the enemy made no further serious resistance; all of them turned and fled, except only the Persians, who, in scattered groups, continued to fight against the Greeks who were still pouring in through the breach in the barricade.

Of the Persian high officers two, Artaÿntes and Ithamitres, who were in command of the fleet, escaped; Mardontes and the army commander Tigranes were killed fighting. The Lacedaemonians arrived with the rest of their division while the Persian troops were still holding out, and took their share in what remained of the fighting. The Greek losses were also considerable, especially amongst the Sicyonians, whose commander Perilaus was killed. The Samians who were serving with the Persians and had been disarmed, seeing right from the start that the result of the battle was in doubt, did all they could to help the Greeks, and the other Ionians, following the Samian lead, deserted their Persian masters and attacked them. The Milesians, as I have said, had received orders to watch the hill-tracks as a precautionary measure to enable them to act as guides to the safety of the hills, in the event of any disaster to the Persians such as in fact occurred. They had also, it will be remembered, been assigned this task for another reason – namely to prevent them from causing trouble in the Persian army; in any case, what they actually did was the exact opposite of their orders; for when the Persians were trying to escape, they led them the wrong way, by tracks which brought them back amongst the enemy, and finally joined in the slaughter and proved their bitterest enemies. Thus this day saw the second Ionian revolt from Persian domination.[46]

The Athenian troops distinguished themselves more than any others in this battle, and the most conspicuous amongst them was Hermolycus, the son of Euthynus, a champion all-in wrestler. Some years later, when Athens was at war with Carystus, he was killed in action at Cyrnus, in Carystian territory, and was buried on Geraestus.[47] After the Athenians, the greatest distinction was won by the men from Corinth, Troezen, and Sicyon.

When most of the enemy forces had been cut to pieces, either 106 in the battle or during the rout, the Greeks burnt the Persian ships and the fort, having first removed everything of value, including a number of money-chests, to a place of safety on the beach. They then sailed for Samos, and on their arrival there held a council upon the future of Ionia. The idea was to remove the Ionians and resettle them in some part of Greece which was under their own control, and to abandon Ionia itself to the Persians.[48] They did not think it was possible to be for ever on the watch in order to protect Ionia, and at the same time there was little hope, failing such perpetual vigilance, of the Ionians escaping Persian vengeance for their revolt. It was accordingly proposed by the Peloponnesian leaders to turn out the Greeks who had supported Persia and settle the Ionians in their commercial centres; the Athenians, however, strongly disapproved; for they had no wish to see Ionia depopulated, quite apart from their feeling that Peloponnesians had no right to discuss the future of Athenian colonists. They expressed their disapproval with great vigour, and the Peloponnesians gave way. Thus they brought into the confederacy the Samians, Chians, Lesbians, and other island peoples who had fought for Greece against the foreigner; oaths were sworn, and all these communities bound themselves to be loyal to the common cause. This done, the fleet sailed for the Hellespont with the purpose of destroying the bridges, which, it was supposed, were still in position.

The small remnant of the Persian force which had escaped 107 destruction and taken refuge in the hills of Mycale, now made its way to Sardis. During the march Darius' son Masistes, who by chance had witnessed the disaster, had words with Artaÿntes, the general. He abused him roundly, and, to crown all, told him his leadership was worse than a woman's, and that there was no punishment too bad for the hurt he had done to the king's house. To call a man 'worse than a woman' is the greatest insult one can offer a Persian;[49] so Artaÿntes, after listening for a while, drew his scimitar in rage and would have killed Masistes but for the prompt action of a certain Xenagoras. This man – he was a Halicarnassian and the son of Praxilaus – was standing behind Artaÿntes and, seeing him about to rush forward, caught him round the middle and dashed him to the ground, thus giving time to Masistes' bodyguard to get into a position to defend him. This action won Xenagoras the favour not only of Masistes himself but also of Xerxes, whose brother he had saved; and he was rewarded for it by a gift from Xerxes of the governorship of the whole province of Cilicia.[50] Nothing else of interest occurred during the march. The army ultimately reached Sardis, where the king had been ever since his retreat from Athens after the defeat at Salamis.

108   During his stay at Sardis Xerxes fell in love with Masistes' wife, who was also there.[51] He sent her various messages, but without success, and at the same time was unwilling to resort to compulsion out of respect for his brother Masistes. The woman was well aware of this, and no doubt her knowledge that Xerxes would not dare to force her, helped her to hold out against him. Xerxes, therefore, gave up his other ways of approach, and arranged a marriage between a daughter of Masistes and this woman and his own son Darius, under the impression that by this means he would be more likely to get her. The betrothal took place with all the usual ceremonies, and Xerxes left Sardis for Susa. At Susa he received the girl – whose name was Artaÿnte – into his own house as his son's bride, with the result that he forgot the mother and transferred his affections 109   to the daughter – now the wife of Darius. This time his passion was successful. But as time went on the connection came to light in the following way: Xerxes' wife Amestris gave him a long robe, of many colours and very beautiful, which she had woven with her own hands. Much pleased, he put it on, and, still wearing it, went to visit Artaÿnte – who pleased him no less, with the result that he told her to ask for anything she fancied as a reward for her favours, and he would assuredly grant it. Artaÿnte, who was doomed to come to a bad end, together with all her house, asked in reply if the king really meant to give her whatever she demanded, and Xerxes, never suspecting what the

request would be, pledged his word to do so. Thereupon she boldly demanded the robe. Xerxes did everything he could think of to get out of giving it, simply because he was afraid of Amestris, who already guessed what was going on and would now, he feared, find her suspicions confirmed. He offered her cities, gold in unlimited quantity, an army – a thoroughly Persian gift – under her sole command; but all in vain – nothing would do but the robe. So he gave it her, and she, in great delight, put it on, and gloried in wearing it.

When Amestris found out, as she soon did, that Artaÿnte had the robe, it was not against her that her anger was directed. On the contrary, she thought that the girl's mother, Masistes' wife, was the person responsible for the whole trouble, and consequently plotted her destruction. She waited for the day when her husband the king gave his Royal Supper – a ceremony which occurs once a year, on the king's birthday. The Persian word for the supper is *tycta*, a word equivalent, in the Greek language, to *perfect*; it is the one occasion in the year when the king anoints his head and gives presents to the Persians. Then, when the day for the supper came, she asked Xerxes for her present – Masistes' wife. Xerxes, who understood the reason for her request, was horrified, not only at the thought of handing over his brother's wife, but also because he knew she was innocent. But Amestris persisted – and, moreover, the law of the Supper demanded that no one, on that day, might be refused his request; so at last, much against his will, Xerxes was forced to consent. Then, having told his wife to do with the woman what she pleased, he sent for his brother. 'Masistes,' he said, 'you are my brother and Darius' son; in addition to that, you are a good man. Do not live any longer with your present wife – I will give you my own daughter instead. Marry her: part with your present wife – I do not approve of your keeping her.'

'My lord,' replied Masistes in astonishment, 'this is indeed a strange proposal! What is the use in your telling me to get rid of a wife who is the mother of grown-up sons and daughters – one of whom you married to your own son – and who is, moreover, everything I could wish for, and to marry your daughter instead? No, sire; I will do neither of these things, proud though I am that you should think me worthy of your daughter. Do not, I beg, force this request upon me; but let me live with my wife in peace. You will find another man as good as I am for your daughter.'

Xerxes was angry at this reply. 'Very well, then,' he cried, 'I will tell you, Masistes, what you have done for yourself: I no longer offer you the chance of marrying my daughter – nor will you live another day with that wife of yours. Thus may you learn to accept a proffered gift.'

'Master,' said Masistes, 'you have not killed me yet!' And without another word he left the room.

112   Meantime, while Xerxes was talking to his brother, Amestris sent for the soldiers of the royal bodyguard and had Masistes' wife horribly mutilated. Her breasts, nose, ears, and lips were cut off and thrown to the dogs; then her tongue was torn out
113   and, in this dreadful condition, she was sent home. Masistes, who knew as yet nothing of what had happened, but suspected mischief of some sort, hurried to his house; and when he saw his wife's fearful injuries, at once he took counsel with his sons and with them and certain other friends set off for Bactria, with the intention of stirring up revolt in the province and of so doing serious harm to the king. He would, I think, undoubtedly have succeeded had he had time to reach the Bactrians and Sacae; for he was greatly beloved by both, and was, moreover, governor of Bactria. But Xerxes discovered his purpose and sent an armed force in pursuit, which caught him on the road and killed him together with his sons and all the men under his command. So ends the story of Xerxes' passion and the death of Masistes.

114   The Greeks who sailed for the Hellespont from Mycale, after being delayed for a time by foul winds at Lectum, reached Abydos and found, contrary to expectation, that the bridges had already been broken up – to destroy them had, indeed, been the chief purpose of their coming. In these circumstances Leotychides and his Peloponnesians thought that the best thing to do was to return to Greece, but the Athenians under their commander Xanthippus determined to stay where they were and make an attempt upon the Chersonese. Accordingly, after

the departure of the Peloponnesians, they crossed thither from Abydos and laid siege to Sestos. This town was the most strongly 115 fortified place in the district, and as soon as the news got about that the Greek fleet had arrived in the Hellespont, men from neighbouring towns came into it for refuge; amongst them was the Persian Oeobazus, who came from Cardia, where he had stored the cables used in the construction of the bridges. The town was held by its own native Aeolians, but there were Persians in it too, and a large number of their allies and dependants. The governor of the district for Xerxes was one Artaÿctes 116 – a terrible fellow, as clever as he was corrupt. By a pretty piece of deception, during Xerxes' march to Athens, he had got possession of the treasures of Protesilaus, son of Iphiclus, which were at Elaeus in the Chersonese, where the tomb of that hero stands, surrounded by a plot of sacred ground.[52] There was much here of great value, gold and silver cups, bronze, rich garments, and other things which had been offered at the tomb, and Artaÿctes stole it all. Actually, he tricked Xerxes into giving it to him, by saying: 'Master, there is the house of a Greek here who made war on your country and met the death which he deserved. Give me his house – it will be a lesson to men hereafter not to do as he did.' It was only to be expected that these words should easily persuade Xerxes to give him the 'house' – for he had no suspicion of what was really in Artaÿctes' mind. Artaÿctes was right, in a certain sense, in saying that Protesilaus made war on the king's country; for the Persians consider that the whole of Asia belongs to them, and to their reigning king. So the request was granted, and Artaÿctes removed the treasures to Sestos and turned over the sacred enclosure to agriculture – and, what is more, whenever he visited Elaeus on subsequent occasions he used to have intercourse with women in the sanctuary.

So now Artaÿctes was blocked up in Sestos by the Athenians. He was not prepared for a siege and had not expected the arrival of a Greek army, which consequently caught him unawares. As 117 the siege dragged on into the autumn, the Athenians, impatient at their long absence from home and their failure to take the place, pressed their generals to abandon the enterprise, but they

refused to do so until either the town fell or they were recalled
by the government in Athens. So the troops had to put up with
118 their hardships. Inside the town, the besieged were already
reduced to the direst extremity – even to boiling and eating the
leather straps of their beds. When these, too, gave out, the
Persians, with Artaÿctes and Oeobazus, made their escape under
cover of darkness, letting themselves down from the wall at the
back of the town, where the enemy lines were weakest; and on
the following day the men of the Chersonese signalled to the
Athenians from the bastions to let them know what had happened, and opened the gates. The greater part of the Athenian
force thereupon went in pursuit of the fugitives, while the
remainder took possession of the town.

119   Oeobazus managed to reach Thrace; but there he was caught
by the Apsinthian Thracians who offered him, as their manner
is, as a sacrifice to Pleistorus, a local deity. The men with him
were killed in another way. Those who accompanied Artaÿctes
left the town later, and their small party was overtaken by their
pursuers not far from Aegospotami. They made a stout fight of
it, but all of them, in the end, were either killed or taken prisoner.
The prisoners were tied up and taken back to Sestos, Artaÿctes
120 and his son amongst them. There is a story current in the
Chersonese that one of the prisoners' guards was roasting salt
fish when the fish began to jump and struggle on the coals, as if
they had been freshly caught. Everyone came crowding round
to see this extraordinary sight; but Artaÿctes called the sentry
who was cooking the fish and told him not to be alarmed. 'This
prodigy,' he said, 'has no reference to you, my Athenian friend.
It applies to me: Protesilaus of Elaeus is telling me that though
he is as dead as dried fish, he yet has power from the gods to
punish the man who wrongs him. Look now; I am willing to
pay him a hundred talents in compensation for the treasure I
took from the shrine, and I will pay the Athenians two hundred,
on condition that they spare my life and the life of my son.'
     Such was Artaÿctes' offer; but Xanthippus, the Athenian
commander, refused to accept it. The people of Elaeus wanted
their revenge for Protesilaus, and urged his death; moreover
Xanthippus' own feelings were in sympathy with them. So they

took him to the spit of land where Xerxes' bridge had been –
or, as some say, to the hill above the town of Madytus – and
there they nailed him to a plank and hung him up. His son was   121
stoned to death before his eyes. This done, the fleet set sail for
Greece with all sorts of stuff on board, including the cables of
the bridges, which the Athenians proposed to dedicate as an
offering in their temples. And that was all that happened during
the course of the year.

This Artaÿctes who suffered death by crucifixion had an   122
ancestor named Artembares; and he it was who made the Persians a proposal, which they readily accepted and passed on to
Cyrus.[53] 'Since,' they said, 'Zeus has given empire to the Persians, and among individuals to you, Cyrus, by your conquest
of Astyages, let us leave this small and barren country of ours
and take possession of a better. There are plenty to choose from
– some near, some further off; if we take one of them, we shall
be admired more than ever. It is the natural thing for a sovereign
people to do; and when will there be a better opportunity than
now, when we are masters of many nations and all Asia?'

Cyrus did not think much of this suggestion; he replied that
they might act upon it if they pleased, but added the warning
that, if they did so, they must prepare themselves to rule no
longer, but to be ruled by others. 'Soft countries,' he said, 'breed
soft men. It is not the property of any one soil to produce fine
fruits and good soldiers too.' The Persians had to admit that
this was true and that Cyrus was wiser than they; so they left
him, and chose rather to live in a rugged land and rule than to
cultivate rich plains and be slaves to others.

THE END

Glossary

Archon one of a board of nine magistrates at Athens.

Barbarian a non-Greek; the term was originally not pejorative, although over time the Greeks began to think of themselves as culturally superior to the barbarians.

Colony an independent settlement sent out by a mother-city; once established, the colony was expected to be self-sufficient. Colonies were sent out throughout Greek history, but the great age of Greek colonization extended from c. 750 to 550 BCE.

Deme a village of Attica; see V. n. 34.

Ephor one of a board of five Spartan magistrates who served annually and who had the general responsibility for running the business of the Spartan state.

Guest-Friendship a ritualized friend(ship); a relationship between guest and host by which one man would extend his protection to an outsider visiting his community; guest-friendship involved reciprocal gift-giving and was formalized and hereditary; it was under the protection of Zeus *Xenios* (Zeus, God of Guest-Friendship, whom Croesus invokes at I. 44).

Helot a state slave of the Spartans; see III. n. 20.

Hero a mortal divinized after death, to whom sacrifices and honours are paid. In Hesiod the heroes are an intermediate generation between gods and mortals.

Hoplite a heavily armed warrior; hoplite armour was introduced into Greece from the Near East in the course of the seventh century (see I. n. 68). A hoplite fought in a line, a phalanx, holding a large round shield (*hoplon*) in his left hand and a thrusting spear in his right. Each hoplite's shield protected the man on his left, and it was therefore essential that the soldiers maintained their formation in the line.

Mother-City the city responsible for sending out a colony; it usually provided the equipment and the founder for the colony.

Ostracism an Athenian procedure whereby a member of the community was exiled from Attica for ten years; the procedure was designed to prevent one man from becoming too influential; a man ostracized was still entitled to the fruits of his property, which was not diminished or harmed while he was in exile.

Penteconter a fifty-oared warship; superseded by the trireme.

Perioeci the inhabitants of Laconia who dwelt around Sparta; unlike the helots they had local autonomy but followed the Spartan lead in foreign policy and accompanied the Spartans on their military campaigns. Since Spartan society was wholly militaristic, the *perioeci* practised all crafts and trade necessary for the Spartan community.

Trireme a warship manned by 170 rowers, who were stationed in three banks on each side; each trireme also had a complement of marines on board to serve as fighting men.

Tyrant a sole ruler of a state, usually distinguished from a 'king' (although Herodotus sometimes uses the terms interchangeably) because the tyrant did not come to power by hereditary right. Tyrants are to be found throughout Greek history, but we sometimes speak of an 'age of tyranny' (mid-seventh–late sixth centuries BCE) when most of the Greek city-states (Sparta being the great exception) were ruled by tyrants. Yet these tyrannies, although passed from father to son, rarely lasted longer than two generations. In Asia Minor the Persians installed tyrants to rule their Greek subjects but the move was unpopular (see V. n. 14).

UNITS OF MONEY AND DISTANCE

1. *Money*. It is impossible to translate the units of Greek money into contemporary equivalents. As a guide, one drachma was the daily wage for a skilled worker or a rower in the Athenian navy in the fifth century BCE. One drachma was equal to six obols. For larger numbers of drachmas the Greeks used minae and talents:

    1 talent = 60 minae = 6000 drachmas = 36,000 obols

2. *Distances*. De Sélincourt has translated most measurements into English feet and miles; occasionally he uses the term furlong (c. 220 yards) for the Greek *stade* (c. 200 yards), but for longer distances he converts the measurement into an English equivalent.

Structural Outline*

The following is intended to assist the reader in following the thread of Herodotus' narrative.

Boldface type indicates major structural units.

Indentations are used to mark off important sections of the work.

→ indicates a chronological move backwards by Herodotus.

↔ indicates an event contemporaneous with the preceding.

ETHNOGRAPHIES are denoted by small capitals.

I. pref.	Author's name and city; contents of work and purpose in writing
I. 1–5	**Preliminary matters**
I. 1–4	Origins of the quarrel between Greeks and barbarians: seizings of women in Europe and Asia
I. 5	Dismissal of those accounts; Croesus the first to injure Greeks
I. 6–94	**Account of Croesus, king of the Lydians**
I. 6–29	→ History of the Mermnadae from Gyges to Alyattes
I. 8–14	Gyges becomes king by murdering Candaules

---

* There are numerous structural outlines of Herodotus' *Histories*: see Jacoby 283–326; Myres 118–34 (particularly elaborate, arguing for 'pedimental' (like a temple) structure); Immerwahr (1966) 329–62; Waters (1985) ch. 8; and S. Cagnazzi, 'Tavola dei 28 logoi di Erodoto', *Hermes* 103 (1975) 385–423.

Chronology

1. LYDIAN KINGS

According to I. 6–7 the Heracleidae ruled for 22 generations, 505 years; they ruled in succession up to Myrsus and his son Candaules (Myrsilus), who was murdered by Gyges of the Mermnadae. Thus the rule of Lydia passed from the Heracleidae to the Mermnadae; but vengeance in the fifth generation was promised.

King	Length of reign	Herodotus' dates	Dates as in Kuhrt
(Heracleidae	505 years	1221–716)	
Gyges	38 years	716–678	680–652
Ardys	49 years	678–629	652–630
Sadyattes	12 years	629–617	630–610
Alyattes	57 years	617–560	610–560
Croesus	14 years	560–547	560s–540s

Croesus defeated by Cyrus; rule of Lydia passes to Persia.

2. MEDIAN KINGS

King	Length of reign	Herodotus' dates	Dates as in *CHI*
Deioces	53 years	700–647	727–675
Phraortes	22 years	647–625	674–653
Scythians[1]	27 years		652–625
Cyaxares	40 years	625–585	624–585
Astyages	35 years	585–550	584–549

Astyages defeated by Cyrus; rule of Media passes to Persia.

[1] H. includes their rule in that of Phraortes.

3. PERSIAN KINGS

King	Length of reign	Dates of reign
Cyrus	29 years	559–530
Cambyses	8 years	530–522
Rule of the Magi		522–521
Darius	35 years	521–486
Xerxes	21 years	486–465/4
Artaxerxes I	40 years	465/4–425/4

4. EGYPTIAN PHARAOHS[1]

Pharaoh	Dynasty	Dates of reign	H. ref.
Min/Menes (Narmer or Aha)	I	c. 3000	II. 99
Cheops (Khufu)	IV	2596–2573	II. 124
Chephren (Khafre)	IV		II. 127
Mycerinus (Menkaura)	IV		II. 129
Moeris (Amenemhet III)	XII	1844–1797	II. 101
Sesostris (Senwosret I and III)	XII		II. 102ff.
Pheros (?)			II. 111
Rhampsinitus (Ramesses)	XIX/XX	1305–1069[2]	II. 121
Asychis (Seshonq)	XXII	945–924	II. 136
Anysis	XXIII (?)	818–715[3]	II. 137
Dodecarchs	XXV	780–664[4]	II. 147
Sabacos (Shabaka)	XXV	716–702	II. 137
Sethos (?)[5]			II. 141
Psammetichus (I)	XXVI	664–610	II. 153
Necos (Necho II)	XXVI	610–595	II. 158
Psammis (Psammetichus II)	XXVI	595–589	II. 158
Apries	XXVI	589–570	II. 161
Amasis	XXVI	570–526	II. 162
Psammenitus (Psammetichus III)	XXVI	526–525	

Psammenitus defeated by Cambyses; rule of Egypt passes to Persia.

[1] Included here are only those pharaohs mentioned by Herodotus. Names in parentheses are their Egyptian names.

[2] Rhampsinitus is an amalgamation of the Ramesses pharaohs; the dates are for the XIXth and XXth Dynasties.

[3] Since Anysis may represent the kings of the XXIIIrd Dynasty, the dates are for the entire Dynasty.

[4] The dates of the XXVth (Kushite) Dynasty overlap with those of the XXIIIrd because of their occupation of Egypt.

[5] See II. n. 77.

5. SPARTAN KINGS

For the two royal lines, see Herodotus VI. 52 with n. Dates are only approximations.

Agiad branch		Eurypontid branch	
Leon	590–560	Hippocratides	600–575
Anaxandrides II	560–520	Agasicles	575–550
Cleomenes I	520–490	Ariston	550–515
Leonidas	490–480	Demaratus	515–491
Pleistarchus[1]	480–459	Leotychides II	491–469

[1] As Pleistarchus was under-age, his place was taken by the regent Pausanias.

6. SELECTED EVENTS, 650–479 BCE

Date	Greece and the West	The Near Eastern Kingdoms	H. ref.
c. 650–620	Spartans fight Second Messenian War		III. 47
632	Cylon attempts tyranny in Athens		V. 70–71
c. 630	Foundation of Cyrene		IV. 150–58
c. 625	Periander succeeds Cypselus as tyrant of Corinth		V. 92f–g
612		Fall of Nineveh; end of Assyrian power	I. 106
c. 600		Foundation of Naucratis in Egypt	II. 178
594/3	Archonship of Solon at Athens		
561	Pisistratus attempts tyranny at Athens (first attempt)		I. 59
560	Alliance of Sparta and Tegea	Croesus becomes king of Lydia	I.67–8/I. 26
550		Cyrus defeats Astyages of Media	I. 128
546	Pisistratus' third attempt at tyranny (successful)	Fall of Sardis; defeat of Croesus by Cyrus	I. 62–4/I. 84
	Sparta defeats Argos		I. 82
539		Cyrus defeats Nabonidus; takes Babylon	I. 188–91
530		Cambyses succeeds Cyrus as Persian king	II. 1
528/7	Pisistratus dies; tyranny passes to his son Hippias		
525		Cambyses conquers Egypt	III. 11
c. 523	Sparta and Corinth attack Polycrates of Samos		III. 44–57
522	Death of Polycrates	Bardiya (Smerdis) revolts (11 March); death of Cambyses; Bardiya killed by Darius (29 September)	III. 124–5/III. 61–88

Date	Greece and the West	The Near Eastern Kingdoms	H. ref.
521	Cleomenes becomes king of Sparta		V. 39
519	Cleomenes invades central Greece, Plataea allies with Athens		VI. 108
514	Harmodius and Aristogiton murder Hipparchus at Athens		V. 55–6
512		Darius conquers Thrace	IV. 118; V. 2
510	Spartans assist Athenians in ousting Hippias		V. 62–5
508/7	Reforms of Cleisthenes at Athens		V. 66; 69
505	Athens and Aegina begin to war		V. 79–90
499		Ionia revolts from Persia	V. 28–38
	Aristagoras asks Sparta and Athens for help		V. 49–51; 97
		Ionians defeated at Lade; sack of Miletus	VI. 6–22
494	Trial of Miltiades for Chersonese tyranny		VI. 104
c. 492	Darius demands submission of Greek states		VI. 48
491	Persians attack Greece; enslave Eretria		VI. 94–124
490	(September) Battle at Marathon		
489	Death of Miltiades		VI. 136
486		Egypt revolts from Persia	VII. 1
		Darius dies; Xerxes becomes king (November)	VII. 4
485	Gelon becomes tyrant of Sicily	Egyptian revolt put down	VII. 155/VII. 7
483/2	Athens uses Laurium silver to build up its navy		VII. 144
481	Greeks establish league against Persia; Athens and Aegina make peace; Greeks send embassy to Gelon of Sicily		VII. 145–62

Date	Greece and the West	The Near Eastern Kingdoms	H. ref.
480	Persians attack Greece; (September) battles at Artemisium and Thermopylae; Athenians evacuate Athens		VII. 108– VIII. 22
	Battle of Salamis (end of September)		VIII. 40–112
	Xerxes retreats, leaves Mardonius in charge		VIII. 113–20
479	(Winter) Mardonius in Thessaly makes overtures to Athens		VIII. 121–44
	(Spring) Mardonius invades Greece, burns Athens		IX. 1–15
	Persians defeated at Plataea and retreat		IX. 15–89
	Persians defeated at Mycale; Ionians join Greek league		IX. 90–106
479/8	(Winter) Athenians besiege Sestos; expel Persians		IX. 114–21

Abbreviations

The following abbreviations are used in the Notes and Further Reading.

1. ANCIENT AUTHORS AND TEXTS

Herodotus is cited throughout as 'H.' and cross-references are always given by Book and chapter number. Other abbreviations for ancient authors are: *Il.* = *Iliad*, *Od.* = *Odyssey*, Aesch. = Aeschylus, Plut. = Plutarch, Thuc. = Thucydides; *Ath. Pol.* = *The Athenian Constitution* (in Greek *Athenaion Politeia*), traditionally ascribed to Aristotle; *Mal. Her.* = *On the Malice of Herodotus*. Fragments of ancient authors are cited according to the standard editions, which may be found in the *Oxford Classical Dictionary* (Oxford ³1996).

2. MODERN WORKS

Works cited only once in the Notes have full bibliographic information where they are cited. Books cited frequently have only the author's last name; where there are multiple works by an author, the name and date of publication in parentheses is given. These works may be found in the Further Reading, §4. The most commonly cited works are abbreviated as follows:

AESH B. G. Trigger, B. J. Kemp, D. O'Connor and A. B. Lloyd, *Ancient Egypt: A Social History* (Cambridge 1983)

AH H. Sancisi-Weerdenburg and A. Kuhrt, eds., *Achaemenid History. Proceedings of the Groningen Achaemenid History Workshop*, i. *Sources, Structures and Synthesis* (Leiden 1987); ii. *The Greek Sources* (1987); iii. *Method and Theory* (1988)

AJP American Journal of Philology

ANET J. B. Pritchard, *Ancient Near Eastern Texts relating to the Old Testament*, 3rd ed. with a supplement (Princeton 1969)

Ant. Class. L'Antiquité Classique

BICS Bulletin of the Institute of Classical Studies

CA Classical Antiquity

CAH The Cambridge Ancient History

CB Classical Bulletin

CHA The Cambridge History of Africa

CHI The Cambridge History of Iran, Vol. 2: *The Median and Achaemenid Periods* (Cambridge 1985)

CJ Classical Journal

CP Classical Philology

CQ Classical Quarterly

CW Classical World

Fornara C. W. Fornara, *Archaic Times to the End of the Peloponnesian War* (Translated Documents of Greece and Rome, 1), 2nd ed. (Cambridge 1983). References are to document not page numbers

G&R Greece & Rome

HSCP Harvard Studies in Classical Philology

HW W. W. How and J. Wells, *A Commentary on Herodotus*, 2 vols (Oxford 1912, repr. 1921)

JHS Journal of Hellenic Studies

Pedley J. G. Pedley, *Ancient Literary Sources on Sardis* (Cambridge, Mass. 1972). References are to document not page numbers

TAPA Transactions and Proceedings of the American Philological Association

YCS Yale Classical Studies

Notes

BOOK ONE

1. The preface serves as title-page and general table of contents. H. begins with his name and city as his predecessor Hecataeus had done, and as his successor Thucydides was to do (I. 1). He announces his work as a 'display of inquiry' and this is true in two senses: (i) the narrative that follows is the result of H.'s inquiry and the work is what he has discovered; (ii) the narrator, more than any other ancient historian, is acutely aware of his own contribution to the history he here presents, calling attention to himself as inquirer, collector, informer, editor, and judge of native accounts and received traditions: see Dewald (1987). Finally, in saying that he does not want the deeds to be without their fame (*kleos*) he is alluding to Homer (cf. *Iliad* IX. 189), indicating that one of his functions will be the bestowal of praise (Introduction §2). This does not mean that H. is a panegyrist; rather, his work by its very presentation has a sense of wonder and admiration for the deeds to be narrated, especially in the section that will deal with the Greek and Persian conflict.

2. The Red Sea is the term used by the Greeks for the Southern (Indian) Ocean or any of its gulfs; here it refers to the Persian Gulf.

3. H. traces the conflict back to its legendary roots, the seizures of Io, Europa, Medea and Helen. Despite the claim that the account rests on 'learned Persians', the account here is thoroughly Greek (on this and other difficulties here see Fehling 50–57). The stories themselves are thematically important because they treat: (i) the Europe–Asia conflict, which reaches its climax in the Persian Wars, and (ii) the importance of retributive justice (*tisis*) which H. sees as an important principle of historical action (Introduction §4).

4. Jason and the Argonauts sailed to Colchis on the Black Sea in search of the golden fleece. They were assisted by the Colchian king's daughter,

Medea, who in other versions fell in love with Jason; but it is necessary for the framework of H.'s story here that Medea be thought to have been captured.

5. H. refers here to the Trojan War and the Greek expedition, led by Agamemnon and Menelaus, to reclaim Menelaus' wife Helen. H. returns to the Trojan War at II. 113.

6. The dismissal of the early accounts of Greek–Persian conflict is followed by H.'s true starting point, Croesus the king of Lydia, whom H. 'knows' to have been the first to injure the Greeks. The conclusion of this section is also important, for H. here introduces another of his important themes, the mutability of human fortune (Introduction §4). In the phrase 'cities of men' there is an allusion to Odysseus, who 'saw many cities of men and came to know their minds' (Od. I. 4), and indeed much in the early books centres around H.'s travels and reporting of foreign and marvellous lands (like Odysseus' narration of his adventures in Od. IX–XI). On Homer and H. see Introduction §2.

7. The Lydian kingdom of central Anatolia was the first monarchy to come into contact with the Greeks; its capital was Sardis. On the Cimmerians see n. 13 below. For the alliance of Croesus with Sparta see I. 69–70. On the portrait of Croesus in H. see Immerwahr (1966) 154–61; Evans (1991) 44–51; H.-P. Stahl, 'Learning Through Suffering?', YCS 24 (1975) 1–36.

8. 'Candaules' was a sacral title, 'Myrsilus' his proper name.

9. 'even for a man' is an explanatory comment for H.'s Greek audience, since the Greeks exercised and competed in athletic games in the nude. Cf. Thuc. I. 6.

10. Gyges (Guggu) is attested as king of the Lydians in Assyrian records, according to which he was inspired by a dream to seek the Assyrian king's help against an invasion of the Cimmerians in the 660s or 650s. The wealth of Gyges was well known to the Greeks and is mentioned by the poet Archilochus (F 19 West = Pedley 40). His accession to the throne appears elsewhere in Greek literature, although it is uncertain whether any of the other versions are earlier than H. Particularly interesting is a papyrus fragment of a tragedy, which had the murder of Candaules and the accession of Gyges as its theme: for the text and discussion see D. L. Page, A New Chapter in the History of Greek Tragedy (Cambridge 1951); see also J. Evans, 'H. and the Gyges Drama', Athenaeum 43 (1955) 333–6. For other versions see Pedley 35–6. On the thematic importance of this opening story see Flory 29–38. For Gyges and the dynasty, see Kuhrt ii. 567–70.

11. This is H.'s first reference to Delphi, the temple of Apollo in central

Greece, and the most important oracle in the Greek-speaking world. Both the oracles and the Delphians themselves (cited explicitly at I. 20) are sources of the first rank for H. On oracles see Introduction §4; for Delphic traditions about Croesus see H. I. Flower (cited Introduction n. 54).

12. Midas, known from Assyrian records as 'Mita', was active in the late eighth century. He was an aggressive king who had frequent dealings, often hostile, with his neighbours to the east, but his reputation among the Greeks was favourable. His dates of rule are c. 738–696, and the Greek tradition states that he died by suicide when the Cimmerians invaded. On the kingdom of Phrygia see *CAH* III². 2. 622–43. This Midas is separate from the mythical Midas of the golden touch (mentioned at VIII. 138), with whom he is sometimes confused.

13. The Cimmerians (the 'Gomer' of Genesis 10.2, Ezekiel 38. 6, *et al.*) dwelt on the shores of the Black Sea, and were probably a Thracian people. H. says at IV. 11 that they were chased out of Asia by the Scythians and settled 'on the peninsula where the Greek town of Sinope now stands' (i.e. in Asia on the southern shore of the Black Sea), although H. adds that they took the wrong route. He also mentions their attack on Ionia (I. 6), which was, however, only a plundering raid. Their invasion began under Gyges, not Ardys, as H. has it here: see *CHI* 91–109.

14. According to H. here, the campaign of Lydia against Miletus occurred over the reigns of Sadyattes and his son Alyattes; since the latter, by H.'s chronology, reigned 617–560, the attack on Miletus should be dated 622–612.

15. Arion is said to have flourished in the late seventh century, although some scholars think he is wholly a figure of legend. He came from Methymna on the island of Lesbos, which is why the Lesbians are cited for confirmation. Tarentum is located in the 'instep' of Italy; Taenarum is a cape on the tip of the more westerly peninsula of Laconia. HW (i. 64) point out that coins at Tarentum and Corinth, as well as later coins from Methymna, show heroes riding on dolphins. For doubts about the entire story see Fehling 21–4; contra, Pritchett (1993) 16–25; on the thematic importance, see S. Flory, 'Arion's Leap: Brave Gestures in H.', *AJP* 99 (1978) 411–21.

16. Croesus came to the throne in 560 and began his attack on Ephesus c. 555; H. does not say how long his conquest of the Ionian and Aeolian cities took, but he seems to suggest that it was accomplished quickly.

17. The story, which explains why Croesus attacked the Greeks of Asia Minor but not the islanders off the coast, contains the historical

explanation: that the Lydian cavalry was formidable but their navy non-existent.

18. The meeting of Croesus and Solon centres around differing concepts of human happiness and fortune. H. had said at the outset (I.5) that human prosperity never abides long in the same place, and Solon here provides the theological explanation: God is envious and likes to trouble mankind (32). See Introduction §4 and Immerwahr (1966) 156. The encounter is usually rejected on chronological grounds, since Croesus ruled 560–546, and Solon is said to be away in the aftermath of his law-giving activity at Athens, which is dated either to his archonship (594/3) or at the latest to 580–570 (so Hignett (1953) 316–21). There is a later tradition that dated Solon's travels after Pisistratus' seizure of power (561/60); this could make a meeting with Croesus possible, but we should then have to abandon the tradition that Solon died in 559/8, since one year or so seems too little time for Solon's travels, not only to Croesus here but also to Amasis of Egypt (I. 30) and Philocyprus, ruler of Salamis (V. 113).

19. Pausanias (X. 5. 13) says that the temple of Apollo burned down in 548. See further at V. 62.

20. On Croesus' gifts to Delphi, see H. Parke, 'Croesus and Delphi', *Greek, Roman and Byzantine Studies* 25 (1984) 209–32. Theodorus of Samos (fl. 560–520) was a famous architect and sculptor; he is mentioned again as the maker of Polycrates' ring (III. 41). On Croesus' bowl see J. Griffiths, *Festinat Senex* (Oxford 1988) 5–23.

21. It is not uncommon for H. to say that he knows something but will not state it; these intentional silences spring from religious scruple (II. 3, 65), or suppress alternative versions which are unreliable (I. 95), or suggest unwillingness to 'immortalize' (by inclusion in the work) scandalous behaviour that does not deserve fame (so here and at II. 123, IV. 43).

22. Amphiaraus was an important Boeotian hero: his oracle was at Oropus but his sanctuary was near Thebes; see also VIII. 134.

23. The 'mule on the throne' is explained at ch. 91. On the ambiguity of oracles and their need for human interpretation see Introduction §4.

24. The Pelasgians were assumed to be the early inhabitants of Greece; they were supplanted in most places by the people of Deucalion's son, Hellen (the 'Hellenes'). When a people claimed to be indigenous (as did the Athenians and the Arcadians) it had to be assumed that they were Pelasgians, although they somehow changed when absorbed into the Hellenic people (57). See Lloyd ii. 232–4, who calls them 'largely a figment of the Greek imagination'; R. McNeal, 'How did the Pelasgians become Hellenes?', *Illinois Classical Studies* 10 (1985) 11–21. By

contrast, the Dorians, who took their name from Doris, son of Hellen, wandered throughout Greece until they finally settled in the Peloponnese; they connected their wanderings with the mythical accounts of the descendants of Heracles, the Heracleidae, who returned to claim their rightful position as lords of the Peloponnese. Thucydides (I. 12) dates this to 80 years after the Trojan War. Modern historians divide on whether the myth represents an actual historical occurrence: for the argument that it does, *CAH* II². 2, ch. 36; against, see A. M. Snodgrass, *The Dark Age of Greece* (Edinburgh 1971) 299–313; for a brief history of the various positions held by moderns, see R. Drews, *The Coming of the Greeks* (Princeton 1988) 203–13.

25. Two important points emerge from H.'s account of Pisistratus: (i) the struggle was regional in nature with three party leaders (coastal villages led by Megacles, son of Alcmaeon; inland/plain led by Lycurgus, son of Aristolaides; men beyond the hills led by Pisistratus, son of Hippocrates); (ii) Pisistratus had difficulty in establishing his tyranny. The three attempts should be dated to c. 560 for the first and second, and c. 546 for the third. The other important ancient source on Pisistratus and his sons is *Ath. Pol.* 14–16, partly dependent on H., which should be consulted. On his tyranny see Andrewes ch. IX; Forrest (1966) 175–89; Hignett (1952) 110–23; *CAH* III². 3. 392–416. H. returns to the sons of Pisistratus at V. 55.

26. For Cylon and the curse see V. 70–71 with n.

27. *Ath. Pol.* 15. 2 adds some details about the exile in Eretria that are not in H.

28. On the Alcmaeonids under Pisistratus' rule see VI. 123.

29. The ancient tradition is unanimous that the Spartans owed their good government (*eunomia*) to Lycurgus, but he is a shadowy figure, dated anywhere from the ninth to the seventh century (sources collected in Fornara 2). He was almost certainly responsible for the military reorganization of Sparta, but the office of ephor appears to be later than his reforms. See further Michell 19–28; Forrest (1968) 40–68; Cartledge (1979) 133–4; Murray (1993) ch. 10.

30. In the aftermath of its enslavement of Messenia (see n. at III. 47) Sparta set its sights on Tegea in Arcadia. This war is dated by H. to the reigns of Leon and Agasides, i.e. c. 580–560, and its conclusion to the reigns of Anaxandrides and Ariston, i.e. c. 560–550. For a fragment of the treaty originally set up on the River Alpheus see Fornara 27. On the importance of the wars with Tegea for Spartan history see Forrest (1968) 73–6; Sealey 83–4; Cartledge (1979) 137–9. The desire for a hero's body arose from the belief that heroes remained powerful after their death and could continue to bring benefit to the place where they resided. For their prominence in H. see E. Vandiver, *Heroes in H.: The Interaction of Myth and History* (Frankfurt am Main 1991).

31. This treaty between Lydia and Sparta was made c. 548/7.

32. As H. describes it here, the Cappadocians inhabit the southern shore of the Black Sea east of the Halys. From Sinope on the south coast of the Black Sea to the Mediterranean is c. 350 miles through mountainous terrain, so H.'s estimate as a 'five days' journey' is an underestimate.

33. The date of this eclipse is 28 May 585. Thales is the earliest of the 'Seven Wise Men', although some have doubted that the Greeks at this time could have predicted an eclipse.

34. Syenessis is the royal title of the kings of Cilicia; Labynetus is the Greek form of Nabonidus, the last king of the neo-Babylonian dynasty. On his rise to power and career see Roux 381–7; *CAH* III². 2. 243ff; and Kuhrt ii. 598–603. Cyrus defeated him in 539: see below, chs 188–91.

35. The crossing of rivers is a significant action in H., almost always an act of *hybris*, for it represents humans overstretching the limits imposed by God and nature: see Introduction §4.

36. This sentence is an explanation by H., because Lydians were later famous for their luxury and effeminacy: see ch. 155.

37. Argos in the northeast corner of the Peloponnese was the most powerful city after Sparta, with whom the Argives were in frequent conflict. In the early seventh century under their tyrant Pheidon the Argives were strongly expansionist (see Andrewes 31–42) and are said to have defeated the Spartans at Hysiae, but this is controversial: see Tomlinson 79–85.

38. It is curious that H. narrates something so unusual without comment: why Meles' concubine should have borne him a lion is not explained.

39. We do not know what happened to Croesus when Sardis fell or how he died. The Chronicle of Nabonidus (*ANET* 306) says, 'Cyrus marched to Lu– [= Lydia?], killed its king, took his possessions, and garrisoned the town.' This would indicate that Croesus died in the siege of Sardis, but the reading 'Lydia' seems unlikely (see Lewis (1984) 588–9). Croesus' fall is the subject of a famous red-figure vase now in the Louvre and an ode by Bacchylides dated to 468 (*Odes* 3. 23–62 = Pedley 124). On the vase, Croesus sits atop a pyre and seems to give orders for his own immolation; in Bacchylides Croesus tries to commit suicide but is saved by Apollo who carries him and his family to the land of the Hyperboreans as a reward for his piety. For more see J. Evans, 'What Happened to Croesus?', *CJ* 74 (1978) 43–60.

40. The Branchidae were the priests of the oracle of Apollo at Didyma (the name H. uses at VI. 19), some ten miles south of Miletus. See ch. 157 below.

41. The tomb of Alyattes has been identified with one of the mounds north of the plain of the River Hermus; its measurements are slightly less than those given by H. Hipponax (F 42 West = Pedley 280) perhaps refers to it when he mentions a 'tomb of Attales' (= Alyattes?). The lake of Gyges, already known to Homer (*Il.* II. 864–6), is to the north of the tombs.

42. The earliest coins of the Aegean are indeed from Lydia, dated to c. 625–600, and made from electrum, the alloy of the gold and silver panned from the rivers of Lydia. For the importance of early coinage see Murray (1993) 237–40.

43. 'Tyrrhenians' is the Greek name for the Etruscans, and H. is our earliest source. Here they are portrayed as Lydian colonists, a tradition mostly accepted in the ancient world except by Dionysius of Halicarnassus, who argued (*Roman Antiquities*, I. 25–30) that they were an indigenous Italic population. The question remains open: see M. Pallottino, *The Etruscans* (Harmondsworth ²1975) 64–81.

44. On the figure of Cyrus in H. see Immerwahr (1966) 161–7; Waters (1971) 49–53; Evans (1991) 51–6.

45. By H.'s own calculations, Assyrian rule of Upper (i.e. east of the Halys) Asia would have begun c. 1220. For a modern account of this powerful and ruthless early empire, see Roux 282ff and Kuhrt i. 349–65.

46. H. here describes a ziggurat; the outer walls at Athens were 60 *stades* (c. 7$\frac{1}{2}$ miles) according to Thuc. II. 13.

47. H. has here compressed a long historical process into the lifetime of a single ruler (*CHI* 80–83), but the 'description makes sense, both typologically and chronologically' (ibid. 89–90). H. puts Median independence too early, however: it should be c. 670, and its guiding force was not Deioces but Phraortes. Deioces, usually associated with the Daiaukku of Assyrian sources, was governor of an area in Media; he rebelled unsuccessfully, was captured, and exiled to Syria by Sargon II in 715 (*CHI* 80–83). See also Kuhrt ii. 654–6 (who is cautious about a Median 'empire').

48. Phraortes has been identified with Kastariti, the governor in the central Zagros and leader of an anti-Assyrian coalition. He, not Deioces, freed Media from Assyrian control; and it was Cyaxares, not Phraortes, who conquered the Persians: see *CHI* 210.

49. The Assyrians of Nineveh: as opposed to the Babylonians whom H. calls the Assyrians of Babylon; see below, n. 70.

50. On Cyaxares, the great military ruler of the Median empire, see *CHI* 121–2; the attack on Nineveh occurred in 614.

51. The 'female disease' is probably impotence, but other interpretations (such as pederasty) have been proposed. The 'Enarees' of Scythia (IV. 67) are androgynes.

52. Scythian domination was longer than the 28 years (ch. 106) of H.; see *CAH* III². 2. 564–8.

53. The fall of Nineveh in 612 (on which see Roux 372–7; Kuhrt ii. 544–6) and the end of Assyrian power shook the world of the Ancient Near East and its reverberations were felt as far away as Greece. The promise here is unfulfilled; there are two others at I. 184 and VII. 213. See Introduction §1 and n. 75 below.

54. The story of Cyrus' birth follows the folktale motif of the unwanted child saved from death who returns to claim what is his; the motif is known from the stories of Moses, the Akkadian king Sargon (*ANET* 119), Oedipus, Romulus and Remus; and for another example in H. see V. 92.

55. The dog was sacred to the Persians (see ch. 140) and it may here represent divine protection.

56. On the identification of these Persian tribes see *CHI* 238–9. At Pasargadae (25 miles northeast of Persepolis) extensive archaeological excavations have revealed many treasures: summary at *CHI* 838–55 with plates 5–7.

57. Since Astyages was betrayed by his own troops, Cyrus' victory entailed collaboration on the part of the Median nobility; see Cook 27 for a summary of other ancient accounts.

58. H. alone among Greek sources refers to this revolt of Medes against the Persians. It can be dated to 520 and is referred to by Darius in his Behistun inscription (on which see III. n. 25).

59. The Persian ethnography that follows is somewhat idealized; for the consistency of Persian action throughout the *Histories* with the portrait of them here see Immerwahr (1966) 184–8.

60. The Persian Zeus is Ahuramazda, the creator god who made earth, sky, man and human happiness. Mylitta (Mullittu) is an epithet of Ishtar. Alilat is probably from Al-Alahat = 'the goddess', sometimes identified with Athena. H. is wrong about Mitra, who is male; Ahuramazda, Anahita and Mitra formed the triad of gods worshipped by the Persians at this time. On Persian religion in general see Cook ch. XIV.

61. Persian names end in 's' only in their Greek transliteration, which shows that H. did not know Persian. For Persian names in H. see O. K. Armayor, *Ancient World* 1 (1978) 147–51.

62. For a brief summary of the scholarly debate about the Magi and their function in Persian religion see Cook 154–5; *CHI* 696–7.

63. As a Halicarnassian, H. knew this story from his city's point of view; Halicarnassus was probably excluded because of its mixed Greek and Carian stock: see HW i. 121; S. Hornblower, *Mausolus* (Oxford 1982) 14 n. 69.

64. At Athens the Apaturia was the festival of the phratries (brotherhoods): see Burkert 255–6.

65. Excavations at Smyrna (modern Izmir) have revealed an important town of the seventh century surrounded by a large wall (illustrations at *CAH* III². 3. 202 and 443). The town was destroyed by Alyattes c. 600 (see I. 16).

66. Alalia (modern Aléria) is located on the east coast of Corsica opposite the coast of Etruria, a busy site for commercial activity. The date of its founding was c. 545. The naval battle mentioned here, of c. 540, was a seminal event in Greece's attempt to colonize the west: see Boardman 214–16; *CAH* III². 3. 142–3. A Cadmeian victory, like the better known 'Pyrrhic victory', is one gained at a high price.

67. Bias of Priene was accounted one of the Seven Sages; proposals to relocate the Ionians appear also at V. 106, 124, VI. 22 and IX. 106. Thales of Miletus is called Phoenician because he was descended ultimately from Cadmus (on whom see II. 49). His proposal clearly has Attica in mind with its demes (villages) and one central government at Athens.

68. The Carian triple contribution is not supported by modern archaeology. The change to hoplite armour among the Greeks (the 'hoplite revolution') was an importation from the Near East in the early seventh century: see A. M. Snodgrass, *Early Greek Armour and Weapons* (Edinburgh 1964); on the social and political consequences, Murray (1993) chs 8–10. See also Osborne 162–4, 175–6.

69. The Caunians lived on the south coast of Caria, though they were distinct from the Carians.

70. For H.'s account of Babylon see J. MacGinnis, 'H.'s Description of Babylon', *BICS* 33 (1986) 67–86, where H. is valued for accuracy. On Babylon in general see Kuhrt ii. 573–622. H. speaks of Babylon as if it were an Assyrian city, but it was not. In 612 a coalition of Babylonians, Medes and Scythians destroyed Nineveh, and it was after this that Babylon, under the Chaldaean (also called neo-Babylonian) dynasty, achieved its greatest power. The collapse of Nineveh had been preceded by a decade or so of struggles between Assyria and Babylon. It was Nebuchadrezzar (604–562) who made Babylon the marvel that H. describes. His ambition brought him to Syria and Jerusalem, where

he is well known from his dealings with the Jews: see 2 Kings 24–5 and Daniel 1–4. It was against his son Nabonidus that Cyrus marched (below, ch. 188).

71. The measurements of the wall (approximately 350 feet) are extraordinarily high; for the site of Babylon, with aerial photograph and plan of the city, see Oates 144–9.

72. Babylonians were famous for their brick-making ability (e.g. Genesis 11. 3) – so much so, in fact, that the bricks were plundered by later invaders, and thus nothing of the outer wall at Babylon remains (Oates 145). The 'hundred gates' are a Homeric echo (*Il.* X. 383); in fact there were eight (Roux 391ff.).

73. Bel = Marduk. In the Babylonian epic of creation, the *enuma elish*, Marduk, son of Ea, is born (like Athena) full-grown. He fights Traniat and her army of monsters, and once victorious is recognized as the greatest of the gods, and the other gods build Babylon for him. His temple was Esagila, a complex of buildings within the city. H. here describes the ziggurat, Etemenanki, which lay north of Esagila. See Roux 385; Oates 156–8.

74. H. is somewhat confused here: the statue taken by Xerxes was that of Bel (Marduk) after the revolt of Babylon c. 480 (not mentioned by H.). Since Bel was emblematic of an independent Babylonia, Xerxes' removal of it was a political act, showing his abandonment of the union between Persia and Babylon. Cyrus, on the other hand, had portrayed himself (Cyrus Cylinder, *ANET* 315–16) as chosen by Marduk himself to benefit Babylon.

75. There is no 'History of Assyria' in H.'s text as it has come down to us, and there seem to be three possibilities: H. never wrote it; he wrote it and incorporated it into his work but it has been lost (it is suggested that it would have followed the account of Darius' capture of Babylon at III. 150–60); he wrote it as a separate work and it did not survive. For different viewpoints see HW i. 379–80; R. Drews, *AJP* 91 (1970) 181–91; J. Macqueen, *CQ* 38 (1978) 284–91; Powell 19–23.

76. Semiramis is Shammuramat, queen of Assyria and wife of Shamshi-adad V (824–810), regent perhaps during the first years of her son's reign (Adadnirari III, ruled 810–782), though this is no longer generally accepted: Kuhrt ii.491. In later Greek accounts (e.g. Diodorus II. 5ff.) she is known for her beauty, power and licentiousness, but there is nothing of this in H., who reserves his admiration for Nitocris.

77. The name Nitocris is not found in eastern sources. What is attributed to her here is actually the work of Nebuchadrezzar. Nor has the village of Ardericca been found; the story smacks of the fantastic.

78. The story is thoroughly Greek, and represents a tradition hostile

to Darius. No tombs have been discovered near the gates of Babylon, and the presence of a dead body would have polluted the gate for a Persian.

79. Labynetus = Nabonidus: see n. 34 above.

80. The fall of Babylon is recorded in the Nabonidus Chronicle (*ANET* 306), which says that the city fell without a battle; it is clear that there was treachery, perhaps because of the discontent aroused by Nabonidus, particularly towards the priestly caste who may thus have welcomed Cyrus. It is likely too that the large Jewish community at Babylon assisted Cyrus' entry into the city; after its fall Cyrus returned the Jewish exiles to Jerusalem, with orders for the temple there to be rebuilt (Ezra 6. 3–22). When Cyrus entered Babylon in triumph, he prohibited looting and established Gobryas (Ugbaru) as Persian governor. For a brief summary of the entire action see *CHI* 408–12. The story of the diversion of the river is not to be accepted (HW i. 390). For the 'second' capture of Babylon see III. 150–59.

81. For Babylon under Persian rule see Oates 136–9; Roux 406–12; *CHI* 529–87.

82. On irrigation see Oates 11–12, 193–4; the 'swipes' are the *shadoufs*, levers 13–15 feet long on a post 3–4 feet high with a bucket at one end and a weight at the other.

83. This type of boat is still used on the Euphrates, but their capacity as given here (c. 130 tons) is greatly exaggerated.

84. The Massagetae are a nomad population living in Sogdana to the east of the Caspian Sea between the rivers Oxus (Amu Darya) and Jaxartes (Sir Darya). On the territory see Cook 194–5.

85. The Araxes may be the Aras, which rises in Armenia and empties into the Caspian Sea.

86. The 'tree' is a type of Indian cannabis, from which hashish is extracted; cf. IV. 74–5.

87. Alone in antiquity H. argued that the Caspian was a sea, not (as Hecataeus and others argued) a gulf of the Northern Ocean. The Caspian is c. 750 miles long and 280 miles wide. H.'s measurements in days are probably inaccurate, although the length is the more serious error, attributable to the fact that the northern part of the Caspian was the least well-known.

88. For H., Cyrus' last campaign beyond the known world is his ultimate act of *hybris*, stretching his dominions too far (cf. Tomyris' words at 206). See Introduction §4.

89. On the possible identity of Tomyris, see Cook 37, 235 n. 32.

90. Only H. records this death of Cyrus. According to Ctesias (F 9 Jacoby), Cyrus was wounded in battle against the Derbici, was brought

back to camp, and before dying appointed Cambyses as king, encouraging his family to love one another. In Diodorus (II. 44) Cyrus is taken prisoner and crucified by the Scythian queen. And in Xenophon (*Education of Cyrus* VIII. 7) he dies at home surrounded by family and friends. H. does not explain how Cyrus' body was returned home. His tomb at Pasargadae (Boardman 103; *CHI* pl. 5; Cook pl. 1) is much discussed by later Greek writers; for a description see *CHI* 838–41; D. Stronach, *Pasargadae* (Oxford 1978) 24–41.

BOOK TWO

1. Egypt had allied with Croesus between 555 and 546 and this alliance had included Babylon. After the Persians' defeat of Croesus and Babylon they turned their eyes to Egypt. On Cambyses' position on the eve of the conquest see Olmstead 86–7. The date of the invasion is May/June 525: Lloyd ii. 3.

2. The Phrygians invaded Asia Minor some time after 1200 and had established a strong kingdom, comprising the Anatolian plateau west of the Halys; their kingdom was destroyed by the Cimmerians in the early seventh century: see I. 15.

3. Memphis is on the west bank of the Nile, some fifteen miles south of modern Cairo. Hephaestus is the Egyptian Ptah, a craftsman god; for the site see *AESH* 319.

4. Thebes (Luxor) is on the east bank of the Nile; on the west bank was the City of the Dead. Luxor has some of the most spectacular ancient ruins including Karnak (about which H. is strangely silent). Heliopolis is Kom el Hisn, c. $7\frac{1}{2}$ miles northeast of Cairo. It was the centre of the worship of the sun god Re (= Helios, thus its name in Greek), on whose characteristics see Lloyd ii. 15–16. Why the priests here are described as 'most learned' may be related to the 'tree of life' which grew there, and on which 'the goddess Seshat and the god Thoth wrote the names and the years of the kings of Egypt at the time of their coronation' (Lloyd ii. 17).

5. Unlike the Greeks who lengthened the year with intercalary months, the Egyptians had a year of fixed length, 12 months of 30 days plus 5 added at the end to equal 365. But since the year is actually $365\frac{1}{4}$ days, the Egyptian civil calendar moved throughout the solar year, sometimes so much askew that winter festivals were celebrated in summer. The Egyptians also had a lunar calendar (which H. seems not to know) used for cult purposes: see further E. Bickerman, *Chronology of the Ancient World* (London and Ithaca [2]1980) 40–43.

6. Zeus, Poseidon, Apollo, Hera, Athene, Artemis, Ares, Demeter, Hephaistus, Aphrodite, Hermes and Dionysus.

7. 'Egypt to which the Greeks sail' includes the Nile delta and as far south as Lake Moeris.

8. 60 *schoeni* = 3600 *stades* = 450 miles; the actual measurement from Plinthine to Lake Serbonis is c. 300 miles.

9. By H.'s measurements, from the coast to Heliopolis is c. $187\frac{1}{2}$ miles (1500 *stades*), and from Pisa (another name for Olympia) to Athens $185\frac{1}{2}$ miles (1485 *stades*). Lloyd (ii. 47) estimates the first distance at c. 150 miles, the second at c. 165 miles.

10. 4860 *stades* = c. 600 miles; the actual distance is c. 450 miles.

11. From the Mediterranean to Thebes is c. 615 miles; from Thebes to Elephantine is c. 140 miles.

12. The 'Red Sea' is the Indian Ocean; the 'very long narrow gulf' is our Red Sea.

13. In fact, the labour involved in the irrigation and cultivation of Egypt was enormous: see *AESH* 326–7.

14. H. now moves to the definition of what constituted Egypt. The arguments are of varying value, designed mostly to show the inconsistency of the 'Ionians'.

15. 6120 *stades* = c. 756 miles; the actual figure is 760–800 miles.

16. On the oracle of Ammon see ch. 42.

17. The inundation of the Nile fascinated the Greeks for centuries, and H. was neither the first nor the last to contribute to the debate. The three reasons he gives and rejects (the holders of these views are in parentheses) are: (1) north – Etesian – winds block the water's flow into the Mediterranean (Thales); (2) the Nile flows from Ocean, a body of water circling the earth (Hecataeus); (3) melting snows in the summertime drain off into the Nile's source (Anaxagoras of Clazomenae; this view appears also in Aeschylus and Euripides). The actual cause of the Nile's flooding is the monsoon rainfall of the Ethiopian plateau, which drains off into two rivers (the Blue Nile and the Atbara) and provides 90 per cent of the Nile's water at the height of the flood (Lloyd ii. 91–3).

18. The Nile's sources were the other great problem in antiquity. The various views are summarized by Lloyd ii. 107–10. Sais (modern Sa el Hagar), c. 10 miles northeast of Naucratis, was well known to the Greeks. The priest 'of Athena' is perhaps a 'Scribe of the Treasury of Neith' (Lloyd ii. 111).

19. Elephantine, the Egyptian 'Ivory Town', is at the first cataract of the Nile; see *AESH* 99–100 = *CHA* i. 686–7; it is the most southerly part of Egypt that H. claims to have visited.

20. This is the first mention in an ancient text of the capital city of the Ethiopians. Modern Ethiopia is confined to Abyssinia, but in antiquity the name 'Ethiopians' was applied to all the people south of Egypt; H. distinguishes several groups among them; here they are the Nubian kingdom of Kush. Meroë is located between the fifth and sixth cataract of the Nile; on the site, see *CHA* ii. 216–19. It became the capital c. 590 (*CHA* ii. 218). For more on Meroë see Burstein 127–46, 155–64; P. Shinnie, *Meroë. A Civilization of the Sudan* (London and New York 1967). Zeus here is Amun, much honoured by the Nubians; there is no evidence of special worship of Dionysus (= Osiris), although the people of Meroë did worship other gods: Shinnie 141–6.

21. The story is told at fifth hand (H. – Cyrenaeans – Etearchus – Nasamonians – wild young men), a remarkable distance even by Herodotean standards; on the maintenance of credibility by the author see Fehling 98–9.

22. The great river is thought by some to be the Niger, but Lloyd (ii. 138–9) follows R. Carpenter in arguing for the Bodele Depression northeast of Lake Chad, now dry. The small men are the Pygmies.

23. On Egypt in H. see Introduction §2; on monuments as justifying lengthier treatment of a people, see III. 60.

24. Hieroglyphs are, in fact, most often written right to left, but H. here is enjoying a pun in the Greek: the Egyptians write *epi ta aristera*, 'to the left', but maintain that they write *epidexia* 'rightly' ('rightwards' might get across the sense of the pun in English, since English maintains the association of the right hand with correctness); while they claim that the Greeks, who write *epi ta dexia*, 'to the right', write *eparistera*, 'leftly', i.e. 'wrongly'.

25. On the clean marks see at III. 28.

26. The goddess is Isis.

27. Probably Chonsu, the son of Amon-re and Mut, whose name, connected with the word for 'travel through', would have suggested the wanderings of Heracles.

28. The Ammonians dwell at the Siwa Oasis, the site of the famous oracle of Zeus. In addition to Egyptians and Ethiopians, there would also have been native Libyans.

29. Lloyd (ii. 201–2) believes that H.'s Egyptian Heracles here is Shu, who was sometimes identified with Chonsu. H. argues that there were two Heracles, the god and the hero whose father was not Zeus but Amphitryon; of this 'hero' Heracles the Egyptians have no knowledge.

30. In the *Iliad* Heracles is referred to as the son of Zeus (XIX. 98ff.) and the son of Amphitryon (V. 392). Amphitryon and Alcmene were descendants of Perseus and thus (see ch. 91) Egyptian.

31. Poseidon was god of the sea, the Dioscuri (Castor and Pollux) the patrons of sailors.

32. For the twelve Greek gods see n. 6 above. But no group of twelve gods in Egypt is known, and H. has been misled by his zeal to make everything Greek Egyptian. The Eight Gods (Ogdoad) created the Nine Gods (Ennead): Re-'Atum, Geb, Shu, Tefnut, Nut, Osiris, Isis, Nephthys and Seth.

33. The temple is that of the Phoenician god Melqart.

34. H. echoes his predecessor Hecataeus here; not coincidentally, he is here, like Hecataeus, criticizing a 'foolish' Greek story: that the Egyptian king Busiris invited Heracles to Egypt, feasted him, and then attempted to sacrifice him. For an illustration of this extremely popular theme see Boardman 150.

35. Pan is the Egyptian Ram of Mendes, who was not, however, one of the eight gods.

36. Dionysus is Osiris, the Moon (Selene) is Isis.

37. On phallic processions in honour of Dionysus see Burkert 103–5. On Melampus see IX. n. 18.

38. Cadmus was the father of Semele, the mother of Dionysus. There is little to suggest that there was any Phoenician migration to Boeotia.

39. Since Poseidon is an Indo-European god, H.'s statement is wrong. Perhaps he is so associated with the Libyans because his wife in some accounts is named Libya, and his son is represented as a Libyan king. Heroes were, for the Greeks, an intermediate group between gods and men; they frequently had one divine parent, and some were divinized (e.g. Heracles) and given a place among the gods. The heroes loom large in the Greek victory over Persia, and they appear frequently in H. Cf. I. n. 30.

40. Stone blocks with a portrait of Hermes on top and an erect phallus in the middle were frequently to be seen in public spaces and before private residences. H. is correct that they originated with the Athenians.

41. On these gods and their rites see Burkert 281–5.

42. 'Four hundred years' before H. is mid-ninth century. The earlier poets he alludes to are Orpheus and Musaeus. Hesiod is generally dated to the eighth century. As for Homer, the *Iliad* may be tentatively assigned to c. 750, the *Odyssey* c. 700, although a centuries-old oral tradition lies behind these poems, and the identity and exact role of 'Homer' continue to be keenly debated.

43. On the problems in this account of oracles see Fehling 65–70.

44. The god is Osiris; he is named at ch. 42 and is called Dionysus at ch. 47; perhaps the suggestion here of a mystery performance makes H. reticent.

45. The phrase 'get to know' is ambiguous here and could be translated 'have intercourse with', which would explain H.'s transition in the next chapter to the subject.

46. The name 'crocodile' comes from *kroke* (pebble) and *drilos* (lizard), an example of the Greek habit of using diminutive language for something grand: cf. 'pyramids' = 'wheat cakes'. As it appears in H. the crocodile is a paradoxical creature: see Benardete 54–5. Contrary to what H. says, the crocodile does have a tongue and it can move its lower jaw.

47. The description of the hippopotamus represents the nadir of Herodotean zoology. Clearly, he saw neither the real thing nor pictures of it, and his description is based purely on its Greek name, which means 'river-horse'.

48. Hesiod (F 304 Merkelbach-West) had called the phoenix long-lived, and Hecataeus included a description of it in his work (F 324a Jacoby). The story that H. tells here is not corroborated by any Egyptian evidence.

49. It was once thought that these flying snakes were locusts (still maintained by Pritchett (1993) 27–9); more likely, they were suggested to H. (or Hecataeus) by the portrayal on Egyptian monuments of snakes with wings; to this may have been added some information on the flying lizard (*draco volans*) of Southeast Asia: see Lloyd ii. 326–7; cf. Isaiah 30. 6 for mention of flying serpents in Egypt.

50. 'Linus' is the personification of the Greek *ailinos*, a mourning cry meaning 'woe to us', interpreted as meaning 'woe to Linus'. No Egyptian equivalent for him has been found, and the name 'Maneros' cannot be recognized in an Egyptian source.

51. This method is not quite astrology, since not until Roman times was it connected with the stars. The poets are Hesiod, Orpheus and Musaeus.

52. The 'innumerable doctors' may be influenced by Homer, *Od.* IV. 231–2, where the Egyptians are described as 'of the race of Paiëon', the legendary healer.

53. Chemmis (Panoplis in later writers) = Arabian Akhmûm, not the floating island described in ch. 156, but the city north of Thebes on the east shore of the Nile. H. identifies Perseus with the Egyptian Horus; he is linked to Egypt by the story of the daughters of Danaus, who fled Egypt and took refuge in Argos; the story is told in Aeschylus' *Suppliants*. The sandal is a reference to the flying sandals that Perseus obtained from Hermes.

54. Here begins the first of two historical sections organized by the thread of those pharaohs whom H. considers noteworthy; he will speak

of their monuments (usually pyramids) and any stories that may have attached to them; he will also treat great deeds or works emanating from the various rulers. The first section (99–142) treats the pharaohs from Min to Sethos, and the source is identified as 'what the Egyptians themselves say'; the second section (147–82) treats the Dodecarchs to Amasis. In this latter section (which is more accurate than the former) H. reports 'what the Egyptians and everyone else say'.

55. Min = Menes, to be identified with Narmer or Aha; see *AESH* 50–55 = *CHA* i. 527–32.

56. Much of the story of Nitocris is folktale and legend, although Lloyd (iii. 13–15) defends her historicity. Moeris is Amenemhet III (1844–1797). For the lake see ch. 149.

57. H.'s Sesostris is an amalgamation of the Twelfth Dynasty pharaohs Senwosret I and Senwosret III, with some absorption of the historical Rameses II. The idealization of this pharaoh probably represents genuine Egyptian tradition (Lloyd iii. 16–17), although Greek contamination and interpretation are also present.

58. There is no evidence that the Egyptians ever did this; for a valiant attempt to explain see Lloyd iii. 20–21; see also West (1985) 298–300.

59. This passage is enormously controversial. Colchis, the legendary home of Medea, is on the Black Sea. What H. means by 'black skins and woolly hair' has been much debated: if H. is saying that the Egyptians are Negroes, then there might be some doubt that he ever went to Egypt. On the other hand, if *melangchroes* can 'denote any colour from bronzed to black' (Lloyd iii. 22), then H. may be saying only that the Egyptians were dark compared to the Greeks. See Lloyd *ad loc.*; Pritchett (1982) 258–62, (1993) 12–16. On the difficulties of the argument see Fehling 17–20. The entire discussion has been further complicated by recent arguments that the ancient Egyptians were black. It may be worth noting that Assyrian reliefs sometimes depict Egyptian captives with woolly hair and African features: see *CAH*, plates to Vol. III (1994), no. 51. (I owe this observation to Mr Robert McLeman.)

60. This figure still stands at the Karabel Pass, south of the road from Smyrna to Sardis. It is c. 8 feet high; the spear is held in the left, not right, hand; the bow is on the right shoulder. H.'s inscription is most likely a Greek invention, for the writing (Hittite, not Egyptian) was probably indecipherable in H.'s time. See West (1985) 300–301; Pritchett (1982) 267–80, (1993) 106–12. A stele of Sesostris is possibly mentioned by the poet Hipponax (F 42 West = Pedley 280). Memnon was king of the Ethiopians.

61. The statues here are probably those of Rameses II at Mit Rahineh, two colossi of granite (originally 32 feet) and limestone (originally 42 feet).

62. The story of Darius is most likely apocryphal, since Darius was in Egypt in 518 and his Scythian expedition was between 516 and 511. Nevertheless, a statue of Darius discovered at Susa in 1972 (Cook pl. 15) has an inscription that states: 'This is the stone statue which Darius the king ordered to be made in Egypt, so that he who should see it in the future should know that the Persian man holds Egypt.' Why it was at Susa is uncertain; see Lewis (1984) 589–90.

63. Pheros = Pharaoh. Egyptian reliefs frequently portray the king spearing a hippopotamus in the water, thus representing his defeat of the forces of chaos. Pheros' search for a faithful woman is a folk-motif, and the account here in general is an amalgam of Greek and Egyptian elements: Lloyd iii. 39.

64. The foreign Aphrodite is Astarte. H.'s story of Helen which follows is a rationalized amalgamation of Menelaus' adventures in *Od.* IV and the lyric poet Stesichorus' famous *Palinode* (F 15 Page), in which the poet stated that Helen herself stayed in Egypt while her image went to Troy. Clearly H. here is giving a performance piece, a type of one-upmanship of Greek tradition and a further 'improvement' on the story as the Greeks had had it before him. That the Egyptian priests told him this version is extremely unlikely, the more so as he uses them here and in his later discussion of the Trojan War (chs. 118–20) to buttress a conclusion of his own, that 'great offences meet with great punishments at the hands of God'. This passage is much discussed: see Lloyd iii. 46–7 (tracing it to Hecataeus); Fehling 59–65 (H.'s own invention).

65. The three Homeric passages are respectively *Il.* VI. 289ff., *Od.* IV. 227–30, and IV. 351–2.

66. Rhampsinitus is based on the pharaohs of the Nineteenth and Twentieth Dynasties, with a generous admixture of legend and folktale. See Lloyd iii. 52.

67. The unnamed writers are the Pythagoreans and the Orphics, who probably did not owe their doctrine of the transmigration of souls to the Egyptians.

68. The Pyramid Builders, Cheops, Chephren and Mycerinus, belong to the Fourth Dynasty and are chronologically displaced; they belong in the earlier group of the 300 kings (chs 100–101).

69. Cheops (Khufu) ruled 2596–2573. His pyramid is the First, or Great Pyramid at Giza. H. is close to the actual measurements of the sides, which are approximately 750 feet; the present-day height is 480 feet, but the pyramid today lacks its casing, and so would have been higher in antiquity.

70. The Egyptians used not cranes but ramps, some of which survive.

71. No evidence exists that any inscriptions of the sort were carved by pharaohs on their pyramids. The '1600 talents' is evidence enough of the falsity, since the Egyptians did not have a money economy. For attempts to explain the misunderstanding (unless perhaps H. himself is jesting) see HW i. 229, who rely on errors in H.'s memory – which ill-suits the author's emphatic 'I remember distinctly'.

72. Chephren (Khafre) built the Second Pyramid at Giza, c. 700 feet on the sides and c. 470 feet high; it is about 10, not 40, feet shorter than Cheops' pyramid, but the latter was taller in antiquity (above, n. 69), so H. may be correct. Some have seen a parody of this remark in Aristophanes, *Birds* 1130 (performed in 415 BCE).

73. Hollowed cow statues with headless images inside were used in the worship of Isis and Osiris (and Saïs was a centre for this): Lloyd iii. 79. The twenty statues perhaps played a role in the ritual; but the story of the missing hands stretches probability (Fehling 129).

74. The pyramid of Mycerinus (Menkaura), grandson of Cheops and son of Chephren, is the third pyramid at Giza, not 280 feet high (ch. 134) but c. 350 feet. On Mycerinus' cult and pyramid complex see *AESH* 92–4 = *CHA* i. 679–81.

75. Asychis is Sheshonk (or Shoshenq) I (945–924), of the Twenty-Second Dynasty. H. has returned to the time period he abandoned at ch. 124 when he began on the Pyramid Builders. The tomb has not been discovered, although remains of his have been found in Memphis.

76. Anysis may represent the kings of the Twenty-Third Dynasty. Sabacos is the Nubian Shabaka of the Twenty-Fifth Dynasty; the first Nubian invasion of Egypt was led c. 750 by Kashta. Sabacos ruled 716–702, a part of the Kushite dynasty that ruled Egypt c. 780–656; on this dynasty see *AESH* 242–6 = *CHA* i. 889–93.

77. No Egyptian pharaoh known as Sethos occurs at this time; the invasion of Sennacherib occurred in the reign of Shabataka, Sabacos' successor, when Egypt was still ruled by Kush (H.'s Ethiopians).

78. Sennacherib became king in 704 on the death of his father Sargon II; in 701 he attacked Phoenicia and Palestine (which had revolted) and defeated an Egyptian army sent to assist the revolt. He is thought to have invaded Palestine again later and to have planned an invasion of Egypt; the battle is narrated at 2 Kings 19.35, where an angel of the Lord attacks his host. In H. another marvel (although not divine) saves the Egyptians. The campaign is sometimes rejected by historians, and the story may have been invented around the statue; the form of the

statue's address is Greek, not Egyptian. See Roux 319–21; *CAH* III².
2. 109–11.

79. This is the first of four references to H.'s great predecessor Hecataeus (see Introduction §3), and the passage is much discussed. For those who believe in the historicity of the event, it marks an important moment in Greek self-consciousness, as Hecataeus is forced to recognize the vastly superior antiquity of the Egyptians, who can point to 341 generations to Hecataeus' paltry 16. It is consequently assumed that H. is here mocking his predecessor and contrasting his own sophistication with Hecataeus' naïveté. Some, however, have challenged the plausibility of the entire episode: for discussion see Lloyd iii. 107–10; Fehling 77–86; West (1991) 174–90.

80. H. resumes the thread of Egyptian history from Sethos and ch. 141; from here to the end of Book II, the narrative derives from Egyptian and Greek traditions (see ch. 154 where H. explains the difference in the tradition).

81. The twelve kings (Dodecarchs) represent the disorganized state of Egypt during the Assyrian and Ethiopian occupations (Twenty-Fifth to Twenty-Sixth Dynasties).

82. Petrie identified the Labyrinth's enormous foundations (1000 × 800 feet) to the south of the pyramid of Amenemhet III (= Moeris) at Hawara in the central Fayoum; for a sketch see Lloyd iii. 122. The Lake is usually identified with the Birket Quarum in the northwest Fayoum, but this is today neither large (c. 34 miles) nor man-made. The statues (c. 40 feet high, of Amenemhet III) were not in the middle but on the east end of the Lake. For a spirited argument that H.'s description of the Labyrinth and Lake Moeris owes more to Homer and Greek influences than to Egyptian architecture, and that such works never existed except in the Greek imagination, see O. K. Armayor, 'The Influence on H.'s Story of the Labyrinth', *CB* 54 (1977–8) 68–72; id., *H.'s Autopsy of the Fayoum: Lake Moeris and the Labyrinth of Egypt* (Amsterdam 1985). A full collection of the evidence, together with illustrations, is in C. Obsomer, 'Hérodote, Strabon, et le "Mystère" du Labyrinthe d'Égypte', in: *Amosiades. Mélanges offerts à Prof. Claude Vandersleyen*, ed. C. Obsomer and A.-L. Oosthoek (Louvain-la-Neuve 1992) 221–333.

83. The Egyptians had bronze but they did not have hoplite armour. Psammetichus' use of Carians and Ionians was of cardinal importance in the development of Greek ties with Egypt. For the Greeks in Egypt see Austin (1970); Boardman 111–15; *CAH* III². 3. 1–56.

84. See IV. 159. Apries' expedition to Cyrene fell c. 571/70: see *AESH* 343–5.

85. There has been much discussion of the chronology of Amasis' revolt: an Egyptian stele of Amasis, though not without bias, orders events differently, and refers to two battles not one; in this account Apries is killed in the fighting and buried honourably by Amasis. Lloyd's reconstruction is that Apries was defeated in the first year of his reign (570), went into exile, returned in 567 with a force of Babylonians, and died in this second defeat. The site of Momemphis is uncertain; Lloyd opts for Kom el-Hisn (iii. 182).

86. The warrior class were in origin Libyans who had been settled in Egypt by Rameses II (1290–1224) and III (1194–1163). On social structure in Egypt see *AESH* 188–94 (= *CHA* i. 835–41), 299–301. The Spartan system was completely militaristic, and all crafts and trade were done for the Spartans by the *perioeci*, the people surrounding Sparta whose states were nominally free, although they followed the Spartan lead in foreign policy and accompanied them on all their campaigns; see Mitchell 64–75. No greater contrast could be found than with Corinth, which was home to many craftsmen; see Salmon 163–4.

87. The god is Osiris. The lake at Delos, c. 325 × 225 feet, was well known to the Greeks (Theognis I. 5–10), not least because tradition recorded that at this lake Apollo and Artemis were born.

88. A stone block with Amasis' name has been found at Saïs, but the marvels described here cannot be confirmed by the paltry remains.

89. Two horizontal colossi are still at Memphis, both of Rameses II, the larger being 42 feet.

90. Naucratis was an extremely important trading post (*emporion*) in the Delta on the Canopic branch of the Nile; Greek presence probably precedes Amasis and begins c. 615–610; see Austin (1970) 23ff.; Boardman 118–33 (with many good illustrations); Murray (1993) 228–31; *CAH* III². 3. 37–43. Archaeological evidence suggests that the sanctuaries of Aegina, Samos and Miletus all predate the Hellenium.

91. On the Amphictyons see n. at V. 62.

BOOK THREE

1. H. here resumes the thread of his Persian narrative, which had been delayed by the digression on Egypt. Cambyses was the elder son of Cyrus and Cassandane, the younger being Bardiya, whom H. calls Smerdis. Cambyses had been with his father at the siege of Babylon in 539 BCE, and accompanied his father on the Massagetae expedition, but was then sent back with Croesus (I. 208). Cambyses ascended the throne in August 530. His attack on Egypt was no doubt the result of its alliance with Lydia against Persia (I. 77). On the portrayal of Cambyses in H. – he stands in stark contrast to his father – see Immerwahr (1966) 167–9; Waters (1971) 53–6.

2. For Typhon see II. 144, where he seems to be identified with Seth. Typhon was a monstrous creature blasted by Zeus into Tartarus or other locations, including Mt Etna in Sicily. H. puts him under Lake Serbonis (modern Sabkhat al-Bardawil), a lagoon east of the Delta.

3. This is the first of two digressions on the Arabs (the second is at 107–13). The term 'Arabs' was used for the nomadic tribes between Egypt and the Euphrates.

4. No great river exists in Arabia; HW i. 258 suggest this is a distorted version of a subterranean watercourse in West Asia.

5. It does in fact rain in upper Egypt, but not much.

6. It is difficult to believe that a generation after the battle (at least), H. actually saw widely separated heaps of skulls still lying on the battle-field; the observations about the relative hardness of the skulls may be related to the roughly contemporary tract *Airs, Waters, and Places*, which ascribes the hardness and softness of bodies to climate (see also IX. 122 and n.): see Fehling 28–30. The battle at Papremis was in 462/1; Inarus was a king of Libya and the leader of an Egyptian uprising that began at the accession of Artaxerxes I; see Thuc. I. 104.

7. On the mutability of fortune see Introduction §4; 'on the threshold of old age' is a Homeric phrase.

8. These incidents also come from the Egyptian revolt under Artaxerxes (n. 6 above). Suicide by drinking bull's blood is common enough in ancient literature (so one tradition about Themistocles: Plut. *Themist.* 31), the more surprising in that the drink is not fatal, as could easily have been demonstrated (one assumes).

9. These 'long-lived' Ethiopians (largely figures of legend) dwell to the south of the Kush kingdom (II. n. 20). The 'Table of the Sun' may be a misunderstanding of the Egyptian story of a 'meadow of offerings' at which the souls of the dead feast (so HW i. 261), or it may be a combination of the stories of Ethiopian banquets which the gods frequent in Homer (*Il.* I. 423–4; *Od.* I. 22–5 *et al.*) with the image of Ethiopia as a land of the Sun (so Asheri 235). The temple known as the 'Temple of the Sun' at Meroë is probably that of the lion-god Apedemek: *CHA* ii. 223.

10. Carthage was a colony of Phoenicia.

11. Although the story of the bow is hardly historical, it may be connected with the Egyptian designation of Kush as 'Nine-Bows': *CHA* ii. 223. Only Smerdis is able to draw the bow, and only a little (ch. 30).

12. The Ammonians are the Libyans who dwell around the oracle of Zeus at Ammon, the site of the Siwah oasis. See further IV. 181.

13. Apis is the sacred bull of Memphis, associated with Ptah and Osiris; he had his own enclosure, the *Apieum*. Epaphus was the son of Zeus and Io.

14. The 'sacred sickness' is epilepsy; some modern historians think Cambyses may have suffered from alcoholism or syphilis.

15. On the Cabiri see n. at II. 51.

16. The fragment of Pindar reads: 'Custom, the king of all / of mortals and immortals, / leads, justifying that which is most violent / by its very powerful hand.' This passage is sometimes seen as an example of the tolerant attitude of H. towards other lands, a type of cultural relativism. H. may indeed be tolerant, but the point in Pindar seems to be that custom is a tyrant, compelling people to behave in a certain way. On this passage see Benardete 80–81; Immerwahr (1966) 319–22; S. Humphreys, *Arethusa* 20 (1987) 211–20; J. Evans, '*Despotes Nomos*', *Athenaeum* 43 (1965) 142–53. See also VII. 104 with n.

17. Polycrates became tyrant in Samos c. 535: see Andrewes 117–22; Shipley 74–80.

18. This explanation fits in with H.'s beliefs about prosperity (Introduction § 4); for a brief summary of modern views on the termination of this alliance see Lloyd iii. 238–9.

19. H. seems here to be having a little fun with the laconic Spartans, who were notorious for their parsimony with words.

20. The Messenians were the Spartans' western neighbours; they were subjugated by the Spartans at an early date, and became enslaved to the Spartan state. They were known as 'helots' and the Spartans practised many forms of state-sponsored terrorism to keep them in check (see Fornara 13). They nevertheless required constant watching, and the omnipresent fear of revolt was an important factor in the Spartans' unwillingness to be long away from the Peloponnese. This reference in H. is probably to the Second War with Messenia in the mid-seventh century; noteworthy is that the Spartans and the Messenians are both supposed to have received overseas help in the war (Fornara 12A); on the helots in general see Cartledge (1979) 160–77, 347–56 (all the ancient sources translated); Michell 75–84.

21. For the bowl see I. 70.

22. Periander inherited the tyranny of Corinth from his father Cypselus (see V. 92) c. 625; the ancient tradition about him is almost uniformly hostile. On his rule see Andrewes 43–53; Salmon 197–205. Corcyra (modern Corfu) is off the northwest coast of the Greek mainland. It was a colony of Corinth, sent out in 734 (the same year as Syracuse),

and it often engaged in power struggles with its mother city; see III. 49 and V. 92. Epidaurus, on the mainland opposite Corcyra, was a colony of the Corcyreans.

23. On Pitana see IX. 53 with n.

24. On H. and Samos see Introduction §1; for a similar justification for a lengthened account see II. 35. On the three works mentioned here see Shipley 76–9.

25. Here begins the story of the false Smerdis, the revolt of the Magi, and the accession of Darius. We are fortunate to have a Persian source for the incidents narrated here, a trilingual (Elamite, Babylonian, Old Persian) inscription set up by Darius at Behistun (Bisitun, c. 20 miles east of Khermansah) and discovered by H. C. Rawlinson in 1836. The inscription was also set up around the Persian empire; copies of an Aramaic version have been found and have been used to supplement the Behistun version. We do not know whether a Greek text ever existed in Asia Minor, which could have been used by H. A full English translation is available at Frye 363–8; illustrations at *CHI* pls 34–5 and Cook pl. 7. There are some important differences between the inscription and H.'s account: in the former, the revolt of the Magus Gaumata (H.'s false Smerdis) is supported by the people; Cambyses dies by his own hand; and then Darius and the six conspirators (see ch. 70 with n.) kill Gaumata at Nisaya in Media. H., however, does not mention the people in the revolt, has Cambyses die of an accidental wound (chs 64–6), and has the Magi killed in the palace after Prexaspes' dramatic speech and leap. We may suspect that both H. and the Behistun inscription have – for different reasons – simplified a complex series of events. Each source reduces the events to a series of personal motives, and ignores any larger political, social or economic causes. The oddness of the story, particularly the likeness of the usurper Gaumata/Smerdis to Cambyses' brother Bardiya/Smerdis, has led the majority of scholars to believe that Darius in fact killed the brother of Cambyses and usurped the Persian throne: see further Kuhrt ii. 664–5. For the relationship between H. and the Behistun inscription see *CAH* IV². 53–63; the fullest treatment is J. M. Balcer, *Herodotus and Bisitun. Problems in Ancient Persian Historiography* (Wiesbaden 1987).

26. The name Patizeithes is not found in Persian sources; nor are the circumstances here possible, since there is no homonymy in the Persian account: Cambyses murders his brother Bardiya, and the Magian pretender whom Darius defeats is named Gaumata. The Greek tradition rendered both as Smerdis.

27. The story of the earless Magus can only have arisen among the

Greeks, for it depends on a belief that the Persian king's ears could not ordinarily be seen. In Greek art the ears of the Persian king are indeed concealed beneath his tiara, but in Persian art (and life), by contrast, the ears of the king are visible. In the Behistun relief the ear of the Magus Gaumata could still be seen in the early part of the twentieth century.

28. The Behistun inscription accords with six of the conspirators: Vindafarna (Intaphernes); Utana (Otanes); Gaubaruva (Gobryas); Vidarna (Hydarnes); Bagabukhsha (Megabyxus); the one name that does not agree is Ardumanish, whom H. gives as Aspathines.

29. This famous set of speeches, known as the 'Constitutional Debate', is not accepted by modern scholars as historical. It seems to have been suspect even to H.'s audience, since he anticipates objections. His remarks, nevertheless, suggest that a tradition about a Persian debate already existed before H.; otherwise, why would he say that some of the Greeks refuse to believe it? (Some see the remark as a comment on the reaction H. had got when he recited this debate in public; it would thus be evidence not of any earlier tradition, but of public readings by H.) If we adduce here VI. 43, where H. again refers to this incident, it seems clear that the disbelief is not that a discussion took place – this the Greeks, with their love of words, would never have doubted – but that any Persian would ever have advocated popular government. Although the historical value may be small, the exchanges here are quite important as the earliest examples of a long tradition in Greek thought on the merits and shortcomings of the various forms of government, distinguished by how many hold power: one (monarchy), few (oligarchy), or many (*isonomia*, translated here as 'popular government'; its meaning is 'equality before the law', and it is an earlier term than *demokratia*, whence our 'democracy'). The discussion is interesting in that it is concerned more with criticisms than benefits of each form of government, and each speaker chooses his own as the least problematic of the three he considers. In the end, not surprisingly in view of ch. 38 above, the Persians choose to maintain their own custom of monarchy, and, appropriately enough, this is urged by Darius. On the value of this debate in the study of Greek political thought, see T. A. Sinclair, *A History of Greek Political Thought* (London 1951) 33–42; for the possible debt to Protagoras see F. Lassère, 'Hérodote et Protagoras: le débat sur les constitutions', *Museum Helveticum* 33 (1976) 65–84. On the thematic importance of this passage in H. see Benardete 85–7; Lateiner ch. 8.

30. No monument of this sort had been discovered, nor should we expect that it will, given the portrait of Darius' rise to power in the

Behistun inscription. Murray (1987) 115 suggests that H. preserves here a trace of the Persian custom of horse divination.

31. This catalogue is an important source for Persian imperial administration, although how H. acquired it is uncertain: the possibilities are that it existed in a previous text, perhaps that of Hecataeus (cf. V. 36, where Hecataeus enumerates the Persian resources) or some other early author of Persian history; or that H. acquired it from an oral source, a Persian or some Persian official in Asia Minor; or (least likely) that it is a free invention by H. For a brief discussion of the matter see *CAH* IV². 87–91; Cook 81–2; on Persian catalogues in H., see Armayor (1978b).

32. For the long-lived Ethiopians, and Cambyses' attack on them, see ch. 25 above. The Ethiopians on the Egyptian border are the people of Kush.

33. Aristotle, *Hist. Anim.* III. 22 (523a 18) corrects H.'s analogic deduction.

34. H. is right about the reversed genitals, wrong about the legs.

35. The gold-digging ants have a long history in writers after H.; that the tradition is Indian is suggested by the *Mahabharata*, which speaks of 'ant gold', and some have suggested marmots or badgers as the animals meant (HW i. 289); S. West has called attention to M. Peissel, *The Ants' Gold* (London 1984), where the author notes the practice of plundering the burrows of the ant *Arctomys himalayanus* as a way of getting the highly auriferous earth which the ants loosen as they tunnel.

36. Linen or cotton, which grows rather on a bush than a tree; these Indians are outfitted in their native wear at VII. 65.

37. On the flying snakes see II. 75 with n.

38. The passage is interesting as an attempt by H. to extend the principle of *tisis* (see Introduction §4) to the animal kingdom, where the death of the male by the female is avenged by the offspring – a popular theme in Greek myth.

39. The description of the carts and the tails is based on a pun found also in Pindar, *Pythian* 2. 167–9.

40. H. is not particularly well informed on Western Europe, nor were the Greeks in general. Spain had been treated by Hecataeus, but only in a superficial manner: see Pearson 34–8. The Eridanus was mentioned by Hesiod and Aeschylus. The Tin Islands were identified by the ancients with Scilly or with Britain in general. For a good summary of what H. knows, see J. Alonso-Núñez, 'H. on the Far West', *Ant. Class.* 56 (1987) 243–9.

41. For the Arimaspians and the gold-guarding griffins see IV. 27.

42. A similar remark occurs in Sophocles' *Antigone* 905–12, where it has been the subject of enormous controversy. Sancisi-Weerdenberg 30–31 sees in this story a reflection of the pressure that women in sixth- and fifth-century Iranian society were subjected to, between the claims of their own family and that of their husbands – a conflict mitigated in this story by Darius' granting to the woman both her brother and her son.

43. On the political events (including piracy and aristocratic dissatisfaction) that form the background to Polycrates' murder see Shipley 90–96.

44. A similar story is told by Thucydides (VI. 46), where the deceivers are the Segestans and the deceived the Athenians.

45. For an analysis of the story of Democedes see A. Griffiths, 'Democedes of Croton: a Greek Doctor at Darius' court', *AH* ii. 37–51, who concludes that it is 'largely fictitious'; contra, Austin (1990) 299.

46. On H.'s apparent sarcasm, Shipley 103 notes: 'The remark . . . may have a real content, implying that the Samians failed to use Maeandrius to protect themselves against Persia.'

47. In the Behistun inscription Darius speaks of two revolts of Babylon; the first is dated to October 522 and was ended in December with Darius present. After his departure there was a second revolt in August 521, which was put down in November by Intaphernes, who impaled the renegade king Arakha and his supporters. H. seems to know of only one siege lasting 20 months, but this cannot be reconciled with the Behistun inscription; and H.'s account is highly dramatic, with its centre occupied by the selfless Zopyrus. See *CAH* IV^2. 129–33; Cook 55.

48. Self-mutilation as a means of winning over a besieged city owes something to the Greek epic cycle. Odysseus is said to have done it at Troy (*Od.* IV. 244ff.), as is Sinon (in the *Little Iliad*, but best known from Virgil, *Aen.* II. 65–198), who persuaded the Trojans to bring the wooden horse into their town.

49. In the Behistun inscription, Darius says that he killed 2497 of the army of the rebel king Arakha.

50. It has been suggested that the younger Zopyrus, grandson of the traitor at Babylon, may have been a source for H. when he was in Athens (so J. Wells, *Studies in Herodotus* (Oxford 1923) 95–111), but this is very uncertain: see Lewis (1985) 105–6. There is, by the way, no evidence to suggest that Zopyrus was ever made governor of Babylon.

BOOK FOUR

1. The first part of Book IV (1–144) consists of an extended account of the Scythians, a heterogeneous people who inhabited the area around the Black Sea; some were nomads, some agricultural; native Thracians too would have been present, and some of these will have been included in those whom the Greeks called Scythians; but even among the ancients there were differences over who were and who were not Scythians. Although Hecataeus treated Scythia in his work, H. seems to have improved on him greatly (Pearson 62–6), and H.'s account remains the most important ancient source about them: for modern treatments see *CHI* 149–99; *CAH* III². 2. 560–90; Boardman 256–64. In H. the Scythians receive more treatment than any barbarian nation except the Egyptians, to whom they form a strong contrast: to take but a few examples: they claim to be the youngest nation, while the Egyptians claimed to be the oldest; their nomadism and movement contrast strongly with the permanence and fixedness of Egypt and its monuments; the Scythians have no record of the past at all, unlike the Egyptians who maintained the most careful account of their past. For more see Benardete 99–121; Redfield; Hartog.

2. See I. 103–6.

3. The Greeks of Pontus will have been one of H.'s main sources on the Scythians. The earliest Greek colony (from Miletus) in the Pontus area is Sinope on the south coast of the Black Sea; its foundation date is controversial, perhaps as early as the eighth century, certainly by the seventh. Another important site was Olbia at the north of the Black Sea at the mouth of the Bug (Hypanis), founded in the late seventh century, also by Miletus. For the many others see *CAH* III². 3. 122–30.

4. On the Cimmerians see I. 15 with n.; the Cimmerian Bosphorus is the narrow strait (modern Kerch) leading from the Black Sea to the Sea of Azov.

5. H. is our main source of information on Aristeas; his date is difficult to establish: see J. Bolton, *Aristeas of Proconnesus* (Oxford 1961) 3ff.; for a reconstruction of his poem, ibid. ch. 4. There is also much of value in W. Burkert, *Lore and Science in Ancient Pythagoreanism* (Cambridge, Mass. 1972) 120–65.

6. Modern equivalents for H.'s Scythian rivers: Borysthenes = Dniepr; Hypanis = Bug; Tanais = Don; Ister = Danube. The Maeotic Lake = Sea of Azov.

7. The sleep of six months' duration may be a confused reference to the long night of the polar winter.

8. The reference is to *Od.* IV. 85.

9. Hyperboreans means 'those living beyond the north wind'; they had been mentioned in the Homeric Hymn to Dionysus (vii. 28–9); by Pindar (*Olympian* 3. 16); by Hesiod (F 150 Merkelbach-West) who called them 'rich in horses'; and they were treated at length in Aristeas' poem *Arimaspeia*.

10. According to Greek tradition, Anaximander of Miletus (610–540) created the first map; his pupil Hecataeus (who may have followed his teacher) is the one being attacked here, since his map certainly had a circumambient Ocean. In his account of the Argonauts he had them sail up the Phasis (on the eastern Black Sea) to the Ocean and then around Ocean to the Nile, and down the Nile to the Mediterranean. H. criticizes the symmetry of Europe and Asia in these early maps, but he uses the same method when describing the course of the Nile at II. 33. On early maps see O. A. W. Dilke, *Greek and Roman Maps* (London and Ithaca 1985), ch. II.

11. 'The Arabian gulf' here = the Red Sea; 'Red Sea' below = the Persian Gulf.

12. This detail, disbelieved by H., is correct, and has been taken as evidence of an early circumnavigation of Africa (Libya) some time around 610–595 (the reign of Neco); some scholars, however, maintain a scepticism by noting (among other things) that the detail could be inferred from existent geographical knowledge. Unlike the later attempt by Sataspes under Xerxes (ch. 43), Neco's men travelled the most favourable route, down the east coast of Africa, up the west coast and then through the Straits of Gibraltar (Pillars of Heracles).

13. The small men are the Pygmies; see II. 32.

14. The Alpis and Carpis rivers cannot be identified.

15. 'Very properly' because *Papaeus* suggests to H. *pappas*, Greek for 'father'.

16. On the 'Enarees' see I. 105 with n.

17. Scythian graves are among the most spectacular finds of modern archaeology; for accounts and photographs see M. I. Artamonov, *Treasures from Scythian Tombs* (London 1970); S. I. Rudenko, *The Frozen Tombs of Siberia* (London and Berkeley 1970); *From the Lands of the Scythians* (New York, Metropolitan Museum of Art exhibition 1975); *Scythian Gold. Treasures from Ancient Ukraine* (Walters Art Gallery and San Antonio Museum of Art Exhibition 1999).

18. The Scythians 'howl with pleasure' because of the intoxication brought on by the hemp (cannabis).

19. Anacharsis became a famous figure in later Greek literature, ranked among the Seven Sages. In H. he and Scyles represent the importance of maintaining native customs and the danger of travelling between cultures: see Hartog 62–84.

20. The 'Mother of the Gods' is Cybele (called Cybebe at V. 102), and Cyzicus was an important centre of her worship. See Burkert 177–9.

21. Sitalces was king of the Odrysians in Thrace and his father Teres was the one who established their power (Thuc. II. 29). He came to the throne c. 450, and was famous for his betrayal of Spartan envoys en route to Asia in 430: see VII. 137.

22. Presumably this was dedicated at the end of the Persian wars in 479, but H. does not mention it again.

23. There is much disagreement whether such a bowl could have been manufactured given ancient technology; the debate may be followed in Armayor (1978a) 49–57; Pritchett (1982) 42ff. HW (i. 331) note as curious that H. does not mention the bowl at Delphi which he claimed was the same size: see I. 51 with n.

24. The Cyrenaean rocks were the gateway to the Black Sea; they are described in Od. XII. 61 as 'wandering'.

25. The Black Sea is 720 miles long (c. 650 miles where H. claims to have measured) and 380 miles wide (270 miles in the narrower east part where H. claims to have measured). The length of the Bosphorus is c. 20 miles; the Hellespont is 33 miles. In giving his measurements H. is unclear whether he himself sailed and measured it; or only calculated from measurements given to him.

26. See West (1985) 296.

27. On Salmoxis, see Hartog 84–109; M. Eliade, *Zalmoxis. The Vanishing God*, trans. W. Trask (Chicago and London 1972).

28. H. is describing the 'heel' of Italy: Brundisium (modern Brindisi) is on the Adriatic coast, Tarentum (modern Taranto) is on the Gulf of Tarentum.

29. Androphagi means 'man-eaters', Melanchlaeni 'black cloaks'.

30. This is a reference to the legend of werewolves.

31. In the war between the Greeks and the Amazons, Heracles attempted to win the girdle of the Amazonian queen Hippolyte; the battle was traditionally assigned to the River Thermodon in southern Cappadocia. See next note.

32. It is clear from this that H. has assumed from the martial skill of the Sauromatian women that they must be descended from the Amazons. On the Sauromatians see *CHI* 189–90.

33. The reference is to the Scythian invasion of Asia (I. 103–6); for H. and retribution see Introduction §4.

34. Donkeys can, of course, be found in cold climates.

35. This communication by objects can be paralleled in oral societies from very different places and times: see S. West, 'The Scythian Ultimatum (Herodotus IV. 131, 132)', *JHS* 108 (1988) 207–11.

36. On Miltiades see VI. 34–9.

37. On H.'s attitude towards the Ionians see V. n. 14.

38. The remainder of Book IV (145–205) is concerned with Libya, by which H. means Africa to the west and northwest of Egypt, and especially the peoples at Cyrene and Ammon. H. prefaces his account of the colonization of Cyrene (c. 630) by the people of Thera (which begins at ch. 150) with an account of Thera's colonization by the Spartans. Theras the founder takes with him some of the Minyae, the descendants of the crew of the *Argo*, whom the Spartans were intending to put to death. For the Greeks in Libya see *CHA* ii. 114–16; on Cyrene's colonization and site see Boardman 153–9; *CHA* ii. 107–10. Lemnos is an island in the Aegean southeast of Thasos; for the Pelasgians see I. 58 with n.

39. The name 'Oeolycus' means 'lone wolf'.

40. As presented by H. the motivation for the colonization of Cyrene is largely driven by the Delphic Oracle which first brings up the idea. But the causes of Greek colonization were many; most often, hunger attendant on population increases necessitated a dispatch of a portion of the population (cf. ch. 151, a seven-year drought), but other pressures existed also: see *CAH* III². 3. 157–9; Murray (1993) ch. 7. An inscription from Cyrene of the fourth century survives, which claims to contain in it the original oath sworn by the colonists: see Fornara 18 with references there.

41. An alternative tradition (Fornara 17) claims that Battus went to the oracle because of civil disturbance in Thera: his own party had been worsted, and he asked the oracle whether he should attempt to return or found a colony.

42. The story probably refers to the great amount of rainfall (rare in North Africa) in Cyrene.

43. On the revolt against Apries see II. 161.

44. Darius' 'Darics' were widespread in antiquity and famous for their purity.

45. Since the Garamantes in ch. 183 have chariots and hunt, it is assumed that the name of the people here in the text is corrupt.

46. Greek armour came not from the Egyptians but from the Near East: see I. 171 with n.

47. The 'lumps of salt' here are a slight misconception of the oases of North Africa. That of Ammon is the oasis of Siwah, which Alexander the Great later visited to confirm his divinity (Arrian, *Anabasis* III. 3–4). It is twenty, not ten, days from Egyptian Thebes. The Fountain is a volcanic spring. For Zeus Ammon see II. 42.

48. 'Troglodytes' ('cave-dwellers') are yet another branch of Ethiopians; they have been identified with the Tibboos.

49. A reference to the Sahara.

50. H. says at II. 77 that the uniformity of seasons is a reason for the health of the Libyans.

51. The *aegis* was a goatskin used not only by Athena but also by Zeus and Apollo in Homer to bring storms, ward off enemies, and instil fear. From the sixth century on it became a regular attribute in representations of Athena: see Burkert 140.

52. 'Beast-eyed men' are mentioned in Aeschylus; 'wild men' and 'wild women' are thought to be gorillas; 'dog-headed men' are perhaps the baboons: see HW i. 366.

53. Cyrauis is modern Cercina.

54. The narrative is now resumed from ch. 167.

BOOK FIVE

1. H. here resumes the narrative of the Persian attack on Thrace from IV. 144. Perinthus is west of Byzantium on the north shore of the Propontis. The Paeonians are an Illyrian tribe dwelling north of Macedonia.

2. The Thracians dwelt 'in an extensive area stretching from the Euxine (Black) Sea to the neighbourhood of the Axius (Vardar) and from the Aegean Sea to the Transdanubian lands' (*CAH* III². 2. 591). On the Thracians see ibid. 591–618, and on their portrayal in H., D. Asheri, 'H. on Thracian Society and History', in: *Hérodote et les Peuples non Grecs* (Geneva 1990) 131–69. For their artwork see I. Marazov, ed., *Ancient Gold: The Wealth of the Thracians* (New York 1998).

3. See IV. 93ff.

4. The Trausi's beliefs in the benefits of death find echoes in remarks elsewhere in H.: see I. 31, VII. 46.

5. The practice described here is suttee.

6. There is something of the inverted world of Egypt here (see Introduction §2), since branding in Greece was the mark of a slave, whereas agriculture was the most highly honoured activity. Perhaps, as with Egyptian customs, this description should be taken with a grain of salt.

7. The 'little horses' of the Sigynnae are ponies. Dressing 'in the Median fashion' means with trousers and jacket.

8. Myrcinus is on the east shore of Lake Cercinitis, near the Strymon, and not far from the coast. The area was rich in natural resources: see ch. 23. A later settlement was known as Nine Ways, and sixty-one years after Histiaeus, the Athenians (Thuc. IV. 102; additional sources at Fornara 62) established the colony of Amphipolis.

9. Transfers of population were not uncommon in antiquity; their causes were complex, not personal: see N. Demand, *Urban Relocation in Archaic and Classical Greece. Flight and Consolidation* (Norman and London 1990) 165ff.; on transfers of population in H. see ibid. 34–44.

10. The Alexander mentioned here is the son of Amyntas, and he ruled c. 498–450; for his genealogy see VIII. 139. On his role in the *Histories* see E. Badian, 'H. on Alexander I of Macedon: A Study in Some Subtle Silences', in S. Hornblower, ed., *Greek Historiography* (Oxford 1994) 107–30.

11. As HW (ii. 7) point out, this request is not in keeping with what we know of oriental attitudes towards women. The story is an example of the *hybris* of the Persians and the *nemesis* that falls upon them; and it emphasizes the danger of transgressing custom.

12. See VIII. 137–8 which is merely a family legend.

13. For the court of the Persian king see Cook 132–46, esp. 144–5.

14. H. here begins the narrative of the Ionian revolt (499–494), which lasts (with digressions) until VI. 32. H. is our sole literary source for this important event in Greek history. His narrative of (as usual) personal intrigue and motivation can, with some effort, be made to yield an acceptable political and historical picture, although this is of no concern to H., the extent of whose political motivation is the natural expectation that states wish to be free. As H. portrays it, the Ionian Revolt is the outcome of the failed attempt by Aristagoras (nephew and son-in-law of Histiaeus, who is detained at Susa by Darius) to win over Naxos for the Persian king, and his subsequent fear for his loss of influence with the Persian governor Artaphernes. The failure to take Naxos is itself the result of a personal quarrel between Aristagoras and the Persian general Megabates. Modern scholars, by contrast, see the following as important in encouraging the Ionians to revolt: (i) desire for greater political participation by the majority of the people in the city-states, and resentment towards the Persian-supported tyrants (cf. ch. 37 where Aristagoras promises popular government, and Mardonius' action at VI. 43 with n. there; cf. also Histiaeus' words at IV. 137); (ii) Ionian resentment at Persian usurpation of their former mercantile power; (iii) disruption of trade by the constant wars of conquest under Darius; (iv) resentment at paying Persian tribute. For modern accounts see Burn 193–217; *CAH* IV². 461–90; Austin (1990) focusses on Persia and the Ionian tyrants. An excellent map of the important sites in the revolt is at Burn 194. It must also be noted that H. in general is not sympathetic to the revolt, which might be expected given remarks made elsewhere in his history (I. 143; IV. 142; VI. n. 5). This prejudice, which seems at odds with his usual impartiality, has been variously explained: some put it down to his origins in Dorian Halicarnassus, some to contemporary Athenian propaganda against their Ionian kinsmen and subjects.

15. For Pausanias' treason in the aftermath of the Persian wars see Thuc. I. 128ff., who gives the substance of a letter (128) in which Pausanias proposes to the king to marry the king's daughter.

16. On Hecataeus see Introduction §3; for his portrayal here as a 'wise adviser' see West (1991) 184–7.

17. See I. 92.

18. These generals may have been on the Athenian model, elected annually and thus limited in their period of power; see *Ath. Pol.* 61. 1–2.

19. Anaxandrides had been king in the time of Croesus: see I. 67, from which point H. is picking up the thread of his account of Sparta.

20. The Ephors had wide discretion to punish whomever they wished, including the king; trials of kings were held before the Ephors, the council of elders (*gerousia*) and the other king: see Macdowell 127–30.

21. Dorieus colonized the area c. 514 and was driven out c. 512.

22. On heroes see II. n. 39.

23. Cleomenes in fact reigned c. 520–490; see HW ii. 348 for an attempt to explain H.'s error.

24. On Greek maps see IV. 36 with n.; for an illustration of what Aristagoras' map may have looked like, see Myres 36.

25. The comparison of Greek (especially Spartan) poverty with eastern wealth is pointedly displayed at IX. 82; and cf. IX. 122 for similar temptations.

26. For this main artery of the Persian empire see Olmstead 299–301; Cook 108 notes possible archaeological evidence of a packed gravel road some 20 feet wide, of the sixth century or later.

27. H. here resumes his account of Athenian history from I. 64. Hippias and Hipparchus are Pisistratus' sons, and the family is collectively known as the Pisistratidae (or Pisistratids).

28. The popular Athenian belief that Harmodius and Aristogeiton liberated Athens from tyranny by murdering Hipparchus is confirmed

by contemporary drinking songs (Fornara 39A). H. and Thucydides (I. 20, VI. 53–9) are agreed, however, that Hippias, not Hipparchus, was tyrant when Hipparchus was murdered. The cult of Harmodius and Aristogeiton did not keep the Athenians from recognizing the role that Sparta played in the liberation of Athens: see Thomas 242–57. Cf. Thuc. VI. 59; Fornara 39B.

29. H. is correct that the alphabet was introduced into Greece by the Phoenicians and that their alphabet was the model for the Greeks' own. He is unaware, however, that the Greeks were illiterate for some three centuries after the fall of Mycenaean civilization c. 1100; thus the time of Cadmus around the Trojan War is far too early as a date for the introduction of writing to Greece. There is much debate about the exact time that alphabetic writing (the Mycenaeans used a syllabary script, not seen again in Greece) appeared in Greece: perhaps the first half of the eighth century is not too far off. See *CAH* III². I. ch. 20; Murray (1993) 92–101. On this passage in general see West (1985) 290–93.

30. Leipsydrium is a fort on the spur of Mt Parnes, north of the deme Paeonidae (not Paeonia as H. has it); cf. *Ath. Pol.* 19.

31. The Amphictyons were the governing body of the oracle of Apollo at Delphi; members included Thessaly, Boeotia and Phocis; the temple burned down in 548, and the Amphictyons appealed for help in rebuilding as far as Egypt (II. 180); for additional sources see Fornara 40.

32. The Pisistratids were allied with Argos (*Ath. Pol.* 19. 4), which would have given the Spartans a stronger motive than H. suggests here (see *CAH* IV². 301–2); the date of this attempt is 511.

33. Pisistratus secured his tyranny in 546 (I. 59) and ruled until his death in 528/7; his son ruled from 527 to his expulsion, which *Ath. Pol.* (19. 6) dates to the archonship of Harpactides, i.e. 511/10.

34. On the struggle and reforms of Cleisthenes see also the account in *Ath. Pol.* 20–21. The portrait painted here is of factional strife among aristocrats (see I. 59 with n.), which broke out again after the expulsion of the tyrants. Cleisthenes took the radical step of taking the people into his party; what exactly this consisted of and how he did it are still imperfectly understood, but there is no doubt that he gave or promised to the common people a say in the government in exchange for their support, and by so doing deserves the title of the founder of Athenian democracy. Before the reforms of Cleisthenes, the Athenians, like all Ionians, were divided into four kinship tribes; the smallest unit was the *phratry* (brotherhood), membership in which conferred citizenship. Cleisthenes' ten tribes, by contrast, were artificial creations, designed

to ensure that each tribe should have approximately one-third of its members from the coast, one-third from the city (Athens and its immediate surroundings) and one-third from the plain; thus the regionalism that had led to severe conflict before would be gravely weakened. In place of membership in a *phratry*, citizenship was now dependent on being a member of a *deme* (village), a unit which most likely predates Cleisthenes. Since demes could vary greatly in size, Cleisthenes arranged different numbers of them within each tribe so that each tribe would be roughly equal in total population. For accounts of his activities see *CAH* IV². 303–46; Forrest (1966) 190–203; Hignett (1952) 124–58. Finally, Ajax was chosen because of his identification with the island of Salamis off the coast of Attica. Since Athens was involved with Aegina for decades over the control of the island, Cleisthenes' choice indicated that he considered the island by right to belong to the Athenians.

35. Cleisthenes of Sicyon (in the northern Peloponnese) ruled c. 600–570; see Andrewes 58–61. The story was that Adrastus had been expelled from Argos and gone to Sicyon, participating in the expedition against Thebes. Since Adrastus is dead, Cleisthenes is trying to make the hero withdraw his support or 'presence' from Sicyon. On the importance of a hero's body see I. n. 30.

36. Dorian cities were arranged into three tribes, the names of which H. gives here. Cleisthenes' humiliation of them and the elevation of his own non-Dorian tribe to 'rulers of the people' may indicate a 'tyranny with a racial prejudice' (Andrewes 59), but the names may have been merely nicknames (so HW ii. 35). For more on Cleisthenes of Sicyon see VI. 126–30.

37. H. is wrong that there were ten demes in every tribe; see n. 34 above.

38. Cylon's attempt at tyranny is the earliest event we know from Athenian history. Thuc. I. 126 also relates the story of his attempt, adding details not in H. On the whole matter see Sealey 98–9; Forrest (1966) 145–6; Andrewes 84; Hignett (1952) 67–74. What the naucraries were is uncertain: see Rhodes 151–3.

39. In view of their later claims to be the defenders of Greek liberty, it is understandable enough that the Athenians did not wish to dwell on this advance to Persia. A. Kuhrt, 'Earth and Water', *AH* iii. 91–9, lays great stress on this disavowal by Athens and sees it as a major reason for the Persian attack.

40. The Corinthians change their minds because they realize that Cleomenes wishes to reinstate tyranny at Athens: see the speech of Sosicles at V. 92.

41. The Persian fire is a reference to the burning of the Athenian acropolis in 480 and 479: see VIII. 53 and IX. 13.

42. Athens' quarrel with Aegina may have been economically motivated, since Aegina was wealthy and powerful in the years before the Persian wars; for the background see Murray (1993) 224–6.

43. There is a pun in the Greek here, since 'eagle in the rocks' (*aietos en petresi*) bears a resemblance to 'Eëtion from Petra' (*aetion ek petres*).

44. The Greek word for 'chest' is *cypsele*.

45. A reference to Corinthian anger with Athens, which precipitated the Peloponnesian War: see Thuc. I. 119–24.

46. Periander's mediation occurred 600–590.

47. The narrative is resumed from ch. 55.

48. This is an echo of *Il.* V. 62, XI. 604, meant to add dramatic weight and a sense of foreboding; cf. Thuc. II. 12 for a similar echo of Homer.

49. On these relocated Paeonians see chs 12–16.

50. The war between Chalcis and Eretria for the Lelantine plain occurred in the late eighth century; Thuc. (I. 15; additional sources at Fornara 7) calls it the first pan-Hellenic war since each side received outside support.

51. Athens' speedy withdrawal from the Ionian Revolt is difficult to explain: Macan (1895) i. 253 suggests that the Athenians would have had concerns at home with Aegina and Chalcis; Burn (201) suggests the rise in Athens of a peace party which wished to atone for the damage done to Persia.

52. On Myrcinus see n. 8 above.

BOOK SIX

1. The real reason was so that he might escape from Susa: see V. 36.

2. Histiaeus here reveals that Aristagoras' declaration of popular government (V. 37) was, as H. had said there, merely for show. The blockade of the Hellespont would most harm Miletus who had extensive trade with her colonies on the Black Sea.

3. Histiaeus' words at IV. 137 show what these tyrants owed to Persia; see also Austin (1990).

4. This consisted in breaking through the enemy line, quickly turning, and ramming the opponent's defenceless side.

5. Prejudice against the Ionians here raises its head and 'justifies' the Samian treachery in the next chapter. As Macan (1895) i. 277 points out, this portrait is largely influenced by Athenian propaganda of H.'s own day, in which the Athenians justified their supremacy over Ionia

by contrasting their own skill with their kinsmen's laziness; their naval victory at Salamis with the Ionian failure at Lade: see Thuc. I. 74–5, and for a similar indictment of laziness I. 99. Macan points out that the Ionians were good sailors, had already been victorious in one battle and owed their ultimate defeat at Lade not to cowardice but to Samian treachery.

6. When he had declared popular government: V. 37.

7. See ch. 77.

8. H. elsewhere calls Didyma 'Branchidae'; see V. 36 for its wealth and I. 92 with n.

9. Phrynichus, an older contemporary of Aeschylus, produced this play in 493. It has been suggested that what touched the Athenians was not only the sufferings of Miletus but also the tacit or explicit reproach for the Athenian withdrawal from the Ionian cause (see V. 103).

10. The Sicels are the natives of Sicily, as opposed to the Greeks who in the eighth and seventh centuries had colonized much of Sicily.

11. Thasos was rich in gold (see ch. 46), which was no doubt the object of the expedition.

12. Atarneus is inland from the coast and directly opposite the island of Lesbos.

13. This procedure may be the same as that described at III. 149, but would seem unlikely, if not impossible, in the mountains and clefts of the Aegean islands.

14. For the Lydian conquest see I. 6; for the first Persian conquest by Cyrus see I. 141ff. But it should be noted that Croesus did not conquer the islands (I. 27) and that Cyrus received the voluntary submission of the islanders without actually conquering them (I. 169).

15. Contrary to what is said here, the elder Miltiades (to distinguish him from the Miltiades of the time of the Ionian Revolt) may have been sent out by the Pisistratids because they trusted his loyalty in the Chersonese, an important area for Athens later and perhaps already in the tyrants' time (CAH III². 3. 404–5). The tradition of Miltiades' enmity with the tyrants might be a later invention after their fall when alliance with them would have been dangerous.

16. This dispatch must be between 527 and 510; for the murder of the father see below, ch. 103.

17. This account seems contradictory with IV. 137 (and see next note) where Miltiades wants to assist the Scythians in destroying Darius. If we assume that he fled two years after he was sent out from Athens and returned two years before the events now being narrated, we have an exile c. 511–496. But this is a confused passage and H. makes his exile seem a rather brief affair. On the whole question see Burn

208–9, 218–19. The conquest of Lemnos (ch. 140) is probably to be dated to this exile.

18. This strongly suggests that the story of Miltiades' betrayal at the bridge (IV. 137) is unfounded, since the Persian king was not likely to protect and honour the son of a rebel.

19. Since the Ionian cities in H.'s time paid tribute to Athens, not Persia, the statement is surprising.

20. On the conference of the seven conspirators see III. 80 with n. there. Mardonius' actions here in the spring of 492 can be seen as an attempt to pacify Ionia and keep it friendly in the rear as he advanced towards the Hellespont and thence against Athens and Eretria. On dissatisfaction with Persian-supported tyrants see V. 28 with n.

21. According to V. 75, the Spartans had made a law at the time of their expedition in support of Isagoras (507) that both kings might not campaign together. For the conclusion of the episode see ch. 73. H. now moves to an account of the double kingship at Sparta and the kings' privileges (52–60) and on to the birth, upbringing and deposition of Demaratus (61–72).

22. The Spartan dual kingship was unique, representing the amalgamation of two communities and two royal houses (on its development, see Cartledge (1979) 104–8); that the houses were not of the same blood is suggested by their separate burial grounds: Murray (1993) 161; Forrest (1968) 28–9.

23. Who these writers were is uncertain.

24. On the Spartan *gerousia* or council of elders see Michell 135–40. Thuc. in a famous passage (I. 20) criticizes the view that the Spartan kings each had two votes. The criticism is thought to refer to H. but H.'s words are ambiguous; the translation given here assumes that H. does not say that the kings each had two votes.

25. The three divisions of the Lacedaemonians are here meant: Spartiates (full Spartan citizens); *perioeci*, the free inhabitants around Sparta (see II. n. 86); and helots, the slaves of the Spartan state (III. n. 20).

26. On the mourning for a king's death in Asia, see VIII. 99–100.

27. Flute-players were important because the Spartan army marched to their music in order to preserve the strict formation of the hoplite phalanx: see Thuc. V. 70. The cooks, who accompanied the army (IX. 82), prepared the common messes which were so important in Spartan life: see Michell 281–6.

28. The sanctuary of Helen at Therapne, c. 2 miles northeast of Sparta, is probably the same as the temple of Menelaus.

29. Demaratus means 'prayer of the people'.

30. At this midsummer festival of Apollo (*Gymnopaidia*) naked boys

and men engaged in ritual combat to honour the god: see Burkert 263.

31. D. Boedeker, 'The Two Faces of Demaratus', *Arethusa* 20 (1987) 189 points out the parallels between Demaratus' birth and Heracles'. And see next note.

32. On Demaratus' revenge see Boedeker (previous note) 190–91; for Cleomenes' eventual madness and death as retribution for his actions against Demaratus see ch. 84.

33. This war of c. 494 may have been Sparta's attempt to bring Argos into the Peloponnesian League (so Sealey 199) or simply to neutralize her (Tomlinson 95–6).

34. For a similar misunderstanding based on homonymy see Cambyses at III. 63–4.

35. For this attack see V. 81.

36. The Athenians expelled the Aeginetans in 431, the first year of the Peloponnesian War: Thuc. II. 27. The exiles then went to Thyrea where they were destroyed in 424 (Thuc. IV. 57).

37. Sophanes also fought at Plataea in 479: see IX. 74–5.

38. For the previous expedition around Athos see ch. 44; the failure to take Naxos precipitated the Ionian Revolt (V. 28 with n.).

39. Persian tolerance towards native religions was an important aspect of their rule (see Cook 148–9). In Isaiah 45. 1, Cyrus is called 'the Lord's anointed' because he gave orders to rebuild Jerusalem and the temple after he conquered Babylon in 539; and Darius' protection of Apollo is well documented in a letter (Fornara 35) to one of his governors, chastising him for taxing land sacred to Apollo, adding that the governor is 'ignorant of my ancestors' attitude to the god, who spoke all truth to the Persians'.

40. Thuc. II. 8 claims that the sole earthquake at Delos occurred a little before the Peloponnesian War. Each historian's insistence on the uniqueness of 'his' earthquake makes the accounts irreconcilable.

41. On these 4000 see V. 77.

42. Marathon, one of the most distant demes of Attica, is c. 26 miles from Athens. For a good map of the environs see Burn 244. On the campaign, which retains its romantic glow even today, see Burn 236–56; Hignett (1963) 55–74; Lazenby 45–80.

43. On the elder Miltiades (uncle of the younger and founder of the Chersonese settlement) see chs 34–8.

44. For the pursuit of Miltiades see chs 40–41. Whether the Athenians were truly affronted by Miltiades' tyranny in the Chersonese or whether this was simply a pretext for his political opponents is uncertain.

45. The name of the runner is also given as 'Philippides'. From Sparta

to Athens is c. 140 miles, so the distance covered in two days was quite great. According to a later tradition Pheidippides is also supposed to have run the 26 miles from Marathon to Athens to announce the Athenian victory; this is the supposed origin of the modern marathon race, but see F. J. Frost, 'The Dubious Origin of the "Marathon"', *American Journal of Ancient History* 4 (1979) 159–63.

46. Sparta was celebrating the Carneia, during which time the Dorians abstained from warfare: see Burkert 234–6.

47. According to Thuc. III. 68, the incidents here occurred 92 years before the destruction of Plataea in 427, thus 519/18. Some scholars think the date should be c. 509/8 to fit better with Cleomenes' presence in central Greece during his interference in Athenian politics following the expulsion of the Pisistratids (V. 70–76), but the two incidents may be unrelated.

48. The polemarch in H.'s own time had lost all military function, so H. must explain his presence here. Burn (246) accuses H. of anachronism, stating that the polemarch was commander-in-chief until 487. But Rhodes in his commentary on *Ath. Pol.* (cf. *CAH* IV². 516 n. 1) follows H.'s account; on this reconstruction, H. is correct that there was a daily rotating 'presidency' of the ten generals (ch. 110). Callimachus was depicted on the painting of the battle of Marathon in the Painted Stoa in Athens (Pausanias I. 15. 3–4; for this painting as a source for H. see E. Francis and M. Vickers, 'The Oenoe Painting in the Stoa Poikile and Herodotus' Account of Marathon', *Annual of the British School at Athens* 80 (1985) 99–113), and the remains of a dedication by Callimachus have been found (Fornara 49).

49. It is clear that there was a tradition that the Athenians waited before attacking the Persians at Marathon. H. has Miltiades wait for the command, but the Athenians were probably waiting for the Lacedaemonians (Lazenby 57–9). Why they eventually attacked is variously interpreted. One idea holds that the Persians were embarking their cavalry on to the ships for a surprise attack on Athens, and while the cavalry was off the scene, the Athenians and Plataeans attacked (so Burn 247, but this is based on the Suda, a late source (text at Burn and Fornara 48), and has little to recommend it: Lazenby 59). Alternatively, the decision is seen as more politically than militarily based, because there was a danger that some of the Athenians might collude with the Persians, which would explain the divided counsels of the generals and the 'rot' referred to by Miltiades in ch. 109, and which necessitated prompt action (so Sealey 191). Finally, there is the possibility that the *Persians* attacked and the Athenians were thus compelled to fight (Lazenby 61).

50. It is difficult to believe that any army could maintain formation for one mile on the run; the Athenians must have advanced briskly and then, at about 200 yards, charged at full speed (so HW ii. 112). The reason for their haste was to get under the range of the Persian archers (Lazenby 67).

51. Another son of Euphorion, the tragedian Aeschylus, also fought at Marathon, and recorded this in his epitaph (Pausanias I. 21. 2).

52. The Athenians had probably marched out to Marathon using two different routes, one of 35 kms, the other of 40 (*CAH*² IV. 507), and presumably they would have hurried back to the city by these same routes. Given the distance, however, even of the shorter of the two routes, it has been doubted that the army, after a long battle, could have made such a journey on the same day. More likely they arrived on the following day. The Persian ships needed to traverse c. 70 miles from Marathon to Phalerum (Athens' main harbour until the building of Piraeus in the 470s), which would also take about a day.

53. More trust should be put in the number of the Athenian dead than of the Persian, since the Athenian names were recorded in an inscription on the burial mound on the site (Pausanias I. 32. 3). The number of Persians killed has been calculated (by H. or the tradition before him) as 100 for every 3 Athenians (192 ÷ 3 = 64 × 100 = 6400), as demonstrated by H. Avery, *Historia* 22 (1973) 757 and W. F. Wyatt, ibid. 25 (1976) 843–4.

54. According to Aelian, *Varia Historia* vii. 38, Epizelus was also on the painting in the Stoa Poikile (above n. 48), and he must therefore have been a well-known figure even before H.

55. As the distance between Athens and Sparta is c. 140 miles, the feat of the Spartans is amazing.

56. Ch. 122 has been left out of the translation; most editors consider it an interpolation.

57. The fragment of an Athenian archon list (Fornara 23) has shown this to be untrue, for in the year 525/4 Cleisthenes, an Alcmaeonid (perhaps the democratic reformer), was archon; this confirms *Ath. Pol.* 16. 9, which says that the Pisistratids solidified their rule by winning over the leading families of Athens. There is no reason to doubt, however, that the Alcmaeonids later played a leading part in expelling the tyrants.

58. On the liberation of Athens see V. 63; Thuc. VI. 59 agrees that it was the Lacedaemonians and the Alcmaeonids who ended the tyranny at Athens.

59. This digression (to ch. 131) on early Alcmaeonids comes at an unusual time, even for H. who is fond of digressions. D. Gillis, *Collab-*

oration with the Persians (Wiesbaden 1979) 45–58 sees it as 'in the nature of a diversionary action' (51), a ruse by H. to paper over the weakness of his defence; but the piece is hardly pro-Alcmaeonid: see Thomas 264–72. For attempts to explain the thematic relevance of these stories see Benardete 176–80; Immerwahr (1966) 125–6.

60. On Cleisthenes of Sicyon see V. 67; on what the following story reveals of the aristocracy in archaic times, Murray (1993) 212–13.

61. Since Xanthippus (father of Pericles) had married into the Alcmaeonid clan before this prosecution, his attack on Miltiades (of the rival Philaid clan) has been seen as politically motivated. The date of Miltiades' attack on Paros is c. 489, and the trial may have been in the same year. It is also thought that the account of Miltiades' sacrilege, coming so soon after the defence of the Alcmaeonids, is evidence of an Alcmaeonid source trying to tarnish the reputation of the victor at Marathon; cf., however, Fornara (1971) 54 n. 33.

62. The Pelasgians were thought to be the original inhabitants of Greece: see I. 56–8 with n.

BOOK SEVEN

1. The battle of Marathon was in autumn 490, so Darius' preparations took from 490 to 487. The revolt of Egypt occurred in 486 and was put down in 485.

2. On Demaratus see VI. 61–72.

3. On revenge as a motivating force in H. see Introduction §4. In Mardonius' description of Europe as a beautiful place we are perhaps to see a clever lie, since H. elsewhere contrasts Persian opulence with European poverty (see IX. 82).

4. Xerxes' speech is an excellent illustration of the compulsion exerted by custom (*nomos*), on which see III. 38 with n. His remarks on Persian expansion mirror well the imperialistic tone of many Persian inscriptions; they have also been interpreted as an allusion to Athens' own imperialism during H.'s time: see K. Raaflaub, 'Herodotus, Political Thought and the Meaning of History', *Arethusa* 20 (1987) 221–48.

5. Mardonius' earlier expedition is narrated at VI. 43ff.

6. Artabanus here assumes the role of 'wise adviser' (Introduction §4); C. Pelling, 'Thucydides' Archidamus and Herodotus' Artabanus', in: *Georgica. Studies . . . George Cawkwell*, ed. M. Flower and M. Toher (London 1991) 120–42.

7. For the conference at the Danube see IV. 136–42.

8. The failure to be buried is a Greek horror; according to I. 140, mutilation by dogs and birds was a part of Persian burial practice. This is the first prophecy of Mardonius' ultimate fate; a second appears at VIII. 114.

9. In the Behistun inscription (III. n. 25) Darius gives his genealogy as Hystaspes–Arsames–Ariyaramnes–Teispes–Achaemenes. H. has two ancestors named Teispes between whom fall Cyrus the Great and his son Cambyses. Reconciliation of the two traditions is difficult and complicated by the propagandistic nature of the Behistun inscription: see Cook 8–10; *CHI* 209–10.

10. Xerxes' dream has been the subject of many discussions. It is modelled on the deceptive dream of Agamemnon in *Il.* II. Its function here is to assure that Xerxes does not waiver from his original intent, i.e., to invade Greece, and in that sense the dream is essential to the working out of destiny, just like some others in H., which bring about 'that which must happen': see Immerwahr (1954) 33ff.

11. The four years of preparation are 484–481; the expedition from Greece sets out from Sardis in spring 480.

12. H.'s magnification of Xerxes' forces not only emphasizes the final chapters of the Persian Wars against Greece, but also by comparison with previous expeditions – especially that of Troy – reveals H.'s emulation of and challenge to Homer (see Introduction §2).

13. Later writers in antiquity ridiculed H.'s account of the Athos canal, but cuttings compatible with his account have been found; for an illustration see Lazenby 95. The alteration of the natural world is an act of *hybris*: see Introduction §4 and below, ch. 24.

14. A later writer, Demetrius of Scepsis, says the canal was 100 feet wide.

15. For the conclusion of this story see ch. 38.

16. On these incidents see IX. 116–21.

17. H. is emphatic here about the megalomania of Xerxes; the reader has a sense of the king's madness and foreboding as Xerxes yokes together the two continents and transgresses the limits of Asia.

18. For the skill involved in the building of the bridge see *CAH* IV². 527–32 (map at 531).

19. Kings in H., like the historian himself, frequently desire to see marvellous things: Darius the Cynaean rocks and the Black Sea (IV. 85), Xerxes here Troy, and at ch. 128 the mouth of the Peneus: for the phenomenon, see M. Christ, 'Herodotean Kings and Historical Inquiry', *CA* 13 (1994) 167–202. His desire to see Troy is yet another allusion to Homer. The panic that overtakes the army here may be a foreshadowing of their ultimate destruction.

20. For similar statements on death as preferable to life see I. 31, V. 4.

21. Cf. Aesch. *Persians* 792–4: '*Darius*. For the land itself is their [i.e. the Greeks'] ally. *Chorus*. What do you mean, "their ally"? / *Dar*. It destroys excessive numbers by starvation.'

22. A reference to the Scythians.

23. For the Ionians in Scythia see IV. 139–42; in Xerxes' expedition the Ionians are not a factor until the final battle at Mycale (IX. 103–4), although the Greeks still made the effort to neutralize them: see Themistocles' ruse at VIII. 22.

24. Fehling (247–8) suggests that Aesch. *Persians* 980 ('counter of tens of thousands') may be the origin of H.'s description of Xerxes' method of counting. As HW ii. 151 point out, the enumeration of the army is likely to have taken place before this, probably at Sardis where it mustered.

25. This catalogue of Persian forces (chs 61–88) is enormously impressive and adds majesty and, we might say, a sense of invincibility to the Greeks' opponents. Described in their exotic and at times fantastic native costumes, they convey visually the power of the enormous and polyglot Persian empire. Contrast with the poor and un-exotic Greeks is strongly implied. It has been suggested that not all of the nations here described would have participated in this expedition, and H. is here giving, perhaps from some written source or official document, the strength of the Persian army on paper; but others suspect that since the king himself was present, it was necessary for all the nations to accompany him. Armayor (1978b) has argued that much of the information here cannot be reconciled with Persian reliefs and that the catalogue derives not from any Persian record (official or otherwise) but from Greek sources and ethnography; for a complementary approach using different evidence see Lewis (1984) 597–602.

26. 'Pisidians' is a modern conjecture for a lacuna in the text.

27. This number for ships agrees with Aesch. *Persians* 341–3, but H. brings the total number of ships up to 3000 by adding transports and other boats (ch. 97).

28. Artemisia, first introduced here, is a marvel (a woman fighting men), a wise adviser and a loyal ally of Xerxes. As ruler of H.'s Halicarnassus, we may assume that stories about her were frequent in the city where H. grew up. For her other appearances and exploits see VIII. 68–9, 87–8, 101–3; on her importance in H. see R. Munson, 'Artemisia in H.', *CA* 7 (1988) 91–106.

29. On laughter as a forerunner of destruction see D. Lateiner, 'No Laughing Matter: A Literary Tactic in H.', *TAPA* 107 (1977) 173–82. The conversation between Xerxes and Demaratus encapsulates some

of the most important themes in H., especially that between slavery and freedom (Introduction §2). The Persian king cannot understand how the Spartans will behave bravely unless someone is compelling them (as H. always emphasizes of the Persians), and Demaratus' answer that the Spartan 'commander' is Law (*nomos*) is completely unconvincing to the king. But Demaratus' words form a clever commentary on H.'s approval of Pindar's remark that *nomos* is a king (III. 38 with n.).

30. The Greeks drove the Persians from Sestos (IX. 118) and Byzantium (Thuc. I. 94, 128) in 478, from Eion in 476 (see next chapter) and from the Thracian Chersonese after the battle of Eurymedon in 469 (Plut. *Cimon* 14).

31. This oracle was well known to the Greeks, and, to judge by H.'s unusual remark here, fantastic or exaggerated stories must have been told by some of the Greeks about its method of divination.

32. On Nine Ways see V. n. 8.

33. The long-horned oxen are aurochs.

34. Therma was the site of Thessalonica (modern Saloniki), founded by Cassander in 305 BCE.

35. H. refers to the burning of Attica in 480 and 479 (VIII. 53; IX. 13).

36. For prostration (*proskynesis*) as a Persian custom see I. 134.

37. This incident, narrated by Thuc. (II. 67), occurred in 430. It is the latest event mentioned by H.

38. Writing in the early years of the Peloponnesian War, H. knows that defence of Athens will be disliked because Athens had become 'the tyrant city', ruling with an iron fist an empire of Greek states. Although this is indeed a strong defence of Athens, it will also have carried a sting of reproval, since contemporaries cannot have failed to notice the change that scarcely two generations had wrought: Greece's great saviour was in the present her great enslaver; see also VIII. 144. On the whole topic see Fornara (1971) 45–6, 84–6; for a study of the argumentation of this passage, N. Demand, 'Herodotus' Encomium of Athens: Science or Rhetoric?', *AJP* 108 (1987) 746–58. We should not overlook, however, the obvious conclusion to be drawn from H.'s remarks: that most people in his time thought that the Spartans had saved Greece in the Persian Wars. (I owe this 'obvious' point, which is often overlooked, to Michael Flower.)

39. The mention of the oracles now leads H. to his account of them here. But when did the Athenians consult them, and did they establish a policy before or in light of them? See VIII. n. 14.

40. Themistocles had been archon in 493, and some have seen a slight in H.'s use of 'recently' here in the year 480; but see Fornara (1971) 68. That Themistocles was the architect of Greek victory in the

campaigns of 480 could not be doubted, even by the usually jealous and suspicious Greeks: see VIII. 123–5.

41. *Ath. Pol.* 22. 7 dates this to 483/2; the mines at Laurium in southern Attica were farmed out by the Athenian state for an annual percentage of the revenues. In the present or perhaps preceding year the discovery of a rich vein of silver meant a windfall for the Athenian state. On the mines see R. J. Hopper, 'The Mines and Miners of Ancient Athens', *Greece and Rome* 8 (1961) 138–51. On the long-standing conflict between Aegina and Athens see *CAH* IV². 339–40.

42. The modern name given to this group of states is the Hellenic League of 481. Its purpose, of course, was to resist the Persians, probably for as long as necessary. The leading states of Sparta and Athens would have been the prime movers, although Sparta, as the greater power, was given the supreme command by land and sea. The members of the confederacy can be known from the Serpent Column dedicated at the end of the wars (see IX. 81 with n.), although at the outset the League will also have included city-states that later during the actual campaign switched to the Persian side. See P. A. Brunt, 'The Hellenic League against Persia', *Studies in Greek History and Thought* (Oxford 1993) 47–83.

43. Argos was the second power in the Peloponnese after Sparta and its differences with Sparta will have made her reluctant to join any league in which Sparta played the leading role. H. relates three traditions about Argos which range from divinely sanctioned neutrality to open treason (152 ad fin.). He expresses no opinion, but his story of each nation's sufferings seems to exculpate Argos, and his remark that the Argives were 'not the worst offenders' (ch. 152) is almost certainly a snide reference to the Thebans.

44. Callias was in Susa, it is thought, in order to negotiate a formal peace between Athens and Persia in 449. This 'Peace of Callias' is an endlessly debated topic in Greek history, but it belongs to Greco-Persian relations after the period treated in H.'s history. See Sealey 278–82.

45. On the Syracusan tyranny see Andrewes 129–36; for a detailed account of the events of the following chapters see *CAH* IV². 757–76.

46. Menestheus (*Il.* II. 550–56).

47. A gloss follows in the text: 'The meaning of his remark is as follows: as the spring is the most excellent part of the year, so his army was the best part of that of the Greeks. And so he likened Greece deprived of his army to the year with spring removed.' Aristotle twice (*Rhet.* I. 7; III. 10) ascribes these words to a funeral oration by Pericles in which he remarked that the loss of the young men in the war was 'as if the

spring had been taken from the year'. The sentiment seems more appropriate there than in Gelon's words in H.

48. Some manuscripts read 'from'; the events are narrated at VI. 23.

49. A tradition later than H. held that Persia was in alliance with Carthage (Diod. XI. 1) but this tradition is variously interpreted by moderns; see Burn 306 with n. 30; Cook 107 ('it can hardly be coincidence'); CAH IV². 773–4 ('a myth').

50. On the Corcyraeans see III. 48 with n.; since they were often at loggerheads with Corinth, their mother-city, they may have hoped for a Persian victory whereby they could profit at Corinth's expense.

51. Iapygia is Apulia (modern Puglia) in southern Italy. The battle occurred c. 473.

52. On the Aleuadae see ch. 6.

53. The Spartan king was the usual military leader but on distant or less important campaigns the leaders might be polemarchs, the highest Spartan officers (V. 66).

54. On Alexander see V. 17–22.

55. For Tempe and Xerxes' route via Gonnus see the map at Burn 340.

56. For the topography of Thermopylae see HW ii. 207–9; Burn 409–11; map at Burn 408; Lazenby 133. Like Marathon, Thermopylae retains its romantic glow, in this case because of the selfless devotion of Leonidas and the 300 Spartans. For modern treatments of the battle see Burn 406–22 (with good remarks on H.'s presentation); Hignett (1963) 105–48; Lazenby 117–50.

57. The Artemisium is on the northwest coast of Euboea.

58. The name means 'lion'.

59. The numbers are (as usually in ancient authors) wildly fantastic. There is no way of knowing the size of Xerxes' forces; for estimates see Burn 326–32; Lazenby 90–96. The early tradition, as we can see from one of the markers at Thermopylae (ch. 228), was 3 million; H. tries to be more precise and inspire confidence with his 2,641,610.

60. Darius thus follows the Persian custom praised by H. at I. 137.

61. The story, familiar from Sophocles' Trachiniae, is that Heracles put on a poisoned garment given to his wife Deianeira by the centaur Nessus. At once Heracles became engulfed in flames and perished.

62. The text here says '420 miles' which cannot be right; most suspect corruption in the manuscripts.

63. On the Amphictyons see V. n. 31.

64. Throughout H.'s narrative the Peloponnesians wish to fall back below the Isthmus of Corinth in order to defend the Peloponnese; such a move would leave central Greece – Phocis, Locris, Plataea and Athens – to its fate.

65. On Spartan comportment before battle see Xenophon, *Constitution of the Lacedaemonians* (translated as *Spartan Society* in the Penguin *Plutarch on Sparta*) 11. 3; 13. 8.

66. H. does not keep his promise; when Ephialtes was proscribed and murdered we do not know, but it is not likely to have been much after 479.

67. On the Spartan prohibition against leaving their post see Demaratus' words at ch. 104.

68. Plutarch (*Mal. Her.* 31), in one of the few places where he scores a hit against H., finds fault here for the treatment of the Thebans. Retaining people of doubtful loyalty in such a situation would have weakened Leonidas' position. H. here has fallen for the anti-Theban propaganda that was rife in Athens before and during the Peloponnesian War. Diodorus (XI. 4.7) says that the Thebans with Leonidas were members 'of the other party', i.e. the one that was opposed to Persia. For Thebes' actions in the Persian wars see Demand 20–27.

69. The struggle for the body of Leonidas has epic associations: see the struggle for the body of Patroclus at *Il.* XVII. 274–5.

70. H.'s troops from the Peloponnese number 3100 in his army list (ch. 202).

71. On his conduct there see IX. 71.

72. This attack on Plataea (spring 431) is the opening action of the Peloponnesian War: see Thuc. II. 2–6, who says that there were 'rather more than 300' Thebans, led by Pythangelus and Diempous.

73. The seizure of Cythera by the Athenians in 424 (Thuc. IV. 53) may have suggested to H. this strategy for a 'wise adviser'. There is also a tradition that the Athenian general Tolmides had taken the island in 456/5 (Pausanias I. 27. 5; cf. Thuc. I. 108) but there is no evidence that he pursued the strategy that the Athenians in 424 did.

74. Cf. VII. 181 and VIII. 92 for Persian generosity towards brave foes.

75. This final chapter, because of its unusual style and vocabulary, is regarded by some scholars as a late addition. If it is by H., the point at which he presumably would have placed it is ch. 220, since Demaratus' information was the occasion for sending to Delphi.

BOOK EIGHT

1. Since Sparta was the great power in Greece at the time of the Persian Wars, it was only to be expected that she would provide the commander-in-chief. Athens indeed may have wanted the naval command, but H. is here misled by later Athenian naval greatness to assume (anachronistically) that she was the obvious choice in 480. It was, in fact, the Persian Wars and their aftermath that saw the rise of Athens to command of the seas.

2. For this incident, which belongs to the immediate aftermath of the Persian Wars, see Thuc. I. 95; H.'s expression here suggests that he, like Thucydides, saw the deprival as a way for Athens to achieve a goal long in the planning.

3. This story of bribery (also at Plut. *Themist.* 7) is likely to have been invented later, after Themistocles had been ostracized and fled to Persia (Thuc. I. 135–8). The story is improbable enough (HW ii. 237) but understandable, given Themistocles' later reputation for greed (on which see Plut. *Themist.* 5).

4. According to Pausanias (X. 19. 1–2), the Amphictyons set up a statue of Scyllias and his daughter because they loosened the cables of the Persian ships which then suffered much damage in the storm.

5. This technique, with bows outward in a circle, was designed to prevent the ships from being rammed in the side, the usual way to disable a trireme.

6. For divine action as an element in historical action see Introduction §4.

7. Cleinias is the father of the infamous Alcibiades of the late fifth century; he died in 447 at the battle of Coronea, after which time his son became the ward of Pericles.

8. Plutarch (*Mal. Her.* 34; *Themist.* 8) says that Artemisium was a victory for the Greeks, quoting as evidence a line from Pindar ('where the brave sons of Athens planted the shining cornerstone of their freedom') and a dedicatory inscription at the site of Artemis Prosoea. H. is correct that the battle was indecisive, but 'Pindar was surely right to see a chink of light amidst the gloom' (Lazenby 150).

9. Themistocles says 'on your account' because it was to help the Ionian Revolt that the Athenians had sent twenty ships (V. 97–8).

10. This story of Xerxes' ruse is very doubtful, and is probably meant rather to display the king's character.

11. It is uncertain when this battle took place; Pausanias (X. 1. 3–9) has a fuller account and a description of the statues (X. 13. 7).

12. This oracle had been consulted by Croesus (I. 46); more surprisingly, in view of what is said here, the Persians consult it again a few months after the events described here: see ch. 134.

13. The attack on Delphi is unlikely to be true, for most of the Amphictyons (see V. n. 31) had by now joined Xerxes' forces, and Mardonius explicitly says that the Persians will refrain from attacking Delphi (IX. 42). For various modern attempts to maintain the tradition

see HW ii. 246–7; Hignett (1963) 445–7; Parker, cited above, Introduction n. 43. In Diodorus (XI. 14) a violent storm dislodges the rocks, but this is an obvious rationalization.

14. In 1960 an inscription was discovered at Troezen which purports to be the decree of Themistocles stipulating the evacuation of Attica and outlining a strategy of fighting the Persians at Artemisium and Salamis (Fornara 55; text and discussion at Burn 364–77). The decree, which would have been passed before the Persians actually invaded, seems to conflict with H.'s account of the actions that led to the decision to fight at Salamis. In the decree, the decision to fight at Artemisium and Salamis, as well as the evacuation of Attica, have been previously agreed upon as Athenian (or Greek) strategy; whereas H. here says: (i) that the Peloponnesians' failure to appear in central Greece necessitated a sudden proclamation by the Athenians to evacuate; and (ii) the fleet had no intention of fighting at Salamis until Themistocles tricked them into doing so (chs 75–6). On the whole, scholars have preferred H.'s narrative to the decree, even if the decision to evacuate Attica cannot have been as abrupt as in H. (Lazenby 111–14). For an analysis that attempts to reconcile H.'s narrative with the Themistocles decree, see M. Henderson, 'The Decree of Themistocles', *Acta Classica* 20 (1977) 85–103. For accounts of the battle of Salamis see Burn 449–71; Hignett (1963) 193–239; Lazenby 151–97.

15. For the contingents at Artemisium see ch. 1.

16. This is the only time H. dates by an Athenian archon; the date is 480.

17. On the wooden wall see VII. 142.

18. Not much is known about Mnesiphilus: his name has turned up on pot sherds used for ostracism, and Plutarch (*Themist.* 2) makes him Themistocles' teacher in politics (an inference from this passage?) and a student of Solon's. Although Fornara (1971) 72 n. 19 sees his introduction as 'calculated to give dramatic emphasis to the crucial moment at Salamis, not to deprive Themistocles of credit', most scholars would agree with Hignett (1963) 204 that it is 'manifestly a spiteful invention to deprive Themistocles of the credit for his originality and insight'. In any case the story is unhistorical and should be rejected; note that Themistocles does not even use these arguments at ch. 60.

19. Siris is located on the River Siris (modern Sinni) between Sybaris and Tarentum on the 'instep' of Italy.

20. The ship is sent for their images; it arrives at ch. 83.

21. The Mother and Maid are Demeter and Persephone; for their festival see Burkert 285–90.

22. On Artemisia see VII. n. 28.

23. The text of H. reads: 'they have been subject to Argos, being Orneatae and *perioeci*'. The exact meaning of this is unclear: see HW ii. 260; on the site of Ornea, see Tomlinson 38–40.

24. This tradition of a secret message to the king is found also in Aesch. *Persians* 355–71. (All the relevant passages about Salamis from Aeschylus are quoted and analysed in Burn ch. XXI.)

25. Cf. Aesch. *Persians* 447–53.

26. The clearest, but hardly the only, expression of belief in oracles by H.; see Introduction §4. On Bacis see Burkert 117.

27. Aristides was ostracized in 483/2 (*Ath. Pol.* 22. 7); according to this same work (22. 8) all exiles were recalled in 481/80, in view of Xerxes' invasion, and ordered to live within the limits of Geraistus (on Euboea) and Scyllaeum in Troezen. The 'Themistocles Decree' (above, n. 14) orders all exiles to return and wait at Salamis until the people shall have decided what to do with them (lines 44ff.). As Burn 351 (cf. Plut. *Themist.* 11) points out, exiles from Greece had a habit of appealing to Persia for reinstatement in their home cities, so the recall of exiles was intended to lessen this possibility.

28. On this tripod see IX. 81 and n.

29. Cf. Aesch. *Persians* 401–5.

30. H.'s account of the movements at Salamis is quite skimpy; more is provided by Aesch. *Persians* 412ff., quoted and discussed at Burn 462–7.

31. Cf. Aesch. *Persians* 465ff.

32. On Pytheas see VII. 181.

33. The story of the Corinthian flight is almost certainly an invention of a later time when Athens and Corinth were enemies. Plutarch (*Mal. Her.* 39) cites numerous inscriptions attesting Corinthian presence, but even without these there is little to recommend H.'s report of hearsay. It may be, as HW ii. 267 note, that the son of Adeimantus, Aristeus, one of Athens' bitterest enemies in the Peloponnesian War (Thuc. I. 60, 65), retroactively besmirched his father's heroic activities.

34. Cf. Aesch. *Persians* 532ff.

35. Themistocles was ostracized c. 472, and while in exile was accused of treason; he decided not to return to Athens but fled to Persia to the court of Xerxes' son Artaxerxes I (Thuc. I. 135–8); it was no doubt this later action that gave rise to the story here and at ch. 75.

36. Themistocles' rapaciousness, like his wiliness, was legendary; he may indeed have made some money from these sieges, but there is no doubt that the alliance itself demanded retribution from those who had supported the Persians.

37. The number 300,000 is as inaccurate as earlier numbers for Persian forces; for estimates of Mardonius' forces see Hignett (1963) 267–8 (c. 60,000 men).

38. On laughter as a sign of impending destruction, see VII. 105 with n.; this is the second 'prophecy' of Mardonius' ultimate fate; the first is at VII. 10h.

39. For a similar (exaggerated) account of the destruction of the retreating army, see Aesch. *Persians* 480ff. The evidence that Xerxes' army did not suffer greatly in the retreat is at Lazenby 206.

40. Pausanias (X. 14. 5) says that this was a statue of Apollo.

41. Belbina is a small island south of Sunium at the entrance of the Saronic Gulf. Themistocles uses it as an example of a small place of no repute.

42. The text is sometimes emended from 'two' to 'seven' to agree with Pausanias III. 1.

43. On Xanthippus see VI. 136; after his prosecution of Miltiades, Xanthippus was ostracized in 484, but recalled in the general amnesty at the time of Xerxes' invasion.

44. H. may mention this Herodotus because he is a friend or relative.

45. H. exaggerates Greek timidity: the Spartans well knew where Samos was, since they had sent an expedition there during Polycrates' reign (III. 39ff.), and the Athenians had gone to Sardis not twenty years before.

46. On Apollo Ptoiüs see Demand 61–2.

47. For the circumstances surrounding this marriage see V. 21.

48. On the historical origin of the Macedonians see the brief summary at *CAH* III². 3. 273–85. The three brothers motif appears also in the story of the origin of the Scythians (IV. 5) and belongs to the realm of folktale.

49. A reference to Athens' despatch of ships to assist the Ionian Revolt (V. 97–8).

50. The Athenian speeches both to Alexander and to the Lacedaemonians have a great nobility, and have been adduced by some as yet further proof of H.'s pro-Athenian bias. But as Fornara (1971) 56–7 points out, the words are heavily ironic in the early years of the Peloponnesian War (when H. was reciting and writing his history) because the Athenians at that time ruled an empire of fellow Greeks and had not hesitated, despite 'the community of blood and language', to enslave or destroy whole communities (see e.g. Thuc. I. 98 (enslavement of Scyros); 114 (expulsion of Hestiaeans)) – not to mention that at the start of that war both Sparta and Athens, in their search for allies, looked to Persia (Thuc. II. 7).

BOOK NINE

1. Xerxes' capture of Athens occurred in September 480, Mardonius' in June 479.

2. The story became famous and is told by later writers, where the man's name, however, is Cyrsilus, not Lycidas.

3. Plutarch (*Aristides* 10) says that the embassy was Aristides' idea and the envoys sent were Cimon, Xanthippus and Myronides, but these details are of questionable value (Burn 505 n. 49).

4. The Hyacinthia was celebrated in honour of Apollo and the beautiful youth Hyacinthus, whom Apollo had accidentally killed. The ceremony, described by Pausanias III. 19. 3, usually took place in early summer.

5. H.'s story of Spartan delay is unusual; Chileus is placed here for dramatic effect, since (as HW ii. 289 point out) the Spartans did not need a Tegean to explain obvious strategy to them.

6. The eclipse occurred on 2 October 480.

7. The 'secret' march may have been done at night to keep Sparta's enemies, especially Argos, in the dark about Spartan activity (so Burn 506); by the time the Argives knew what was happening, it was too late (see their speech to Mardonius in the next chapter).

8. For the position of Mardonius' camp see the map at Burn 508.

9. H. rarely names individuals whom he has met (II. 55, III. 55, IV. 76 are the only other examples), and he perhaps does it here because of the extraordinary nature of the conversation related and its aura of prognostication. The speech itself sums up many of H.'s themes throughout the *Histories*: divine ordinance; failure to believe warnings; and the contrast between freedom and subjection to the will of others. It makes a striking prelude to the battle – in H.'s eyes the most glorious ever: see ch. 64 – that finally drove the Persians from Greece. On Attaginus' later fate, see chs 86–8.

10. On Phocian and Thessalian enmity see VIII. 30.

11. The positions of both Greeks and Persians may be seen on the map at Burn 518.

12. These particular Persian customs are not mentioned at I. 131–40; H. notes that the Egyptians shave their heads as a sign of mourning (II. 36).

13. For the desire of seeing a splendid enemy dead, see *Il.* XXII. 369–75.

14. The narration of the early Athenian exploits becomes a regular

feature of public funeral orations at Athens. The Athenian claim to have fought 'alone' at Marathon becomes standard in later oratory, and ignores the assistance of the Plataeans (VI. 108).

15. Forty-six nations corresponds to Xerxes' host (VII. 61–80), but it is unlikely that all the nations fought at Marathon. The speech and the contest for the wing are usually dismissed as unhistorical but see Hignett (1963) 312–13.

16. Of the 10,000 Lacedaemonians, 5000 were Spartiates (ch. 10) and 5000 were *perioeci* (ch. 11).

17. On the classes of Egyptians see II. 164–5.

18. Melampus ('Black Foot') of Pylos was a famous prophet already known to Homer (*Od.* XI. 285ff.; XV. 225ff.). When the women of Argos refused to worship Dionysus, and the god sent madness upon them for this affront, the Argives summoned Melampus from Nestor's court to teach the women the Dionysiac mysteries.

19. The battles of Tegea and Dipaees occurred c. 473–470; not much is known of them. The battle at Ithome against the Messenians is described in Thuc. I. 101–3 (cf. Fornara 67), and dates to c. 465–460; and Tanagra occurred in 457 (Thuc. I. 107–8).

20. Neither the date nor the circumstances of Hegesistratus' capture are known.

21. Mardonius here, by ignoring the warnings from the sacrifices of Hegesistratus, fulfils what the Persian at the Theban feast had said would happen (ch. 16).

22. Mardonius' words here conflict with the account of a Persian attack on Delphi in the previous year (VIII. 39 with n.).

23. This narrative of troop movements is ridiculed by Plutarch (*Mal. Her.* 42) and usually dismissed as unhistorical (see the arguments at HW ii. 308); the incident reflects poorly on the Spartans and may betray later bias; on the possible strategy involved here see Hignett (1963) 317; cf. Burn 528–9.

24. Pitana, a suburb of Sparta on the River Eurotas, was the burial-place of the Agiad kings; H. claims to have visited it (III. 55). The existence of a Pitanate regiment is explicitly denied by Thucydides (I. 20) but H. may mean only that it came from Pitana, not that it was an 'official' regiment; cf. Cartledge (1979) 255–6.

25. Dramatic but inaccurate: voting pebbles were used at Athens, not at Sparta, where voting was by acclamation (Thuc. I. 87).

26. Pausanias' delay may have been militarily motivated by his desire to engage the Persian infantry fully for a battle at close quarters; by doing this he would neutralize the Persian superiority in cavalry: HW ii. 314; Hignett (1963) 336; Burn 530, 538. Lazenby 241 sees no

strategy at work and accepts the story as in H. that Pausanias was waiting for favourable omens.

27. On the oracle see VIII. 114.

28. Aeimnestus probably died in the helot revolt at Ithome: see n. 19 above.

29. H. has not previously mentioned the burning of this sanctuary of Demeter at Eleusis.

30. Anti-Corinthian and -Megarian prejudice may again be at work here. The contemporary poet Simonides spoke of the Corinthians at Plataea as 'holding the centre' (Plut. *Mal. Her.* 42); see further Burn 536–8 and (more cautiously) Hignett (1963) 338–9; for a defence of H., see Lazenby 244.

31. On Aristodemus at Thermopylae see VII. 229–31. His 'rushing forward' would have been little appreciated by the Spartans, who prided themselves on their order and discipline.

32. The war referred to is the Peloponnesian War. What H. says of the Spartans' attitude towards Decelea is true only of the first portion of the war (the so-called Archidamian War, 431–421); in 413 the Spartans occupied it to the great destruction of the Athenians (Thuc. VI. 19).

33. H. has already mentioned Sophanes' victory at VI. 92 (a rare repetition); the battle with the Edoni may be dated to an Athenian attempt to occupy Thrace c. 465. More details at HW ii. 319.

34. The story is meant to contrast Greek and barbarian practice (as does ch. 82 that follows); anti-Aeginetan bias is again in evidence here.

35. The tripod was melted down by the Phocians c. 354; the base, on which were carved three intertwined snakes (not one snake with three heads as H. says), was removed from Delphi by the Roman emperor Constantine in the fourth century CE and brought to his new capital Constantinople (Istanbul), where it still stands in the ancient hippodrome (*At-maidan*) without its snake heads (one of which is in the Istanbul museum). On the coils of the snakes were engraved the participants in the war. The text is at Fornara 59. Not all the names agree with H.'s account and some were inscribed after the monument was dedicated. See the tabulation at HW ii. 323; for discussion see Hignett (1963) 435–8.

36. Pausanias (V. 23. 1–3) describes this statue and gives the list of peoples on it; but they are not the same as those on the serpent column or in H.

37. These are marvels (see Introduction §2) and included here for their own sake; cf. H.'s interest in Persian and Egyptian skulls at III. 12.

38. The manuscript reading of *irees* ('priests') is altered in many texts to *irenas* ('youths', i.e. Spartan youths between the ages of 20 and 30)

on the strength of a late lexicographer's assertion that the latter word occurs in H. But this is not likely here and we should keep the manuscript reading. HW ii. 235 suggest that H. has misunderstood and that the three graves were of the Spartiates (full Spartan citizens), *perioeci* and helots.

39. A later construction by the Aeginetans is indeed possible, but H.'s conclusion that they were not there for the battle is likely to have been influenced by the anti-Aeginetan feelings of his Athenian informants.

40. H. picks up the story from VIII. 132; the Persian fleet was stationed at Samos to forestall an uprising in Ionia after the Persian defeat at Salamis. Mycale is a promontory directly across from Samos. Modern treatments of the battle are: Burn 547–51; Hignett (1963) 255–60. That the battle occurred on the same day has been doubted; see the suspiciously similar synchronism at VII. 166.

41. 'Hegesistratus' means 'leader of the army'; Leotychides cuts him off lest the Samian say something unlucky.

42. This Apollonia (there are many others) is located north of Corcyra on the River Aous on the coast of Illyria; it was a Corinthian colony (Thuc. I. 26). On this story of Euenius here and its thematic importance, see A. Griffiths, 'Euenios the Negligent Nightwatchman (Herodotus 9.92–6)', in R. Buxton, ed., *From Myth to Reason?* (Oxford 1999) 169–82.

43. For Themistocles' ruse see VIII. 22.

44. According to VI. 19–20, all the men who survived the Persian destruction of Miletus were settled by Darius on the Tigris; HW ii. 330 point out that H. must have exaggerated the destruction, since the Milesians here appear as benefactors to the Greeks.

45. A later rationalized version of this incident has Leotychides invent the story that the Greeks had been successful at Plataea in order to encourage his men at Mycale to fight bravely. There is no value in this. H. obviously likes the story because it proves again 'that the hand of God is active in human affairs' (Introduction §4).

46. As the last 'historical' action, the battle of Mycale brings the wheel full circle as Ionia is liberated a second time; for H. had begun his work with Croesus, who had first subdued Ionia (I. 5, 26–7).

47. Athens' attack on Carystus occurred c. 472 (Thuc. I. 98).

48. For earlier proposals to evacuate Ionia see I. n. 67.

49. Because bravery is their greatest good (I. 136).

50. Some editors amend the text to 'Lycia' because Xenophon (*Education of Cyrus* VII. 4. 2) says that Cilicia was ruled by native princes until c. 400.

51. H.'s history ends with three episodes of great thematic importance:

Xerxes' passion; the crimes of the Persian governor Artaÿctes; and Cyrus' advice to the Persians. Each of these episodes in a different way rounds off the story that H. had begun with Croesus' attack on the Ionian Greeks. The end of the *Histories* has recently been the subject of important studies: J. Herington, 'The Closure of Herodotus' *Histories*', *Illinois Classical Studies* 16 (1991) 149–60; J. Moles, 'Herodotus Warns the Athenians', *Papers of the Leeds Latin Seminar* 9 (1996) 259–84; C. Pelling, 'East is East and West is West – Or Are They?', *Histos* 1 (1997), electronic publication; and C. Dewald, 'Pickled Heroes, Wanton Kings and Gnomic Founding Fathers: Reading the End of Herodotus' *Histories*', in *Classical Closure: Reading the End in Greek and Latin Literature*, eds. D. H. Roberts, F. M. Dunn and D. Fowler (Princeton 1997) 62–82.

The tale of Xerxes' passion for Masistes' wife gives us our last view of the hybristic king and in it he appears partly as the tyrant ruled by lust and partly as the hapless victim of his own passion, who is unable to control his desires or the machinations of the one who uses him. His story in many ways parallels that of Gyges with whom the *Histories* open (I. 8–12): the motif is that of the destructive promise, the reason for the action taken is revenge, the guiding force is a woman, and the man is bound by necessity to commit some evil: see E. Wolff, 'Das Weib von Masistes', *Hermes* 92 (1964) 51–8. Sancisi-Weerdenburg 28–9 thinks that the story may conceal a tradition that Masistes tried to rebel from Xerxes and seize the kingship for himself.

52. Protesilaus was the first Greek to land on the shore of Troy (*Il.* II. 701–2), and it is not accidental that H. has chosen this incident with which to end his work. The Trojan War had been the great European–Asian conflict until the time of the Persian Wars, and H. has attempted to portray these wars as the culmination of that conflict. Destruction (*nemesis*) here catches up with Artaÿctes, as Protesilaus has his vengeance (*tisis*) for the sacrilege against his temple. H. even here repeats that 'the Persians consider that the whole of Asia belongs to them', the almost exact words with which he had begun his narrative of European–Asian conflicts (I. 4). On the thematic importance of this final incident see D. Boedeker, 'Protesilaos and the end of Herodotus' *Histories*', *CA* 7 (1988) 30–48, who sees in Artaÿctes' story 'a broader justice directed against the entire armada, which, like Artaÿctes, had entered into forbidden territory' (45).

53. The concluding story of the *Histories* brings back upon the stage Cyrus the Great – the man who had won the Persians their freedom and with whom no Persian could ever compare himself – in an anecdote that encompasses many of the themes of the work, especially those of

poverty and wealth, closely related to freedom and despotism. There is some minor inconsistency with I. 126, where Cyrus promises the Persians 'a thousand pleasures . . . without ever turning your hands to servile labour', and with I. 207, where Croesus speaks to Cyrus of the luxuries that the Persians enjoy. Yet having shown in the previous story of Protesilaus the role of the divine and the importance of retribution, H. here wishes to emphasize the importance of a national character, which is shaped not only by the natural environment of a people (Introduction §2) but also by human institutions and customs (III. 38 with n.; see also Redfield 113–15). And so the portrait of the rough Persians under Cyrus is somewhat idealized. Some scholars think that the work is unfinished; they cite this ending (considered by some unusual) and H.'s three unfulfilled promises (see Introduction §1), and assume that he would have continued his work to a later point. These objections may be valid, but it can hardly be denied that H.'s conclusion – with the Persians finally driven from Greece, with the Greek Protesilaus obtaining his revenge (previous note) and with the warning that freedom demands vigour – is brilliantly realized, and manifestly suited to all that has gone before.

Index

PENGUIN ⓟ CLASSICS

The Classics Publisher

'Penguin Classics, one of the world's greatest series.' JOHN KEEGAN

'I have never been disappointed with the Penguin Classics. All I have read is a model of academic seriousness and provides the essential information to fully enjoy the master works that appear in its catalogue.' MARIO VARGAS LLOSA

'Penguin and Classics are words that go together like horse and carriage or Mercedes and Benz. When I was a university teacher I always prescribed Penguin editions of classic novels for my courses: they have the best introductions, the most reliable notes, and the most carefully edited texts.' DAVID LODGE

'Growing up in Bombay, expensive hardback books were beyond my means, but I could indulge my passion for reading at the roadside bookstalls that were well stocked with all the Penguin paperbacks ... Sometimes I would choose a book just because I was attracted by the cover, but so reliable was the Penguin imprimatur that I was never once disappointed by the contents.

Such access certainly broadened the scope of my reading, and perhaps it's no coincidence that so many Merchant Ivory films have been adapted from great novels, or that those novels are published by Penguin.' ISMAIL MERCHANT

'You can't write, read, or live fully in the present without knowing the literature of the past. Penguin Classics opens the door to a treasure house of pure pleasure, books that have never been bettered, which are read again and again with increased delight.' JOHN MORTIMER

READ MORE IN PENGUIN

In every corner of the world, on every subject under the sun, Penguin represents quality and variety – the very best in publishing today.

For complete information about books availabale from Penguin – including Puffins, Penguin Classics and Arkana – and how to order them, write to us at the appropriate address below. Please note that for copyright reasons the selection of books varies from country to country.

In the United Kingdom: *Please write to* Dept EP, Penguin Books Ltd, Bath Road, Harmondsworth, West Drayton, Middlesex UB7 0DA

In the United States: *Please write to* Consumer Services, Penguin Putnam Inc., 405 Murray Hill Parkway, East Rutherford, New Jersey 07073-2136. *VISA and MasterCard holders call 1-800-631-8571 to order Penguin titles*

In Canada: *Please write to* Penguin Books Canada Ltd, 10 Alcorn Avenue, Suite 300, Toronto, Ontario M4V 3B2

In Australia: *Please write to* Penguin Books Australia Ltd, 487 Maroondah Highway, Ringwood, Victoria 3134

In New Zealand: *Please write to* Penguin Books (NZ) Ltd, Private Bag 102902, North Shore Mail Centre, Auckland 10

In India: *Please write to* Penguin Books India Pvt Ltd, 11 Community Centre, Panchsheel Park, New Delhi 110017

In the Netherlands: *Please write to* Penguin Books Netherlands bv, Postbus 3507, NL-1001 AH Amsterdam

In Germany: *Please write to* Penguin Books Deutschland GmbH, Metzlerstrasse 26, 60594 Frankfurt am Main

In Spain: *Please write to* Penguin Books S. A., Bravo Murillo 19, 1°B, 28015 Madrid

In Italy: *Please write to* Penguin Italia s.r.l., Via Vittoria Emanuele 451a, 20094 Corsico, Milano

In France: *Please write to* Penguin France, 12, Rue Prosper Ferradou, 31700 Blagnac

In Japan: *Please write to* Penguin Books Japan Ltd, Iidabashi KM-Bldg, 2-23-9 Koraku, Bunkyo-Ku, Tokyo 112-0004

In South Africa: *Please write to* Penguin Books South Africa (Pty) Ltd, P.O. Box 751093, Gardenview, 2047 Johannesburg

SEUTONIUS

The Twelve Caesars

'Too many rulers are a dangerous thing'

As private secretary to the Emperor Hadrian, Suetonius gained access to the imperial archives and used them (along with eye witness accounts) to produce one of the most colourful biographical works in history. *The Twelve Caesars* chronicles the public careers and private lives of the men who wielded absolute power over Rome, from the foundation of the empire under Julius Caesar and Augustus, to the decline into depravity and civil war under Nero, and the recovery that came with his successors. A masterpiece of anecdote, wry observation and detailed physical description, *The Twelve Caesars* presents us with a gallery of vividly drawn – and all too human – individuals.

Robert Graves's celebrated translation, sensitively revised by Michael Grant, captures all the wit and immediacy of Suetonius' original.

'Graves has given us *The Twelve Caesars* in a good, dry, no-nonsense style ... Suetonius, in holding up a mirror to those Caesars of diverting legend, reflects not only them but ourselves: half-tempted creatures, whose great moral task is to hold in balance the angel and the monster within' Gore Vidal

Translated by ROBERT GRAVES
Revised with an introduction by MICHAEL GRANT

HOMER

The Iliad

*'Look at me. I am the son of a great man. A
goddess was my mother. Yet death and inexorable
destiny are waiting for me'*

One of the foremost achievements in Western literature,
Homer's *Iliad* tells the story of the darkest episode in the Trojan
War. At its centre is Achilles, the greatest warrior-champion of
the Greeks, and his refusal to fight after being humiliated by his
leader Agamemnon. But when the Trojan Hector kills Achilles'
close friend Patroclus, he storms back into battle to take revenge
– although knowing this will ensure his own early death.
Interwoven with this tragic sequence of events are powerfully
moving descriptions of the ebb and flow of battle, of the domestic world inside Troy's besieged city of Ilium and of the conflicts
between the gods on Olympus as they argue over the fate of
mortals.

E. V. Rieu's acclaimed translation of Homer's *The Iliad* was one
of the first titles published in Penguin Classics, and now has
classic status itself. For this edition, Rieu's text has been revised,
and a new introduction and notes by Peter Jones complement
the original introduction.

Translated by E. V. RIEU
Revised and updated by PETER JONES *with* D. C. H. RIEU
Edited with an introduction and notes by PETER JONES

HOMER

The Odyssey

*'I long to reach my home and see the day of my
return. It is my never-failing wish'*

The epic tale of Odysseus and his ten-year journey home after
the Trojan War forms one of the earliest and greatest works of
Western literature. Confronted by natural and supernatural
threats – shipwrecks, battles, monsters and the implacable
enmity of the sea-god Poseidon – Odysseus must test his bravery
and native cunning to the full if he is to reach his homeland
safely and overcome the obstacles that, even there, await him.

E. V. Rieu's translation of *The Odyssey* was the very first
Penguin Classic to be published, and has itself achieved classic
status. For this edition, Rieu's text has been sensitively revised
and a new introduction added to complement his original
introduction.

**'One of the world's most vital tales ... The Odyssey remains
central to literature' MALCOLM BRADBURY**

Translated by E. V. RIEU
Revised translation by D. C. H. RIEU
With an introduction by PETER JONES

VIRGIL

The Aeneid

'I sing of arms and of the man'

After a century of civil strife in Rome and Italy, Virgil wrote *The Aeneid* to honour the emperor Augustus by praising Aeneas – Augustus' legendary ancestor. As a patriotic epic imitating Homer, *The Aeneid* also provided Rome with a literature equal to that of Greece. It tells of Aeneas, survivor of the sack of Troy, and of his seven-year journey: to Carthage, falling tragically in love with Queen Dido; then to the underworld, in the company of the Sibyl of Cumae; and finally to Italy, where he founded Rome. It is a story of defeat and exile, of love and war, hailed by Tennyson as 'the stateliest measure ever moulded by the lips of man'.

David West's acclaimed prose translation is accompanied by his revised introduction and individual prefaces to the twelve books of *The Aeneid*.

'The most truthful translation ever, conveying as many nuances and whispers as are possible from the original' *The Times*

'Sweet prose, clear and clean and dancing like a mountain stream, as here . . . West opens the window and the winds bring life into Virgil's body' *Wall Street Journal*

Translated with an introduction by DAVID WEST

PLATO

The Last Days of Socrates

*'Nothing can harm a good man either in life or
after death'*

The trial and condemnation of Socrates on charges of heresy
and corrupting young minds is a defining moment in the history
of Classical Athens. In tracing these events through four dialogues, Plato also developed his own philosophy, based on
Socrates' manifesto for a life guided by self-responsibility.
Euthyphro finds Socrates outside the court-house, debating the
nature of piety, while *The Apology* is his robust rebuttal of the
charges of impiety and a defence of the philosopher's life. In
the *Crito*, while awaiting execution in prison, Socrates counters
the arguments of friends urging him to escape. Finally, in the
Phaedo, he is shown calmly confident in the face of death,
skilfully arguing the case for the immortality of the soul.

Hugh Tredennick's landmark 1954 translation has been revised
by Harold Tarrant, reflecting changes in Platonic studies, with
an introduction and expanded introductions to each of the four
dialogues.

Translated by HUGH TREDENNICK *and* HAROLD TARRANT
With an introduction and notes by HAROLD TARRANT

PLATO

The Symposium

'I've realized how great and wonderful a god Love is, and how his power extends to all aspects of human and divine life'

In the course of a lively drinking party, a group of Athenian intellectuals exchange views on *eros*, or desire. From their conversation emerges a series of subtle reflections on gender roles, sex in society and the sublimation of basic human instincts. The discussion culminates in a radical challenge to conventional views by Plato's mentor, Socrates, who advocates transcendence through spiritual love. *The Symposium* is a deft interweaving of different viewpoints and ideas about the nature of love – as a response to beauty, a cosmic force, a motive for social action and as a means of ethical education.

Christopher Gill's translation retains all the drama and humour of the Greek, bringing the historical figures to life. His introduction discusses aspects of classical Athenian life shown in *The Symposium* and provides thoughtful examinations of the individual speeches.

'Translated in bright modern English by Christopher Gill'
PETER STOTHARD, *The Times*

A new translation with an introduction and notes by
CHRISTOPHER GILL